Real Estate Economics

Also by Ernie Jowsey

MODERN ECONOMICS (with Jack Harvey)
URBAN LAND ECONOMICS (with Jack Harvey)
ONE HUNDRED ESSAY PLANS FOR ECONOMICS

Real Estate Economics

Ernie Jowsey

Principal Lecturer in Applied Economics, Built Environment,
Sheffield Hallam University, UK

First published 2011 by
PALGRAVE MACMILLAN

Palgrave Macmillan in the UK is an imprint of Macmillan Publishers Limited,
registered in England, company number 785998, of Houndmills, Basingstoke,
Hampshire RG21 6XS.

Palgrave Macmillan in the US is a division of St Martin's Press LLC,
175 Fifth Avenue, New York, NY 10010.

Palgrave Macmillan is the global academic imprint of the above companies
and has companies and representatives throughout the world.

Palgrave® and Macmillan® are registered trademarks in the United States,
the United Kingdom, Europe and other countries.

ISBN 978-0-230-23320-1

This book is printed on paper suitable for recycling and made from fully
managed and sustained forest sources. Logging, pulping and manufacturing
processes are expected to conform to the environmental regulations of the
country of origin.

A catalogue record for this book is available from the British Library.

A catalog record for this book is available from the Library of Congress.

For Mop, Cinders and Fishboy
You've got to laugh

Contents

Boxes, Figures and Tables

Boxes

Figures

Tables

Preface

This book is intended to be of use to undergraduate and professional students of real estate, land and property, housing, planning and applied economics. It may also be of interest to anyone working in the broad fields of real estate, property management, estate management, land surveying, construction urban planning and property development.

The structure of the book is very straightforward: it is in five parts, covering twenty-two chapters in total. The five main parts are:

Part I The Economic Framework: providing some generic economic background to enable readers new to economics to engage with subsequent material.

Part II Land and Property in the Economy: explaining the way that the real estate market works and its imperfections.

Part III Property Development: explaining the economics of the development process, cost-benefit analysis, planning regulation, construction, sustainable development and contaminated land.

Part IV Land and Property Investment: explaining UK investment in land and property, UK commercial property, the nature and relative size of international real estate markets and globalization of the UK real estate market.

Part V The Government and Real Estate: covering regional policy in the UK and Europe, how government policy impacts on real estate, and the nature of taxation of real estate including full consideration of land taxes.

As is the nature of economic modelling, perfect market models are constructed and then real world imperfections are introduced. Diagrams have been used where they help explain points made and boxes are included to provide examples and illustrations of interest to anyone working or studying in land and property.

Acknowledgements

The author and publishers wish to thank the Energy Saving Trust (http://www. energysavingtrust.org.uk) for permission to use their data.

Every effort has been made to trace all copyright holders, but if any have been inadvertently overlooked the publishers will be pleased to make the necessary arrangements at the first opportunity.

Part I
The Economic Framework

The Scope of Economics

After studying this chapter you will be able to:

- explain the meaning of 'allocation of resources';
- define opportunity costs;
- use a production possibilities curve as an analytical tool;
- distinguish between positive and normative economics;
- explain the nature, scope and limitations of economics.

Why we need to study real estate economics

Land and buildings are scarce resources and it is essential, therefore, that they are used as efficiently as possible. As a result, economists apply economic analysis to formulate the necessary principles for the efficient use of land resources and to suggest ways in which the existing allocation can be improved. Conventional microeconomics has a limited ability to analyse the effects of time and space in relation to property. It is often assumed that all economic activity occurs at a single point in time and that consumption occurs at the time of the transaction. Real estate assets, however, because of their long life, their location and their heterogeneous character, are traded in markets that differ significantly from those of other commodities.

One's property must be preserved and, as the philosopher John Locke put it:

> The great and chief end, therefore, of men's uniting into Commonwealths, and putting themselves under Government, is the preservation of their Property.
>
> Government has no other end, but the preservation of property. (John Locke 1632–1704)

The Scottish philosopher and economist Adam Smith also wrote about the foundation of property-holding for economic well-being. He wrote of individual self-interest and of deriving 'a revenue from a stock which is larger than necessary for immediate consumption'. Smith devoted a considerable part of the 'Wealth of Nations' to 'the rent of land' and also said

> The property which every man has in his own labour as it is the original foundation of all other property, so it is the most sacred and inviolable. (Smith 1776, 121–22)

Property ownership represents a significant part of any economy, and the property industry employs a large proportion of a nation's workforce, directly or indirectly. Property ownership is important in both public and private sectors; and across many areas including commercial, retail, industrial, residential, recreation, tourism and government. The ways in which property is acquired, funded, held and managed vary greatly and affect the performance of property as an asset and in its role of providing services. Property ownership involves many other industries and economic agents such as legal practices, real estate agencies, property management, construction and maintenance, professional consultants, tenants, landlords, financial institutions and investors, all of whom need to understand the economics of real estate.

An understanding of real estate markets is essential for anyone working in any of the areas mentioned above. But it is also necessary in order to make sensible decisions regarding one's own property and wealth. A better understanding of real estate economics in a national and international context is the overriding aim of this book.

Box 1.1   Property professionals

It could be asked why there is a need for property professionals such as property managers and estate agents. In the markets for other goods such professions do not generally exist, so what is it about real estate that makes it necessary to have professional people dealing in its interests? The answer lies in the nature of real estate itself.

Most real estate has a functional use and an asset value. This makes it both a consumer (or producer) good and an investment. For both of these it will require ongoing maintenance. For apartment blocks careful management may be necessary by a property manager or management agent. They will manage ongoing maintenance, longer term or unforeseen expenses such as replacement of lifts or stairways, care of grounds and common areas and health and safety requirements such as fire exits and access for emergency vehicles.

Most units of property have special characteristics, making valuation difficult – some interests such as freehold ground rent can be accurately assessed – others, such as location, state of repair and so on, are subjective, requiring expert valuation. Individual properties (even in the same area) have their own characteristics, making at least some part of a valuation subjective and this means that costs of obtaining knowledge are not absolutely certain.

Where knowledge is difficult to obtain, valuers and agents provide specialized functions which are important for the working of the market (availability and type of property, negotiations, finance, insurance and so on). In addition, the most appropriate method of sale can be advised, such as:

Private Treaty which allows flexibility in lotting (boundary determination) and is cheap – but negotiations may drag on and even fail.
Public Auction can lead to an immediate contract (if bidding exceeds the reserve price) and is suitable if the property is difficult to value because of special characteristics.
Tender by sealed bid allows confidentiality and should capture the value of any unique quality (for example where one potential buyer has a great interest) – but some buyers may be reluctant to bid 'blind'.

The difficulty of obtaining knowledge necessitates payments for professional advice and, together with legal fees and stamp duty, this adds to costs of property transactions and to the time taken to complete them. Estate agents often get a bad press – even being accused of obtaining more money for their own properties than for their clients in *Freakonomics*. The internet may change the information position of course: the vast majority of house buyers use the web for research. Anyone selling a home can get online and gather their own information about sales from sites such as landregistry.gov.uk, rightmove.co.uk, houseprices.net and mouseprice.com. The information has been set loose (Levitt and Dubner, 2005).

The economic problem: limited resources but unlimited wants

In comparison with all of the things we want, our means of satisfying those wants are quite inadequate. Just think of all the things you would buy if your income was larger – new clothes, a better car, exotic holiday and so on. On a global scale, if everyone on earth was to live at the same standard of living as people in the USA, three planets would be needed!

This is 'the economic problem' – unlimited wants and very limited resources. The difficulty can never be completely overcome. But what we can do is to make the most of what we have – in other words to *economize*. Each household has to make the most of its limited resources and the word 'economics' is derived from the Greek word meaning the management of a household. The person doing the weekly household shopping has to make decisions as to what to buy in order to obtain the maximum satisfaction for the family. Certain goods – those regarded as necessities, such as bread, tea, milk and fuel – are purchased in regular quantities almost by habit; but spending would vary on them if their prices changed significantly. Many goods compete for the money in the household budget; beef or chicken for Sunday lunch, peas or broccoli? New potatoes are cheaper this week, so more will be bought.

Everyone has to economize. Students have to make sure their funds last the term. Businessmen have to decide on quantities of raw materials and labour to buy; or whether to hire transport or buy a lorry. Even Bill Gates must decide how to allocate his time!

Let us assume that a property developer has alternative possibilities on a plot of land

Detached houses	Apartment blocks
40	0
30	10
10	30
0	40

The developer's production possibilities can be shown in a production-possibility curve, as shown in Figure 1.1.

The straight line production possibilities curve (*PPC*) in Figure 1.1 represents the trade off between detached houses and apartment blocks facing this developer. She cannot build 40 of each because she does not have the resources and so that combination lies outside the PPC and is unattainable. Of course, the actual combination decided upon will be influenced by demand for detached houses and apartments in the market and almost certainly by planning conditions.

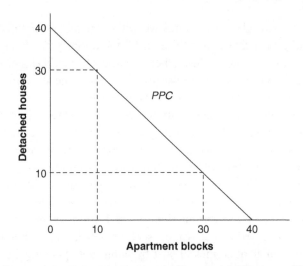

Figure 1.1   A straight-line production-possibility curve (PPC)

Governments also have to decide how their resources or funds are allocated. More on defence might mean less for the health service. Less on roads might mean more can be spent on the health service, but might lead to more road traffic accidents. Better schools, roads and hospitals may be needed but all are competing for the limited revenue that can be raised from taxation. Extra houses, new roads and conservation or wildlife areas – all are claiming a share of the limited land available. In all these instances and many more, the government has the task of making the most of national resources.

We can illustrate the economic problem as follows. Suppose that country X produces only agricultural produce and manufactured goods and that it can, with all its resources fully employed, produce, during a year, the following alternative combinations (in unspecified units):

Agricultural produce goods	Manufactured goods
100	0
80	25
60	40
40	45
20	48
0	50

By plotting these alternative combinations we obtain another production-possibility curve (Figure 1.2) This shows the various combinations of agricultural produce and manufactured goods attainable by country X with its limited resources and given technology.

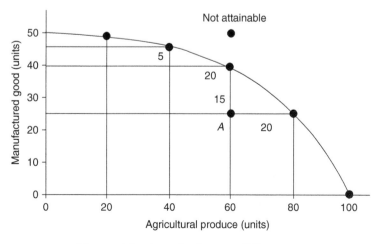

Figure 1.2 A production-possibility curve

The figure shows that, with its limited resources, country X can produce either 100 agricultural produce or 50 manufactured goods, or a combination of both. Any larger output is outside the curve and unattainable.

Nevertheless, as resources are transferred to manufacturing from agriculture, an ever increasing quantity of manufactured goods has to be given up to obtain an extra 20 units of agricultural produce. For instance, when 40 agricultural units are produced, the opportunity cost of an extra 20 is only 5 manufactured goods, whereas when production is 60 agricultural units the opportunity cost of a further 20 is 15 manufactured goods.

The reason is that resources are not equally suited to producing agricultural produce and manufactured goods. For instance, factory workers would need training in farm work, while land, tractors and so on, would have to be worked more intensively. The result is that this production-possibility curve is concave to the origin and the slope gets steeper as one moves along it from left to right.

Scarcity forces us to economize. We weigh up the various alternatives and select that particular assortment of goods which yields the highest return from our limited resources. Modern economists use this idea to define the scope of their studies. But since there is no one definition which is completely satisfactory, ours will be kept as simple as possible: *Economics is the study of how people allocate their limited resources to provide for their wants.* Economics is a social science. This follows from the fact that economics studies how people act. As we shall see, this puts it at a disadvantage compared with the physical sciences which examine various aspects of man's environment. Economics is closely concerned with the findings of other sciences. Because economics studies human behaviour, it must, in reaching conclusions, refer to other branches of study, particularly psychology, sociology and politics. The alternative, advocated by some economists, of restricting economics to pure scientific analysis, curtails its usefulness.

Economics selects a particular aspect of human behaviour. But, although economics is closely connected with such social sciences, it is distinguished from them by its concentration on one particular aspect of human behaviour – choosing between alternatives in order to obtain the maximum satisfaction from limited resources. This narrower approach is an improvement on Professor Alfred Marshall's definition – 'a study of mankind in the ordinary business of life' (Marshall, 1890) – because this, as it stands, would embrace all forms of human activity.

In effect, the economist limits the study by selecting four fundamental characteristics of human existence and investigating what happens when they are all found together, as they usually are. First, the ends of human beings are without limit. Second, those ends are of varying importance. Third, the means available for achieving those ends – human time and energy and material resources – are limited. Fourth, the means can be used in many different ways: that is, they can produce many different goods.

But no one characteristic by itself is necessarily of interest to the economist. If, for instance, you have two wants and you cannot choose between them, you are between a rock and a hard place, and you will never get as far as the problem of allocating resources between them. Similarly, 'free' goods are of no interest to the economist since resources do not have to be allocated to obtain them although sometimes a free good such as air can become an economic good because of pollution – in Tokyo, vending machines sell clean oxygen at street corners. Nor is the mere scarcity of means necessarily of significance. Where resources can be used only in one way, for example, lichen-bearing volcanic land in Iceland for rearing sheep, they do not, although scarce, have to be 'economized'. Using such land for sheep does not mean that the owner has less of other things. Its use, therefore, does not give rise to any problems and the economist is interested only in the relatively minor point of determining the earnings of such land. Only when all four characteristics are found together does an economic problem arise.

The market economy

Economies are based on specialization and division of labour in order to increase production. This necessitates the exchange of goods and services in markets using money to facilitate the exchange. A multitude of markets coordinate millions of individual decentralized economic decisions. The term 'market economy' means a system where buyers and sellers are solely responsible for the choices they make. A free market gives absolute power to prices to determine the allocation and distribution of goods and services. These prices are determined by the forces of supply and demand for commodities. Where demand falls short of the supply of a commodity, the price will fall and when the supply is inadequate to meet the demand for a good or service, prices will rise. A fully free market economy is also characterized by free trade without any 'tariffs' or 'subsidies' imposed by the government. The role of government in a free market economy is limited to controlling law and order and to providing certain 'public goods', such as national defence, that would not otherwise be provided (see Chapters 20 and 21). A feature of the free market economy is that only people with sufficient income and wealth have the ability to purchase goods and services. People with low incomes may be unable to purchase basic needs such as food and shelter and great inequality in the distribution of resources may result.

A market or 'free market' economy uses signals from prices to guide decisions on resource allocation to produce goods and services. This is something of a miracle in a modern complex economy – when you go to the supermarket on Friday evening in the hope of buying a corkscrew, to your amazement there is one there! And at a price you are willing to pay. How did the supermarket know? Adam Smith, a great Scottish economist from the eighteenth century described the ability of the market to deliver goods and services where they are demanded and in the right quantities as an 'invisible hand' that guides the economy. If each consumer is allowed to choose freely what to buy and each producer is allowed to choose freely what to sell (and how to produce it), the market will settle on product distribution and prices that are beneficial to all. This is because self-interest will lead consumers and producers to engage in behaviour that benefits the community. Efficient methods of production will be adopted in order to maximize profits. Low prices will be charged in order to undercut competitors. Investors will invest in those industries that are most likely to maximize returns, and withdraw capital from those that are less efficient in creating value. Workers will train for the most rewarding careers. All of these effects will take place dynamically and automatically. So, in a market economy:

- Individuals act in their own self-interest;
- Prices act as signals to guide decisions of producers and consumers (see Figure 1.3);
- Incomes are earned by selling services, or by selling goods produced, or by selling the services of property owned.

There is no direction of labour; people are free to work wherever they choose.

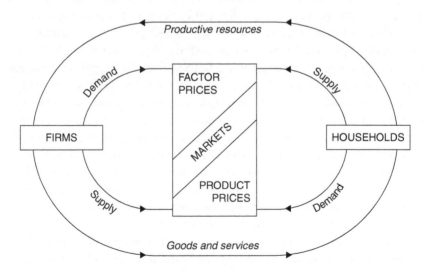

Figure 1.3   The allocation of goods and services through the market economy

The command economy

Another system of resource allocation is central planning in a 'command economy' (sometimes called a 'planned economy'), in which resources are allocated by government in a way that Karl Marx believed would lead to a more equal and fairer distribution of resources. In centrally planned economies, however, without competition and prices to guide decisions, many problems occurred and shortages of many goods arose because the estimates of the planners were poor. In the former Soviet Union (command economies tended to be communist) there were often shortages of basic necessities and surpluses of goods that few people wanted. And because the state guaranteed employment, there was little incentive to work hard with the result there was 'hidden unemployment' (someone employed but with very little work to do). The quality of goods produced was often very poor because production quotas were for quantity produced rather than quality. Even the environment was harshly treated in command economies – perhaps in pursuit of output targets at any cost.

The mixed economy

In reality, all economies have some mixture of central control and market determination, although in some relatively undeveloped societies behaviour may be determined by custom and tradition. The proportion of free market behaviour (private sector) relative to central control (public sector) varies from one economy to another and can change over time in any economy. The USA has more market determination than many other world economies and certainly less central control than China, where free markets have only recently begun to make inroads into the economy. The UK has a mixed economy where the government takes an active part in overcoming the defects of the market economy. The private sector comprises those firms that are privately owned and is responsible for approximately three-quarters of national production. The government creates laws of ownership and contract and provides law and order through the courts to enforce these laws.

In areas where the free market does not work very well, such as in protecting people from hardship caused by poverty, the government intervenes to correct 'market failure'. Provision of certain 'public goods' such as national defence and a police force must also be provided by government because the private sector could not provide them adequately. Another market failure occurs where firms impose costs on others by their economic activity. This is known as an externality and an example would be air pollution from a chemical company. People are affected as an external effect (outside of the market) of private production.

The public sector, comprising government departments and agencies, local authorities and 'quangos' (quasi autonomous national government organizations) is significant and its share of GDP varies with the nature of the political party in power. It is common for governments to intervene in economies in order to influence macroeconomic objectives such as the level of prices or employment or economic growth. In particular the government is concerned with the inherent instability of the market economy and its cyclical booms and recessions, which it is arguably easier for the government to influence if the size of the public sector (which it directly controls) is large. For all these reasons all modern economies are mixed economies although the extent of government involvement varies greatly.

Positive and normative economics

Consider how the particulars of different estate agents describe the same room: the first, 'the living room is 4.5 metres by 3.5 metres', the second, 'the living room is deceptively spacious'. One can be verified by measuring; the other is a matter for the eye of the beholder. This leads us to the distinction between positive and normative economics. Positive economics limits itself to statements that can be verified by reference to the facts. Thus, the observation that: 'the UK's real national income in 2009 was larger than in 2004', is a positive statement. In other words, positive economics holds that any hypothesis formulated should be testable against empirical evidence.

Normative economics, on the other hand, appreciates that in practice many economic decisions involve subjective judgements; that is, they cannot be made solely by an objective appraisal of the facts but depend to some extent on personal views in interpreting facts. Thus the statement that 'the UK's national income in 2010 should have been larger than it was' is a normative statement. As soon as we introduce the words 'should' or 'ought' we are making subjective valuations, or normative statements. Because in practice the distinction between positive economics and normative economics is often blurred, opinion is divided about the exact scope of economics, and so it is instructive to examine their nature in more detail.

Positive economics

Positive economics considers that economics can claim to be a science only if it is strictly scientific in its approach, eschewing normative judgements and adopting scientific methods.

First, it does not attempt to set out criteria for determining what is good or bad, what ought or what ought not to be – any more than physics attempts to say that liquids are 'better' than solids. It is concerned only with positive statements and with the consequences of certain actions. That is why, for instance, the economist must accept ends as given, expressing no opinion as to whether those ends are 'good' or 'bad'. On the other hand, he must point out that individual ends have economic implications for society as a whole. A man, for instance, may decide that he wants to get drunk every day. Here the economist must point out the full cost of this end – the cost to the man of getting drunk, plus the cost to society if he eventually becomes a charge on the National Health Service as an alcoholic. Nor is the economist concerned directly about the physical aspects of the limited means – the mechanical principles of the plough, the chemical properties of the soil or the biological characteristics of the seed. Both ends and resources are accepted as given. The subject of study is how people mobilize these resources to achieve their ends and how efficient are the methods which they choose.

Second, economics science has a particular object in view – the establishment of principles, propositions, theories or generalizations stating the relationship of one thing to another. In this it goes beyond descriptive economics, which concentrates on a mere description of an economy – its institutions (such as, firms, banks, government organizations), its population, its system of taxation and so on. But studies ended there could hardly be termed 'scientific'. While descriptive economics is desirable, indeed necessary, it merely describes the mechanism. What we really want to know is how the mechanism operates.

That is the task of analytical economics, which sets out to establish general principles about the way in which an economic system works. In discovering these principles, economics makes use of the methods of other sciences. These methods are induction and deduction.

In the inductive approach, the economist observes facts, classifies those facts and then tries to observe any causal relationship between them. For instance, he may discover that the price of eggs falls in the spring. This would be connected with the increase in the supply of eggs at that time of the year, and from this a generalization can be established that an increase in supply, other things being equal, leads to a fall in price. The weakness of the inductive approach is that the scientist can never be sure that the principles established are one hundred per cent foolproof. Hence, whenever possible, he will try to substantiate by deduction what has been discovered by induction.

With deduction, the economist starts from hypothetical assumptions (frequently referred to as postulates). Then, by a process of logical reasoning, he derives propositions from these assumptions. This is often termed 'model-building'. The sequence is as follows:

1. The economic phenomenon to be explained is selected. Certainly, if the analysis is to be useful, the problem must be of practical significance.
2. The initial assumptions are made. These should be as close to reality as possible. But, although he is concerned with human behaviour, realistic assumptions are not impossible. In the main he is interested in market,

not individual, reactions. Dealing in large numbers means that patterns of behaviour emerge. Of course, the economist has to simplify initially, confining himself to broad assumptions from which he can obtain only broad generalizations.

Later, the assumptions can be changed according to particular circumstances, and the conclusions modified accordingly.

3. Logical reasoning establishes what follows from the assumptions. Let us take a simple example. The economist wishes to discover what price will prevail in a market. He makes three assumptions:
   - there is a high degree of competition, on the basis of price, among buyers and among sellers, and between buyers and sellers;
   - more will be demanded the lower the price;
   - more will be supplied the higher the price.

   Demand and supply thus move in opposite directions for a given change in price. The conclusion the economist comes to is that the price of the good will settle where the amount supplied equals the amount demanded. Any other price will not be a settled price. If it is above, there will be more offered for sale than is demanded. Stocks will pile up, and some suppliers will lower their prices. As the price falls, so more will be demanded, and this will go on until demand equals supply. Similarly, when the price is below that where demand equals supply, shortages lead buyers to offer higher prices. As the price rises, so more will be supplied, and this goes on until demand equals supply (see Chapter 2). He has thus built up a model showing how price is determined in a market – a very useful piece of economic theory.

   By modifying the assumptions, the economist can make the model closer to real life or show how changes in the economic system work. For instance, suppose that, as a result of an advertising campaign people's tastes change so that they want more of the good at the market price than formerly. At the original price, demand now exceeds supply. As before, this will cause the price to rise and supply to expand until a new price is arrived at where once more demand and supply are equal.

4. As far as possible, propositions derived by deduction are tested by observed data. Often, however, such tests will prove impracticable, if not impossible, to undertake. For instance, the economist may be predicting outcomes which have no past parallels; he has therefore to await events before he can test the validity of his propositions.

   If the principles established are not disproved by such testing, they can be used to predict what will happen in particular instances, for they show how the different parts of a system are related to one another. It should be noted, however, that such forecasts are not unconditional statements of what will occur. The nature of an economic proposition is simply of the form 'if this occurs, then such and such will result'. For example, if demand increases then, other things being equal, price will rise (see Chapter 2). When we apply general principles to particular cases, we are in the realm of what is often called applied economics.

It is this power to predict which enables firms and governments to plan with some degree of accuracy. The theory of price, for instance, would enable a building firm to make a useful forecast of the effect of an increase in the demand for houses on bricklayers' wages. Or, if there were widespread unemployment in the economy, a knowledge of the principles determining the level of activity could suggest appropriate measures which the government might take to reduce it.

Normative economics

Normative economics, or 'political economy' as economics was originally called, accepts the analytical methods of positive economics in formulating theories. But it considers that the rigid scientific stance adopted is defective in two main ways.

First, it holds that it is virtually impossible to avoid value judgements. For instance, since facts have to be used to test hypotheses, the selection of those facts depends on the judgement of the economist who may unconsciously let his individual bias creep in. Again, in holding that the preferences and ends of individuals in a society are the ones that count, it overlooks that the state may have different ends. Thus the state may ban certain drugs because their abuse can result in ill-health and crime, incurring costs to society, but which drugs are banned involves a value judgement by the state. Finally, in evaluating growth over a period, the economist holds that 'more is better'. However, this view is based only on a consensus opinion, and is thus a value judgement. In any case, even though there may have been an increase in income per head of the population over time, we have no objective measure of welfare to assess whether people are obtaining more satisfaction.

Second, and more fundamental, economics is rather sterile if not applied to policy objectives. Positive economics, by restricting itself simply to predicting all the relevant consequences of alternative policies, ends up by 'sitting on the fence'. In contrast, the earlier economists have pursued their studies chiefly because of the social benefits which can result. 'The compelling motive that leads men to economic study is seldom a mere academic or scientific interest in the movements of the great wheel of wealth. It is rather the sense that, in the world of business and of labour, justice stands with biased scales; that the lives of the many are darker than they need be. In these things lies the impulse to economic investigations.' (Pigou, 1913).

Thus the normative economist, while still seeking to solve problems as scientifically as possible by following the techniques of the positive economist, applies the results to suggest the course of action which appears to be economically more efficient than the others. In doing so, he enters the region of value judgements.

It also means that, because economics studies human behaviour, the economist's judgement is enhanced by taking into account the findings of other social sciences. For instance, most people would consider that the economist should have something to say on the question, 'Should income tax be made more progressive?' But the reply would have to be along the following lines: 'The tax yield would almost certainly increase; but higher-income groups might not work so hard'. While I can suggest theoretical reasons for this, you should also consider what the psychologist has to say. Furthermore, the pattern of consumption may change as the rich have less income to spend. For possible social effects, consult the sociologist. Finally, it will also help in making incomes more equal. That concerns me in that it may increase the proportion of total income spent – but ethics and politics have most weight in deciding whether greater equality of incomes is desirable.'

Microeconomics and macroeconomics

Microeconomics

A study of the price system is largely concerned with:

1. how the supply of a particular good or service is related to the demand for it;
2. how the demand for a particular factor of production is related to its supply.

As we shall see, this relationship of demand to supply is based upon prices established in the different product and factor markets (see Chapter 2). Since it is largely a study of the decisions of individual consumers and of individual firms in particular markets – small parts of the economy – it is usually referred to as microeconomics (from the Greek word *mikros* meaning 'small'). Thus if we ask ourselves what forces determine the price of tomatoes, the rent of a house in London, or the wage of a Birmingham bus driver, we are dealing with microeconomic questions.

Macroeconomics

However, in addition to studying how resources are allocated to different uses, we have to consider the level at which resources as a whole are being employed; that is, the overall level of activity. This gives rise to a series of 'general' questions. How can the total of consumers' demand in the economy change? How do firms in total respond to such a change in demand? What brings about changes in the general level of prices? We are now looking at variables in the aggregate – the aggregate flow of income, aggregate investment, aggregate wages, and so on. Such questions are the concern of macroeconomics (from the Greek word *makros* meaning 'large').

Sustainable development

Resource allocation decisions may seem very complex in the current time period, but imagine the difficulty of allocating resources efficiently over time. The problem of 'inter-temporal' resource allocation has been considered by environmentalists who feel that the present generation should take into account the well-being of future generations in their decision making. The principle of 'inter-generational equity' has become a cornerstone of the principle of 'sustainable development' which can be defined as 'development that meets the needs of the present generation without compromising the ability of future generations to meet their needs'. Questions then arise such as: should we use all North Sea oil reserves now or leave some for people in the future? And if the present generation increases carbon-dioxide emissions by burning fossil fuels in pursuit of economic growth, will this mean catastrophic consequences for future generations through global warming?

There are differing views as to how to allocate resources efficiently and fairly over time. The free market view argues that self-interest will ensure sustainability because, as resources become scarce, their price will rise encouraging conservation and development of substitutes. The social-efficiency view is that social costs and benefits should be considered in decision making and not just the private interests of consumers and producers. In this approach, greater importance can be given to future generations and sustainability. The conservationist view suggests that the economic system should not pursue greater consumption and economic growth because it will lead to environmental degradation. The Gaia approach is the strongest advocate of sustainability. This argues that humans should look after the planet's resources and ensure that the land they leave for their descendants (and other species) is in at least as good condition as they found it.

Box 1.2   The term 'sustainable development'

The most commonly used definition of sustainable development (from the Brundtland Commission at the United Nations in 1983) is

> development that 'meets the needs of the present without compromising the ability of future generations to meet their own needs' (WCED, 1987).

The term has been criticized because it is vague, and different versions have arisen as a result – weak sustainability, strong sustainability and deep ecology. Broadly the concept encourages the current generation to manage natural, man-made and social capital for the welfare of their own and future generations and so as to leave the world in no worse condition than they inherited.

The limitations of economics

Economists face two major difficulties:

Economists cannot experiment

The task of a science is to formulate laws describing what will happen when there is a change in a given set of circumstances. The physicist and chemist can conduct their investigations by experimenting under controlled conditions in a laboratory. But because economists are dealing with human behaviour rather than with physical properties, their laboratory is effectively the real world.

It is impossible to isolate a group of consumers or business people in a test-tube to see how they would react to a given change. The most the economist can usually do as regards consumers' behaviour, for instance, is to take a sample survey which will suggest how groups as a whole will behave. The economy is subject to continuous change, and so conditions cannot be held constant while the effect of one particular measure is observed. Because the economy is so complex, no body of economists could follow through all the results of any given change and any measurements are usually approximate. Because of these difficulties, economists can only be approximate in their investigations in real life. Nevertheless, the information available is increasing and becoming more precise, through, for example, market research and government statistical enquiries. Thus economists' predictions are likely to gain in accuracy.

Economists cannot directly measure welfare

Since satisfaction, like love or pain, is personal to the individual, there is no absolute scale for measuring welfare. So the economist, using the best approximation, works on the principle that, because two loaves are better than one, an increase in goods represents an increase in welfare. Even so, he cannot measure

---

Box 1.3   A classroom economics experiment

Although economists cannot experiment on a large scale, small experiments in microeconomics are possible. Here is one example:

The instructor should bring an ice-cold can of lemonade to class on a warm day and ask how many students are prepared to pay 10 pence for it; how many 20 pence; how many 30 pence and so on.

Draw up a table of results (price and quantity demanded) and then a graph which will be a demand curve.

Then assume the day is much hotter and repeat the experiment. The demand curve should shift to the right showing increased demand because tastes have changed.

all goods. If he gives a value to the vegetables grown in gardens or to do-it-yourself repairs to cars, should he not logically include also something for housewives' cleaning and cooking services? Because it is impossible to know where to draw the line, the economist simplifies matters by confining attention to those goods which are exchanged against money. Since all these have a 'price' it is possible to make use of exact measurement and total dissimilar goods in terms of the common standard. Nevertheless, the economist must be careful to include any costs or benefits which are not allowed for by an individual in making a decision. Or, if the project is so large that it is likely to have external effects elsewhere, for example a proposed new airport or motorway, a cost-benefit analysis may have to be used to cover these full effects (see Chapter 11).

Summary

Economic systems must determine what to produce and the most efficient way to produce it. Market economies rely on the price system to allocate resources, and it usually does this very efficiently, although there are instances of market failure to deal with:

- community goods (or public goods);
- imperfect competition;
- imperfect knowledge;
- externalities;
- instability.

In command or planned economies the state estimates resource requirements and allocates resources accordingly. Estimating wants is very difficult, however, and mistakes are frequent. There are also problems of reduced incentives and authoritarian control in such economies.

Chapter 1: review questions

1. Why do property professionals exist?
2. What are the main aims of any economic system?
3. What are the advantages and problems of market economies?
4. What are the advantages and problems of command (or planned) economies?
5. Why are most of the world's economies mixed economies?
6. What is meant by sustainable development?

2

Economic Efficiency

After studying this chapter you will be able to:

- explain the concept of Pareto optimality;
- define and illustrate economic efficiency;
- show how the price system can bring about economic efficiency;
- assess the efficiency of real estate markets.

Welfare and economic efficiency

This chapter uses indifferent curves or isoquants to investigate the concept of economic efficiency. Those new to economics may find these concepts a little difficult but it is worth persevering in order to grasp fully the different meanings of the word efficiency and then to apply the concept to the real estate market as we do in Chapter 3.

Maximizing welfare

We can start with the proposition that society's aim is to maximize its welfare. Two factors which will influence welfare are: (a) the way society uses its limited resources; and (b) the distribution of income between members of society.

The first is the subject matter of positive economics; it is possible to analyse it scientifically. Economic efficiency is achieved when society has secured the best allocation of its limited resources, in the sense that the maximum possible satisfaction is obtained.

The second, the distribution of income, does not lend itself to scientific analysis. The reason is that satisfaction, like love and pain, is personal to the individual and cannot be measured on any objective scale. Taking a small amount of income from the rich man and giving it to a poor man may increase welfare, since the former's loss may be little compared with the latter's gain. But we can never be sure: since we cannot measure welfare cardinally (on a measurable scale), interpersonal comparisons are impossible. Thus, while distributional efficiency is necessary to maximize welfare, it cannot be dealt with scientifically, and decisions on income redistribution ultimately rest with the politician.

This book is concerned with economic efficiency, with particular reference to the allocation of land resources. This does not mean that we shall ignore the redistribution of income. Politicians carry out such redistribution in the field of real property, both directly through taxation, for example, income tax and inheritance tax, and indirectly by intervening in the free operation of the price system, for example, by rent control and subsidies to social housing. What the economist has to point out is how such redistributive measures may impinge on the efficient allocation of resources. The politician can then weigh the balance of advantage.

Pareto optimality

In discussing economic efficiency, therefore, the economist side-steps the distributional problem which may result from a reallocation of resources. He does this by adopting the narrow Pareto-optimality condition: *welfare is maximized when no one can be made better off without somebody else being made worse off.* Thus any improvement in economic efficiency which involves nobody losing will represent an increase in welfare. Efficiency in the use of resources is often called Pareto optimality or Pareto efficiency in honour of the Italian economist Vilfredo Pareto (1848–1923) who first introduced this concept.

For instance, in Figure 2.1 we start from the initial income position X, with A's income equal to OA and B's equal to OB. A movement to Y would represent an increase in welfare for both A and B; a movement to Z would increase B's welfare without reducing A's. Both Y and Z therefore represent Pareto improvements. It is impossible, however, to say whether position R represents an overall gain or loss, since A's income has increased but B's has fallen.

Conditions necessary for Pareto optimality

The weakness of the strict Pareto-optimality condition is that its application is restricted to only those cases where there are gainers but no losers resulting from the reallocation of resources. Even so, it does enable us to specify three conditions which must be fulfilled simultaneously for the efficient allocation of resources. First, no improvement can be achieved by an exchange of goods between persons, that is, there is *exchange efficiency.* Second, no increase in output can be obtained by producers substituting one factor for another, that

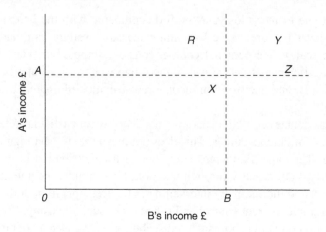

Figure 2.1   Pareto and non-Pareto improvements

is, there is *factor-combination efficiency*. Third, from the maximum overall output of goods which can be obtained from society's limited resources, that assortment is produced which gives society the greatest possible satisfaction, that is, there is *economic efficiency*. We shall examine each in turn.

We can simplify this analysis by assuming: a) resources consist of a limited quantity of land and capital; b) two goods are produced, food and manufactured goods.

Exchange efficiency

Figure 2.2 (a) and (b) represent the 'indifference maps' of consumers A and B respectively. Each indifference curve shows combinations of food and manufactured goods which yield equivalent satisfaction, and the further the indifference curve is from the origin, the greater the satisfaction obtained, as shown by the unspecified units, *10*, *15* and so on. Note that the indifference curve is convex to the origin. This denotes a diminishing marginal rate of substitution, an increasing amount of one good having to be given up in order to obtain an additional unit of another. It assumes that there is no 'conspicuous consumption' when people buy goods simply to impress others.

We can depict the preferences of A and B in an 'Edgeworth box' (see Figure 2.3). B's indifference map is rotated 180°, so that the origin is O_B. The length of the vertical side of the box denotes the maximum food available to be exchanged, and the horizontal side the maximum amount of manufactured goods.

Suppose A and B commence with an initial distribution at K, where A has $O_A f$ food and $O_A m$ manufactured goods, and B has $O_B f$ food and $O_B m$ manufactured goods. K is not a Pareto-optimal situation. A could move along his indifference

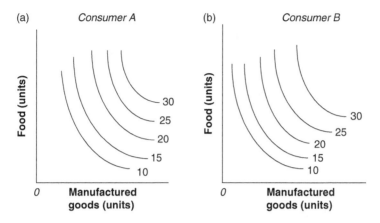

Figure 2.2 Indifference maps of consumers A and B

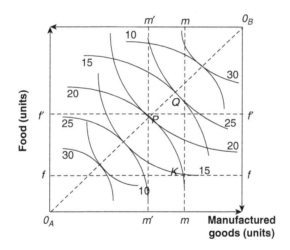

Figure 2.3 Efficiency in exchange

curve substituting food for manufactured goods until he reached the point *P*, where, being on the same indifference curve *20*, he would feel no worse off. On the other hand, this exchange increases *B*'s satisfaction, putting him on a higher indifference curve *20* (from *15*) where he has $O_B f'$ food and $O_B m'$ manufactured goods.

Had *A* been the more skilful bargainer, position *Q* could have been reached, and here *A* would have been on curve *25* without *B* being worse off. In practice, they are likely to end up somewhere between *P* and *Q*. What is important to note, however, is that a Pareto-optimal position will be achieved only when the marginal rate of substitution between any two goods is the same for each consumer, as at *P* and *Q* where their indifference curves are tangential. Indeed, it is possible to find such a point for all combinations of food and manufactured goods. A line joining these points is known as a 'contract curve' (the dotted line between O_A and O_B), and Pareto optimality will only hold provided that the division of available goods between consumers is on this curve.

Factor-combination efficiency

We can use the same technique to specify an efficiency condition for combining factors of production. In Figure 2.4 (a) and (b) we have isoquants showing how two factors, land and capital, can be combined to produce given quantities of food and manufactured goods respectively. Note that the isoquants are convex to the origin. This denotes a diminishing marginal rate of *technical* substitution between factors, an increasing amount of one factor being needed to compensate for the loss of a unit of the other factor if the same quantity of output is to be produced.

Again, these isoquant maps can be combined in an Edgeworth box by rotating the manufactured-goods origin through 180° (see Figure 2.5). The length of the vertical side represents the amount of capital available, and the horizontal side the maximum amount of land.

Assume initially that production is at N, with $O_F l$ land and $O_F k$ capital used to produce 25 units of food, and $O_M l'$ land and $O_M k'$ capital used to produce 20 units of manufactured goods. N is not an efficient situation. By transferring land from food to manufactured-goods production and capital from manufactured goods to food production, we can move to C (with a net gain of 15 units of manufactured goods), or to D (with a net gain of 10 units of food), or to an in-between position (showing some net gain of both manufactured goods and food).

Thus a Pareto-optimal position will be achieved only when the marginal rate of technical substitution between factors is the same in each use and for all producers. As before, we can obtain a contract curve (the dashed line AE in Figure 2.5) joining all points for all combinations of land and capital where this condition holds. Pareto optimality requires that, according to the assortment of goods required, factors must be combined on the appropriate point on the contract curve, otherwise society can be better off by a reshuffling of resources.

Economic efficiency

From Figure 2.5 we can derive the various combinations of food and manufactured goods which it is possible to obtain from the limited supply of land and capital. These outputs are achieved only if land and capital are combined efficiently: that is, each combination of land and capital must be found on the contract curve.

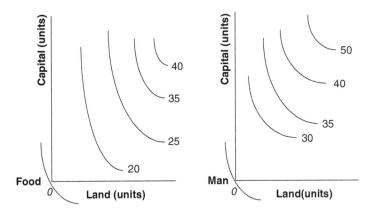

Figure 2.4 Combinations of land and capital to produce food and manufactured goods

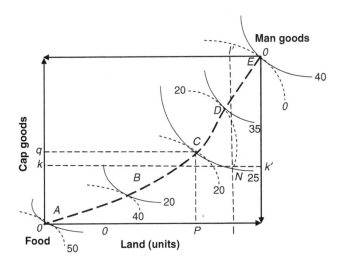

Figure 2.5 Efficiency in factor combination

For the various points A to E on the contract curve, we obtain the following outputs:

	Food (units)	Manufactured goods (units)
A	0	50
B	20	40
C	25	35
D	35	20
E	40	0

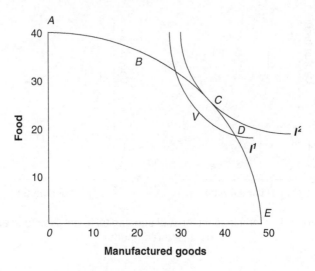

Figure 2.6   The production-possibility curve and society's preferences

Figure 2.6 graphs these outputs, smoothing them in the curve *AE*. This represents a production-possibility or transformation curve for this society. Any point within the production-possibility curve, for example *V*, is not a Pareto optimum because it is *technically* inefficient, as more of both goods can be obtained with the limited land and capital resources.

But while *technical efficiency* is a necessary condition for Pareto optimality, it is not sufficient. *Economic efficiency* requires that the actual product-mix is the one which gives society maximum satisfaction. We therefore have to relate the production-possibility curve to society's preferences.

Ignoring the conceptual difficulties involved, let I^1 and I^2 represent two indifference curves of society. While a product-mix *D* is on the production-possibility curve, it does not maximize society's welfare, since by producing more food and less manufactured goods a higher indifference curve I^2 can be attained at *C*, where the indifference curve and production-possibility curve just touch. We therefore have a third condition of Pareto optimality: consumers' marginal rate of substitution between products shown by the indifference curve must equal the marginal rate of transformation between products shown by the production-possibility curve.

Achieving the conditions of economic efficiency

Alternative methods

In our model, society maximizes welfare when 25 units of food and 35 units of manufactured goods are produced. Thus in Figure 2.5 the optimum allocation of resources is achieved when O_{Fp} land and O_{Fq} capital are used to grow food, and the remainder produce manufactured goods.

Broadly speaking, there are two methods by which the above resource allocation can be carried out: government direction and the price system. While the former can overcome certain defects in the price system, for example the external effects (social benefits and social costs of private decisions could be 'internalized', see Chapters 11 and 12), it faces formidable difficulties. Not only does it have to assess people's preferences, but it has the gigantic administrative task of allocating resources in the optimum proportions to produce the goods and services preferred.

In contrast, the price system assumes that the individual is the sole judge of his welfare and that, both as a consumer and as a producer, he acts through markets to maximize that welfare. Economic efficiency is achieved through Adam Smith's 'invisible hand'. As we shall see, however, this will only apply when many rigorous conditions prevail. Nevertheless, since, in Britain's mixed economy, most decisions are taken through the price system, we shall concentrate on this.

Pareto optimality through the price system

Exchange efficiency is achieved by the consumer relating his preferences to market prices in order to maximize satisfaction from his limited resources. In a perfect market a single price is established at which food and manufactured goods can be exchanged. In Figure 2.7 the distance of the line *FM* from the origin indicates the limit of consumer *A*'s resources, his budget line. The slope of this budget line reflects the relative prices of food and manufactured goods. Consumer *A* could spend all of his money on food and reach point *OF*, or all of his money on manufactured goods and reach point *OM*; or buy some combination of both goods on the budget line *FM*. Consumer *A* will maximize his

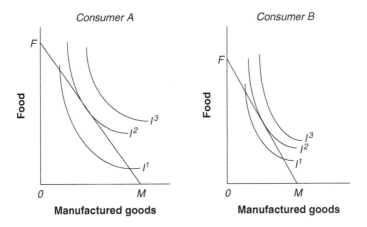

Figure 2.7 Consumer equilibrium

welfare when the budget price line touches the highest possible indifference curve. Here the marginal rate of substitution of food for manufactured goods is equal to their relative prices.

But since there is a single market price at which food exchanges for manufactured goods, and consumer *B* adopts the same course, it follows that the marginal rate of substitution of food for manufactured goods is the same for each consumer. Thus the condition for exchange efficiency is satisfied.

Put in Marshallian terms, (after Alfred Marshall, 1842–1924) the equilibrium condition in spending on goods occurs when, for all consumers:

$$\frac{Marginal\ utility\ of\ food}{Marginal\ utility\ of\ manufactured\ goods} = \frac{Price\ of\ food}{Price\ of\ manufactured\ goods} \qquad (2.1)$$

A similar argument can be applied to factor combinations – *technical efficiency*. Individual producers combine land and capital to obtain maximum output from a limited budget. Demand and supply in the factor market will establish a price at which land and capital are exchanged, the demand for each factor being dependent upon the price of the finished product. The food producer therefore employs those quantities of land and capital where the marginal rate of technical substitution equals their relative price. But since there is only one price at which land exchanges for capital, and since the manufactured-goods producer adopts the same profit-maximizing course, it follows that the marginal rate of technical substitution of land for capital is the same in the production of both food and manufactured goods. Thus the condition for factor-combination efficiency is achieved.

Put in Marshallian terms, the equilibrium condition in combining factors occurs when, in all uses and for all producers:

$$\frac{Marginal\ physical\ product\ of\ land}{Marginal\ physical\ product\ of\ manufactured\ goods} = \frac{Price\ of\ land}{Price\ of\ manufactured\ goods} \qquad (2.2)$$

How *economic efficiency* is achieved through the price system is more easily explained by translating the production-possibility curve into Marshallian terms.

As we have seen, there is a single price in the market at which food is exchanged against manufactured goods. The production-possibility curve shows, for any combination, the rate at which food can be transformed into manufactured goods. This transformation rate can be referred to as the *opportunity cost*, which, in perfect competition, is reflected in marginal costs (given no external costs). Thus the rate of transformation at any point on the production-possibility curve equals:

$$\frac{Marginal\ cost\ of\ food}{Marginal\ cost\ of\ manufactured\ goods} \qquad (2.3)$$

However, in perfect competition, a farmer growing food will produce that output where the price of food (P_f) equals the marginal cost of a unit of food (MC_f). Similarly, the output of manufactured goods will be where the price of manufactured goods (P_m) equals the marginal cost of a unit of manufactured goods (MC_f).

Since we are dealing with equalities, we can divide the first equation by the second, giving:

$$\frac{P_f}{P_m} = \frac{MC_f}{MC_m} \qquad (2.4)$$

That is, the relative price of food and manufactured goods is equal to the marginal rate of transformation between food and manufactured goods. But equilibrium for both consumers A and B is where the relative price of food and manufactured goods is equal to the marginal rate of substitution of manufactured goods for food. Thus the condition for economic efficiency is fulfilled.

In the simple Marshallian formulation, by combining (2.1) and (2.4), we have:

$$\frac{MU_f}{MU_m} = \frac{P_f}{P_m} = \frac{MC_f}{MC_m} \qquad (2.5)$$

Conditions necessary for economic efficiency through the price system

In the above outline of the working of the price system no assumptions were made. This was done deliberately in order not to interrupt the flow of the main argument. Our analysis, however, implicitly assumed that certain conditions held: particularly all the strict requirements of perfect competition; the absence of 'spillover' benefits and costs (often referred to as 'externalities'); and the ability of the market mechanism to supply all goods and services, provided that society is able and willing to pay the necessary costs. We shall examine each in turn.

Perfect competition

For market prices to reflect both consumers' satisfaction and producers' costs, certain conditions must exist:

A perfect market

There must be a perfect market, so that any price differences are quickly eliminated. Consumers and producers must seek to maximize utility and profits
respectively and, in doing so, be unhampered by legal and other constraints.

Perfect knowledge

There must be perfect knowledge, in that consumers are aware of any price differences which temporarily exist in the market, and entrepreneurs aware of any
super-normal profits being made by other firms, the costs of producing different outputs, production costs using different techniques and so on. Moreover,
there should be no costs of obtaining knowledge, no ostentatious buying and no
'brainwashing' advertising. Even such 'static' assumptions as these are impossible in real life. But the difficulties are magnified when allowance is made for
dynamic conditions – something outside the simple price-mechanism model.
Dynamic conditions, for instance, produce uncertainty about the size of future
demand, the nature of competitors' plans and changes in government policy.
Where market facts are deficient, personal assessments have to be made. Since
these are likely to be subject to degrees of inaccuracy, Adam Smith's 'invisible
hand' which automatically brings about the desired adjustments in the economy only acts in practice through a process of trial and error.

Only if the first and second conditions are fulfilled, will there be common
prices throughout the market for each product or factor of production.

P = MR = MC

Producers maximize profits by producing that output where marginal revenue
equals marginal cost ($MR = MC$). But this will only represent economic efficiency if marginal revenue equals price ($MR = P$), since production must proceed to the point where the satisfaction which the consumer derives from an
additional unit of the good equals the cost to society of producing that unit, that
is $P = MC$.

However, price will only equal marginal revenue under conditions of perfect
competition (see Figurec 2.8(a)). Here the producer is a 'price-taker', accepting
the market price as given. For this situation to occur there must be many producers each supplying so small a quantity to the market that no single producer can
influence the market price. Furthermore, there must be freedom of entry into
the industry. Similar conditions must apply in selling factors of production.

In contrast, where there is imperfect competition, marginal revenue is less
than price. Suppose that a monopoly exists with cost and revenue conditions, as
indicated in Figure 2.8(b). Basic theory of the firm suggests that it would produce an amount OM_1, at a price OP_1, whereas in a competitive market (in long-
run equilibrium) OM would have been produced at a price of OP. The latter
equates marginal cost with price which conforms to the wishes of consumers as
expressed through the price mechanism. Under monopoly, too little is produced
at a high price. The demand for factors of production in this particular activity

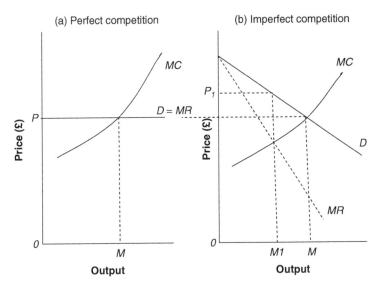

Figure 2.8   Equilibrium output under perfect competition and imperfect
competition

is lower than it would be in the absence of monopoly, and so there is a distortion
of factor prices – which has its repercussions on more competitive sectors of the
economy. Thus monopolistic forms of organization are suspected of exploiting
consumers, though a final decision can only be made after possible advantages,
for example, economies of scale, are taken into account.

Increasing costs

For perfect competition to exist, the *MC* curve must be rising to cut the horizontal demand curve from below (see Figure 2.8(a)). However, certain industries, chiefly those that have to produce on a large scale, have decreasing costs
(a falling *MC* curve) at the relevant part of the demand curve. This means that,
to obtain an equilibrium output, the *MR* curve would have to be downward-
sloping in order to cut the *MC* curve (Figure 2.9). Thus at the equilibrium output (*OM*), price (*OP*) is greater than marginal cost (*OC*) and so the conditions
of economic efficiency are not fulfilled.

Perfect mobility of the factors of production

The price system operates imperfectly if factors of production do not move in
response to changes in relative prices. Transport costs and housing costs, for
example, restrict mobility. Above all, any movement takes time, and this is
particularly so with land resources, since buildings have a long life.

   Immobility may also give rise to imperfect competition and super-normal
profits, for example, allowing the owner of a site vital for a proposed development to exercise monopoly powers.

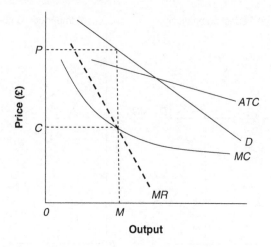

Figure 2.9   Equilibrium output under conditions of decreasing cost

Weaknesses of the price system

Externalities: spillover benefits and costs

In the market, private consumers and producers seek to maximize their own benefits and profits. However, this assumes that their decisions impose no indirect benefits or costs on others. In practice, this is often not so, especially in the use of land resources. For example, flowers in people's gardens give pleasure to passers-by or the design of a new house may destroy the architectural harmony of a whole street. In the decision-making process allowances should be made for such spillover benefits and costs.

Community goods and services

The pure price system implicitly assumes that all economic goods are capable of being priced in the market, but this is possible only if the enjoyment of a good or service can be confined to those people willing to pay for it. With some goods and services, such as defence, street-lighting, common land and National Trust open spaces, it is impossible or impractical to exclude non-payers, since anybody can be a 'free-rider'. Goods from which the community benefits, therefore, have to be provided collectively and financed, not by charging individuals as they use them, but by subscription (for example, the Royal Society for the Protection of Birds), by advertising and sponsorship (for example, commercial television) or, more usually, by taxation (for example, defence, street-lighting, common land). Indeed, as we shall see in Chapter 21, a Pareto improvement may be effected by providing collectively, rather than privately, goods where exclusion *is* possible.

Box 2.1 Are home ownership subsidies Pareto optimal?

Owner-occupied housing has sometimes been deemed a merit good or even a public good. Herbert Hoover's affirmation of the need for encouragement of home ownership 'at all times' came in 1932 at the fiercest stage of the Great Depression. Others, such as Margaret Thatcher in the UK have argued that homeowners make better citizens and contribute to improved communities. Why people who rent their homes cannot offer the same contribution to the community is not made clear, but existing homeowners, homebuilders, mortgage lenders and local authorities have all seized on the idea that subsidizing home ownership is 'Pareto optimal'. It may not be, however.

Subsidies for home ownership – in the form of remission of mortgage interest, lower mortgage borrowing rates derived from government guarantees for mortgage lenders like Fannie Mae (The Federal National Mortgage Association FNMA) and Freddie Mac (The Federal Home Loan Mortgage Corporation FHLMC), in the USA, and exemption from capital gains tax on the homeowner's primary residence in the UK have long benefited those who own homes at the expense of those who do not. Moreover, the subsidies to home ownership contributed to the bubble in the housing market that burst so spectacularly in the credit crunch of 2007–8 arguably making everyone worse off no matter what their housing tenure.

There is certainly a case for saying that home ownership should not be considered deserving of government subsidies even without the bubble collapse for a simple reason: Those who receive the subsidy get to capture the benefits in the form of home prices that are higher than they would otherwise be without government support. Anyone renting who then wants to buy must pay a higher price. The subsidies make homeowners better off while they make renters worse off. They are, therefore, not Pareto optimal.

Resource allocation over time

The analysis of economic efficiency above is essentially a purely static theory. Economic decisions also span time, so that a choice has to be made between present and future benefits. For example, the decision to designate land as a National Park must involve consideration not only of the present community's preference, but also of the probable preferences of future generations. This involves accuracy in estimating such future benefits and costs, and is thus likely to conflict with our previous condition of perfect knowledge. Consideration of allocating resources over time, however, will be postponed to Chapter 11.

The distribution of income and unemployment

The price system only operates within the existing distribution of income. There are as many Pareto-optimal situations as there are possible distributions of income. But, as we have seen, redistribution of income is ultimately a political decision.

In addition, the price system cannot guarantee full employment, while decisions are influenced by inflation expectations. With the first, government action is demanded politically; with the second, miscalculation can distort resource allocation.

The allocation of real estate resources

The discussion above implies that the market economy is unlikely to be fully efficient in allocating resources. On the other hand, allocation by government decisions in a 'command economy' can present even greater problems. At least the market system does start with the advantage that economic decisions are based on prices which reflect, albeit somewhat imperfectly, consumers' preferences and relative costs.

This points to the compromise of a 'mixed economy'. This uses the price system as the basis for allocating resources, but, recognizing its defects, relies on the government to provide, as far as possible, the conditions necessary for its efficient functioning.

Allocation of real estate resources is still mainly through the price mechanism of a market economy. In the next chapter there is a discussion of the efficiency of this.

Summary

Society's welfare is influenced by economic efficiency and the distribution of income between members of the society. Economic efficiency is achieved when society has secured the best allocation of its limited resources. And economists adopt the very limited welfare criteria of Pareto optimality: welfare is maximized when no one person can be made better off without somebody else being made worse off. Pareto optimality requires

- exchange efficiency
- factor-combination or technical efficiency
- economic efficiency

The price system can achieve these types of efficiency if these conditions are met:

1. A perfect market
2. Perfect knowledge
3. Price = Marginal Revenue = Marginal Cost
4. Increasing costs
5. Perfect mobility of factors of production

So the free market and the price system can achieve economic efficiency if these conditions are met. There may be problems, however, with externalities, community goods and services, allocation of resources over time and the distribution of income. As a result, all economies are mixed economies, with allocation of most resources by the price mechanism, but with government intervention to try to correct the imperfections. Land and property resources are also allocated in this way.

Chapter 2: review questions

1. Illustrate with a diagram and with examples a Pareto improvement and a non-Pareto improvement.
2. Use a production-possibility curve to illustrate the concept of economic efficiency.
3. What are the conditions necessary to achieve economic efficiency through the price system?
4. What reasons are there for economic efficiency not to be achieved in the world of property?
5. What are externalities? Give examples from the property sector.

Part II
Land and Property in the Economy

3 Real Estate Markets

After studying this chapter you will be able to:

- Explain the term 'real estate';
- Define and illustrate property rights;
- Explain the unique features of real estate;
- Assess the efficiency of real estate markets;
- Describe the latest developments in real estate markets.

Why 'real estate'?

The term 'real estate' is a legal term in several countries, for example in the USA, the UK, Canada and Australia. It encompasses land and anything permanently affixed to it such as buildings. Real estate is property that is fixed in location and is sometimes called 'realty'. In law *real* means related to a thing (from the Latin *res* for thing), as opposed to a person. The essential difference is between immovable property (real estate) which could transfer title along with land; and movable property which a person could retain title to. The oldest use of the term would appear to be in about 1666 and it may be that the use of the phrase real estate was reinforced by the idea that all property belonged to the crown or was 'royal' or real in Spanish as in Real Madrid (again originally from the Latin word *rex* meaning king).

In Britain 'real property' refers to a particular type of good – land, or resources embodied in land. The point is that neither is physically movable. This characteristic distinguishes it from labour and capital and from other goods. Although land resources are not movable, property can be owned by some person or institution. And of course, exchanges take place. Thus the real property market is simply the arrangement by which buyers and sellers of virgin land, agricultural estates, industrial buildings, offices, shops and houses are brought together to determine a price at which the particular property can be exchanged. Sometimes the market is formal (for example, auctions advertised nationally), sometimes informal (for example, introductions by estate agents or deals between principals). Indeed, it is not possible to distinguish the means by which people are informed from 'the market'. Much real property is advertised in journals (such as the *Estates Gazette*) and newspapers, all of which can therefore be said to be part of the market. In other words, 'the real property market' is an abstract term aggregating all transactions in real property throughout the country. Even so, it is possible to distinguish sub-markets for different types of property, for example, prime shop properties and for different geographical areas, such as City of London office blocks or houses in a given locality. Each fulfils the basic functions of a market although sometimes perhaps imperfectly.

Real property rights

What the real property market actually deals in is 'property rights', often referred to as 'interests'. In this, however, it is no different from any other market. I may, for instance, go to a Ford dealer and purchase a car. In this case the car is handed over to me and I am given the exclusive right to drive it as long as I wish, and even to part with that right by selling it to somebody else. Alternatively, I could hire a car from Hertz. Here my right to drive the car would be restricted to a specified period and subject to conditions regarding damage, and so on. In the first case there is little formal definition of my right: the car is simply handed over to me upon payment for it. On the other hand, when I hire a car my restricted rights are more likely to be clearly defined in a written agreement which, by implication, also excludes Hertz from letting anybody else drive the car during the specified period.

Similarly with real property – here it is not possible to hand over land and buildings in the same way as would be the case with movable goods. It is much more obvious, therefore, that it is 'rights' which are dealt in, especially as, accompanying the transaction, there is a written statement defining the exact rights which are being transferred. In short, the real property market deals in the rights relating to real property rather than in the land and buildings themselves.

With real property, too, the separation of rights is more usual than with personal property. The largest collection of rights which a person can hold in real property is 'fee simple absolute': that is, the unencumbered freehold. But all the rights inherent in the ownership of 'fee simple absolute' can be separated and transferred individually to other people. Thus a lease may be granted to a person to erect a building on a plot of land and to enjoy the rights to this building and land for a 99-year period on payment of a specified yearly sum to the lessor. Provided the terms of the lease are fulfilled, the lessor's rights are, for 99 years, now restricted to the receipt of a freehold ground rent. The freehold has thus been divided into two interests: the leasehold and the freehold ground rent. In any given land resource different people may have many different rights – for example, a freehold ground rent, a head-lease, a sub-lease, a mortgage, a rent charge and so on.

It is worth noting that the exact rights transferred can be finely adjusted according to the individual preferences of the seller or buyer, for example, by a restrictive covenant. Such a fine differentiation to meet the individual preferences of sellers and buyers is achieved automatically through the free-market mechanism and is reflected in prices.

Four aspects of real property rights need emphasis. First, within his rights the 'fee simple absolute' owner can possess, use, abuse and even destroy his real property. He can sell rights in such a way as to restrict their future use (for example, by covenant), or he can bequeath them to distant heirs. Even so, his rights are limited: 1) he can only use his property subject to other people's property rights (for example, easements may exist giving other persons 'ancient rights', or the right to take drains or pipe water across his freehold interest); 2) he is subject to the legal restraints imposed by planning restrictions, building regulations and similar legislation.

Second, an interest comes into existence simply because a bundle of certain rights is wanted. But no rights would be wanted unless their owner could exclude others from them. What, for example, would you give for fishing rights in a country where poaching was no offence and suffered no penalty? Thus the concept of *rights* is essentially a legal one: it presupposes that there is a government authority that will, if necessary, protect the rights vested in the owner. Moreover, being a legal concept, a right must be clearly defined. This implies limitations to the right. Thus a right is merely exclusive, not absolute or unlimited. In fact, different rights are really only differences in 'exclusiveness'.

Third, where rights are well defined and the costs of negotiating and enforcing contracts are small compared with the benefits of the transaction, an exchange system based on prices works smoothly. Economic theory tends to assume these conditions. At times, however, the failure to define rights unambiguously may lead to economic inefficiency. Thus it is generally felt that persons with low income should enjoy some form of housing subsidy. In practice, however, this right has not been made explicit.

Fourth, because real property is durable, the rights existing in real property have a long time-scale. Moreover, no problem of storing such rights exists, though there may be management costs. Real property rights, like stocks and shares, are therefore demanded as investment assets (see Chapter 16). Indeed, the real property market can now be regarded as a part of the wider investment asset market, its significance in this respect having increased in the years up to the 'credit crunch' recession.

The real property market

The main economic agents in real estate markets are:

- Owners – pure investors who do not live, or work, in the real estate they own; normally they rent out or lease the property to the users.
- Owner-users – both owners and consumers; they live in the residential property they own or work in the commercial property they own. They may view the property as both a consumer good and investment good.
- Renter – pure consumers paying a rental fee to use the property.
- Facilitators or property professionals – including banks, building societies, real estate brokers, estate agents and lawyers that facilitate the purchase and sale of real estate.
- Developers – providing new real estate to the market by preparing greenfield land or previously developed land as a new development.
- Renovators – supplying refurbished improved real estate to the market.

There are several unique characteristics of real estate markets, which include the following.

Heterogeneity

Real estate property is heterogeneous, meaning that every unit is unique in terms of its building, condition, financing and location. Even on large housing estates where the design of many houses is the same, the houses are in different places and at the very least they get slightly different sunshine and shade and are a slightly different distance to bus stops and so on. This makes assessing value and prices difficult.

Durability

Buildings can last for decades, even centuries (Egyptian pyramids for thousands of years) and land is virtually indestructible. As a result, there are two parts to real estate supply – the stock of existing buildings and the flow of new real estate onto the market. In most of the developed world the stock is about 98 per cent of the market and the flow of new development only about 2 per cent. The way that the two parts of supply interact is analysed in Chapter 5.

High transaction costs

Property purchase costs much more than most other types of transaction. These costs include land transfer taxes, search costs, legal fees, estate agent fees and possibly moving costs. In the UK these can be 2–6 per cent of the sale price for the seller (they can be considerably more in other countries).

Time-lags

Delays occur due to the length of time it takes to obtain planning permission for new supply, and to finance, design and construct new property. This can mean prolonged periods of excess demand or excess supply and a real estate market that is rarely in equilibrium.

Speculation

Because property can be both a consumption good and an investment good, speculation about prices can create instability in the real estate market. The speculative effect can mean that when property prices are rising, more property is bought (contrary to what we would expect from the laws of demand). This is because investors are speculating that prices may rise further and they want to obtain some of the profits. In addition, for homeowners who see their property purchase as a consumer good to be lived in – they will want to buy into the market (get onto the property ladder) before prices rise. These influences can exacerbate cyclical movements in the real estate market – booms are made bigger and downturns made worse by speculation (see Box 3.1).

Box 3.1   Singapore acts to prevent property market speculation

In September 2009, the Singapore National Development Minister, Mr Mah Bow Tan announced measures to reduce speculation in the property market. Among these measures to 'temper the exuberance' of the market will be the immediate withdrawal of the interest absorption scheme and interest-only loans being offered for purchases of uncompleted property developments. Under the interest absorption scheme, developers pay the interest on home loans instead of buyers until the project receives its Temporary Occupation Permit (TOP). For interest-only loans, a borrower only pays the interest and defers repayment of the principal to a later date. Mr Mah told Parliament that both schemes could encourage speculation in a buoyant market as they lower instalment payments in the initial years.

Pointing out that property purchases are a major long-term financial commitment, the national development minister said the removal of the interest absorption scheme and interest-only loans will help home buyers make careful decisions. The immediate withdrawal of the interest absorption scheme will only affect new projects and not those which had been offering the scheme until the announcement. As for interest-only loans, these will be disallowed with immediate effect. Singapore's actions come as some Asian governments warn of speculative bubbles in real estate markets and said they

---

Box 3.1 continued

may take steps to cool an overheated market. For instance, Bank of Korea said it would lift interest rates if home prices climbed further. Mah's announcement in Parliament caused property stocks to fall sharply, with City Developments falling as much as 5.6 per cent, CapitaLand fell 3.4 per cent while Keppel Land was down 4.3 per cent.

Box 3.2 Location, location, location

You can buy a fantastic property in the wrong location. You can change the structure, remodel it or alter the layout but you can't move it. It's attached to the land.
   The best locations are often considered to be:

In the catchment area of a good school – because homebuyers with (or planning to have) children are willing to pay more for a property which entitles their children to go to a school with a good reputation.
Close to water or green areas – for recreation and for visual amenity.
Homes with a view – a panoramic city view can command a premium price as can views of mountains, the sea or even golf courses.
Near transport links – a property within easy commuting distance of a major city can command a high price. Being close to the fastest train lines into London is a clear advantage.
Near entertainment or shopping or health care – people prefer the convenience of being able to walk to shops, theatres or the health centre and are prepared to pay for it.

   Poor locations are considered to be:

Near to industries causing negative externalities – such as congestion or pollution. For example, properties near chemical works can suffer unpleasant smells when the wind is in a particular direction. Homes close to petrol stations or busy road junctions are undesirable.
Under flight paths or close to railway lines – the noise may be reduced using double or triple glazing but it remains in the garden or on the balcony.
In areas of high crime rates – obviously people want to feel safe from burglary, drug dealing, 'joy riding' and mugging. Crime statistics can, therefore, be important.
In economically depressed areas – where there is high unemployment other social problems may also be present, which lessen the desirability of the neighbourhood.
Near hazards – real or imagined danger from nuclear power stations, landfill sites, power lines, mobile phone masts or farms can put people off a property.

Immobility

Real estate stays where it is. Buyers come to the property rather than the property going to them. As a result there is no physical market place for real estate. It is often said that the three most important features of a property are 'location,

location and location' on the grounds that the property can be altered but where it is cannot be changed.

Are real estate markets efficient?

Since a defective market mechanism will impair the efficiency with which resources are allocated through the price system, we have to ask: how efficient is the real property market in registering changes in demand and supply through their effect on price? In an efficient market we could expect the market to be in equilibrium most (if not all) of the time. This would mean the market clears or demand equals supply.

In Figure 3.1, D is the demand curve for residential property or houses. It slopes downward from left to right because more houses will be demanded at lower prices – people will buy rather than rent if it becomes cheaper to buy – and fewer houses will be bought at higher prices. S is the supply curve for houses. It slopes upwards from left to right because more houses will be supplied to the market at higher prices – house builders will see that they can make more profit as prices rise and will respond by building more, thus increasing supply.

The point where the two curves cross is the point where demand equals supply in the market. At this point the market price P brings forward supply equal to Q and demand equal to Q. The market 'clears', that is, there is no excess of supply or excess of demand. The market is in equilibrium. In an efficient market, demand equals supply at the market price and the market clears, as in Figure 3.1. There are many reasons why this may not, in fact, be the case in the residential property market and these are considered in Chapter 5.

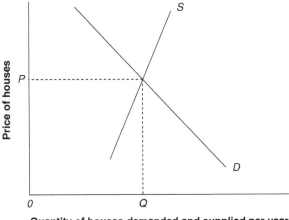

Figure 3.1 Demand and supply of residential property

Consequently if the real property market is efficient there would be no prolonged periods of excess demand or excess supply. However, any observer of the cyclical nature of the real estate market in most market economies would recognize that this is not the case – in the upswing or boom there is a period of excess demand and in the downswing or recession there is a period of excess supply.

The efficiency of a market depends on both technical and economic characteristics.

Technical characteristics

Physical conditions should ensure that price differences for the same commodity within the market are eliminated easily and quickly. This comes about by buyers moving to the cheaper parts of the market and sellers moving to the dearer. This requires that both buyers and sellers must have up-to-date knowledge of price differences and base their actions solely on price. Moreover, dealing costs should be small relative to the value of the transaction.

With the real property market, certain factors not only make it difficult to obtain up-to-date knowledge but lead to dealing costs being relatively high. As regards the first, knowledge tends to be obtained infrequently and is limited geographically. Most occupiers (as distinct from investors) move in response to changes in family circumstances, income or business conditions. Only rarely do they move for the sole purpose of making a gain from a price or rent difference. Moreover, with occupational interests, buyers tend to have a demand which is essentially local, either because their knowledge of the prospects of their business is confined to a particular district or because, as workers, they have to be within easy travelling distance of their place of work. On the other hand, for a holiday or retirement residence people in Britain may compare prices in Cornwall, Spain or the Bahamas. Here the cost and time involved in travelling to work no longer count.

Land and property owners may be unaware of changes in value – they may be aware of prices rising or falling in the market generally, but not sure of the extent to which their individual property is affected. In an efficient market all the information currently available is capitalized into the price of the object being traded (for example shares on the stock market). In principle the price of every characteristic of any property, such as its heating system or size and condition of garden, is known and the price paid for the property is the aggregate of these prices. There is evidence to suggest, however, that predictions of the price paid that should be achieved for a property are inaccurate by about 10 per cent (and that 10 per cent can be above or below the prediction, so the variation is in fact, greater than 10 per cent).

Valuers in the property market can only predict a range within which a property might sell; the actual price is affected by the negotiating abilities of buyers and sellers. Moreover there will always be some adjustment for differences in location (no two properties have an identical location) and all properties differ in some way, consisting of different bundles of characteristics. Economic factors may also affect prices – factors affecting the market (which can change very quickly), for example a rise in petrol prices may depress the price of rural properties; as well as factors affecting the buyer or seller such as a change in their perception of job security.

Nor can paying for advice completely overcome this difficulty of lack of knowledge. Because of differences of location, size, construction and age, most units of real property have special characteristics, making 'grading', the most efficient form of description, difficult. Of course, some interests, such as freehold ground rents, can be described accurately. Others, such as houses, shops, offices or industrial premises, may have labels attached according to the physical characteristics of the structure (for example, high-rise or low-rise, in good repair or in need of modernization, a large or small number of units) or by location (such as city centre or suburban, London or provincial). Indeed, it is possible to say fairly accurately what price a special location, such as Oxford Street, will fetch. Yet even within these 'grades' individual properties have their own characteristics. Their great heterogeneity means that a professional valuer cannot *fully* assess their respective merits. To some degree, therefore, his valuation is subjective. Thus, unlike transport costs, costs of obtaining knowledge are not absolutely certain, and a purchaser would normally go to the trouble of making a personal inspection and discussing with his adviser the weight to be given to special characteristics.

This does not, however, diminish the role played by valuers and agents in the property market. Indeed, where knowledge is difficult to obtain, their specialized functions assume an even greater importance for the smooth working of the market, since they provide information on the availability, type and price of properties, assist or conduct negotiations, arrange finance and insurance and collaborate with conveyancers.

Furthermore, the professional adviser can suggest the most appropriate method of selling a property. Whereas *private treaty* allows flexibility in lotting and is cheaper, negotiations may drag on and even fail. In contrast, if bidding exceeds the reserve price, *public auction* affords an immediate contract. Moreover auction is particularly suitable where a property is difficult to value because of special characteristics, while competitive bidding may push the price above that expected. On the other hand, careful lotting is necessary, as renegotiation is difficult once particulars have been published, and for the buyer there may be the costs of prior survey, legal advice and financial arrangements.

Tender by sealed bid has advantages additional to those of auction. The buyer can be selected on identity as well as price, while confidentiality may be attractive. Above all, where a property has a unique quality – for example, for a developer marrying different sites – the price paid may include consumer's surplus (the total value that buyers place on the property). However, the risk is that some prospective buyers may be reluctant to 'bid' blind so that the successful bid is below the price which could have been achieved at auction.

The imperfection of the property market gives real estate agents a role to play. They provide information to buyers and sellers. Their role is often criticized because they may only be able to predict a price range rather than a particular price – but this is a reflection of the inefficiency of the market itself rather than of agents. They may prefer to undervalue in order to get a quick sale (and only slightly reduced percentage fee) rather than price highly but have to wait some time for their income. Indeed, as mentioned in Chapter 1, in *Freakonomics* (Levitt and Dubner, 2005), a study is quoted which suggests that real estate agents keep their own homes on the market for an average of 10 days longer than their clients and sell for 3 per cent more than they sell their clients' homes!

The difficulty of obtaining knowledge necessitates payments for professional advice which, together with legal fees and stamp duty, add to the expense of property transactions and cause them to take longer to complete compared with those in stocks and shares. Even so, transaction costs are, in principle, no different from the costs usually incurred in transporting goods within the market. Thus they have the same effect as transport costs: if they are highly relative to the value of the commodity dealt in, they tend to separate markets geographically, or at least, to reduce their sensitivity to small changes in demand and supply.

In practice, therefore, 'the real property market' is an omnibus term covering a number of separate markets. Moreover, whereas some markets are quite distinct (such as urban housing and Scottish grouse moors), others are closely related and overlapping (for example, houses and shops can be sold for both occupation and investment). Some, where institutional investment demand dominates, are national (even international) in coverage, for example, offices and prime shop property. Others, where demand is local, tend to be divided geographically (such as owner-occupied houses and seaside hotels). Additionally, even within these markets, differences in rent persist, changes in demand not being fully effective until leases have expired.

Nevertheless, all markets and sub-markets have this in common – the commodity traded in is *real property rights*, even though such rights can take a variety of forms.

Another indicator of efficiency would be low transaction costs so that exchanges can take place quickly and efficiently. Clearly, there are high transaction costs (and often considerable delays) in most real property markets. The nature of the legal system in force in a particular country plays a large part in this. It seems that countries with a French-style legal system (where the use of lawyers is mandatory) have significantly higher transaction costs than those with a German, English or Scandinavian origin legal system. 'Roundtrip' transaction costs mean the total costs of selling and buying a residential property. The four main costs are:

1. Registration costs: fees incurred in registering the property with the appropriate authority (the Land Registry in England and Wales and the Registers of Scotland).
2. Real estate agent fees for marketing, matching buyers with sellers and negotiating price.
3. Legal fees paid for conveyancing (the preparation of documents transferring property from one owner to another).
4. Taxes including stamp duty in the UK or sales and transfer taxes elsewhere, sometimes including VAT.

In the UK, roundtrip transaction costs are quite low at around 5 per cent while at the other end of the scale in Russia and Bulgaria they are around 25 per cent (see www.globalpropertyguide.com). In Bulgaria, VAT is charged on the sale of existing properties which is unusual. In Italy and France transaction costs are around 17 per cent, while in Sweden and Norway they are only about 5 per cent. In Australia and New Zealand transaction costs are about 4 per cent. Of course these costs can vary widely even within a country. Often professional fees can be negotiated, especially if the fee is normally a percentage of the sale price as is common in the UK.

Economic characteristics

In addition to its physical features, we must examine the market's economic characteristics, particularly in the extent to which competition prevails. We have to ask: is there freedom of entry into the market? Does the market consist of many buyers and sellers, each so small that no one can exert monopsony (one buyer) or monopoly powers?

Generally speaking, there is freedom of entry into real property markets, resulting in many buyers and many sellers. But we must also recognize that certain conditions allow an owner to gain some monopolistic control. Such conditions are: 1) the geographical divisions of the market lead to imperfect competition between local markets; 2) the imperfection of the capital market may prevent some would-be buyers from borrowing the large sums required for certain purchases, such as multi-storey office blocks; 3) the spatial fixity of real property puts certain site-owners in a strong position relative to a buyer. Consider, for instance, a developer who has purchased every freehold interest except one for a given project. The owner of the outstanding site can exploit his monopoly power by demanding a price far in excess of that paid for the other sites, and so virtually secure all the developer's super-normal profit from the scheme.

Dealings in real property interests

The main categories of property interests are:

1. *Freeholds* (FHs) involve the holder in the full financial risks of owner-ship, and if rents rise through inflation, a freehold interest provides a hedge against inflation.
2. *Leaseholds* occur where a freeholder grants a lease for a number of years, during which time he parts with some of his equity interest in exchange for a premium and/or for a regular fixed money income. Thus leaseholds are equivalent to fixed money interest-bearing bonds, though they assume a greater equity interest as the lease nears its reversion date.
3. *Freehold ground rents* (FGRs) are paid on long leases of undeveloped land. Certainty of payment means that FGRs are similar to an investment in gilt-edged securities.
4. *Mortgages* are long-term money loans against the security of property. Since interest and capital repayment in money terms are fairly certain, mortgages can be regarded as almost equivalent to debentures and medium-term government bonds.

Occupiers demand property either for *use*, as a consumer good (such as a house, garage, mooring rights), or as a producer good (such as a shop, farm, office, factory). As a consumer good, property is wanted for the satisfaction it yields directly, and demand varies with tastes, income and so on. As a producer good, the demand is derived from the contribution it makes to production, and thus depends upon its marginal revenue productivity. It should be noted that occupiers are found in both the private and public sectors. Thus government departments and defence forces require offices, land, warehouses and so on,

---

Box 3.3 Commonholds

Commonhold as a form of ownership was introduced in 2002 in the UK as a new way of owning a building divided into flats or commercial units. A 'commonhold association', acquires the freehold interest and, instead of a lease, a 'commonhold community statement' governs the rights and obligations of the owners of the units. Each owner has a vote in the association which determines service charges, repairs and so on.

  This form of ownership would be advantageous when the majority of owners wish to have their building demolished – if leaseholders have long leases this can be a big problem if one or two object. With a commonhold arrangement, a majority vote would allow the development to go ahead.

  There are, to date, very few commonhold schemes. This is probably because people (and lenders) are unwilling to invest in an untried system.

but their transactions are supervised by a coordinating agency, the Office of Government Commerce (OGC).

Investors regard property primarily as a *store of wealth*, an alternative to other types of investment asset. But, as we shall see in Chapter 16, investment demand cannot be completely separated from occupation demand. Not only is investment in real property possible because some occupiers prefer to rent rather than to buy their premises, but the amount of rent paid will affect the capital value of the interest.

In discussing the functions of the market we give examples from both occupation and investment dealings since they differ in the major considerations affecting demand and supply.

Functions of the real property market

In any market the price of a good reflects current conditions of demand and supply. But the market does more than *indicate*. Because buyers and sellers respond to these price signals, it also *motivates*. In short, the price system functions through the market. Thus we can break down the functions of the real property market as follows.

Allocate existing real property resources and interests

Because land resources are scarce (that is, not unlimited in supply), they have to be allocated between the various uses and people wanting them. This is achieved by arriving at the *equilibrium* market price – the price which equates the resources (or interests) being offered for sale with what people wish to buy. Thus the market reflects preferences and allocates available supply accordingly. It is important to note, however, that analysis tends to assume static conditions in a perfectly competitive market.

Indicate changes in demand for land resources and interests

If, for instance, house-occupiers switch their demand from rented to owner-occupied houses, this will be shown (see Figure 3.2), other things being equal, by a relative rise in the price of houses for owner-occupation, *up* from OP to OP_1 *(a)*, compared with houses for renting, *down* from OR to OR_1 *(b)*.

Increases or decreases in demand result mainly from changes in the following

1. *Expectations of future yields* resulting from, for example, a change in the price of the final product (where land is a factor of production), a possible switch in government policy (for example, relaxation of rent control or less

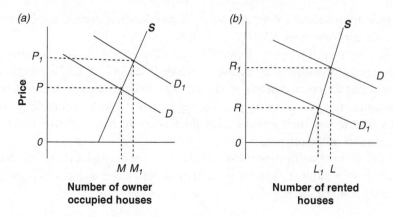

Figure 3.2   A change in demand from rented to owner-occupied houses

restrictive planning) or expected changes in the rate of growth of the economy or in the rate of inflation;
2. *Taxation*, for example, tax concessions to owner-occupiers but not to renters,
   favourable treatment of charities (where relief from income tax leads them
   to favour high-yield rather than growth assets);
3. *Income or tastes*, so that a resource or interest becomes more desirable for
   personal reasons – for example, more leisure increases the demand for golf
   courses and bowling and fishing facilities;
4. *Institutional factors*, such as the costs of transferring assets being altered, or
   funds becoming more difficult to obtain in an imperfect capital market.

Induce supply to adjust to changes in demand

The supply of interests in real property can change by:

- *Developing real property*, either by the adaptation of existing buildings or by
  constructing new buildings. Thus, in Figure 3.2(b) as demand switches from
  rented to owner-occupied houses, the price falls to OR_1, and supply contracts
  from OL to OL_1, LL_1 being sold for owner-occupation (expanding supply
  there by MM_1). Eventually, new equilibrium prices are established, OP_1 in
  the owner-occupied market and OR_1 in the rented market.
- *Changing existing interests*, with no physical alteration in the property.

These amalgamations and separation of interests are continually taking place
in all sections of the real property market in response to people's preferences. A
property developer, for instance, has often to marry the FGRs and the shop leases
on a given site in order to secure the freehold for development. Similarly, an agricultural estate may be formed out of many separate farms. On the other hand,

---

Box 3.4 Property interests

For example, assume that, initially, freeholds are selling at £200,000, whereas similar 99-year leases are making £160,000 and their FGRs are just over £4,000. An increase in the demand for freeholds drives up their price to £240,000. Dealers could now buy FGRs and leaseholds separately, marry the two, and make a profit upon sale of the single freehold. As a result, the prices of FGRs and leaseholds (through the increased demand) would rise, and that of freeholds (through the increased supply) would fall. This would continue until a new set of equilibrium prices had been established, say freeholds £220,000, leaseholds £170,000 and FGRs £5,000. On the other hand, an increase in the demand for leaseholds and FGRs could lead to the division of freeholds.

   Assuming a yield of 7 per cent in the example above, calculate how much profit could be made by buying the leasehold for £160,000 and the FGR for its capital value then combining them and selling the freehold for £240,000.

   [Hint: the capital value of the FGR equals the annual payment multiplied by 1/yield and your answer should be around £22,000.]

---

interests may be separated. A property company may originally have intended to retain the whole of the freehold interest in a development. But a rise in demand, resulting in a higher price for freehold investments, may induce it to sell a part-share to an institution, reinvesting the proceeds in a new development.

Of course, such changes take time to complete, and are subject to the imperfections of the real property market. Moreover, efficient adjustment to changes in demand and supply assumes that all interests are divisible and that there is a perfect capital market. Neither is true. Office blocks come in large 'lumps' (though the emergence of property bonds, property unit trusts and 'securitization' has helped to overcome this difficulty). Imperfections of the capital market may prevent a full response to preferences regarding interests. Thus if a building society will not give a mortgage on a freehold flat in the centre of a town, the would-be purchaser could be forced to go to a modern semi-detached house in the suburbs. Or if the government is seeking to reduce its spending, the OGC, its agency, may be forced to lease premises instead of buying outright. Finally, government restrictions on supply (such as planning controls) or interference with the price mechanism (such as rent control) obstruct the efficient operation of the market economy. Thus an equilibrium situation takes a long time to be achieved, by which time new factors are likely to have arisen, producing a change of direction towards a new equilibrium.

Indicate changes in the conditions upon which land resources can be supplied

Improved techniques in constructing high-rise buildings, for example, may make flats cheaper compared with low-rise houses and flats. Thus in Figure 3.3

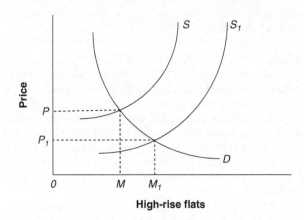

Figure 3.3   The effect of a change in the conditions of supply
on price

the supply curve moves from S to S_1. This is signalled in the market by a fall in
the price of high-rise flats from OP to OP_1.

Induce demand to respond to changes in the conditions of supply

As a result of the fall in the price of high-rise flats, demand for them expands from
OM to OM_1 (see Figure 3.3). Demand for low-rise houses therefore decreases from
D to D_1 (see Figure 3.4) with an actual contraction in supply of MM_1. These changes
simply illustrate the fact that prices of substitutes move in the same direction.

'Reward' the owners of land resources

Rewarding the owners of land resources is a by-product of the market. Such
rewards are of two main kinds.

First, there is the return on capital invested. When a person looks for a
certain return without risk (for example, FGRs) then the return corresponds
closely with the opportunity cost – what his capital could have earned in the
best alternative (such as government stock). There is therefore little 'profit' element in such a return.

But the yield from a land resource usually extends far into the future. Being
a fixed factor, its reward is dependent upon demand and is thus largely in the
nature of 'economic rent'. It can be high, for example, to people who own land
banks before an increase in demand; or it may be negative, for example, to
builders who have bought land banks before a slump. In short, this second type
of reward, 'super-normal profit', arises because of the risk attached to any fixed
factor.

Box 3.5   City living UK

The fashion for 'city living' accommodation led to a big rise in prices for city-centre apartments in the UK in 2006 and 2007. New entrants to the buy-to-let market were also keen to buy and the average cost of flats/maisonettes rose to £175,776 at the peak of the boom in January 2008 (source: Land Registry). Developers were rushing to build city-centre apartments in many cities including Liverpool, Leeds, Manchester and Birmingham with a corresponding big increase in supply.

Then came the downturn; by May 2009, the average flat was worth £141,565, a fall of 19.5 per cent (source: BBC.co.uk). In Birmingham average prices declined by 17 per cent; in Manchester by 17.1 per cent; in Leeds by 16.3 per cent and in Liverpool by 12.6 per cent.

Apartment developer City Lofts called in administrators in July 2008 as its developments in Liverpool (City Lofts, Half Tide Dock) and Sheffield (City Lofts, Sheffield) stalled (source: Construction News).

Allsopps estimated that new build city-centre flats sold at auction lost 45 per cent of their value when sold within 3 years.

For many city-centre developments where would-be buyers pulled out this meant that the developers collapsed, as at the Thames Tower development in Leicester where the developer was Brampton Asset Management (Leicester) Ltd. According to law the would-be buyers (many of whom had paid a deposit but were now unable to get a mortgage) could be pursued by the administrators and forced into completing the sale. Instead of simply taking the deposit and selling the apartment to someone else some developers are trying to force customers to keep to contract and pay the full agreed sale price.

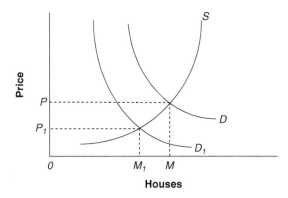

Figure 3.4   The response of demand to changes in the conditions of supply

The function of the real property market is to establish a pattern of prices and rents so that, given sufficient time (the long period), land resources are allocated according to their most profitable ('highest and best') use relative to other land resources. This occurs because competition in the market induces owners to switch resources to that use which yields the highest net return. For example, agricultural land is used for housing, a house is divided into flats or changed to offices, and, in time, sites are cleared for redevelopment. The market, in allocating resources between competing uses, establishes patterns in land use and land values.

Of course, efficiency of the market economy may be impaired because the conditions stipulated in Chapter 2 do not hold. But, given competitive conditions, the creation of different interests in real property is the response to differences in individual preferences. Although we have illustrated the argument in terms of the main forms of interest, we must recognize that there is a wide variety of interests meeting individual preferences, for instance, through restrictive covenants. When looked at in this way, we have to acknowledge how well the market performs its task, allowing just a small change in price to reflect individual preferences. In contrast, the state is likely to be rigid, so, for example, council tenants may not be able to keep a dog in their apartment or paint the front door to the colour of their own choice even if willing to pay slightly more rent. And, even more important, if land is taken over by local authorities, how will it be allocated among its different uses to obtain the maximum net benefit possible?

Summary

The real property market deals in property rights or interests. The main categories of property interests are:

1. Freeholds
2. Leaseholds
3. Freehold ground rents
4. Mortgages

Economic agents in real estate markets include: owners, owner-users, renters, property professionals, developers and renovators.

Real estate has a number of unique features including: heterogeneity, durability, high transaction costs, delays in production, speculation and immobility.

The technical and economic characteristics of real estate markets can lead to some inefficiency.

The functions of the real property market are:

- To allocate existing real property resources and interests
- To indicate changes in demand for land resources and interests
- To induce supply to adjust to changes in demand
- To indicate changes in the conditions in which land resources are supplied
- To induce demand to respond to changes in the conditions of supply
- To 'reward' the owners of land resources

The overall function of the property market is to establish a pattern of prices and rents which results in land resources being allocated according to their most profitable ('highest and best') use.

Chapter 3: review questions

1. What is the origin of the term 'real estate'?
2. Why is the real estate market unlike the markets for other commodities?
3. Explain why the unique features of real estate can lead to inefficiency in the real estate market.
4. Why are transaction costs relatively high for real estate deals?
5. What are the different methods of selling property?

4 Land and Property Price Determination

After studying this chapter you will be able to:

- Analyse how change in land prices relative to other factors affects demand for land
- Explain how commercial land rents are determined
- Illustrate how changes in supply of land take time
- Assess the implications for taxation of the concept of economic rent
- Analyse the relationship between housing stock and the flow of new building
- Describe the possible advantages of land value taxation

Land as a whole

Undeveloped land, or 'pure' land, refers solely to natural resources and space. Thus land as a *whole* – that is, the earth's land surface – can be regarded as being fixed in supply. Increasing such land by reclamation from the sea involves so much investment of capital that it is more appropriate to view it as an addition to capital goods rather than to land.

This idea of land as a whole being fixed in supply has been important in past discussions of cost and value. With man-made commodities, including capital goods, price is a function of demand and supply and, in so far as supply is influenced by cost of production, price itself is influenced by cost. But since land as a whole is a fixed supply provided by nature, the earnings of 'pure' land are determined solely by demand.

Thus in Figure 4.1 *POMN* represents the earnings of land when demand is D, and P_1 *OML* when demand is D_1. In fact, however small the earnings, the total supply of land is still the same. We can say, therefore, that its opportunity cost is zero. Hence all the earnings of land as a whole are an excess over opportunity cost. They represent *economic rent*, that part of the earnings of a factor which results from it having some element of fixity

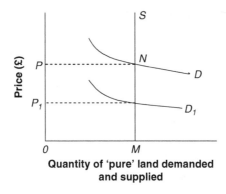

Figure 4.1 Economic rent

Box 4.1 Reclaimed land

Although the reclamation of land from the sea is extremely expensive and requires vast amounts of resources, it has been successfully achieved where land is at a premium. Notable examples include Rio De Janeiro which is largely built on reclaimed land, parts of New Orleans, a major part of Helsinki, Back Bay in Boston, East Coast Park and Changi airport in Singapore and Hong Kong international airport. Over 20 per cent of the Netherlands lies below sea level and the Dutch parliament recently approved plans for a massive tulip-shaped island of over 247,000 acres.

The world's three largest man-made islands have been constructed off the coast of Dubai in the United Arab Emirates where there are seven major reclamation projects that create 520 kilometres of new shoreline. These include: Palm Jumeriah, Palm Jebel Ali, Palm Deira, The World (300 islands at a total cost of $1.8 billion), Dubai Maritime City and the Burj Al Arab hotel. Palm Jebel Ali is intended to be home to an estimated 1.7 million people by 2020.

Critics of such resource-intensive projects claim that they cause considerable environmental damage to marine life and corals, and that the practice of building on sea sand makes buildings vulnerable to earthquakes. Reclaimed land is liable to sinking because of the difficulty of compacting the sand and draining off water. As a result many buildings on reclaimed land suffer subsidence damage. Japan's Kansai International airport, built on an artificial island in 1994 has sunk by more 38 feet requiring expenditure of more than $2 billion on repairs.

---

of supply (in economic terms, the return arising because supply is not perfectly elastic).

Certain points should be noted about the economic rent of land:

1. To say that the earnings of land are a surplus over opportunity cost does not mean that payments do not have to be made for land. Price still performs the vital function of rationing scarce supply among *competing* uses. This is

necessary to ensure that, in each location, land is put to its most profitable use according to the preferences of consumers and society.

2. It follows from (1) that the supply of land can never be regarded as fixed from the *viewpoint of any one use* (unless it really can only be used in one way). Additional supplies can always be bid from other uses if the proposed new use has a higher value than the existing use.

3. The productivity of land can usually be increased in response to additional demand by using it more *intensively* by the addition of capital.

4. The fact that the earnings of land as a whole are entirely demand-determined is important from the point of view of taxation – land will still be there, no matter how high the tax. In other words, a tax on pure land has no disincentive effect on the supply of land. Economic rent can be taxed away entirely. This is the basis of taxes on land, such as petroleum revenue tax, a development land tax covered later in this chapter.

Nevertheless the following points must be remembered.

- Unless all forms of land use are taxed equally, the pattern of land use will be distorted. Whether such distortion is on balance good or bad can only be decided by: (i) a comparison with the inevitable distortions produced by alternative taxes; (ii) its connection with spillover benefits and costs; (iii) one's political views.

- Costs of production include normal profit – that is, what is necessary to keep the entrepreneur in the current line of production. But the size of normal profit may be blurred, and taxes may overlap super-normal profit and fall on normal profit. Thus, as first proposed, the petroleum revenue tax was too high, and oil-drilling companies threatened to withdraw from further operations since it cut into the normal profit required to cover the risk involved. The government therefore had to modify its proposals.

The commercial rent of land

Commercial rent is simply a periodic payment for the hire of land. Normally, there is competition for land between the different potential users. The rent of land, therefore, as with other factors of production, is a price which is determined, in the absence of any government interference, by the interaction of demand and supply.

Let us assume that:

1. the land under discussion is homogeneous;
2. buyers are only interested in maximizing private utility or money returns;
3. conditions of demand and supply do not change – for example, in sources of raw materials, transport facilities, public utilities, building technology;

4. a long-period situation prevails, in that firms can vary the quantities of all factors employed;
5. the output at which profits are maximized is known.

Here we are concerned with *occupation* demand, either as a consumer good or as factor of production. We shall concentrate on the latter.

In order to maximize profit, the equilibrium output must be produced at the minimum possible cost. The demand for land as a factor of production is a *derived demand* – it is wanted for the contribution it can make to a final product. Moreover, it has to be combined with other factors, labour and capital, to produce the goods that are wanted. Thus the quantity of land which a firm demands depends upon: (i) its productivity; (ii) its price relative to other factors and (iii) the price of the final product.

In determining the demand curve for land, therefore, there are three main problems:

1. How does a change in the price of land relative to other factors affect the demand for land?
2. How will a change in the productivity of land in a particular use affect demand?
3. How will a change in the price of the product affect the demand for land in that use?

The isoquant technique can be applied to solving these problems. In Figure 4.2 EP_{10} and EP_{20} are isoquants showing all the different combinations of land and capital which will yield outputs of 10 and 20 units of accommodation respectively. According to the profit-maximizing output (which we will assume to be EP_{20}), there will be a minimum given outlay on factors of production. Spent wholly on land it would buy OL units; spent wholly on capital it would buy OC units. The slope of the budget line CL indicates the relative prices of land and capital.

The cost-minimizing factor combination for the EP_{20} level of output is OM

$$\frac{Price\ of\ Land}{Price\ of\ capital}$$

land plus OP capital. Any other combination would yield less than 20 units of accommodation (that is, it would fall below EP_{20}). At A the marginal rate of technical substitution of land for capital equals:

If the profit-maximizing output had been EP_{30} a larger money outlay would have been required, but, given the same land and capital prices, the slope of the budget line would remain unchanged. Here the cost-minimizing point would be D.

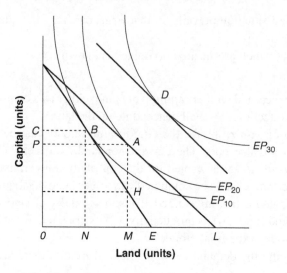

Figure 4.2   The optimum combination of factors of production

The following points should be noted.

1. If the price of land were to rise so that the same money outlay as before now buys only *OE* land, it will produce a new budget line *CE* and a new cost-minimizing combination of *ON* land plus *OQ* capital. Thus the rise in the price of land has had two effects: (i) more capital is now combined with less land than before; (ii) because less land can be bought with the given outlay, the level of output has been reduced from 20 units to 10 units of accommodation.

2. An increase in the productivity of land will produce a new isoquant for 20 units, as shown by the dashed line EP'_{20} (see Figure 4.3). The same output (20 units) can now be produced for a smaller minimum outlay – the budget line is nearer the origin – by increasing land from *OM* to *OS* and by decreasing capital from *OP* to *OR*.

3. The smooth continuity of the isoquant denotes that factors are infinitely divisible; with land, this means that the homogeneous plots are infinitely small. Moreover, our analysis assumes that the quantity of land can be adjusted. Suppose, however, that when the price of land rises from *CL* to *CE* (Figure 4.2) the quantity of land remained at *OM*. This would produce a new position at *H* (only *HM* capital could be afforded on the given budget), with a product of something less than EP_{10} (say 8 units of accommodation) because land is having to be employed too extensively.

4. Suppose, through an increase in demand, that the price of the standard unit of accommodation rose. The new profit-maximizing output would now be larger than EP_{20}, say EP_{30}. At this output more capital and more land would be demanded even at the same relative prices.

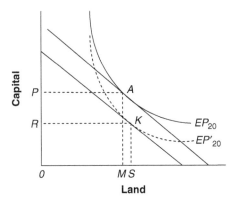

Figure 4.3   The effect on the demand for land of an increase in its productivity

We can sum up by saying that a fall in the price of a factor (in this case land) will lead to an extension of demand (the demand curve slopes downwards), whereas an increase in its productivity or an increase in the price of the product will lead to an increase in demand for the factor (the demand curve moves to the right). The sum of the demands for land of the individual firms will give the industry's demand for land.

The equilibrium market price or rent

Concerning supply, when the rent for land in a particular use rises, it will be surrendered by less profitable uses. In short, the higher the price, more will usually be supplied; there is an upward-sloping supply curve (see Figure 4.4). The interaction of demand and supply will give an equilibrium market rent *OR* for this type of land. Competition will have ensured that at this rent it goes to the highest and best use.

Note that when there is any degree of supply elasticity, that is, the supply curve is not vertical, then the land (or other factor of production) has an alternative use in which it could earn transfer earnings. In the long run the supply schedule of many factors of production is highly elastic, so there is little or no economic rent. For land, inelastic supply is normal and so economic rent exists. With inelastic supply as in Figure 4.4, most of the earnings of land are economic rent, however, and this has implications that will be considered later in the chapter.

Non-homogeneous land and economic rent

So far we have assumed that all land is the same or 'homogeneous'. We shall now relax this assumption. In practice, land varies in quality. Thus *agricultural land* differs in fertility, climate, altitude, topography and accessibility to the market.

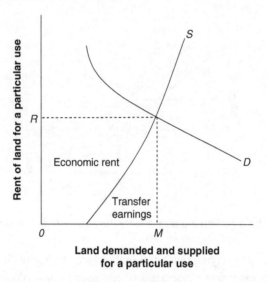

Figure 4.4   The determinants of the commercial rent of land

Consider a piece of land which produces eight tonnes of wheat per hectare. There will be less fertile land, but, we will assume, such land will still be used for growing wheat provided it yields four tonnes per hectare. This latter land just earns its *transfer cost*, the minimum it has to earn to keep it in its present use, and is thus said to be marginal as regards wheat-growing. In contrast, the eight tonne land yields four tonnes per hectare above the marginal land; this extra yield is an *economic rent* resulting from its greater fertility.

The same argument applies to *urban land*. Different characteristics such as, accessibility, the physical condition of the site and institutional restrictions (development plans and covenants), give rise to differential rents. As Tim Harford pointed out in *The Undercover Economist* (Harford, 2006) two things determine the rent on prime locations such as coffee bars at busy railway stations: the productivity of the site (in terms of footfall) and the value of that productivity (which is high because rush-hour customers are willing to pay a high price for coffee – they are 'price-blind' when in a hurry).

Economic rent accrues to any factor which is fixed in supply, and is determined by demand. Thus if the demand for shops in a district increases, an existing shop let on a lease earns a *profit rent* until the next rent review. This profit rent is economic rent, and can be capitalized in the form of a premium should the lease be sold.

The pricing of land resources

Whereas land refers to natural resources, land resources can be defined as the total natural and man-made resources over which possession of the earth's

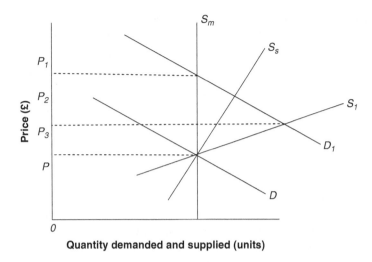

Figure 4.5 The effect of time on the conditions of supply

surface gives control. That is, land resources are equal to the natural content of land plus any improvements attaching to, or incorporated in, the land. Indeed, when we talk about a transaction in land, we are usually referring to land resources. In agriculture, for instance, land would normally include the farm-house and buildings, the fences and water supply, while a freehold residence is the land plus all the fixtures on the land – the house, conservatory, fish-ponds, swimming pool, fences and so on.

Price in the market is determined by demand and supply. In economic analy-sis it is usual to allow for the fact that changes in supply take time by dividing time into three main periods (see Figure 4.5).

In the 'momentary' period, no adjustment of supply is possible (S_m). In the 'short period' supply can be altered by engaging more variable factors (S_s). Eventually, however, supply can be increased by adding to fixed capital, thus combining the factors of production in their best proportions (the 'long period', S_l). Thus if demand increases from D to D_1, the price of the product changes from OP to OP_1, OP_2 or OP_3 (corresponding respectively to the above periods).

The dominance of stocks over flows

While not incorrect, the general analysis of the formation of price over time suffers from two main weaknesses when applied to individual goods.

1. The time taken to achieve the long-period situation varies
The full response of supply to a rise in the price of buildings usually takes a very long time. The various interests in a site required for redevelopment

have to be amalgamated (usually by acquiring leases), planning permission has to be obtained and any compulsory purchase orders subjected to time-consuming procedures. This means that, when applying the usual time-period analysis to land resources, we have to recognize that for a considerable period of time we are virtually dealing with a fixed stock. Thus changes in demand will tend to be more significant than changes in supply in determining market price.

2.   No allowance is made for the size of stocks of existing goods relative to flows of new goods coming on to the market
With most goods we do not have to pay much attention to this. Because their life is relatively short, existing goods (the stock) have to be replaced frequently by new supplies (the flow over a period). This is true even of consumer durable goods, such as washing machines, refrigerators and motor cars.

Take cars, for example. Other things being equal, any increase in the demand for cars will, in a free market, push up the price. Extra imports may help to meet this additional demand. But if manufacturers consider that the higher price is likely to be permanent, they will eventually add to plant so that the supply of cars coming on to the market increases. This flow of new supplies will be significant relative to the supply coming on to the market from existing *stocks*, and will thus be a main determinant, with demand, of price.

But the position is somewhat different with certain goods, for example, ships, aircraft and land resources. Because such goods are so durable, stocks of them accumulate over time. As a result, new flows on to the market (additions, say, per annum) are small or insignificant in comparison with the supply to the market coming from existing stocks. As a result, *new* supply has relatively little influence on price; for all practical purposes, supply from old stock dominates the market.

Two qualifications, however, should be made. First, it is the turnover of old stock which is really significant (see below). Second, over the years accumulated flows affect the size of stocks, and have their effect in this way. But the possibility of this is very limited in developed city centres.

In the very short run, supply is perfectly inelastic. It takes time for supply to respond to a rise in price – this means that for some time the stock of land/buildings is fixed. This means that changes in demand will tend to be more significant than changes in supply in determining market price. Additions (flows) of stocks of land/buildings are small compared to existing stocks and so new supply has relatively little influence on price (in the UK there are approximately 25 million owner-occupied houses, but only about 180,000 new build each year – and only 100,000 in 2008 and maybe only 80,000 in 2009!)

Price is therefore largely determined by demand; new supplies follow this price rather than have much influence in determining it. The position is summarized in Figure 4.6.

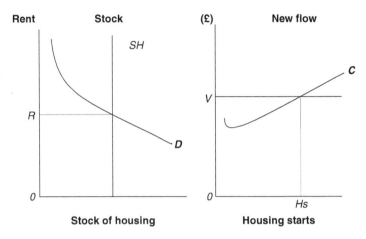

Figure 4.6 The dominance of stocks in housing

The initial price, R is determined by supply of existing stock SH and demand D.

This rent translates into value V by discounting cash flows. Then value is compared to construction costs C to determine whether profitable opportunities exist for developers – while V is greater than C this is the case and so Hs is the maximum number of housing starts. In the next period SH shifts to the right by the amount Hs.

An increase in demand for housing D to D' in Figure 4.7 will lead to either an increase in price R to R' or an increase in numbers built Hs, or a mixture of the two.

If deterioration reduces the housing stock (say, after a slum clearance programme), then the price of existing stock could rise – or more likely there will be an increase in new starts in the housebuilding sector. The situation is illustrated in Figure 4.8.

Since buildings have a long life, the stock of *owner-occupied* housing units in the UK is approximately 25 million. The turnover of this stock (about 5 per cent or 1,250,000 units) is large relative to the flow of *additional* units being produced each year, about 180,000 in a normal year. Indeed in areas such as Greater London, which are surrounded by a green belt, most houses coming on to the market are from the existing stock of houses.

In such a situation demand determines the price of houses. For example, let us assume an increase in the demand for living accommodation. In the short run, existing dwellings are used more intensively, for example, by a decrease or disappearance of the number of vacant dwellings, an increase in subtenancies, a doubling-up of families, an increase in the number of persons per room. Eventually, this will cause the prices of owner-occupied houses and rents of existing accommodation to rise.

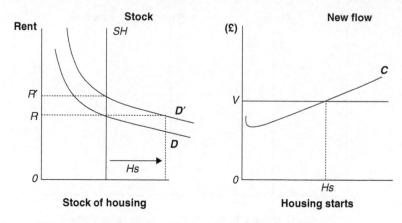

Figure 4.7   The effect on price and new starts of an increase in demand for housing

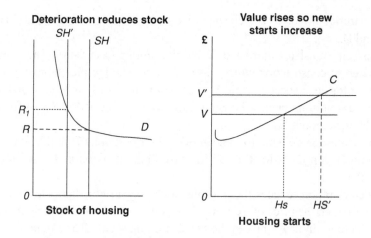

Figure 4.8   The effect of some deterioration of the housing stock

But since the flow of new houses on to the market is insufficient to affect significantly the supply, this higher price of existing houses will represent the price of *all houses* in the market. Any newly built house which comes on to the market will be sold at the higher price. In other words, the price of new houses is determined by the price at which existing houses sell.

Land prices are determined by property prices in an unconstrained market (that is, a market without planning constraints). The price paid for land for new housing is thus the residual between what the new house will sell at (determined by the demand for old houses) and what it costs to build, including normal profit. Take, for instance, a builder bidding for a spare site in London on which to erect a house. Suppose similar old houses are selling for £240,000, and

> **Box 4.2** UK housebuilding
>
> At the peak of UK construction activity, in the late 1960s and early 1970s over 400,000 houses were being built per year. This rate dropped steadily and by the 1990s, the average annual rate was 190,000 houses per year. Increasingly new buildings are being constructed on land that has been previously developed (brownfield land – see Chapter 15). The percentage of developments taking place on brownfield land rose from 55 per cent in 1981 to 61 per cent in 2004 (DETR policy is 60:40 brownfield to greenfield sites and local authorities are required to consider using previously developed land before releasing greenfield sites).
>
> The average rate of net gain in UK dwellings 1981–2006 was 194,584 per year. In 2007 it was 193,000; in 2008 it was 101,000; and in 2009 only 80,000 (forecast by NHBC). The new Coalition Government of 2010 has allowed councils to abandon building targets and more than 14,500 planned new homes in Aylesbury Vale, Winchester, Newmarket and Moreton-in-the-Marsh have been stopped.

that he estimates that it will cost him £160,000 (including his normal profit) to build. He can therefore afford to bid £80,000 for the land and indeed will have to do so if he is to secure it in competition with other builders.

Because houses take time to build, this is a situation which exists in all localities in the short period. Where building land is available, however, the high price offered for existing and, therefore, new houses will encourage builders to erect new houses, and this will continue so long as the cost of new houses on to the market will be sufficient to influence the stock of houses, and the price of old houses will tend to fall. This is most noticeable in districts where the supply of building plots is plentiful, for example, in new towns, overflow towns (Swindon, Ashford and so on) and the fringe land of certain towns where planning permissions have been freely given to permit expansion. In the long period, therefore, these new flows affect the price of old houses, and when the prices of old and new houses coincide, the cost of building new houses does affect the price. But it may take a very long time before this situation happens and, where cities are surrounded by green belts which cannot be built on, the price of houses will tend to be dominated by demand.

The price of land and property

It is sometimes stated that the high cost of land is responsible for high house prices, thus limiting home ownership. Our analysis gives little support to this view. In fact land prices are determined by property prices in an unconstrained market. An increase in demand for houses causes the price of old houses to rise. This enables builders to bid more for land – up to the difference between what they can sell a new house for (the price of similar existing houses) and the cost of building (including normal profit). Thus, if the price of houses rose to

£350,000 and building costs remained unchanged at £160,000, £190 000 could now be paid for the land.

Of course, to the individual builder, the price of land is a cost; as with building components, he has to pay the going competitive market rate to obtain it. But the view that land prices should be controlled because they push up the price of houses is incorrect. After examining the underlying factors it is clear that it is the demand for houses which determines the price of land from the point of view of builders as a whole.

Empirical support of the above analysis is contained in the *Digest of Building Land Prices* (Estates Gazette, 1974). In 1972 the average price paid for land on housing estates was £25,000 an acre. In the last quarter of 1973 it had fallen to £21,000, and builders who had acquired land banks at 1972 prices were showing a loss. The reasons for the fall in land prices were the fall in house prices and the rise in costs. The *Digest* comments that current conditions make it clear 'that land prices are determined by house prices rather than the other way round' – an example of the inductive method of establishing an hypotheses as opposed to our deductive method.

Three other points should be noted.

1. It is what could be the builder's super-normal profit which represents the maximum he can bid for land. Unless this is sufficient to attract land from its next-best use, such as agriculture, he cannot build.
2. Since the price of land is determined by the demand for housing, controlling its price artificially would not result in house prices falling.
3. Instead, the surplus return would simply go to somebody other than the landowner, for example, the first purchaser, or local authorities who acquire land compulsorily at existing use values. Furthermore, it would upset the allocative function of the market whereby the equilibrium price ensures that scarce land goes to its highest and best use. Artificially low prices, maintained by some form of price control, would lead to a 'wasteful' demand for land in less profitable uses.
4. As the price of houses rises, land costs form a greater proportion of that price. Thus, in our earlier example, when the house sold for £240,000, the land cost formed one-third of that price; when the house price rose to £350,000 through increased demand the land cost rose to more than one-half.

Building costs and property prices

Similarly, we have to ask whether a rise in *the cost of building materials and labour* will put up the price of houses in the short period. The answer is that, where building land is earning an economic rent (that is, its price is above its 'transfer' or next-best use), a rise in building costs has no effect on the current price of houses. Since the supply of houses comes mainly from existing stock, their price in the market is determined by demand. A rise in building costs therefore simply means that the builder has a smaller margin to bid for the land. So if houses in an area are selling for £400,000 and building costs (including the builder's normal profit) are £160,000, the maximum bid for the land would be £240,000; if building costs rise to £200,000, then the maximum bid is only £200,000.

Price changes support this argument. Whereas in 1987–8 average construction costs rose by approximately 10 per cent, the price of new dwellings rose by 28 per cent, and the price of housing land by 33 per cent as builders acquired land in anticipation of a future rise in house prices. On the other hand, in 1989–90 when the price of new dwellings fell by 3 per cent and construction costs by only 1 per cent, the price of housing land fell by 12 per cent as builders had to release surplus land acquired in the previous 2 years.

The effect of a rise in the *rate of interest* must be considered from the viewpoint of both the builder (whose costs are increased) and the house purchaser. On the supply side, the builder has to pay more for his overdraft, but this will affect only what he can bid for the land, not the house price. It is on the demand side that the rise in the rate of interest has the major effect – the higher cost of borrowing on mortgages leads to a decrease in demand, and thus the price of houses will tend to fall!

Tax implications of economic rent

The government can impose a tax on land resources up to the level of economic rent they earn and this will make no difference to their supply. As long as the tax is not so large that it removes all economic rent (which includes normal profit sufficient to keep the land in its present use) and also eats into the transfer earnings of the land, it will not affect the use to which the land is put. In this respect land is no different from any other factor of production. Where a factor of production has any inelasticity of supply, there will be economic rent and that rent can be taxed without forcing the factor into an alternative use. So for an entertainer who is very highly paid, such as Madonna, her earnings are mainly economic rent and her transfer earnings are the amount that she could earn in an alternative occupation, say teaching. Even if Madonna is taxed very heavily, she is unlikely to quit her entertainment career and go into teaching instead. The economic rent can be taxed without affecting the allocation of resources.

Henry George (1839–97) in his book *Progress and Poverty* published in 1879, argued that natural resources including land belonged to the nation and that land rent created nothing of value and so could become the source of all taxation (his single tax). It should be noted, however, that land resources include capital. If the tax should be so large as to overlap the transfer earnings of capital or normal profit, further building will not take place. Hong Kong is perhaps the best example of the successful implementation of a high land value tax (LVT). The Hong Kong government generates more than 35 per cent of its revenue from land taxes, and keeps its other tax rates low. Singapore and Taiwan also operate land taxes. LVT can raise substantial sums without damaging the economy. It broadens the tax base and produces very predictable returns in contrast to more volatile taxes made on profits. The supply of land is very inelastic, and its value does not fluctuate so much if the speculative element is removed. It is also easy to collect because the authorities need only registers of owners and a valuation of the land. It is hard to evade, because land cannot be hidden (or transferred into tax havens abroad). The cost of collecting some taxes is very high, but a land tax is a low cost tax. Because LVT is cheap to impose and a reliable revenue raiser, it can reduce the need for other taxes. A land tax reduces speculation because it imposes a cost on holding land in unproductive use while waiting for its value to increase. This should have the effect of returning land to productive use. Furthermore, it may reduce urban sprawl because it reduces the number of vacant lots in a city.

In Figure 4.9 the effects of a land value tax are illustrated. The tax reduces the return to the producer *OPNM* (the 'producer surplus') by *LPNK* but does not affect market price. LVT is payable regardless of whether or how well the land is actually used, and because the supply of land is perfectly inelastic, market land rents depend on what tenants are prepared to pay rather than on the costs of landlords, and so LVT cannot be passed on to tenants. An argument for LVT is that it will not deter production or distort market mechanisms as other taxes do. LVT is considered in more depth in Chapter 22.

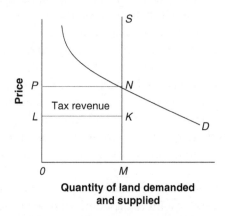

Figure 4.9   The effects of a land value tax

Box 4.3 Taxation of North Sea oil

The term 'land' in economics includes all natural resources. Oil from the North Sea became economic to produce after the OPEC price rise of 1973. The earnings of the oil companies are considerable and much of them consist of economic rent. Petroleum Revenue Tax (PRT) is a special petroleum profits tax assessed on a field-by-field basis with all fields treated equally irrespective of ownership. PRT was charged initially at a rate of 45 per cent on the value of oil and gas produced. The tax regime imposed a high effective marginal rate by the combination of PRT and corporation tax; and also allowed substantial tax deductions for development costs. The tax base broadly equates to revenue receipts less the expenditure incurred in developing and operating the field. PRT was introduced to capture economic rent from the more profitable fields. The UK government has to balance its desire to secure as much as possible of the proceeds from the oil for its citizens, with the need to encourage oil companies to invest in exploration and production. Figure 4.10 is a simple illustration of the situation.

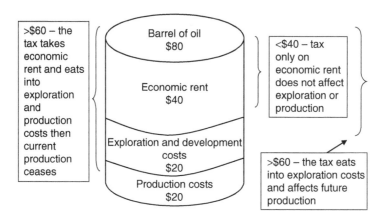

Figure 4.10   Taxation of the economic rent from North Sea oil

Summary

Land as a whole can be regarded as fixed in supply, although this is not true from the viewpoint of any one use. As a result, all the earnings of land as a whole are an excess over opportunity cost or 'economic rent'.

A fall in the price of land will lead to an extension of demand (the demand curve slopes downwards); while an increase in the productivity of land, or an increase in the price of the product of land, will lead to an increase in demand for land at all prices (the demand curve shifts to the right). Supply of land for a particular use will be increased as its price increases (the supply curve slopes upwards).

Changes in supply take time and so the supply curve of property becomes more elastic the longer the time period. The commercial rent of land is determined by the interaction of demand and supply and competition ensures that at this rent the land is put to its most profitable use.

Property and land resources are durable and so stocks of them accumulate over time. As a result, new supply is a small proportion of the total stock and, therefore, has little influence on price. Prices are then largely determined by demand.

Chapter 4: review questions

1. Are land resources fixed in supply?
2. Why would a tax on pure land have no disincentive effects on the supply of land?
3. Explain, using a diagram, how supply of property can become more elastic in the long run.
4. Why are there long lags in property supply?
5. Explain why it is efficient to tax economic rent.

5

Residential Property Markets

After studying this chapter you will be able to:

- Explain why housing supply is dominated by the stock of existing houses;
- Describe the main objectives of government housing policy;
- Explain the short-term and longer-term effects of rent control;
- Show how housing policies have changed in the last 50 years;
- Analyse the effects of the 'credit crunch' on UK housing.

The provision of housing through the market economy

The housing market is concerned with the relationship between households and dwellings. A *household* is defined as 'two or more persons living together with common housekeeping, or a person living alone who is responsible for providing his or her own meals'. A *dwelling* is a building, or part of a building, which provides structurally separate living accommodation.

In the private sector, owner-occupied houses are built according to the price which people are able and willing to pay for them. Demand will depend upon the price of the house, the prices of other goods and services (particularly near-substitutes), the level of income, the distribution of wealth and tastes. Supply responds automatically to this demand; the number and type of houses supplied depends ultimately on the equilibrium price determined in the market. The determination of price by demand and supply in the market was illustrated in Chapter 3, Figure 3.1.

In contrast, in providing housing according to needs, the public housing authorities regard housing as a social obligation. Consequently, price signals are either inadequate or non-existent. This increases the difficulties of decision making because the authorities first have to estimate the number of households seeking accommodation according to the sizes of family units, the ages of their members, their location, their preferences for houses or flats and so on. And since houses are very durable some consideration must be given to future requirements. Then the authorities have to decide on the standard required for an adequate housing unit, and then get the dwellings built either by private contractors or by their own, directly employed, staff.

The task of estimating needs is made more difficult in the public sector because there is no price system in operation to provide reliable criteria. Thus rents charged by local authorities are less than the open-market rent. This means that demand exceeds supply, and the only indication of needs thrown up by this restricted-price system is the number of households waiting their turn on the housing list.

The dominance of the standing stock

An essential feature of housing is that, except over very long periods, we are dealing with a stock; in 2009, the 25 million dwellings in Great Britain increased by only 120,000, the lowest level of completions for 64 years. Even if the construction industry could raise its annual output by a third (which would be a considerable achievement), the average yearly rate of increase in the standing stock would only rise from 0.66 per cent to 1 per cent.

The 'stock' nature of housing has important implications for housing policy.

1. In the short period (which may be many years) the only immediate solution to the problem of a housing shortage is to restrict demand to the limits imposed by the fixed stock.
2. In fully developed urban areas, the price of old houses determines the price of new houses. Thus the land price is a residual, and high land prices do not restrict the supply of housing.
3. If 'needs' are not covered by the number of dwellings available, resources must be diverted into house construction. An example of this being done is the plan to build 200,000 new homes in the south-east announced by the deputy prime minister in February 2003. This is part of a £22 billion plan to reverse a 30-year decline in housebuilding and to channel government money into housing and communities.

The quantity of new housing supply is determined by the cost of inputs such as land and labour, the price of the existing stock of houses and the technology of production.

The process by which the housing stock is increased through the price mechanism was described in Chapter 4 and will now be re-examined here.

In Figure 5.1 the stock of housing supply is shown in the diagram on the left and the flow of new housing (housing starts) is in the diagram on the right. Rents (R_1) are determined by the interaction of demand for housing (D) and the

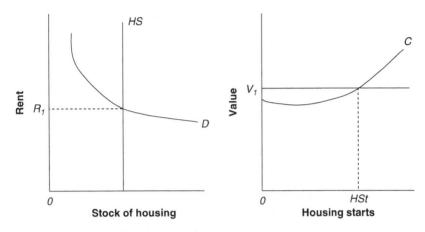

Figure 5.1 Housing stocks and flows

supply of the existing housing stock. The rent is translated into value (V_1) by discounting cash flows (multiplying rent by year's purchase). If values are sufficient to allow developers to make a profit above construction costs (C), then the number of housing starts (HSt) adds to the stock of housing in the next time period, shifting HS to the right.

Consideration of the housing market model shown in Figure 5.1 should enable other possible changes to be analysed. For example, if demand for housing increases in the left hand diagram, then the demand curve shifts to the right and rents increase. As a result, value increases in the right hand diagram and this allows more housing starts adding to the stock of housing (HS) in the next period.

If construction costs increase, shifting the cost curve C up in the right hand diagram, then there will be fewer housing starts and this will eventually reduce the housing stock. And if there is deterioration of the existing housing stock then HS will shift to the left in the left hand diagram, increasing rents and values and prompting more housing starts in the right hand diagram.

Equilibrium in the distribution of the standing stock

We shall assume that housing is occupied either by tenants or owner-occupiers. This means that there are three parties: tenants, landlords (who can be regarded as investors) and owner-occupiers.

The standing stock will be allocated between tenants and owner-occupiers according to preferences expressed through *demand* in the market for renting as opposed to owner-occupation. While the overall demand for housing depends mainly on long-term factors, the choice between renting and owner-occupation will be influenced by the rent charged compared with the cost of mortgage repayments, the desire for independence from a landlord, pride of homeownership, possible capital gain and so on.

Let us assume that: (i) initially the stock of dwellings is randomly distributed between renters and owner-occupiers irrespective of preferences; and (ii) there is perfect competition both in the housing and capital markets.

Because, among other reasons, there may be little difference between the rent charged and mortgage repayments on a house, some renters may seek to become owner-occupiers. On the other hand, some owner-occupiers may wish to sell and rent, preferring immediate capital. Since the stock was initially distributed randomly, households will now trade in the market to achieve their preferred positions. Suppose people show a higher preference for renting compared with owner-occupation. Prices of owner-occupied houses would fall, while rents paid by tenants would rise. Landlords would therefore buy owner-occupied houses and rent them out. This increase in rented accommodation would mean that rents would fall until eventually equilibrium between renting and owner-occupation was established, rents being somewhat higher than in the initial situation.

Two further points can be made. First, assuming that a landlord seeks to pay off his interest and capital within 40 years, the rent he expects would, other things being equal, be equivalent to mortgage repayments where the term of the mortgage was 40 years. Second, since we have assumed perfect competition in the capital market, such a rent produces a long-term equilibrium situation, for the landlord will be obtaining the going rate of return on capital with no alternative investment offering a higher yield.

Suppose now that there is an overall increase in the demand for housing as opposed to other goods. Let us assume, too, that this increased demand occurs in the rented sector. Rents will rise and so will the yield to landlords. In the short term, landlords buy owner-occupied houses, renting them to tenants. But the yield on housing as an investment is now higher than the return on alternative investments. In the long term, therefore, landlords would provide the capital for building new rented housing. Eventually, with the additional supply, rents would fall back, and this would continue until equilibrium was restored.

In practice, the model must be varied for real life conditions, as follows:

1. Mortgages are usually shorter than 40 years, so that initial repayments are higher than rents.
2. On the other hand, rents will be higher because of additions for items often ignored by the owner-occupier: (a) normal profit and administrative costs; (b) possible adverse changes in government policy (c) the costs of repairs (the owner-occupier often doing these himself) and (d) a sinking fund to recoup capital (the owner-occupier's main concern being that the house will last his lifetime).
3. A part of the rented market may be 'frozen' or affected by the government, for example, 'social' housing.

4. Finance may not be available for would-be owner-occupiers, especially the aged and those in the very low-income groups.
5. Imperfections of the market mechanism and immobilities, such as leases for fixed terms, mean that it takes time to achieve equilibrium.
6. Legislative provisions, such as rent control, may, on the one hand, force people into owner-occupation, and, on the other, deter landlords from renting out accommodation.
7. The pattern of taxation and allowances benefits the owner-occupied sector.

It should be noted, however, that the rate of interest will not affect the division of the housing stock between renting and owner-occupation, since capital value adjusts to yields as follows. If we ignore the repayments of capital and the cost of repairs, the monthly rent paid would, as we saw above, equal yearly interest charges on the *capital* value divided by 12. Now if the rate of interest falls, the capital value of an investment in rented houses rises, just as it does with other investments, such as bonds. Thus the total interest charge which has to be paid on the purchase of a house remains the same, so that rents are not changed. Since owner-occupiers will have to pay this higher capital value when purchasing a house, a fall in the rate of interest will similarly leave them in the same position.

The above, however, must be subject to the proviso that, in the long term, a fall in the rate of interest is likely to encourage investment in housing, since it would be particularly beneficial to investments whose yields extend far into the future, and thus increase their profitability as compared with shorter-term investments.

Finally, it is important to remember that: (a) the market allocates housing within the existing distribution of income; and (b) in practice, because it takes time to build houses, the short period for housing is so long that for some time it is accommodation within the existing stock which is competed for. Thus for the poorer households only the older, low-quality housing is affordable, indeed often by more intensive occupation. In the long period, however, growth in income and in the housing stock should enable them to spend more on housing and 'filter' upwards as the better-off move into new houses.

The advantages of the free market system in the provision of housing

Until the First World War, housing was provided almost entirely through the price mechanism, with 80 per cent of all dwellings rented, 10 per cent tied and 10 per cent owner-occupied. Local authority housing was virtually non-existent.

Such a free market in housing has advantages:

1. Some accommodation is always immediately available, the quality enjoyed being determined by the rent people are able and willing to pay.
2. Within their income limitation people can exercise choice in housing according to their preferences. Therefore, if one landlord will not allow them to keep a dog, they may try to find another who will, though perhaps at a higher rent.
3. Where the stock of accommodation is small compared with households, rents rise and people are forced to economize on space, possibly by doubling up with other families. In the short term, using available accommodation more intensively is the only possible solution.
4. High rents stimulate the conversion of large houses into separate flats and new construction, eventually enabling low-income households to filter upwards.
5. No complex and expensive government machinery is necessary to build and allocate dwellings or to supervise day-to-day maintenance.

Housing policy

The above model indicates how housing can be provided by the market economy and, indeed in the UK today, the private sector accounts for 76 per cent of all housing, mostly through owner-occupation. What, therefore, are the economic grounds for government interference?

First, there is uneven distribution of income, some people having insufficient means to secure adequate housing by bidding in the open market.

Second, there are significant external costs, ignored by both households and landlords, of bad housing. Some households may not allocate sufficient income to housing, preferring other goods, such as cars, holidays abroad and so on. Landlords may boost current net income by neglecting repairs. As a result, slums develop, giving rise to ill-health, delinquency, vandalism and other social problems.

Third, the government may consider that people generally underestimate the satisfaction they would obtain from extra housing. Thus housing, like education and social insurance, is treated as a 'merit' good, being encouraged by subsidy or provided directly through the public sector.

Fourth, public intervention is often necessary to accelerate new building, the renovation of dwellings and the elimination of slums. This is the problem of the speed of adjustment to equilibrium.

Unfortunately, much current housing policy has to be directed to rectifying mistakes made by past governments. Worse still, it is dominated by political considerations, which, as we shall see, have thwarted the formulation of a consistent policy and have ignored basic economic principles. In any case, there will always be a 'housing problem' for the same reason that there will always be an economic problem – resources are scarce relative to wants. Can economic analysis help to ensure that the limited resources devoted to housing go as far as possible?

Difficulties of framing a housing policy

In treating housing as a 'social good', governments find little difficulty in stating the ultimate objective of housing policy: that everyone should have a decent home with a reasonable choice of owning it or renting (HMSO, 1973). But while admirable in sentiment, such an aim glosses over the difficulties of framing an actual policy. What, for instance, do we mean by a 'decent home'? The answer involves a subjective judgement, with policy tending to be based on 'needs' rather than on 'demand'. Moreover, the concept of what is adequate changes over time as people's incomes increase and technical improvements, such as central heating, come about. Policy has, therefore, not only to define what is currently 'decent', but also to decide to what extent *future* minimum requirements should be anticipated. Thus spreading resources thickly on a limited number of houses by councils building to very high standards must be balanced against the fact that it extends the time that many people have to continue living in wretched conditions.

Again, choice in housing means that dwellings should be sufficient in number and variety to enable people to exercise their preferences of tenure as between buying and renting and, within the tenure, of location, space, number of rooms, design and whether the house or flat is furnished or unfurnished. Such choice promotes people's freedom, eliminating petty rules as to how they use their home and providing increased mobility. Here the price system can play an important role by reflecting such preferences (admittedly within the existing distribution of income) and stimulating production in response to them. What the government has to recognize is that without some form of subsidy, poorer households could not obtain a 'decent home' through the market.

Objectives of a housing policy

As a first approach, we can state the potential role of the government as follows.

To obtain the optimal use of existing housing resources

At any time there is a given stock of housing to meet current needs. Often governments have been so preoccupied with new building programmes that present stock has been neglected by being allowed to remain unoccupied or to fall into disrepair. As we shall see, the policy of rent control contributed largely to both types of neglect.

To ensure adequate housing for all households

Longer-term policy must aim at improving housing conditions. Consideration must be given to individual preferences as regards tenure, type and location of dwellings. Furthermore, policy must allow for a surplus of dwellings over households in order to: (i) provide a 'pool' so that people can change homes, (ii) allow substandard houses to be replaced and (iii) cover ownership of second homes.

To be responsible for the housing needs of special groups

Certain people, such as the elderly, disabled people and mentally handicapped, must have housing requirements coordinated with the welfare services, for example, through sheltered accommodation or specially designed or adapted housing.

To guide the future requirements and location of new housing

New housing should be so located as to take account of current shortages, employment opportunities, future changes in demand, the existing infrastructure and overall strategic plans. Because planning permission to build is now necessary, the government has to estimate likely requirements for at least 15 years ahead, ensure the capacity of the housebuilding industry to provide them and to decide where these new houses shall be located.

To influence the policies of local authorities in allocating housing

If, as seems likely, dwellings for long-term renting will, for the foreseeable future, have to be provided largely by councils and housing associations, the government must ensure that certain groups, for example those who have just moved into a new area, are not hopelessly handicapped in obtaining a rented dwelling by the method of allocation, such as the points system.

UK government intervention in the housing market

Rent control

An active state housing policy really began with the Increase of Rent and Mortgage (War Restrictions) Act 1915. This controlled the rents of lower-rated unfurnished dwellings at the August 1914 level, except for rate increases or improvements. Security of tenure, necessary to make rent control effective, was given to occupiers.

Although originally introduced as a purely temporary expedient, rent control eventually became the keystone of government housing policy, and the remnants still linger today as there was no political consensus on phasing it out. For the provision of housing, Labour governments seemed to be biased against the private landlord and favoured expanding the public sector. In contrast, Conservative governments promoted increased owner-occupation with its possible political advantage. Thus instead of a long-term and coherent housing policy, what emerged was a succession of *ad hoc* expedients, for example 'fair' rents and 'reasonable' rents, and frequent changes in subsidies for public sector building and the owner-occupier. It follows, therefore, that the starting point of any explanation of the current housing situation must be an examination of rent control, the economic principles it flouts and the consequences which follow.

While rent control may be acceptable as a short-term expedient in an emergency, it has serious weaknesses when employed as the corner-stone of an ongoing policy. In the short term there is a fixed stock of dwellings, *OM* (Figure 5.2). Let us assume that initially this fixed stock is 'rationed out' by a market rent, *OR*, which equates demand and supply.

Now assume that, through additional household formation, demand increases from *D* to *D*$_1$, but rent is controlled at *OR*. In a free market, rent would rise to *OR*$_1$. This higher 'price' would ration out the existing stock of housing among all households seeking to rent according to the emphasis they place on house space compared with other goods. Where rent remains controlled at *OR*, however, two results follow. First, landlords cannot secure the extra economic rent, *R*$_1$ *RTY*, arising through the increased demand for a fixed supply. Second, persons *who are already occupying a rented dwelling can*, through security of tenure, continue to occupy it at the current rent. The difficulty is that there has been no rise in rent to cause the existing stock to be used more intensively. Some households do double up with relatives, but demand continues to exceed supply, broadly by *MM*$_1$, forcing those who can afford it to become owner-occupiers and those who cannot to fall back on the limited public sector. Hence, rent control does not solve the short-term housing problem.

Rent control also has the effect of allocating housing arbitrarily and often unfairly. With a free market mechanism the existing stock of accommodation

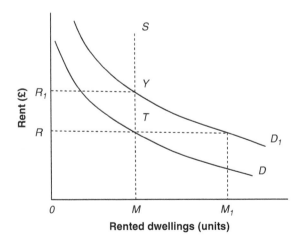

Figure 5.2 The effect of rent control in the short period

is allocated by the equilibrium market rent, for this is the 'price' where demand just equals supply. This rent would be determined by people bidding in the market, reflecting their preferences and income constraint.

Whenever the price system is rejected, some other means of allocating supply has to be used. Thus the government can divide the limited stock of a good into 'fair' shares which are rationed out. But because of the relatively small flow of new dwellings on to the market, such a method is not suitable for allocating housing. For instance, when petrol was in short supply in 1979, rationing would have been possible, since new flows were constantly coming on to the market. As the size of these flows changed, the ration could be varied. With housing, however, people are occupying the fixed stock; they cannot be turned out in order to implement the principle of 'fair shares'.

Initially, therefore, the housing stock is allocated randomly, simply on the basis of possession. And even where private landlords relet dwellings, many carry out their own 'rationing', preferring to let to companies rather than to private individuals.

Rent control also decreases the supply of privately rented dwellings. In the long period the supply of dwellings would extend in response to a higher free market price, but rent control obstructs this functioning of the price system. Indeed, supply tends to decrease. First, dwellings may be underutilized, for example through old people retaining the same accommodation although their children have left home (because they have a controlled low rent). Second, as rented dwellings become vacant, they are sold in the higher-priced owner-occupier market. Third, as repair costs rise relative to rents, houses deteriorate or remain substandard.

The above can be demonstrated diagrammatically. In Figure 5.3, in the short period (with S_s) when demand increases to D_1, the rent would rise from OR_c to OR_1; but in the long period it would settle at OR_2, with supply extended by MM_2. With rent controlled at OR_c, demand exceeds supply by MM_1. Successive short-period reductions in supply, however, eventually give a new long-period supply curve of SL_1, with excess demand of $M_3 M_1$.

A further problem of rent control is that it distorts other prices within the housing market. Households who cannot find dwellings to rent are forced to turn to the uncontrolled owner-occupied sector of the market. This drives up the price of owner-occupied houses. Thus those who are not fortunate enough to obtain rent-controlled dwellings are forced to pay a higher 'rent' than if the whole market were completely free. Rent control redistributes income in an arbitrary way. There is no guarantee that households having a rent-controlled dwelling are more deserving than those who are forced to become owner-occupiers at higher house prices. Indeed, some who cannot afford to buy, for example, the poor, newly-weds and those just starting work, are penalized the most. Just as random is the redistribution of income between tenants and landlords especially when prices generally rise

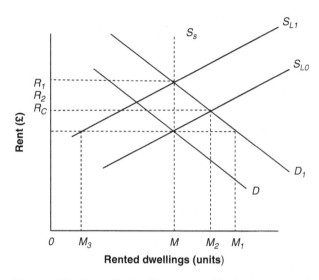

Figure 5.3 The effects of rent control in the long period

over time. In 1961, Cullingworth's survey of Lancaster (Cullingworth, 1963) showed that one-half of the landlords were over 60 years of age, owned only one house and had an average weekly income (including net rents) of less than £10 a week.

Rent control has also given rise to several undesirable 'spin-off' effects. First, by perpetuating shortages, it fostered demands for further rent control – for example to furnished dwellings. Second, to match the 'subsidy' which controlled tenants enjoy at the expense of landlords, the government introduced subsidies for owner-occupiers and council tenants. Third, the resulting shortages led to a policy which is need-orientated rather than demand-orientated. Fourth, the artificially low rents produced by rent control and housing subsidies have influenced the man-in-the-street's view as to what is a 'reasonable' or 'normal' rent.

Furthermore, once subsidies are in place, those receiving them resist their removal. Thus both the Rent Act 1957 (which aimed at some decontrol of rents) and the Housing Finance Act 1972 (which switched local authority housing subsidies from tenants generally to only those needing them) met with such opposition that both policies were dropped by subsequent Labour governments.

A major problem of rent control is that it distorts the allocation of resources. One advantage of the price system is that given perfect competition and the existing distribution of income, it allocates resources so that marginal private benefits equal marginal private costs. This, unless there are externalities, is an optimum allocation which is thwarted by rent control.

Moreover, a policy directed to low rents over 60 years influenced people's views as to the proportion of income it is reasonable to spend on housing. Thus when rents rise, people looked for government help; in contrast, when car prices rise, they accept the rise and pay the higher price. As a result, insufficient resources are attracted into the rented sector.

In the public sector, increased subsidies, necessary if rents are not raised when costs are rising, add to government borrowing. As a result, local authority housing suffers when cuts to grants have to be made (as in 1993–6). Labour mobility is also hampered by rent control. Because the 'subsidy' implicit in rent-controlled housing is attached to the dwelling, not to the person, it is lost on moving (unless it can be capitalized by inducing the landlord to pay a money sum for possession). Consequently, workers find it difficult to move geographically.

Finally, rent control involves considerable administrative costs and bureaucracy. For example, rent officers are required to determine 'fair rents', and rent assessment committees to hear appeals.

Controlled rents coupled with *security of tenure* have been highlighted as the main causes of the emasculation of the private-rented sector, and eventually measures were taken to remove these obstacles. The Housing Act 1980 introduced: (a) *assured tenancies* for *newly-built* privately rented property, with rents *market-determined* but tenants having security of tenure, and (b) *shorthold tenancies*, with registered *fair* rents, but security limited to an agreed fixed term. This was merely the first step, with the fair rent condition being finally abolished in 1987 for shortholds.

It was the Housing Act 1988 which finally produced deregulation. For all new lettings within the newly termed *independent rented sector*, covering both private and housing association lettings, rents can now be freely negotiated between landlord and tenant. Thus in the private-rented sector, rents should tend towards the market clearing rent. Housing associations, however, seek to ensure that low-income households just above the housing benefit eligibility level can afford adequate accommodation, and so set a rent which, while covering their costs, is reduced by the subsidy.

From 15 January 1989, the Act introduced two new types of tenancy: the *assured tenancy* and the *assured shorthold tenancy*. Under the *assured tenancy* provisions, there are no rent controls, while security of tenure provisions are much more favourable to the landlord. At the end of a fixed-term tenancy, a statutory periodic tenancy arises, and the landlord can apply for possession or renew the tenancy at an agreed rent. If the rent is disputed it is determined by a local Rent Assessment Committee (RAC) as being the going *market* rent for that type of accommodation. If the landlord wants possession he must serve the prescribed notices and obtain a court order. Grounds for possession are divided into those over which the court has no discretion (such as substantial arrears of rent) and those where it can make an order only if it considers it reasonable to do so.

With an *assured shorthold tenancy* the rent is negotiated at the market level as with the assured tenancy, but it is easier for the landlord to repossess the premises at the end of the agreed term. This could not be less than six months, and the notice stating that it is a shorthold tenancy had to be served before entry. Here, provided the stipulated conditions, including at least two months' notice, have been fulfilled, the court *must* make an order for repossession at the request of the landlord when the fixed term comes to an end.

The Act also encouraged the letting of rooms by affording no statutory protection for tenants who share living accommodation with their landlord (that is, he must live in the house himself). Thus there is no appeal to a RAC, and no court order is necessary to obtain repossession.

But many long-standing tenants still enjoyed the protection afforded by the Rent Act, 1977 – a 'fair rent' which eliminated the 'scarcity' element as determined by a Rent Officer or RAC, and security of tenure for both the original tenant and a first, or even a second successor, where a wife or child has been living as a member of the family for the previous six months or more.

However, although the Act did not take away any rights which the tenant enjoyed on 14 January 1989, it speeded up the disappearance of regulated tenancies by curtailing rights of succession: (i) the minimum qualification of residence for a member of the tenant's family to succeed was increased from six months to 2 years, and (ii) where the first successor was not the tenant's spouse, the second succession is abolished.

In practice, because a landlord could obtain repossession under an assured shorthold tenancy, its use predominated, and so the Housing Act 1996 made it the standard form of tenancy. It also gave more freedom to the market by removing the 1988 requirements of pre-tenancy notice and the minimum six months' letting term. The tenant can, however, demand a statement of the tenancy conditions.

Thus rent negotiations in the independent rented sector are now little different from those in any other market. Nonetheless, rent control still lingers on with some residual protected tenants whose 'fair rent' is determined by a Rent Officer. As of 1 April 2009, the functions of The Rent Service (TRS) transferred to the Valuation Office Agency (VOA).

Housing subsidies

When the Conservative party under Mrs Thatcher came to power in 1979, many aspects of the housing situation were bound to conflict with their private enterprise philosophy – rent control, lack of individual freedom of choice in housing and a public sector whose management was not only often inefficient, but whose scale of spending was embarrassing to a government whose macroeconomic policy embodied a reduction in public expenditure. Their strategy, therefore, was to develop a housing system based almost entirely on the private sector, believing that efficiency in the allocation of resources devoted to housing could be best achieved by using the market as far as possible. This would allow: (a) consumers to express their choice, and (b) supply to respond accordingly. The first needed a transfer of subsidy from the dwelling to the occupier; the second, the ending of rent control.

Subsidies enable certain households to enjoy services below the cost of providing them through the free market. Such a broad definition covers:

1. the transfer of income from landlords to tenants by rent control;
2. tax concessions enjoyed by owner-occupiers;
3. direct subsidies, consisting of:
   - central government grants to local authority housing accounts and to the housing corporation;
   - housing benefits to tenants on low incomes;
   - renovation grants.

Subsidies have two broad objectives. First, they can be used to redistribute income more equitably, a decision which rests ultimately on a subjective judgement. Second, they can allocate more resources to housing than would be available through the market economy to cover, for example, the external costs of inadequate housing. However economics can suggest conditions which, as far as practicable, subsidies should observe.

First, any subsidy should be given in such a way that consumers can obtain the highest possible satisfaction from a given subsidy expenditure. Where the objective is to enable a consumer to enjoy a minimum standard of housing, a subsidy can either provide more income or reduce the price of housing. The former would appear to be the more efficient method, since it enables the consumer to exercise choice – to buy his or her preferred combination of housing and other goods, effectively enabling the achievement of a higher level of satisfaction. With a reduction in the price of housing relative prices are distorted. Leaving the consumer free to choose how to spend their income supplement, however, might mean they do not spend more on housing, preferring instead to spend it on other goods. It might, therefore, be necessary for society to implement a selective housing subsidy, such as housing benefit, rather than a neutral income supplement.

Second, if the main reason for a housing subsidy is inadequate income, it should be flexible with respect to changes in income (so that it can be stopped if income increases). Again it follows that the subsidy should be attached to the person and not to the dwelling.

Third, the selectivity of any subsidy should be kept under review. The purpose of selectivity is to influence the allocation of resources. Thus housing subsidies are selective as between: (i) housing and other goods; (ii) housing association and private-rented housing, the former being supported by government grant and (iii) slum clearance and housing generally, the former attracting higher subsidies. This means that subsidies have to be adjusted to reflect changes in housing needs and for new policy requirements based on experience. For example, a switch from rebuilding to restoring inner-city dwellings can be promoted by reducing general housing subsidies in favour of improvement grants.

Fourth, public expenditure on housing should be related to the financial resources available, particularly with the government's other commitments, such as defence, health and education and the general extent of government borrowing.

Like housing policy, subsidies evolved piecemeal. Apart from those enjoyed by the owner-occupier, they were applied on the supply side. Exchequer grants to local authorities enabled councils to charge rents at less than the economic cost, and irrespective of tenant's income. In the private sector, landlords provided a virtual subsidy to rent-controlled tenants. In short, the criteria suggested above were not observed.

From 1979, the policy of switching from supply-based to demand-based subsidies, therefore, was on firm ground. In 1982 rent rebates were incorporated in a new *housing benefit*. But the change by which the subsidy would target the person rather than bricks and mortar was really effected by the Social Security Act 1988. Henceforth the housing benefit would be paid to tenants in both the public and private sectors to allow them to afford a rent which matched their needs. This would allow tenants to exercise their preferences regarding housing and could be adjusted with changes in their income.

In the very short term, the supply is fixed at OM (Figure 5.4). A housing benefit limited to PP_1 per unit is given to all qualifying tenants. Rent therefore rises to P_1, the market rent for all would-be tenants including those whose income is above the limit to qualify for housing benefit.

In the long term, supply can respond to the higher rent and a new equilibrium is established at a lower rent OR, but with more accommodation OM_2. The

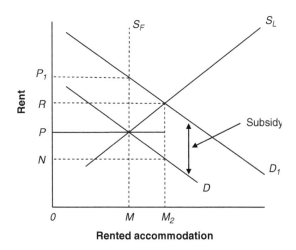

Figure 5.4   The effects of housing benefit

total subsidy now being paid equals $RN . OM_2$ of which $RP.OM_2$ represents the benefit received by landlords.

It can be seen from this that as the quantity of rented accommodation demanded and supplied increases as a result of the subsidy, the cost to the authorities (number of rented dwellings times the subsidy) increases. What was not foreseen, however, was the escalation in the total housing benefit bill from £3.6 billion in 1988 to £8.4 billion in 1993/4. In 2008, 4.6 million people received housing benefit (HB) in the UK, at an annual cost of around £11.5 billion (approximately 1.5 per cent of GDP; much higher than other European countries) Since public sector housing was occupied predominantly by the old and disabled, single-person households and others on low income, 60 per cent of public sector tenants received housing benefit. Moreover, as it covered the difference between the asking rent and need, there was little incentive for the tenant to negotiate with the landlord or to economize on accommodation. In addition, high rents (especially in the London area) often gave rise to a 'poverty trap' for low-income families who, as a result, refrained from increasing their income in case it triggered a reduction in their housing benefit.

Pressure was put on local authorities to monitor rents to ensure that they do not exceed the local level, and so prompt tenants to negotiate with landlords. But it was not thought logical to impose a global limit to government spending on housing benefit because that would undermine the whole strategy of providing housing through the market by regenerating the private-rented sector.

The new coalition government of 2010, as part of its plans to reduce the public sector deficit, announced restrictions on housing benefit. Rents will only be paid at 30 per cent of the local average and capped at £400 per week for a four bedroom and £250 for a one bedroom home. Anyone out of work for over a year will lose another 10 per cent in housing benefit and the value of housing benefit will only rise by Consumer Price Index (CPI) inflation every year, which is likely to mean an effective fall in value as rents and house prices rise by a greater percentage.

Household tenure in the UK

The private-rented sector

The demand for rented dwellings comes mainly from persons:

1. unable to qualify for a mortgage; or
2. waiting to purchase; or
3. frequently moving on account of their work.

Thus renting is an important alternative to buying.

Whereas in 1914, rented and tied dwellings comprised 90 per cent of UK housing, by 1951 this had shrunk to 50 per cent, and by 1997 to 9 per cent. There has been a slight recovery (probably because of the rise in house prices between 1996 and 2007 making houses unaffordable to first-time buyers) so that in 2009 the private rental sector comprised 10.6 per cent of UK households. This loss of privately rented dwellings (Table 5.1) was largely the result of rent control. Because rents did not keep pace with inflation, management and maintenance costs left a net return which was uncompetitive compared with alternative investments. Furthermore, in contrast to other forms of tenure, the private-rented sector received no subsidies. Above all, security of tenure compounded the landlord's disadvantage, for he was locked into his investment until vacant possession was eventually obtained or the property sold on the market at a loss in real terms.

Renting private accommodation through the market enables tenants to exercise their preferences within their income constraint. It is flexible, and facilitates mobility. With one exception, rent control brought this to an end. The exception was furnished accommodation, which was not subject to control: so for persons waiting to purchase or moving frequently, such accommodation could be found. Consequently, the Rent Act 1974, by bringing furnished accommodation within the provisions of rent control, was a measure of extreme folly as this small safety-valve ceased to operate almost overnight.

Two further inducements to increase supply were also introduced by the government on the supply side. First, under the *Business Expansion Scheme* (BES) a taxpayer who bought new shares in a qualifying company could claim income tax relief on the amount invested and pay no capital gains tax on first disposal of the shares provided they had been held for 5 years. The company had to offer assured tenancies for a period of at least 4 years. Properties had to be unlet at the time of acquisition, with a maximum capital value of each dwelling of £85,000 (£125,000 in Greater London) to avoid concentration on the young urban professional (yuppie) end of the market. Assured shorthold tenancies were excluded because the purpose was to encourage the long-term provision of rented property. In its early years the BES scheme was highly successful. It was estimated that by the beginning of 1989 over £100 million had been raised

Table 5.1 Changes in tenure distribution 1914–2001, UK (%)

	1914	1947	1963	1983	1993	1997	2001
Owner occupied	10	26	45	58.8	66.4	68	69
Rented privately	90	61	27	10.7	9.7	11	10
Rented from:							
Housing association	–	–	–	2.3	3.7	5	7
Local authority or new town corporation	–	13	28	28.1	20.1	16	14

Source: www.communities.gov.uk: Survey of English Housing Preliminary Report, 2007–08.

under BES assured tenancy schemes, often to purchase repossessed properties from building societies. But for the most part, investors were more interested in making a short-term tax-free capital gain rather than renting their properties long-term. Thus the scheme was brought to an end in December 1993.

Second, from 1997 an occupier who lets a furnished room(s) in his main residence can enjoy tax relief of up to £4,250 a year. This level of tax relief has not been increased despite the average level of rents increasing by 110 per cent since 1997.

After a period of deregulation flowing from the 1988 and 1996 Acts the private-rented sector has grown from 8 per cent to 10.1 per cent of households in 2001 and to 14.2 per cent in 2010. This is an increase from 2.1 million to 3.1 million homes. Almost 20 per cent of households in London are private tenants. The Housing Act 2004 introduced specific provisions to enable local authorities to work to secure improved management arrangements and property conditions within the sector. Since 28 February 1997, all new tenancies for less than £25,000 per annum are 'assured shorthold tenancies', unless the contract specifies that the dwelling is being let on an 'assured' tenancy. (Tenancies above £25,000 per annum can be entirely freely contracted). The assured shorthold tenancy gives the tenant security for an initial six months, even where the contract is for six months or less, unless the tenant has breached one of the standard grounds for possession. After that, the landlord need only give two months 'notice requiring possession' to remove the tenant. No reason need be given for requiring possession.

Rents can be freely negotiated when the contract is signed. If the tenant subsequently thinks his rent is higher than is being paid by other tenants for similar properties, he can go to a rent assessment committee, which will assess a market rent. However, UK law gives the tenant no protection against retaliatory eviction (after two months' notice) by the landlord.

A strong housing market, high demand for social housing, the emergence of the 'buy-to-let' landlord, demographic changes and an increasingly mobile society, mean that the role of the private-rented sector in meeting housing need is increasingly important in the UK.

Public sector housing

By the end of the nineteenth century concern over the effects on health of bad housing had led to tentative steps towards dwellings being provided by local authorities. But the policy did not gather momentum until after 1919 when, because of the neglect of building during the previous war years, the Town and Country Planning Act required local authorities to prepare plans for providing housing to meet local needs. It was thought that, once the construction industry had fully recovered, public housing would be necessary only for the 'needy' – the poor, old and sick – and for slum clearance.

But the decline of the private-rented sector, meant that the deficiency in low-cost rented dwellings had to be made good by the public sector. However, in implementing policy, rents charged had to be comparable with those of similar dwellings in the *rent-controlled* private sector. This rejection of the market mechanism meant that local authority housing had to be: (a) provided and allocated on the basis of 'need', not demand; and (b) subsidized.

For most authorities, demand exceeded supply and so their housing activities were, with the support of subsidies, extended. Thus waiting lists contained not just those on low incomes but others who simply preferred to rent at a subsidized level rather than buy. Such bypassing of the market mechanism creates difficulties in allocating the limited supply – as the difference between 'need' and 'demand' indicates.

Housing Need measures the extent to which existing accommodation falls short of that required to provide each household with accommodation of a minimum specified standard irrespective of ability to pay. Making such an estimate, however, is not easy. For one thing, projections of households are based on such variables as marriage rates and the size of family, both of which depend upon changes in income and social attitudes. For another, 'need' is more than the difference between aggregate households and aggregate dwellings, since both have to be subdivided and related to size and location. Census returns and statistics from the Registrar General provide the basic data.

Above all, determining the 'minimum specified standard' presents practical and conceptual difficulties. How do we measure accommodation standards – by the family unit or by area per person? In fact, we should concentrate on the needs of the different types of family. For instance, a family of six requires less space than three households each consisting of two persons, while two adults and two young children differ in their housing needs from one adult with three grown children. However, since it is impossible to forecast for such refinements, requirements are usually calculated on the basis of so many square feet or rooms *per person*.

Similarly, what standard should be specified? Although this is basically a subjective decision, it has to be related to the overall level of income. Moreover, in formulating building plans, a decision has to be made on whether to aim at a standard to overcome current overcrowding or a future standard which allows for income growth. When there is deficiency of housing, the former tends to be paramount. In the long term, however, when only replacement is called for, it is important to anticipate future standards.

To obtain the number of *households*, the existing population is projected for the target year according to age and sex by applying birth and death rates and allowing for external migration. How many households a given population will form, however, depends upon the marriage rate, the proportion of young people who live separately from their parents, and the number of old people who go to live with their children or are admitted to institutions. In addition, an attempt must be made to classify households according to size by applying statistics relating to the size of the completed family. Finally, since dwellings cannot be moved physically, an estimate should be made of the regional location of households in the target year. Naturally, the more distant the target year, the more inaccurate are forecasts likely to be, since data are influenced by changes in the level and distribution of income, immigration policy, internal migration and so on.

Ideally, policy should aim at providing housing units of sufficient quantity and quality and in the right location for the households estimated. The stock of *dwellings* has to be estimated for the target year, taking into account new building, demolition, renewals and conversions, all of which are affected by changes in the rate of growth of national income. In addition, the quality of dwellings – in terms of age and standard amenities – and their location are important. Finally, not all the stock will be occupied by a separate household. Some 4 per cent is likely to be vacant to permit mobility, while 1 per cent will be held for second homes, a figure which is likely to rise as real incomes increase.

Housing Demand refers to an economic concept, *effective demand* – what people are willing and able to pay for housing. We are therefore concerned with: (a) preferences at a *price*, and (b) the conditions of demand – the level of income, income distribution, household formation, the rate of interest, the price of substitutes, government policy, changes in tastes, expectations of future price changes and so on. Demand, therefore, is an expression through the price system of people's preferences for different types of housing. In contrast, where housing is allocated arbitrarily according to 'need', there may be some loss of satisfaction because a household occupies more subsidized housing than they would have chosen via the market and the taxpayer suffers loss of welfare by footing the bill.

Estimating demand for housing as a guide to *future policy* is far from easy. One method is to apply past statistical relationships between demand and house prices, rents, interest rates and so on. The difficulty here is that the same relationship may not hold in the future, since the conditions of demand change over time. Another method is through direct enquiry, but this has limitations. Not only do people restrict their estimates of demand to two or 3 years ahead, thereby providing little guide for long-term policy, but such estimates tend to be related to the artificially low rents to which households are accustomed.

The growth in the importance of public sector housing during the twentieth century is shown in Table 5.1. From 13 per cent of total housing just after the Second World War it had risen to 31 per cent by 1980, when the UK stock of local authority and new town properties reached a peak of 6.5 million.

The figures for 2008 for England only (statistics for Scotland are now separate) show a fall in the owner-occupied percentage to 68.3 per cent. Owner-occupation peaked at 70.9 per cent in 2003. In 2008 social rented tenure in England was 17.7 per cent and private-rented was 13.9 per cent.

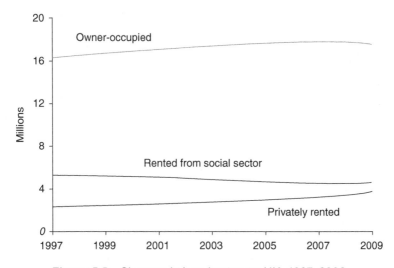

Figure 5.5 Changes in housing tenure UK, 1997–2009
Source: www.communities.gov.uk: Survey of English Housing Preliminary Report, 2007–08

Since 1997, as can be seen in Figure 5.5, there has been a slight decline in the social rented sector (from 5.3 million households to 4.5 million).

The owner-occupied sector

Table 5.1 shows the relative growth in owner-occupied housing: from 10 per cent in 1914 to 26 per cent in 1947, 56 per cent in 1980, and 69 per cent in 2001. It peaked at 70.9 per cent before the downturn of 2007–9 and has fallen back to around 67 per cent. Although the shortage of houses to rent undoubtedly forced many to buy, it was not the sole cause. With rising incomes among skilled and semi-skilled workers, houseownership was often a first preference. Aspiration to do as well as neighbours and relatives gave it further impetus. Furthermore, schedule A income tax on the imputed income of the house owned was abolished in 1963. But the 'subsidy' of mortgage interest tax relief remained unaffected until 1974, when it was limited to the first £25,000 borrowed. It was not finally abolished until 2000. Above all, finance on favourable terms was available through the expanding building societies. For most people, a house can be bought only by borrowing for a comparatively long period. This was possible because: (a) the house secures the loan; (b) building societies specialized in this type of finance, and were the main providers (see Chapter 18, Table 18.2).

Building societies originated in Birmingham in 1775 when a group of working men formed a society to build houses and allocate them on completion. This background may still exert some influence on their policies with recognition of 'social' obligations in lending to first-time buyers at the lower income end and to housing associations. Their success was based on their ability to compete for small short-term loans from private savers by careful attention to their convenience and preferences and by overcoming the risk inherent in borrowing short and lending long by proven financial stability. Such retail short-term loans meant that they could compete by lending at a lower rate of interest than banks. Nor did they have to compete with each other because they operated a cartel through the Building Societies Association to fix both lending and borrowing rates.

As a result, demand for mortgages usually exceeded supply. This allowed societies to impose conditions which reinforced other policies, chiefly safety of capital. Thus, they showed a preference for certain types of property, in particular brick-built, freehold, three-bedroom houses of traditional design, and on these they were prepared to grant a 90 per cent mortgage. Only when the rise in the price of houses forced first-time buyers to settle for cheaper types of dwelling, particularly flats, did the building societies relax this preference.

This dominant position of the building societies influenced the shape of owner-occupied housing. First, since the purchase of most houses was through building-society mortgages, speculative builders concentrated on the type of house likely to attract a mortgage, particularly the two-bedroom or three-bedroom house of traditional design. Second, their condition of a mortgage that there be no sub-letting without approval reduced a possible source of rented accommodation.

The private enterprise philosophy of the 1979 Conservative government under Prime Minister Margaret Thatcher, meant a change to the development of a housing system based almost entirely on the private sector. The market was to be used to allow consumers to express their choices and to enable supply to respond accordingly. It was decided to reduce local authority housing expenditure (both capital and revenue) and to privatize much public housing. Local authorities were forced to raise rents on their public sector housing and although an increasing part of the higher rents was supported by housing benefit, the overall effect was to redirect subsidized rents from tenants in general to those most in need.

The Housing Act 1980 contained 'right-to-buy' (RTB) provision which gave local authority tenants discounts of between 33 and 50 per cent of market value. Sales rose sharply to a peak of 207,050 in 1982. They fell back to 145,121 by 1990. By 1998, over 1.6 million of Great Britain's 6.5 million stock of public sector dwellings had been sold at an average price of £22,000 (£33,000 in Greater London). In 2007–8 there were 19,360 RTB sales and in 2008–9 just 7,300 at an average discount of £25,410 on an average price of £107,250.

In favour of the RTB policy it is argued that it:

1. enabled tenants to fulfil their aspirations of becoming owner-occupiers and liberated them from perpetual dependence on council housing:

2. resulted in risk and management and maintenance costs being transferred from the local authority to the new owner;
3. reduced government subsidies by scaling down new council housebuilding; and
4. helped in reducing the PSNCR through the privatization proceeds (which in fact exceeded those of British Telecom).

But opponents argue that it:

1. decreases the supply of housing available for letting to those most in need:
2. reduces the range of council housing available since the better houses are those more likely to be sold;
3. could lead to management and long-term development problems on a housing estate through the diversification of ownership and tenures.

With the object of improving the quality of management, privatization also took the form of encouraging local authorities to transfer houses to housing associations, while tenants were given the right, providing a majority do not vote against it, to change landlords to a housing association or other approved persons. In fact there has been little take-up of this option.

It is unlikely that a future government would reverse what has proved to be a popular and successful policy. But, with enforced sales at a discount, there would seem little point in councils building further houses to rent, although marginal additions may be obtained at little cost via 'planning gain' (see Chapters 12 and 22).

Nevertheless, with a current stock of nearly 5 million dwellings, local authorities still have an important role to play in providing a residual tenure for those in social need – clearing slums, accommodating the homeless, providing for special groups such as the aged and disabled (for example, through sheltered accommodation). More thought, too, can be given to improving the quality of management.

Housing association dwellings

In addition to the RTB scheme, since 1997, the Right to Acquire (RTA) scheme gives eligible housing association tenants a statutory right to purchase the property in which they live at a discount, generally between £9,000 and £16,000 depending on the local authority area in which the property is located. RTA only applies to properties built or acquired by housing associations, both charitable and non charitable, with public funds from 1 April 1997 onwards. (Properties transferred from a local authority to a housing association after 1 April 1997 are also eligible).

Some properties are exempt from RTA including those in small rural settlements and sheltered housing. Existing housing association tenants should get advice from their landlord to determine whether their house qualifies for RTA.

To be eligible for the Right to Acquire scheme, a tenant must occupy a qualifying property, have spent a minimum period as a public sector tenant, and live in a self-contained flat or house which is their only home. The minimum period for those who were tenants before 18 January 2005 is 2 years. This was extended to 5 years for new tenants from 18 January 2005 by the Housing Act 2004. The Homes and Communities Agency (HCA) provides grants to cover the discount offered to the purchaser.

Now that councils are no longer building new houses, the government has fallen back on housing associations as the main, though still inadequate, source of low-cost rented dwellings – now referred to as 'social housing'.

Housing associations are private sector voluntary bodies set up to provide housing on a non-profit basis. Altogether in the UK there are about 2,000 registered associations owning over 1.45 million dwellings (some 5 per cent of the total housing). Most are quite small, nearly one-half managing fewer than 25 houses; but there are some 75 which own over 2,500 houses apiece.

The Housing Corporation (established in 1964) provides over half their capital, the government allocating it a yearly Housing Association Grant (HAG). The remaining finance is obtained from local authorities, building societies, banks, institutions (such as the Norwich Union), housebuilders (such as Barratts) and even lenders through the euro-bond market. The Housing Corporation also monitors and audits the activities of housing associations registered with it.

Traditionally, the activities of housing associations complemented those of local authorities by providing accommodation in stress areas and for special groups, such as single people, the elderly and disabled people, where obtaining mortgages for owner-occupation could prove difficult. For instance, dilapidated houses in the inner cities were acquired, converted into flats or hostel accommodation, and brought up to standard with the help of a renovation grant.

But now that local authorities no longer build new houses, the provision of socially affordable rented dwellings has been largely taken over by housing associations. Indeed some local authorities have handed over the residue of their housing estates to them. The government, considering that they offered more efficient and sensitive management, increased HAG support and relaxed restrictions on their borrowing. As a result they have been able to integrate with the greater lending power of building societies to expand their activities. Thus in addition to rented accommodation, housing associations now provide low-cost owner-occupied dwellings, often on a shared-equity basis, in cooperation with building societies who thereby still retain some of their 'social' tradition.

The original aim of the government was for housing associations to provide an extra 50,000 low-cost units a year at 'affordable' rents made possible through HAG finance. But this has been cut, in line with other government spending. As a result rents have had to rise (now being based on the capital value of the dwelling). For the three-quarters of their tenants who qualify for housing benefit, this is not too serious but for others the 'affordable rent' objective has been undermined. Nevertheless, provided they can continue to attract private capital, housing associations are still the most likely providers of long-term (as opposed to shorthold) *rented* accommodation on an assured tenancy basis.

The owner-occupied sector

Owner-occupiers were the main beneficiaries of the Conservative government's policy between 1979 and 1997 and the sector has expanded from 56 per cent in 1980 to 69 per cent in 2001, with UK numbers rising from 12 million to 16.7 million over the same period. The main contributory factors were: (a) the 1.5 million. former local authority and new town tenants who had exercised their right-to-buy; (b) tax concessions; (c) the rapid growth in the economy and in personal income during the mid-1980s; (d) an increase in the availability of mortgages.

The policy of relating subsidies to need was *not* applied to owner-occupation. Indeed in 1983 the ceiling for mortgage interest relief was raised from £25,000 to £30,000, and not until 1991 was it limited to the standard rate of income tax and subsequently reduced in stages until its abolition in 2000. There was no discrimination in favour of the small, first-time buyer even though he was more likely to be on a low income. The freedom from capital gains tax, which also remained, had some justification, since the owner also took the risk of a loss.

The growth of the economy and of personal incomes coincided with the freeing of financial markets which released funds for house purchase. There are two main mortgage sources, (i) banks, (ii) building societies.

Banks

Table 18.2 (see Chapter 18) shows the advance of the *banks* since 1985 as lenders for house purchase. Factors contributing to this are:

1. The greater sophistication shown by depositors in investing their funds encouraged banks to compete by offering savings accounts with a high rate of interest.
2. The emphasis from 1981 onwards of controlling credit through the rate of interest permitted an upsurge in the banks' deposits. One outlet for funds was that of loans for house purchase.
3. The building societies were slow in changing their rather rigid financial requirements in granting mortgages. In contrast, the banks competed through the terms offered, especially at the higher end of the market, for example, by a uniform rate irrespective of the size of the loan.
4. Banks recognize that borrowers through a low-start mortgage may eventually use other customer services.

Today it is not only the commercial banks that have realized that homebuyers are good business. Merchant banks, foreign banks (for example, America's Citibank), and a new National Home Loans Corporation have all increased competition by entering the market.

Building societies

Such competition forced the *building societies* to realize that they would have to compete by marketing mortgages – for example, by advertising and offering low-start mortgages. They also had to compete more fiercely with the government, banks, insurance companies, unit trusts, and so on, for depositors' funds. Moreover, depositors today are more aware of alternative investment opportunities and are more ready to switch their funds even for short periods if this appears to be advantageous. This was noticeable in the privatization issues when subscribers drew heavily on their deposits. Again, with no capital gains tax on gains of under £7,700 (2002), investments in equities are more attractive for the small investor. In order to compete, societies introduced bonus rates to attract longer-term loans, issued cheque books to substantial depositors, and so on.

But it was the Building Societies Act 1986 that transformed the building societies from a 'movement' pursuing social goals to an 'industry' with sights set on financial targets. Until then, their response to the new competition from the banks had been restrained by legal restrictions imposed in recognition of their mutual status and their exclusion from the normal supervision of financial institutions. The Act extended the powers of the building societies, enabling them to: develop an integrated house purchase service covering, for example, estate agency, surveying, insurance and conveyancing; offer new types of loan, such as first-step index-linked, equity-linked and shared-ownership mortgages; own subsidiary companies and land; participate directly in the provision of housing by owning and developing land; provide a full range of personal banking services and, usually through specialist firms, advise on life insurance, pensions, unit trusts, stocks and shares, inheritance tax and school fees; borrow on the wholesale money markets; make unsecured loans up to £10 000 to individuals and, from 1993, acquire assets other than residential mortgages and conduct business other than mortgages up to 25 per cent and 15 per cent respectively of their total assets.

Borrowing on the wholesale markets enabled the societies to obtain additional funds and to even-out fluctuations in the flow of retail savings which now occur more frequently as the popularity of unit trusts and ISAs ebbs and flows.

This wide extension of the functions of building societies has involved considerable capital expenditure in new technology so that only societies, which are powerful financially or have a strong local connection can survive. The Abbey National and Halifax for example, now operate as banks, the Cheltenham &

Gloucester has been taken over by Lloyds TSB, and the Nationwide and the Derbyshire have amalgamated.

One question that has to be asked is: what directions will building societies take once the owner-occupied sector of the housing market becomes saturated? There are a number of possibilities, for example:

1. forming their own subsidiary companies to provide social housing for first-time purchasers, sheltered housing for the elderly and in conjunction with housing associations, affordable rented accommodation;
2. extending their traditional skill in obtaining retail funds to provide residential mortgages in the wider EU, where the proportion of owner-occupation is on average less than half that in the UK; and
3. providing finance to the commercial and industrial property markets.

The Conservative government's housing policy was based on the long-term improvements which would be effected by market forces. But it glossed over the immediate problems: homelessness; the 3 million dwellings unfit or in a state of serious disrepair; the special needs of the aged, and the physically and mentally disabled. Although local authorities were saddled with these responsibilities, and in 1990 were free to specify *housing renewal areas* and given power to acquire land and effect improvements, they were not provided with adequate funds.

Instead the Thatcher government supported the flagship of its housing policy – owner-occupation – with mortgage interest relief at an annual cost to the Exchequer of £6 billion, and this grew with increased owner-occupation and eventual rises in the rate of interest. Phasing out this subsidy would have allowed funds to be switched to the housing needs of the poorer sections of the community and to the provision of affordable rented accommodation through housing associations.

Nor was it appreciated that a housing policy based on housing benefits, the provision of rented accommodation by housing associations, and owner-occupation can only be followed within the framework of overall monetary policy. When this failed, the flagship was blown seriously off course, as follows.

By the end of 1988, the annual rate of houseprice inflation was as high as 33 per cent nationally, and in some regions even 50 per cent. Price is determined by the interaction of demand and supply. But, as we saw in Chapter 4, because the supply of houses is inelastic, their price is largely demand-determined. The following all played a part in increasing demand:

1. After the restrictive anti-inflation policies of the early 1980s, the Thatcher government took the reins off the market economy, and the GNP grew at an annual rate of 4 per cent. People, especially young executives, had more spending power, and much of this found its way into the housing market.

2. The cost of borrowing for a mortgage fell progressively as the Chancellor reduced base rate in stages from 14 per cent in January 1985 to 7 per cent in May 1988.

3. After 1985 credit control was relaxed, more significantly with 'Big Bang' in 1986. Competition between the main lending institutions – building societies, banks and foreign banks – led to easier mortgage terms, even the building societies throwing aside their traditional caution regarding a safe loan-to-earnings ratio. Borrowing of 95 per cent, and even 100 per cent, of the price of a property became possible.

4. The effect of easier credit was reinforced by the 1988 Budget, which reduced the standard rate of income tax from 27 to 25 per cent, and the higher rate from 60 to 40 per cent.

5. The 1988 Budget announced that, as from 1 August, *multiple* mortgage tax relief (enjoyed by each mortgagee of a joint house purchase) would be abolished. This created a stampede for mortgage funds to beat the deadline, particularly from first-time buyers. House prices rose, initially at the lower end of the market, but eventually having a ripple effect upwards.

6. Details of the proposed replacement of the rates by the poll tax increased demand for higher-priced houses, for which the new tax was usually less than the rates, especially where households did not exceed two adults.

7. The government's policies of a 'property-owning democracy' and the 'right-to-buy' added thrust to the desire for houseownership as the only alternative to the shrinking rented sector.

8. A long-term factor – the increasing flow of inherited wealth resulting from the past growth in homeownership by the present 65-year plus age group – began to make itself felt. This was estimated to have amounted to £8 billion in 1988.

9. Expectations of a continued rise in house prices often led to spending on a house being regarded as an excellent investment asset which could be obtained by borrowing against a small deposit. That is, houses were demanded by owner-occupiers for 'investing' in as well as for living in.

In retrospect, the government was too late in recognizing the latent inflationary pressures. The easier credit of 1986–8 and the cut in income tax took place just when monetary policy should have been tightened. Aggregate demand was already more than sufficient to sustain the level of growth that could be achieved without causing an uncomfortable pressure on prices. In June 1988, the government had to raise base rate by 1 per cent to 8 per cent. However, as rising prices had gathered their own momentum, further successive increases in base rate brought it up, by October 1989, to 15 per cent.

The recession, which followed, had a traumatic effect on the housing market. By 1991 unemployment had risen to 2.25 million and was continuing to rise.

Mortgage rates rose in sympathy with base rate. Not only could potential new owner-occupiers not afford to buy, but recent buyers found that interest payments could not be covered as earnings fell, perhaps because of redundancy.

By 1992 over 290,000 households were over six months in arrears with their mortgage payments. Repossessions followed: there were 75,000 in 1991, and though they gradually fell, there were still 34,000 in 1998. The government's 1992 response of making £750 million available to housing associations to buy 20,000 houses was hardly significant in view of an estimated 200,000 forced vacancies. Repossessions also severely aggravated the problem to local authorities of homelessness, which in the United Kingdom rose from 70,000 in 1979 to over 178,000 in 1991.

From their peak in the third quarter of 1989, house prices fell by 14 per cent in 2 years, and continued to fall, averaging 17 per cent by 1994 (Nationwide House Price Index) and by as much as 30 per cent in London and the south of England. Thus an estimated 15 million buyers (70 per cent of whom were first-time), who entered the market in 1987–9 when prices were high, were locked into a situation of *negative equity* (estimated in 1995 at £7.5 billion), where the proceeds of a sale are insufficient to pay off the mortgage debt.

The gloom was prolonged by the shock of the recession on consumer confidence. One incentive to spend was eliminated by the virtual ending of price inflation. But far worse was the uncertainty regarding job security, as competition forced firms to streamline their operations and cut back on production. Potential new buyers were reluctant to take on a mortgage, as is shown by the fact that the houseprice/earnings ratio fell from 4.56 in 1988 to 2.81 in 1994.

The fall in house prices bottomed out in late 1993, but not until 1995 did they start to recover, at first hesitantly, but accelerating between 1996–7, especially in London and the south-east.

The rate of price increase slowed in 1998, reflecting concern of a possible downturn in the economy following the financial crises in south-east Asia, but by early 1999 prices had improved sufficiently to remove the overhang of negative equity. Returning confidence, lower mortgage rates following the fall in base rate to 5 per cent, and a shortage of houses coming on to the market brought about an acceleration in price increases so that in the UK as a whole they increased by 25 per cent 1993–9 and in south-east England by over 33 per cent. In 2002 alone house prices rose by more than 22 per cent in England and Wales. The average houseprice in early 2003 was £145,251 and in Greater London it was £241,838.

Although the housing market cannot be held responsible for the general inflation which forced the government to take disinflationary measures in 1988, it did play a major part. Early on, it had shown itself sensitive to important changes in demand, and the government should have acted sooner once the price signals flashed up. Nor can the lending institutions, too, be absolved from a large part of the blame, for their lending was imprudent, to say the least. It should not be necessary, for instance, for an individual building society to have to make provision

---

Box 5.1   Home Information Packs, 2007–10

Home Information Packs (HIPs) were introduced in 2007 in England and Wales. The aim was to speed up the house-selling process by obliging sellers to provide much of the required conveyancing information when properties are first put up for sale. The packs were paid for by sellers and contain property information, title deeds, and local searches.

The energy performance certificate (EPC), which ranks the energy efficiency of a home with A to G ratings (see Chapter 14), has been retained (it was European Union legislation) and must be produced by the seller within 28 days of putting a home on the market. Each EPC costs about £60.

The burden of paying about £200 for searches from local authorities and search companies will now fall on house buyers, which could add to costs for first-time buyers.

HIPs, which were mandatory for anyone selling a home, have been dogged by criticism. Estate agents have long complained they add red tape to the selling process, while sellers have grumbled about the £200–£400 price tag attached to the packs. Many prospective sellers were discouraged from testing the housing market because they had to spend money up front on the HIP.

The National Association of Estate Agents welcomed the news of their abolition in May 2010, saying that HIPs had 'failed to benefit homebuyers and actively discouraged sellers'. Homeowners would again be able to 'test the market', a practice that had almost disappeared in the 3 years that HIPs were in force.

However, the announcement will mean that thousands of people who trained as home inspectors and relied on the packs for their income would probably lose their jobs. There are between 3,000 and 10,000 people whose livelihoods depend on HIPs, according to the Association of Home Information Pack Providers.

---

in its annual accounts of over £100 million against bad debts. What happened between 2005 and 2009, however, showed that lessons were not learned and that financial institutions and governments were not sufficiently cautious about the links between the housing market and the overall economy.

The credit crunch and UK residential property

In the years 2004–7 there was exceptionally high liquidity in world financial markets. This contributed to a UK surge in investment in commercial real estate. Cheap borrowing meant property was a self-financing investment (interest rates approximately 6 per cent and prices rising by 10 per cent per annum). There was unparalleled demand for housing in the UK as a result of population increase and a rise in the number of single-person households. The sustained growth of the UK economy fuelled this rising demand, which, combined with insufficient delivery of new stock, led to considerable demand-pull inflation of house prices. This was sufficient to inflate average prices at the peak to six times average income. Mortgages were issued at high-loan-value ratios and at unprecedented multiples of household income, sometimes with few rigorous credit or personal checks. In the UK money was transferred from equities into property and by the end of 2007 more than 60 per cent of Britain's wealth was tied up in property (residential housing: £4,314 billion; offices and factory buildings: £699 billion).

Unfortunately, this over-exposure to risk in the property sector of the UK was about to be threatened by the collapse of the US subprime mortgage market in mid-2007. The expression 'subprime' appropriately suggests less than the best and does, in fact, describe risky mortgage lending as US lenders had allowed themselves to get carried away on a speculative property 'bubble' and had considerable exposure to high-risk debt. (suffering approximately $400 billion losses). A slow down in the US economy was accompanied by a credit squeeze and a decrease in property values. The USA cut interest rates to try to boost the economy but this had no positive impact and there were early signs of recession. The global nature of financial markets resulted in a ripple across the financial sector worldwide and the consequent lack of liquidity in the global banking system caused a slow down in most western economies, and property values began to decrease.

In the UK, initially, there was resistance to interest rate cuts because of inflationary risks from oil and food price rises. There was a loss of confidence in credit markets and a 'run' on the Northern Rock bank in late 2007 as a result of reduced short-term lending on the LIBOR (London Inter-Bank Offer Rate – the interest rate that the banks charge each other for loans) market. This was followed in early 2008 by problems for other UK banks – the Bradford and Bingley (over exposed in the 'buy to let' sector) – Royal Bank of Scotland and HBOS. Fears arose that these banks and others were on the verge of collapse.

In the USA, the Federal National Mortgage Association (nicknamed Fannie Mae) and the Federal Home Mortgage Corporation (nicknamed Freddie Mac) had to be rescued by guarantees from the government, followed by Lehman Brothers who became the world's biggest corporate bankruptcy at $639 billion. In addition, the insurance industry giant AIG had to be bailed to the tune of $85 billion by the US Federal Reserve. The Bank of England estimated that the world's financial firms lost £1.8 trillion ($2.8 trillion).

The financial markets were now extremely nervous and but for unprecedented UK government intervention further bank failures would have followed. According to the Governor of the Bank of England, total UK government support for the banks will be £1 trillion (or £1,000 billion). As a result, public sector debt reached unprecedented levels and with tax revenues reducing in the recession, confidence in the pound was hit and it fell in value.

All of this meant difficult lending conditions and the tighter finance affected businesses, consumers and the housing market. There was greatly reduced development and construction activity as highly leveraged investment activity was curtailed. As lending conditions tightened in 2008 and loan-to-value ratios were reduced, the UK listed property sector including REIT's experienced major falls in share prices.

The tight credit conditions meant greater risk sensitivity and rental projections were more cautious while assumptions about end value of completed developments were revised downward. Developments not yet started were subject to revised development appraisals. and substantial pre-letting commitments were being sought before commencement of development. Overseas funding was sought by developers, for example the 'Shard of Glass' development at London Bridge required Qatar finance.

There was oversupply of commercial space and contraction of commercial and residential demand as employment fell. The average UK houseprice in January 2008 was £184,203; by September 2009 it had fallen to £158,337 (a decline of 14 per cent). Nevertheless, in the previous decade from 2000 to 2009, average houseprice growth in England and Wales was 117 per cent and 68 per cent in real terms (after allowing for inflation).

There was a considerable rise in the number of flats or apartments built during the first decade of the century. This was driven by changes in planning rules, the rise of buy-to-let, and the search for swifter returns by housebuilders. From 2000 to 2008 the proportion of newly-built homes that were flats rose from just over 15 per cent to almost 50 per cent. In contrast, detached housing fell from 45 per cent to less than 15 per cent. This trend increased the supply of new homes and meant that over the decade, old houses grew in value by more than new houses. The buy-to-let boom was driven by the bubble in easy and cheap credit, but when that came to an end with the credit crunch, the fall in price for city-centre flats was more pronounced than for other forms of housing with prices in some cities falling by 50 per cent.

House prices in the UK stabilized in 2009, finishing the year slightly higher than at the start. Savills predicts that inflation-adjusted house prices will rise by 40 per cent in the decade to 2020. This compares with 49 per cent in the 1970s, 43 per cent in the 1980s, 14 per cent in the 1990s, and 68 per cent in the 'noughties' (2000–2009).

Future provision of housing

Policy for future housing is concerned with two main issues: (a) expanding the existing stock, and (b) providing the type of dwelling preferred by different households within their income constraint. Each will be examined in turn.

Projections of future housing requirements are based mainly on underlying demographic factors and trends in household formation. For decades in the UK, housing supply has failed to keep up with the demand for more homes and the needs of a changing demographic population – more people are choosing to live alone and people are living longer.

New households are projected to increase by, on average, 252,000 each year between now and 2031 (see Table 5.2). This has led to significant problems of affordability, particularly for those seeking to buy their first home.

In March 2004, Kate Barker, an economist and a member of the Bank of England Monetary Policy Committee, presented a 'Review of Housing Supply – Delivering Stability: Securing our Future Housing Needs'. The Barker Review had the following objectives:

- to achieve improvements in housing affordability in the market sector;
- a more stable housing market;
- location of housing supply which supports patterns of economic development; and
- an adequate supply of publicly funded housing for those who need it.

The Barker Review said that Britain urgently needed to build up to 140,000 extra houses a year if supply is to keep up with demand. Between 70,000 and 120,000 of those homes should be provided by the private sector, while around 23,000 should be social housing units. In addition, planning authorities should make it easier for developers to build new homes in areas of high demand – house prices in the UK had doubled between1995 and 2004 and many people were unable to get a foothold onto the housing ladder.

There was also a lack of affordable or social housing, particularly for key workers. The problem of high house prices was compounded by the shortage of houses being built. (In 2001, housebuilding fell to its lowest level since

Table 5.2 UK household formation 1971–2031

Year	England	UK	Average household size
1971	16012 000	19027 000	2.84
1981	17362 000	20727 000	2.65
1991	19165 000	22886 000	2.45
2001	20522 000	24553 000	2.37
2011	22748 000	27209 000	2.28
2021*	25439 000	30310 000	2.19
2031*	27818 000	33002 000	2.13

*Projections

Source: Department of Communities and Local Government: www.communities.gov. uk/documents/statistics/pdf/1172133.pdf.

1924 excluding the war years). The report put much of the blame on the UK's planning authorities, finding that the system is complex and takes an 'unacceptably long' time. The report calculated that refusals for planning permissions in major housing developments increased from just 15 per cent in 1996–9 to 25 per cent in 2002. Land is scarce in the UK and this is exacerbated by tight restrictions relating to green belts, development densities and the priority development of brownfield sites. In addition, developers often have planning obligations in the form of Section 106 (Town and Country Planning Act 1990), sometimes known as 'planning gain' which require developers to offset the potential external effects of proposed developments by providing a monetary contribution, again increasing costs and reducing the viability of schemes.

The report also pointed out that if housebuilding was to flourish in the UK, skills shortages were likely. At the time of the report more than eight out of ten construction firms reported skill shortages – even modest growth would require 70,000 new workers.

In recent years, the housebuilding industry has responded well to the challenge of increasing housing supply, with supply in 2007/08 reaching 207,500 additional homes – an increase of 59 per cent compared with 130,000 in 2001/02. This was the highest rate of housing supply since 1977. The credit crunch and resulting recession hit house construction hard, however, and the number of new houses constructed in 2009 was only 80,000. It remains to be seen how the industry recovers when the economy begins to grow again.

The tenure trend from 1997 to 2008 confirms a limited resurgence of the private-rented sector. This can be seen in Table 5.3.

In 2007, Prime Minister Gordon Brown promised to build 3 million affordable homes by 2020 to help reduce the housing waiting list which was approximately 5 million but these plans were completely derailed by the recession. The Royal Institute of Chartered Surveyors (RICS) suggested that the only way to deal with the housing problem was to renovate empty homes. However, government spending cuts in 2010 threaten to reduce housebuilding. The Homes and Communities Agency (HCA) has had £230 million cut from its budget

Table 5.3   UK housing tenure 1997–2008

Year	Owner occupiers thousands (%)	Social renters thousands (%)	Private renters thousands (%)	Total
1997	13629 (68.5)	4170 (21.0)	2078 (10.5)	19877
2000	14339 (70.5)	3953 (19.5)	2029 (10.0)	20320
2004	14677 (70.7)	3797 (18.3)	2284 (11.0)	20758
2008	14628 (68.3)	3797 (17.7)	2982 (13.9)	21407

Source: Department of Communities and Local Government: www.communities.gov.uk/.../ housingengland2006-07.

Box 5.2 Why are house prices so high in the UK?

Many people in the UK complain that houses are too expensive, making it difficult for first-time buyers to get on to the 'property ladder'. Over time, the average price of a house has risen greatly – from around £600 in 1911 to more than £160,000 in 2010. But, of course, wages have also gone up and the prices of other goods have risen with inflation as well. According to *The Economist*, the country with house prices that are most over-valued in 2010 is Australia (61 per cent over-valued), followed by Hong Kong (53 per cent), Spain (50 per cent) and Sweden and France (39 per cent). This conclusion was arrived at by comparing the current ratio of house prices to rents with its long-term average. In the UK by this measure house prices are 34 per cent over-valued.

There are several reasons why UK houses are so expensive:

- Demand exceeds supply – increased population, increased household formation, a trend to home ownership, increasing incomes, low interest rates (since 1992) and greater mortgage availability have all increased demand for houses while there are restrictions upon supply.
- Constraints on housebuilding – there is a shortage of land in densely populated areas, strict planning regulation, greenbelt land cannot be built on, a lack of social provision of housing for political reasons. These factors all mitigate against new housebuilding.
- Speculation – housing has consistently been seen as a good investment. Over the long term prices have risen making home owners wealthier. With only two short-lived exceptions house prices have risen since the 1970s (hence the expression 'safe as houses').
- Renting is expensive – rents are high because demand exceeds supply for rental properties also, and people regard rent paid as 'dead money' while expenditure on house purchase is, at least in part, an investment.

---

and is putting on hold spending decisions on social housing projects and its Kickstart programme, which invests in restarting mothballed private housing developments. The Kickstart programme was announced in the 2009 budget in an attempt to help housebuilders who halted construction in the midst of the recession. Some £400 million was spent in 2009 allowing construction of 9000 homes.

Once the economic recovery is under way, the main problem will be determining where the extra dwellings will be built – on 'greenfield' or 'brownfield' sites? Current government policy has environmental objectives of preserving the countryside and reducing car journeys in favour of public transport.

The volume housebuilders in particular prefer large developments on new greenfield sites, mostly agricultural land, where they can achieve economies of scale and are untroubled by the possibility of contamination, as can occur with brownfield sites. However, the National Land Use database (NLUD) shows that there are insufficient brownfield sites to accommodate all the houses required. Actual policy, therefore, is a compromise of: (a) a target of 60:40 brownfield to greenfield sites; (b) a sequential test introduced by a 1999 draft PPG3 (housing) whereby local authorities are required to consider using previously developed land and buildings before releasing greenfield sites. The government claims that it has met and exceeded the 60:40 target in recent years, but critics point out that development on gardens in residential areas is counted as brownfield, when in fact it is previously undeveloped land (see Chapter 14).

Improving substandard housing has become a key part of the government's plans to increase the amount of affordable housing available. The Empty Homes Agency estimates that there are 840,000 empty homes in the UK. In addition, the National Land Use Database figures show that an additional 420,000 homes could be created by converting disused commercial premises such as former public houses and rooms above shops. Potentially these could provide over one-third of the government's target of 3 million.

The government has introduced three initiatives to encourage this:

- reduced VAT on refurbishing a property (from 17.5 per cent to 5 per cent) on properties vacant for 2 years rather than 3 years, as previously;
- local authorities are being encouraged to reduce the 50 per cent rebate from council tax or business rates for empty properties;

local authorities are being offered the same rewards for bringing a property back into use as they would for building a new property.

The government has plans for four new 'eco-towns' as part of a scaled-down initiative. They are Rackheath, Norfolk; north-west Bicester, Oxfordshire; Whitehill Bordon, east Hampshire; and the china clay community near St Austell, Cornwall. The four locations have been whittled down from an original list of fifteen, many of which were deeply unpopular with local residents and also with environmental campaign groups who accused the Government of using the idea to get round the planning process and build on greenfield countryside. The four proposed new settlements announced in 2009, which will have up to 20,000 homes each and will be the first new towns built in Britain for more than 40 years, were among the least controversial in terms of countryside destruction. The towns would include smart meters to track energy use, community heat sources and charging points for electric cars. Parks, playgrounds and gardens would make up 40 per cent of their area. The proposed affordable homes would take their energy from the sun, wind and earth, with residents able to sell their surplus energy into the grid. Their development would be coupled with strict rules on public transport, with all homes located within ten minutes' walk of bus, train or tram services.

The government had announced plans to create hundreds of thousands of homes in ten 'carbon neutral' communities. But the zero-carbon developments – some earmarked on open countryside – have caused protests and a legal challenge.

Schemes at the four confirmed sites are proposed or broadly supported by local authorities, according to the government. However, the developments – including 4,000 homes on the disused airfield at Rackheath, near Norwich, and 5,000 in the Cornwall eco-town – must still go through the planning process. Construction should be under way by 2016, later than originally envisaged.

Other suggestions for sites for new dwellings include:

1. increasing building intensity on urban residential land;
2. considering a change from industrial land use to residential where possible;
3. developing urban fringes by creating village communities of around 1,000 dwellings – similar to Prince Charles' prototype of Poundbury on the edge of Dorchester;
4. infilling, with limited extension, of existing rural villages even in the face of 'not in my back yard' (NIMBY) opposition.

Overview of residential property markets

In many economies, credit markets and housing markets are very important to the working of the whole economic system at the national and regional level. Housing wealth plays a very important role in the macroeconomy and in the distribution of welfare and incomes. Housing is both an investment asset and a consumer good providing services and this differentiates it from other assets. The role of housing as collateral varies from country to country depending on the state of development of their financial institutions. Increased access to credit via equity release increases the impact of changes in house prices on consumption.

House prices are determined by the interaction of supply and demand. On the demand side, income, interest rates, credit availability, demographics and expected appreciation of prices are of major importance (Muellbauer and Murphy, 2008). On the supply side, land use planning controls, the tax system and the structure of local government are important influences.

Houseprices can 'overshoot their fundamentals' because of speculation and there is evidence that in many countries housing markets are not efficient. Houseprice expectations contain an element based on the extrapolation of recent gains and the UK evidence supports this.

Summary

Housing supply in the UK is essentially the stock of existing houses which is added to by new build of less than one per cent per annum. This makes the market very demand determined. Free markets in housing are efficient and lead to availability and choice of accommodation. In addition, supply responds in a variety of ways to rises in rents, for example by conversion of large houses into flats.

Governments have persistently intervened in housing markets since 1900 because:

- inequalities in income mean that some people cannot afford adequate housing;
- there are external costs of poor housing;
- families may not purchase the amount or quality of housing which society thinks is desirable (housing is a merit good);
- public intervention may be necessary to speed up the response of supply to an increase in demand.

Government intervention in the form of rent control has occurred since 1915. It contravenes several economic principles and has led to short-term and long-term problems in housing markets and has contributed to changes in the tenure distribution of UK housing.

The owner-occupied sector of the housing market has expanded from 10 per cent in 1910 to 68.3 per cent in 2008. There are a number of reasons for this including the greater availability of finance through the building societies and banks, favourable government policy towards homeownership and the general increase in affluence of the population.

The credit crunch of 2007–8 began in the subprime mortgage market in the USA and led to a global financial crisis and recession. The UK housing market was badly hit with mortgages difficult to obtain, house prices falling, many homeowners consequently suffering negative equity and the house construction industry contracting markedly.

The number of households in the UK is projected to increase by almost 6 million by 2031 and the government has announced its intention to facilitate the building of 3 million affordable homes by 2020. The number of houses constructed each year would have to increase considerably in order to address these issues.

Chapter 5: review questions

1. Why is housing supply very inelastic?
2. Is there any economic justification for government interference in housing markets?
3. Explain the economic arguments against rent control.
4. Describe the changes in UK household tenure distribution since 1900 and give reasons for the main changes.
5. Why did house prices in the UK rise strongly between 1997 and 2007?
6. Why did the period of houseprice rises come to an end in 2007?

6

The Cyclical Nature of Real Estate Markets

After studying this chapter you will be able to:

- Explain the relationship between business cycles and real estate markets;
- Describe three clear property cycles in the UK since 1970;
- Describe the events leading up to the credit crunch recession of 2007–9;
- Assess the common features of real estate crashes in the 1970s, early 1990s and 2007–9.

Business cycles and property cycles

In all developed economies there are regular cyclical fluctuations in output, employment and incomes. In periods of macroeconomic stability, the cycles are subdued and manageable; at other times cycles are severe with consequences for other sectors. These trade or business cycles repeat periodically and investors and market analysts need to predict cash inflows, sales, rents, vacancy rates and so on. Business cycles are fluctuations in aggregate economic activity with expansion in many sectors at the same time, followed by contractions in many sectors at the same time – they vary in duration from one to 12 years.

At the top of the cycle, when GDP peaks, is a boom – industries become fully utilized and bottlenecks begin to appear, putting upward pressure on prices. In a downturn or recession, consumption, investment and employment fall and business expectations become negative. A severe recession could lead to a depression which is characterized by heavy unemployment, a low level of consumer demand and surplus productive capacity plus low business confidence. In a recovery, employment, incomes and consumer spending all begin to increase. Business expectations improve and investment increases. The business cycle is illustrated in Figure 6.1. The long-term trend line rises over time because of economic growth.

Figure 6.1 is a simple diagram of a trade or business cycle. The time between any two points at the same stage of the cycle is the period of the cycle. The

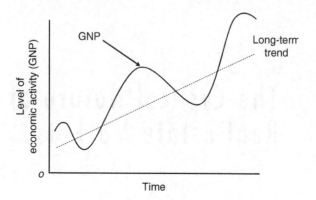

Figure 6.1   The business cycle

amplitude is given by the height of a peak above the trend line or of a trough below it. Characteristics of business cycles include:

- Fluctuation of economic activity (usually measured by national income) around a secular trend;
- Variation in periodicity and amplitude;
- Most indicators show systematic cycles;
- Business cycles occur in all market economies.

Property cycles are recurrent but irregular fluctuations in the rate of all property total returns, which are also apparent in many other indicators of property activity, but with varying leads and lags against the all-property cycle (RICS, 1994). In real estate markets, housing, commercial, retail and industrial sub-sectors are subject to periods of booms and slumps – cycles take place over longer/shorter periods of time and their impact on prices and activity varies. All developed countries have a property cycle which is closely linked to GDP and the business cycle and fluctuations in the UK property market between 1962 and 2000 were related to, but not identical to, movements in the economy generally. Property cycles include: building, development, rental and investment cycles and they can be identified by many variables: rents, returns, vacancy rates, yields and so on (Barras, 1994).

Short cycles of 4–5 years are created by business cycles, operating on the property market through occupier demand. Long cycles of 9–10 years are generated by the exceptionally long production lags in property development, creating a tendency for supply to outstrip demand in every other business cycle. Long swings of up to 20 years are associated with major building booms which may generate significant urban development.

Explanations for the occurrence of property cycles tend to provide reasons which are endogenous (from within the property sector) and exogenous (from the macroeconomy). Endogenous reasons can arise from successive and changing patterns of excess demand and excess supply, changes in rents and vacancy rates, and expectations of inflation. Periodic and reversing excess demand and excess supply mean the property market is rarely in equilibrium. Short cycles are driven by fluctuations in demand for office space (related to 3–5 year business cycles) and by production lags between start and completion of office projects. The sequence of events is: *increased demand – delay – shortages – rising rents – more new building – speculation (bandwagon effect) – completion – excess supply – falling rents – little development.* Exogenous influences on the property sector include: fluctuations in income, employment, flows of funds, rates of interest, exchange rates, changes in government policy and so on.

An RICS (1994) study *Understanding Property Cycles* described three submarkets of the commercial property market:

- Demand for commercial and industrial property is a derived demand (firms need property as a factor of production) – changes in aggregate demand affect the demand for property by firms as they decide to expand or contract their activities.
- In occupier markets, cyclical demand factors, including consumer spending, financial and business services and manufacturing activity, influence rental values.
- In investment markets, property is an asset amongst competing assets, and the proportion of a portfolio held in property will be influenced by:
  - values and potential of rival assets, for example, bonds
  - inflation
  - the rate of interest
  - the need for portfolio 'balance'

The different property cycles have different causes and starting points and there is interaction between them. They may either strengthen or dampen one another, for example, a short-term boom generated by a rapid rise in rents, coinciding with the upward phase of a medium-term cycle, would cause a more dramatic boom.

A strong business cycle upturn coinciding with a shortage of available property may be the starting point of a cycle. This causes rents and capital values to increase, and this encourages new development. Further speculative developments are financed by an expansion of bank credit. A major building boom results but, because of the nature of the construction industry it takes time for supply to reach the market and so rents continue to rise. By the time the new developments are completed the business cycle may have begun to turn downward, causing falling demand for property. Thus, just at the point when supply is increased, demand is falling and the result is reduced rents and values. This leads to a property slump characterized by depressed values, high vacancy levels and widespread bankruptcies in the property sector.

The effects of the slump may well last through the next business cycle because the surplus property means there is no shortage in the upturn. When the next long cycle of development begins it will tend to be demand-driven with little speculative development because the banking system is still struggling with debt problems from the previous slump. This would tend to lead to major property booms occurring in every second long cycle of development and every fourth business cycle (although economic and political events are likely to interrupt such a regular pattern).

The three major boom/slump cycles in the UK in the last 40 years (the 1970s, the late 1980s and 2007–9) were the result of strong demand growth, supply shortages and credit expansion acting together. In each of the three cycles the government and/or the banks pursued expansionary monetary policy (Barber boom 1972/3, Lawson boom 1987/8 and the property bubble created by US and UK banks 2004–7).

In each of these 'bubbles' an upswing in the business cycle was added to by relaxation of credit restrictions. The upswing in demand meant existing space was quickly occupied and rent and capital values soared – easy credit fuelled a speculative boom. When the economy went into recession, over-supply of property caused a plunge in rental and capital values (see Figure 6.2).

The UK real estate market 1945–79

During the war years, what was left of the construction industry could do no more than carry out first-aid repairs to those bomb-damaged buildings still capable of being put to effective use. As a result when the war ended the industry was faced with the mammoth task of reconstructing whole city centres and rebuilding on derelict bomb sites.

The demand for new buildings opened up opportunities for a new breed of property developer, some of whom had originated as estate agents and had the foresight to acquire derelict sites at bargain prices. Initially their activity followed the traditional principle: if the prospective yield of the finished building exceeds the rate of interest at which finance can be borrowed, there is the possibility of profitable development. The shortage of modern office and retail buildings resulting from the war, together with a low rate of interest, meant that their profits were high and attracted other developers.

On completion, the developer could choose either to retain the development or to sell it on to an institution, chiefly an insurance company or pension fund. Both were seeking prime properties for their investment portfolios to take advantage of rising rents and to provide a hedge against an increasing rate of

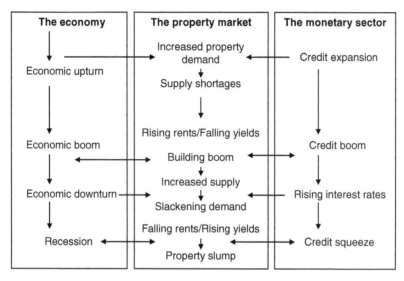

Figure 6.2   The links between the property cycle, the economy and the monetary sector

Source: Adapted from Barras (1994).

inflation. Initially institutions bought from a developer on a long lease. Later, seeking a share of the profits, they provided the funds for the construction period on a profit-sharing arrangement or even formed a joint company with the developer.

There were only occasional and minor hiccups in the upward trend of property prices, usually because the government, to reduce imports, had to raise base rate. In 1964, however, it resorted to physical control of new office developments in London and Birmingham, because the very large increase in office developments had adverse impacts on planning and housing. To constrain developers, they had to apply to the Board of Trade for an office development permit (ODP). This control was in addition to any application for planning permission and had the effect of increasing rents as it constrained office development. In 1972, the Heath government decided to expand the economy and the money supply was increased. Much of this new money found its way into the property market via the clearing banks, which could now compete openly with the merchant banks. Between 1970 and 1973 bank lending increased from £71 million to £1,332 million, with most of the increase going to property companies.

There was no lack of demand, the institutions were willing to buy all completed developments. Not only was 3.5 per cent an acceptable rate of return on prime property investments but, with a shortage of office space for occupation purposes, rents doubled within 2 years, thereby enhancing capital values still further. Between 1964 and 1974 the value of the Centre Point office block in London soared from £10 million to around £60 million, even though it remained empty.

The price of property freeholds, however, now contained a large element of speculation, with loan repayments not covered by rents in the expectation that deficits could be safely rolled over until covered at the next rent review. The first check on optimism occurred in November 1972 when, as part of its strategy to combat inflation, the government froze commercial rents and, the following summer, a steep rise in the world oil price gave a further twist to inflation and a loss of confidence in sterling. The government's growth policy came to an end and the rise in interest rates which followed was catastrophic for developers. Buildings under construction fell in value, the situation being aggravated by rising construction costs and completion delays. Worse still, depositors with the fringe banks withdrew their money since they could obtain higher returns elsewhere, for example, in local authority short-term loans. These banks could, therefore, no longer roll over loans to developers.

The problems worsened when the rent freeze was renewed. The institutions now reappraised property as an investment, for continually rising rents, upon which their policy had been founded, appeared doubtful. The crisis in confidence, as institutions stopped buying, engulfed both developers and banks, particularly the fringe banks. While property prices were rising, the liquidity risk of borrowing short and lending long for property development and acquisition seemed negligible. Now, when the banks wanted their money back, borrowers could not sell the property against which they had borrowed. But the banks themselves had been far too liberal as regards 'deficit-financing' by property companies – lending, for instance, at 14 per cent on controlled residential property showing a current yield of less than 5 per cent. As property prices tumbled, even the original lending base of four-fifths' valuation was not covered.

Many major developers and property companies failed. But, in order to protect depositors and the integrity of the banking system as a whole, most of the fringe banks were rescued by a support operation, known as the 'Lifeboat', mounted jointly by the 'Big Four' clearing banks and backed by the Bank of England.

Anti-property sentiment produced two further blows. First, in December 1973, to deal with the windfall profits made by developers, a development charge on first lettings was imposed. This was a tax on capital gains before they were realized, but it was so ill-defined, it would suggest that the Conservative government did not really know what it was doing. Second, in March 1974 a new Labour government came to power. Residential rents were frozen, and there was no easing of the restrictions on business rents and as a result, an orderly property market ceased to exist.

What the government had failed to realize when introducing its various measures was the extent to which property had become a vital part of the UK financial structure. The collapse in property prices involved a large part of the City. Not only could insurance companies pay less in bonuses on life and annuity policies but also pension funds could not keep pace with inflation. The value of the assets of many banks also fell. Thus the liquidity crisis in property affected Stock Exchange optimism and share prices tumbled, Worse still, this loss of confidence occurred when world events were revealing the underlying weaknesses of the British economy.

The assumption behind the creation of the Bank of England's 'Lifeboat' was that the crisis was simply a short-term one of confidence: given breathing-space, properties could be sold off in an orderly manner, and confidence restored. But throughout 1974 high interest rates necessitated increased borrowing by the secondary banks, and this forced the sale of property. Thus the government, following pressure by the Bank of England and the institutions, announced in December 1974 that control on business rents would end. This partially lifted uncertainty surrounding property values, and confidence in first-class property as an investment was gradually restored. The property collapse of 1973–4 has been described in some detail because important lessons could have been learned from it. Instead, in less than a decade, the same basic mistakes were being repeated. The reader may well have recognized similarities with subsequent property collapses.

The UK real estate market 1980–9

As the institutions once more began to buy prime properties, an orderly property market was re-established by the end of 1975. But the secondary market remained dull, largely because many development and property companies were still selling to repay the banks. In addition, the banks themselves were following a much more conservative lending policy, reinforced by the Labour government's strict control of the money supply.

As to development, finance was still available – at a price – for base rate remained high. The difficulty lay in finding projects to give a profitable return on a borrowing rate of around 15 per cent. Moreover, apprehension about future profitability resulted from; (i) doubts as to whether rents would continue to rise at their previous rates, (ii) the uncertainties resulting from the Community Land Act 1975, (iii) the introduction of the development land tax, 1976, and (iv) the recession shortly after the Conservative government under Margaret Thatcher took over in 1979.

The demand for property recovered strongly from the mid-1980s onwards. This was the result of: (a) the rapid rate of growth in the economy; (b) expansion in the service industries; (c) the demand for large modern offices to house information technology equipment and Stock Market personnel following Big Bang in 1986; (d) the relaxation of planning controls; (e) changes in the User

Classes Order 1987, and the advent of business parks, science parks, out-of-town shopping centres and retail warehouses; (f) the explosion of consumer credit and spending. It all added up to a major increase in the demand for space and in rental growth, inducing investors to buy buildings at ever-lower yields in anticipation of this continuing.

Initially the banks followed a fairly cautious lending policy, usually limiting loans to about 65 per cent (80 per cent on rare occasions) of the value of the property and for a period of no more than 5 years, with actual advances geared to various stages in the completion of the project. Covenants were tailored to the risk-exposure they were prepared to accept and to provide an 'exit' should the development turn sour for some unforeseen reason. The individual development loan was usually in the range of £5–£20 million.

One important feature of development schemes in the 1980s was the vast increase in their complexity and size: London Bridge City, Broadgate and Canary Wharf, were all over 2 million square feet of office space. While a loan of £100 million would be considered on its merits, few banks would accept this degree of risk-exposure on their own and so they usually invited others to join in funding the project. Such a syndicate also allowed small banks to participate in high-quality developments. As a rule of thumb, banks also limited their risk by restricting their loans on property to some 30 per cent of their total lending, with development funding accounting for about half the property portfolio. Sometimes, as an alternative, risks were spread by insuring the 'top slice' of loan where this was above 60 per cent.

In Chapter 9 there is a description of the conventional method of financing property development through forward funding by an institution. Usually the development was pre-let, thus making it a sound investment even before construction started. Often the buyer was the same institution which had provided the initial finance, for insurance companies and pension funds were eagerly seeking an equity interest in first-class property, especially easily managed office blocks which, with rising rentals, provided a hedge against inflation and real growth. Property companies, too, often retained some of their developments to increase income from their own investments.

From the early 1980s, however, the institutions became less enamoured with property as an investment and so had no need to seek prime properties for their portfolios. Instead they considered that shares had better growth prospects (which proved true of the early 1980s but meant that they missed out on the property boom of 1985–9). Pension funds, for instance, reduced the proportion of their assets in property from 21 per cent in 1979 to 9 per cent in 1989.

However, the withdrawal of the institutions from financing commercial development did not bring about a decline in construction activity, for the void was filled in various ways, chiefly by the banks where a number of factors induced them to follow a less-cautious lending policy. The government's

change in the method of monetary control (from minimum liquid asset requirements to varying the rate of interest) allowed them to expand their deposits, and
financing property development provided a welcome home for their surplus
funds. Moreover, the removal of controls on exporting capital by the world's
leading economies allowed overseas banks and their financial conglomerates,
particularly US and Japanese, to offer loans. In contrast, the merchant banks, so
severely mauled in 1974, largely confined their participation to pure investment
lending and underwriting, and avoided holding any major element of development debt in their own loan portfolios.

Not only did the replacement of the institutions by the banks in financing
development represent a move from investment-led to debt-financed development, but the approach and nature of the developer also changed. With the earlier developer the building was pre-let and the long-term investor was in place
before construction started.

In contrast, the 1980s developer, often an individual rather than an institution, had as many projects in the pipeline as he could obtain finance to initiate
them and during the early part of the boom he found little difficulty in managing to sell at a profit – the bank would then be repaid, and further projects
embarked on. Such a developer-trader flourished in the ethos of Thatcher free
enterprise.

Proposed projects brought forward by ambitious developers met a ready
response from the banks, who competed with one another and with foreign
rivals by designing new loan packages. The role of the banker changed from
that of conservative risk-manager to a target-achieving seller of loans, with the
loan officer rewarded with bonus payments. 'Limited recourse loans' restricted
the banks' ability to recall debt, and going even further, 'non-recourse loans'
isolated a particular project from the overall financial profile of the borrower,
for example, debt and covenants existing on other projects. This really meant
that a parent company could not be called upon to cover any default on a loan
by an offshoot company formed simply to carry out a particular development.
In effect, the lender, not the borrower, took all the risk and was the loser if the
development turned sour.

To make it easier for developers to obtain funds, merchant banks were
joined by other financial intermediaries – specialists in 'structural engineering
finance'. By 'creative finance' and 'mezzanine' finance, loan schemes were tailored to obtain the maximum initial finance, usually by allowing the difference
between interest payments and rental returns to be carried over to the next rent
review when it could be paid out of higher rents.

As an alternative method to bank lending in raising capital, preference shares
were offered to investors. If successful, this source was more attractive than
selling ordinary shares at a heavy discount, for this diluted the equity portion.

In effect, financial deregulation liberalized capital and delivered a decade-
long bull market. Between 1985 and 1990 yearly bank lending to property

companies increased in money terms from £7 billion, to £38.9 billion with overseas investors (mostly American and Japanese banks) providing some 40 per cent. By 1990 the banks' total property debt amounted to approximately £500 billion, yet property analysts had previously cautioned that an excess of space over demand, particularly in the office sector, could develop.

The UK real estate collapse 1989–91

Just as there were special factors which stimulated the boom, so other conditions arose which triggered the slump. The banks had looked at property development solely from the supply side, treating developers not as entrepreneurs, but as manufacturers of floor space. Scant regard was thus paid to the fact that they were lending in a highly speculative market. If, say, the interest charged is 15 per cent and the yield from rents 6 per cent, even if loans cover only 70 per cent of the value of the property, it still leaves a shortfall if rents do not go on rising. Then asset cover is diminished as capital values decline, and the banks find that the escape routes provided by their loan covenants including collateral are insufficient to avoid a loss.

Such a check on rental growth occurred both on the demand and the supply sides. The rate of inflation started to rise, almost doubling to 7.7 per cent between 1987 and 1989, causing workers to seek wage rises in excess of this. The rate of interest was raised in stages, the banks' base rate reaching 15 per cent in October 1989. This had the effect of halting firms' investment plans and squeezing consumer demand, especially as house mortgage rates rose to 15.4 per cent.

Nor was there any follow-through in demand to the expansion of financial services following deregulation in 1986. Confidence was eroded by the stock market crash in October 1987, and later the general economic recession reduced demand for both workers and office space, especially in the City of London. The levying of VAT on rents of new buildings added to the gloom for banks, building societies and insurance companies, since they were unable to reclaim it. Furthermore, the introduction of the Uniform Business Rate in 1990, although phased in, left many firms, especially retailers, with smaller profits. Moreover, such profits had already been squeezed by the downturn in consumer spending and wherever it was possible, therefore, retailers cut back on their existing floor space.

The situation was aggravated on the supply side. Just as demand was falling, new floor space, both retail and office, was coming on to the market as developments in the pipeline were completed. Thus by the end of 1991 some 30 per cent of the City/Dockland office stock was vacant. Office rents fell by over 20 per cent, and the gloom spread to the retail sector. The decline was most marked in London and the south-east, but also rippled outwards. When a highly speculative market exists, anything which administers a shock to confidence has a disproportionate effect, especially when the market, as with property, is highly sensitive and responsive to monetary conditions. The result, therefore, was a cumulative slump in which the housing market was also caught up (see Chapter 5). Developers were left with expensive land banks and unfinished buildings on their hands. The reader may well have recognized similarities with previous and subsequent property collapses.

Some property and development companies played for short-term relief from their cash-flow problem by capitalizing interest payments below the line in order to avoid showing a serious fall in profits in their annual accounts. But this 'creative accounting' and any restructuring of borrowing could only afford a breathing space while alternative sources of long-term funds were investigated. The trouble was that half-completed buildings, and even buildings that could not be let, were unsaleable. The resulting fall in asset values left developers with insufficient cover for their borrowing with the banks. Thus the choice for the banks was whether to call in the receivers for interest defaulters and to write-off losses or to restructure loans in order to protect the funds already committed until the climate for selling completed developments improved. Generally, though a few major companies were forced into bankruptcy, the banks followed the restructuring course, but at a price to the borrower.

The 1989–91 property market collapse was very severe. But its basic causes were essentially similar to those of the market's failure in 1973–4, thereby underlying the rather cynical observation that 'the only thing we learn from history is that we learn nothing from history'. If instead we are to profit from past experience, it is important to recognize the circumstances which can eventually give rise to market instability.

First, the over-optimistic expectations of developers were supported by borrowed funds, but the loans advanced were only short-term. Thus to cover a construction period of 2 or more years, it was absolutely essential that they could be rolled over.

Second, the lending institutions failed to adhere to the recognized principle of sound banking – not to borrow short in order to lend long without adequate security as cover for regaining liquidity. All lenders – secondary and merchant banks in 1971–5 and the clearing and foreign banks in 1985–9 – failed to recognize the vulnerability of their loans to the inadequate security provided by unfinished or unlet buildings. In comparison, the developer-trader or a company buying property by deficit-financing had little more than the lender's money to lose should there be a downturn in the market. Insurance companies, too, by underwriting mortgage indemnity policies, were party to the over-lending, and building societies provided funds for commercial development although they had little real experience in this field. Thus the lending institutions were exposed to unforeseen shocks: the world reaction to the rise of the oil price in 1973 and the hike in interest rates to curb mounting inflation in 1989.

To a large extent the banker's lack of caution was inexcusable for in 1987, 2 years before the property market collapse, Lloyds Bank economists had predicted in their *Economic Bulletin* a deteriorating economic situation ahead which would result from a serious balance of payments problem. Nor should it have been necessary for the Governor of the Bank of England to warn the banks in October 1989 that their £40 billion lending on property looked excessive. More heed should also have been given to property analysts who were cautioning that an excess of space over demand, particularly in the office sector, could develop in the near future. Nor can valuers be held blameless, for they failed to appreciate the inadequacy of relying on historic comparables instead of making some attempt to suggest likely future relevant economic trends similar to those covered by analysts of Stock Exchange securities.

But the major responsibility for both collapses rests with the governments in power at the time. Both expanded monetary demand in pursuit of growth. Yet they failed to recognize the resulting incipient inflationary pressure and had no effective or coherent policy to deal with it before it got out of hand.

The 1972–3 measures of the Heath government – a rent freeze and a development charge which bit into normal profit – were inadequate, ill-defined and, above all, misguided in that they failed to appreciate the major part played by the property industry in the overall functioning of the economy. Nor did the Labour government, which took over in March 1974, help to restore confidence with its antipathy towards property and its proposals to rationalize land by a Community Land Act.

Similarly the seeds of the 1989 collapse were sown in Lawson's 1988 budget. Fearing deflationary consequences from a collapse in security prices on Wall Street, he cut income tax. In the event Wall Street quickly recovered, and his decision simply added to an already surging aggregate monetary demand.

The UK real estate market 1991–9

Apart from 1973–4, the property industry in 1985 had enjoyed 40 years of growth, underpinned by increasing real incomes, inflation, rising rents and the expansion of pension and life insurance funds looking for long-term investment. But, with the 1990 crisis, property entered uncharted waters against a background of static real income, unemployment of 2.75 million, a developing world-wide recession, a government determined to hold down inflation by adjustments in the rate of interest, and institutions already switching from property to other assets in their investment portfolios.

The immediate effects of the collapse have been described. But it also altered many of the basic conditions upon which property development and investment had hinged over the previous 40 years. It is to a consideration of some of these more important repercussions that we now turn.

A revision of the institutions' view of property as a long-term investment

The annualized return on a property holding depends on the rent received and the acceptable yield in competition with substitute investments. Thus if the rent rises and the competitive yield remains unchanged, there is an increase in capital value which, added to the rent, gives the annualized rate of return on the original cost. In the recession, rents fell and yields rose. From 1991–4 and after 1997 the reverse yield gap (the amount by which the yield on gilts exceeds that on property) disappeared. For secondary properties it was possible to obtain a margin of earning capacity above the cost of borrowing.

Attention then focused on the fact that the demand for property is derived from the use to which it is put. In short, occupation demand became a crucial element in the value of a property. In the boom, large office developments in particular seem to have been prompted more by their yield as an investment, with supply responding more to the availability of finance than to the likely demand of potential tenants. In addition, too little weight was given to the illiquidity of property or to the fact that much of the new office supply would be tied to a single industry – financial services. Even before the downturn, many institutions had started to reduce the property content in their investment portfolios, considering that equities offered better long-term prospects – the property crisis reinforced this view. Thus the Church Commissioners, following a 20 per cent drop in the value of its £1.5 billion commercial property portfolio together with losses on its development programme, decided to reduce its property weighting from 70 per cent to less than 50 per cent.

Moreover, with the government apparently determined to hold the rate of inflation at 2.5 per cent, the inflation hedge attribute, which applied particularly to retail properties, was of far less significance. By 1993 *net* institutional investment in property had fallen to £500 million, only a quarter of what it had been in 1982.

From the mid-1990s property made a sustained recovery. Nominal returns were close to their long-run average at 12 per cent per year, but inflation-adjusted returns of over 9 per cent have only been bettered at the high point of the 1980s' boom.

Revision of the lease structure

The typical 'institutional' lease prior to 1989 was the 25-year full repairing and insuring lease with 5-year rent reviews on an upward-only basis. Such a lease on a prime property let to a good covenant presented an institution – for example, a life insurance company – with a secure long-term investment for meeting future commitments together with a hedge against inflation.

With rents rising consistently, such terms were acceptable to a tenant since strong competition for properties meant that, should there be a wish to end occupation, the lease could easily be assigned, often for a premium. Furthermore, against this background, the lessee was willing to concede *'privity of contract'* (that is, the original lessee is liable for fulfilling the terms of the lease even after assignment, should the new occupier default).

The 1990 collapse of property changed the relative strengths of landlord and tenant, for with supply of all types of property exceeding demand, negotiating strength moved in favour of the tenant. Thus, at best, rents tended to remain static, the over-rented being protected from falling only by the upward-only condition; at worst, the tenant, hit by recession, was forced into liquidation, leaving the landlord with empty premises and a difficult letting situation ahead.

Consequently, on renewals or new leases the tenant was able to exploit his/her improved negotiating position. New leases were usually for a shorter period of about 15 years, with a possible fitting-out and rent-free period, and rent reviews and even break-clauses every 5 years – a useful negotiating ploy at a rent review as it threatens the landlord with a possible rent void should the tenant quit.

The fall in rents also meant that many properties on earlier leases were 'over-rented': this focused attention on 'privity of contract'. With rising rents, possible default by the new tenant was acceptable since the property could soon be re-let, possibly at a higher rent. Now it could result in the assignor being landed with a considerable financial liability. The Landlord and Tenant (Covenants) Act 1995, therefore, limited liability to the first assignment only. What are the likely possible effects of this new type of lease on property investment?

First, there is a change of emphasis on criteria. At one time it was considered that the virtue of a property depended on location, location, location. Now the security of the covenant – the tenant's standing and his ability to pay the rent and to fulfil other conditions such as repairs and insurance which the lease stipulates – have an enhanced importance.

Second, the new lease may have reduced the willingness of institutions to invest in property. The lower security offered together with the added uncertainty through the occupier's exposure to a harsher economic background may have strengthened the trend towards reducing the proportion of portfolio funds held in property.

New sources of finance for property development

The withdrawal of the banks from development finance meant that developers have had to go into the market in search of funds. There were two major problems. First, how could property companies which were just keeping their heads above water fund their debt to avoid sinking into liquidation? Second, in view of the vast amount of capital now required for so many modern development projects, what changes in the nature of the debt are necessary to attract lenders?

Short-term finance

One source was to tap the money markets direct by issuing *commercial paper*. This is a very short-term IOU sold by the borrower at a discount on the commercial paper market where there are investors looking for a home for surplus cash. The period could be for 40 days to three months, though by rolling-over on the market it could be regarded as a medium-term source of finance up to £50 million. As commercial paper is unsecured, the standing of the borrower is very important.

Longer-term finance

In order to bridge the period from the start to the completion and sale of the project, a developer could contact a specialist finance firm who might be able to arrange the necessary bridging loan for non-speculative, preferably pre-let, projects. Thus with a *'defer and accrue'* plan the lender agrees to advance, say, 85 per cent of the value on completion, possibly with the rate of interest 'capped' – that is, the ceiling is fixed, but not the bottom. The developer knows exactly what he can spend and may, if he so wishes, hold on to the property as an investment. This type of funding might be more suited to a building society wanting comparatively little risk.

Where a bridging loan is not available, a property company could find that its only option is to appeal to shareholders to provide funds through a *'rights issue'*. This dilutes capital and is thus not really a satisfactory method for a property company, which in normal circumstances should be able to finance property acquisition and development by debt, with profit going to shareholders.

A *sale and leaseback* (see Chapter 9) would be preferable and could be tailored to suit the future requirements of the property company. The seller realizes the capital tied up in his property in exchange for a stream of rental payments. The purchaser, possibly a bank, has no wish to hold on to the property indefinitely. Although provision will be made for periodic rent increases, the bank is quite willing to include an option to re-purchase the property at, say, 5-year intervals. The bank has the benefit of tax allowances on capital expenditure, and these allowances can be set off against profit from other business. The cost of funds charged to the borrower can thus be kept relatively low.

Convertible mortgages offer another alternative whereby the borrower provides the lender or investor with equity in the scheme in return for a higher loan advance and reduced obligations. The amount of equity at stake is determined by the investor's required internal rate of return and the expected level of capital growth offered by the property.

Many modern development projects are so large that the finance required presents difficulties regarding size and illiquidity. Thus an alternative which is currently gaining favour is for the finance to be provided by some form of *syndicate*. A syndicate can be formed for a specific project, with each member accepting the risk and sharing the profit according to the size of this contribution.

'*Unitization*' of a property goes one step further, its value being divided into a number of small units and often covering different projects. By buying units the investor can spread his risk, while liquidity can be achieved by selling units on the market. The main drawback is the difficulty and cost of frequent valuations. The method developed in the USA for raising the large amount of capital required for modern projects is *securitization,* for example, through Real Estate Investment Trusts (REITS). In essence, this involves segmenting the mortgage into bonds carrying different levels of risk in order to appeal to the preferences of as many different types of investing institutions as possible. In doing so it gives access to global markets, being particularly suitable to the Japanese, for example, who wish to lend while avoiding as much risk as possible. Yet at the same time there is the possibility of considerable flexibility, for different types of bond can be packaged according to the requirements of the buyer. As a result, although large sums can be raised, the weighted average cost of the financing is lower.

Furthermore, the issuer may be able to finance a number of projects in one securitized offering. Since bonds are tradable, in the way that bank debt is not, they offer greater liquidity. Indeed as property securitization in Europe grows, eventually a global securities market is likely to develop. Finally, although most of the debt is packaged in the form of bonds, the developer retains the freehold and therefore full management control. This allows him to exploit his expertise and market knowledge to obtain the growth which accrues to the equity interest. *Property bond funds* and *Real Estate Investment Trusts* (REITs) have become popular in the UK since 2007 for private and institutional investors as they offer a high-profit, low-tax investment vehicle via a broad property portfolio which is traded on the stock market (see Chapter 16). As yet, however, the UK does not allow mortgage REITs although this may change as the banks lobby to be able to offload bundles of mortgage debt.

An extension of valuation objectives

Until recently valuation technique has concentrated almost exclusively on ascertaining the current open market value (OMV) of an individual property by comparing its location, physical characteristics, rent, covenant and other tenure conditions with those of fairly similar properties having a recently traded price. This emphasis on an individual appraisal of a property based on historical data recognizes the fact that, though to a degree each interest may be uniquely different from others, there are often characteristics which afford a measure of substitutability. Even so, such a valuation is limited by the infrequency of transactions and the paucity of information regarding those which do take place, thereby depriving the valuer of essential market evidence for lettings and rent reviews.

In contrast, there is, within the broad types of stocks and shares, a large measure of homogeneity. Moreover, through frequent dealings on the Stock Exchange and modern information technology, investment analysts are provided with an up-to-date valuation of each individual share, bond, and so on. Furthermore, knowledge is now worldwide. Nor is the current price of an interest based solely on the merits of its past performance: the microeconomic factors of demand and supply in its particular market and changes in the macroeconomic variables of the wider economics will also affect its price. Both micro and macro considerations play an important role in the securities market. In short, the current price also reflects an assessment of the risk from all possible changes which can occur in the future.

The collapse of the property market in 1989 caused valuers to reflect on the part they played in fuelling the preceding boom. Their OMVs were based on the assumption that the economic conditions underlying the price of comparables would remain constant. As a result some valuations were so inaccurate that they gave cause to legal redress. Should more weight have been given to the implications for property of wide shifts in the economies of the UK and the world at large?

Consequently, what is now being mooted is that the valuer of property (which is, like securities, a long-term investment) should similarly make an estimate of future price movements, even to the extent of containing within his report a sensitivity analysis. In short, he must go further than the micro-level analysis of individual market returns of comparables, to view the wider shifts and currents in the major economies of the world, as already happens in the world market in securities. Indeed this requirement is already recognized in the newer concept of the 'estimated realization price' (ERP) which, while still requiring precise definition, does hint at an assessment of the possible risk element in property's future price movement.

The demand for land and real property is closely related to the level of real national income and the cost of borrowing. With houses, demand depends mainly on the level of monthly personal income relative to mortgage repayments. For commercial and industrial property, demand depends on net profitability; that is, it is a derived demand, similarly dependent on the current level of income and on the cost of borrowing.

To be more specific, consideration would, for example, have to be given to the rate of growth of national income, the success of anti-inflation policy, possible changes in the rate of interest, the ability of firms to maintain and increase exports, and the government's likely attitude to tax levels and the type of tax favoured. Such important questions must be based on reasoned analysis.

It is essential, therefore, that valuers of real property have a knowledge of how the level of activity is determined, how the main macro-variables are related and how changes in them can affect the economy as a whole. Such knowledge provides insight into the current position, and from there some peering into the future is possible. The objective cannot be complete accuracy – even the Treasury model cannot achieve this. Rather it should indicate possible future cyclical movements, and the application of macroeconomic theory to information currently available should reduce the margin of error. As external circumstances change over time, so the forecast needs to be amended. Cyclical booms and slumps affect the rate of development and the allocation of funds to the property sector. An expanding economy will probably require new factories, warehouses, shopping facilities and improved housing. Similarly an increase in the inflation rate may prompt the government to raise the rate of interest, and bring into question whether the present level of activity can be sustained.

The market boom, 2000–7

Since 2000, investment markets in the UK have been dominated by the fall in the stock market, giving successive years of negative returns on equities for

---

Box 6.1   Canary Wharf as an illustration of the 1989–91 cycle

The history of Canary Wharf epitomizes the nature of the crisis and the subsequent recovery. The construction of this office tower block, the flagship of the docklands regeneration complex, was nearing completion when the demand for offices collapsed. The interest payments incurred by its parent Canadian company, O & Y, forced it into liquidation, and the creditor banks, led by Lloyds, had little option but to administer the complex.

A fall in City of London office rents, increased demand from an expanding financial services sector and bargain purchases by Japanese and German investors in particular brought stability to the London office market. At an initial rental of £18 per square feet, Canary Wharf was therefore able to let its own offices as they were completed.

The rise from 1993 of office rents in general enabled Paul Reichmann, the developer of Canary Wharf, to obtain new overseas backers and buy back control from the banks. It must be emphasized that the Canary Wharf complex was part of the scheme to regenerate the dockland area, with the government providing aid in tax concessions and improvements in the infrastructure (including the extension of the Jubilee Line) at an estimated £2,650 million. Today 7 million square feet out of the complete scheme of 13.5 million have been completed, and major tenants are coming forward at rents approaching £40 per square foot in order to secure the rate-free concession before the Enterprise Zone status comes to an end. The City of London now recognizes Canary Wharf as a major competitor.

The Canary Wharf scheme was expected to break even by 2000. This prospect enabled Paul Reichmann in March 1995 to float on the open market 25 per cent of the equity, at a price which valued Canary Wharf at £2.3 million.

the first time since 1973–4. One consequence of the stock market slump was that until 2007 property ranked as the UK top asset class performer over the previous 9 years.

The UK largely escaped the economic downturn experienced elsewhere in the world in the early years of the new millennium. This was, in part, due to high demand in the UK, partly financed by large-scale equity release as property prices continued to rise. The economic boom in the economy saw 40 successive quarters of economic growth from 1997, and the UK had one of the highest economic growth rates of the major developed economies during that time and certainly the strongest of any European nation.

Population growth of about 2 million also contributed to increased demand for property in the UK during this period. And the trend towards more single-person households and an ageing population with increased life expectancy also added to demand and the pressure on prices. Greater availability of mortgages from the financial institutions also increased demand for property. In terms of demand and supply analysis (which is admittedly rather static to represent such a dynamic range of factors) the situation is represented in Figure 6.3.

Despite the limitations of Figure 6.3 it does illustrate the effect of a considerable increase in demand – for the reasons described above – when supply is inelastic. Supply is inelastic (meaning that it can not be increased easily in response to increased demand and prices) because the construction of new property takes time and, more importantly, requires planning permission (see Chapter 13). The result of this increased demand and inelastic supply is a significant increase in property prices from P_1 to P_2.

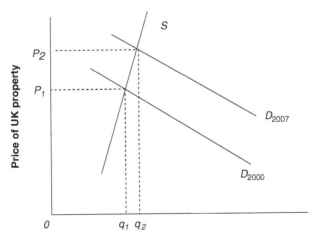

Figure 6.3   The property market 2000–7

The credit crunch recession, 2007–10

A 'credit crunch' is a severe shortage of money or credit in the economy. It has happened before in the UK and other economies but the severity of the world-wide 2007–9 credit crunch is without equal. This remarkable credit collapse was triggered by events in the USA – a housing boom was slowed and then halted by interest rates rising from 1 per cent to 5.35 per cent between 2004 and 2006.

House prices rose in real terms in most OECD countries except Germany, Japan and Switzerland over the 11 years from 1995 to 2006. They rose by 180 per cent in Ireland, 133 per cent in the UK, 105 per cent in Spain, 90 per cent in Australia, 99 per cent in France, 104 per cent in Sweden, 93 per cent in the Netherlands, 69 per cent in the USA and 52 per cent in Canada (Kim and Renaud, 2009).

The boom in house prices was driven by historically low interest rates and a lack of perceived returns on stock markets following the crash of the stock market in 2000. Following the share slump, changing perceptions of relative returns on assets caused investors to switch holdings of assets in favour of property. As investors switched preferences from stocks to property, rising prices of houses generated expectations of further rises in property values, fuelling additional speculative demands. US investors were prepared to buy houses they would rent out at a loss, just because they expected prices would keep rising. Economic activity was stimulated by the investment in new houses and associated purchases (carpets, curtains, furniture, insurance, lawn mowers and so on): 69 per cent of US households are homeowners. The 'wealth effect' meant that people felt richer because their property values had increased and so they spent more – either from their savings or by equity extraction borrowing.

US banks relaxed lending criteria in order to give mortgage loans to people with poor credit histories. Increasingly, little or no documentation of a borrower's assets, employment and income was required for a loan (this is known as self-certification of income in the UK where similar things were happening). The National Association of Realtors (NAR) said that 42 per cent of all first-time buyers and 25 per cent of all buyers made no down payment on their home purchase in 2004. These were high-risk loans and have become known as 'subprime' (that is, not the best) lending. These subprime mortgages along with other loans, bonds or assets were bundled into portfolios known as Collateralized Debt Obligations (CDOs) and sold to investors around the world, thus providing a transmission mechanism for the crisis to go global when the bubble burst.

In the UK, between 1996 and 2007, house prices rose by an average of 187 per cent (London 240 per cent). The average UK house price rose from £62,453 to £194,500 (average of 10.6 per cent per annum.) Over the same period: stock prices rose by 4.6 per cent per annum; nominal earnings by 4.2 per cent per annum. and retail prices by 2.6 per cent per annum. The UK housing market recovery from 1996 was due to:

- low interest rates relative to long-term averages (currently 0.5 per cent and 20-year average is 7.3 per cent),
- high employment levels (employment up by 770,000 over the 3 years 2004–7),
- demographic factors – population increase – more 1 person households and so on.

A housing 'bubble' is characterized by rapid speculation in house values until they reach unsustainable levels relative to incomes or rents or some other economic fundamentals. Housing bubbles may occur in local, national and now global real estate markets. There may then be a decrease in house prices that results in many owners ending up in a position of negative equity – a mortgage debt higher than the value of the property (see Chapter 5).

Many commentators have said that no one foresaw the bursting of this bubble and economists took a blow to their reputations when it did burst with such calamitous consequences. It is not true, however, to say that it was not foreseen or predicted. The *Economist* magazine said, in 2005, that rising property prices helped to prop up the world economy after the stock market bubble burst in 2000 and it estimated that the total value of residential property in developed economies rose by more than $30 trillion over the previous 5 years, to over $70 trillion: an increase equivalent to 100 per cent of those countries' combined GDPs. The *Economist* said that the rise looked like the biggest bubble in history (*Economist*, 2005).

The International Monetary Fund (IMF) has pointed out that housing price 'busts' are less frequent than stock market busts but they last twice as long and their consequences in terms of output loss (fall in GDP) are twice as large (IMF, 2003).

The slowdown in US house prices that occurred once interest rates rose was likely to have severe consequences. Homeowners, who had taken out loans when interest rates were low, began to default on their mortgages. Default rates rose to record levels and the effects were felt across the financial system because of the CDOs that had been sold worldwide. The first sign of trouble came on August 9th 2007 when French bank BNP Paribas told investors they could not take money out of two of its funds because they could not be valued as a result of 'complete evaporation of liquidity in the market'. This meant that the banks had stopped lending to each other.

The European Central Bank pumped more than 200 billion euros into the banking system to improve liquidity. The US Federal Reserve and other banks around the world also began to intervene, recognizing that the liquidity crisis threatened to cause a recession. In September 2007, Northern Rock, a UK bank

---

Box 6.2   Jingle mail

This term was first used to describe the surprise mailings that mortgage lenders received following the crash of 1990–1. This term resurfaced during the housing and sub-prime mortgage collapse, which began in 2006. In the USA, 'jingle mail' is a situation where a homeowner mails his or her house keys to a mortgage lender due to an inability to meet mortgage payment obligations and a lack of equity in the property. If a homeowner has negative equity and feels the entire loan is a lost cause, they may choose to walk away from the property altogether and rent, despite damage to their credit rating. US law makes it difficult for a bank to pursue borrowers for an unpaid mortgage loan following foreclosure (repossession).

The situation in the UK is different because the debt stays with the borrower even after repossession. If a UK borrower has negative equity of, say £25,000, and cannot keep up the mortgage payments and the bank or building society repossesses and sells quickly in a poor market, the proceeds may fall short of the mortgage amount on the property by, say £35,000. The borrower, despite the loss of the property, still owes the shortfall to the mortgage provider and can be pursued for it for 12 years after repossession. This provides a powerful incentive in the UK to keep up mortgage payments and wait for house prices to recover to restore your wealth rather than walking away from your negative equity.

Repossessions in the UK have not been as great as feared during the credit crunch recession. Arrears and repossessions have increased since in 2007, but far more slowly than expected. In 2007 there were 25,900 repossessions, and in 2008, 40,000. In 2009, 46,000 properties were repossessed and more than 180,000 mortgages finished the year with arrears of 2.5 per cent or more of the outstanding mortgage balance. Each of these is, of course, a personal tragedy and the effects can take decades or even a lifetime to overcome. But so far the extent of mortgage defaults in the UK has not been as severe as might have been expected for three reasons:

• the temptation to walk away is not so great when the debt follows you as described above;
• low interest rates have helped people to maintain payments; and
• although house prices have fallen by about 20 per cent since their peak, they have recovered quickly to a situation of modest increase giving homeowners hope that their negative equity will be removed (see Chapter 5).

---

that had a business model of lending long on mortgages and borrowing short-term from the financial markets rather than financing its lending from savers' deposits, found that it could no longer borrow. It was granted emergency financial support from the Bank of England, but on 14th September Northern Rock depositors withdrew £1 billion in a 'run on the bank', something not seen in the UK since the mid-nineteenth century.

In October 2007, Swiss bank UBS and US bank Citigroup announced losses of more than $3 billion each related to subprime debt. Citigroup announced further losses of $40 billion within 6 months. UBS lost $37 billion. Merrill Lynch (later taken over by Bank of America for $50 billion) announced a loss of $7.9 billion. Interest rates began to fall in the USA and UK by December and the US Federal Reserve coordinated action by five leading central banks around the world to bail out the banks with loans.

In January 2008, MBIA a major bond insurer, announced $2.3 billion losses from subprime exposure. In February, the UK government announced it would nationalize Northern Rock. JP Morgan Chase bought Bear Stearns for just $240 million – a year earlier before two of its hedge funds collapsed it was valued at $18 billion.

In April, the IMF warned that losses from the credit crunch could be more than $1 trillion. The UK housing market began to see falling prices and 100 per cent mortgages were withdrawn. The Bank of England announced a £50 billion scheme to allow banks to swap risky mortgage debts for safe government bonds. Several banks announced rights issues to raise funds and Barclays received funds from the Qatar Investment Authority. The UK FTSE stock market index fell 20 per cent in July 2008.

The two largest US mortgage corporations, Fannie Mae and Freddie Mac were bailed out by the US government in September 2008: they could not be allowed to fail as they were owners or guarantors of $5 trillion worth of home loans. The UK government announced a 1-year rise in stamp duty exemption from £125,000 to £175,000 to try to help the housing market where prices were by now falling rapidly.

In September 2008, Lehman Brothers became the world's biggest corporate bankruptcy ($639 billion). AIG, the biggest US insurer was rescued by a package worth $85 billion from the Federal Reserve which constituted an 80 per cent stake – effectively nationalization. In the UK, Lloyds TSB took over HBOS, Britain's biggest mortgage lender for £12 billion and Bradford and Bingley, which had lent heavily in the buy-to-let market, was nationalized. European banking and insurance company Fortis was partially nationalized and Dexia was rescued.

In October 2008, governments and central banks around the world began to take unprecedented measures to rescue their financial sectors. $700 billion was pledged in the USA. The Financial Services Authority (FSA) in the UK agreed an increase to £50,000 in the amount of deposits that it would guarantee. Germany announced a 50 billion euro bail out for Hypo Real Estate. Iceland took control of Landsbanki, its second largest bank, and interest rates across the developed world were cut. The G7 group of leading industrialized nations announced a plan to unfreeze credit markets. The UK government announced rescue packages worth £37 billion for Royal Bank of Scotland, Lloyds TSB and HBOS – again, effectively nationalization.

In November, the IMF approved a $16.4 billion loan to Ukraine. The Bank of England reduced base rate to 3 per cent, the lowest rate since 1955. The IMF approved a $2.1 billion loan for Iceland. Rescue packages worth hundreds of billions of dollars are announced by the USA, and the European Commission – the Eurozone, the UK and the USA were all in recession.

In December 2008, interest rates in Europe and the UK are cut again and in the USA they fall to between zero and 0.25 per cent – the lowest since records began.

In January 2009, the Bank of England cut its base rate to 1.5 per cent and Eurozone rates fell to 2 per cent. The Irish government decided to nationalize Anglo Irish Bank. The IMF announced that world economic growth would be only 0.5 per cent in 2009, the lowest since 1945. In March, the US Federal Reserve said it would buy almost $1.2 trillion of debt to help boost lending and promote economic recovery. Also in March, the UK base rate was cut to 0.5 per cent, the lowest since records began in 1694, and they would stay at that level well into 2010.

At the G20 summit of the world's largest economies held in London in April 2009, it was agreed to tackle the crisis with measures worth $1.1 trillion. The UK budget predicts a fall in output of 3.5 per cent in 2009 and a budget deficit of £175 billion.

In June, the OECD predicted a fall in output of 4.1 per cent for 2009 in the 30 most industrialized nations (http://news.bbc.co.uk). The United Nations has revised its 2009 world output projection to a fall of 2.6 per cent – the worst recession since the Second World War (UN, 2009).

In the UK, GDP fell by a record 5 per cent in 2009. Property is a major part of the UK economy and the recession has had a big effect on values, investment and occupational take up. Tighter finance affected businesses, consumers and the housing market and there has been greatly reduced development and construction activity as well as a curtailment of highly leveraged investment activity. Lending conditions have tightened and loan-to-value ratios have been reduced because of greater risk sensitivity. The UK listed property sector, including Real Estate Investment Trusts (REITs), has experienced a major fall in share prices. There has also been a significant reduction in new construction: rental projections are more cautious and assumptions about the end value of completed developments have been revised downward. Developments not yet started have been subject to revised development appraisals and substantial pre-letting commitments are being sought before commencement.

Overseas funding is being sought by developers, for example, the 'Shard of Glass' development at London Bridge has Qatari finance. There is over-supply of commercial space and contraction of commercial and residential demand as employment falls. The average house price fell from £184,203 in January 2008 to £158,337 in September 2009, and in 2010 mortgages were difficult to obtain and unemployment was high. The FSA Mortgage Market Review in October 2009 made the following recommendations

- Imposing affordability tests for all mortgages and making lenders ultimately responsible for assessing a consumer's ability to pay;

Box 6.3   Common features of three UK property crashes:
1973–4; 1989–91; 2007–9

- Over-optimistic developments supported by borrowed funds
- Lenders borrowed short and lent long without adequate security (e.g. Northern Rock)
- Lenders were exposed to unforeseen shocks:
    the oil price rise in 1973
    the inflation and subsequent interest rate rise in 1989
    the US sub-prime crisis in 2007.

- Banning 'self-certification' mortgages through required verification of borrowers' income;
- Banning the sale of products which contain certain 'toxic combinations' of characteristics that put borrowers at risk;
- Banning arrears charges when a borrower is already repaying and ensuring firms do not profit from people in arrears;
- Requiring all mortgage advisers to be personally accountable to the FSA;
- Calling for the FSA's scope to cover buy-to-let and all lending secured on a home.

The global banking system suffered instability due to the long-term credit boom, higher risk lending with uncertain asset credit quality and systemic problems with global interbank lending.

The major difference and to some extent saving grace of the latest property recession is that there have been low interest rates – historically low in the USA and UK. This has meant fewer repossessions than would otherwise have been the case and a more favourable business climate. The massive extent of government rescue packages and £200 billion of quantitative easing in the UK could, however, increase inflation and if that were to lead to an increase in interest rates to combat it, the consequences for real estate could be disastrous.

Summary

In all developed economies there are regular cyclical fluctuations in output, employment and incomes. In periods of macroeconomic stability, the cycles are subdued and manageable; at other times cycles are severe with consequences for other sectors.

Property cycles are recurrent but irregular fluctuations in the rate of all property total returns, which are also apparent in many other indicators of property activity, but with varying leads and lags against the all-property cycle.

Explanations of why property cycles occur tend to provide reasons which are endogenous (from within the property sector) and exogenous (from the macroeconomy). Endogenous reasons can arise from successive and changing patterns of excess demand and excess supply, while exogenous influences on the property sector include: fluctuations in income, employment, flows of funds, rates of interest, exchange rates, changes in government policy etc.

There have been three pronounced property cycles in the UK in the last 40 years: 1973–4; 1989–91; 2007–9 and they have sufficient common features to suggest that speculative real estate bubbles are likely to recur. The severity of the latest credit crunch downturn confirms the global nature of interrelated real estate and financial markets.

Chapter 6: review questions

1. Why are business cycles likely to influence real estate markets?
2. What causes property cycles?
3. Explain how monetary policy plays an important role in real estate cycles.
4. What is meant by the expression 'speculative property bubble'?
5. In what ways does the credit crunch recession of 2007–9 differ from previous boom and bust cycles in real estate?

Part III
Property Development

7
The Development Process

After studying this chapter you will be able to:

- Explain how and why development takes place;
- Explain the functions of a developer;
- Show how development takes place for economic reasons and how it ensures efficient use of land resources;
- Illustrate different methods of development project evaluation;
- Explain the economic rationale for intensity of site use;

The nature of development

Over time, the demand for land resources changes, brought about by changes in the size, income and tastes of the population, the rate of growth of economic activity, and methods of transport, techniques of production and distribution. On the supply side, existing buildings wear out or become less suitable for present use, and the cost of constructing new buildings or adapting old buildings changes. Development is the response to such changes.

Indeed, the development process may itself be dynamic: one development generating development elsewhere. Thus a houseowner who gives his property a face-lift may stimulate his neighbours to do likewise. As a result, demand increases for nearby houses which can be improved, and eventually a whole neighbourhood may be upgraded, a process often referred to as 'gentrification'. Similarly a comprehensive replacement of large houses by blocks of flats can lead to the redevelopment of a shopping centre in order to serve the needs of the increased population.

As a result of such changes in the conditions of demand and supply, some structural change of buildings is usually necessary. This may take different forms:

1. *modification of the existing building* through refurbishment (for example, new office or shop layouts) or conversion (for example, houses divided into flats, offices converted into residential apartments);
2. *redevelopment*, where existing buildings are demolished and replaced by new ones;
3. *new development* through outward expansion on undeveloped land (for example, suburban housing).

All these usually require planning consent. As a rough yardstick, therefore, development covers those projects which entail planning consent.

In the *private sector* development is carried out by (i) occupiers, (ii) specialist developers, or (iii) by financial institutions, property companies or construction firms working through the price system.

The advantage to the occupier of initiating his own development is that he obtains a building which is tailor-made to his individual requirements. But development involves know-how and highly specialized skills not usually found in the main business of the occupier, and only a few firms are large enough to have their own property division responsible for development. Most occupiers wishing to develop their own property, therefore, compromise by employing a specialist developer, such as Bovis. They submit a specification of their requirements for a building, and the developer endeavours to meet these on previously agreed terms. Irrespective of whether the development is carried out by the occupier or a specialist developer, the same basic decisions and calculations have to be made, for (given competition) each has to pay the full opportunity cost in order to secure a site.

Public-sector development accounted in 1998 for 8.3 per cent of total development, but the percentage varies from year to year. Most public development decisions are taken on a mixture of political, social and economic grounds. Public development therefore tends to fluctuate both with the politics of the government in power and the current overall requirements of its stabilization policy. In Chapters 7–10 we concentrate on commercial development in the private sector, analysing in particular how it functions within the price system.

Functions of the developer

The commercial developer may be defined as an entrepreneur who provides the organization and capital required to make buildings available in anticipation of the requirements of the market in return for profit. This definition emphasizes that the developer is essentially an 'entrepreneur' accepting the risks of producing for an uncertain demand. Consideration of his functions will reveal not only his major problems but also the risks involved.

Recognizing the potential for development

In essence this means (i) estimating future demand for alternative uses of existing land resources (see below), and (ii) calculating the cost of building for new uses. From among these different uses he must choose the scheme which will produce the maximum net return subject to the constraints involved: for example, the availability of finance, planning and building requirements and legal restrictions in the title or use of the land.

His initial assessment will cover the physical nature of the site (soil-bearing, drainage, slope), the availability locally of adequate construction capability, and, if residential, social amenities (schools, shops, health services and so on) and environmental aspects (open spaces, trees, compatible land uses nearby).

Thus the developer bears the uncertainty of the scheme. On the demand side, returns may be less than estimated, the result, for example, of economic depression, increased taxation or new rival projects. On the supply side, planning permission may be delayed, construction costs escalate or the cost of finance rise.

Assembling the site

This involves buying the proprietary rights over the land as they become available until the whole site has been assembled. But there may be difficulties in acquiring certain interests which exploit the monopoly power inherent in their unique situation. As we shall see in Chapter 10, this can involve collaborating on a partnership basis with the local authority – but with some loss of profit to the developer.

Again he may, by improving accessibility, enhance the value of a site. Usually this involves providing a road. But British Gas and Bud Developments paid much

---

Box 7.1   The costs of property development

Depending on the scope of the development project, the costs of property development and construction may include:

- Land/building acquisition costs
- Construction or refurbishment costs
- Stamp duty
- Professional/legal fees
- Architect, engineering, quantity surveyor, specialist consultants as required)
- Finance costs
- Interest
- Selling and marketing expenses
- Contingency allowance

of the £50 million extra cost of diverting the extension of the Jubilee Line to take in Greenwich so that a derelict 276-acre site there could be developed profitably.

Assembling the site and the actual construction both take time. This exposes the developer to a possible fall in the profit estimated; for example, the government may restrict office development or construction costs may escalate. Moreover, he has to allow for certain costs additional to those of acquiring the land and construction. These additional costs can be divided into *ripening costs* and *waiting costs*.

Ripening costs arise through holding land in anticipation of profitable future development. They cover the interest on capital tied up, plus any speculative element which has been paid for the land above its current use value in the hope that eventually planning permission for a higher use will be forthcoming. Waiting costs are incurred, even when the land already has planning permission, because construction takes time and it is necessary to span the period before revenue from the development is received. Such costs, therefore, include professional fees and interest on stage payments.

Obtaining the necessary planning permission

This involves negotiating with the local authority to secure the most profitable scheme. After checking the statutory development plan and other documents, such as Planning Permission Guidance Notes (PPG) of the Department of the Environment (ODPM), the developer will probably make contact with the local planning officer. Not only will this acquaint him with the authority's thinking, but it can be a valuable public relations exercise in that it indicates a willingness to cooperate. Naturally the developer will seek the maximum possible flexibility in the planning conditions in order to meet the requirements of prospective purchasers or tenants. On the other hand, since interest charges on finance for the site are accruing, he may be forced to compromise in the interests of speed.

The authority may provide a *planning brief* for the specific site or group of related sites. This indicates probable constraints and the authority's requirements regarding density, layout, building type and materials. Often these views are the result of previous unsuccessful planning applications. Alternatively, the brief may accompany the *outline* planning permission in which case it is really a *design brief*, since it covers the design details which have to be submitted within 3 years.

Arranging the finance

The developer must arrange short-term finance to cover the development period, and long-term finance if the development is to be retained as an investment. Development finance is considered further in Chapter 9.

Getting the project built

Organizing the factors of production efficiently is a key role of the developer. Land, labour and capital are required for any development and their coordinated input into the project is vital if costs are not to overrun. This includes extra costs through delays in construction or modification of the original design, unless this is unavoidable.

Arranging the first letting or sale of the development

The developer may retain the whole or part of the development. Retention of a development provides asset backing for future borrowing and a steady rental income which serves as a cushion against *a slump* in receipts *from new developments*. On the other hand, the developer has now to manage the property, becoming in part a property company. In practice, the decision on retention may hinge on the availability of finance. For instance, an insurance company might only lend for a commercial development on condition that upon completion it obtains the freehold interest.

Box 7.2   The visionary role of the developer

In their basic role, commercial real estate developers serve as an intermediary between the construction companies that build the buildings and the businesses that use them. Developers help businesses to provide the optimum value in location, function and cost. Developers ensure that newly constructed real estate meets the clients' needs. Real estate developers are sometimes property managers as well, maintaining facilities and thus allowing their tenants to focus on driving profits. By liaising between builders and space users, real estate developers play an extremely important role in controlling expenses and in improving efficiency and effectiveness for all parties involved.

Some real estate developers are visionaries, looking years – even decades – beyond the present to determine what buildings will be needed, and where. They imagine a commercial building, an industrial park, a hotel or shopping centre, or even an entire commercial district in a currently undeveloped area by looking into the future and projecting what tomorrow's businesses and consumers will need. Real estate developers are entrepreneurs who seek out an opportunity and make it happen, in the process improving communities, towns and cities.

Notable visionary property developers include:

- John Raskob and Al Smith who wanted to create the world's tallest building and did so with the Empire State Building in New York in 1931;
- Walt Disney who had the idea for the world's first theme park (near Los Angeles in 1955) despite considerable scepticism from the banks and his own company;
- Victor Gruen, a Viennese architect who was responsible for the world's first modern shopping mall at Northland near Detroit in 1951.

With large projects, these functions are likely to be performed by a team of specialists consisting of an architect, quantity surveyor, letting agent, and so on. At their head is a project manager, who may be the developer himself. Indeed, today, insurance companies and property bond funds may not only supply the finance for development but also fulfil the uncertainty-bearing role of the developer by directly employing such a team to find, plan and carry out development schemes.

The rationale for development

Development is necessary to ensure the efficient use of land resources. In the main, the life of a building ends not because the structure is physically worn out but for *economic* reasons. Sometimes operating costs exceed revenue and, because there is no alternative use, the structure is abandoned, as, for example, in the case of Cornish tin mines and many UK coal mines after 1992. More usually the site can be used more profitably. As we shall see, the developer who can put a site to its most profitable use can make the highest bid for it. Thus, given a competitive price system, land resources are used to their greatest efficiency. However, it is important to note that the developer's bid is based solely on his private benefits and costs. Externalities may justify government interference in the development process.

The first question the developer asks is: will the value of a replacement building exceed the value of the present building plus the cost of rebuilding? If so, redevelopment will be profitable. In order to arrive at this fundamental decision, the developer has to:

1. choose between development projects;
2. estimate demand for different developments;
3. decide on the quality of the building;
4. calculate how intensively the site shall be developed;
5. estimate costs of the development
6. estimate how much he can bid for the site;
7. obtain finance;
8. decide whether to develop alone or in partnership with a local authority.

Choosing between development projects

The development of land resources involves present capital expenditure in return for an anticipated flow of future benefits. Where, as usually happens, capital funds are limited, or where only one development is possible on a given site, projects are said to be 'mutually exclusive'. It is essential, therefore, to choose the project whose value exceeds the cost of the factor inputs used by the greatest amount. This means that projects have to be 'ranked'. Ranking, however, poses problems. First, with different projects, benefits are received and costs incurred at different points of time. Second, the future is uncertain. Third, benefits and costs, particularly in the public sector, may be difficult to measure. In this chapter we concentrate on methods of dealing with the first two difficulties. Chapter 11 considers the third.

Capital projects can differ as regards

1. initial outlay;
2. phasing of capital expenditure;
3. size of expected yields;
4. timing of future yields;
5. certainty of yields; and
6. estimated life and terminal value (if any).

Table 7.1 illustrates four hypothetical projects. It is assumed that (i) such projects are competing alternatives; (ii) all have the same initial expenditure which covers the total cost of the project; and (iii) there is no terminal value. But they differ as to the size and timing of expected yields. To simplify, we deal in terms of future net annual revenue (NAR), that is, the gross annual return (for example, from rents) less annual management, maintenance and repair costs. *NAR*s are assumed to be net of tax and to accrue at the end of each period.

Evaluation method one – comparative cost

Here a straight comparison is made between the initial capital costs of projects – which may be the determining factor when funds are limited. Even if profits are likely to be much better from a more ambitious development, if the developer cannot raise the finance to proceed then a smaller project may have to be undertaken. Otherwise the comparative cost method suffers from the obvious weakness that it fails to take into account the size and timing of *NAR*s; all

Table 7.1   Differences in capital projects

Project	Initial capital cost (£000)	NAR (£000)			Terminal value
		Year 1	Year 2	Year 3	
A	100	50	50	50	Nil
B	100	100	10	–	Nil
C	100	–	50	120	Nil
D	100	100	50	–	Nil

projects in Table 7.1, for example, being rated equally because their initial capital cost is £100,000 in each case.

Evaluation method two – cut-off period

This method chooses a period by which the initial cost must be recouped. If in our example this period were 2 years, all projects except C would be acceptable, preference being given to D on account of its higher total yield. The difficulty is that project C is rejected solely because returns, although considerable, accrue late in its life. Nevertheless, using a cut-off period to choose D could be justified – for example, if D hinges on an innovation which cannot be protected by patent and is likely to be copied by other firms within 2 years or if political uncertainty or financial constraints necessitated recouping the initial cost within 2 years.

Evaluation method three – pay-back period

With this method, investment options are ranked according to how long income yields take to recoup the initial outlay. In our example, both B and D achieve pay-back in *Year 1*. This method can be justified where there is uncertainty with future cash returns: for example, for either a small firm lacking diversity or where obsolescence of equipment is marked, then a possible quick exit must be borne in mind. But it fails to take account of: (i) differences in the timing of yields earned before the pay-back date or (ii) yields earned after the pay-back date. On the latter count, for instance, D is obviously superior to B.

Evaluation method four – average rate of return

A *net* average rate of return is obtained by adding the NARs, deducting the initial capital outlay, dividing by the number of years, and expressing this net average yield as a percentage of the initial outlay. This gives:

$$D = \frac{150 - 100}{2} \times \frac{100}{100} = 25 \text{ per cent} \tag{7.1}$$

and

$$C = \frac{170 - 100}{3} \times \frac{100}{100} = 23 \text{ per cent} \tag{7.2}$$

This method has two main disadvantages. First, it depends upon the number of years chosen. If, for instance, in *Year 3*, *D* had an NAR of 20, it would cease to rank above *C*, although its overall profitability had increased! Thus the method produces a bias in favour of short-term investments having high yields. Second, it ignores the pattern of yields, higher earlier NARs being treated the same as low later ones.

The major criticism of the above methods is that they fail to take into account both the number and the timing of yields. Other things being equal, the greater the number of NARs, the more profitable the investment. Similarly, early NARs have the advantage that they can be reinvested. The number and timing of yields are allowed for by the *net present value* and the *internal rate of return* methods described below.

Evaluation method five – net present value

Here the future NARs of the investment are discounted at a target rate of interest to give their present value. The net present value (NPV) of the project equals the sum of these discounted NARs minus the capital cost of the project. For example, if we take 8 per cent as the rate of interest for discounting, the present values of the NARs of project *A* are:

$$\frac{50}{1.08} + \frac{50}{(1.08)^2} + \frac{50}{(1.08)^3} = 128.9 \qquad (7.3)$$

Thus the net present value is 28.9.

Ranking the above projects according to NPV would give: *C* (38.1), *D* (35.5), *A* (28.9) and *B* (1.2). All show positive NPVs and are therefore acceptable, but if borrowing was subject to a limit, the rule would be: accept all schemes from the highest *NPV* downwards until the capital budget has been exhausted. In general,

$$NPV = \sum_{t=0}^{t=n} \frac{B_t}{(1+i)^t} - \text{capital cost} \qquad (7.4)$$

where *B* is net benefit (NAR), *i* is the target rate of discount and *t* the life of the project in years. A project is profitable where NPV > 0.

It should be noted that:

1. The NPV of a particular investment depends upon the rate of discount used: the higher the rate of discount, the lower will be the NPV.
2. Where projects differ in their patterns of NARs, the ranking of projects can depend upon the rate of discount chosen. For example, comparing projects *C*

Table 7.2   NPV at rates of discount of
8 per cent and 20 per cent

	Discount: 8%	Discount: 20%
C	38.1	4.2
D	35.5	28.0

and *D* for rates of discount of 8 per cent and 20 per cent gives the information contained in Table 7.2.

The reason for the reversal of ranking when the rate of discount increases to
20 per cent is that NARs for *C* are realized later in the project's life, and the
higher rate of discount penalizes later benefits more heavily. Alternatively, we
can explain the situation by considering the rate of interest at which earlier
NARs can be reinvested to provide a sinking fund to cover the cost of the
project. Since project *D* has earlier NARs, raising the rate of interest at which
these can be reinvested means that eventually they outweigh *C*'s larger, but
later, NARs.

Evaluation method six – internal rate of return (yield)

This method involves finding that rate of discount at which all future NARs
from the project would have to be discounted to make their sum equal to the
initial capital cost. More generally:

$$\sum_{t=0}^{n} \frac{B_t}{(1+r)^t} = K \tag{7.5}$$

where *B* = net benefits, *r* = the IRR, and *K* = the initial capital cost.
    For example, for project *A* we have:

$$\frac{50}{1+r} + \frac{50}{(1+r)^2} + \frac{50}{(1+r)^3} = 100 \tag{7.6}$$

where *r* equals the IRR.
    This is found either by solving the equation for *r* or, more practically, by trial
and error using valuation tables. Thus using PV of £1 tables (single rate, no
tax), discounting at a rate of 24 per cent gives a PV of £99.1 (too high a rate),
while 23 per cent gives £100.6 (too low a rate). The rate to give PV of exactly
£100 can be obtained by interpolation: it is 23.38 per cent. A similar process
gives the IRR for the other projects: *B* = 8.5 per cent, *C* = 22 per cent, *D* = 37
per cent.

The advantages of the IRR method are:

1. No rate of discount has to be specified (as with NPV), since r is determined by expected NARs.
2. It conforms with the more usual business practice of comparing rates in order to assess profitability. All projects are profitable if their IRRs are greater than the appropriate borrowing rate of interest. But if projects are mutually exclusive or there is a budget constraint, they have to be ranked, which can still be done according to their IRRs.
3. No substantial recalculations are necessary should the cost of borrowing change.
4. It is easier to take account of risk than with the NPV method since the margin between the IRR and the appropriate borrowing rate of interest will indicate whether there is sufficient to cover risk.

Nevertheless, where a choice has to be made between different projects, the IRR ranking may differ from the NPVs. This happens where the NPV is calculated at a low rate of discount, for here, in comparison, the IRR discriminates against later-benefit projects, as follows. Since the IRR is calculated for an NPV = 0, it must always be greater than a rate of discount which produces a positive NPV. We can illustrate this by calculating the IRRs for projects C and D from Table 7.1. D (37 per cent) ranks above C (22 per cent). This confirms the NPV ranking (Table 7.2) for a rate of discount of 20 per cent of D (28 per cent) and C (4.2 per cent). The reason is that a 20 per cent rate of discount is fairly close to the IRRs.

However, a discrepancy arises when the rate of discount diverges considerably from the IRRs. At a rate of discount of 8 per cent, C (38.1 per cent) is ranked above D (35.5 per cent) see Table 7.3. To guard against such a discrepancy when using the IRR method, the correct procedure would be to compare the *incremental* yields of C and D – their different cash flows. D has an NAR of 100 in *Year 1*, whereas C has an NAR of 120 in *Year 3*. That is, with C, an effective outlay (income forgone) of 100 yields 120 in 2 years' time. This is equivalent to a yield of 9.5 per cent, whereas D's initial 100 can only earn the market rate of 8 per cent when reinvested. Thus C is preferable to D.

Calculation of an incremental yield is also necessary when the capital costs of projects differ. If one scheme is cheaper but has a higher yield, it is necessary to calculate the incremental (marginal) yield on the additional sum invested. For example, if there were no constraints on borrowing at 10 per cent and only one building could be erected on a site, it would obviously be more profitable to invest in a project costing £15 million and yielding 15 per cent than one costing £150,000 and yielding 100 per cent! On the other hand, allowance would have to be made for the tendency of risk to increase with the size of an investment.

The conclusion is that we should test projects by both NPV and IRR methods to ensure that they do not differ. In general, the NPV method is safer. In effect it chooses the market rate of interest at which to invest early benefits, whereas the IRR assumes that early benefits can be reinvested at the rate of return on the project, a somewhat higher (and more doubtful) figure.

Allowing for risk and uncertainty

So far we have treated expected future benefits and costs as if they will actually occur. In practice, however, they are not certain and, in assessing projects, allowance has to be made for the risk of forecasts being wrong. How should this be done?

In economics it is usual to distinguish between *risk* and *uncertainty*. With the former there is a known probability distribution. With uncertainty (which arises, for instance, through a change in consumer demand or a change in technology), the 'law of large numbers' does not apply. However, the methods described below, with the notable exception of the application of probability distribution, apply equally to both risk and uncertainty.

Most methods in general use can best be described as 'rule of thumb'.

1. For very risky projects, a *cut-off period*, for example, 3 or 4 years, can be adopted (see above).
2. A *percentage addition* to costs or a *percentage reduction* in benefits can be made where these are uncertain. In practice, however, this method really provides only for overoptimism, and there are risks apart from this.
3. A *risk premium* can be added to the discount rate when calculating present values. That is:

$$NPV = \sum_{t=0}^{t=n} \frac{B_t}{(1+i+p)^t} - \text{capital cost} \qquad (7.7)$$

where p is the risk premium. Not only is this method simple, but it also penalizes distant returns, where uncertainty is considered to be greater, more heavily. However, this presents difficulties because: (a) it is unlikely that risks are so orderly as to be constant in each year; (b) the risk premium penalizes projects where benefits are mainly received late in life; and (c) it gives the decision maker no guide as to how large the premium should be.

Where the IRR method is used, it has to be judged whether the estimated yield provides sufficient margin to cover the risk involved.

More systematic ways of allowing for risk are:

4. Applying the mean of the *probability distribution* for the different risks involved, for example, the probability of a building project exceeding the stipulated completion date. The difficulty here is that while two distributions can have the same mean, they may differ significantly in their dispersions.

5. Making a *sensitivity analysis*. For example, where there is doubt over the exact rate of discount which should be applied to future NARs, different discount rates can be used to indicate how a change in the rate would affect the viability of the project. The method can be applied to other variables, such as occur in construction costs or changes in the future rate of inflation. It is thus possible to highlight the more sensitive variables and the degree to which the profitability of a project could be affected by even minor variations in a single component of the total calculation. On the other hand, a sensitivity allowance is limited in the number of variables it can embrace for otherwise the range between the best possible outcome and the worst could be so wide as to provide little real guidance to the decision maker.

6. For uncertainty, *rule of choice* can be formulated for different degrees of certainty. The rule chosen depends upon whether the planner is optimistic and can afford to take risks, or whether he is pessimistic and cannot take a chance on possible bankruptcy. In the former case the rule would allow him to maximize the possible return, while with the latter he would seek the best possible minimum return.

For example, Table 7.3 gives possible outcomes at different degrees of optimism for two different projects, A and B. Thus the most optimistic outcome for A is 14 and the most pessimistic is 4, whereas for B the most optimistic is 17 and the most pessimistic 2. It is likely that a large firm (such as Wimpey) having many projects or capital reserves can afford to be optimistic. It therefore adopts a policy of 'maximax' by choosing project B. On the other hand, a small firm with fewer projects and less capital reserves would have to take a more cautious view. If an NPV of £4 million is necessary to cover building costs,

Table 7.3   Uncertainty and the returns on projects

Project	Possible NPV's (£m)		
	Optimism		Pessimism
	Best	Medium	Worst
A	14	7	4
B	17	8	2

it must choose project A, since the worst possible outcome of B could lead to bankruptcy.

While 'games theory', of which the above is an example, may provide no definite solution to the problem (as for the large firm above), it does allow the developer to consider uncertainty possibilities in a logical form.

Estimating demand

The NPV of a development indicates to the developer the likely value of the completed project. Since the NPV depends upon the stream of future NARs, demand for the type of building and its operating costs both now and in the future have to be estimated. The problem of estimating demand for a small, single development differs somewhat from that of a city-centre project. We can illustrate this by concentrating on shop developments.

Single development

With a single development, a guide to the likely selling price can be obtained from current market information. If, for instance, enquiries from estate agents reveal that, in the same shopping area, a prime shop unit with vacant possession sells for £200,000, the developer has a yardstick for his own project, since this price has been reached in a market where buyers and sellers have taken into account present and estimated NARs. Similarly, a recently agreed market rent of, say, £16 per square foot of shopping space would reflect the current NAR.

The developer would adjust such prices to her own particular project by allowing for differences in location, nearness to multiples, complementarity with similar shops, occupation rates (if a specialist shop) and features such as layout, storage facilities and staff accommodation. Consideration would also have to be given to the possibility of similar new developments rivalling hers in the near future. Some indication could be obtained by an examination of the development plan and of the register of outstanding planning consents and current applications.

Other adjustments could cover how quickly the type of shop sells or lets and the adaptability of the layout to selling different goods as demand changes or to introducing new techniques of retailing.

City-centre projects

In the past, shopping areas have developed along high streets on a shop-by-shop basis. But post-war new town projects, comprehensive redevelopment of city centres and suburban growth of the more prosperous towns have necessitated planning the size and layout of shopping areas in advance.

The developer has first to estimate the overall demand for shopping facilities, both current and future. The major influence will be the number of people likely to fall within the catchment area of the shopping centre. Furthermore, the structure of this catchment population must be analysed as to its age, composition, household formation rates and socio-economic groupings. Census information should help with these details.

Other influences on demand include the current national economic climate and the possibility of future changes in the rate of growth, inflation, the interest rate and government policy. And, since the value of a shopping complex relies heavily on the economy of its immediate location, a similar analysis must be carried out for both the region and the town, especially regarding the level of employment, whether the employment has a stable base or is largely dependent on one industry or employer, and the likelihood of future expansion through the influx of new industries. One approach to estimating the demand for a shopping centre and its power to attract retail spending from other centres is as follows.

The size of the *shopping space* must be related to estimated overall demand for shopping facilities and the extent to which there is a present deficiency. In practice, this demand is usually expressed in terms of the *total value of retail turnover*. From turnover in existing shopping centres, a floor-space ratio (FSR) for each particular type of shop can be obtained, using the formula:

$$FSR = \frac{\text{Units of floor space}}{\text{Turnover in current prices}}$$

This known FSR can then be applied to the forecast retail sales of the new shopping centre: floor space required = FSR × forecast retail sales. Since each type of retail shop will have a different FSR (jewellery, for example, with its low physical turnover will have a lower FSR than groceries), the total floor space requirement will be an aggregate of the floor-space requirements of all shops in the shopping area calculated according to their individual FSR.

While this technique can provide a rough guide to estimating shopping space, it has three main weaknesses. First, it depends on the accuracy of the forecast of total retail turnover. Second, the 'units of floor space' in the formula will itself be dependent on shop rents. If these are high, increased turnover may be met by more intensive use of existing floor space rather than by adding to it. Third, the method ignores the power of a new shopping centre to attract customers from a rival centre.

Reilly's (1931) law of retail gravitation covers this last problem. Examining shopping habits in the USA in the 1920s, W.J. Reilly concluded that, as a general rule, two cities will attract retail spending from the area between them in direct proportion to the size of the city's population and in inverse proportion to the square of the distance to the city from any particular point in the area between. Thus a city of 320,000 population located four miles from the intermediate area will attract twenty times as much trade from it as a rival city of 49,000 located seven miles away; that is:

$$\frac{320\,000}{16} : \frac{49\,000}{49} = 20:1 \tag{7.9}$$

We can apply the theory to estimate the retail catchment area of a city. Supposing we have a smaller town of population P_1 and a larger town of population P_2, there would be some point between them where a household would be indifferent whether it shopped in town one or town two (see Figure 7.1). According to Reilly's law, the location of such a point is determined by the formula:

$$\frac{P_1}{(d_1)^2} = \frac{P_2}{(d_2)^2}, \text{that is} \frac{\sqrt{P_1}}{d_1} = \frac{\sqrt{P_2}}{d_2} \tag{7.10}$$

But $d_1 + d_2 = D$, the distance between the two cities, so the last expression can be written:

$$\begin{aligned}
d_2\sqrt{P_1} &= (D - d_2)\sqrt{P_2} \\
&= D\sqrt{P_2} - d_2\sqrt{P_2} \\
d_2\sqrt{P_1} + d_2\sqrt{P_2} &= D\sqrt{P_2}
\end{aligned} \tag{7.11}$$

Dividing through by $\sqrt{P_2}$, we have

$$d_2 \frac{\sqrt{P_1}}{\sqrt{P_2}} + d_2 = D$$

$$d_2 \left(\frac{\sqrt{P_1}}{\sqrt{P_2}} + 1 \right) = D \tag{7.12}$$

$$d_2 = \frac{D}{\frac{\sqrt{P_1}}{\sqrt{P_2}} + 1}$$

Thus d_2 locates the watershed of city P_2 as regards its 'pulling power' relative to P_1 and is defined once we know D, P_1 and P_2.

Although this crude formulation illustrates the basic technique for evaluating shopping developments, refinements are necessary. Because a city's power of attraction rests on spending power rather than on just its population size,

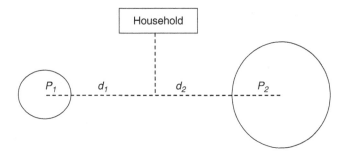

Figure 7.1   Reilly's law of gravitation

consideration has to be given to the composition of the population (for example, by age group and working proportion), its earning capacity (for example, whether they are skilled workers), government subsidy policy within the district and the spending habits of different income groups. Ease of transport between the intermediate area and the centre is also relevant.

More important, dynamic factors must be taken into account. Thus some allowance would have to be made for future population growth. Above all, a new, large shopping centre may generate its own growth. For example, specialist shops may so enhance the reputation of such a centre that it will grow more rapidly than smaller centres in the area.

Not only the size but also the *layout of a new shopping centre* must be planned carefully. With a single shop development, the subsequent provision of a municipal car-park nearby or the opening of a 'big name' store next door would increase revenue-earning capacity.

In contrast, with a comprehensive city-centre development, such externalities are under the developer's control. That is, externalities can be 'internalized' to maximize the value of the total area. This means relating the shopping area to public transport and car-parks, and then siting shops in order to secure *complementarities*, sometimes referred to as 'special accessibility' or agglomeration economies.

Such complementarities arise because retailers of a certain type can achieve enhanced turnover by trading next to or close to retailers of a similar or compatible type or even of a completely different nature. It is therefore essential to secure the optimum 'tenant mix' (sometimes referred to as 'merchandizing') by planning the size, shape and location of shops in order to maximize the value of aggregate turnover, for this in turn should maximize rentals.

The developer is likely to start from the key retail outlet, such as the department store or supermarket. Secondary magnets, such as banks and the Post Office, are then located, and multiples positioned between them. The object is to generate movement of shoppers around the whole centre by avoiding the creation of dead spots through the concentration of too many important magnets in one area. The remaining space is then allocated to the specialist shops, such as jewellery, shoes, cameras and clothing, having regard to their complementarity preferences. Thus food stores prefer to be located together, with the specialist shops, such as delicatessen and patisserie, being close to the supermarket. Other trades, such as stationers, hairdressers, florists, restaurants and toy shops, are less demanding, but they add colour and variety to the centre and so have to be carefully located in order to secure the overall objective.

Since different types of shop have different requirements for window space (cameras, jewellers), show space (furniture), customer-circulating space (clothiers) and storage space (hardware stores), merchandizing demands detailed planning in advance, especially if there is to be flexibility to meet future changes in requirements.

Mixed-use developments

This can mean either that a number of single-use buildings with a different business focus are built on a site, or that a building (or buildings) are occupied by different types of users. Costs for such developments are likely to be higher because the structures and regulations are more complex than for single-use developments and leases can be of varying lengths. Even so, such developments have a number of advantages because they can improve revenues, for example by incorporating retail space in residential or office blocks, and they can be more sustainable in that, if several uses are catered for, they reduce the need for travel from the development. Mixed-use schemes may be considered more risky by investors, however, who prefer single-use, single-tenant, premium properties. In addition the planning process is more complicated with mixed-use schemes and consequently slower and more costly.

Optimum construction outlay

Revenues are determined not only by the use to which a site is put but also by the capital outlay on the building erected. Questions to be answered are:

1. What refinements should be incorporated in the building?
2. To what extent should higher initial capital costs be incurred in order to save future maintenance costs?
3. How intensively should the site be developed?

As we shall see, the answers to these questions all hinge on the principle of equating marginal revenue and marginal cost. More specifically, any addition to construction outlay must be at least covered by the addition to NPV from the resulting higher net revenues. When deciding on refinements, such as lifts and air-conditioning in offices, the basic question is: how much will such refinements add to revenue? If the enhanced NPV exceeds the cost of installation, such refinements should be incorporated.

For most buildings there will be some possibility of trading off higher initial construction costs against reduced maintenance costs. Again, the same marginal principle applies: if higher initial building costs lead to lower future maintenance costs, NARs will be greater than for a building costing less. We therefore have to choose that combination of construction costs and discounted NARs which will yield the highest NPV and the rate of interest and expectations of future wage-rates would be major determinants. A high rate of interest penalizes projects whose returns are received further in the future, such as a building with initial capital costs. Thus a high rate of interest operates in favour of a low-capital/high-maintenance building. On the other hand, maintenance costs tend to be labour-intensive, and if wage-rates are expected to increase more than other factor rewards it would give an advantage to the more expensive, low maintenance-cost building.

However, over and above these considerations, the imperfection of the capital market may impose a budget restraint so that a cheaper building has to be erected.

The intensity of site use

Buildings as the addition of capital to land

As well as determining the best use of a site, the developer has to decide how intensively it should be developed. If, for instance, the most profitable use of a large suburban site is for housing, to what density should the houses be built? Or, if an office block is to be built in a city centre, how many storeys upwards (given no government restrictions) should it go? In economic terms: how much capital shall be combined with the site?

Although the two decisions – most profitable use and capital-intensity of development – are arrived at simultaneously, we shall simplify the analysis by assuming that the best use has already been determined, confining the immediate discussion to capital spending on the actual building.

Combining capital with a fixed supply of land

Since we are dealing with a particular site, we can regard land as a fixed factor. To simplify the explanation, we shall assume that the project has a life of 1 year and that all returns are received at the end of the first year. (The obvious example of this in practice would be where a non-renewable 1-year lease is held on a vacant site).

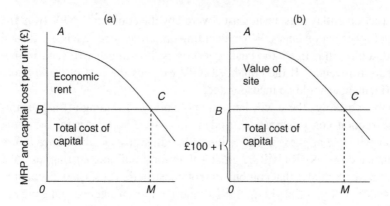

Figure 7.2   Applying capital to a fixed site

The problem now resolves itself into the familiar one of applying units of a variable factor, which we shall term 'capital', to a fixed factor, land. It is assumed that:

1. All costs of developing the site – material and labour costs, ripening and waiting costs, legal fees and normal profits – are capital costs.
2. The capital unit may be an unspecified physical amalgam of materials and labour with the return and cost likewise unspecified (see Figure 7.2(a)). Alternatively, we can be more precise, defining the capital unit as £100-worth of capital factors, with the cost of this unit for the year thus being £100 plus the going rate of interest (see Figure 7.2(b)).
3. There is perfect competition in both the capital and product markets. Thus all the capital the developer requires can be obtained at a given price, and the product sells at a given price per unit. The latter means that the marginal physical product curve can be regarded as the marginal revenue product curve since MRP equals MPP times the price per product unit whatever the output. The MRP is *net*, operating costs having been deducted.
4. A site is being developed for offices, with one suite of offices occupying one storey. It is assumed that the height of the office suite makes no difference to the rent, and so, following from (3), each suite lets at the same rent.
5. There are no government controls on height, and developers are free to bid for the site.

As extra units of capital are applied to the fixed site, the law of diminishing returns eventually comes into operation, and the MPP of capital falls. This is because building upwards incurs extra costs; for example, a more expensive substructure is necessary, labour costs per unit rise with height, and lifts and fire escapes have to be provided. Thus the return on given additions to capital eventually decreases, giving a downward-sloping MRP curve (see Figure 7.2). Since all capital can be obtained at a given price (assumption [3] above) the *MC* curve is horizontal.

Development of the site will take place up to the point where marginal revenue equals marginal cost: that is, to where the MRP of a unit of capital equals the cost of a unit of capital (*OB* in Figures 7.2(a) and 7.2(b)). The building reaches its optimum height, that is, the development is complete, when *OM* units of capital have been applied to the site.

The amount that can be paid for the site

In Figure 7.2, total proceeds of the development will be *AOMC*, and the total capital cost *BOMC*. In practice, the developer will have plans of the optimum building to be constructed, and he can obtain preliminary cost estimates based on these plans. In addition, he will have to cover waiting and ripening costs, extra costs arising from the operation of escape clauses, overheads and normal profit. All costs will be included in *BOMC*. Thus the maximum which he can pay for the land is the residual, *ABC*.

Further conclusions follow from our assumptions and analysis.

1. If offices were the only, or the best, use to which the site could be put, *ABC* would represent the demand price for the site. Thus if the site were 1,000 square metres in size, its demand price would be £*ABC*/1,000 per square metre. *Competition among developers would ensure that this price was in fact bid.*
2. Suppose, however, there was an alternative use (for example, a department store) with greater productivity. This would be shown by the higher *MRP'* curve (Figure 7.3) giving a larger residual surplus. The developer who

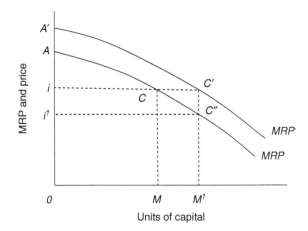

Figure 7.3 The effect of changes in the productivity of capital or in the rate of interest on the height of a building and on the site value

recognized this use could bid more for this site. Thus competition ensures that the site goes to its most profitable use, for this has the largest residual surplus.

3. Competition also ensures that the site is developed upwards to the point where $MR = MC$, where ABC, the bid for the site, is a maximum. Thus, not only does the site go to its most profitable use, but the type of building upon it is the one which secures the highest possible yield – having regard to the cost of alternative sites (see below).

4. A *higher building* and a *higher site price* will result either from a rise in the MRP of capital or from a fall in the rate of interest.

   A rise in the marginal revenue productivity of capital from MRP to MRP' (Figure 7.3) could occur through: (i) an increase in the marginal *physical* product as a result of improved techniques (such as self-service selling) or increased productivity of the construction industry; (ii) higher revenue – for example, from increased prices of the existing product supplied by the building or from a new higher use as the demand for another good increases or planning permission is granted. The height of the building increases from OM to OM^1.

   A fall in the rate of interest would lower the cost of each capital unit – for example, from Oi to Oi^1 again increasing the height of the building from OM to OM^1 (using the MRP curve).

   Similarly, the *price of the site* will rise from AiC to $A'iC'$ when MRP rises to MRP' or from AiC to Ai^1C' when the rate of interest falls to Oi^1.

5. From the viewpoint of the individual developer, land is a cost; he has to pay the competitive market price in order to obtain it. His argument therefore runs as follows: 'The higher the price of land, the more I have to economise in its use. Thus a site has to be used more intensively by applying more capital per square metre. High land prices have caused high buildings.'

While this may be quite true from the viewpoint of the individual, our analysis of the *land market as a whole* turns the argument on its head: (i) where demand, as reflected in the rent attainable, is high, the use capacity of land is high; (ii) this means that a highly intensive use of land is profitable; and (iii) because high building is profitable, land values are likely to be high.

If we relax the assumption that the project has a life of only 1 year (and the price of capital and the price of the product do not change over time) yields can be discounted back to their present value according to the year in which they are obtained and then added together. The area $AOMC$ in Figure 7.3 then represents the value of the aggregated discounted yields throughout the estimated life of the project.

Building higher versus building wider

By building higher, the developer is in effect saving on the cost of land. But diminishing returns mean that the cost of obtaining a given addition to revenue increases. Therefore, the developer will only build an extra storey so long as this is cheaper than acquiring extra land. In other words, there is a 'margin of building' in terms both of intensive use (adding an extra floor) and of extensive use (adding extra land).

Let us suppose that the demand for office suites in a district increased. A developer could respond either by adding a storey to a building or by building a ground-floor suite on undeveloped land. The course of action adopted would be that which costs less to produce a given addition to revenue.

In practice, competition for land for different uses will ensure that, in the long run, in an efficient market, development everywhere will be pushed to the point where the marginal return to capital is equal to the marginal cost of capital for every site. Thus in Figure 7.4, plots of land of the same size are developed for (a) the city-centre site by the addition of capital OM_a, and for (b) the suburban site by the addition of OM_b. In the first case, the rent is ABC, and in the second $A'B'C'$.

To sum up, it is the strength of demand, represented by MRP (Figure 7.4) which determines simultaneously both land prices and density. In a large city there is likely to be greater demand than in a small city and so buildings are likely to be higher in the centre of large cities than in the centre of small cities – see Figure 7.5.

Values of land in the centres of cities rise in response to increasing demand. Both land rents and building heights tend to be highest at the city centre.

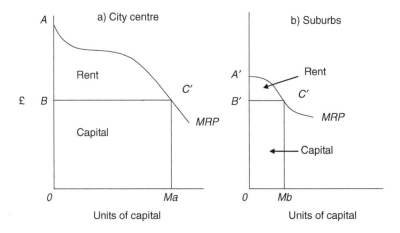

Figure 7.4   Intensive and extensive use of land

Box 7.3   The world's tallest buildings

The fortunes of the Burj Khalifa (formerly Burj Dubai) may not look so good after the downturn in Dubai's property sector in 2008–9, but other iconic tall buildings in the past have survived completion in a recession to go on to great success. In the 1930s the Empire State Building in New York was known as the 'Empty State Building' and Canary Wharf in London's Docklands (started in a boom and completed in recession) was not fully let for several years.

Tallest buildings

1. Burj Khalifa, Dubai, 2010, 800 metres plus
2. CN Tower, Toronto 1974–5, 553 metres
3. Taipei 101, Taipei, 2004, 509 metres
4. Shanghai World Financial Center, Shanghai, 2008, 492 metres
5. Petronas Towers, Kuala Lumpur, 1998, 452 metres
6. Willis Tower, Chicago, 1974, 442 metres
7. Jin Mao Building, Shanghai, 1999, 421 metres
8. Two International Finance Centre, Hong Kong, 2003, 415 metres
9. CITIC Plaza, Guangzhou, 1996, 391 metres
10. Shun Hing Square, Shenzhen, 1996, 384 metres

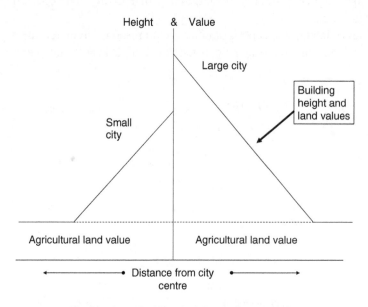

Figure 7.5   Building height and land values

The choice of development project

Where only one project is possible on a given site, the developer has to choose the one which is most profitable – that which yields the highest NPV. The answers to the questions considered above will provide the essential data for comparison purposes – the expected NARs from different projects, how NARs fall as the height of the building increases, the initial capital cost and subsequent maintenance costs.

Having done their calculations, developers compete with each other to obtain the site. The developer who can recognize the most profitable use (often described as the 'highest and best use') can make the highest bid. As a result, given perfect knowledge, a competitive price system and no external costs or benefits, the site is used in the most efficient way.

Summary

Development takes place in response to changes in the demand and supply of land resources. It includes modification of existing buildings, complete redevelopment and new development on greenfield sites. Development is an important part of overall UK investment and a significant part of GDP.

Developers perform a range of functions, acting as entrepreneurs who recognize development potential and bear the risks of the project. A variety of different methods are available to developers to enable them to evaluate development projects. The developer's decision on intensity of site use is subject to the law of diminishing returns – in effect, units of a variable factor (capital) are applied to a fixed factor (land) up to the point where the MRP of a unit of capital equals the cost of a unit of capital.

Chapter 7: review questions

1. What factors influence the decision to redevelop land and buildings?
2. What are the main functions of the developer?
3. Explain the basis of a project evaluation based on net present value.
4. Explain how risk and uncertainty can be coped with in evaluation of development projects.
5. Use a diagram to explain what determines the intensity of site use in a development project.

8

Redevelopment

After studying this chapter you will be able to:

- Explain how the timing of redevelopment is an economic decision;
- Show how changes in property demand can affect rental income;
- Show how changes in property supply can affect operating costs;
- Explain how a change in the rate of interest is likely to affect the development decision.

The timing of redevelopment

Where land is already developed by having a building on it, fixed capital is embodied in the land. Such capital has no cost in the short period; as a result, redevelopment to a new use, which requires expenditure of further capital, usually occurs only after a considerable period of time.

In general terms, redevelopment takes place when the present value of the expected flow of future net returns from the existing use of the land resources becomes less than the capital value of the cleared site. We have therefore to calculate the present value of the land resources in their current use and compare this with the value of the cleared site. Our method of arriving at both values follows the present value method. It is assumed that over the period under consideration there is no change in the value of money (that is, no inflation). But it should be noted that the rate of discount used for calculating present values has, over the last 10 years, been related to an interest rate which tries to keep the yearly inflation rate at 2.5 per cent.

It must be emphasized that we are seeking to establish a *capital* value. Since this depends on the *net* returns expected to be earned in future years, such returns must first be estimated and discounted to the present and then aggregated in order to arrive at the present capital value.

The net annual return (NAR) during any given year of the life of a project is the difference between the gross annual return (such as the rental received) and

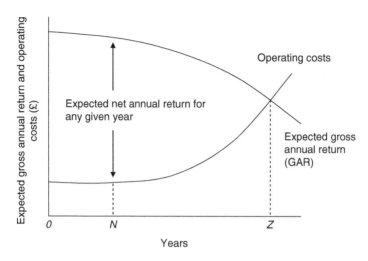

Figure 8.1 Gross annual returns and operating costs over time

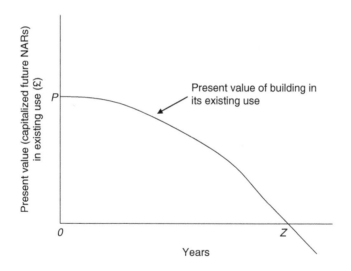

Figure 8.2 The present value of land resources over time

the operating costs (including repairs and maintenance). Since we are dealing with the future, both the gross annual return (GAR) and the operating costs are estimates – shown diagrammatically in Figure 8.1.

As the years go by, GAR is likely to decrease because: (i) where there were super-normal profits accruing to the initial development, they will encourage similar developments, and this will lower future returns – for example, from rents; and (ii) expectations are subject to greater uncertainty and risk the further one looks ahead. Offsetting these, complementary developments may come along, thereby exerting an upward pressure on rents.

In contrast, operating costs rise as the years go by because: (i) the structure deteriorates physically; and (ii) the older the building, the less adaptable it is to new technical requirements, such as modern office machinery and parking for shopping by car.

The NARs for the whole of the future life of the building have to be discounted to the present and then aggregated in order to obtain the present value of the land resource in its current use (see Figure 8.2).

In Figures 8.1 and 8.2 NAR and present capital value both become zero after OZ years. If no redevelopment has taken place by then, the land resources are left derelict, as with old coal mines and Welsh slate quarries. This can be summarized as:

$$P = \sum_{t=i}^{n} \frac{R_i - O_i}{(1+r)^i} \tag{8.1}$$

where:

1. P = value of property in current use
2. n = period when GARs can be earned in current use
3. R_i = GARs from i to year n
4. O_i = operating costs, excluding depreciation, from i to year n, and
5. r = rate of discount

The value of the cleared site

At any one time, the value of the cleared site is equal to the present value of the most profitable alternative use *less* the cost of clearing the site and rebuilding for this new use (see Figure 8.3).

The present value of the most profitable alternative use is obtained by the procedure used for calculating the present value of the current use: (i) the future NARs in the best alternative use are calculated; and (ii) these NARs are discounted to the present and aggregated to give a capital present value, DD_1 in Figure 8.3.

It will be observed in Figures 8.2 and 8.3 that in year 0, when the existing building was constructed, the present value in the current use (OP) was greater than the present value in the new alternative best use (OD). It was for this reason that the land went to its current use. From then on, however, the value of the alternative use (DD_1) rises. This occurs for two main reasons. First, changes in the conditions of demand and supply (discussed later) mean that a new building, being specifically designed for the new use, will earn higher NARs. Thus an old office building will give way to one that is air-conditioned and has the structure and space suitable for modern office equipment. Second, any new building would probably have a longer time horizon than the old building

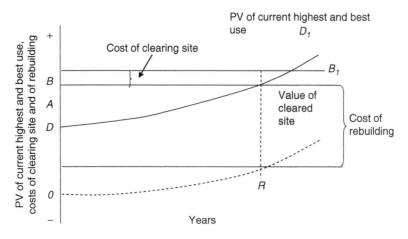

Figure 8.3 The value of the cleared site

(which has already run a part of its life) so that there would be more future NARs to aggregate to obtain its present value.

From the present value of the best alternative use at any one time, we have to deduct: (a) the cost of demolishing and clearing the site (*AB* in Figure 8.3); and (b) the total cost of rebuilding for the new use, including ripening costs and normal profit (*OA*). For simplicity, we have assumed that costs (a) and (b) both remain constant over time. BB_1 represents the sum of (a) and (b).

The present value of the cleared site is thus the difference between DD_1 and BB_1 in any given year. In year *O* the value of the best alternative use would be only just below that of the chosen current use, for then each was competing for a cleared site. However, once a site has been allocated to a given use and has had a building erected upon it, any new use has the additional handicap of demolishing and rebuilding. Thus, until year *R* the value of the cleared site is negative.

Using the previous notation, and assuming that *R'* and *O'* to refer to the best alternative use, and

1. *C* = the value of the cleared site
2. *D* = the cost of demolition and clearing the site
3. *B* = the cost of rebuilding to the new best use, we have:

$$C = \sum_{t=0}^{n} \frac{R_i' - O_i'}{(1+r)^i} - D - B \qquad (8.2)$$

By combining Figures 8.2 and 8.3 in Figure 8.4, we can show when redevelopment takes place. From year *R* the value of the cleared site is positive and

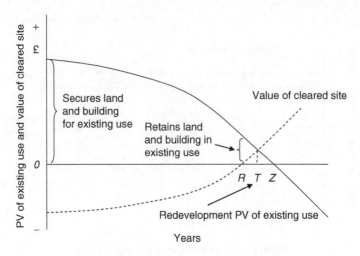

Figure 8.4 The timing of redevelopment

increasing and eventually in *T* exceeds the present value of the building in its current use. Thus redevelopment takes place in year *T*, when *C = P* (the value of the cleared site equals the current use value).

It should be noted that in year *T* the building is still *technically* efficient, for it can earn a NAR until year Z. However, in year *T* it becomes *economically* inefficient because resources can be switched to a new use having a greater value. Thus we can define the economic life of a building as that period of time during which it commands a capital value greater than the capital value of the cleared site.

The rate of redevelopment

The diagrammatic model used so far can be used to analyse all redevelopment situations. By way of illustration, we shall examine the *rate* of redevelopment. The rate of redevelopment will depend upon changes which occur over time in the relationship between:

1. the present value of the existing use of the land resources;
2. the present value of the best alternative use;
3. the cost of rebuilding.

It will be accelerated if (2) increases relative to (1), or if the cost of rebuilding falls. It will be retarded if opposite changes occur. What we have to consider, therefore, are the factors affecting (1), (2) and (3).

Present value depends upon expected future NARs and the rate at which they are discounted to the present. This rate will be common to both existing and alternative uses. We can thus concentrate on the NARs of each, the difference between GAR (*rentals*) and *operating costs*. Rentals are concerned largely with changes on the demand side, operating costs with changes on the supply side.

Changes on the demand side affect rental income. Let us assume that the current site in the city centre consists of large residential houses and the best alternative use is that of offices.

A change in the *demand for large city-centre houses* can arise through changes in:

1. tastes (such as a switch in preferences towards flats or smaller suburban houses);
2. real income (for instance, people tend to move outwards to more spacious gardens as their income increases);
3. the distribution of income (for example, higher taxation of the rich forces them to vacate expensive city-centre houses);
4. the price of substitutes (such as cheaper suburban houses);
5. transport costs or facilities (for example, fare increases or the building of a motorway or underground railway);
6. mortgage terms;
7. complementary activities (such as new schools or golf courses in the suburbs);
8. government policy (for example, making planning permission to convert large houses to flats conditional upon the provision of off-street parking).

Similarly, rents from offices, the alternative use, would be affected by changes in both occupation and investment demand. Thus, a rise in *occupation demand* for professional services or for offices in city-centre positions would increase rents, while government dispersal policy would tend to decrease them. But since NARs depend largely on *expected* future rentals, *investment demand* would increase the capital value if such rentals were expected to increase. In other words, the current yield on offices would be capitalized at a lower rate for investment purposes, thereby increasing the capital value of offices.

Changes on the supply side also affect operating costs. Essentially, the same considerations apply to both houses and offices, but we shall illustrate the former. With houses, operating costs may change because: (i) maintenance costs and repairs change – for example, builders' charges may rise, or repairs may be curtailed (as, for instance, in the twilight zones of towns); (ii) technical improvements may allow conversions to a more intensive use, so small apartments may become economically viable as a result of cheaper partitioning and the development of compact units incorporating a sink, refrigerator and electric cooking facilities; and (iii) government policy may alter – for example, improvement grants will reduce conversion costs, whereas more stringent fire-precaution regulations will increase them.

Renovation or clearance?

Buildings are maintained, repaired and improved throughout their economic life. At some point a decision must be made as to whether to renovate in order that the building can continue to provide useful services, or to clear it and rebuild or redevelop the site. If the decision is taken to renovate or refurbish the

---

Box 8.1 Manchester city centre redevelopment

On Saturday 15 June 1996, a 3,300 lb bomb exploded in Manchester city centre injuring 220 people and causing immense physical, social and economic damage. It was the largest peacetime bomb ever detonated in Britain, and as a result 50,000 square metres of retail space and 25,000 square metres of office space needed to be reconstructed. Four hundred businesses within a kilometre of the blast were affected and 40 per cent never recovered. Insurers paid £411 million in damages although estimates of the total costs are between £700 million and £900 million.

From the start it was decided not merely to repair and reinstate what had been damaged, but to adopt a much more radical approach – turning the adversity into an opportunity to re-plan and rebuild the heart of the city centre. The first major step forward was the launch of an international design competition to produce a master plan which would set out a vision for the new city centre and act as a guide for the rebuilding programme.

The plan chosen was designed by EDAW, a North American urban planning consultancy. The rebuilding was made possible by a dedicated 4-year funding package and the close support of key public and private funding partners. It was felt to be important to strengthen Manchester's role as a regional centre in a European and global context and to offer a quality of life and an urban environment that is attractive for all those who want to live, work, shop and be entertained in the city centre. Manchester's predominant role as the retail and business centre of the wider region needed to be preserved. The city centre needed to provide additional investment opportunities to attract new activities while the distinctive quality of its architectural and historic urban fabric was to be preserved and further enhanced so as to contribute to the city's future success. Five listed buildings such as the Corn Exchange and Royal Exchange were badly damaged by the bomb. One of the first priorities for Manchester Millennium, working closely with English Heritage and others, was to ensure a programme of meticulous repair and conservation of these listed buildings.

The bulk of the rebuilding was finished by the end of 1999 at a cost of £1.2 billion, although some was not completed until 2005. The northern end of the Arndale Centre was demolished as was Cannon Street and the Arndale bus station. Cannon Street was overbuilt with a new part of the shopping complex and reborn as New Cannon Street. At either end is Exchange Court and the Wintergarden. A major new store for Next was created facing the Urbis Museum, completing the regeneration of the Millennium Quarter and Exchange Square. Manchester now has the largest Marks and Spencer store in Europe and also Selfridges and Harvey Nichols. There are 5,000 residential properties in the city centre and imaginative landscaping has provided many public spaces including the newly developed Piccadilly Gardens.

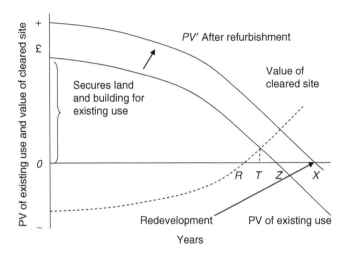

Figure 8.5 Renovation or refurbishment delays redevelopment

building, the objective must be to raise the present value of future revenues or net annual returns (NARs) by more than the cost of the refurbishment. NARs would increase because future rents in the refurbished building would be higher and because operating costs are likely to be lower, especially if (as is increasingly the case) refurbishment also includes energy saving and possibly energy-generating measures such as the fitting of solar panels or wind turbines.

Renovation or refurbishment would delay clearance and redevelopment as illustrated in Figure 8.5.

In many cities the economic life of large old houses has been extended by renovation or conversion into apartments. Inner city areas can thus maintain the appearance of former grandeur, at least from the facades of such buildings, while internal modification and refurbishment provides smaller, more modern accommodation. Further issues concerning historic buildings are considered in Chapter 10.

The effect of a change in the rate of interest on the rate of redevelopment

A change in the rate of interest is unlikely to have equivalent effects on both the present and alternative use.

First, at any given time a part of the physical life of a building has passed. Thus the years of future yields are fewer, and its present capitalized value is less. In contrast, the next-best-use building has not yet begun its life, so that there are more yields to be capitalized. This means that a rise in the rate of interest will favour the present use since it applies to fewer future yields. In other words, it will reduce the value of the next-best use more than that of the

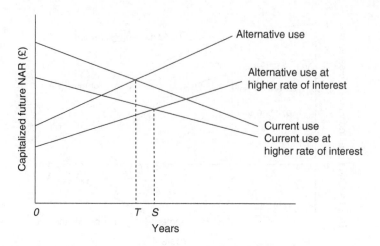

Figure 8.6 The effect of a rise in the rate of interest on redevelopment

current use. Second, a higher rate of interest will increase ripening and waiting costs, thus decreasing the present capital value of the next-best use.

Figure 8.6 illustrates how, for the above reasons, a rise in the rate of interest brings about changes in the position of the capital-value curves of the present and next-best uses. The net result of a rise in the rate of interest is to retard redevelopment from year T to year S; a fall in the rate of interest would tend to accelerate it.

Third, in addition to a rise in the rate of interest, the imperfection of the capital market may mean that certain forms of development may encounter additional penalties. Therefore, house purchasers tend to rely more on borrowed funds than do insurance, industrial and property companies. For instance, insurance companies have a net inflow of premium income, while large firms can usually borrow temporarily from a bank when the rate of interest seems high, funding the loan later when the long-term rate has fallen. In contrast, house purchasers will find that a higher rate of interest will reduce the maximum loan available through the building societies' and banks' income/repayment ratio constraint on lending.

The effect of a change in building costs on redevelopment

Redevelopment will be accelerated by a fall in real building costs because this will increase the value of the cleared site (raising the alternative use curve in Figure 8.5 and bringing forward redevelopment). Such a fall may occur through increased productivity in the construction industry or improved technology, for example, in the building of high-rise office blocks. In contrast an increase in building costs – perhaps because material costs go up or wages rise – will retard redevelopment (lowering the alternative use curve in Figure 8.5 and delaying redevelopment).

Box 8.2   Wembley stadium redevelopment

When the FA (via Wembley National Stadium Limited WNSL) awarded the contract to build Wembley to Multiplex, it seemed as though they were on to a winner. The Australian company said it could complete the stadium for under £500 million but eight difficult years later the eventual cost of the stadium was at least £827 million.

The aim of the new Wembley stadium project was to design and build a state-of-the-art national stadium, unlike any other in the world, to be the home of English football and to host large events such as Cup Finals, music events and athletics. The new stadium is eventually expected to become an icon, in the same way as the old stadium with the twin towers. These have been replaced by the arch, which is not just a cosmetic feature; it supports the north roof and a sizeable area of the south roof. The old stadium was closed in 2000 and demolished in 2002. Construction of the new stadium began in October 2002. In order to overcome financial concerns over the new stadium, the parties involved came to an agreement on a fixed-cost contract. This made provision for a building cost of around £352 million, with total project costs of £757 million.

The new Wembley stadium is a good example of the problems that can occur with fixed-price contracts. Under such an arrangement, the client is protected from exposure to budget over-runs or delays in construction. That risk is borne by the main contractor. The stadium will be linked to Wembley Park Station (London Underground) via Olympic Way and also Wembley Central Station via the White Horse Bridge. The design (50-year design life) of the new stadium is both functional and architecturally significant. Sir Norman Foster designed the arch and the roof structure, with the remainder of the stadium being designed by architects Foster and Partners and HOK Sport. By using retractable roof panels, which retract to the south, it allows as much daylight and ventilation to reach pitch level as possible.

Several construction problems have been highlighted during the project. The first was a problem between Multiplex and the steel contractor Cleveland Bridge. Cleveland Bridge quit the project in 2004 shortly before the arch was raised because they did not believe they would be paid for materials and there were irreconcilable difficulties between the two parties. The problems resulted in two high-profile court cases where the two companies have sued each other for breach of contract (Multiplex sued for £45 million and Cleveland Bridge sued for £22.5 million to recover what it believed it was owed). As of June 2006 the courts had found in favour of Multiplex because of breach of contract, but Cleveland Bridge is appealing.

The second problem involved a temporary roof support rafter, which fell by over half a metre in March 2006. This resulted in the evacuation of 3,000 construction workers and delayed work while inspections and reports were carried out. The project was started again shortly afterwards. Later in March 2006 a third problem came to light. The sewers under the stadium had buckled due to ground movement. Remedial work was put into action for this and is currently nearing completion.

Multiplex (now owned by Brookfield Europe) is estimated to have absorbed cost over-runs of £300 million (although they are pursuing engineering consultant Mott MacDonald for £253 million in the courts). Multiplex claim changes in the design were responsible for the project being late. Cleveland Bridge Company lost over £26 million and so far legal costs are around £65 million.

Other factors affecting the pace of redevelopment

If we relax the assumptions of a perfect market and perfect competition, then real world conditions may affect the pace of redevelopment.

1. Imperfect knowledge, immobility of factors, or just inertia, may mean that it takes time for profitable redevelopment to get under way.
2. Imperfections of the capital market may affect the type of development. For instance, houses may be built instead of a block of flats because selling the former on completion gives the developer an earlier cash flow.
3. Legal restrictions, such as a covenant prohibiting the building of a particular type of shop, may postpone redevelopment until another type of shop becomes competitive with the current use.
4. There may not be perfect competition in the supply of sites. Thus publicly owned land might not be offered for sale, while some owners of sites essential to the complete development exercise their monopoly power in the price they demand
5. Government policy, particularly as regards planning, may prevent redevelopment for certain uses. On the other hand, the exercise of compulsory purchase powers may make it easier to combine interests and so accelerate development – for instance, for slum clearance. Other examples of government policy affecting the rate of development are taxation policy (for example, residential and commercial buildings cannot be written off as depreciation), improvement grants (which encourage the modernization of owner-occupied or rented, older, residential properties), and the Leasehold Reform Acts of 1967, 1993 and 2002 (which, by enabling owner-occupiers to purchase the freeholds of their leasehold interests, have made it virtually impossible to retain estates intact for future comprehensive redevelopment).

Summary

Redevelopment takes place when the expected value of the expected flow of future net returns from the existing use of land resources becomes less than the capital value of the cleared site. The rate of redevelopment depends on the relationship between the present value of the existing use, the present value of the best alternative use and the cost of rebuilding. An increase in the rate of interest is likely to retard development because its effect on present values of the alternative use will be greater than its effect on the present value of the current use.

Market imperfections, such as legal restrictions or planning regulations may mean that in the real world redevelopment is not as efficient as the theories presented indicate.

Chapter 8: review questions

1. Why are operating costs of buildings likely to rise over time?
2. Why are property returns (rents) likely to decrease over time?
3. Explain the determinants of the rate of redevelopment of land resources.
4. Show how demand changes can affect the rental income from a property.
5. Show how supply changes can affect operating costs of a property.
6. Explain why a rise in the rate of interest is not neutral in its effects on the present value of existing and alternative uses of a land resource.

9

Development Finance

After studying this chapter you will be able to:

- Explain what is meant by 'creating an interest' in real property;
- Describe how imperfections in real property markets affect property development finance;
- Describe the main sources of short-term finance;
- Describe the main sources of long-term finance.

Principles of financing real property development

Development needs finance: (i) to cover the development period; and (ii) to purchase the finished development either for occupation or to hold it as an investment. The former is usually referred to as a 'short-term' or 'bridging' loan, and the latter as a 'long-term' or 'funded' loan. There are thus usually three main participants: (a) the *borrower*, that is, the developer (who may also be the long-term holder); (b) the *lender of short-term finance*, such as a clearing or merchant bank; and (c) the *provider of long-term finance*, usually a bank or institution such as an insurance company or pension fund.

The method of raising finance, whether short-term or long-term, is based on the principle of creating an interest in the real property. The owner can use the property simply as security for a bank loan (which can be regarded as a short-term mortgage). Alternatively, he can sell a definite interest. For instance, the owner of the 'fee simple absolute' of a particular property may lack the capital necessary to develop. He might obtain this against a rent charge. Or the owner-occupier of a shop or farm may wish to raise additional working capital. He could do this by 'sale and leaseback'(explained later in this chapter). The creation of an interest enables the lender to obtain an income from a property without having to occupy it.

The essential point to note is that, for the person creating the rent charge or selling and leasing back his property, the form chosen represents, *other things being equal*, the most preferred way of raising capital. Similarly for the lender: the particular interest created, a rent charge or leaseback, represents the best way of using capital. However, 'other things being equal' assumes that in the market: (i) there are a number of competitive lenders; and (ii) there is always a 'price' represented by the rate of interest at which a would-be borrower can obtain funds as an alternative to selling an interest.

In practice, these conditions do not hold. First, the borrower may be faced with a monopoly lender, as occurs, for instance, with the small developer who has to rely mainly on a bank. Thus a speculative builder might find that the conditions of a loan are more or less the same from all banks, being limited to 1 year only. As a result, he has to watch his cash-flow position carefully. This may even force him to build houses, which can be sold as they are completed, rather than a block of flats.

Second, property often consists of 'large lumps', an office block costing, say, £50 million to build and a city-centre redevelopment considerably more. In such cases finance is usually secured by negotiation between principals, and the precise terms will reflect their relative strengths in bilateral bargaining.

Third, government policy may influence the terms of a loan. For example, the switch to using base rate changes as the major weapon for suppressing inflation could mean that lending on variable rate terms is preferred, with a loan at a fixed rate having to carry a risk premium to cover a possible future rise in base rate. Similarly, taxation affects property finance. Corporation tax and capital gains tax leave smaller profits for ploughing back into future developments. Exemption from income tax means that leaseholds have advantages for certain purchasers, such as charitable trusts, while capital gains tax may discourage 'sale and leasebacks'.

Thus the main effects of these market imperfections are:

1. Interests may be created which would not have been had the market offered alternative sources of finance. Thus a sale and leaseback may be preferred to a mortgage simply because it provides finance to the full value of a property as opposed to only two-thirds.
2. Particular conditions can be imposed by the lender as an alternative to charging a higher rate of interest.
3. Since funds cannot always be obtained when needed or on terms which suit the borrower, finance plays an important role in the timing, quantity and type of development undertaken.

A study of property development since 1945 reveals no hard-and-fast ways by which capital is raised. Rather, it demonstrates the ingenuity of developers in obtaining funds as conditions have changed in the capital market, usually as a result of changes in government policy. Thus in the 1960s when the 'Big

Four' banks were required to limit their lending, property developers turned to merchant banks, foreign banks and even finance companies who had previously specialized in hire purchase.

Sources of capital also change as the requirements of lenders change. This may be due to a policy adjustment – for example, insurance companies sought equity interests with the introduction of 'with-profits' policies. On the other hand, it may simply be the result of an adjustment in an institution's portfolio of assets. Thus, as a hedge against inflation, a pension fund may increase its lending for property development in return for a part-share in the freehold interest. This means that a developer should organize facilities with three or four alternative sources.

What follows, therefore, is simply a broad survey of the different arrangements which may be made to raise finance. In practice, new devices are continually being invented to meet changes in market conditions. Indeed, each project tends to attract its own financial structure, the exact terms being finely tailored to suit the particular preferences of both borrower and lender (see Table 9.1).

Table 9.1   Sources of capital for development

Source of capital	Method	Advantages	Disadvantages
Finance by cash/ assets	- paid before acquisition - paid after acquisition - paid by instalment	- certainty - no ongoing liability - retain control of development	- drain on resources - can affect cash flow - restricted to own cash/ assets
Finance by loans	- bank/institutional loan - issuance of shares/ bonds / futures/ options/ REITs	- steady cash flow - risk sharing default option/ prepayment option - tap-in any opportunity - better control of quality and asset specificity	- liability / possibility of liquidation - cost of loan (depends on credit rating) - collateral at risk
Finance by sub-letting land interests	- sale and leaseback - joint venture (PPP/PFI) - Build-Operate-Transfer (BOT) - Build-Own-Operate-Transfer (BOOT) - sale of land promises (e.g. naming rights/ roof-top antenna/ external wall advertisement)	- no cash drain - ultimate ownership of land retained - own the development with no construction and operation costs - risk sharing - can attract value-added developers and increase profits	- loss of control of land interests - high asset specificity (the investments made to support a particular transaction have a higher value in that transaction than they would have if they were redeployed for any other purpose) - moral hazard (may act differently if risk is reduced) - quality of development affected

Property developments are often one-off projects that can be undertaken using a company specifically incorporated for the project – a single purpose vehicle (SPV) that can be wound up when the project is completed. The revenues from the development tend to be received towards the end of the project when the work is completed and units are sold, so the funding is often for a long period of time. Selling before completion ('off-plan') can bring in revenue earlier, but to do this a discount must be offered.

Finance for property development generally operates as an interest-only, draw-down facility to finance development as required. Often the interest on a development loan is capitalized during the development period, with the entire loan, inclusive of interest charged, being repaid upon the sale of the development and or the refinance of any residual debt.

Short-term finance

A developer needs *short-term* finance for the development period in order to purchase land, meet ripening and waiting costs and pay the building contractor and professional consultants. The period usually extends from one to 3 years, but for comprehensive developments it can be much longer. With the latter, the developer may rely on rolling over short-term loans; more usually, longer-term finance from the institutions will be required from the start. The distinction between short-term and long-term finance in property development reflects *risk*. The greatest risk is during the construction period, the least when the building is completed and occupied. There is thus a difference in the terms and rate of interest charged.

In many respects short-term development finance can be likened to the working capital of industry, for such capital covers the production period until the finished good is sold. Thus the sources of short-term finance for development tend to be similar to those for businesses in general. Short-term finance is obtained mainly from the banks – the clearing banks, merchant banks and the UK subsidiaries of foreign banks. All are concerned with the liquidity, security and profitability of the loan.

Collapses in the property market in 1973, 1990 and 2008 have highlighted the risk to a bank of being locked in as a lender of 'project finance', where the sale of the finished building is the sole means of repayment. The tendency now, therefore, is to put more emphasis on *liquidity*, that is, regaining quickly the money lent should there be a collapse in the property market.

First, therefore, the bank assesses the development company's capability and financial background. Has it a record of previous successful developments? Has it managed to retain some of these? If so, what is its gearing and overall cash flow? Can it be relied upon to complete the project?

> **Box 9.1** Lending criteria for property development finance
>
> Lenders will look at a number of areas when considering if they will provide finance for a development project. These may include:
>
> - Experience as a property developer
> - Financial strength of the developer
> - How much equity is brought to the project
> - The location of the proposed development
> - The profit potential of the development
> - Builder experience and capacity
> - Project management team experience
> - Type of development (residential housing, apartments, commercial or mixed use)
> - Level of pre-sales/pre-leases
> - Ability to cover cost over runs
> - Exit strategy

The quality of the project will also be examined for its location, design, and so on – but, more importantly, for its saleability in a weak market. And, where a loan is offered, it will be structured to the nature of the project (for example, site assembly, working capital for construction), and limited from 1 to 3 years. Thus a loan for an industrial warehouse development would be for a shorter period than a loan for an office block, since the former usually takes less time to complete. The object is to give the borrower sufficient flexibility, while still exercising a measure of control over the project.

For security, a *clearing bank* limits the loan to about two-thirds of the cost of the development, usually determined by its own valuer. This may present a difficulty for a small entrepreneur, such as a housebuilder or minor office developer with few supporting capital resources, so that he is advised by the bank to consider less costly and risky projects such as refurbishments. Any super-normal profit could provide the equity for more ambitious schemes later. Alternatively, where his own bank declines to lend, there is just a slight possibility that a loan can be arranged through a *property insurance broker.*

In contrast, the well-established property company is at an advantage. Not only may its existing property holdings provide collateral, but net revenue from them may cover interest payments on the new loan. Even so, it will limit its collateral as far as possible since uncommitted property can be used to support later borrowing. Where a loan is confined to the specific project it is known as a 'non-recourse' loan; where other assets of the company or parent company can be called upon, it is a 'recourse' loan. usually the final agreement lies between these two – a 'limited recourse' loan.

A large property company may wish to form a subsidiary company to carry out a particular development, but limiting its equity commitment to an initial

5 per cent of the finance required. A bank would advance, say, 80 per cent of 'senior debt'. The balance of 15 per cent – 'mezzanine debt' – could probably be obtained by arranging cover against loss with an insurer who specializes on loans secured against commercial property.

Loans from a bank can be by either overdraft or term loan. Whereas the overdraft is cheaper, a term loan gives the developer greater security. But with both, the rate of interest can fluctuate. A developer may therefore prefer to raise short-term finance through a *merchant bank*, whose lending limits may be up to four-fifths of the value. Although the interest rate charged may be a little higher, it can be fixed for the whole period of the loan, enabling development costs to be forecast more accurately.

As regards *profitability*, it must be recognized that, whereas the institutions, the ultimate purchasers, base security on the completed and occupied buildings, the banks have to base theirs on their assessment of the project and their knowledge of the developer. This risk must be reflected in what it earns over and above the 'opportunity cost' of a safe return on the money market. Moreover, unless there is some provision for varying the rate charged, this risk margin can be eroded should short-term interest rates rise.

Longer-term development finance

Since construction finance on a 2-year basis presents difficulties for major developments such as a shopping centre or a large office block, it is now usual for the institutions to provide long-term finance from the start. Similarly, when the developer is building for an occupying institution, the latter may make all the financial provision. This financing of the development process by the institutions has been encouraged by the increasing competition to secure prime property investments, and their provision of development finance may hinge on there being some degree of equity participation in the completed building. The actual arrangement may, therefore, take many forms, with an increasing degree of final equity, as follows.

Priority yield

The institution agrees a minimum yield with the developer of, say, 6 per cent. If the developer's ability is such that he can achieve a yield of 7.25 per cent, the institution allows him to keep the capitalized 1.25 per cent difference as his profit. Should there be a yield in excess of 7.25 per cent, the institution would require a share to enable it to relate risk to profit. Priority yield provides a high incentive for the developer to keep costs to a minimum and to let the project as quickly as possible.

Sale and leaseback

The basis of the leaseback is that the freehold, with the benefit of planning consent, is sold to an institution, which then advances the development costs at a fixed rate of interest. If the development is not let within, say, six months of completion, the developer receives a balancing payment in return for either entering into a leaseback or providing a leaseback guarantee at an agreed base rent. This balancing item represents the developer's profit and is based on a certain yield to the institution of about 7.5 per cent. If costs rise or completion takes longer than expected, the developer makes up the difference from his balancing item.

Once letting to an occupational tenant is achieved, the lease is surrendered or the guarantee extinguished. Thus this form of a sale and leaseback is somewhat akin to a mortgage. If the rent secured is in excess of the base rent, provision is made for the institution to share in the enhanced value.

Profit erosion

A variation of the straight leaseback is the profit-erosion method. Where the developer is reluctant to commit himself to a potential 25-year-lease liability, he stakes his profit by agreeing to the institution's drawing the base rent from the balancing item. If the balancing payment is exhausted, the developer's interest ceases and the institution takes over full letting responsibility. Since under this method the institution accepts a greater risk, it requires a slightly higher yield.

Cooperation between the developing company and the occupying institution

If the developing company has a successful record, an institution may accept fuller participation in the project, providing both the short-term and long-term finance. The institution acquires from the developer a legal interest in the site, grants him a licence to build and meets the development costs. In return, it receives interest on the sum advanced and, when complete, occupies the building at a rent calculated on an agreed percentage of the total cost of development.

Joint company

The developer and the lending institution can form a joint company, shares being held in agreed proportions. This enables the institution to acquire a major equity interest in modern developments which may be in short supply. Moreover there is a secure return on the finance advanced. On the other hand, only interest payments are a deductible item in assessing corporation tax, so

---

Box 9.2   Sale and leaseback in the UK

Sale and leaseback is now often used by established companies to raise funds. It was once regarded as last-resort borrowing. As the name suggests sale and leaseback refers to an agreement that allows a company to release equity in an asset while still being able to use that asset. If a cash injection for business expansion and growth into a new market is needed, then rather than take on the added burden of additional debt, cash can be raised from the asset and it can be leased back from the company to which it is sold.

Property is becoming more important in corporate decision making, and financial decisions on property, such as the use of off-balance sheet finance, are increasingly being driven by the accountancy function rather than by the in-house property team. Attachment to corporate property ownership has softened, with the recognition of the often significant funding potential within assets where value has often appreciated significantly over recent years.

There is no immediate shortage of investable property in the UK, where the ratio of freehold to leasehold property in corporate ownership is significantly higher than in the USA. This type of arrangement can be used with buildings and specialist equipment. For premises, sale and leaseback can offer a very profitable company significant tax advantages. For example they could sell their asset to another company in their group and the lease payments would then become an allowable tax deduction.

Advantages

- Sale and leaseback allows a company to gain access to money tied up in valuable business assets.
- It frees up capital to fund merger and acquisition activity or to reallocate to core activities. The asset can still be used even if it is no longer owned.
- Tax benefits are realized by offsetting lease costs as an operating expense.
- The seller remains in day-to-day operational control of the property.
- Transfers property value risk to a third party on a fully transparent basis

Disadvantages

- The asset is no longer owned by the company, thereby weakening its balance sheet.
- There may be better ways to gain access to the funds either by refinancing or by securing a loan using that asset as collateral.
- The long-term costs of the premises are likely to be greater than if they remain in ownership of the company

Some prominent UK Sale and Leasebacks

- Travel Lodge   £400 million (2004 to Prestbury)
- Debenhams   £495 million (2005 to British Land)
- IBM   £120 million plus (2005 to Highcross)
- Tesco   £636 million (2005 to Consensus Business Group and Morley Fund Management)

that dividends on shares are reduced by the tax. This is a disadvantage to non-tax-paying institutions such as pension funds and charities.

Direct development by the institution

The tax disadvantage of the joint company has in recent years induced many institutions to accept the full risk of carrying out developments themselves. Usually a developer/consultant is engaged and paid a project management fee, calculated either as a fixed percentage of the construction cost or related to the eventual profit of the project. Not only does this allow the institution to influence the design and specification of the property and the quality of the tenant but, as the property is being obtained at source, it is likely to show a 1–1.5 return above current market yields.

Long-term investment finance

With short-term finance being quite expensive, the developer will start building as soon as possible after the site has been acquired and get the building completed quickly. He is then able to realize his profits, either by selling the development or holding it as an investment.

A developer who realizes all his profit as soon as possible by selling the completed project is, in reality, a property trading company: ideally, he would sell during the construction period. Suppose, for example, that the development is an office block with a capital cost of £4 million. A merchant bank makes the developer a short-term loan of £3 million, leaving him to find £1 million (including interest) from his own resources. The developer finds a tenant and pre-lets at a rent of £500,000 a year which, on a 10-year-purchase basis, gives a capitalized value of £5 million. He can now sell the project as an investment to an institution on an initial payment, with the balance being paid as the development proceeds, giving him a profit of £1 million. However, it is likely that a successful property development company will wish to retain some of its better developments, or at least an interest in them, as an investment. To do this, it needs some form of 'holding' agreement in the development finance arrangements and long-term finance.

Finance can be divided broadly into *equity capital* and *loans*. Equity capital is obtained by ploughing back profits or by selling shares. Except for well-established and fairly large companies, the former is unlikely to provide sufficient capital to purchase developments of high value. On the other hand, raising capital by the sale of shares is really open only to a public company, and usually a minimum of £50 million must be raised to make a public offer or 'rights issue' an economic proposition. Though this sum may present no obstacle to a successful developer, equity financing has three main disadvantages.

First, the cost of this type of finance depends largely upon the current popularity of property-company shares on the stock exchange. If these are selling on a low-yield basis relative to fixed-interest-bearing bonds, new equity can be obtained on favourable terms and give owners of existing shares a capital gain. But the opposite may apply, especially at a time when the company requires funds urgently.

Second, since shares carry voting rights, increasing the number of shares could mean that the control of the company passes out of the hands of the original owners and makes it more difficult to contest a hostile takeover bid.

Third, property companies are particularly suited to 'high-gearing', that is, having a high proportion of fixed-interest loans to ordinary shares. Since rents are regular, fairly certain and (with inflation) likely to rise, fixed-interest charges are covered by a steady income flow. Moreover, the property itself provides security for the loan. The alternative of raising funds by increasing the number of shares, referred to as diluting capital, simply means that any rise in profits has to be shared with the additional shareholders and is therefore only used to the extent that loan finance is unavailable or that too high a gearing may be detrimental to the share price.

Yet though a straight loan in money terms is preferred by a property company, the imperfections of the capital market may restrict its choice. For instance, to guard against inflation, many institutions may lend only on some form of equity-loan basis (see below), while the smaller company will probably find it advantageous to work through a specialist *property finance broker* having close connections with insurance companies and other lending institutions. He deals with specific propositions on a fee-paying basis and advises on the relative merits of the different offers of finance for the proposed project.

Since long-term finance is secured on completed buildings, capital is much safer. Moreover, the margin between interest payable and rental income provides an indication of the security of the loan. Therefore, long-term finance is usually available on easier terms than short-term development finance and is tied closely to the current yield on long-term government securities.

Mortgages

Ideally, a developer would prefer to obtain a straight loan from an institution, covered by a mortgage on the completed development. At one time it was usual for the capital to be repaid at the end of the mortgage period; nowadays, in order to protect themselves against inflation and rising interest rates, lending institutions tend to require periodic repayments of the loan which can then be reinvested.

The difficulty for the developer is that he may not have a sufficient cash flow to cover the interest charge plus the capital repayments, especially as the latter are not chargeable to income for taxation purposes. Thus whether a mortgage loan is feasible depends upon, (i) the timing of future revenues with respect to outgoings, and (ii) how the lender requires repayment of capital. Figures 9.1 and 9.2 illustrate two possibilities.

In Figure 9.1 the developer's flow of revenue is quite adequate for servicing the loan, and this in spite of the fact that the lender requires repayment of the capital by equal amounts during each year of the loan.

In Figure 9.2 the borrower has negotiated more favourable terms. With equal yearly sums to cover both interest and capital repayments, the latter is smaller at the beginning of the loan. In spite of this, however, the developer's cash flow is insufficient to service this total yearly sum simply because,

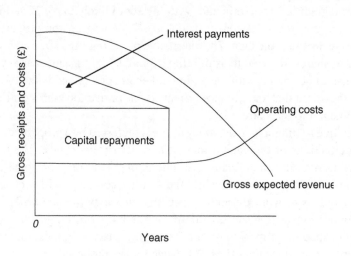

Figure 9.1   Viable mortgage terms

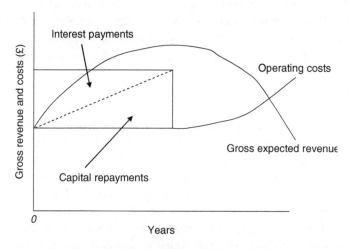

Figure 9.2   Mortgage terms not viable

in relation to required interest payments, gross revenues are small in the earlier years of the project, though they are expected to increase over time, either through increased demand for this type of development or through inflation.

In practice, the deficiency in cash flow may be substantial. If, therefore, the developer does not already have income from other property to cover the shortfall, he has to rethink his financing along one of the following lines. These alternatives, used to avoid early capital repayment, are usually acceptable because they offer the lending institution some form of equity participation as an inflation-hedge, the extent of this involvement depending largely on the requirements of its investment portfolio.

Mortgage debenture

An advance is made against the security of a particular property but with the lender having a recourse against the assets of the company or parent company. This advance is usually limited to two-thirds of the value of the *completed* development, but capital repayment is not required until the end of the loan period. While such a straight loan may suit the borrower, it provides no inflation-hedge. Lenders may therefore add some form of equity-participation condition, such as the option to convert the debenture into share capital at a future date. Alternatively, the return on the loan may be in the form of a rent charge.

Rent charge

A rent charge simply gives the lender a charge on the rents of the property. This can provide an inflation-hedge by linking the charge to rising rents, but legal remedies for non-payment are less satisfactory than for a mortgage or lease. If the rent charge is unpaid, the lender may enter into possession and collect rents until the debt is recovered, when the property reverts to the owner. With a mortgage or lease, however, proceedings can be taken for forfeiture should the tenant persistently fail to fulfil his commitments.

Government sources of capital

Apart from the private-sector sources of finance described above, government funds are also available. *Regional Selective Assistance*, partly funded by the EU's structural funds can cover up to 15 per cent of the cost of buildings in Assisted Areas. The *Regional Development Agencies* can draw on the *Single Regional Budget* to promote local forms of regeneration. In the remaining *Enterprize Zones*, new and existing firms enjoy exemption from general rates and 100 per cent capital allowances for corporation and income tax for expenditure on industrial and commercial buildings (see Chapter 20). In housing, housing associations obtain capital through the Housing Corporation, while renovation grants for dwellings over 10 years old are available to owner-occupiers, landlords and tenants subject to a financial resources test.

Summary

Short-term development finance is required to cover the development period. Long-term development finance is required to purchase the finished development either for occupation or to hold it as an investment. The method of raising finance depends on the creation of an interest in real property (such as a rent charge). Sources of short-term development finance include clearing banks, merchant banks and foreign banks. Long-term finance comes from institutions (such as insurance companies), the occupying institution, equity capital (obtained by selling shares) and in some circumstances from government funds.

Chapter 9: review questions

1. What are the main sources of short-term development finance?
2. Describe the types of arrangement that may be entered into by developers in order to obtain long-term finance.
3. Explain why 'sale and leaseback' arrangements might be affected by changes to stamp duty on commercial leases which were made in the 2003 budget.
4. Explain the advantages and disadvantages of raising development finance by selling shares.
5. What is meant by 'high gearing'?
6. Why are property development companies suited to high gearing?

10

Urban Regeneration and Urban Problems

After studying this chapter you will be able to:

- Describe the advantages and disadvantages of urbanization;
- Evaluate 'green belt' policy;
- Explain policies to deal with 'overspill' and 'urban sprawl';
- Describe the factors that contribute to the quality of the urban environment;
- Explain problems of urban decay in inner cities;
- Show how pollution impacts upon the quality of the urban environment;
- Explain policies which may be used to reduce pollution problems;
- Assess the different methods which have been employed to address the urban traffic problem.

Urban growth

Cities begin for many reasons: for example, defence, trade or as political or religious centres. Whatever the reason, economic forces are likely to reinforce the original impetus. Initially growth was associated with industrialization, which generated more intensive use of existing buildings, changes in their use and outward expansion.

More recently, urban growth in developed countries has taken four main forms. First, there has been urban renewal, usually with much taller buildings. Second, there is inter-urban competition resulting in the movement between cities as some grow (for example, Greater London) and others decline (for example, Glasgow). Third, with the rise in income and the development of fast and convenient transport, particularly the motor car, there has been a movement of population from the inner and older parts of the city to the suburbs and outlying towns and villages, so that the sharp distinction which once existed between 'town' and 'country' tends to be diminishing. Fourth, a hierarchy of urban centres has evolved, differing in size and importance – provincial, regional, national and international.

In 1998, the UK government set up the Urban Task Force, chaired by Lord Richard Rogers, to report on the state of England's cities and to propose measures to reverse decline and promote an "urban renaissance". The report (DETR, 1999) was widely hailed as a way forward, recognizing that without urban regeneration on a spectacular scale, the British economy and social fabric would gradually come under threat. Shortage of land, wasteful low-density building, growing polarization, regional decline, congestion and environmental damage, inner-city decline and abandonment of the worst affected neighbourhoods, could all be tackled through a more coherent approach to city recovery.

The basic Keynesian model – the determination of the income of the national economy – can be used to explain the growth (or decline) of the urban economy. Changes in the total income of the urban area will result in changes in its level of business activity and employment.

Figure 10.1 shows a simple income-flow model for an urban economy. Households derive income from local firms, external employments and government transfers. A part of this income goes to the government in direct taxation. The remaining income is spent on local output or on goods and services from outside the area (a part going in indirect taxes to the government) or is saved. Some savings (including undistributed profits) may not be invested within the urban area, thus leading to a fall in income.

Urban growth depends upon the size of net money inflows and the extent to which income is spent within the town. If money inflows ('injections') increase – for example, through increased 'exports' of goods to places outside the area or through external factor employment – the income of the urban area will expand. The extent of the resulting urban growth will depend upon the proportion of the additional income which is spent on internally produced goods. The greater this marginal propensity to consume on local goods, the greater will be the 'urban multiplier'. Thus if c is the marginal propensity to consume on local goods, the multiplier will be $\dfrac{1}{1-c}$. For instance, if this marginal propensity to consume were 0.66, the multiplier would be 3; if it were 0.25, the multiplier would be only 1.33.

A principal weakness of the Keynesian approach when applied to urban growth is the lack of statistics available at a local level. Moreover, the Keynesian approach cannot predict when a change in causative activities will occur or explain why any activity, serving other than a local market, chooses to locate in a particular urban area. It is a demand-side theory, which does not incorporate the possibility that local bottlenecks may prevent additional supply. Indeed supply-side policies are likely to be particularly important at the urban level.

Finally, the Keynesian theory tends to ignore the dynamic nature of urban growth. For instance, urbanization itself, by increasing opportunities for specialization, increases the output of goods and services. This rise in real income

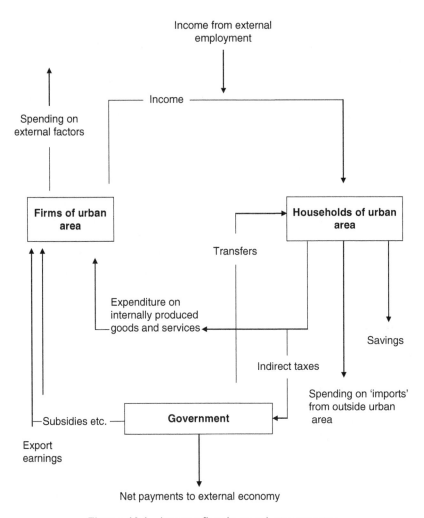

Figure 10.1   Income flow in an urban economy

leads to an increase in demand, with the enlarged market stimulating still further specialization. These extensions of economic opportunities attract new firms and labour, and so on.

Initial growth and decline of cities can both be traced to changes in the conditions of demand or supply. For example, on the demand side we can note a change in tastes, the income-elasticity of demand for the goods produced, the development of substitutes. On the supply side, there may be new competitors from outside, a change in the transport network, the exhaustion of local mineral or oil deposits, automation replacing traditional local skills and such technical change as the substitution of oil and gas for coal in the generation of electricity and in supplying power and domestic heating.

But while growth of an urban area may be adversely affected by a decline in the initial employment base or simply halted as the external costs (such as traffic congestion, air pollution) of further urbanization exceed its benefits, neither of these may necessarily lead to progressive decline. While the very size of the urban area may have already stimulated diversification through the development of new industries, also influential are the human and political factors. Some cities may have a steady supply of industrial leaders and a dynamic regional authority which responds to the challenge by introducing new industries with the aid of government grants.

Thus the real reasons for growth and decline are probably a complex blend of external economic change and the extent to which firms and local authorities are able and willing to seize opportunities that arise, or to create them if they do not. No theory which ignores the human element, the dynamism of differing institutions, the effect of government policies and other factors on the supply side of the urban economy can be wholly satisfactory.

Advantages and disadvantages of cities

Advantages

A large urban area permits the following.

Specialization

The transport developments of the industrial revolution were vital to the process of urbanization. First, by bringing food from distant areas they allowed agricultural labour to be released for urban jobs. Second, by improving the mobility of goods and factors of production they extended the market. This allowed greater specialization both between economic units within the urban area, and between urban areas themselves. For example, where a commodity is demanded by only 5 out of 1,000 inhabitants, and a demand for 1,000 goods is necessary to employ a specialist, a firm supplying the urban area needs a population of 200,000 if the advantages of specialization are to be obtained.

Large-scale production

If the working population is half the total population and only one-fifth have the skills required by a particular firm employing 10,000 workers of whom one in ten has to be skilled, a town of 100,000 people would be necessary. Nevertheless, a new firm would probably have to import its own highly skilled specialist staff. As the city grows in size, more highly skilled staff become available, thus attracting other firms and producing further economies of concentration. In this way urban growth feeds itself.

Complementarity between activities

Activities may be complementary to one another, either vertically, such as merchanting and financial services, or horizontally, such as specialized repair facilities for office equipment. A large urban area may be necessary to bring such firms together. Vertical complementarity allows greater efficiency: for example, manufacturers can often obtain components from local producers, reducing the size of stocks which have to be carried. Horizontal complementarity means that a more complete range of services is available.

Like specialization, complementarity is a function of the size of the market. The larger the market, the greater is the possibility for producing specialized goods and services and for interaction between firms.

General external economies of agglomeration

As an urban area grows, external economies arise in both production and consumption through the concentration of many types of activity. Even firms in different trades benefit from the larger market, access to large and well-organized labour markets, specialist commercial facilities and improved transport. For people generally, a large urban area can allow specialized amenities – such as clubs, churches and cultural societies – to develop, and offers a wide range of job choice, shopping outlets and educational, medical and recreational opportunities.

Economies in the use of public services

As cities grow, economies of scale occur in the provision of basic public utilities and services, such as transport, water, gas, sewerage, refuse collection and libraries. Intra-urban transport facilities also become more extensive, thereby facilitating further growth of the urban area.

The disadvantages of cities

Growth in the size of the city can eventually give rise to disadvantages and agglomeration diseconomies, as follows.

Higher transport costs

Offices and shops, attracted by the accessibility of central locations, gradually replace residential uses, people being forced to seek housing in the suburbs. Thus while employment increases in the centre, there is an increasing separation of workplace and homes, adding to the cost and inconvenience of commuting. Eventually the town centre may lose its long-established functions as a 'market place' or as a 'meeting place': that is, it ceases to be the commercial and social heart of the urban area.

Traffic congestion

As the urban area expands and offices in the centre are built higher, traffic congestion increases. Indeed this may eventually result in a fall in central land values, since accessibility diminishes with the saturation of the transport network.

Increased pollution
Pollution as urban areas expand takes various forms – noise, smoke and over-crowded housing in the centre, urban decay in the transitional zone as commercial development is anticipated, suburban sprawl along the main road and rail routes, the loss of open space for recreation and the despoilment of the surrounding countryside.

The development of a 'town versus country' conflict
People living in rural communities feel that their own way of life and traditions are under threat from the numerically larger urban communities whose interests are largely city-based. For example, demands for the 'right to roam' and the abolition of hunting are seen as the city-dwellers' failure to fully appreciate farmers' difficulties in protecting crops and livestock and in controlling vermin – a view which found a collective 'hands-off' expression in the formation of a pressure group, the 'Countryside Alliance'.

Optimum city size

The foregoing discussion highlights the fact that cities are built on a complex of 'externalities' associated with locational proximity. Some are 'good', such as defensive strength; others 'bad', for instance, increased pollution, noise and congestion, and the cost of eliminating these eventually outweighs the benefit of the 'good' as the city expands. This suggests that there is a point beyond which an urban area should not expand. It is necessary therefore to consider how the relationship between costs and benefits (internal and external) changes as the total population of the city grows. This is depicted in Figure 10.2.

The average cost per head curve, AC, includes all costs – private (the cost of land and labour), public (the cost of local government services) and social (the cost of congestion, pollution, and so on). It is likely that average cost falls initially as the population increases, but eventually rises as agglomeration diseconomies occur. The minimum average cost point P_m has often been taken to be the optimum city size, but this view fails to allow for the benefits of growth for both households and firms. As the city grows, average benefits per head are likely to increase but at a diminishing rate, giving the curve AB.

We can derive the marginal-cost (MC) and marginal benefit (MB) curves from the average cost and average benefit curves. Marginal analysis thus gives an optimal city size of P_o. However, this could be maintained only if there were restrictions on further growth since at P_o AB exceeds AC by RT, thereby encouraging migration into the city until size P_e has been reached.

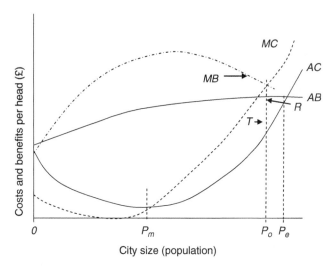

Figure 10.2   Optimum city size

In practice there is no *single* optimum city size. First, each 'central place' within the urban hierarchy performs its own range of functions, and the smaller town would find it difficult to take over the specialized functions of the larger city. Second, average costs per head are a function of the optimum use of land as well as of growth. Third, optimum city size will change with transport costs, the level of income and building technology. In contrast to these dynamic influences, the concept tends to be static in nature.

These weaknesses do not mean that the concept has no practical use. For instance, when planning a new town there must be some notion of its ultimate size, while the idea of a green belt stems from the view that the expansion of the urban area should be halted.

The problem of 'overspill'

The growth of the town gives rise to two broad types of problem: (i) finding living space for a growing population; (ii) improving the existing urban environment by dealing with inner-city decay, pollution, traffic congestion and poor housing conditions. These issues are considered in this chapter.

Living space for a growing population can be found by: (i) redeveloping the central area at higher densities; and (ii) developing suburban communities or even new urban communities away from the city. Although there has been some redevelopment of city centres, central sites for housing and new road systems are so costly that the policy is only feasible if large public funds are available. Furthermore, it is often impossible to provide for the growth of population except by outward expansion. It is therefore the latter approach which has been favoured over the past 50 years. This approach means that part of the existing population, part of any natural increase and part of any unplanned immigration has to be accommodated outside the existing built area.

Without planning restraints a town may expand by suburban development. As shops and offices take over central sites, people move outwards to the suburbs. In this they have been helped by new road construction and increased car ownership. Moreover, with the rise in real income, they can trade off extra transport costs against more spacious living.

Although most suburban dwellers still travel into town to work, employment opportunities have developed in the suburbs as industry and commerce locate there. Factors stimulating this movement to the suburbs include: (i) transport improvements, such as new road systems; and (ii) improved communications, such as the telephone and, more recently, computer-based information technology for handling and transmitting data. Both have enabled firms to decentralize their paperwork.

But although suburban development has advantages from the health point of view, it can have serious defects. Early expansion was uncontrolled and the result was haphazard *urban sprawl* in successive rings of suburbs. Moreover, housing often outstripped the provision of communal buildings and services, leaving such communities without valuable amenities and lacking centres for social interaction. Sometimes, too, the spread took the form of *ribbon development* progressing along each side of a main highway and far into the countryside. Thus rows of low-density semi-detached houses and bungalows were frequently accompanied by new factories, wayside cafés, roadhouses, garages, billboards and so on. Ribbon development was dictated by a desire to save on costs of road development, but it only contributed further to the traffic congestion these roads had been built to relieve.

In certain cases, where several towns were expanding, coalescence occurred, thus forming *conurbations*.

The external costs (costs outside the market, such as costs of traffic congestion) of suburban sprawl have been recognized and a more planned approach has since been followed, so that a considerable part of an increase in a city's population is now settled outside the urban area. Policy for transferring this 'overspill' population, preferably with supporting employment, has taken three main directions:

Green belt land, to contain suburban spread;
New towns, to settle surplus population and industry outside the urban area and whose size and layout are planned from the outset;
Expanded towns, to take the surplus to selected towns which are within reasonable distance and in a position to respond favourably to rapid growth.

Box 10.1   UK conurbations

A conurbation is an urban area comprising a number of cities, large towns and suburbs that, through population growth and physical expansion, have merged to form one continuous urban and industrially developed area. There are many examples of conurbations throughout the United Kingdom due to urban sprawl. In particular the area around Greater London can be thought of as one large conurbation.

A conurbation (or metropolis in North America) can encompass one or more cities but also includes suburban districts, towns and villages which are not necessarily urban in nature, yet which are dependent on the city or cities, most notably for employment. The city has a very large travel to work area or commuter belt. The larger an urban area becomes, the more likely it is to combine with or absorb outlying towns and villages.

When new towns were built in the UK they were strategically placed in proximity to existing cities and towns. As the new towns evolved and their suburbs became increasingly developed, the fringes of these new towns often merged with the peripheries of existing towns and cities. Land near to the transport routes between towns becomes prone to development, and this also encourages urban sprawl. London, Birmingham, Manchester, Bristol, Liverpool, Edinburgh and Glasgow all have large conurbations around them.

Green belt land

Early attempts to limit urban concentration consisted mainly of controlling the density of development. However, this did not prevent urban sprawl through suburbanization or neighbouring towns merging with one another, and so the notion developed of establishing a girdle of rural land encircling an expanding urban area. Some form of such a 'green belt' would:

1. check the further growth of the built-up area;
2. prevent ribbon development;
3. maintain a town's identity by preventing neighbouring towns from merging;
4. preserve the character of historic towns, such as Oxford, Cambridge, York, Norwich;
5. prevent the loss of agricultural land by wasteful urban spread;
6. provide adequate outdoor recreational facilities within the reach of the townsfolk;
7. reduce air pollution and conserve the environment generally;
8. assist urban regeneration.

Therefore, a green belt is not just an attempt to combat growth but rather a means of shaping the expansion of a city on a regional scale. This it does by reducing employment in the heart of the conurbation by encouraging the growth of towns which, though partly dependent on the city, enjoy their own independence by providing adequate local employment, shopping facilities, and entertainment and recreational opportunities for their own inhabitants.

The idea of a metropolitan green belt first came to prominence in the 1930s, but not until the Town and Country Planning Act 1947 were county councils given power to designate land for green belts. Today around 12 per cent of England's land surface is covered by green belt land.

Over the past 50 years, green belts have succeeded in confining urban sprawl. More than that, they have provided a pleasant environmental background for the development of new towns. Indeed they have served to concentrate attention on the need to regulate future town expansion. Nevertheless, criticisms occur (as might be expected when such diverse interests as those of conservationists, developers and planning authorities are directly concerned).

First, implementation of policy has revealed defects of:

1. adding to the problem of congestion by forcing development in existing urban centres;
2. failing to ensure that the land is put to recreational use or even made accessible to the public;
3. not preventing development from bridging the green belt, thereby creating problems for effective village planning.

Second, commuting across the green belt reduces the efficiency of transport systems and adds to the cost, time and strain of getting to work. Third, green belts have contributed to the spiralling increases in land values in the urban conurbation. However, since the price of land here is mainly determined by the price at which existing houses sell, it would require a massive release of land to lower the price of houses and therefore of land (see Chapter 5).

Fourth, developers claim that, within existing green belts, there are still sites, for example, of redundant hospitals around London, which do not serve the objectives of a green belt, and these should be released for development. Fifth, present government policy lacks coherence, with the result that many appeal decisions appear capricious. For instance, past decisions could be used to justify the 'very special circumstances', such as job gains and site decontamination, which could override green belt controls. Sixth, a more flexible strategy is desirable to allow housing and associated functions especially on green belt land which has little environmental merit or recreational potential. Instead of a continuous green belt, there would be a number of wedges serving as 'green lungs' through which the city could 'breathe'.

Nevertheless the 1994 PPG 2 (amended 2001) indicates that, in spite of pressure from developers, the government is still committed to restraining building in green belts for purposes other than agriculture, forestry, outdoor sport, cemeteries and other uses appropriate to a rural area.

New towns

Green belts simply limit the outward expansion of large urban areas; the problem of housing the overspill population still remains.

Early overspill schemes were left to private entrepreneurs – for example, Robert Owen (New Lanark, 1816), George Cadbury (Bournville, 1879), Thomas Neve (Port Sunlight, 1888), and Ebenezer Howard (Letchworth, 1903, and Welwyn Garden City, 1920). Public policy dates from the New Towns Act 1946, which provided for the development of new towns. The idea was that such towns should be established as self-contained communities for working and living. The principal aim was that they relieve the 'overspill' housing problem, but some, such as Aycliffe and Peterlee in County Durham, were developed as growth centres for the area.

Under the Act, the Secretary of State for the Environment designates the appropriate area and appoints a development corporation having powers to acquire by agreement or compulsory purchase the necessary land or property. In reality, a New Town Development Corporation is a statutory speculative builder with the job of building a town, attracting customers, selling and letting real estate and services and showing a return on capital just like any commercial undertaking. Indeed, to encourage the professional and higher-income groups to a new town, the corporation may sell freehold sites on which private enterprise can build individually designed houses.

The building of a new town means providing houses and all the associated developments, shops, churches, clinics, estate roads, parks, factories, offices and other buildings or services essential for the development of towns. For each 10,000 persons to be housed in a new town it has been estimated that some 525 acres are needed to provide the urban facilities commensurate with modern planning standards. The necessary capital is advanced from central government funds to be repaid over a period of 60 years from the proceeds of the development. The approval of such advances depends on the ODPM and the Treasury being satisfied that the projects are financially sound. Since the Minister's consent is also required for proposed land acquisitions and development, he has strong powers of control. Altogether, 31 new towns have now been established.

The sources of income from which the capital advanced can be recouped are the rents charged on premises erected and the sale of freehold or leasehold sites and properties. The most profitable revenue-earners are the factory sites, shops, public houses, and similar premises. In many cases the corporation will build the factory or shop and lease to a tenant; in others, the site is leased and the buildings are constructed by private enterprise. Though the corporation receives statutory subsidies for overspill housing, no profit is made on rents of the low-cost housing.

When the corporation has substantially achieved its purpose of creating a balanced community – this should normally take about 15 years – it is wound up and its assets transferred to a central agency, the Commission for New Towns, which is responsible for estate management and any development during the period of consolidation. This has already happened with many of the original new towns, such as Crawley, Hatfield, Hemel Hempstead and Welwyn Garden City.

The size of new towns

New towns must be large enough to become independent, self-contained, self-supporting communities. With this in mind, and taking into account such factors as acceptable internal densities and the proximity of homes to places of work, the town centre, schools and open countryside, an upper limit of 50,000 population was accepted by the New Towns Act 1946.

It has since been realized that such a town is too small. Full social provisions, an adequate range of complementary and competitive shops, and a comprehensive choice of employment and of employees could barely be obtained in a town with so small a population. Further, the full economies of scale in development and in the production of goods and services could not be realized. Only if small new towns were sufficiently close to major cities could their populations benefit from services and facilities not found locally or commute to a wider range of job opportunities within the larger urban area. But such a development could be contrary to the principle of self-sufficiency. Hence the latest generation of new towns – Warrington, Milton Keynes, Northampton, Telford and Peterborough – all have ultimate projected populations ranging from 190,000 to 350,000. Unlike many earlier new towns, they have been located close to motorways.

But can we specify an 'optimum size' for new towns as a whole? In practice, the possible size of a new town depends upon its regional setting – the distribution of population, industry, roads, means of transport, public utility services, and so on. Only a very large new town might expect to compete successfully as a shopping centre against the established retail centres of other urban areas in the region. It is important, therefore, to ensure that a new town is located correctly within the urban hierarchy and not within the commercial and social hinterlands of existing towns of a higher order.

Conversely, new town development should not have significant adverse repercussions on lower or similar order towns. It may be difficult to quantify the effects of new development on other towns in the region but an attempt should be made so that steps can be taken to minimize the adverse effects of disturbing the urban hierarchy.

As regards industrial development, planning must again be in the regional context, both in the short and medium term. Initially when the new town is small, it will have to overcome the pulling power of larger established industrial towns. Thus rapid industrialization is necessary if development programmes are to run to schedule. It must be recognized that a fully integrated industrial structure within the new town itself can only be achieved in the long term.

Therefore, the precise population of a new town when it is fully developed cannot be predicted accurately, since it is impossible to know all the factors that might influence the future situation. But it ought to be possible to forecast the order of magnitude – whether, for example, it will be approximately 200,000 or 350,000.

In general, a new town's size and land uses should be planned to be as flexible as possible, allowing 'natural' development in response to the interplay of demand and supply. The difficulty, however, is that, as the town grows, changes in land uses for profit-making purposes in response to changing demand conditions tend to be slow, piecemeal and costly, resulting in such problems as urban blight and twilight areas. One object of town planning is to prevent such problems arising. Furthermore, while private land uses change with time in response to market forces, they have to do so within a rigid framework of public land use.

Eco-towns and future overspill

The government gave the go-ahead in July 2009 for the construction of four eco-towns (from an original shortlist of fifteen), offering 10,000 homes overall, which, it hopes, will showcase environmentally friendly living in the UK. The settlements, to be built by 2016, will include the latest in energy efficiency measures, numerous cycle routes and easy access to public transport. The eco-town plans include use of smart meters, community heat sources, charging points for electric cars and zero-carbon schools, shops, restaurants and public buildings.

However, despite the government's renewed commitment to achieving zero-carbon new homes by 2016, the homes in the proposed eco-towns will only have to meet at least level 4 of the Code for Sustainable Homes (zero-carbon homes would be level 6). This has led to accusations that the proposals are simply a way for volume house builders to get around planning regulations.

The four eco-town locations are Whitehill Borden in Hampshire; the China Clay Community at St Austell, Cornwall; Rackheath in Norfolk; and northwest Bicester, in Oxfordshire. Each site will be allocated a share of £60 million for their 'green' infrastructure. The eco-towns are designed to tackle Britain's housing shortage in a sustainable way.

Because of the fall in the rate of increase in the population of the UK and the increased emphasis on the regeneration of inner-city areas, new towns are likely to receive less attention in the future. Recent increases in immigration and in the number of single person households may change this, but recent announcements of new housing development indicate expansion of existing towns in the Thames Gateway, Stansted-Cambridge and Milton Keynes areas. Thus while existing new towns are likely to be built up slowly to their planned size, no further new towns are planned at present.

For the same reasons, there is likely to be less emphasis on formal 'over-spill' arrangements. The movement of population out of the central areas of the larger conurbations – especially London – is proceeding much faster than had been expected, and has begun to alarm those local authorities that are losing population. Too rapid a run-down of population may create problems, for example, because it is unbalanced in that the younger, more vigorous and more affluent leave in disproportionate numbers.

Although this does not mean the end of urban planning, the emphasis shifted from sweeping 'greenfield' schemes to the smaller-scale regeneration of old urban areas and to developing districts of 'patchy' development while retaining existing communities. Furthermore, wider car ownership has also meant that people can spread into scattered rural dwellings.

Problems of urban areas

The same economic factors which stimulate outward growth also create problems within the older built-up area – urban decay, economic decline, pollution, inadequate conservation, traffic congestion and neglected housing. These problems arise because: (i) a built-up area can only adjust slowly to changes in the conditions of demand and supply; and (ii) as the size of the urban area grows, the external costs of more concentration on the centre increase and multiply. Therefore, though such problems are common to most large towns, they are particularly severe in the conurbations, such as London, Glasgow, Liverpool, and Birmingham.

It must be emphasized that the problems of the *urban* area are really only part of those of the wider environment. A wealthier, car-owning urban-dweller enjoying more leisure requires recreational facilities for playing golf, unspoiled countryside over which to ramble, uncontaminated beaches, theme parks, airports, and so on. But there is often a clash of interests – for example, between ramblers and farmers, urban waste disposal and country dwellers, and national parks imposing restrictions on certain agricultural techniques. How are such clashes of interest to be resolved – through the price system or by government decision or by a combination of both?

As we saw in Chapter 7, over time buildings deteriorate, while changes in the conditions of demand and supply necessitate a change in the use of land resources. The price system responds to such changes. A building will be demolished and replaced by a new one when the present-use value is less than the value of the cleared site. But while the price system can perform satisfactorily for comparatively small changes in land use, problems arise with comprehensive urban renewal, whether that be city centre redevelopment or the regeneration of 'twilight' zones and slum areas.

In the city centre, the limited space available means that the effects of changes in the conditions of demand and supply are accentuated. For example, because any increase in demand for central offices has to be concentrated on a relatively small area, high-rise building soon becomes economically viable and redevelopment proceeds apace.

While much of this city centre redevelopment takes place through the price mechanism, there are disadvantages, most of which stem from the inherent defects of the market economy. First, certain redevelopment may be thwarted by a key site-owner who uses his 'monopoly' power to extort a high price for his interest. Second, renewal may be delayed by the need to wait for leases to expire in order to bring all interests affected within a single ownership. Third, external benefits of conserving aspects of the city centre may be overlooked by developers seeking relatively short-term gains. Fourth, not all possible complementarities may be secured, for example, linking new shops with such public services as bus termini, libraries, municipal offices, and so on. Fifth, private enterprise has to work within the existing infrastructure and this may not be efficient, particularly with the road layout.

As a result, some overall control of city centre redevelopment is necessary, either through planning control (see Chapter 13) or, more directly, by the city authority undertaking redevelopment itself or in partnership with a private developer. Such redevelopment takes two broad forms: (i) piecemeal restoration, adaptation and rebuilding; and (ii) comprehensive redevelopment.

Piecemeal redevelopment allows the widest possible individual participation, since the necessary finance is smaller and more readily obtained. Moreover because it takes place within the existing pattern of land ownership, it is cheaper and usually avoids the complex political, social and legal problems which arise when people and workplaces are forced out. Above all, it maintains continuity with the past and preserves the distinctive character of the city centre by retaining buildings of historical, architectural or aesthetic appeal. This gives the citizens themselves a community identity. The major difficulty, however, lies in reconciling the historical street system with the needs of modern motor transport. The most usual solution is for the city authority to convert the old high street into a pedestrian precinct and to provide off-street car-parks as close as possible. At the same time one-way traffic flows are introduced to facilitate movement within the city centre, while new bypass roads are constructed to take through traffic.

Comprehensive redevelopment has been followed where city centres were devastated by wartime bombing or where resolute city authorities have decided that urban decay is so extensive that the most satisfactory solution is to make a clean sweep. Such redevelopment allows complete planning of the whole area in order to integrate all the activities of the city centre for both accessibility and the environment. However, some flexibility must be incorporated into the overall scheme to allow for future adaptation in response to changes in the conditions of demand and supply.

Problems of inner-city areas

Unlike the city centre, where redevelopment proceeds fairly quickly and the difficulties are mainly those associated with traffic congestion, the inner-city area, which begins at the edge of the central business district and spreads out to engulf mainly pre-1914 housing, tends to continue to suffer from economic decline, physical decay and social disadvantage. Again these problems are largely associated with the defects of the price system – the immobility of resources, imperfect knowledge, and the existence of external costs which do not enter into private decision making.

In the inner city, renewal responds only slowly to a falling demand for traditional uses of buildings. Middle-income families move to the suburbs or outside the built-up area in order to enjoy more space. Old factories and workshops close as production moves to modern factories on the outskirts of towns. Docks become redundant with the decline in sea transport and the growth of containerization. Warehouses, often on a number of floors, become unsuitable for modern storage methods and are often inaccessible to large lorries.

Whereas factories and warehouses tend to lie derelict, the life of houses may be prolonged by adaptation or transfer to new uses, such as multiple occupation by low-income families or conversion to hostels for homeless people. Furthermore, in an effort to maintain net returns from property in the short term, operating expenses (for example, of common services) are pruned and essential maintenance (such as roof repairs, guttering and painting) neglected. This postpones redevelopment. Furthermore, even where factories and warehouses are demolished, the sites may be used temporarily as scrap-metal yards, car-breaking premises, off-street car-parks and so on. Worse still, the site may be left derelict while a decision is made on the form of redevelopment or while other sites are acquired.

The problem is aggravated by the fact that existing owners will not risk capital in improving their properties, since the intentions of adjacent landlords are unknown. With shops and houses boarded up, buildings neglected and land lying derelict, the shabby environment contrasts with better conditions elsewhere, making the areas unattractive to the people who live there and to new investment in housing, industry and commerce. In short, physical decay creates external costs, which, by increasing cumulatively, give momentum to the process and result in *slums*, where all the characteristics of degeneration are concentrated in their worst forms in particular neighbourhoods.

The inner-city area often has a higher rate of unemployment than the rest of the city area and the decline in manufacturing industry and the rationalization of plant has hit the inner city particularly severely, especially as new firms prefer peripheral locations where lower rents permit ground-level production and ring roads give better accessibility. Technological changes have also brought about a decline in the old service industries, with the railways being replaced by road transport and the docks moving down river or being changed by containerization and warehousing, too, is no longer needed near railway termini or ports. Though the skilled manual workers tend to follow their employment opportunities outwards, the unskilled remain, often augmented by immigrant workers. The new offices and service industries provide few job opportunities for unskilled manual workers.

The inner city often exhibits signs of physical decline also. Although many of the worst slums have been cleared and replaced by modern dwellings, much remaining accommodation consists of old houses in multi-occupation and lacking basic amenities. To some extent rent control was responsible, for it prevented landlords charging a rent sufficient to cover even essential upkeep (see Chapter 5). Often, too, the inner-city area suffers from an inadequate or neglected infrastructure, especially in roads, transport services, school buildings, open spaces and recreational facilities.

Largely as a result of the high level of unemployment and the lack of job opportunities for married women, inner-city areas tend to have a high concentration of poor people, but the exodus of the skilled worker has added to the relative poverty of the inner-city area. Since he cannot afford to become an owner-occupier, the unskilled worker is reluctant to leave his existing low-rent accommodation. Furthermore, many families have no wage-earner, while those less able to cope in society – the mentally ill, the alcoholic, the drug addict and the social misfit – tend to find refuge in these areas. Nor is the environmental background conducive to educational achievement. Standards are lowered by poor home conditions, often leading to truancy and drop out from school, delinquency, vandalism and other behavioural problems. In many cases there are problems of coping with ethnic minority communities – language difficulties, racial discrimination and at times even open hostility from those already living in the area.

Policies for renewal of inner-city areas

A policy to deal with the problems of the inner city must start from four salient features: (i) the general aspect of physical decay; (ii) the poverty of its inhabitants; (iii) its economic function of providing cheap housing close to employment opportunities; and (iv) an outward movement of both households (particularly those of the skilled, better-off worker) and firms, to newer areas. As we have seen, all four are interrelated. The degeneration of the area gathers momentum as unemployment and social problems increase and the infrastructure becomes more inadequate and shabby. Government action is essential if the vicious circle in which the inner-city area finds itself is to be broken.

Until the 1960s, policy in Britain concentrated on the physical aspect, with whole areas being bulldozed and completely rebuilt. Precedence was given to providing working-class dwellings to a high density in tower blocks. Commerce and industry were encouraged to go to the suburbs, new towns, and development areas, for example, by the Location of Offices Bureau, or indirectly forced to do so through Office Development Permits and Industrial Development Certificates.

However, the weaknesses of such a policy were eventually appreciated, as the time taken to rebuild (and at a lower density) created an overspill population which had to be directed to outside dormitory estates, expanded towns and new towns. And it failed to recognize that over the centuries the inner city had developed an organic mixture of uses and had become a centre of complex linkages, providing accommodation near the city centre and neighbourhood employment in local industries. Firms, too, were mostly small in size and labour-intensive, employing craft skills to make products where quick alterations in design are necessary in response to frequent changes in demand. Such firms need to be located near their customers, still with low overhead costs. Thus while the bulldozing did provide better housing, firms which were driven out failed to return, so that the problem of physical degeneration was replaced by the new one of a largely unskilled population without employment opportunities, isolated in tower blocks and deprived of its old sense of community.

It became accepted that a purely physical approach to the problem was unsatisfactory and that the correct policy was renovation and gradual rebuilding, accompanied by environmental improvements, the dispersal of the concentration of poverty and ignorance, and economic resuscitation by encouraging rather than hindering the growth of small industry. Thus the White Paper, *Policy for the Inner City* (DOE, 1977) set out three major themes for strengthening the economic and social structures of the inner cities while improving their physical environment:

1. maintaining a sizeable, stable and balanced population in the inner area;
2. securing a thriving economic community, particularly of small businesses; and
3. carrying out the foregoing aims with an emphasis on rehabilitation and infill rather than by wholesale clearance and redevelopment.

The Conservative government initiated an Urban Programme to tackle the problems of the inner cities. *Enterprize Zones* were introduced in 1981, and funding was increased with *Urban Development Grant*, 1982, and with

Box 10.2 London docklands regeneration

In the 1980s, in an effort to reverse the process of inner city decline, the UK government set up Urban Development Corporations (known as UDCs). The aim of these UDCs was to regenerate inner-city areas with large amounts of derelict and unused land by taking over planning responsibility from local councils. These UDCs had the power to acquire and reclaim land, convert old buildings and improve infrastructure through the investment of government money. These UDCs also attracted private sector investment through offering companies reduced taxes and other benefits and, in doing so, they promoted industrial, residential and community developments.

During the nineteenth century, London's port was one of the busiest in the world, but by the end of the 1950s it was in signficant decline with many of the docks derelict and abandoned. In response to the resulting social, economic and environmental problems, the London Docklands Development Corporation (LDDC) was set up in 1981. Whilst the LDDC was responsible for the planning and redevelopment of the Docklands areas, other organizations have also been involved in the redevelopment process, these included:

- national government –they created an Isle of Dogs Enterprise Zone in April 1982 – offering incentives such as grants, reduced rates and so on,. to encourage private investment;
- property developers – responsible for building large office blocks (for example, Canary Wharf);
- a local housing association, which obtained home improvement grants;
- conservation groups;
- Newham Council.

There has been £7.7 billion in private sector investment including financial and high technology firms, TV studios and newspaper offices at the prestigious Canary Wharf complex. There are more than 2,700 businesses trading and major new roads including the link to the M11 as well as the building of the City Airport in the former Royal Docks with more than 500,000 passengers a year. Unemployment fell from 14 per cent to 7.4 per cent with a doubling in numbers of businesses. The opening of the Docklands Light Railway in 1987 was a significant transport innovation – it now carries 35,000 passengers a week.

The docklands regeneration included schemes to improve the environment such as:

- a network of pedestrian and cycle routes through the area with access to the river and dock edge through waterside walkways;
- the creation of pedestrian bridges;
- the creation of new open spaces (150 hectares);
- a water based Ecology Park and London's first bird sanctuary at East India Dock Basin – one of 17 conservation areas set up;
- the planting of 200,000 trees;

As a result the area has now received many awards for architecture, conservation and landscaping.

the *Urban Regeneration Grant*, 1987. The philosophy behind these grants was to make schemes commercially viable for developers by providing grant aid equivalent to the shortfall in the development appraisal. In assessing schemes, an anticipated gearing of 1:4 (£1 of public money to £4 of private money) was the guideline, and this was achieved. A succession of new schemes and replacement grants followed, usually linked with regional regeneration.

As early as 1949, it was recognized that the quickest way to provide dwellings for families in the lower-income bracket is, where practicable, to carry out essential repairs to the existing stock in order to make it suitable for habitation. Consequently, much renovation of housing in city centres was supported by *improvement grants*, later termed *house renovation grants*.

These discretionary grants for repairs and mandatory grants for providing standard amenities (hot water supply, bath and so on) were made available for tenants, private owners, local authorities and housing associations. In addition such a policy, as opposed to wholesale rebuilding, helps to preserve local communities. In 1980 the conditions of grant were marginally relaxed. The result was that between 1980 and 1984, the take-up of grants by private owners and tenants more than trebled.

Since 1990, however, grants have been means-tested, reflecting the principle that subsidies should be targeted on the person rather than on the property. This has meant that only people on very low income can qualify, although those on state social security benefits can obtain the full cost. For landlords the test of resources is the expected increase in income, and possibly in the capital value, which would result from the renovation. This is in keeping with the move towards market rents (see Chapter 5). But the result of these more rigid financial conditions has been that the number of grants for renovation fell from 320,000 in 1984 to 71,000 in 1987, recovering to around 100,000 in 2001. The situation currently is made more complex by the separation of statistics since Scottish devolution. In England the New Deal for Communities Programme spent £427.3 million between 1999 and 2008 on housing and the physical environment to reduce gaps between 39 deprived neighbourhoods and the rest of the country. In Scotland, dicretionary grants and loans are available from local authorities as well as practical assistance, information and advice. Local authorities have the power to designate as a Housing Renewal Area any area with a concentration of houses that are substandard. In 2002 the Scottish Home Condition Survey showed that in the owner-occupied sector 27 per cent of houses and 40 per cent of flats had at least one element in a state of urgent disrepair (meaning that if repair is not carried out, the fabric of the building would deteriorate further or health and safety would be placed at risk). The Housing (Scotland) Act of 2006 took steps to raise standards in the private sector and in 2008–9 repair grants worth £52.2 million were made.

Pollution

Pollution is not a new phenomenon. In the sixteenth century, for instance, the shortage of wood led to coal, mainly from Newcastle, being used for fires in London. The resulting smoke that hung over the capital provoked such a public outcry that eventually the burning of 'sea coles' was prohibited by Act of Parliament. Nor is pollution confined to urban areas of advanced industrialized societies. For example, rural Indian villages have untreated sewage flowing into watercourses and garbage rotting in the streets.

What is new is the recognition of the *problem* of pollution. On the one hand we have the recent rapid industrialization of the western world. Economic growth has brought:

> the most notorious by-product of industrialisation the world has ever known; the appalling traffic congestion in our towns, cities and suburbs ... the pollution of the air and of rivers with chemical wastes ... the destruction of wild life by indiscriminate use of pesticides, the change-over from animal farming to animal factories, and visible to all who have eyes to see, a rich heritage of natural beauty being wantonly and systematically destroyed. (Mishan, 1967)

On the other hand, people are now enjoying a standard of living where they can afford to question whether material growth is not being achieved at too high a cost to the environment. Pollution has become a problem because it is now felt that something can and should be done about it. Paradoxically, though economic growth may cause pollution, growth may be an essential prerequisite of environmental improvement. Economic poverty often compels us to accept visual squalor, poor buildings and pollution. It is prosperity which enables us to buy a better environment. In this way the EU's excess production of foodstuffs has made it easier to switch attention to preserving the landscape.

Pollution occurs when, directly or indirectly, humans introduce damaging waste matter into the environment. While residual waste is created in consumption (for example, household waste, scrapped consumer durables, litter), it is pollution resulting from production which is more serious (for example, acid rain, smoke, gases, toxic chemicals, pesticide contaminants, liquid effluents, noise, oil spillages) for it affects the whole of the environment – land, sea and the atmosphere. It is harmful to human health, for example, through carbon monoxide fumes; to agriculture, for example, resulting in lower yields or poorer quality; to buildings, such as in corrosion of stonework; to amenity, such as causing damage to fish, fauna and flora; and to the life of the whole planet through the 'greenhouse' effect produced by carbon dioxide discharged into the atmosphere.

Two aspects of developed economies give particular significance to pollution by waste. First, much waste could be avoided if it were not for the self-indulgent extravagance of modern society. The 'throw-away' mentality simply discards non-degradable waste, for example plastics, car tyres, radioactive material, with little regard for their ultimate disposal. Second, since much waste is derived from non-regenerating basic inputs, for example fossil fuels and minerals, society must show greater willingness to conserve such resources, for example by reducing car use and by recycling.

Everybody can recognize evidence of pollution but the economist, however, must have a precise definition. Present-day concern is with the increasing environmental pollution resulting from population and economic growth. Both production and consumption leave unwanted residuals – smoke, poisonous chemicals and gases, noise, household waste and so on. Some, such as carbon dioxide gas, can be transformed by the environment into harmless or even beneficial materials (such as oxygen). But this takes time, and *pollution occurs when the flow of residual emissions and waste exceeds the natural environment's capacity to absorb them.* Indeed pollution may even reduce the environment's ability to assimilate waste.

Although technological developments stimulate growth, it could be that new technology will allow growth, while containing pollution. Such developments could take the form of: (a) substitute products which are more environmentally friendly, for example, degradable containers; (b) greater efficiency in production to reduce waste; (c) on-site treatment of controlled disposal of waste, for example, desulphurization of gases by power stations, catalytic converters on cars; (d) the replacement of coal and oil with 'greener' sources of energy, for example, natural gas, wind, tide.

But while such technical developments are likely to occur eventually, what is 'sustainable pollution' must be assessed in the context of the current technology employed. It is here that economic analysis can contribute to a solution of the problem by suggesting and examining a range of broad options.

Control of pollution

As we have seen in previous chapters, the economist emphasizes *marginal* decisions. While everybody likes clear air, pure water, a peaceful environment, clean pavements, roads free from congestion, and so on, pollution abatement incurs costs. Thus the choice is not the simple one between clean air and polluted air, but between various levels of dirty air. In short, we have to apply the marginal principle and accept that level of pollution where the cost of further abatement exceeds the extra benefit which results.

In most cases pollution represents external costs. The right to peace and quiet, the right to enjoy a landscape unspoiled by electricity pylons, the right to swim

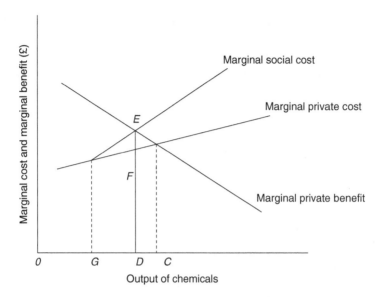

Figure 10.3   Efficient output with external costs

from an oil-free beach are not private legal rights that can be easily enforced. Often, therefore, no *private* cost is incurred for infringing those rights. Thus in Figure 10.3 if there is no cost to a chemical manufacturer of discharging effluent into the river, he will produce chemicals up to the point *OC*. But when we take into account the poisoning of fish, the destruction of vegetation which provides a habitat for insects and birds and the overall loss of visual beauty for ramblers, such spillover costs have to be added to private costs to obtain the aggregate social cost. This means that while *OC* is the efficient level of production for the chemical manufacturer, the *socially* efficient level of production is *OD*, because here marginal social cost equals marginal social benefit (assuming marginal private benefit equals marginal social benefit). In other words, if more than *OD* is produced there is a misallocation of resources.

Difficulties occur in devising and applying an appropriate policy to control pollution, however. First, although the costs of pollution control can be measured in money terms, the benefits are 'intangibles', having no price tag since they are not traded in the market. Take as an example the chemical factory which discharges effluent into a river. While the value of the fishing rights lost can be measured by market information, the value of the loss suffered by birdwatchers and ramblers has no direct market price. This means that the technique of shadow pricing, with all its weaknesses, has to be employed (see Chapter 11).

Second, most economic assessments of damage are made after the pollution has occurred. But adjustments in response to such pollution may already have been made. For example, the broccoli yield in a market garden may be

20 per cent below that which could have been expected in a clean-air environment. Yet this loss would understate the damage if, in an environment originally free from smoke, more profitable tomatoes would have been grown. In practice, it is extremely difficult to ascertain and measure this 'adjustment factor'.

Third, since pollution occurs in different forms, circumstances and scale, it is necessary to apply different policies to deal with the problem.

Pollution control policies

'Greening' public opinion

Publicity drawing people's attention to the nature of the pollution problem by the government and pressure groups, such as the Green Party and Friends of the Earth, has had remarkable success in recent years. Households have become waste-recycling conscious and global climate change has become part of everyday conversation whenever there is a prolonged spell of hot weather.

Firms have responded. Pilkington Glass, for instance, encourage managers to integrate environmental responsibility in all business decision making, covering such matters as waste and emission reduction, recycling waste and energy saving. Similarly, B&Q and Homebase have pledged to supply only goods made with timber from sustainable forests, with the sources being monitored.

Creating an environmental protection agency

Externalities arise because of non-existent, ill-defined or unenforceable private property rights. To overcome this, it may be possible to create an agency in which these property rights are vested, in effect internalizing externalities in order to maximize benefits and minimize costs. For example, the Environment Agency coordinates drainage, water supply, waste disposal and angling interests in the UK and the Environmental Protection Agency in the USA is committed to protecting human health and the environment.

Market negotiation

If a 'market' in the pollution can be established, the optimum amount of pollution can be arrived at. Suppose a garden owner wishes to burn all his rubbish at the weekend when his neighbours just want to enjoy sitting in their gardens. They could negotiate with the burner to burn at some other time, either by arrangement or at a price. In the latter case, the externality is being 'priced'.

The same principle could apply on an international scale. Brazil could be paid not to clear her equatorial rain forests, and Sweden already assists Poland in reducing acid rain, because the acid rain from Poland damages Sweden.

Usually, however, if the market is to be used to control pollution there must be incentives to avoid pollution by conserving energy or to reduce pollution by the controlled disposal of waste products.

Direct regulation imposing a maximum level of pollution

The government decides what each polluter must do to reduce pollution, and enforces it under penalty of law, for example, environmental conditions of planning, no discharge of oil waste by ships within so many miles of the coast. Such a policy, however, provides little incentive to install anti-pollution devices so that the specified standard becomes the target, involves constant inspection, and tends to impose national (sometimes international) standards instead of allowing for different local circumstances. On the other hand, the policy does allow the polluter to find the cheapest means of achieving the specified maximum.

It should be noted that rigid control is essential where: (a) pollution is a threat to existence, such as blue asbestos dust in workshops; and (b) pollution is cumulative and becomes dangerous at a certain level, such as cadmium absorption by the soil.

Subsidizing the reduction of pollution

Where it is impossible or too costly to identify the polluters (for example, litter louts) the government itself takes responsibility for pollution control, the cost being covered from taxation. Alternatively, the government may decide that specific compensation is adequate to deal with the particular pollution, especially where this is localized. Thus in clean-air zones, people are given subsidies to install smokeless fuel appliances. On the other hand, losers may be compensated, for example, grants to provide double glazing to reduce noise from aircraft. The difficulty is that such public schemes simply mean that polluters are passing on the cost to the taxpayer. Often, therefore, where polluters can be identified, control has to be enforced through individual penalties imposed by the courts, for example, for dropping litter or polluting watercourses.

Alternatively, the government could seek to reduce pollution by directly subsidizing: (a) the development of new techniques to reduce pollution or save energy; (b) the production of cleaner substitutes for example, a reduced tax on unleaded petrol or (c) the recycling of waste, such as bottles.

Taxing pollution

A charge or tax according to the level of pollution seeks to ensure that the 'polluter pays'. In terms of Figure 10.3, a tax of *EF* would induce the factory owner to limit his production to *OD*. Such a policy has the merit of flexibility, and is thus particularly desirable where the benefits can only be ascertained by trial and error or where the aim is to achieve a progressive reduction in pollution since charges can be adjusted accordingly. Moreover, charges have the effect of 'internalizing externalities': once the tax is set, the polluter can respond to it as he chooses. Thus a profit-maximizing polluter would install his own pollution control to the point where the marginal cost of doing so was less than the tax saved. Furthermore, the proceeds of a tax can be used to compensate those losing by the residual pollution. Finally, in as much as the charge raises the price of the product, the actual consumer now pays the full opportunity cost of production – a fairer solution than passing on the external costs to society at large.

Even so, a charges policy has its limitations. First, a tax can only be imposed if the individual polluter can be identified. Second, there is the problem of *how* to tax. If it is on units of output, such as tonnes of nitrate fertilizer, the larger producer pays more as his pollution is likely to be greater. But this does nothing to encourage a reduction in the pollution *per unit*. If, however, the degree

---

Box 10.3   Green infrastructure

Natural England and the Commission for Architecture and the Built Environment (CABE) claimed in 2009, at the Park City Conference, that a strategically planned network of high quality green spaces and other environmental features could improve health, cut climate emissions and create jobs. Urban areas could be transformed into healthier, wealthier and more pleasant places if green infrastructure received a fraction of the investment given to 'grey' projects such as roads and airports.

They further claim that the money budgeted for road building over 5 years would provide one thousand new parks, and the funds to widen the M25 would provide 3.2 million street trees. Trees are important because:

- asthma rates for children fall 25 per cent for every extra 350 trees per sq km;
- for every 5 per cent of tree cover added, water run-off is reduced by 2 per cent;
- a treeless street is 5.5°C (10°F) warmer than a tree-lined one in hot summers;
- property in treeless streets is worth 18 per cent less than buildings in roads that have trees.

Green Infrastructure can provide many social, economic and environmental benefits close to where people live and work including:

- Places for outdoor relaxation and play;
- Space and habitat for wildlife with access to nature for people;
- Climate change adaptation – for example flood alleviation and cooling urban heat islands;
- Environmental education;
- Local food production – in allotments, gardens and through agriculture;
- Improved health and well-being – lowering stress levels and providing opportunities for exercise.

of pollution can be measured, for example, the quantity of toxic waste being discharged into the river, and taxed accordingly, there would be an incentive to install an anti-pollution device. Third, there are distributional implications if the product whose price rises is one which is bought mainly by poor persons, though the proceeds of the tax can be used to compensate. Fourth, if a country imposes a tax unilaterally, for instance, on the burning of fossil fuels, it may give an unfair advantage to its foreign competitors.

Tradeable permits

Suppose in Figure 10.3 that output represents the aggregate of all chemical firms on a given river. The government decides to limit pollution to *GD (note there is no pollution before output level G)*. Each firm is given a licence to emit a share of *GD*. If the government wishes to raise revenue (equal, say, to *EF*), it can sell or auction the licence. The essence of these pollution permits is that they can be traded on the 'permit' market. Those firms having a high cost of reducing emission will want to buy permits from the efficient firms who sell them for more than it costs them to abate. This method provides an incentive to those who sell permits to install equipment which reduces pollution. At the same time, it uses the market to cover much of the regulation required. One difficulty is that as firms become more abatement-efficient, the supply of permits coming on to the market will increase, and their fall in price will allow inefficient firms to buy them. In this case, the government could itself buy on the market and, by retiring permits, keep up the cost of pollution.

Conservation

Conservation is only one aspect of the larger problem of the quality of the human environment in the midst of change. It is not limited to mere preservation but seeks creative continuity by promoting vitality of use of the environment while ensuring that change is sympathetic to the quality of life of both present and future generations. In the use of land resources, conservation has particular significance with regard to green belts, national parks, conservation areas, public bridle-ways and footpaths, common land and parks, nature reserves, National Trust property and buildings of special architectural and historic interest.

Because, in essence, conservation is synonymous with the optimum use of resources over time, it reflects many of the problems concerned with investment in general. But, largely on account of the distant time-horizon involved and its far-reaching effects on the community at large, there are special aspects of conservation which make it unsuitable to be left entirely to market forces – difficulties of estimating future conditions of demand and supply, choosing an

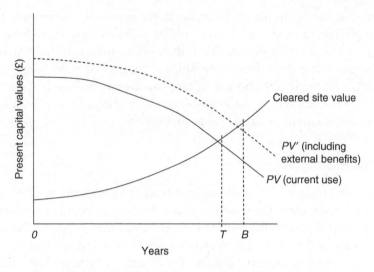

Figure 10.4   Adjustments to the present value of a historic
building for different uses

appropriate discount rate, allowing for externalities and the possible irrevers-
ibility of wrong decisions. We can illustrate this by analysing the problem of
preserving historic buildings, but the approach is applicable to the conservation
of 'cherished land', such as national parks, green belts and conservation areas,
where development could, in practice, be virtually irreversible.

If left to market forces, the demolition of a historic building would take place
in Year T (Figure 10.4) where the present values of the current use and of the
cleared site are equal.

The question we need to consider is: on what grounds may *economics* justify
interference with this market solution? In Chapter 8 the general case for redevelopment was considered, but the assumptions made there need to be qualified
when considering a historic building.

Forecasting demand often has to start from the position where even *current*
demand is not priced, as with, for example, the aesthetic appeal of a historic
building. Some 'shadow' pricing with all its weaknesses has therefore to be
substituted. Even then, though forecasts can be made regarding future population and income, it is difficult to predict how increased leisure will affect tastes.
For instance, there may be a swing from viewing historic buildings to foreign
travel. Above all, the estimate of net annual revenues (NARs) from which is
derived the present value of the historic building, may ignore 'option demand'.
Where decisions are irreversible (as with the destruction of a historic building),
many people would pay something just to postpone such a decision (because
they value the option to visit it at some time in the future). The difficulty lies
in quantifying such 'option demand', but its existence is evident in the fact that
many people subscribe voluntarily to the National Trust and the World Wide

Fund for Nature, for example. The rest enjoy the option as 'freeriders', but their demand should also be included. Such higher NARs would give a higher present value curve, for example, *PV'* (Figure 10.4), and postpone demolition to year *B*.

Second, in practice we cannot point to a unique rate for discounting NARs. Furthermore, because the rate of social time-preference is lower than that of private time-preference (see Chapter 11), a present value derived from the lower rate of discount appropriate to the social time-preference would be higher than one based on a rate of discount which merely reflected *private* time-preference. Thus the present value curve for a historic building should be higher, for example, *PV'* in Figure 10.4. Furthermore, NARs measure only private assessments of benefits and costs. Thus external benefits, such as the pleasure which the view of a historic building gives to passersby, are ignored. Again this would produce a higher present value curve, such as *PV'*.

Finally, knowledge is not perfect, especially when we are dealing with the future. Thus a decision to demolish a building may be based on a defective assessment of the future conditions of demand and supply. This is not serious when we are dealing with *flows*, such as the services provided by offices, since new offices can always be built if demand increases in the future. But demolishing a historic building diminishes a *stock* which cannot be replaced. The situation is illustrated in Figure 10.5.

In period *t*, the historic building has a low value, *OH*. On the other hand, an office block would command price *OP_t*. Over time, however, the value of the historic building increases relatively to that of offices. This is because, with higher incomes and more leisure, people take a greater interest in historic buildings. Increased demand means that in period *t + 2,* the price of the

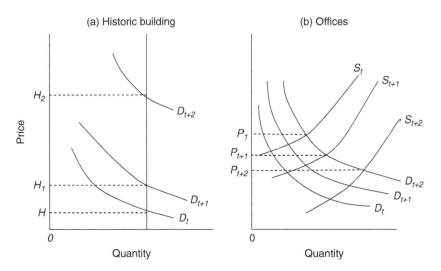

Figure 10.5 Changes in the future relative prices of historic buildings and offices

historic building has risen to OH_2. On the other hand, the demand for offices is not likely to increase so quickly, income-elasticity of demand being lower. Moreover, with technological improvements in construction, the supply curve shifts to the right over time. As a result, in period $t + 2$ the price of offices falls to OP_{t+2}.

The situation is transferred to Figure 10.6. We can assume that the price of the office block in period t gives a cleared-site value of FD, so that demolition of the historic building and redevelopment of the site as offices has become a viable economic proposition. Eventually, however, the value of the historic building starts to rise, while the rate of increase in the value of the cleared site declines. Indeed, if demolition in year D could be prevented, by year E the present value of the historic building once again exceeds the value of the cleared site.

The above analysis suggests that the government must intervene in the free operation of the price system in order to preserve historic buildings. Its action can take a variety of forms.

First, the building could be brought under public ownership. Such a policy would usually be followed where the cost of excluding freeriders would be prohibitive, for example, Hadrian's Wall. Equally important, it would allow welfare to be maximized and public ownership would automatically allow external benefits to be internalized.

Second, the historic building could be left in private ownership but a subsidy given through repair grants or inheritance tax concessions on the grounds of the external benefits conferred. Such a subsidy would increase NARs and so raise the present value (as shown by the curve PP in Figure 10.6). However, there are difficulties. Many external benefits cannot be quantified, while shortage of funds could mean that the subsidy was insufficient to raise the present-use value curve permanently above the cleared-site curve, so that demolition is only postponed unless other action is taken.

Third, any building of special architectural or historic interest may be 'listed'. This means that it cannot be altered or demolished without the consent of the local planning authority. Although this gives protection against positive acts of demolition, it may not cover destruction by the neglect of the owner. Such neglect occurs because high maintenance costs result in negative NARs. Even though in such circumstances the local authority can appropriate the building, there is reluctance to do so since the cost of maintenance now falls on public funds. Thus, in practice, 'listing' in year D may be only a 'stopgap' measure, bridging the years between D and E (Figure 10.6) until increased NARs raise the value of the historic building above that of the cleared site. More frequently, 'listing' simply imposes a prohibition on demolition until an alternative policy can be formulated.

Fourth, giving permission for the building to be adapted to a more profitable use provides such a policy. Thus stables may be converted into a dwelling, and

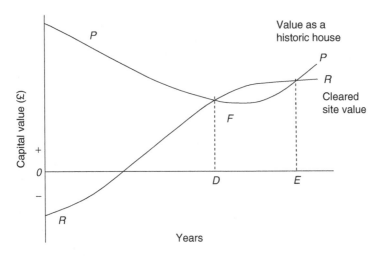

Figure 10.6 Methods of preserving a historic building

houses into offices. This has the effect of increasing NARs and thus raising the present value curve so that it is above the cleared-site curve. This change of use could take place in year *D* and the present value curve PP would shift upwards from that point (Figure 10.6).

In consenting to a change of use of a historic building, the objective of the authorities must be to retain as many of the original features as possible. Thus some flexibility of building regulations is necessary, for example, in height of rooms, window space and even fire precautions. As in Figure 10.5(a) the distinctive character of the converted building may produce increasing rentals over time, for example, for prestige reasons, so that not only is it preserved but there is no charge on public funds.

Urban traffic

Since the mid-twentieth century, motor transport has increased accessibility for both resources and people through the mobility, flexibility and convenience it affords: it has therefore contributed to the improvement of living standards. Unfortunately, as the use of road vehicles has increased, the benefits they afford have been progressively diminished by external costs. The greater mobility afforded by the car has enabled workers to live some distance from their place of employment and has been a major cause of urban sprawl. Moreover, people still have to travel from the suburbs to the city centre for work, shopping and leisure activities. Whereas traffic increases as we approach the centre, road capacity decreases. The resulting concentration of traffic imposes environmental costs on non-car users by CO_2 pollution, noise, the danger of accident, visual blight, inconvenience to pedestrians and loss of time to bus travellers. More than that, the expansion of motor transport has led to the demand for road space exceeding supply so that one road-user imposes on other road-users the extra costs of congestion – higher fuel consumption, reduced speed and time spent in traffic jams. Indeed, the problem becomes more acute as income and population increase and the use of cars and commercial vehicles expands.

The major external cost is congestion, for this undermines the chief advantage – accessibility – which motor transport affords. It is necessary, therefore, to analyse the problem and to consider possible ways of dealing with it.

Two salient points should be noted. First, it is basically a peak-hour problem, confined to approximately five hours a day on fewer than 250 working days of the year. Second, it is largely the result of the increased use of the private car for journeys to work. The former tends to restrict the amount of investment which can be profitably undertaken in the transport system. The latter indicates that some effort should be directed towards making the road-user pay the full costs (including external costs) of taking his vehicle on the road.

Bearing these principles in mind, actual policy can follow six main lines:

Do nothing and suffer the externalities

Some people argue that trying to improve movement on the roads is self-defeating: the easier it is to travel, the more people use their cars. As congestion increases, there comes a point where the cost in terms of wasted time and frustration is such that motorists switch to public transport.

But such a policy has snags. First, it provides no *incentive* for motorists to switch to public transport. There should be such an incentive, since those who do switch make travelling easier for those who do not. Second, the high level of congestion envisaged would become a permanent feature, penalizing equally the essential car-users and the optional users, those for whom using public transport would impose no severe hardship. Third, the congestion would affect non-car users, such as pedestrians.

Invest in the construction of more roads

The long-term solution is increased investment to improve the urban environment and the circulation of traffic. This could take the form of comprehensive redevelopment of existing city centres and improved town planning, such as siting industry away from city centres. The main thrust, however, would be to build more roads linking the suburbs and city centre – bypasses also play a part by siphoning off through traffic. It is doubtful, however, whether this would be a complete solution.

1. As it is difficult to impose tolls on short-run roads, these have to be financed from taxation and made freely available to all wishing to use them. But as the amount that can be devoted to public investment in general is limited, roads have to compete with defence, health care, social welfare, the modernization of public transport, and so on. Yet, without direct pricing of road use, there is no precise indication of what people are prepared to pay for more roads and therefore no firm basis for comparing the rate of return with that of alternative capital projects (though CBA may help – see Chapter 11). Therefore, there is no answer to the basic question of whether vast investment in new urban road systems is economically viable, bearing in mind that it is largely to provide for peak-hour travel between the suburbs and the city centre.

2. Investment in roads, as opposed to extending public transport, involves an income redistribution, since public transport is used mainly by poorer persons. The result is that the decision on whether to invest in more roads is eventually a political one and pressure groups in favour may be successful in spite of the very high cost of urban road construction.

3. It would take many years for a complete road network to be built. In the meantime, movements in industry and population and transport developments could change needs considerably. This factor largely accounts for the wide discrepancies between forecasts and actual flows, as in the case of the M25 or the M6.

4. The demand for road space seems to respond to supply, with better roads generating more motor transport. Demand and supply, therefore, are never in equilibrium. This was recognized in 1994 when the government announced a major curtailment of its roadbuilding programme.

This means that we are always faced with a short-term situation of making the best possible use of existing road space.

Impose physical controls to improve traffic flows

Some immediate improvement in traffic flows can be achieved by clearways, reversible lanes, linked traffic signals, bus lanes, mini-roundabouts and so on. Such adaptation of the existing road layout can often be combined with schemes that improve the environment for example, designating pedestrian-only areas, installing traffic-calming measures, constructing culs-de-sac in residential districts or simply restricting the movement of heavy vehicles in residential zones.

In the longer term, attempts can be made to spread the flow of rush-hour traffic over a longer period (such as by staggering working hours) or to reverse the flow (for instance, encouraging offices to locate in the suburbs and the building of out-of-town shopping centres). Nevertheless care must be taken to ensure that the commercial heart of the city is not destroyed as a result. This latter consideration has led to government discouragement of further out-of-town shopping developments.

It must be noted, however, that traffic management can only increase the capacity of the road network when the initial *pattern* of movement is sub-optimal. Even then it only provides a short-term relief from congestion since, unless entry is restrained, improving the traffic flow eventually generates additional traffic.

Restrict parking

Perhaps the greatest advantage of the motor vehicle is the convenience of door-to-door travel. This needs parking facilities. These contribute to accessibility and – by increasing catchment areas – to the prosperity of shopping and business centres. Yet, paradoxically, too many facilities lead to congestion, and so an appropriate balance between parking and movement has to be sought.

Parkers are of two sorts: the 'long-term' parker (the commuter) and the 'short-term' parker (the shopper and the business visitor). The problem is largely one of removing the 'long-term' parker from the streets, so that there will be sufficient accommodation for 'short-term' parkers to pursue their shopping or business activities. The two approaches, 'stick and carrot', are possible – physical control and road pricing. Both involve costs of adequate administration.

Physical controls take various forms, from the restriction of parking to certain days, time, side of street or type of vehicle (such as taxis only) to the complete prohibition of all kinds of waiting, including the loading and unloading of commercial vehicles. Permits may also be issued to give priority to essential users and residents. At one time, planning consents for new buildings stipulated the minimum number of parking spaces to be provided. Present policy for new developments is for planning authorities to exact payment towards their costs of providing car-parks. Furthermore, in order to divert commuters to public transport it is suggested that each private office parking space should be taxed and there are proposals to do this in Nottingham from 2011.

Since physical controls are unrelated to ability to pay, they lack the subtlety of the price mechanism's rationing function. Where parking is possible, charges can be imposed to bring demand into line with the limited number of spaces available. So that street parking should be confined to short-term parkers, it is usually linked with the physical control of limiting the time which can be spent at any one bay.

Kerbside parking has to be supplemented by off-street parking, especially for the long-term commuter. Since the cost of this is high, it is more likely to be provided where meter charges are also high. Local-authority car-parks are mostly hardstands and tend to be for short-term parkers only. Multi-storey and underground garages are expensive to build. Since demand drops off at night, they are largely dependent financially on there being sufficient daytime parkers to pay the relatively high charges. If these, however, encourage commuters to travel by public transport, there is a net benefit to the community through reduced congestion and less cost of road construction. This would justify any shortfall in revenue being underwritten by the local authority.

The provision of cheaper parking for shoppers and other short-term parkers has also to be considered, especially in the light of current government policy of protecting the vitality of city centres by restricting new out-of-town shopping developments. But without massive local-authority subsidy, such parking cannot be provided in the city centre. This suggests that 'park and ride' arrangements will have to be the preferred solution.

Use the price system to allocate existing road space

The principle of allocating limited parking space by charges can also be applied to moving vehicles by imposing a tax to reduce the use of vehicles and so relieve congestion.

In addition to his running costs, the private motorist allows for the time his journey will take. The greater the traffic flow, the longer this time. There is thus a rising cost curve, *MPC* (Figure 10.7). The demand curve, *D*, also takes account of this time factor: the greater the congestion, the longer the time journey, so that demand falls as the intensity of traffic-flow increases. Thus, left to the private motorists' decisions, the flow of traffic will be *OP*, where private marginal cost equals marginal benefit (price).

But while the private motorist allows for the time-cost of a heavy traffic-flow, the very fact of his taking his car on the road will add to the time-cost

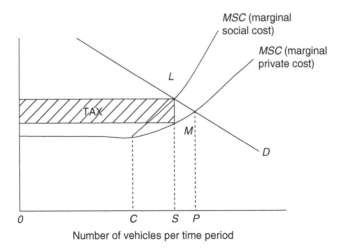

Figure 10.7   Allowing for the external cost of congestion

of others. Congestion can be defined as occurring when the private use of his car by a motorist 'impedes' the movement of other road-users, that is, at *OC* (Figure 10.7). There is a marginal social cost which, if added to the marginal private cost, gives the curve *MSC*. Applying the principle that output should take place where marginal social benefit equals marginal social cost, the economically efficient flow of traffic would be *OS*. This could be achieved by imposing a charge equal to *LM*. Ideally such a charge should reflect the time, miles covered on the road, the degree of congestion, the size of car and the location and direction of the journey in relation to the city centre. The difficulty lies in devising a single tax which covers all these requirements and is practical.

Imposing tolls on certain roads discriminates against the poor essential motorist, especially where no suitable alternative route is available. A high motor vehicle licence, by raising fixed costs, simply penalizes car ownership rather than congestion costs. A petrol tax reflects only mileage and size of car, and is thus unfair to the country dweller.

The most appropriate method of charging is to fit each car with a meter which would electronically register 'units' as certain control points were passed. These control points could be located more closely to each other as the city centre was approached, and the number of units could be varied according to the time of day. Even so, a congestion charge does not take account of the degree of congestion or the extent of use within the congestion area.

On 17 February 2003, a congestion charge was introduced in Central London. It is one of the world's largest and most ambitious plans to tackle urban congestion and involved an initial £5-per-day charge for vehicles entering the Inner Ring Road charging zone (£8 since July 2005). The congestion charge zone was extended into parts of West London in 2007.

Some economists consider that an additional advantage of such road pricing is that it would establish 'road values' and thus rates of return to guide future road investment. But metering faces difficulties.

1. Though it is economically valid and technically possible, it is only practical if the cost of installation, the periodic reading of the meter and the payment of charges are accepted by the motorist. The costs of administration and enforcement could be high.
2. Since this meter does not catch the parker, there would have to be additional parking charges.
3. It raises a distributional problem in that the wealthier motorist would be able to travel on the now uncongested roads, while the poorer *non*-motorist would enjoy better public transport. The relatively low-income motorist, who would now have to resort to public transport, would lose most. But why should the price mechanism be unacceptable on account of income differences in the road price market and not elsewhere in the economy?

4. Unless *MC* pricing is imposed in all sectors of the economy and, in particular, on all modes of transport, an optimal allocation of road use will not be achieved.
5. It has to be decided how the tax yield should be disposed of. Returning it to motorists would simply increase their income so that they could reclaim the road use they have given up.

Use the existing road system more efficiently through a better distribution of the means of travel

We have to consider the respective merits of the private car and public transport from both the demand and supply sides.

On the demand side, the car affords a convenient door-to-door means of transport and, in comparison with public transport, is comfortable. It also affords flexibility with traffic jams avoided by the choice of alternative routes and does not involve frequent stops to collect passengers. In contrast, public transport may be irregular, and incur the discomfort of standing. Its great merit is speed, especially with long-distance rail travel. Moreover, the method of charging for car travel as opposed to public transport favours the former. Much of the car's costs are fixed costs – the initial purchase price, the motor vehicle tax, insurance, and so on. The cost of actually using the car – the variable cost – is the cost of fuel and wear and tear (though motorists are inclined to ignore the latter). Thus the private motorist adopts what is virtually a marginal-cost basis of pricing.

In contrast, apart from any subsidies given, fares on public transport have to cover both fixed and variable costs; that is, the fare per mile tends to equal *average* total cost. The price system cannot yield an efficient allocation of resources between private and public transport when different principles are adopted as the basis of pricing.

Moreover, since fixed costs, particularly for the railways, are high, public transport tends to operate under conditions of decreasing cost. This means that the principle of marginal-cost pricing cannot be used if total costs are to be covered (Figure 10.8). Instead public transport seeks to cover total costs by price discrimination, charging higher fares to passengers whose demand is least elastic. Such passengers tend to be commuters and business people – and higher fares simply induce them to switch to travelling by car. The alternative is to make good the shortfall (*PFLN* with price *OP* in Figure 10.8) by government subsidy.

On the supply side, consideration has to be given to the respective cost patterns of the car and public transport. Figure 10.9 shows that when a relatively small number of passengers have to be coped with, the car has a cost advantage. Since the initial fixed costs to put a car on the road are so small compared with

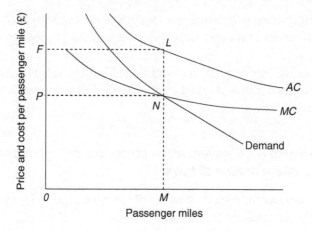

Figure 10.8 The effect of high fixed costs on public transport

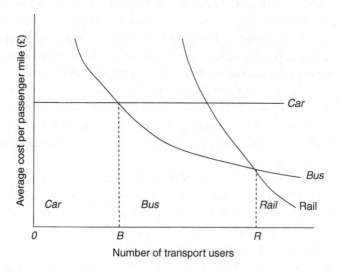

Figure 10.9 Difference in average costs per mile of car, bus and rail transport

the bus and train, for exposition purposes average cost per passenger can be regarded as constant.

However, as the number of passengers increases, the higher fixed costs of the bus are spread more thinly, so that eventually at *OB* average cost per passenger mile falls below that of the car. Rail transport has to incur even higher fixed costs in maintaining tracks, stations, expensive rolling stock, and so on, and so costs per passenger mile are only below those of the bus at a high level of passenger use, *OR*. In addition, development density should be high so that the number travelling from a single station is large. Hence urban rail travel is limited to very large cities.

One further point should be noted: the bus is more flexible in use than the train both in routeing and in dealing with small variations in the number of passengers. In its turn, the car is more flexible than the bus, especially for cross-commuting to employment in suburban offices, and so on.

It must again be emphasized that while the bus and train have a *cost* advantage over the car in dealing with passenger-users above *OB* and *OR* respectively, relative prices for each mode of travel will also depend upon demand. It may be that people's preference for car travel is so high its price would indicate that this mode should prevail even when the number of transport-users is high.

Policy for traffic congestion

The above analysis suggests that on *cost* considerations rush-hour travel is most economically provided by public transport, since this follows the predominantly radial flow to the centre and causes less congestion per passenger carried than the private car. The logical first step, therefore, would be to tax the private car-user as described earlier. This tax, supplemented by funds from general taxation, could be used to subsidize public transport. The subsidy would:

- enable public transport to cover its fixed costs;
- recognize the 'fall-back' or 'option' benefit which everybody enjoys simply from there being public transport facilities available if needed;
- reward public transport-users for the external benefits conferred by not increasing road congestion and other environmental costs, and
- redistribute income in favour of the poorer sections of the community who are most dependent on public transport.

In addition, price discrimination could be introduced into the fare structure to allow for differences in the time and direction of travel so that passengers travelling in the direction of the traffic flow during the rush hours pay more.

But there are difficulties. First, the policy is dependent upon the extent to which travellers would respond to the change in relative prices and switch to public transport. People seem very reluctant to leave their cars, and public transport is regarded as an inferior good. In other words, there is a low price-elasticity of demand for the private car and a high income-elasticity of demand. Indeed, it can be argued that the decline in the use of public transport is a result more of inconvenience and discomfort (such as draughty bus stops and overcrowding) than of cost. If this is so, in fairly affluent societies, more convenient and better transport even at *higher* prices would attract more customers than cheaper transport of the traditional type.

Second, the efficiency and equity of public transport subsidies have to be considered. If one aim is to make public transport cheaper for those on low incomes, then some form of income supplement would be more efficient. Furthermore, a subsidy financed by general taxation is unfair to the person who does not use public transport.

There are many approaches to the traffic problem and considerable controversy as to the most appropriate 'mix' of policies. A system which relies on any *one* mode of transport, or on one single approach, is unlikely to be satisfactory. There is a need for facilities which permit all types of transport: walking, cycling (through the provision of cycle tracks or lanes), car, minibus, bus and rail transport.

The cost of providing new roads to cater for the increasing number of private motorists may be such that some form of congestion tax may have to be imposed. But eventually an integrated city system could be introduced, with some flexibility to allow for individual preferences. The car would be used to get people from places where demand was insufficient to justify the fixed costs of providing public transport. Such people would be taken to collecting points from which they could transfer to public transport, as with 'park and ride.' In the absence of adjustments through the price system, methods of diverting travellers to public transport will have to be effected by physical controls, such as banning cars and goods vehicles from certain areas, rigorously extending and enforcing parking restrictions and creating bus lanes. In the long term, large cities may find that the solution to their traffic problems lies in building new underground railways.

Finally, the traffic problem cannot be solved in isolation from the location of urban activities. In the long run, one of the most effective ways of dealing with it may be to reduce the need for travel by organizing cities in a more sustainable way so that workplaces and residences are nearer to each other.

Summary

Economic forces generate growth in urban areas and the Keynesian model of national income determination can be adapted to explain the growth of urban areas. It is likely that a combination of economic influences determines the size and growth of urban areas.

Advantages of urbanization include:

- specialization of labour;
- external economies;
- large-scale production;
- economies of public services;
- complementarity between activities.

Disadvantages of urbanization include:

- higher transport costs;
- traffic congestion;
- increased pollution;
- antipathy between town and country dwellers;
- Policies to deal with 'overspill' of urban populations include green belts, new towns and expanded towns.

Inner-city areas or twilight zones arise because the urban area can only adjust slowly to changes in the conditions of demand and supply, and because the larger the city, the greater the external costs of concentration are likely to be. Problems of economic decline, physical decay and social disadvantage are interrelated and need to be addressed using a combination of policies to maintain a balanced population and improve the local economy, and through physical improvement rather than wholesale redevelopment.

Pollution occurs when the flow of residual emissions and wastes exceeds the natural environment's capacity to absorb them. The costs of pollution are often external to the market and therefore require government intervention in a variety of forms in order to deal with them.

One of the major external costs of urban areas is congestion caused by traffic. Various possible solutions to this problem have been tried around the world, including investment in roads, management of traffic flows, restrictions on parking and road pricing. There is great interest in the Central London congestion charge, which will almost certainly be adopted by other cities if it continues to be successful.

Chapter 10: review questions

1. What factors determine optimum city size?
2. Why is it necessary to regulate suburbanization or 'urban sprawl'?
3. Explain the rationale for green belts around expanding urban areas.
4. Describe the future of overspill arrangements (or alternatives) in the UK.
5. Why is there a 'prisoner's dilemma' type problem in improving a property in an inner-city area?
6. Describe the types of problem that occur in inner-city areas.
7. What policies are available to attempt to reduce pollution problems?
8. Explain, using a diagram, why the market is unlikely to preserve historic buildings.
9. What policies are available to attempt to alleviate traffic congestion in urban areas?

11

Cost-benefit Analysis of Development Projects

After studying this chapter you will be able to:

- Explain the concept of potential Pareto improvement;
- Describe the principles of cost-benefit analysis;
- Explain the limitations of cost-benefit analysis;
- Analyse the difficulties of choosing an appropriate discount rate;
- Give examples of use of CBA in actual land-use decisions.

UK public-sector development

Public-sector development amounted to 34 per cent of all development expenditure in 2008. Of this, new housing development expenditure amounted to £3,483 million; infrastructure £7,120 million and other new work £10,646 million. The total of public-sector development expenditure was £21,249 million from a total of all public and private new construction of £62,492 million (ONS, 2010).

Action by the government may take the form of regulation (such as building regulations to reduce fire hazards), taxes or subsidies (such as grants towards the maintenance of historic buildings) or by the government itself providing goods and services. It is with the last that we are chiefly concerned in cost-benefit analysis (CBA). Government responsibility for roads, bridges, airports, parks, amenity land, new urban areas and housing means that decisions have to be made about the allocation of land and land resources. Questions arise such as: is investment in a new motorway justified? Which site should be chosen for a new airport?

The difficulty is that, since many public-sector goods are provided free or below market price, indications of the desirability of investment through the price system are either non-existent or defective. Moreover, allowance has to be made for 'spillover' benefits and costs: for instance, the usual cost-revenue criterion may be inappropriate when there are unemployed resources, as the real cost of government spending to employ them may be zero, especially if there is a strong 'multiplier' effect. The government, too, may have to pay more attention than the private sector to the wishes of unborn generations to achieve inter-generational equity. Therefore, some other basis of decision making usually has to be adopted.

Government decisions may rest mainly on subjective political considerations. For example, in order to obtain a 'social mix', council housing may be provided in an expensive residential area. Such a procedure, however, has serious defects in dealing with public investment. First, the one-person, one-vote principle does not weight votes according to the intensity of welfare gained or lost. Therefore, the simple majority decision might allow two voters marginally in favour of a scheme to outvote one who strongly opposes it, in spite of the fact that the sum of their benefits is less than the costs inflicted on the single opponent. Second, political decisions are essentially subjective. Economic efficiency in resource allocation requires that objective criteria should be used as far as possible. Third, the extension of government involvement in the economy has increased the burden and complexity of public-sector decisions. Many would argue that decentralization of decision making is desirable in order to enable local decisions by local people.

CBA is a technique which seeks to bring greater objectivity into decision making. It does this by identifying all the relevant benefits and costs of a particular scheme and quantifying them in money terms so that each can be aggregated and then compared. In particular, CBA is likely to have its main use in the public sector where

1. price signals are inadequate to guide investment decisions;
2. 'spillover' benefits and costs are important because of the magnitude of the schemes; and
3. the welfare of unborn generations has to be allowed for – for example, by conservation measures.

The role of cost-benefit analysis (CBA)

The object of an economic system is to allocate scarce resources in such a way that society's welfare is maximized (see Chapter 2). But since welfare is subjective to the individual person it cannot be quantified in absolute terms. It follows that only in the narrow Pareto sense – where at least one person is made better off without anyone being made worse off – can we assert that the reshuffling of resources will result in a *definite* welfare improvement. For practical purposes, however, this requirement is too restrictive. Securing benefits for some persons almost invariably incurs costs to others. We can allow for this by saying that a *potential* Pareto improvement exists when those who gain from a change can fully compensate those who lose. The improvement is only 'potential' because the compensation may not, in fact, be paid and welfare may be affected by the inherent income redistribution underlying the change when compensation is not actually paid.

Property development represents a reallocation of resources to increase welfare. In the private sector it takes place through the market system; in the public sector decisions have a political content, but cost-benefit analysis (CBA) may be used to impart objectivity. Whichever method is used, it must be evaluated on the welfare test: does it allocate resources to produce a Pareto-optimal situation? That is, is it one where it is impossible to increase welfare by a further reshuffling of resources?

With the price system, individuals indicate their preferences in the market. The demand curve reflects the benefit expected to be received from different quantities of goods and services. Similarly, the costs of supplying these quantities are shown by the supply curve. Resources are allocated on the basis of the equilibrium price which results. But, as indicated in Chapter 2, the market economy can achieve the maximum net benefit for society only under highly restrictive conditions, and then subject to the existing distribution of income. Because such conditions do not apply in real life and because welfare could possibly be increased by redistributing income there are grounds for government interference in the market mechanism.

The principles of CBA

Since welfare is subjective to the individual, it cannot be measured cardinally in order to aggregate the welfare of individuals. The nearest we can come to surmounting this difficulty is to say that benefits are commensurate with willingness to pay (WTP) in terms of money. This can be justified as follows.

A consumer maximizes benefits from his expenditure when:

$$\frac{MU_A}{MU_B} = \frac{P_A}{P_B} \qquad (11.1)$$

If, for instance, the marginal utility (MU) of the last unit of A is five times that of the last unit of B, he will buy an extra unit of A provided that the price of A is less than five times the price of B. So benefits derived are indicated by WTP, that is, the sum of money which a person will pay for a good or service rather than go without it and the area under a market demand curve

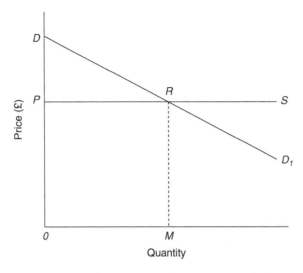

Figure 11.1   Measuring 'willingness to pay' (WTP)

measures aggregate individuals WTP or, in other words, aggregate marginal benefits.

In Figure 11.1, DD_1 is the demand curve. Assume that average costs are constant: the supply curve *PS* is thus perfectly elastic. The price will then be *OP*, and people will buy *OM*. Benefits derived equal *DOMR*, but total expenditure will be *POMR*, giving *consumers' surplus* of *DPR*. Consumers' surplus should therefore be included with benefits, especially with large indivisible projects. But for goods which are bought in quantity in the market, calculating consumers' surplus would involve ascertaining and aggregating each demand curve for each consumer. Because of the difficulties involved in obtaining a complete demand curve, it is usual to value the benefits in terms of total expenditure.

Benefits have to be compared with the costs of obtaining them – that is, the cost of the factors which have to be diverted from the best alternative project (*POMR* in Figure 11.1). In practice, the supply curve may not be perfectly elastic but rising, indicating average cost increases as output expands. Some factors earn economic rent, the aggregate of which is known as *producers' surplus*. This too should be included as a net benefit. But, for practical reasons, costs, like benefits, are measured in terms of quantity times price. If benefits exceed costs, the project should go ahead.

A simple CBA example

Assume that an attractive sandy beach can be reached only by a narrow lane branching off the main road some five miles away. As a result, visitors, even though they are mostly local, find it necessary to travel to the beach by car. No parking is permitted on the approach lane, but the local farmer has converted a field adjacent to the beach into a car park (Harvey and Jowsey, 2004).

A parking fee is charged which the farmer feels makes the most money possible. The car-parking fee is £1, at which 10,000 cars park annually, leaving considerable spare capacity. The only cost, which is incurred irrespective of the number of cars parking, is £2,000 for two attendants employed for four summer months to collect parking fees and clean the toilets. The farmer is currently seeking to sell the car park and is asking £80,000 for it.

The lane to the car park is very narrow and all waiting is prohibited by double yellow lines each side. The council has to employ two wardens, costing £5,000 a year, to ensure that the no-waiting restriction is observed. Nevertheless, frequent hold-ups mean that the return journey averages 32 minutes.

The council estimates that if it took over the car park and made parking free, the cars using the park would increase by 10,000 a year. The increased visitors would require extra toilets costing £20,000, but these could be supervised and cleaned by the existing two men, since they would not be needed to collect parking fees. The extra traffic would also necessitate widening the approach lane at a cost of £170,000. After the road improvements the return journey to the beach would take only 20 minutes. It is estimated that the 12 minutes saved is worth 20 pence per car journey. Moreover, the two traffic wardens would no longer be necessary.

For the council the scheme has a further advantage: enlarging the town's recreation park some eight miles distant at a cost of £50,000 need no longer go ahead, since people are likely to prefer the beach once car parking is free. Finally, it is assumed that there is full employment and no inflation.

In all cost-benefit analysis it is necessary to:

1. *List all relevant items.* These will include spillover effects of the proposal, such as the cost of extra toilets and road-widening, the saving on the extension to the town's recreation park. Care must be taken to avoid double-counting: thus the farmer could not include the loss of his land and the loss of parking fees, because the former is simply the capitalized value of the latter.
2. *Value expected benefits and costs,* deciding whether any allowance is to be made for the more distant future.
3. *Discount the future flow of benefits and costs* in order to obtain their capitalized present value. This involves choosing an appropriate rate of discount (see pp. 149–51).
4. *Appraise the project* by setting off aggregate benefits against aggregate costs. This can be done either according to the Pareto criterion of seeing how different parties gain or lose, or by a direct comparison of additional benefits and additional costs.

The parties to this public investment in a car park are the farmer, the existing parkers, the additional parkers and the taxpayer. What are their respective gains and losses?

- The *farmer* receives £80,000, but loses a net income of £8,000 a year.
- *Existing parkers* save £10,000 a year on fees, and 12 minutes on the return journey valued at £2,000 a year.
- *New parkers* have so far provided no firm indication of the value of car-parking benefits to them. It is therefore necessary to estimate their WTP.

The situation is shown in Figure 11.2.

Since the farmer is a monopolist, his demand curve will be downward sloping; let us assume it is linear. We know that, with free parking, the demand would be 20,000; thus the demand curve cuts the quantity axis at this point. The farmer's marginal revenue curve will also be linear. Because $MR = 0$ at point M, elasticity of demand at A is equal to 1, and therefore $DA = AD_1$; and $OM = MD_1$. We know that all the farmer's costs are fixed costs; thus $MC = O$ up to full capacity of the car park, and therefore MC is coincident with the quantity axis up to this point.

The farmer will maximize his profits by charging car parkers 100 p (OF), appropriate to 'output' OM where $MR = MC$. At this price, there are 10,000 parkers. With free parking total demand would be 20,000 and the WTP of new parkers would be measured by the area AMD_1, equal to £5,000 a year. The saving in time through the road improvements also provides these new 10,000 parkers with an extra benefit of £2,000 a year.

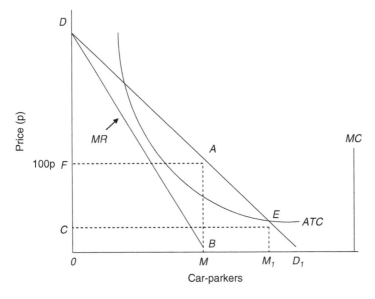

Figure 11.2   Demand for car-parking (at an unnamed beach)

Taxpayers have to bear the costs of the investment: £170,000 for widening the road and £20,000 for the additional toilets. But there are gains: £50,000 is saved through not having to enlarge the town's recreation park, and the two traffic wardens at £5,000 a year will no longer be required; since full employment has been assumed, they can find jobs elsewhere.

Annual future revenues and costs have to be discounted to the present to obtain their current capital value. Let us assume a discount rate of 10 per cent and that these perpetual flows are valued on a 10 years' purchase basis. Assuming a ten-year purchase, we obtain a Pareto balance sheet (Table 11.1).

Since those who gain can compensate those who lose and still show a net increase in benefits of £20,000, the local authority should undertake the project. It should be noted, however, that the viability of the scheme arises only because spillover benefits, chiefly the saving on enlarging the town's recreation park, have been included.

In practice, CBA usually concentrates only on net *additional* benefits and costs (Table 11.2). The net increase in benefits is still, of course, £20,000.

A CBA is itself a commodity having costs and therefore should not be undertaken if these are likely to be greater than the possible net benefits where these are not certain. Even if CBA shows a favourable balance, the project may run up against obstacles. Therefore, the council's car-park scheme above could only go ahead if funds were available. In practice, there may be *budget constraints*. Public-sector borrowing may be limited or financing the scheme through taxation may be difficult. Where there is a budget constraint, projects have to be ranked and available funds apportioned between them so as to secure the maximum net benefit possible.

Table 11.1   A Pareto balance sheet

	Gains (£)		Costs (£)
Farmer			
Sale proceeds	80000	Profit lost	80000
Existing parkers			
Fees saved	100000		
Time saved	20000		
New parkers			
Parking benefits	50000		
Time saved	20000		
Taxpayers		Land	80000
Saving on:			
Town park extension	50000	Toilets	20000
Traffic wardens	50000	Road widening	170000
Total benefits	370000	Total costs	350000

Table 11.2 CBA net additional benefits and costs

	Benefits (£)		Costs (£)
Existing parkers	100 000	Road-widening	170 000
New parkers	50 000	Land	80 000
Costs saved:		Toilets	20 000
Parkers' time	40 000		
Traffic wardens	50 000		
Town's recreation park	50 000		
Total	290 000		270 000

Some projects may be subject to *legal constraints*, involving easements, covenants or even the responsibilities of public bodies as laid down by statutes, for example, for common land. A costly and time-consuming private bill procedure may be necessary in order to proceed with the scheme.

More important, the project may encounter *administrative or political difficulties*. Where more than one local authority or public body is involved, they may be motivated by different interests or political views: for example, the National Trust would probably oppose an electricity scheme which took pylons over land for which it was responsible.

Finally, the project may be opposed on *distributional* grounds, being deemed to benefit the rich to the exclusion of the poor. For instance, if it were located in a prosperous region rather than one of high unemployment, it could conflict with government regional policy.

Difficulties with CBA

The simple example of the car park obscures conceptual and practical difficulties, which are inherent in any CBA. These include:

Allowing for the distributional effects of a project

It would be rare for a public project to qualify on the strict Pareto principle of some gainers but no losers. In the example above, suppose the farmer knows the demand curve, DD_1 (see Figure 11.2). His costs as stated are all fixed, with the average total cost curve a rectangular hyperbola (ATC) and the marginal costs nil up to the point of capacity (MC). Profits are maximized at a parking charge of OF (100p) with the number of cars restricted to OM (10,000), where $MC = MR$. Now assume the council faces the same demand curve and the same cost conditions. It could purchase the site from the farmer and extend car parking to OM_1, charging price OC where revenue just covers the same total costs. This produces a net benefit increase given by the triangle ABE. Moreover, since the farmer has been fully compensated in money, no initial problem of income redistribution arises.

However, in our original example, car parkers, although willing to pay, were given the benefit free, the cost being borne by taxpayers. The former gain; the latter lose. There is thus some redistribution of income.

The difficulty is that the gainers may be rich people having, as is generally assumed, a lower marginal utility of income than poor people (they do not value an extra unit of income very highly). On the other hand, the losers may be poor people with a high marginal utility of income (they do value an extra unit of income highly). In the car-park project, for example, the gainers were car-owners who had sufficient leisure time to take a trip to the beach, whereas the losers, the taxpayers, may include many old people who could ill-afford an increase in their council tax.

Because there is no cardinal measure of utility, we cannot completely overcome this difficulty of income redistribution. But it is possible to deal with it up to a point. If the change in income redistribution is small relative to the net benefit gain, it can be ignored. Alternatively, a weighting system, which will necessarily have an element of subjectivity, can be used. Thus, to assess the welfare of the car-park scheme, we should apply a low weight to the richer car-parkers' benefit and a higher weight to the poorer taxpayers' losses in order to reflect their relative differences in marginal utility of income.

This problem of distributional effects crops up in various forms. Country lovers may lose pleasure through electricity pylons intruding on the landscape. If they are fully compensated, there is no loss of income so the problem of measuring their marginal utility of income does not arise. The difficulty (a frequent one) of identifying such losers means that compensation is not actually paid, and there are thus distributional effects. Similarly, when comparing the benefits of a project to future generations with its costs to the present population, some allowance should be made for the fact that future generations are likely to have a higher income.

Adjusting market prices

Where market prices reflect the true opportunity cost to society of employing resources in a particular way (assuming no externalities), they can be used to estimate the cost of a project. However, in the real world it has to be recognized that prices in the market may not accurately reflect opportunity cost. This may be the result of imperfect competition, indirect taxes and subsidies, or controls which interfere with the free operation of the market mechanism. In these circumstances it is necessary to consider whether some adjustment is both desirable and practical in order to produce a set of *shadow prices* for the CBA calculations.

Considering the problem of imperfect competition first; under perfect competition, price = marginal revenue = marginal cost = the cost of an additional unit of the good to society. Where there is imperfect competition, however, price is higher than marginal revenue, though the latter is still equated with marginal cost. As a result, price exceeds marginal cost which measures opportunity cost to society. Similarly, in factor markets the value of the marginal product at the quantity employed is higher than the factor reward when the firm is a monopsonistic buyer of factors.

Suppose in our example of the car park that the tarmac for the road was supplied by a monopolist. In order to maximize his profits, he would charge price *OP* per tonne (see Figure 11.3). On the other hand, marginal cost would be only *OC* per tonne. We should thus value the tarmac at *OC*, the opportunity cost for this amount.

There are, however, two major difficulties. First, there is the practical one of estimating marginal cost. Second, there is the conceptual problem of the 'second best'. Given that the 'first-best' allocation of resources by marginal-cost pricing in all markets is unattainable, do we ensure a 'second-best' solution by adopting marginal-cost pricing solely in the public sector? We cannot be certain. If, in the existing situation, there is the same degree of distortion between price and marginal cost in all markets, adopting marginal-cost pricing in only one part of the economy could lead to an allocation of resources further from the Pareto optimum. In short, while there may be a single optimum position given all the essential conditions for Pareto optimality, there may be many 'second-best' possibilities, and if only the 'second best' is obtainable in practice we may be making things worse by tinkering with the system in the hope of attaining what is really impossible.

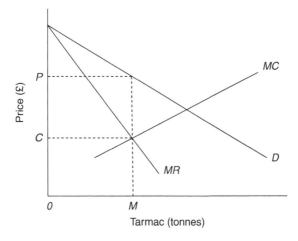

Figure 11.3 A monopolist's price and marginal cost for a given output

It should also be noted that marginal cost is not acceptable when, in a situation of decreasing costs, total costs are not covered. It has been suggested for such a case, therefore, that the principle of a two-part tariff pricing system should be followed, a sum being added to marginal cost by way of a fixed standing charge.

The second issue that necessitates the adjustment of market prices, is where there are indirect taxes, or subsidies, or market controls. Opportunity cost is represented by factor cost (that is, cost *less* indirect taxes, plus subsidies). It is argued that market prices should be adjusted by subtracting indirect taxes (for instance, for petrol saved by the construction of a motorway) and adding subsidies (for example, for the value of agricultural produce lost). The difficulty with this procedure, however, is that taxes 'deducted' in this way should really be 'recouped' on other goods, thereby distorting *their* prices. There is therefore a case for calculating benefits and costs at current market prices.

Similarly, physical controls such as rent control may keep prices below market price. Such controlled prices cannot therefore be used for CBA purposes. Moreover, prices may be distorted by controls elsewhere – for example, through quotas. Suppose, for instance, that a land-reclamation project allowed a dairy farm to be established. In valuing milk it should be remembered that its price is largely the result of the EU's agriculture policy of restricting supply by quotas. Similarly, prices of imports may be artificially lowered by a protection policy aimed at maintaining a higher exchange rate than that which would prevail in a free market.

Although market prices may not reflect true opportunity costs, the obstacles to making the necessary adjustments are formidable. The cost of obtaining the information needed may be too high to be worth while, and consistency in the adjustments made would be difficult to attain throughout both the public and private sectors. Because of such problems, some economists have rejected correcting market prices. Others, however, consider that adopting a straight marginal-cost pricing rule gives consistency to accounting procedures and corresponds more closely to the costs which CBA is seeking to measure.

Pricing non-market goods

Market prices may not be available. This occurs with the following goods.

1. *Community and public goods*, where 'free riders' cannot be excluded (examples are street-lighting, land, radio programmes) or where it is decided to make no charge (for instance, for public parks or bridges). Here the cost is covered by taxation which is unlikely to reflect true 'willingness to pay'.
2. *Intangible externalities*, such as noise and congestion cost, human lives saved, the pleasure derived by passersby from flowers and trees in private gardens or from a walk in a park.

Since both enter into CBA calculations, it is necessary to ascribe notional prices to them so that benefits and costs can be quantified in money terms. But formulating such 'shadow' or 'surrogate' prices faces formidable difficulties, as the following specific examples – recreation, timesavings and human life – reveal.

Firstly recreation; in our example of the car park we were able to estimate the benefits (WTP) of a trip to the beach from an existing market. However, for many recreational facilities – such as the Lake District, Hadrian's Wall, the National Gallery – there has been no previous market. How, then, do we derive a demand curve? One method would be to devise a questionnaire in which people state how much they would be willing to pay for the facility. Nevertheless, difficulties may arise in obtaining a representative sample, while replies may lack accuracy because of respondents' subjectivity.

A second possibility is to adapt prices from a parallel facility where charges are made, for instance, for admission to the grounds of a stately mansion. But for many activities, such as fell-walking, such an alternative is not available.

The accepted method, therefore, is to see how demand varies with travel costs, both in money and time. The greater the distance travelled for such recreation, the greater the travel costs; thus demand should fall with distance. To allow for differences in density of population in the catchment area being studied, the number of trips per thousand of the population for different zones is derived. Suppose the following figures are obtained:

Zone	Trips per 1,000 population
1	300
2	100
3	60

To simplify, let us assume that: (i) travel costs from zone 1 average £1; (ii) an outward movement to zones 2 and 3 each adds £1; and (iii) there are 1,000 people in each zone.

Price (£)	Trips made from zone			Total trips
	1	2	3	
1	300	100	60	460
2	–	100	60	160
3	–	–	60	60

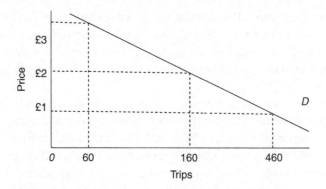

Figure 11.4   The demand curve for recreation

Thus if travel costs represent the price, we can derive a demand curve (see Figure 11.4) as follows:

From the demand curve we can estimate WTP.

This approach, although based on revealed market behaviour (or 'revealed preference'), presents difficulties:

1. What should be the unit priced – whole-day trips, half-day trips or hours spent enjoying the facility?
2. If the car is the main mode of travel, then the number of trips should be related to every 1,000 *car-owners* of the population.
3. Some allowance ought to be made for the average number of persons brought by each car.
4. Where the journey is made by car, the assessment of cost presents problems. If the car is used mainly for business, then only the marginal cost (chiefly for petrol) will be the real cost of the journey. On the other hand, if the car is used exclusively for recreation, a proportion of overheads should also be included.
5. At what price should travel time be valued (see below)?
6. How should costs be adjusted if the actual journey to the facility also gives pleasure?
7. How is the cost to be apportioned if more than one recreation centre is visited on the journey?

Valuing time saved

Transport improvements usually result in reducing the time spent in making a journey. What price do we put on this benefit?

Where it is working time saved, for example, in deliveries by lorry, and it results in extra work being done, the employer's valuation should be accepted: that is, it would include savings on overheads as well as on wages.

However, time saved may simply mean that people get to work quicker, thereby increasing their leisure time. For people who choose how many hours they work, the marginal utility of leisure and work time would be equal, so that again, time saved should be at the earning rate. But for most people a straight choice between an extra hour's work and an extra hour's leisure is not available. In practice, therefore, leisure time has to be valued arbitrarily as a proportion of the earning rate, and in fact 25 to 50 per cent is usually taken as being the value of time saved.

An alternative approach is to take the value, which people put on time, indirectly when they incur higher costs in order to save it. This value may be indicated in different ways:

1. People may pay a higher price for their housing in order to be nearer their work. The difficulty with this is that the higher price may also reflect quality differences or nearness to non-work facilities.
2. The route chosen may reduce time but at a higher cost, such as the toll paid to cross an estuary by ferry. To be accurate, however, the assessment would have to be confined to regular users having perfect knowledge.
3. Car drivers may trade speed against petrol consumption, and so on. However, they may not know the exact extra cost involved, may enjoy driving at speed, or choose their speed for safety considerations.
4. One mode of travel may be faster than another but more expensive – for example, a taxi as opposed to a bus, or the underground in London as opposed to a taxi. Comfort considerations, however, may enter into such a choice.

Some allowance should also be made for the fact that as productivity increases over time so will the wage rate; therefore, the value of leisure time will tend to increase over time.

The value of human life

Such projects as road improvements reduce deaths and accidents; others, such as airports, may increase them for people in the vicinity. How can a money value be given to human life? More specifically, how can loss of life be valued? Here again there are alternatives, each presenting its own difficulties.

First, the present value of future expected earnings can be calculated, with additions for suffering endured and the grief experienced by the family. However, this ignores the consumer's surplus a person enjoys in spending his income.

The second alternative measures the present value of *net* output of the dead person, that is, the flow of future earnings less consumption. This method, however, presents moral difficulties, for it implicitly assumes that society's objective is maximizing total GNP. Fortunately, society does not require a person to justify his existence on economic grounds. People living on state pensions are not disposed of because their death would represent a net gain to society! Society takes into account human feelings.

A third method assesses the value placed on human life by society through its political decisions. For instance, if compulsory safety-belts costing £X saved in total Y lives, the value of human life is at least £ $\sum X / Y$. However, the fundamental objection to this approach is that it is a circular argument: the economist should really be justifying the cost of compulsory safety-belts in terms of the value of lives saved!

A fourth measure is the sum for which a person insures his life; this does not measure the value of life, but simply reflects a man's concern for his family's future in the event of his death. A single person, for instance, might have no life insurance, but still value their life! Or life insurance may simply be the condition for obtaining a mortgage.

A fifth measure may be derived from people doing dangerous jobs. But information about risks may be incomplete and the labour market may be imperfect.

The real difficulty with all these methods is that they break with the criterion for a potential Pareto improvement: that there is still a gain after all losses have been compensated for. The second method highlights this problem, for the fact that society could gain from the death of a retired person arises simply because the latter receives no compensation for the loss of his life. Since such compensation is probably infinite, any project which saved one life would cover its costs!

However, it must be remembered that, in practice, we are not concerned with *one* person's certain death. What we have to compensate for is the extra *risk* of death to which all affected persons are exposed, for example, as the result of the increased traffic of a new airport. Those concerned are: (i) the additional air passengers; (ii) their relatives\ and (iii) people living around the airport. The value of the risk to the first can be disregarded, since it can be assumed that travellers have allowed for this in buying an air ticket. Indeed, for the third group, care must be taken to avoid double-counting, since compensation may already have been carried out through the price system – for example, in a lower price for houses near the airport which has persuaded residents to accept the risks involved. Otherwise, an insurance Figure can be accepted as the necessary compensation required by the second and third groups except that, since people tend to underestimate, this Figure may be somewhat inadequate.

Spillover effects

Spillover effects present practical problems. Which spillovers should be included? The problem of which spillovers should be included is concerned, first, with the difficulty of distinguishing between real changes and distributional effects, and, second, on deciding the cut-off point.

Real changes are those that affect the performance of other inputs (for example, an additional large office building in the City of London could increase traffic congestion and thus lower the efficiency of road transport) or the pleasure of others (for instance, a motorway creates a noise nuisance to nearby residents). Obviously such effects should be taken into account.

Distributional or transfer effects refer to those effects of individual projects which result in shifts in *prices* to other parties. Thus an increased demand by tourists for hotels in London will lead to higher wages of catering workers, not only in hotels but also in restaurants and cafés. Are these effects part of the cost to society of increasing hotel services? Consider what happens. The higher wages of catering workers will cause restaurants and cafés to reduce their demand for them. Each restaurant itself will now earn a lower economic rent, while variable factors will drift to more profitable uses. But what all this means is simply that maximizing consumers' economic welfare has pointed to a better 'basket' of products from a reshuffling of resources. Although painful for some, such readjustments must occur in a changing economy. In any assessment of the costs and gains of public development, there is no reason why the government should consider distributional effects except that, on grounds of equity, it may feel some compensation is called for.

Similarly, does an allowance have to be made for changes in the prices of substitute and complementary goods and services which result from some public development? For example, road and rail transport are to some extent substitute products. If the government, by instituting a new road-building programme, reduced the economic viability of the railways, should this be allowed for in assessing the economic viability of investment in new roads? A private monopolist with many lines of production would obviously take into account such interactions when introducing changes. Should not the government do the same? Quite apart from the obvious difficulty of trying to trace the endless chain of effects throughout the whole field of government action, the answer is not entirely clear. The action of the monopolist may not be the appropriate criterion for the maximization of consumers' economic welfare since there may be other spillover effects which he does not take into account. Thus the government may require the price of North Sea gas to be raised relative to that of wind energy in the interests of, conservation of gas reserves and a long-term fuel policy dependent on renewable resources.

In practice, it may be extremely difficult to sort out real effects from distributional effects. For example, if a bypass road isolates formerly thriving shopkeepers and involves them in loss of trade, does this represent a real cost or simply a transfer item? It could be argued that in this case planning has so affected the locational pattern of shopping services that production potential has suffered because they are now in the wrong place. If we accept this reasoning, such losses must count as real effects which should be included in any reckoning. In most cases these effects are not likely to be of great significance and are often offset by changes in the opposite direction (for example, in the case of the new road, production potential elsewhere may increase through being more advantageously located).

To sum up, the gains and costs of a project should include the value of any real spillovers. But changes in prices which merely reflect relative changes in the conditions of demand and supply are beside the point. Therefore, in choosing between alternative public projects, the government should not act like a giant monopoly, seeking to maximize overall profits from its many activities, but should assess each case on its merits, taking into account real spillover effects. Pure redistribution effects are outside the question of economic efficiency, though the government can make a political decision to allow for them on the grounds of equity.

In considering spillovers there is also the difficulty of deciding the cut-off point and whether any allowance should be made for unforeseen costs and benefits.

If a new motorway is constructed from city X to city Y it may reduce congestion and travelling times for travellers between the two cities and also on routes nearby. The further we go, the more difficult it is to distinguish all beneficiaries. Moreover, certain spillovers have to be decided by reference to what would generally be regarded as 'reasonable'. Thus while environmental spillovers from the motorway would certainly qualify, the envy which some people not owning a car might feel as they saw others using the motorway to get to the seaside would have to be excluded.

Nor can all spillovers be foreseen. The motorways around Los Angeles have saved the white-tailed kite from extinction. The reason is that the shrubs and grass of the broad shoulders and central dividers provide relative safety for mice and lizards, the staple diet of the kite, for no man in his right mind ever sets foot in these areas. Alternatively, there could be unforeseen external costs. The Aswan Dam, for instance, reduced the flow of fish food from the Nile into the Mediterranean, giving rise to the real costs of fewer fish and, by affecting the livelihood of fishermen, having distributional effects. Moreover, since this was not confined to Egyptian fishermen, it raises the problem of whether, in a world where countries are becoming increasingly dependent on one another, spillover effects should be limited to the national economy.

Intangibles

In aggregating costs and benefits, how much weight should be attached to the shadow prices of intangibles compared with true market prices? In so far as there is perfect competition, market prices at factor cost reflect true opportunity costs. In comparison, shadow prices are derived indirectly, and to that extent are somewhat suspect. Should we therefore, when aggregating, treat market and shadow prices equally? The difficulty becomes more real when shadow prices form a high proportion of total costs and benefits. Thus, in our example of the car park, the £70,000 benefits obtained by new parkers were based on an estimated demand curve derived from the price paid by existing car parkers. Should this shadow price represent an overestimate of 30 per cent, the scheme would not be viable. Actual CBAs have shown the crucial margin of error is usually much smaller. Thus, while the Roskill Commission (1970) estimated that the Cublington site for the third London Airport would be £158 to £197 million cheaper than Foulness, only a 1 per cent error in total benefit or total cost figures could have made Foulness the lower-cost site.

Choosing the appropriate discount rate

If we postpone current consumption, resources can be used for investment in capital equipment. This produces greater output in the future: that is, there is growth. The gain is increased future consumption. We can thus speak of a rate at which current consumption can be transformed into future consumption. Starting from consumption C_0 this is shown by the transformation curve TT_1 in Figure 11.5.

However, future consumption is valued less highly than present consumption. This is because (i) people generally suffer from myopia (they have a short

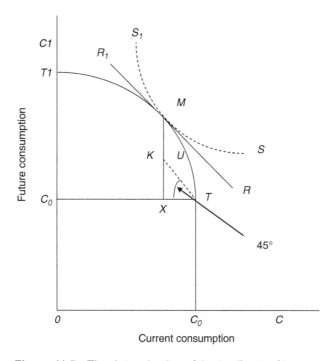

Figure 11.5 The determination of the 'real' rate of interest

time-horizon); (ii) future income is less certain since there is always the risk of death and (iii) future income is likely to be greater than present income, and thus the marginal utility of present income is higher. This preference which people generally have for present as opposed to future consumption is referred to as *time preference*, and is shown by the indifference curve SS_1.

A function of an economic system is to bring people's time preference into line with the actual opportunity cost of transforming current consumption into future consumption. Given a perfect market, perfect competition, perfect knowledge and no externalities, the free market system can produce a rate of interest which achieves this. We shall refer to this as the 'real' rate of interest.

In Figure 11.5 the transformation curve TT_1 shows that if XT is not consumed but invested, consumption in year 1 can increase by MK. That is, the net productivity of capital, k, equals:

$$\frac{MK}{XT} = \frac{MX - KX}{XT} = \frac{MX - XT}{XT} = \text{slope of } TT_1 - 1 \text{ at } X \qquad (11.2)$$

Similarly, SS_1 can be regarded as a society indifference curve between C and C_1. At any point the marginal rate of substitution of C_1 for C is equal to the slope of SS_1. Since, however, people prefer C to C_1, this slope will equal $1 + s$, where s is the weighting to be attached to C compared with C_1. But s is really society's rate of time preference, and so $s = \text{slope of } SS_1 - 1$.

Given our assumptions, the market will produce a unique or 'real' rate of interest, i, represented by the slope of RR_1, which equates the time preference of society (the individuals comprising the market) with the profitability of available investment opportunities. This means that $i = s = k$. In Figure 11.5 equilibrium occurs at M, where TT_1 just touches SS_1 the highest indifference curve attainable by society.

Any other point on TT_1 would put society on a lower indifference curve. Thus point U represents under-investment compared with society's time preference, for the opportunity-cost rate of return is greater than the time-preference rate required. This disequilibrium between investment and saving would cause the rate of interest to fall until there was equilibrium with RR_1 at point M, where the net productivity of investment would be in line with society's time preference.

In practice, however, the conditions necessary for a unique, equilibrating rate of interest are not fulfilled. First, many different rates exist, reflecting differences in risk (the small private company would have to pay a higher rate of interest than a large public company) or in imperfections in the capital market (the only source of funds to the small private company may be a bank, whereas the large company could float a loan on the capital market).

Second, money rates of interest may be affected by monetary influences as opposed to being determined solely by real forces – the return on investment and time preference. Monetary influences would include external pressure on the exchange rate or changes in the demand for money for liquidity purposes. Third, actual money rates of interest may be higher than RR_1, the real rate, because the reward for saving is reduced by taxation and inflation.

With different rates to choose from, which is the most appropriate for assessing public-sector projects? One view is that discounting should be at the rate of interest at which the government can borrow to finance such schemes: that is, the yield on long-term gilt-edged securities. However, the government borrowing rate tends to be low because it is a 'riskless' rate. But public projects such as the *Docklands Light Railway* are not free from risk, and the rate of discount should reflect this. Even if the project is financed from taxation, the opportunity cost is the rate which the taxpayer could have obtained had the money been left with him to invest.

Therefore, it is argued that because resources for investment are not unlimited, the opportunity cost of a public project is the equal-risk project in the private sector which has to be forgone. Therefore, the appropriate rate of interest is what a large public company would have to pay for funds to finance such investment – for example, the current debenture rate. Only if lower risk is inherent in public projects should a lower interest rate be used. It can be argued that this lower risk does in fact exist. Because so many public projects are undertaken, risks are spread: losses on one project can be averaged out by gains on others, so the government in effect carries its own insurance. Moreover, not only are risks spread over projects but also the cost of any error in estimation is distributed among so many taxpayers that the actual risk borne by each is so small as to be acceptable. Therefore, discounting projects at a slightly lower rate than in the private sector is justified.

Apart from allowances for differences in risk between public and private projects, the problem is complicated by time-preference considerations. First, society's time preference is not the same as the sum total of individual time preferences. It can be held that individuals suffer from myopia, or shortsightedness, so that they fail to appreciate how much they would benefit from future as opposed to current consumption. This difficulty is covered where society acts for individuals.

Second, society as a whole is an undying institution, and the government, which is responsible for society's decisions, is therefore concerned with the welfare of future generations, making decisions (as it were) on behalf of those still unborn. Such decisions are of particular importance when a project has an 'irreversible' cost, such as the demolition of a historic building, the destruction of the natural beauty of the Lake District, the complete exhaustion of a mineral stock or the wiping out of a particular species of animal, bird or plant. As the green lobby puts it: 'We do not inherit the land from our fathers; we borrow it from our children.' Thus in comparison with individuals, who have a limited time- horizon, society has a lower time preference.

Both points above therefore give further justification for discounting public projects at a lower interest rate – the 'social time-preference rate' – than that arrived at through the market. Although all the usual methods of allowing for risk and uncertainty in appraising projects can be applied to public-sector schemes, the above discussion suggests that one based on choosing an appropriate rate of interest will be the one usually followed. In practice, governments fix a minimum rate of return which must be achieved for public-sector investment to be acceptable. However, if public projects are discounted at a lower rate than in the private sector, this will divert resources towards public investment because such projects have a higher present value.

Use and limitations of CBA

It is essential, since resources are limited, that public-sector expenditure obtains 'value for money'. The difficulty is that financial criteria may be either non-existent or inadequate for assessing the viability of projects, but CBA is designed to assist such decision making. Public projects often involve the allocation of land resources; therefore, the technique of CBA can be applied to evaluating planning applications, comprehensive redevelopment proposals, motorway construction, the siting of an airport, and so on. In particular, it can ensure that full allowance is made for spillover benefits and costs.

Nevertheless, as our analysis has indicated, CBA runs up against conceptual and practical difficulties. These weaken its effectiveness as a tool for decision making. The following considerations are of particular importance.

First, CBA cannot be used where political decisions dominate. For instance, how much is spent by Britain on defence may depend upon subjective views as to the possible role of the armed forces in support of foreign policy and to what extent such expenditure can be trimmed in order to extend the social services. Similarly, proposals for comprehensive education are advanced, at least partly, on the subjective grounds that they promote a more integrated society, while expensive local authority housing may be provided in areas of high land values, such as Hampstead, in order to achieve a 'social mix'. Although social factors can be identified, it is often impossible to measure them satisfactorily.

Second, CBA may be difficult to apply to certain decisions. Consider, for instance, a local authority which has £2 million to spend on a swimming pool. The decision rests between: (i) one swimming pool of Olympic standards which, while it could also be used by local people, would bring prestige to the town; (ii) three smaller swimming pools, suitable for inter-school galas and (iii) six very small pools specifically designed for children learning to swim. The advantages of each are largely immeasurable by CBA techniques, the result being that councillors will have to decide subjectively by voting at a council meeting. Similarly, a firm CBA decision cannot be applied to a project involving irreversible decisions, such as the survival of a species of animal or plant. In such cases it is impossible to estimate a current economic cost, since it would deny future generations the opportunity to choose.

Third, CBA cannot deal objectively with the redistribution of income which results from a project. Fourth, CBA encounters formidable difficulties both in measuring and aggregating intangibles. Its validity is enhanced as the number of values obtained directly from the market increases, particularly if they are determined under conditions of near-perfect competition.

Fifth, there is always the problem of the cut-off point in deciding the benefits and costs to be included. The viability of a project could rest on this decision, and interested parties may be tempted to extend the cut-off point in order to justify their particular preferences. Finally, what passes as CBA is often in reality merely a 'cost-effectiveness' study comparing different methods of achieving a given end. CBA should not only examine the method of achieving an objective but should compare the likely returns from alternative uses of the same resources. Thus, in the Roskill study, the decision to build a third London Airport had been predetermined; the Commission merely examined the costs and benefits of alternative sites.

CBA provides a rational technique for appraising projects where market information is either non-existent or deficient. But it must not make false claims for objectivity by dealing in precise sums. Though it is an aid to decision making, it is not a substitute for it. Its role is to present systematically all the information relevant to a decision, indicating the weight which can be placed on the accuracy of the calculations submitted. Drawing up such an agenda ensures that the claims of rival pressure groups are assessed and that all the relevant issues are fully debated before the ultimate political decision is taken.

Although CBA, as outlined above, can be used in all public investment decisions, it has particular application to the allocation of land resources, where externalities are likely to loom large. As a result, CBA studies have been undertaken for:

1. the construction of the M1 motorway;
2. London underground's Victoria Line;
3. the siting of the third London Airport;
4. the resiting of Covent Garden Market;
5. town planning: Cambridge;
6. urban expansion: Ipswich;
7. Edgware shopping centre;
8. a Severn barrage for tidal generation of electricity.

A cost-benefit study of a third runway and sixth terminal at Heathrow airport

In assessing the case for London Heathrow airport (LHR) expansion, the Department for Transport (2009) used the technique of cost-benefit analysis as part of its study. As their report puts it:

> In cost-benefit analysis, the relative costs and benefits of a scheme over time are expressed in monetary terms. This incorporates both elements usually expressed in financial terms, such as profit, and those that have to be assigned an estimated monetary value, such as pollution. These costs and benefits over time are discounted over time to give a present value, reflecting the time value of money and uncertainty.

Using cost-benefit analysis, the policy proposals for LHR expansion were assessed on the basis of monetized net benefits: total benefits expressed in financial terms less total costs. The Department for Transport estimated that the monetized net benefit of a third runway and a new terminal from around 2020 is £5.5 billion at 2006 prices.

Criticisms of this cost-benefit analysis were identified as two broad categories:

1. The monetized analysis does not account for various factors. On the costs side, the calculations do not consider the value of lost greenfield and agricultural land, or the community severance implications of the loss of the village of Sipson. Conversely, the calculations also fail to take into account the advantages of potential reductions in flight delays and wider economic benefits through improved productivity and competitiveness as identified in the Eddington Report (Eddington, 2006).
2. The cost-benefit analysis can be criticized on the basis of the estimates and assumptions used by the DfT. Prominent among these are complex models of air passenger demand and greenhouse gas emissions.

It is also important to bear in mind that DfT cost-benefit analysis does not consider the net benefits or costs of alternative potential infrastructure schemes. For example, the investment required for LHR expansion might be spent on a new airport in the Thames estuary, a high-speed rail scheme, or indeed a hospital. Such schemes may also have positive net benefits if considered independently. Understanding the choice between desirable but mutually exclusive results uses the concept of this 'opportunity cost'. In the context of this analysis, it means that projecting a net benefit from LHR expansion does not necessarily imply it is the most efficient allocation of resources.

Table 11.3 Cost-benefit analysis calculations: third runway and sixth terminal from 2020

	Included		Key factors not included
Benefits	Passenger benefits	£9.3bn	Wider economic benefits
	Airport operator	£6.2bn	Reduced delays
	Government (Air Passenger Duty)	£3.7bn	Greater airport resilience
	Air freight users	£0.0bn	
	Total monetized benefits	**£19.2bn**	
Costs	Infrastructure costs	£7.8bn	Landscape and townscape
	Greenhouse gases	£5.4bn	Historic environment
	Noise	£0.3bn	Biodiversity
	Local air quality	£0.1bn	Community severance
	Accidents	£0.0bn	Road congestion and noise
	Total monetized costs	**£13.7bn**	
Net monetized benefit		**£5.5bn**	

Source: DfT, *Adding Capacity at Heathrow Airport: Impact Assessment*, January 2009.

In addition, the impacts of LHR expansion will not be even. Some groups will benefit disproportionately, while others will be negatively affected. Differing opinions of the relative importance of each group will result in differing assessments of the merits of the proposals. Table 11.3 summarizes the components of this figure, together with noting other potential costs and benefits that were not monetized:

Summary

If those who gain from a property development can *in principle* fully compensate those who lose then a potential Pareto improvement has occurred. In the public sector, cost-benefit analysis may be used to determine whether a development will lead to a potential Pareto improvement. In a CBA it is necessary to:

- List all relevant items – including externalities;
- Value expected benefits and costs;
- Discount future flows of benefits and costs using an appropriate rate of discount;
- Assess the Net Present Value of the development – if it is positive then there is potential Pareto improvement.

Difficulties arise at each stage of the CBA and especially in the choice of discount rate (which is often based on market rates of interest by default). Nevertheless, CBA provides a rational technique for appraising developments where market information is lacking.

Chapter 11: review questions

1. Give a property sector example of a potential Pareto improvement.
2. Explain how a cost-benefit analysis is undertaken.
3. Explain the concepts of *consumers' surplus* and *producers' surplus*.
4. Why is it that market prices are not available for certain goods and services?
5. Explain how using a lower rate of discount in the public sector than in the private sector can lead to problems.

12

The Economics of
Planning Regulation

After studying this chapter you will be able to:

- Explain why private sector development may not be socially optimal;
- Show how bargaining between affected parties can, in certain circumstances, resolve externality problems;
- Explain why government intervention, in the form of planning regulation, may be necessary;
- Show how the planning system impacts on the workings of the real estate market in a wide variety of ways;
- Describe the planning procedure;
- Explain the economic impact of planning regulation.

The rationale for planning regulation

The market economy, reflecting numerous individual economic decisions, is not only capable of allocating land among competing uses but, as we have seen with development, does, *given certain conditions*, achieve maximum efficiency, both in the use to which a site is put and the type of building erected. The key phrase, however, is 'given certain conditions' which do not always exist. Markets in real estate are rarely perfectly competitive and there are external factors which distort their operation. Mistaken signals are then sent to market agents creating continuing disequilibrium between supply and demand for land and property. This explains the volatility of the development process which causes new buildings to be under-produced during long periods of recession but to be overproduced during short periods of boom (Adams, 1994). Market failure occurs because land has characteristics of social or community goods although it is owned and traded as a private commodity. Negative externalities such as detrimental effects on a piece of land from an adjacent piece of land are common. Private real estate markets are unable to take account of social costs and benefits, such as congestion costs, where there is over-intensive development or benefits to households from the improvement of neighbouring properties. Developers seek to maximize their profits without taking account of consequent social costs (for example, by intensive development that lacks social or 'green' space). Furthermore, buildings are long-lasting but developers require a return within a relatively short space of time; so costs and benefits over the longer period are substantially discounted in conventional methods of development appraisal. As a result of these issues, the price system may not achieve full efficiency in the allocation of resources. It is appropriate, therefore, if we examine the part played by planning regulation as a means of promoting equity, efficiency and sustainability and in dealing with defects in the market economy.

Dealing with externalities

In the pure market economy, resource allocation is the result of the decisions of consumers and producers who seek to maximize the difference between benefits and incurred costs. We refer to these as *private benefits* and *private costs*.

However, there may be benefits and costs – externalities – additional to those which are the immediate concern of the parties to a transaction and which are not provided for directly in the market price. These benefits or costs *spill over* onto others not directly involved. A firm may decide to build a new factory on a derelict site in a depressed district. In doing so it confers external benefits – tidying up the site and reducing the cost of government unemployment benefit payments. On the other hand, should the factory be built in a predominantly residential district, it would incur external costs of heavy vehicle movement, noise, loss of visual beauty and so on. The full *social benefits (costs)* are, therefore: private benefits (or costs) plus external benefits (or costs). Thus if an economically efficient allocation of resources is to be achieved, externalities, provided they are not too trivial, must be allowed for.

Since the spatial characteristic of land in particular gives rise to considerable 'spillover' costs and benefits, it is appropriate if, before considering planning controls, we examine the nature of these 'externalities' and how they might be dealt with. To simplify, it is realistic to assume that, because the initiators are unable to collect payments from beneficiaries or the sufferers to extract compensation for the extra costs imposed on them, externalities are ignored by private decision makers. This gives rise to a divergence between private net product and social net product.

In Figure 12.1, it is assumed that: (a) there are no external benefits; (b) the price of a house received by a developer is constant, that is, marginal revenue (MR) = marginal private benefit (MPB) = marginal social benefit (MSB) and; (c) the marginal cost (MC) of building a house rises with increased density. On private benefit/

Box 12.1 External benefits of housing improvements

When an individual household spends time and money on house improvements, there may be benefits for other houses in the area. If the improvement makes the general area seem tidier and less run-down, then other households in the vicinity benefit from a positive externality. If several households make improvements the area may be considerably improved and all property values could increase. Of course, this issue could suffer from the problem of 'free riders' – some households doing nothing but still benefiting from the uplift in property values. The benefits of the improvement to the area are non-excludable and if enough households acted as free riders then the improvement would not materialize.

In order to try to encourage the households in the area to engage in individual and, therefore, general improvement, the government or local authority could provide improvement grants in run-down areas. This will be Pareto optimal if the private and social benefits are greater than the private costs to the residents plus the cost of the grants. There is evidence to suggest that subsidizing housing investments produces significant and sustainable external benefits to urban neighbourhoods, and of course, they can be used to reduce the external costs of inadequate housing (health and social problems and so on).

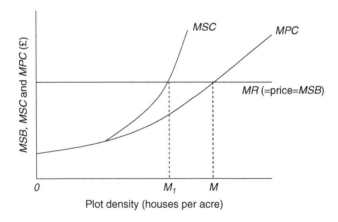

Figure 12.1 External costs and plot density

costs considerations alone, houses would be built to a plot density of M. But more intensive development gives loss of open space and so on. MSC, therefore, exceeds MPC. Plot density should therefore be limited to M_1, in order to achieve optimal development where $MSB = MSC$ (equalizing social benefits and social costs).

A divergence between MSC and MPC merely shows that a problem exists. Further information (using, for example, the techniques of cost-benefit analysis) is required to provide a solution to the problem. That solution can take a variety of forms from public ownership of the activity giving rise to externalities to relatively minor private arrangements, such as the provision of nesting boxes in woodland close to where birds have been disturbed by development.

Where people live in close proximity, some spillover costs are inevitable. Thus town-dwellers limit the open space available to one another and suffer a continuous hum of traffic noise. But people live in towns because of the advantages conferred and these include external benefits, such as agglomeration economies and such benefits of town-life have to be set against the costs. Nor should it be assumed that the price system completely fails to respond to externalities. Consequently, one property developer has responded to *environmental pressures* by providing a barn owl tower in a new office building to house the birds which were previously on the site (Harvey and Jowsey, 2004).

Often externalities are reflected in the market price, so people will pay more for a house in a neighbourhood which has good schools, open spaces, shopping facilities, golf courses and road and rail communications. On the other hand, shops where traffic congestion is a serious problem will command a lower rent because trade will be adversely affected. Similarly with office rents: the necessity of having to pay employees an extra 'London allowance' to offset higher housing and travelling costs makes labour more expensive and induces some firms to seek an alternative location.

Externalities can also be 'internalized' by *private arrangements*: a developer will attract shops to a shopping centre by making prior agreements with key retailers, and arrangements are made to concentrate small firms on industrial estates where they have some mutual interdependence. With residential estates, houses and flats may be sold subject to leases or convenants in order to secure external benefits (such as a satisfactory standard of upkeep, garden maintenance, and so on) or to avoid external costs (for example, excessive noise, car-parking nuisance and so on).

Taking this a stage further, persons adversely affected by a new road proposal, such as routeing the M3 through Twyford Down, Winchester, may subscribe to a *pressure group* to oppose the scheme. More pervasively, some form of private trust, such as the Royal Society for the Protection of Birds or the Woodland Trust, may be established to deal with a general environmental externality.

In practice, neither the market nor private arrangements are likely to be adequate in dealing with externalities. With the price system, there may be heavy frictional costs before a new equilibrium pattern of land values is established. How much congestion has to be suffered, for instance, while the price system solution is attained? Again, passively leaving the price system to deal with externalities may produce an inferior net social product (see below).

Similarly, private arrangements encounter obstacles. Not only may the costs be exorbitant relative to the benefits to be shared, but where 'free riders' cannot be excluded, it may be impossible to organize sufficient collective bargaining

---

Box 12.2 Market provision for externalities by private negotiation

Ronald Coase, a British economist developed the Coase Theorem which suggests that:

> If the two parties to an externality – the sufferer and the perpetrator – can bargain together with zero transaction costs, they will produce efficient use of resources. If either party has a property right (it does not matter which of them) then they can force the other to bargain (Coase, 1960).

This can be seen more easily by example and Tim Harford provides a simple one in *The Undercover Economist*. If my neighbour's tree is damaging my property (perhaps causing subsidence to my house), then if it really bothers me I can pay him to let me cut it down. If she refuses the amount I am willing to offer, then it is reasonable to assume that she values its presence more than I am willing to pay to get rid of the problem. On the other hand I may have a legal right to insist it is cut down because of the damage it is causing. In this case my neighbour can pay me not to enforce my right and I can use the money to underpin the foundations of my house. In either case the tree survives if it is worth more to my neighbour, and is cut down if the problems it is causing are worth more to me. In this case the externality is not really external to the market, because if bargaining can easily take place it is, in fact, brought into the market (Harford, 2006).

---

strength to negotiate effectively. In any case, costs (or benefits) are often so far ranging – for example, the detrimental effects of exhaust fumes – that not all the losers (or beneficiaries) can be identified. Finally, uncertainty and selfishness may prevent a satisfactory solution by private action. However, where the individuals concerned have an identical interest on a specific issue, it is possible to arrive at an acceptable arrangement: owners of the fishing rights on the Hampshire chalk-streams mutually agree to confine weed-cutting to three specified weeks during the fishing season (Harvey and Jowsey, 2004).

Because there are a variety of methods by which externalities can be allowed for in the allocation of land resources, the government can choose according to the particular case. First, it may introduce a pricing system to bring externalities into the reckoning. For example, to deal with congestion, parking meters may be installed, with even local residents charged for reserved parking permits.

Second, taxation and subsidies may take the idea of 'charging' a stage further. Thus it is suggested that prolonged roadworks by gas and water services, which cause serious traffic delays, should be deterred by taxation. In addition, the rating of empty houses can be regarded as a tax imposed to offset the external costs resulting from homelessness and the overall shortage of accommodation. On the other hand, external benefits may be allowed for by subsidies. Government help towards slum clearance and housing falls under this heading (although alternatively it could be regarded as offsetting external costs). Other examples are the contributions and tax concessions made towards the costs of repairing ancient monuments and listed buildings and the sheep subsidies given to hill farmers in order to preserve the fell environment. In both cases, because private costs of upkeep exceed private benefits, rapid deterioration would otherwise result.

Third, externalities may be 'internalized' by the parties concerned combining or by widening the area of control. The National Trust, for instance, harmonizes the interest both of farmers and walkers in order to secure maximum benefits from its Lake District properties.

Fourth, the government may itself assume responsibility for providing certain goods and services. This is usual when externalities are: (a) of national importance, for example, the Environment Agency can coordinate drainage, water supply and angling interests in order to maximize net benefits; (b) so extensive that only government authority can adequately allow for them – for example, providing a major airport; (c) cumulative, for instance, a slum area. Therefore, if left to private enterprise, the clearance of a slum would take place in year P (Figure 12.2). However, a local authority could allow for the external benefits of such complete rebuilding – better health, less juvenile delinquency, an improved road layout and so on. The capital value of such benefits would be added to the private enterprise's value of the best use, moving the cleared site value curve from CC to CC^1 and thus bringing redevelopment forward to year L.

Fifth – and frequently in the subject of land resources – one function of planning regulations is to control externalities through the separation of incompatible land uses: most evident are the consents required by law, currently the Town and Country Planning Act 1990. The defects of the price mechanism may be offset by the government intervening in the market by adjusting its own supply and demand (for instance, by stockpiling agricultural produce and basic materials, locating its own offices in Development Areas,

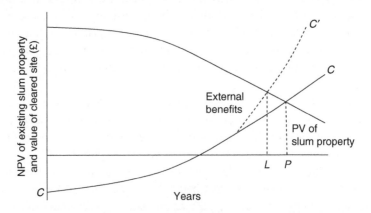

Figure 12.2   Allowing for externalities in slum clearance

or placing orders with firms in areas of high unemployment). Government can also tax or subsidize certain activities (for example, imposing a higher rate poundage on commercial and industrial buildings than on dwellings; subsidizing agriculture through rate relief) or make regulations on a general basis (such as rent control; general building and fire precaution regulations). Why, therefore, should it interfere by planning control, which is basically on a case-by-case assessment?

The first reason is that a centrally determined rate of tax would be general in its application and might not be appropriate for particular cases. Thus the external costs of a proposed development – such as extracting minerals in an area of outstanding natural beauty – may in total be so great that any tax imposed ought to be so high as to prevent such a project from being economically viable. But is it certain that this would happen? It is possible that the rate of tax decided centrally on an average basis would be so low as to enable the mineral extraction to proceed. In this particular case, therefore, the rule that an activity should proceed to the point where marginal social benefit equals marginal social cost would be breached. The difficulty is that the external costs incurred can vary in magnitude from one beauty spot to another for each differs in character and in the number of visitors it attracts. Taxation, however, would be applied to all on the same basis, perhaps even preventing mineral extraction where the beauty spot was of no outstanding quality and so remote that it was hardly likely ever to attract many visitors.

Similar criticisms apply to minimum standard regulations, such as room height, window space, ventilation and safety precautions. Not only do the minimum requirements tend to become the accepted normal standard of provision, but being decided centrally they impose rigidity. With buildings, there must be flexibility to cover individual cases – for instance, a historic building where special features have to be preserved. Indeed, because all developments tend to be heterogeneous in character there is much to be said for controlling on a case-by-case basis rather than by general regulation.

Moreover, when granting planning permission, the local authority can impose special conditions covering the provision of public services, such as access roads and open spaces, a community centre, low-income housing units and so on. Obviously the extent of such possible 'planning gain' through 'section 106' agreements varies from project to project. Planning on a case-by-case basis permits flexibility in the conditions imposed (see pp. 276–8, 465–9).

Finally, while some distributive effects are often inherent even in planning decisions (for example, countryside recreation facilities involving high transport costs benefit the rich more than the poor), intervention by taxation would be far more favourable to the rich, since they are in a better position to pay in order to proceed with a scheme.

For all of the reasons given above, there is justification for planning intervention at local level.

The planning procedure

Current planning legislation for England and Wales is consolidated in the Town and Country Planning Act of 1990. Three further planning-related acts are associated with this principal Act. These four acts are defined as the Planning Acts. Parts of these Acts have been replaced or amended by the provisions of the Planning and Compulsory Purchase Act of 2004. The basic planning law of Northern Ireland is contained in the Planning (Northern Ireland) Order 1991. The relevant Act for Scotland is the Town and Country Planning (Scotland) Act, 1997.

Putting planning controls in place is accomplished in four main stages.

1. *Planning Policy Guidance* notes (PPG) and Planning Policy Statements (PPS) are issued periodically by the Department for Communities and Local Government (DCLG) to indicate important principles which should guide local authorities when they are considering planning applications. They are revised about every 4 years to reflect any change in current government thinking. Examples are PPG 6, proposing the limitation of new out-of-town shopping developments in order to preserve the vitality of town centres, and PPG 13, emphasizing the need to curtail road traffic movements in order to reduce global warming through carbon dioxide emissions.
2. Appeals against a planning decision in England are to the DCLG. They can be by:
   - written statements from both sides where a planning inspector decides after visiting the site;
   - a public enquiry before an inspector, where witnesses can be called and cross-examined;
   - for a major development, appeals are usually 'called in' by the Secretary of State for his own decision.
3. A *structure plan* is drawn up by the county council. This envisages the broad lines of development by designating zones for different types of use. To be successful, a structure plan requires a preliminary *economic study* to assess the area's potential growth, the feasibility of alternative growth strategies, and the extent to which specific projects would be commercially viable within the overall plan. In short, such an economic appraisal at local level provides an objective basis for the physical redevelopment of the area, ensuring that environmental plans relate to an authority's real opportunities and not simply to its subjective development ambitions. To allow for changes in government policy, the structure of local industry, improvements in the road network and technological advances in transport and construction, a structure plan must be reviewed on a rolling basis at regular intervals of about 7 years.
4. A *local development plan*, prepared by the district council, sets out more detailed policies to guide development in its area. In metropolitan areas,

councils produce unitary development plans which combine the functions of structure and local plans. Before any plan is adopted, local people can make representations of objections, usually at a local enquiry.

5. *Planning consent* for a specific development which the developer has to obtain from the local planning authority – the district council – before he can proceed. In contrast to structure plans and building regulations which represent control by general regulation, planning consents are made on a case-by-case basis, though decisions are normally required to conform to the structure plan.

Specific planning issues

Many developers are inclined to view planning controls as being negative, imposing frustrating conditions on their well-researched schemes. But, from the point of view of the community as a whole, planning controls can obtain positive benefits (subject to the condition that these exceed the administrative costs involved in applying them). Such benefits include the following:

Improved knowledge

Decisions influencing the allocation of land resources through the market may be based on inadequate knowledge. At times, it can be argued, people may not be the best judges of their own welfare. For instance, their preferences expressed through the market might make inadequate provision for open space, such as parks and playing fields. Through planning, a paternalistic policy allocates land to such uses. On the other hand, permission to build on cheap land near a motorway may be refused because the authorities consider that prospective purchasers of houses would underestimate the noise nuisance.

In addition, in their present utilization of land resources, individuals might make insufficient allowance for future needs. Governments, however, because they take into account the needs of society, have a longer time-horizon. Therefore, they take measures to preserve buildings which have special architectural or historic interest and designate green belt land around towns. This may be necessary to safeguard amenity land for unborn generations, but it could also increase land values in the present. In Figure 12.3, original land values, shown by the curve *LV*, decrease regularly from the city centre outwards. With the introduction of the green belt, the land value curve shifts to LV^1, showing that the fall in the average value of land in the green belt is more than compensated by the rise in values elsewhere – even in the city centre – since accessibility to recreation and amenity land is now guaranteed. Thus houses adjacent to the green belt command a premium in their price representing this capitalized accessibility value, and this is recognized by the owners who resist any relaxation of green belt controls.

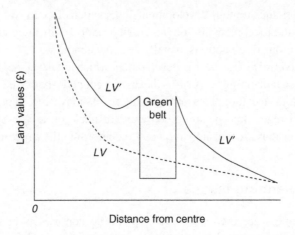

Figure 12.3   The effect on land values of the designation of a green belt

---

Box 12.3   Green belts in the UK

The first green belt was defined by the London County Council in the Greater London Plan of 1944. Soon after, the Town and Country Planning Act 1947 led to the designation of a green belt by the councils around London. It has proved the most popular and successful regional planning policy of post-war Britain.

The green belt soon proved to be very effective in limiting the extent of development. So much so that, in 1955, the Government published a Circular (No 42/55) setting out the purposes of the green belt and encouraging other cities to follow London's example and consider establishing a green belt. The basic objectives of green belt policy have remained unchanged since that time.

The current Government stance on green belts is set out primarily in PPG2. This points out that the Government attaches great importance to green belts, the purposes of which are

- to check the unrestricted sprawl of large built-up areas;
- to assist in safeguarding the countryside from encroachment;
- to prevent neighbouring towns from merging into one another;
- to preserve the setting and special character of historic towns; and
- to assist in urban regeneration by encouraging the recycling of derelict and other urban land.

The PPG states that the use of land in green belts has a positive role to play in:

- providing opportunities for access to open countryside for the urban population;
- providing opportunities for outdoor sport and outdoor recreation near urban areas;
- retaining attractive landscapes, and enhancing landscapes near to where people live;
- improving damaged and derelict land around towns;
- securing nature conservation interests; and
- retaining land in agricultural, forestry and related uses.

Inaccurate forecasts of future demand may also affect the efficient alloca-tion of land resources. For example, in building on a particular site, the devel-oper has a restricted time-horizon. But some consideration should be given to the extent to which demand is likely to grow in the future through population expansion or a rise in incomes. If, in fact, he underestimates future demand, the site will not be developed intensively enough; if he overestimates, it may be difficult to let units at an economic rent. The better information available to planners may avoid such mistakes: for example, through a policy of density control. Similarly, with shopping-space, planning controls may be necessary to prevent too much being provided.

Imperfect knowledge may take the form of having to make decisions without being able to ascertain the investment plans of competitors. This can result in over-supply by the industry concerned and the inability to sell at the expected price. We can illustrate by office development in a city area. In Figure 12.4, D, D_1 and D_2 represent the demand curves for offices at different time periods, and S the long-period supply curve. In period 1, demand increases from D to D_1 but, because it takes some time for supply to expand to OM_1 the number of offices remains fixed at OM. Competition, therefore, leads to higher rents which rise to OP_1. Office developers respond to this higher price, starting to build offices irrespective of the fact that others are doing likewise. When all their build-ing programmes have been completed supply has increased to OM_2. In order to clear the market, price has to fall to OP_2 unless demand increases to D_2 or inferior office accommodation is taken off the market. Here again planning can impose a scheme which coordinates the proposals of separate developers.

Uncertainty arising from imperfect knowledge of the intentions of others in a similar position can affect decisions on land use. This can be explained in terms of 'the prisoner's dilemma'. The police suggest to prisoner **A** that, in return for

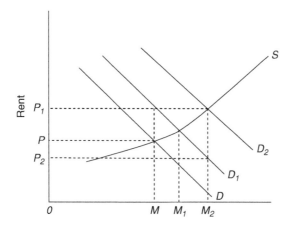

Figure 12.4 The effect of time lags in the supply of offices

confessing and implicating his accomplice **B**, they will do their best to ensure that **A**'s sentence is limited to 1 year's imprisonment, although **B** will get five. However prisoner **A** senses that the police do not have a strong case and that, if neither confesses, there is a chance that they will both be acquitted. He has no means of communicating with **B**, and so his problem is to assess how **B** is likely to react to the same offer. Will he remain silent, relying on **A** to do likewise in order to give them both a good chance of going free? Or will he act selfishly and settle for 1 year, leaving **A** to do 5 years? (The equilibrium solution for this dilemma is the noncooperative one where each prisoner confesses, because no matter what the other decides to do, each prisoner's best individual strategy is to confess). This situation of the prisoner's dilemma can be related to an owner's decision on whether to improve his property in a run-down inner-city area. One owner is contemplating spending £20,000 on improving his property. If the owners of adjacent properties do likewise, there is a beneficial spin-off because the value of all properties would each increase, say by £30,000. On the other hand, if fellow owners fail to renovate their properties, the first owner's expenditure could be largely wasted in terms of adding to the value of his property, since it may eventually have to be demolished. Although the planning authority also does not have knowledge of owners' intentions, it can create greater certainty by policy action – announcing a definite plan to renovate the whole area. This would stimulate owners to improve independently, secure in the knowledge that those who failed to do so would be brought into line.

Finally, it should also be noted that plans for future road developments and general regulations covering structure plans, zoning and building requirements all serve to eliminate much uncertainty, thus providing a framework within which developers can formulate their particular schemes.

Allowance for externalities

The activities of individuals or groups may give rise to spillover benefits or costs to others. As shown earlier, in certain circumstances, externalities may be dealt with by 'internalization' or agreement, or through the market mechanism. But where the total effect of the externality is important but spread so thinly that persons affected cannot be identified for purposes of coordinated action, state intervention is necessary. Those conditions apply in particular to land use. The type of building erected and the use to which it is put affect the welfare not only of neighbours but also of passersby. Thus both the design of the building and its use are subject to public intervention through planning control.

In practice such control tends to concentrate on dealing with undesirable external effects, noise, smoke and congestion. *Zoning*, for instance, restricts land in certain parts of an urban area to a particular use. In doing so, it seeks to eliminate competitive uses of adjacent land, such as factories in residential areas or urban sprawl into the rural countryside. Planning decisions can also prevent the erection of buildings which do not harmonize with their surroundings resulting in a loss of variety in shopping centres or employment outlets.

But planning can also be positive, arranging complementary uses – for example, siting dwellings, schools, shopping facilities, car parks and bus termini in strategic proximity, or encouraging the preservation of a listed building by granting an acceptable change of use.

Dealing with imperfect competition

Local authority planning backed by powers of compulsory purchase provides an overriding authority when the owner of a particular site stands in the way of a comprehensive development. Indeed, once the need for planning has been established, the logical step of allowing the planning authority to exercise powers of compulsory purchase makes coercion more acceptable since the authority has to give reasons. Similarly, the privatized utilities enjoy compulsory purchase powers under their own Acts to acquire private land or rights over it.

Planning powers may also be used to deal with underdevelopment of a site. For instance, the owner of a vacant half-hectare site in a built area may find it more profitable to restrict building to three executive town houses (*OA*, Figure 12.5), whereas the need of the district is for a more intensive development of smaller houses, a development which would result if building were pursued to the perfect competition position *OB* where price equals marginal social cost.

Provision of public and collective goods

The deficiencies of the market in supplying public and collective goods were examined earlier in this chapter. Since the provision of these goods, such as roads,

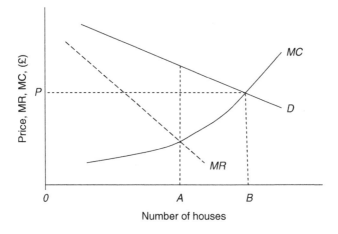

Figure 12.5   Restriction of the supply of houses on a given site by a monopolist owner

bridges, car parks and national parks, must be the responsibility of the state, and because they cover large areas or have location significance, some central planning is inevitable. Indeed, this is all the more essential as there is often a near-irreversibility about land use, either on account of the cost of replacing a building, or the difficulty of unifying the different interests involved. Can we imagine, for instance, Hyde Park being created from an area covered by buildings?

Infrastructure services such as parks, sewerage, schools and water supply, also have to be integrated into a land-use plan for the area.

An overall planning authority has further advantages for dealing with the infrastructure aspects of land use. For example, if a private firm is entirely responsible for a development, it is restricted to working within the existing road scheme, the pattern of which was probably established before the coming of motor transport. In this way the road layout remains configured in an inefficient form. In contrast, cooperation between the private developer and a local authority having planning powers would allow the road system to be altered to meet the needs of modern transport and the environment generally.

Improving the mobility of resources

For various reasons resources may be sluggish in responding to changes in demand or supply as indicated by the market. For instance, an increase in industrial activity in a given area may make it difficult to obtain extra labour because of a shortage of suitable housing in the district. Here the planning authority can help by ensuring that development proceeds in a balanced way, with housing being provided alongside permissions for new factory buildings.

Similarly in a depressed area labour may not wish to move because of social ties. The latter should be recognized by the planners as a benefit to be considered through the provision of an up-to-date infrastructure in the area and by making sites available to small firms.

The redistribution of income

Income redistribution is a political decision rather than an economic one, but problems of income distribution may be inherent in planning decisions. For instance, a householder who sells a part of his garden for development does so because there is a net benefit to him, but, because his action imposes uncompensated costs on his neighbours, they suffer a loss of welfare. Thus while the planning authority may consent to a development on environmental grounds, there can be distributional implications and they may give these some weight.

Indeed planning may go further, redistributing income as an active policy. For example, while there may be economic grounds for earmarking dwellings for essential workers in city centres where the price of land is high, it also allows the poorer members of the community to occupy dwellings at a lower rent than would be established in a free market. More recently, planning control has been relaxed for building 'affordable housing' in rural areas. Furthermore, planning decisions may redistribute income in favour of future generations – for example, by providing land for parks and recreation, preserving green belts and protecting historic buildings.

Delivering sustainable development

The planning system has considerable impact on quality of life – including the size of homes people can afford, the nature of their environment, the employment opportunities and amount of open countryside available to them. The planning system broadly aims to deliver a range of outcomes to help deliver sustainable development (Barker, 2006):

- Economic objectives – planning can provide greater certainty for investors about the likely shape of future developments in a locality or region; it can help deliver public goods such as transport infrastructure; it can promote regional inward investment by supporting regeneration and enabling comprehensive redevelopment where the landowner has monopoly power, for example by compulsory purchase orders.
- Social objectives – positive planning can also help deliver important social objectives, including protecting the vitality of town centres, providing new housing, aiding regeneration, and protecting our historic built environment, in part, via the listing of 370,000 buildings. Planning authorities can play a positive role in shaping our towns and cities through, for example, urban design coding.
- Environmental objectives – there are benefits to the environment more widely, through protecting and enhancing the countryside and natural environment, minimizing the effects of, or influencing the location of, developments that create noise, pollution or congestion and using mitigation measures to limit the flood risk potentially associated with new developments in certain areas.

Criticisms of planning regulation

Compared with taxation (where this is possible), planning lacks flexibility for individual preferences. This applies particularly to zoning through structure plans. For instance, married, female, part-time workers might be excluded from employment by transport costs and the time taken in travelling to a factory in an industrial zone. Thus a firm classified as 'industrial' and relying heavily on such labour might be prepared to pay additional rent (including a tax) for a site convenient for its employees, and this would be justifiable if the extra benefits to the firm exceeded the costs. Moreover, structure plans may impose rigidity since the highest and best use of a land resource can alter over time with income changes and transport developments.

In addition, planning may take insufficient account of certain benefits which exist in the current land-use situation. Thus, in the past, structure plans dealing with the environmental problems of inner-city areas by complete rebuilding have not fully allowed for the loss of job opportunities in small firms which existed through low rents, the higher cost of travelling to work, the extra cost and inconvenience of obtaining odd-job services, the destruction of social contacts, the loss of community spirit and the elimination of variety – for example, in employment, shops and architecture.

Planning also tends to overlook certain repercussions of the controls imposed. For instance, low-density housing requirements may mean that building for the poorer members of the community is confined to those parcels of land available for high-density development, with the result that its price per acre exceeds that of land for rich people's housing. Similarly design guides, such as the old Parker-Morris standards (which specified minimum space standards for new homes in 1961), impose an additional strain on maintaining the stock of second-hand dwellings. Secondary effects also occur when commercial developments are restricted in intensity (for instance, by plot ratios) in order to limit congestion. In practice, the reactions of firms may actually increase movement: for instance, storage may be decentralized but the space vacated occupied by employees, while extra vehicles are usually needed to maintain contact between decentralized offices and the centre. In addition, public transport has to overcome the difficulty of serving more scattered destinations.

Planning also tends to be negative in character. Thus, though it may prevent undesirable results, such as the despoliation of a beauty spot or excessive urban sprawl, planning controls in themselves do not lead to market forces initiating those schemes that the authorities would like to promote. For these, the lead may have to come from the local council which nevertheless must always bear in mind that innovative private developers may propose superior schemes.

It is inevitable that case-by-case examination of applications for planning permission leads to delays in arriving at a decision: delays, which are both frustrating and costly to the developer and wasteful in the use of land resources. Department of Communities and Local Government statistics show that 70 per cent of major planning applications are decided within thirteen weeks, but this Figure is weighted by applications which concern minor changes to large schemes such as erecting a porch or building a garage where the principle and the major issues of development are already established.

Although about 85 per cent of applications are given permission, there are still about 20,000 each year that go to appeal, with a 35 per cent success rate. Delays are more significant when the development is on a large site since alternative schemes have usually to be considered and objectors may force a public enquiry. The Heathrow Terminal 5 Enquiry lasted from May 1995 to March 1999!

While planning policies and processes aim to address market failures, there can also be costs associated with government intervention. Where information is imperfect, plans may under or over-provide for certain non-market goods, while the transaction costs of intervention may be high. There may also be unintended consequences of policy. The planning system, therefore, needs to ensure it tackles market failures in an efficient and effective manner (Barker, 2006). Finally, it must be remembered that the planning process itself uses up resources and so, like other activities, must only be undertaken to the point where the marginal benefit equals marginal cost. It is not therefore appropriate for dealing with only minor faults in the land and property markets.

The impact of planning regulation

There are two schools of thought on the impact of planning regulation: the planning view and the market view.

In the *planning view*, the planning system simply organizes but does not constrain the development of land. Variations in house and land prices are determined by variations in value in the market, not by artificially constrained land supply relative to demand. Additionally planning helps to generate stability over the building cycle by reducing uncertainties – sufficient land is allocated to ensure a 5-year housing land supply on the basis of calculations of need (from demographic projections). The quantity of land required to meet this need over a 5-year period is based on estimates of the rate at which developers will build new houses (by extrapolating from building rates in the recent past). These calculations are revised regularly and so can respond to changing market conditions without imposing unnecessary constraints.

In the *market view*, the planning system constrains what would otherwise be a reasonably responsive supply of land – directly by allocating insufficient land and indirectly by providing a framework in which oligopolistic landowners can reorganize development to increase their incomes from monopoly rents. Planning also increases risks by generating unnecessary time lags in development and by affecting expectations of future values. The costs of planning are seen to include those arising from direct controls, such as restrictions on the density of development and the size and types of houses which may be built, and from changes in the timing of development, which may make it unprofitable when it comes to market, resulting in fewer houses being built compared with a free-market situation (Monk and Whitehead, 1996).

The planning constraint has two effects:

- a greater density of housing development, higher prices, lower quality, less choice and more pressure on already developed areas meaning a reduction in external benefits compared with a free market;
- in the national economy, the land supply constraint leads to reduced labour mobility and inflexibility of supply, ultimately contributing to Britain's lack of competitiveness in world markets.

Planning regulation does increase the price of housing by affecting supply in different locations, by altering densities and the type and mix of houses (compared to market allocation) and by encouraging speculative behaviour leading to market volatility.

It is clear, however, that in the UK, planning regulation has been successful in preventing urban sprawl and in ensuring that less desirable urban land is used before green field sites can be developed. However, planning regulation contributes to a land supply constraint which raises costs, reduces labour mobility and affects production methods, contributing to Britain's uncompetitiveness in Europe and elsewhere (Muellbauer, 1990). Planning makes a difference to economic agents' behaviour and to their expectations but it does not completely replace the market, though it interacts with it.

Though planning seeks to improve the working of the price mechanism, it does have repercussions on the real estate market and on the local economy in the following ways.

The value of an individual site

This can be illustrated by considering how the value of a site is affected by the restriction of building density. In essence, such restriction limits the amount of capital which can be applied to a given site. Thus in Figure 12.6 the restriction of density to *OR* reduces the value of the site from *AIN* to *AIKL*.

The pattern of land values

Planning control – for instance, by zoning – alters the pattern of land values. For example, restricting the amount of land available for offices raises the value of existing office land and therefore of any land, which in the future is given planning consent for offices.

This is illustrated in Figure 12.7. In a free market the price of office land would be *OP*. Where planning controls restrict the supply to *OC*, the price would rise to *OP'*. But since another effect of control would be to free *CM* land for other uses, the price of land for such uses would be depressed.

Overall land values

Maximizing aggregate land values (but allowing for external benefits and costs) is an indication of the optimum use of scarce land resources. Rigid planning control ensures the separation of markets for different uses and this can result in virtually identical adjacent pieces of land selling for vastly different prices. The Uthwatt Committee (1942) considered that planning merely shifted land values from one site to another with no change in the aggregate value.

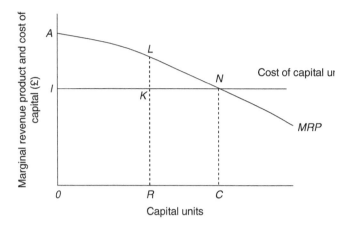

Figure 12.6 The effect of planning control on the value of an individual site

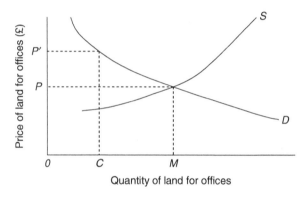

Figure 12.7 The effect of planning on the pattern of land values

But is this so? Suppose that in the redevelopment of a central urban area the town planner considered that more land should be devoted to workers' housing and less to offices and light industry. This means that the affected firms would have to develop elsewhere. But the efficiency of such firms could be impaired if, through moving, they lost important advantages of accessibility to customers and of complementarity with other firms. In such circumstances the increase in land values of the sites to which firms moved would be less than the loss of values in the centre of the town.

Furthermore, it may not be valid to assert that increased social benefits would compensate for the difference. Moving firms to other locations could result in the loss of job opportunities for those workers not wishing to travel longer distances (for example, housewives and part-time workers) and for those too old for retraining. Moreover, the firms that remain may have relied on complementary services from the firms that move, resulting in higher costs to them.

In such ways the value of land in the urban area could fall. Therefore, the town planner cannot assume that his decisions merely shift land values. They can affect aggregate value and hence allocative efficiency.

Distributional effects

Though planning is mainly concerned with the allocation of land resources, it has both direct and indirect distributional effects which may clash with the economic efficiency objective. For example, the owner of land who obtains planning consent for development receives a windfall gain. On the other hand, where a restrictive planning policy forces up the price of land, new purchasers – such as first-time house buyers – lose. Similarly, the grant of planning consent for a large supermarket could harm nearby shopkeepers.

Often the distributional effects are less direct. Where planning covers the provision of public goods – for example, transport developments, parks, schools, municipal golf courses – the tendency is for it to enhance the values of the better-class houses on the urban fringe. Similarly, a low-density plot ratio benefits the richer people who can afford a house with a large garden, while out-of-town hypermarkets or green belt recreation facilities are likely to be used more by people owning cars.

Supplementary effects

Attention has already been drawn to certain repercussions of planning decisions: loss of job opportunities in the city centre, the destruction of social contacts, higher costs of travel, delays which increase development costs. Other supplementary costs include:

1. the bureaucratic machine which has to administer planning;
2. the possibility of planning blight settling on an area subject to proposals; and
3. the growing practice of planning authorities to exact 'planning gain', even in the form of money payments, as a condition of granting consent (see below and Chapter 22).

Nor must we forget that, subject to appeal to the Secretary of State, planning is ultimately controlled at the local level by committees of politically motivated people.

Planning gain

Planning gain is the practice of local authorities to obtain some of the benefits of development for themselves by asking developers to contribute to local amenities or infrastructure in return for the granting of planning permission.

Section 106 (S106) of the Town and Country Planning Act 1990 allows a local planning authority (LPA) to enter into a legally binding agreement or planning obligation with a landowner in association with the granting of planning permission. The obligation is termed a Section 106 Agreement.

These agreements are a way of delivering or addressing matters that are necessary to make a development acceptable in planning terms. They are increasingly used to support the provision of services and infrastructure, such as highways, recreational facilities, education, health and affordable housing.

Matters agreed as part of a S106 must be:

- relevant to planning;
- necessary to make the proposed development acceptable in planning terms;
- directly related to the proposed development;
- fairly and reasonably related in scale and kind to the proposed development;
- reasonable in all other respects.

Some S106 agreements have attracted controversy, being seen as a bribe to authorities to allow development, for example, Oxford City Council's decision to grant planning consent for a leisure centre in exchange for £145,000 worth of road and bridge improvements and a £135,000 upgrade of a distant swimming pool; RJB Mining (the private successor to British Coal) offering to invest £300,000 in community projects in return for planning consent to strip mine a 400-acre site near Blythe in Northumberland and many superstore planning applications.

Whilst Department of the Environment guidelines limit planning gain to matters specifically and directly relating to the proposed development, this does not prevent abuses nor make planning gain deals illegal.

The UK government is putting increasing emphasis on providing affordable housing through the planning system. The aim is to ensure that land is made available, developers make a financial contribution and new housing is built within mixed communities. Ten per cent of total housing completions have been made affordable through S106 agreements and rural exceptions sites policies (about 12,000 units per year). Land availability for residential development is a major constraint to the policy, however, and many sites are too small to reach the threshold at which S106 comes into effect.

Most housing achieved through S106 is in high cost areas of the South East of England, particularly London, where it is likely to be social housing for rent, commonly separated from market housing on the site. By contrast, in the North and Midlands, S106 is used mainly to produce improved tenure and community mix through forms of low-cost home ownership (Crook et al., 2002).

Section 106 does not apply in Scotland and the future for planning gain in Scotland is unclear. As well as issues about the legal framework within which the planning gain system should operate there are significant issues in relation to the funding of planning gain (or developer contribution) packages as a result of the current financial climate. It is accepted in Scotland that the planning system is essential to achieving increased sustainable economic growth and planning agreements can have a limited but useful role to play in the development management process, where they can be used to overcome obstacles to the grant of planning permission.

Planning gain is a controversial subject and there is a more detailed discussion of it in Chapter 22 where it is considered as a substitute for a Development Land Tax.

Summary

Externalities are costs and benefits, which are not taken into consideration in market prices. It may be possible for such externalities to be accounted for by private bargaining arrangements. In most cases, however, it is necessary for governments to intervene in order to ensure that externalities are considered so that a socially optimal outcome is achieved and the planning system is one way in which a government does this.

Planning regulation can be used to cope with a variety of problems such as:

- the need to preserve land resources for future generations;
- urban sprawl;
- factories in inappropriate locations;
- monopoly ownership of land resources;
- provision of public and collective goods.

Among the criticisms of planning control are:

- lack of flexibility in zoning;
- not fully recognizing the benefits of current land use;
- delays in reaching decisions.

Chapter 12: review questions

1. What forms of government intervention are available to cope with externalities?
2. Why are planning regulations necessary?
3. Show, using a diagram, the impact of planning regulations on:
   a) land around a designated green belt;
   b) the value of an individual site for development;
   c) the pattern of land values.
4. Explain the main criticisms of control by planning.
5. Describe the UK planning procedure.

13

The Economics of the Construction Industry

After studying this chapter you will be able to:

- Assess the contribution of the construction industry to the UK economy;
- Assess the efficiency of the construction industry;
- Explain the structure of the UK construction industry;
- Suggest ways in which productivity can be increased in the construction industry;
- Analyse the latest developments in the construction industry.

The nature of the construction industry

In order to achieve consistency in national income calculations, industries are defined according to the Standard Industrial Classification. 'Construction' covers the erection, repair and demolition of all types of buildings and civil engineering structures. Specialist subcontracting finishing trades, such as asphalting, electrical wiring, flooring, plastering, roofing and plumbing are included, as well as the hiring of contractors' plant and scaffolding.

This definition recognizes that building and civil engineering projects, unlike most other industries, are split into the separate operations of design, production and assembly. Architects and surveyors working on their own account are classified as professional services. The manufacture of components and materials, such as bricks, cement, timber, doors and windows, comes under 'manufacturing', and quarrying gravel and sand under 'mining and quarrying'. Therefore, the definition confines the construction industry to the *assembly* process.

Consequently, the contribution of the construction industry to GNP is the value added to the inputs of materials and services from other industries. In 2008 this amounted to £109,716 or 7.57 per cent of GDP and in 2009 to £97,152 or 6.95 per cent of GDP (ONS, 2010). Sometimes, however, the full value of the output of construction firms is used and this includes the cost of materials and components. Such is the basis of measurement of Gross Fixed Capital Formation (expenditure on fixed assets), to which construction of buildings and dwellings contributed £129,716 million in 2008, 53 per cent of the total.

Since the construction industry is concerned mainly with the construction, adaptation and maintenance of buildings, its efficiency is vital to real property.

First, an increase in construction efficiency will tend to accelerate redevelopment, for it is now relatively cheaper to provide a replacement building (see Chapter 8). Second, greater efficiency in construction will lead to a higher proportion of capital being combined with land, as capital, in the form of buildings, is made cheaper relative to land. Therefore, if both factors are variable, capital is substituted for land. In other words, development is more intensive. This is shown in Figure 13.1; increased efficiency means that the price of capital falls from OR to $O'R$, shifting the budget line from RT to $R'T$. Consequently there is a movement to a higher isoquant and more capital, OC', and less land, OL', are employed, and more units are built for a given outlay. Where construction is on a fixed site, a better or higher building will be constructed (assuming no government planning or building limitations).

Greater construction efficiency raises the productivity of capital: in Figure 13.2 the MRP curve moves from MRP to MRP'. Since the price of capital (the rate of interest) does not change, the amount of capital applied to the site increases from OM to OM'.

Third, given no change in the overall demand for accommodation, greater intensity of development will tend to produce increased land values in the centre of the urban region compared with the periphery. In Figure 13.2 the rent that can be offered for a central site rises from AiC to $A'iC'$. In contrast, sites on

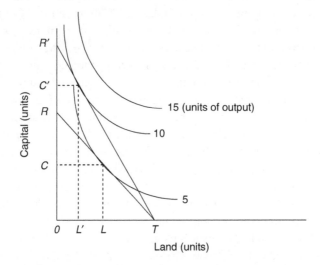

Figure 13.1 The effect of increased construction efficiency on the combination of capital and land in buildings

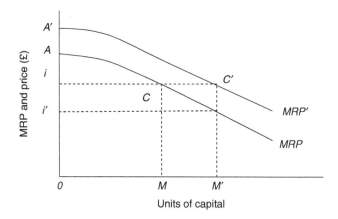

Figure 13.2 Greater construction efficiency raises the productivity of capital

the periphery (which are less capital-intensive) will benefit less from increased construction efficiency. This will be particularly true for office buildings, where high structures are more acceptable, than for shops and factories. Moreover, since with a given demand for accommodation a larger proportion of it will be satisfied by the higher buildings on central sites, the demand for peripheral sites will fall. In other words, the *MRP* curve of peripheral sites moves towards the origin, so that they are either developed less intensively in their current use or put to a lower alternative use.

Conditions of demand and supply in the construction industry

At first sight, certain aspects of the construction industry would appear to indicate inefficiency – cumbersome pricing procedures, a high preponderance of small firms, the distribution of materials through builders' merchants, a large proportion of casual labour resulting in a high level of unemployment, the comparatively small increase in output per worker over time, a low level of mechanization and a failure to adopt modern techniques of mass production.

While some criticism is justifiable, much results from a failure to appreciate the diverse activities of an industry which ranges from large international companies performing all types of work to small, local, repair and maintenance firms. A study of the conditions of demand and supply relating to the industry reveals that its organization is largely the response to economic factors. In other words, the critics are largely confusing technical efficiency with economic efficiency: they focus on the supply side, particularly in production methods, and tend to overlook the special aspects of demand.

There are some important features of *demand*:

1. Because of differences of site, surroundings and users' requirements, most buildings, apart from speculative housing, are 'bespoke', tailor-made to the client's *individual specification*. To a large extent this determines the method of pricing (see later) and reduces opportunities for standardization and thus of mass production.
2. Since buildings are durable, nearly one-half of the value of the output of the construction industry is on *repairs and maintenance* (see Table 13.1).
3. Because the products are mainly capital goods, they are expensive relative to income and are thus usually purchased through borrowed funds. Demand is, therefore, dependent upon the cost of *credit*. As a result, controlling inflation through the rate of interest hurts the construction industry in particular.
4. Demand is particularly subject to *seasonal and cyclical fluctuations*. It tends to be bunched in the spring and summer months. More serious, however, is the effect of periodic recessions since the industry accounts for one-half of Gross Domestic Fixed Capital Formation. As an investment good, industry construction is vulnerable to private-sector fluctuations in demand resulting from changes in expectations, a rise in the cost of borrowing or induced changes related to the level of income (the 'accelerator').
5. *Government policy* is a further cause of unstable demand. Changes in taxes and subsidies can affect the rate of redevelopment. Of far greater significance, however, are the effects of virtually using the construction industry as one of the 'regulators' of the economy. Approximately one-quarter of the work of the industry is for the public sector (see Table 13.2). Thus a

Table 13.1 Value of output in the construction industry Great Britain, 2008–9 (£million; constant 2005 prices, seasonally adjusted)

	Housing new work	Non-housing new work	Housing repair and maintenance	Non-housing repair and maintenance	Total output
2008	18336	44156	23677	23546	109716
2009 (provisional)	14192	40457	21501	21002	97152

Source: www.statistics.gov.uk.

Table 13.2 Value of construction new work Great Britain 2008–9 (£million at constant 2005 prices, seasonally adjusted)

	Public sector	Infrastructure	Private sector	All new work
2008	14129	7120	41243	62492
2009	17075	7811	29763	54649

cut in government spending bears heavily on the construction industry for the major impact is on capital projects such as new hospitals, roads, universities, local authority schools, housing, slum clearance and city-centre developments.

Several distinctive features of the construction industry are also evident on the *supply* side:

1. Not only is it an *assembly industry* but also its operations, like those of agriculture, are *consecutive*. In contrast, most manufacturing industries can carry out all their operations concurrently.
2. Instead of production taking place in a factory, it occurs on the *site* of the *finished* product. This gives rise to problems of protection from the weather, storing materials, moving labour and equipment and supervision of work.
3. For most jobs *the minimum technical unit is small*. Thus a traditional house can be built by two bricklayers, two bricklayers' labourers, two general labourers and a carpenter, with other tasks, such as plastering, electrical work and plumbing, being subcontracted. Even large jobs can be completed by a relatively small labour force by putting out the work to specialist firms, that is, by vertical disintegration.
4. *Labour costs* form a high proportion, between one-third and one-half, of total costs. Skilled labour accounts for just over two-thirds of total labour costs. Furthermore, although construction labour tends to be sheltered from international competition, the casual and cyclical nature of the work results in a high rate of unemployment. This is true even at the top of the boom, since there is often a time lag between the completion of one project and the start of another. As a result, unemployment in the construction industry forms a far higher percentage than unemployment of workers in general.
5. The time lag between the response of supply to a change in demand can be regarded as a built-in mechanism likely to produce short-term fluctuations in activity.
6. Because construction takes time and the final product is usually specific to the customer, the Housing Grants, Construction and Regeneration Act 1996 details the stage payments which must be included in the contract.

Pricing in the construction industry

The construction industry can be divided into two groups: (a) contractors; (b) speculative builders. The nature of pricing the project differs accordingly.

Contractors

Efficient pricing of a project would ensure that the requirements of the client are met at the lowest possible price. To achieve this, the building should be constructed by the most efficient firm at a price which just covers total costs. This implies competition between firms.

It is not easy to assess whether price is competitive. While the estimates of quantity surveyors and the experience of architects on similar projects may provide some guide, comparisons cannot be exact, since most projects are different. To achieve individual pricing on a competitive basis, various methods are used.

Tenders

The most common method is for firms to tender for the contract, the lowest tender, other things being equal, being successful. Certain points, however, should be noted.

1. Competitive conditions in pricing the product require that many firms tender.
2. In considering tenders, account must be taken of the proven efficiency of firms and normally the architect will advise. The ability to complete by a specified date is important. Moreover, under-pricing a project is not always to the advantage of the client. If the contractor runs into financial difficulties, delay results. Worse still, if another firm has to be engaged to complete, it may be in a strong position to exact a high price.
3. Unlike manufactures, construction firms working on a contract are in effect working to a fixed price for their product *before* production commences. Therefore, risk is incurred when tendering, for there is little possibility of adjusting the selling price (as in manufacturing) to cushion the effects of unforeseen difficulties.
4. Since the construction process can cover a number of years, any fixed-price contract is, in time of inflation, fraught with danger. This risk is usually covered by the insertion of a 'rise and fall' clause to guard against cost increases. However, to some extent this reduces the contractor's incentive to shop around for the lowest-priced materials.

Tendering may be on an open-list or a selected-list basis. With *open tender* the project is advertised and any firm which wishes to submit a tender can do so on the basis of the plans and bill of quantities supplied. This method ensures the greatest degree of competition. On the other hand, it does involve firms in unproductive work, as only about 20 per cent of tenders submitted are successful: a cost which is eventually reflected in the price of projects. *Selected-list tender* partly overcomes this defect. A few contractors whose past work has proved their competitiveness and capability are invited to tender. An additional advantage is that time is saved in awarding the contract so that work can start sooner. Provided new firms, especially those with more progressive methods, can be added to the list, and collusion between the fewer firms involved can be eliminated, the selected-list tender method still ensures competition.

Negotiated contract

Although tendering promotes competition, it relies largely on a separation of the design and construction processes. Yet a building may prove just as acceptable, functionally and aesthetically and be constructed at a lower price, when the design allows for the special techniques, skills and equipment of a particular contractor. Such coordination can be achieved through a negotiated contract. With this, a single contractor is chosen for a given project without competitive tendering, and he consults with the architect even at the design stage. Indeed, a negotiated contract may be the only form of pricing possible when the work involves processes that only the particular contractor can carry out. However, because the removal of competition could lead to a higher final price for the project (which can be on a fixed-sum, cost-plus or bonus basis), the selected contractor is usually chosen on the evidence of his previous tenders and work.

A development of the system of negotiating further contracts with a firm, which has proved satisfactory is *serial contracting*. Where other buildings of the same type are to be erected, there is a legal understanding that the firm will be given a series of contracts once the first has been completed successfully. This enables the firm to plan large-scale economies, and should therefore result in keener prices.

Package deal

Instead of appointing an architect, the client may go to a contractor offering an all-in comprehensive service from the design to the complete building at an inclusive figure. Therefore, the package deal is used mainly where a limited choice of design is acceptable – for example, for factories and farm buildings – but it may be extended to offices and local authority housing. The package deal enables the client to be certain of the initial capital cost of the building, and it usually results in greater speed of erection and lower costs. However, these may be partly offset if the client has to engage a specialist surveyor to advise him, or if he requires changes during construction, for then the contractor can largely dictate his own terms.

A variation of the package deal is the *design and construct* contract. The client's professional consultant prepares a brief of the buildings required, often with site layout plans. Each contractor then tenders on the basis of his own design and method of construction for that type of building.

Fee construction: management contracting

Certain contractors, such as Bovis, have introduced a 'fee-construction' arrangement. The contractor and client negotiate a fee for management services, the client covering the construction costs. This reduces the contractor's risks, but brings the client and contractor into a close relationship. Keeping costs to a minimum, however, depends upon the contractor's professional integrity and his hope of further business.

Speculative builders

Speculative builders resemble manufacturers in that they produce buildings, chiefly houses, in anticipation of demand. They are particularly active when demand is rising, and this is reflected in housing starts. The speculative builder's estimate of the selling price of the building will largely determine the bid price for the land. Since the building process takes time, the success of the venture will mainly depend upon the price originally paid for the land in competition with other builders. Rising house prices, with other costs fixed, will increase economic rent on the land, and thus super-normal profit. It must be remembered, however, that the volatility of house prices (often resulting from an unstable financial background) makes speculative building risky owing to the supply time lag. Consequently, many small builders undertake it as a supplement to their main contract work, working on their own speculative project as time allows.

Apart from the physical imperfections of the market, awarding contracts by competitive tender does promote competition, though past experience has revealed some collusion between contractors (see Box 13.1). With the negotiated contract and the package deal, imperfect knowledge and relative bargaining ability may influence the price.

Box 13.1 Collusive tendering

In September 2009, 103 UK construction companies were fined almost £130 million for illegally colluding in bids to secure building contracts including schools and hospitals. The biggest fines were: £17.9 million to Kier Group; £5.4 million to Carillion; and £5.2 million to Balfour Beatty. The Office of Fair Trading (OFT) conducted a 4-year investigation, uncovering about 4,000 tenders that were affected by anti-competitive activities. The firms involved effectively operated a 'cartel', having secretly agreed the prices they would submit during a tender process – a practice known as 'cover-pricing'. In its simplest form, companies that do not have the resources or spare capacity to take on a job but still want to remain on tender lists obtain an inflated price from a rival and submit it in the knowledge that their bid will not succeed. The companies involved had driven up the price of the projects by agreeing to submit artificially high quotes. In at least six cases the companies submitting high tenders were compensated for the cost of tendering. The tendering authority, often a local council, is given a false impression of the level of competition and could end up paying artificially high prices. Some estimates of the amounts overpaid were as much as 10 per cent but the OFT did not put a Figure on this.

Furthermore, it is necessary to emphasize that competitive prices will only prevail if, on the supply side, firms are of optimum size. This requires continuity of work, enabling them to operate at full capacity. It is the lack of such continuity which is one of the major causes of inefficiency in the construction industry.

The structure of the construction industry

Firms in the construction industry vary in size from the large civil engineering/building contractors, often undertaking such types of construction work as roads, bridges, office blocks, shopping centres and speculative housing estates, to one-man labour-only contractors such as bricklayers, plumbers, carpenters and jobbing maintenance firms.

Large construction firms can obtain the advantages of large-scale production. These include technical economies of specialized equipment and linked processes; commercial economies in buying materials; specialization in management, such as their own surveyors and legal experts; the ability to raise finance on cheaper terms; and the spread of risks through diversification into many products, including international contracts. For small or even medium-sized contractors, spreading risks is difficult since a single contract may account for a large proportion of their work.

Nevertheless, the small firm predominates, those with less than twenty-five workers (including the self-employed) covering 96.8 per cent of all firms (see Table 13.3). On the other hand, such small firms account in value for only 29 per cent of total work. Large construction firms with more than 600 employees are only 0.06 per cent of the total number of firms but they account for almost 25 per cent of the value of construction work done.

This predominance of the small firm is a feature of all industries, including manufacturing. However, it is much more marked in the construction industry, a phenomenon common to other developed economies. The reasons are to be found on both the demand and supply sides.

Table 13.3   The size and importance of private contractors in the construction industry, 2008

Size of firm	No of firms	% of total	Value of work (£m)	% of total
Fewer than 25 employees	195891	96.8	7768	28.9
25–114 employees	5631	2.8	6276	23.3
115–599 employees	766	0.38	6164	23.0
600+ employees	119	0.06	6672	24.8
Total	202407	100	26890	100

Demand in construction is characterized by the preponderance of relatively small contracts resulting from the individuality of the product (for example, the single house or extension where the minimum technical unit is small) and the importance of minor repair work. Above all, there are the fluctuations in demand, referred to earlier, which influence firms to remain small and flexible rather than burden themselves with disproportionately high overheads resulting from underutilized specialist equipment.

Supply factors in construction also favour small firms. Since production is on site rather than in a factory, the difficulties of supervision are greater. With a large firm carrying out work on many sites, the difficulties of management control are magnified. As a result, management diseconomies of scale may soon outweigh technical, commercial and other economies. Moreover, vertical disintegration in construction through the employment of specialist firms results from the consecutive nature of the operations and the lack of continuity of the work for specialized equipment. Therefore, we have comparatively small firms contracting for pile-driving foundations, roofing, electrical work, heating and ventilation systems, lift installation, and so on. Such subcontracting has advantages to the main contractor, for (apart from saving on overheads) it makes estimating easier and reduces on-site supervision. On the other hand, it can increase the problem of coordinating the various construction operations.

Finally, as with other types of production, small businesses exist because the owner is prepared to accept a lower return in order to be his own boss. Entry to the construction industry is fairly easy, as many jobs require little capital equipment or, if specialist tools and equipment are necessary, they can be obtained by hiring or subcontracting. Like most other businesses, however, builders find difficulty in obtaining capital to expand beyond a certain size, for their sources are, to all intents and purposes, limited to merchants' trade credit, personal savings, bank overdrafts and ploughed-back profit. Many small builders try to operate on too limited a cash flow, even though progress payments are received on an architect's certificate. Fluctuations in demand can prove financially crippling even for medium and large firms. Consequently, the rate of bankruptcies in the construction industry tends to be twice that of other industries.

Builders' merchants

The builders' merchant is the 'middleman' between the manufacturer of components and the builder. Few merchants now stock a full range of materials and components, and even the large chains hold only those products having a high turnover. Instead we find specialization: (i) stockists of heavy materials, such as bricks, breeze-blocks, cement, sand, aggregates, drain-pipes, and so on; (ii) merchants, including DIY stores such as Wickes and B&Q, handling components for the later construction stages, such as baths, washbasins and kitchen fittings, or for repair work, such as tiles, slates, guttering; (iii) specialist shops dealing in ironmongery, glass, electrical equipment, glazed tiles, door fittings and so on; (iv) local shops concerned mainly with finishing materials, such as wall coverings, paint, standard tiles and fittings, with their main customers being the 'DIY' enthusiasts.

Merchants also vary in size. There are regional chains, such as Jewson Builders Merchants Federation, and large merchants who often supply small merchants and retailers. But the specialist wholesalers and shops mentioned above tend to be small.

For builders' merchants, the cost of ordering, transporting, holding stocks and serving customers is high, for not only are materials and components bulky and often fragile, but many also have only a small turnover. Indeed, it has been estimated that an 18 per cent mark-up margin is required just to cover these costs. In addition, there are cash discounts and normal profit to be taken into consideration, so that the final mark-up on manufacturers' prices varies between 30 and 50 per cent.

Yet, in spite of such charges, builders' merchants continue to exist simply because they perform essential functions which result from the peculiar characteristics of the industry: the large number of small firms, the high proportion of repair work, the consecutive nature of the construction process, and the difficulty of storing materials on site. In short, they represent another form of vertical disintegration in the construction process.

The functions of the builders' merchant can be summarized as follows.

Economizing in distribution

Where orders are small and numerous, it is more economic for manufacturers to distribute centrally through a wholesaler. Thus delivering in bulk to a merchant economizes in transport and clerical work, while it is easier to assess the credit-worthiness of a few established merchants than of individual builders. In his turn, the merchant breaks down the deliveries from manufacturers according to the requirements of the individual builder, usually economizing in transport since one delivery to a builder may contain items from different manufacturers.

Holding stocks

The merchant's function of holding stocks has advantages both to the individual builder and the materials' manufacturer. The builder is provided with an 'off-the-shelf' service, an important consideration where the demand for many jobs, such as repairs, cannot be anticipated, for it saves having capital tied up in storing components. Many merchants extend this service to larger projects. Because the consecutive nature of the building process gives rise to difficulties of storing materials and components on site, the merchant helps by phasing delivery.

Moreover, by holding stocks, the merchant enables the manufacturer to maintain the flow of components during periods of slack demand, thereby helping to stabilize prices. On the other hand, since the merchant does not fulfil the role of the dealer and speculate on future prices, fluctuations in the prices of building materials tend to be less than for agricultural products and minerals. Where materials, such as timber, have to be imported from abroad, the complications of foreign trade are shifted from the builder to the merchant.

Transporting goods

By arranging transport, the merchant relieves the small builder of the need to own a lorry for moving dirty and bulky materials, such as gravel, sand, bricks and heavy components. This allows the small builder to carry fewer overheads, operating merely with a van or even his own car.

Granting credit

Builders are usually given at least a month's credit in purchasing supplies, though a tighter control is exercised when interest rates are high.

Giving technical advice and promoting new products

By dealing with a large number of builders, the merchant knows which materials are successful. Where a builder is free of an architect's specification or, as in jobbing and maintenance work, can use his own discretion, suggestions from the merchant may be helpful. The merchant is often assisted in selling new products by technical information supplied by the manufacturer. On the other hand, there is a tendency for merchants to hold 'conventional' goods, especially where new products are more fragile.

Recent trends in the construction industry have tended to increase direct dealing between construction firms and manufacturers. The increase in the size of construction firms and the growth in the number of large projects, have meant that orders of sufficient size to interest manufacturers can be placed. Indeed, system-building uses components not normally stocked by builders' merchants. More manufacturers, too, are including installation in the price of their products, as with lifts, and heating and ventilation systems. Finally, many manufacturers have developed their own selling outlets – an example is Everest double-glazing which advertises in national newspapers.

High rates of interest can increase the costs of holding stocks. Merchants have often responded by amalgamations to achieve rationalization of activities, while merchant chains tend to stock only standardized products having a short shelf life, leaving it to smaller specialist merchants to hold other products.

Labour in the construction industry

The construction industry employs some 2,095,000 people (September 2009). There is a high proportion of skilled craftsmen (67 per cent) and of male workers (88.5 per cent). The main features of the work-force, however, are the number of one-man, labour-only subcontractors, the high rate of unemployment and the low productivity per worker compared with other industries.

Labour-only subcontracting predominates in housebuilding among carpenters, bricklayers and plasterers, who work either as individuals or in gangs. The main contractor provides the equipment and materials, paying the subcontractor for labour only. The advantages claimed are higher productivity, less site supervision and flexibility. But among other motives for its growth has been the desire of employers to reduce the burden of holiday and redundancy payments and training levies.

This labour-only subcontracting presents certain difficulties. In spite of regulations requiring up-front payment of tax, the government is faced with possible evasion. Because subcontractors work mainly on piece rates, they are unwilling to take on apprentices, the traditional means by which craftsmen are trained. Moreover, there may be uncertainty as to when the work will be performed and a failure to cooperate with other subcontractors. Finally, there is a tendency to neglect safety precautions, to waste materials and, with some gangs, to produce rushed, substandard work.

The rate of unemployment in the construction industry is usually between two and three times that of the economy generally. For instance, the rate of redundancy in the autumn and winter of 1993 was double that of manufacturing. The industry is vulnerable to all types of unemployment except that arising from a contraction of international demand.

Normal (or casual) unemployment results from the high labour turnover as projects are completed. While the small building firm works with a few, but fairly regular, local employees, the civil engineering contractor operates on a national basis, accepting contracts wherever they are available. Only key workers are retained for the different jobs; other workers are engaged locally and are paid off on completion of the project. Both at Christmas and Easter there is usually a two-week lay-off.

Frictional unemployment also occurs, some areas having surplus labour while others are suffering an acute shortage. The problem is not so serious with unskilled labour, but with skilled craftsmen there is both geographical and occupational immobility. Education and training of young workers is discouraged by the small pay differential between skilled and unskilled labour and the high rate of casual unemployment. To overcome the difficulty, the larger contractors try to retain skilled workers on a permanent basis, encouraging workers to go to different sites by travel bonuses and lodging allowances.

The industry is also affected by structural unemployment, resulting from long-term changes in demand for the goods made in a region or changes on the supply side through the introduction of new techniques. When an area is depressed there is less demand for construction work, although, to some extent, unemployment may be alleviated by government regional policy: new industries being attracted to the region by improving the infrastructure and providing modern factories. The construction work-force is therefore given more time to contract by natural wastage. It is cyclical unemployment, however, which hits the construction industry particularly hard since it is producing capital goods (see Chapter 6).

The prevalence of labour-only subcontracting and the high rate of unemployment have led to fragmentation of trade unions, with only about one quarter of the labour force being members. Most of these are employed by large civil engineering contractors and those local authorities that still employ some labour directly.

In the past, it is work on large sites that has suffered the most from poor site performance and industrial relations: various devices have been tried to improve the situation and better working conditions, such as weather protection, heating and lighting, can help, but these are not always practicable. Improvement in the quality of management, especially as regards site supervision, has a greater impact. Personal supervision, where the principal works with his operatives, has been shown to increase productivity by 15 per cent. This, however, is not possible with large civil engineering contracts, and experiments have been made in keeping to a few contractors (avoiding workers being disgruntled by the higher earnings of operatives employed by small subcontractors on piece rates) and reducing the work-force of each site contractor to less than 500. This allows closer supervision, ensuring that materials arrive on time, reduces non-productive time (for example, by better timekeeping), encourages a better team spirit through closer contact between management and labour, and increases effort.

The latter can be promoted by special devices. Where possible, piecework can increase productivity, but allowances have to be made for site difficulties and differences in mechanization, and there must be some underpinning by a basic rate to allow for bad weather. Target-bonus schemes can also be introduced where work can be attributed to specific gangs. The difficulty is that to some extent such schemes can reduce management control over output and, unless all gangs keep in step, the flow of work can be upset. Finally, length-of-service payments may be made in order to de-casualize labour with the object of improving labour relations.

Box 13.2   Health and safety in the construction industry

Despite considerable advances in technology in the construction industry over the last 10 years, it is clear that workplace equipment and machinery are involved in a number of fatal accidents – 72 workers were killed at work in construction in 2007–8 and 1 million days were lost due to workplace injury (0.45 days per worker).

In addition, occupational health remains a serious problem in the construction industry. Thousands of workers die every year from mesothelioma and other occupational cancers and lung diseases. Twenty skilled workers (electricians, plumbers, for instance) die every week from asbestos related disease and 12 more construction workers die every week from silica related lung cancer – 1.7 million days were lost in 2007–8 due to work related ill-health (0.77 days per worker).

One of the reasons put forward for this poor record of health and safety in construction is the large proportion of self-employed workers. The construction industry generally is modelled to provide maximum flexibility. As a result the majority of functions are contracted out and at least 40 per cent of workers are self-employed or part of the Construction Industry Tax Scheme (CIS). The advantages are obvious in that it reduces overheads and probably improves profitability and productivity. The disadvantages are that it becomes more difficult for a safety culture to flourish, worker engagement is weak, employment security and continuity is minimal and skills training is at best patchy.

Many stakeholders, particularly trade unions, some academics and bereaved families, feel strongly that self-employment, whether genuine or bogus, adds to the risk in the industry because self-employment is such a high proportion of the total. In London it is approaching 90 per cent. The self-employed can never be genuine apprentices nor could they take on the role of safety representatives. Some claim that the under-reporting of serious accidents is also because the self-employed tend not to report them as they do not receive benefits. The cost of any permanent injury to a self-employed person is probably met by the state.

Source: Donaghy, 2009.

Productivity in the construction industry

Increased productivity means that a given output can be achieved at lower cost – that is, the supply curve shifts to the right. The introduction of more and improved machines and the training of workers normally increase productivity in all industries over time. Where output per worker is increasing, there is a rise in the Marginal Revenue Product (MRP) curve, and firms could grant a wage increase. This is shown in Figure 13.3.

As marginal revenue productivity rises from MRP to MRP_1, wages of existing workers ON, rise from OW to OW_1. Alternatively, if there were unemployment, extra workers, NN_1, could be employed at the previous wage rate.

But there may be difficulty in apportioning the increased productivity between the workers' efforts and investment in new machines, research, and so on Moreover, increases in labour productivity in the construction industry

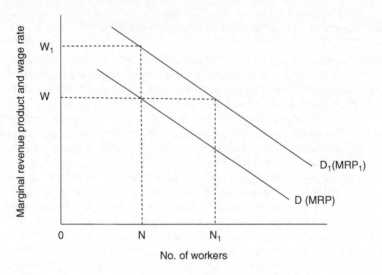

Figure 13.3   The effect on the wage rate of a change in marginal
revenue productivity

lag behind those in the economy generally, largely the result of the low level of
mechanization (see below).

One result of the slower growth in the construction industry's productivity is
that the real cost of buildings tends to increase relatively to costs in general. Thus,
given no change in demand for its products relative to those of manufacturing
industries, an increasing proportion of national resources has constantly to be
devoted to construction. Such reallocation would be accentuated if demand for
construction projects increased relatively to other goods, because (for example)
of a high income-elasticity of demand for houses, shopping facilities, schools
and motorways, or through an increased rate of household formation.

In manufacturing, increased productivity has resulted chiefly from mechanization, innovation and the creation of a large demand permitting mass production. The relatively lower increase in productivity of the construction industry
suggests, therefore, that there has been less progress along these lines. The
average worker in manufacturing uses five times as much capital as the average
construction worker. We have to ask, therefore: why should construction be so
labour-intensive?

Since mechanization means providing workers with tools and power, it
is really a substitution of capital for labour. The extent of such substitution
depends upon: (i) how efficient firms are forced to be through competition;
and (ii) the productivity and price of capital compared with the productivity
and price of labour.

As we have seen, restricted local markets and imperfect knowledge may
reduce competition for construction work. Nevertheless, some 50 per cent (by

value) of such work is covered by fairly large contracts for which national firms compete by tender. Low mechanization is therefore hardly the result of lack of competition.

It is necessary, therefore, to examine relative productivity and prices. Equilibrium will exist when capital and labour are combined to the point where their marginal rate of technical substitution equals their relative prices (see Chapter 2). In Marshallian terms:

$$\frac{MPP_{capital}(K)}{MPP_{labour}(L)} = \frac{Price_{capital}(K)}{Price_{labour}(L)} \tag{13.1}$$

Regarding relative marginal physical productivity, that is, the rate at which MPP_k falls as capital is substituted for labour, we must consider both the short period, where labour is assumed to be the fixed factor, and the long period, where both factors are variable.

The short-period situation is depicted in Figure 13.4, where extra units of capital are added to a fixed supply of labour. Given perfect competition, the slope of the curve reflects substitutability. In project A, MPP_K drops off more slowly as capital is added because capital is a better substitute for labour than in project B. Thus a fall in the price of capital from OC to OC_1 leads to MM_2 extra capital being employed in project A but only MM_1 in project B.

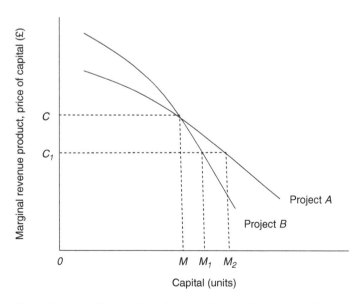

Figure 13.4   The substitution of capital for labour in the construction industry in the short period

In the long period, a fall in the price of capital relative to labour should produce a substitution of capital for labour. But the extent of this substitution will depend upon: (i) how good physically is capital a substitute for labour; and (ii) the extent of the relative price fall.

When we examine the possible replacement of labour by machines in the construction industry we find reasons why it is limited.

First, capital is not a good substitute for labour. Whereas a general labourer is flexible in performing the consecutive jobs on a building site, capital tends to be specific to one process (for example a mini-digger). Nor is capital a good substitute for skilled workers, such as plumbers, carpenters, bricklayers and electricians, who form over one-half of the labour force. Second, the nature of the work of the industry as a whole limits the substitution of capital for labour. Over one-third of all work consists of repairs and maintenance covering mostly labour-intensive jobs. Third, 40 per cent of new construction is high-rise building (mostly offices) where there is already considerable mechanization with capital equipment, such as tower cranes replacing unskilled labour.

In practice, therefore, the substitution of capital for labour is only possible for unskilled labour engaged in low-rise construction, that is, for about half of the labour force engaged in 60 per cent of total *new* work. Such low-rise construction is mainly traditional housebuilding, where, as we shall see, the flexibility of the general labourer, in performing many different jobs necessitated by the consecutive nature of building operations, makes him cheaper than specialist machines, which have a low rate of use. Thus machinery is confined mostly to excavators for foundation-digging and site-levelling, all-purpose transport (such as dumpers and lorries) for moving soil and materials, and powered tools such as drills and saws.

For any given fall in the price of capital, therefore, the substitution of capital for labour would tend to be confined to about 20 per cent of the industry's operations. But, even within this, the conditions of the industry's work are such that the price of capital relative to that of labour tends to remain high. The low utilization rate of specialized machines results from poor site organization, delays and extra wear and tear due to bad weather, and the consecutive nature of building processes. It has been estimated, for example, that site utilization of mixers is 30 per cent, of dumpers 66 per cent, water-pumps 26 per cent and excavators 70 per cent, though this can vary between jobs – cement-mixers, for instance, being more fully employed on road construction. Hiring machines or employing specialist firms for certain processes is not the complete answer to keeping down capital costs. Hiring is relatively expensive and vertical disintegration of processes, for instance, by obtaining ready-mixed concrete from a specialist producer, can increase the problems of dovetailing processes and of site organization. Added to this, the frequent and wide fluctuations in the level of activity in the construction industry increase the risk of expensive machines lying idle.

The low utilization of machines, high wear and tear resulting from bad weather and the necessity of moving machines from site to site, all tend to make capital expensive relative to unskilled labour. This, together with the low physical substitutability of capital for labour, accounts for the low degree of mechanization in the industry.

It follows, therefore, that increased mechanization depends upon a fall in the price of capital relative to labour or a rise in the physical productivity of capital compared with labour. Both are foreseeable possibilities.

First, a relative rise in wages, resulting from trade-union pressure or competition from other industries, would tend to produce a substitution of capital for labour. Thus bricks are now being delivered in packages or on pallets for mechanical handling.

Second, increased mechanization could result if large firms, with their better organization, became more important. For instance, improved organization can reduce the high cost of a tower crane. Similarly, more large-sized contracts such as for new eco-towns or major projects for local authorities, give greater assurance that an expensive machine will be used to capacity.

Third, a movement towards larger components (for example, through off-site prefabrication) or towards high-rise buildings (for example, through the high cost of central sites, greater productivity in high-rise building or the relaxation of height limits) would necessitate cranes, and so on, for lifting.

Finally Winch (1998) considers the tendency towards self-employment in the construction industry since 1970 to have hindered productivity increases.

> The strategic decision to leave control over the detailed execution of work largely in the hands of self-employed labour only gangs, rather than in the hands of management, has a number of implications for the effectiveness of the industry. Costs are higher than they would otherwise be; productivity growth in the construction industry has been relatively slow compared with other industrial sectors, and the productivity of the UK industry is relatively low in comparison to other EC countries. (Winch, 1998)

Innovation in the construction industry

In broad terms, innovation covers new labour-incentive schemes, improvements in organization and the use of standardized components.

The characteristics of the construction industry and the nature of the construction process present formidable obstacles to innovation. The preponderance of small, local firms means that knowledge of new and improved methods does not spread quickly and such firms, particularly housebuilders, are often sheltered from competition. Even for other types of construction, differences in design, location and the degree of subcontracting make comparisons difficult, so that builders may not know whether new methods are cost-effective. Furthermore, with little significant change in the relative cost of factors, wide variations in the level of construction activity and the difficulties inherent in the piecemeal introduction of new methods where production consists of consecutive processes, there is little spur towards innovation. In addition there is an element of risk since faults in a new method (for example, the collapse in a block of flats at Ronan Point in 1968) or in new materials (for example, the deterioration of concrete made with high alumina cement) may not show for some years later.

Improving the organization of the construction project can be examined with reference to the integration of the design/construction process and securing continuity of operations. In Britain construction is marked by the diffusion of responsibility for the finished product. Although design and supervision are the responsibility of the architect, the main contractor is responsible for the actual construction. This division adds to the problems of organization and site management.

Integration of the design/construction process requires the client, architect, quantity surveyor and main contractor to work closely together from the beginning. In this way the particular strengths of the builder can be harnessed and the most economic materials, consistent with the functional design of the building, chosen. The main difficulty of such integration of the complete process is that work cannot be put out to competitive tender. Because construction consists of consecutive processes, careful programming is necessary to ensure continuity of operations, the arrival of specialist firms and materials on time and the best use of machines. However, the programme must have some flexibility. For example, inside work can be kept in reserve against bad weather, initial overtime limited so that there is scope for making up delays, and work outside the main programme, such as on garages and paths, held back in case delays occur through unforeseen difficulties.

Programming the basic processes can be tackled in a number of ways. In its simplest form it may simply mean planning operations around the task which takes the longest time, such as laying the foundations and building the main walls. Or the construction process may be based on ensuring that the minimum technical unit is fully employed – for example, about seven men in building a house, with other operations being subcontracted. A third method is to simplify the construction process by using new materials (such as ready-mixed concrete and lightweight concrete blocks for building), employing specialist firms and incorporating prefabricated units in order to reduce the number of operations on site.

Where the building is large or of a non-repetitive type, *critical path analysis* can be used to secure the efficient coordination of separate activities. Figure 13.5 shows in simplified form how this approach can be applied to the construction of a bedroom-garage extension to a house. The project is represented on

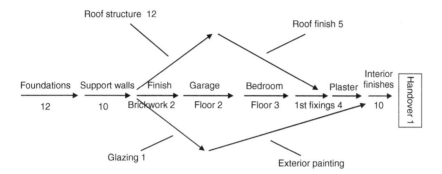

Figure 13.5 Simple critical-path analysis diagram

Notes: (a) figures denote the time (in days) for each activity: (b) total project time = sum of critical activities = 58 days: (c) non-critical activities have a 'float' time e.g. roof finish (4 days), glazing and exterior painting (30 days), brickwork and floors (5 days)

an arrow diagram in which the arrows represent the different activities and the pattern of the diagram shows how these activities must be interrelated. This decides *how* the project must be carried out: all activities represented by incoming arrows must be completed before any of the activities represented by outgoing arrows can start. A second decision will then cover how long processes will take to complete; but it should also be noted that only the critical path activities are worth expediting if an earlier completion is required.

The use of standardized components, such as windows, doors and roof trusses, reduces costs by allowing factory production and eliminating much craft labour on site. Factory-produced components are cheaper because they can be mass-produced with specialized tools; the organization is on a permanent basis and does not need to be set up anew with each move to a fresh site; workers can be provided with cover from bad weather and with heat and light; and expensive skilled labour can be replaced by machines. In addition, the reduction in variety eases the problem of carrying stocks, while interchangeable spares make repair jobs cheaper.

Standardization of components can be carried further by *dimensional coordination*, a systematic method of relating the size of components to facilitate their use together. It is based on a module of chosen dimensions which, in multiples and sub-multiples, provides the required sizes of all components, such as bricks, breeze-blocks, windows, doors, panels and floor slabs, in a logical progression. The advantages of dimensional coordination (which took a big step forward with metrication) are a reduction in the number of components, the elimination of wasteful cutting, and higher productivity through factory production and quicker assembly on site.

The European Union has mandatory standards for materials and products used in construction and listed under the Construction Products Directive. The CE mark of the EU is a declaration by the manufacturer that a product complies with the respective EU directive and is thus standardized.

Box 13.3   Lean construction

Lean construction is a philosophy based on the concepts of lean manufacturing. It is about managing and improving the construction process to profitably deliver what the customer needs.

Lean manufacturing was initially pioneered and developed by the large Japanese car manufacturers. It has been implemented by a number of Japanese, American and European manufacturers with considerable success, and has been widely applied outside the automotive industry.

Lean principles:

- Eliminate waste;
- Precisely specify value from the perspective of the ultimate customer;
- Clearly identify the process that delivers what the customer values (the value stream) and eliminate all non-value-adding steps;
- Make the remaining value-adding steps flow without interruption by managing the interfaces between different steps;
- Let the customer pull – don't make anything until it is needed, then make it quickly;
- Pursue perfection by continuous improvement.

These principles are applied in construction by improving the whole process from procurement through production planning and logistics to final construction. The facility and its delivery process are designed together to better reveal and support customer purposes. Positive iteration within the process is supported and negative iteration reduced. Examples of lean construction techniques are:

- supply chain management,
- transparency of costs,
- elimination of waste,
- benchmarking to ensure best possible production methods and outputs,
- risk management,
- just-in-time delivery of materials to reduce need for storage,
- daily progress reporting,

Lean Construction is particularly useful on complex, uncertain and quick-to-complete projects. It challenges the belief that there must always be a trade between time, cost, and quality.

Source: constructingexcellence.org.uk
See Ballard and Howell (2003), which contrasts lean and traditional approaches to project management; and Salem **et al**. (2006) for a comprehensive evaluation of lean construction techniques.

Standardization and 'industrialized building'

In manufacturing, one way in which costs have been reduced has been through the creation of a mass demand, usually by persuasive advertising. This has allowed the introduction of mass production yielding maximum economies of scale. Nevertheless, while the first requirement for this is a large demand, technical conditions of production must allow the process to be split into many separate operations so that specialist machines and workers can be employed continuously.

The construction industry has been based on what can be described as 'traditional building': that is, materials and components are purchased in the market and then assembled on site into buildings designed for particular or prospective clients. Recent trends have been towards substituting, where possible, 'system building'. This may simply refer to the incorporation in the building design of prefabricated components. More particularly, it may be limited to industrialized building, where (as far as possible) the whole building process from design to the finished product is based on factory techniques.

Industrialized building enjoyed a short-lived boom in the early 1960s, and by 1966 it accounted for 25 per cent of all dwellings (42 per cent of new town and local authority housing). The Ronan Point disaster of 1968, however, produced a reaction against high-rise flats especially in the social disadvantages and certain constructional faults which emerged. Moreover, subsequent recessions in the construction industry have highlighted the risk of over-investment in fixed capital, thereby eroding any competitive advantage enjoyed by industrialized building. Finally, when unit cost controls were imposed in 1967, industrialized buildings could not keep within the prescribed cost maxima.

In essence, *industrialized building* takes the form of designing a building in which the components, such as walls, ceilings, floor panels, cladding, concrete beams, and so on, are repetitive, thus allowing mass production under factory conditions with the advantages described above. Furthermore, since as much finishing work as possible is incorporated into the components, site work can consist mainly of assembly with no further work to be done. By this means it has been estimated that the building of a house can be reduced from 1,800 man-hours by traditional methods to 900–1,300 man-hours by industrialized methods, depending upon the particular system.

There are two main types of industrialized building: (i) 'open,' where the architect uses 'off-the-peg' components to achieve a design acceptable to the client; and (ii) 'closed', where design and components are one system, the manufacturer of the components also being responsible for the erection of the finished building. As far as possible, components are produced in a factory, though with closed systems they may be made on site.

To be successful, industrialized building must be able to compete on costs with traditional building methods. However, costs must be interpreted broadly, allowing for speed of building, subsequent maintenance costs, flexibility for future adaptation and special government aid towards research and development. The extent to which industrialized building can be cost-competitive depends upon conditions of demand and supply.

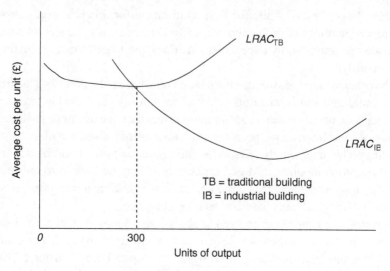

Figure 13.6   The minimum number of units to justify industrialized building

Industrialized building requires a demand which is both large and continuous. Thus in Figure 13.6, in order to secure the lower long-run average cost curve of industrialized building ($LRAC_{IB}$) resulting from design/construction integration, factory production of components and economies of scale, there must be a demand for at least 300 dwellings per period. McCutcheon (1988) identified 300–500 units as the minimum economically efficient production run.

The difficulty is that, in the construction industry, total demand is simply an aggregate of small parcels: apart from new towns and local authority housing, approximately 90 per cent of all contracts are for less than 100 dwellings. Increasing the size of contracts would only be possible if the variety of buildings were restricted to a narrower range. Yet private clients, especially housebuyers, demand a building which is satisfying both functionally and aesthetically, since they feel that they are going to occupy it for a long time. Industrialized building, in contrast, is frowned upon as being uniform, a view mainly derived from the austere appearance presented by local authority flats which were subject to severe cost restrictions.

Demand for industrialized building therefore has to come from those clients where some uniformity of product is acceptable and where the highest and best use of the site is not impaired by the erection of a factory-built construction. This has meant that in the private sector the method has been most successful for factories, hotels, farm buildings, small garages, house extensions and garden sheds. Nevertheless, in the public sector, where 'need' rather then 'demand' is the dominant consideration, industrialized building has been significant in providing dwellings (particularly high-rise flats), schools (for example, the CLASP system – Consortium of Local Authorities Schools Programme), hospitals and universities. Even so, in 1971, their best year, industrialized dwellings accounted for only a third of the total of all new local authority and new town dwellings completed. Approximately 372,000 industrialized dwellings were built between 1965 and 1977 in the UK and there were five main reasons why industrialized building developed (McCutcheon, 1988):

1. Internal technical developments combined with increase in use of similar building types;
2. Government action to ensure large markets in the public sector from the late 1950s to late 1990s (and so greater profits);
3. Theoretical premises related to the benefits of prefabrication;
4. The need to increase labour output in the face of a shortage of craft skills;
5. Fashion.

The decline of industrialized flats was accentuated by the Ronan Point collapse in 1968, which was built using the Larsen Nielsen system. Within the Greater London Council, 29 blocks used the system and 1,108 families had to be rehoused at great expense and inconvenience.

A twenty-first century revival of industrialized building can be seen with the entry of Ikea-Skanska into the market via the 'Boklok' (Swedish for Live Smart). About 800 such homes are built in Sweden each year and the first development in the UK – construction of 119 dwellings consisting of 36 BoKlok apartments, 57 BoKlok houses and 26 LiveSmart@Home dwellings is sited along the Felling Bypass in Gateshead. The company aims to assemble about 500 affordable dwellings per year in the UK by: 'Buying building materials in volume and building a limited but exciting range to maintain high quality and low costs' (LiveSmart@ Home). Each dwelling takes about four weeks to construct on site.

Continuity of demand is a requirement of industrialized building because it involves capital investment, and this is likely to be uneconomic unless there is an adequate work-load over a number of years and here the construction industry faces difficulties. First, particularly with regard to dwellings, the main product of industrialized building, tastes may change, as, for example, with high-rise flats. Second, public-sector construction, the main outlet for industrialized building, fluctuates. Not only do political swings influence public-sector housing programmes, but they are a major victim whenever cuts are made in government spending.

Even if demand is sufficient to justify mass production, the method will only be adopted if it results in a competitive saving in costs of production. Yet, in spite of a government subsidy, industrialized building has failed to gain an overwhelming advantage over traditional methods. The reasons for this are:

• If skilled craftsmen and wet finishers are to be eliminated in the assembly process, the components of factory-built systems must have greater

---

Box 13.4   Bathroom pods

Pre-fabricated bathrooms can be successfully produced in factories where there is plenty of space and the conditions offer the opportunity to fine-tune the assembly process. This means that bathrooms produced in a factory have fewer defects. Economies of scale allow pod makers to research and implement aesthetic or functional innovations and ways of improving quality. On site, bathroom pods will make savings in time because they are faster to install. Time saving may be a critical aspect of the project, particularly in hotels or student accommodation where there is pressure to realize revenue streams.

There are now several makers of pods offering ranges of varying quality. Pods can be specified according to the end use, for example student accommodation, key-worker accommodation or low, medium or high-cost hotel accommodation. Bathroom pods are commonly specified for such applications because of the repeatable nature of the bathrooms and the promise of assured quality.

Research suggests that specifying factory-fitted bathroom pods incurs a cost premium of about 30 per cent compared with traditional bathroom fit-outs. The perceived advantage of the pod is that this cost premium can be offset against the time savings during installation, less re-work, and fewer defects to rectify in use. Traditional bathroom fit-out needs the skills of a number of specialists including plumbers, carpenters, plasterers, wall and floor tilers, electricians and painters. The total time required for these specialists to install a bathroom is estimated at 82 hours. In contrast, a pod requires fewer specialists and takes typically 10 hours on site.

---

dimensional precision than traditional materials. But the greater accuracy of steel, plastics, wood and concrete slabs prepared under high pressure has to be weighed against their higher cost relative to bricks and concrete, especially as they are not as yet fully proven. Since materials account for about 50 per cent of the cost of a building and labour for 33 per cent, a 25 per cent increase in the cost of materials would require a 37.5 per cent saving in labour costs just to break even.

- Factory-produced components increase transport costs through the extra journey of delivering them to the site and because they are usually bulkier and more fragile than the raw materials.
- A higher capital outlay is required, cranes for lifting being essential.
- Industrialized building tends to be inflexible. With traditional building, modifications are usually possible, both in actual construction and in subsequent use. In contrast, changes in industrialized building usually involve interference with the basic design. Therefore, when experience necessitated new fire precautions for hospitals, they could only be incorporated in the industrially designed building at considerable expense.
- There is a tendency for industrialized building to eliminate the competition of tendering, a monopoly seller often being faced by a monopoly buyer with the price depending on their relative bargaining strengths.

• Traditional building can now make use of factory components through dimensional coordination (See Box 13.2).

Rising standards of living and the swing to owner-occupation have favoured traditional building to individual designs. On the other hand, possible future developments could renew interest in industrialized building. These include: higher land prices, which would encourage high-rise building; improved organization and greater continuity of demand; a fall in the price of precision materials (such as plastics) relative to that of the traditional brick and concrete poured on site; a rise in relative wage rates or shortages of skilled craftsmen; a fall in the price of capital; and lower transport costs.

In the immediate future, however, such developments appear to be doubtful. Increases in productivity in the construction industry, therefore, are more likely to come from better labour relations, improved organization and, above all, from the development of designs based on lean construction incorporating, as far as possible, standardized, factory-made components. The extent and speed of such innovations will depend upon the degree to which standardized components prove acceptable and the extent to which fluctuations in the level of demand generally can be eliminated. Harmonization of linear dimensions of

---

Box 13.5 Construction and the 'credit crunch' recession in the UK

Although hit very hard by the 2007–9 recession, the construction industry has held up remarkably well. The government's stimulus package enabled work to continue in social and low-cost housing and new schools and hospitals. As a result, the fall in employment from a peak of 2.3 million in September 2008 was only 186,000. Helped by favourable government action to allow firms to defer tax payments, only 1 per cent of building firms became insolvent in 2009, but this Figure is likely to rise coming out of recession.

There are expected to be cuts in the public sector which accounts for 30–40 per cent of all construction activity, because of excessive government borrowing. This is likely to hit school and hospital building and improvement programmes. PFI contracts (see Chapter 21) are longer term and may not be so badly hit. These tend to be the staple of the big construction firms as 'whole-life' contracts from original design and construction to long-term maintenance.

If public sector spending on construction falls, the private sector may be able to fill the gap. New orders for private housing and commercial buildings increased in the last quarter of 2009, but there is a shortage of mortgage finance working against this. Barratt Developments, one of the major homebuilders has reported losses for three consecutive years.

The market for commercial building is tentative with some developers encouraged by the fall in construction prices of 20 per cent from the peak of the boom. But commercial-property values in central London have fallen by as much as 50 per cent and vacancy rates are around 8.8 per cent in the City and 6.7 per cent in the West End.

both components and design throughout the EU represents an important step in this direction.

Summary

In 2009, the UK construction industry contributed almost 7 per cent of UK GDP and employed more than 2 million people. Its efficiency is clearly of importance to real property since it is concerned with the construction, adaptation and maintenance of buildings. The preponderance of small firms, low productivity and a high proportion of casual labour give an impression of inefficiency, but in fact the demand conditions of the construction industry result in these outcomes. Supply conditions are also distinctive with consecutive operations, production on site, small minimum technical unit size, high labour costs and time lags between demand change and supply response.

Construction is very labour-intensive and this is a major reason for low productivity. Output per worker could be increased by substitution of capital for labour but skilled labour is vital to the industry, and many jobs are relatively small and labour-intensive. Industrialized building was briefly popular in the 1960s, but demand for traditional buildings to individual designs has meant that this 'mass-manufacturing' approach to construction has not really taken off. In the last few years innovations in lean construction and the factory manufacture of component parts of buildings such as bathroom pods have begun to change the nature of some construction processes.

Chapter 13: review questions

1. Why is the efficiency of the construction industry important to:
   (a) the economy;
   (b) real property?
2. Explain the special features of demand and supply which are likely to result in a preponderance of small firms in the construction industry.
3. What is meant by 'collusive tendering'?
4. What functions do builders' merchants perform?
5. How could productivity be improved in the construction industry?

14

Sustainable Development and 'Green Building'

After studying this chapter you will be able to:

- Explain how the built environment can make a contribution to sustainable development;
- Describe the contribution of the UK housing stock to carbon emissions;
- Explain the basic principles of 'green building';
- Discuss methods of greening the existing housing stock.

A sustainable built environment

The often quoted definition of sustainable development as 'development that meets the needs of the present without compromising the ability of future generations to meet their own needs' comes from the United Nations World Commission on Environment and Development report (WCED, 1987) – often known as the Brundtland Report after its chair person. It incorporates the concept of inter-generational equity or fairness to people in the future.

The concept of sustainable development also requires intra-generational equity or fairness to the current generation in the form of relief of poverty and decent living standards in both the developed and the developing world. The built environment and especially the form of world cities has a key role to play in achieving sustainable development and inter- and intra-generational equity.

Sustainable development has a number of practical features that can be implemented directly in policies for the built environment. They include:

- *Environmental limits* should not be exceeded; for example, absorption of waste, protection against radiation, overuse of resources, air quality and so on. The precautionary principle should be adopted where there is any doubt.

- *Demand management* should follow an acceptance of environmental capacity limits; for example, instead of building roads or airports in anticipation of more demand (which is then self-fulfilling) the increase in demand should be managed. This is accomplished for energy through conservation and efficiency measures rather than building new power stations.
  - *Environmental efficiency* – this can be increased by: increasing durability,
  - increasing technical efficiency,
  - avoiding overuse of renewable natural resources (faster than replenishment),
  - closing resource loops by reuse, recycling and salvage,
  - reducing primary non-renewable resource use.
- *Welfare efficiency* means gaining the greatest human benefit from each unit of economic activity. Environmental issues cannot be separated from social issues and the built environment should protect and enhance health.

Equity for people in the current generation (intra-generational equity) because poverty leads to environmental damage. In 2009 for the first time, more than half of the world's population lived in cities according to UN Habitat, the agency for human settlements which produces twice-yearly State of World Cities reports. And the projection is for 70 per cent of world population to be urban dwellers by 2050. Mega-regions have developed where urbanization has spread to join cities together to form continuous urban sprawl often with unbalanced development, income inequalities and slum shanty towns. The largest of the mega-regions is Hong Kong – Shenhzen – Guangzhou, China home to about 120 million people. Other mega-regions have developed in Japan and Brazil and are developing in India, west Africa and elsewhere in the developing world.

The UN-Habitat report in March 2010 described the process of urbanization and 'endless cities' as unstoppable but generally positive because these regions are driving wealth. The top 25 cities in the world account for more than half the world's wealth and the five largest cities in India and China account for 50 per cent of the wealth in those countries. Migration to cities for economic reasons continues at a fast pace and much of the wealth in rural areas comes from people in urban areas sending money back home. The process of urban sprawl, however, is wasteful, adds to transport costs, increases energy consumption, requires more resources and causes the loss of prime farmland.

The biggest threat to sustainable cities comes from inequalities of income. The more unequal cities become, the higher the risk that economic disparities will result in social and political tension. Cities that are prospering the most are generally those that are reducing inequalities.

The ecological footprint of cities is the land required to feed them, to supply their water, to supply their timber and other products and to re-absorb their carbon dioxide emissions by areas covered with growing vegetation. For London, this is at least 50 million acres (which equals the Great Britain land area) or 125 times its surface area of 400,000 acres. If the population of the world lived at the standards of US citizens, then three planets are needed. A typical North American city with a population of 650,000 would require 30,000 square kilometres of land – an area roughly the size of Vancouver Island, Canada – to meet domestic needs alone without even including the environmental demands of industry. In comparison, a similar size city in India would require 2,800 square kilometres (Wackernagel and Rees, 1996), (see Table 14.1).

The high levels of consumption are associated with large amounts of waste and pollution, which are causing health problems and climate change. Changing this is a central objective of sustainable development policies. The built environment can be made more sustainable by achieving targets to reduce its ecological footprint.

Local Agenda 21 is an action plan for the twenty-first century agreed at the Rio Conference in 1992. Its key principle is the importance of local action to achieve sustainable development. Orebro in Sweden has an exemplary range of policies including:

- a bicycle plan to reduce car use;
- a waste sorting plan to increase recycling;
- ecologically designed apartment blocks;
- a transport and housing plan to reduce journeys to work, shops and schools;
- heat and energy to be supplied from renewable sources;
- new construction will use demolition materials and local materials;
- rainwater from roofs collected and used in toilets and gardening;
- cars to be eliminated from journeys to work;
- car parks to be converted to green recreation areas.

Urban planning and design needs to incorporate the principles of sustainable development. Land use planning can be made more sustainable – densities of population are very variable but if the land-use planning system can be used to produce sustainable densities there will be benefits in terms of :

- less fossil fuel burning;
- less green field development for roads and housing;
- less pollution.

Table 14.1 Comparison of consumption levels

	USA	India	World
CO_2 (tonnes/yr)	19.5	0.81	4.2
Vehicles/100 persons	57.0	0.2	10.0
Paper use (kgpa)	317.0	2.0	44.0
Fossil energy (Gjpa)	287.0	5.0	56.0
Fresh water (m³pa)	1868.0	612.0	644.0
Ecological footprint (ha/person)	5.1	0.4	1.8

A graph placing cities according to their population density (x-axis) and gasoline consumption (y-axis) plotted as long ago as 1989 (Newman and Kenworthy, 1989) reveals that the high gasoline and low population density cities of the world are all in North America. The high population density and low gasoline consumption cities were Hong Kong, Moscow, Tokyo and Singapore while European cities are in the mid-range. Houston, Texas is by far the lowest population density/highest gasoline consumption city.

While the situation will have changed somewhat since 1989, it is the relationship between the variables that is interesting. The clear inference is that urban design that addresses population density and mass transport networks is likely to be more sustainable.

The cities of the world, from Katowice in Poland to Dar es Salaam in Tanzania and from Concepción in Chile to Shenyang, China are very different in their environmental setting, the type and level of their development, and the set-up and capacity of their administration. However, most cities have enormous environmental problems in common. Cities also have a firm understanding that solutions

---

Box 14.1   Mega-regions

Hong Kong–Shenhzen–Guangzhou, China, home to about 120 million people and a massive Pearl River Delta Megapolis – which includes half a dozen cities of more than 4 million people each (Guangzhou, Shenzhen, Hong Kong, Dongguan, Foshan, and Jiangmen);

Nagoya–Osaka–Kyoto–Kobe, Japan, expected to grow to 60 million people by 2015;

Rio de Janeiro and Sao Paulo region, Brazil home to 43 million;

There are also fast-growing urban corridors in:

West Africa – 370 miles of urbanization link Nigeria, Benin, Togo and Ghana (Africa now has the highest rate of urban growth in the world – 4.4 per cent against a global average of 2.5 per cent);

India – from Mumbai to Delhi with 54 million residents by 2025;

East Asia – four connected 'megalopolizes' and 77 separate cities of more than 200,000 people each occur from Beijing to Pyongyang to Seoul to Tokyo. Urban areas account for at least 70 per cent of economic growth in East Asia and urban areas will account for 100 per cent of demographic growth in virtually all countries in developing East Asia by 2030. This is already the case in Indonesia, the Philippines, Thailand and China and will be true of Mongolia and Vietnam by 2020.

The developed world's cities have quickly been overtaken. New York–Newark, the world's biggest urban agglomeration in 1950, is now only the sixth largest and will drop to seventh by 2025. While the USA had eight of the world's 30 largest cities in 1950, it now has three, Chicago and Los Angeles being the other two.

The trend is even more pronounced in western Europe. London, the world's third biggest city in 1950 now does not feature in the top 30 list. Paris is the only western European city still in the list, a far cry from 1950 when nine cities of the UK and western Europe were among the top 30.

Source: worldbank.org

to their environmental problems, in order to be effective and sustainable, cannot depend upon external or central government support but must rely upon local technical and financial resources. New approaches to governance and urban management are required from the local public, private, and community sectors.

The contribution of housing to carbon emissions

Climate models have been used by the Intergovernmental Panel on Climate Change (IPCC) to anticipate global warming of 1.4° C to 5.8° C between 1990 and 2100. The main greenhouse gases are:

- CO_2 – from the combustion of fossil fuels (power plants, car exhausts, industry);
- Methane – from animal agriculture, natural gas, rice paddies, landfills.

In addition, land use change, especially deforestation, reduces absorption of CO_2. The need to reduce carbon dioxide emissions and to conserve energy has become urgent and there are three things on which almost all climate scientists are now agreed. The first is that man-made climate change is real. The second is that we need to take action. The third is that, to avert catastrophic effects on both humans and ecosystems, we should seek to prevent global temperatures from rising by more than two degrees above pre-industrial levels (Monbiot, 2006).

Since the UN Conference of 1987, when the definition of sustainable development as 'Development that meets the needs of the current generation without compromising the ability of future generations to meet their own needs' was put forward by Bruntland, the Earth Summit in Rio de Janeiro in 1992 and the Kyoto Protocol in 1997, the UK government has adopted environmental aims and targets. The design, construction and occupancy of buildings have been identified as areas where more could be done to minimize waste and reduce energy consumption as well as providing healthier and safer working and living environments (Keeping and Shiers, 2004).

Global climate change and the need to reduce greenhouse gas emissions necessitates decisive and timely action to improve the energy efficiency and performance of housing (Horne and Hayles, 2008). Reducing the amount of natural resources that buildings consume and the amount of pollution given off is crucial for future sustainability. The energy used in constructing, occupying and operating buildings represents approximately 50 per cent of greenhouse gas emissions in the UK. Emissions from the domestic building stock were responsible for 41.7 million tonnes of carbon (MtC) in 2004 – 27 per cent of total UK carbon emissions (DEFRA, 2006). Domestic energy use represents a large proportion of total national energy use: it has risen from 25 per cent of the UK total in 1970 to 30 per cent in 2001 (Shorrock and Utley, 2003). A standard 4-bedroom house in the UK uses 22,700 Kwh of energy per year and produces 6 tonnes of CO_2. It is clear that too many existing buildings are environmentally inefficient and do not make best use of limited resources such as energy and water. At present rates of improvement, it might take until 2050 before cavity wall insulation is present in all homes for which it is suitable.

As one of the UK's leading industries, responsible for 8 per cent of GDP and employing 1.5 million people, construction can lead the way in integrating sustainable development in all of its activities. Promoting sustainable construction is difficult, however, because of the industry's size and fragmentation. The construction business in the UK is responsible for nearly a third of all industry-related pollution incidents. Construction and demolition waste alone represented 72.5 million tonnes of total UK waste of 177 million tonnes (40.9 per cent) in 2000 (Martin and Scott, 2003).

The rate of construction in the UK is set to increase (assuming the recession of 2008–10 is a temporary or cyclical setback). The Government's *Sustainable Communities Plan* seeks to accelerate the current housebuilding programme and increase the housebuilding target by about 200,000 on top of the 900,000 new homes planned between 1996 and 2016 in the South East. This new emphasis on growth represents an opportunity to shift development towards delivering more sustainable homes and construction. Energy (and greenhouse gas) savings can be achieved by increasing building code stringency (Horne and Hayles, 2008).

The Department for Communities and Local Government published a *Code for Sustainable Homes* (DCLG, 2010). The Code is the national standard for the sustainable design and construction of new homes, which aims to reduce our carbon emissions and create homes that are more sustainable. It set design principles for energy, materials and water usage and to improve health, reduce pollution and minimize waste. The Code measures the sustainability of a new home against nine categories of sustainable design, rating the 'whole home' as a complete package. The Code uses a one-star (least efficient/sustainable) to six-star (most efficient/sustainable) rating system to communicate the overall sustainability performance of a new home and sets minimum standards for energy and water use at each level. It is intended to provide valuable information to home buyers, and offers builders a tool with which to differentiate themselves in sustainability terms.

In July 2007, the Government's 'Building a Greener Future' (DCLG, 2007) announced that all new homes will be zero carbon from 2016. Following up the commitment in the policy statement to consult further on the definition of zero carbon, in December 2008 the Government published 'Definition of Zero Carbon Homes and Non-Domestic Buildings' (DCLG, 2008) This proposed an approach based on:

- high levels of energy efficiency in the fabric of the home;
- a minimum level of carbon reduction to be achieved onsite or through directly connected heat; and

---

Box 14.2 'Green building' principles

Reducing the environmental and human health impact of the construction and operation of buildings involves a number of principles to be applied to building design. These include:

- minimizing energy consumption, using low-energy lighting, natural ventilation, efficient heating systems and solar heat-gain;
- minimizing resource use, particularly water by recycling and re-using systems;
- minimizing waste in construction by recycling and by using efficient processes;
- minimizing the use of toxic materials such as adhesives and solvents using volatile organic compounds;
- siting and structure design efficiency – minimizing site impact on local ecosystems and visual amenity;
- using environmentally friendly building materials such as sustainable forestry timber;
- encouraging sustainable transport usage through urban density requirements, location in relation to public transport and provision of sustainable transport features such as cycle lanes;
- local sourcing of materials;
- generation of on-site renewable energy.

With synergistic design, individual green building technologies can work together to produce a greater cumulative effect.

- a list of allowable solutions for dealing with the remaining emissions (including from appliances).

In the Budget of 2008, the government announced its aim that all new non-domestic buildings should be zero carbon from 2019 – with earlier targets for schools and other public buildings (DCLG, 2009).

The DCLG has established the 2016 taskforce, jointly led by the Minister of Housing and Planning and the Executive Chairman for the Home Builders Federation, to identify barriers to implementation of the zero-carbon 2016 target and put in place measures to overcome them.

The number of certificates issued by the DCLG in 2009–10 according to the Code For Sustainable Homes (post-construction stage) is shown in Table 14.2. The total number of certificates issued at 4,818 from a total of housing completions of 113,420 is unimpressive. And the number of level 6 certificates

Table 14.2 Codes for sustainable homes certificates

Code level	0	1	2	3	4	5	6	Total
Certificates	49	34	75	4326	290	37	7	4818
%	1	1	2	90	6	1	0	100

Source: Communities.gov.uk 20/05/2010

issued – just seven – is derisory given that all new homes should achieve this standard by 2016.

Greening the existing housing stock

Housing is a key aspect of the UK's challenging carbon targets for 2010 and 2050 as buildings contribute half of the UK's CO_2 emissions and UK's homes contribute about 27 per cent of the CO_2 emissions and energy consumption is rising. These CO_2 emissions are attributed to the consumption of fossil fuels for the generation of power and heat, with around 80 per cent for space heating and hot water (see Table 14.3). Energy efficiency has been identified in the Government's Energy White Paper (Department of Trade and Industry, 2003) as the cheapest, cleanest, safest way of reducing carbon emissions. Existing housing may be refurbished to a high standard of energy efficiency and this has clear benefits to occupants through improved comfort and reduced running costs.

Measures to improve the thermal efficiency of the building envelope depend on the type of construction of the building. Insulation, heating and ventilation measures should be considered in a combined package in order to avoid risks of condensation and fumes. There is a range of data and guidance available for the building stock of England and on appropriate thermal improvement measures from the Energy Savings Trust Energy Efficiency Best Practice Programme (EST, 2008).

Energy efficiency savings through improved thermal performance of building fabric could be outweighed by rapid increases in energy consumption from electrical appliance demands. The energy use of lights and appliances is increasing by 2 per cent annually. It will therefore be necessary to promote energy efficient lights and appliances in order to reduce overall consumption, which

Table 14.3   UK household energy consumption by end use

Usage	%
Space heating	60
Hot water	21
Cold appliances	3
Consumer electronics	3
Cooking	3
Lighting	3
Wet appliances	2
Miscellaneous	2

Source: Sustainable Development Commission, 2006

in turn may be met by the lower energy density available from the renewable sources (for instance, solar, wind and biomass).

Except over very long periods, however, we are dealing with a stock of housing in the UK. In 2001, 24.5 million dwellings in Great Britain increased by only 161,900, the lowest level of completions for 54 years. In 2008, the downturn in the housing market in the UK reduced the number of completions to 147,000. Even if the construction industry could raise its annual output by a third (which would be a considerable achievement) the yearly rate of increase in the standing stock would only rise from 0.66 per cent to 1 per cent. A 1 per cent per annum replacement rate for the existing stock would mean that it would take 70 years to replace the entire stock. For comparison, in Australia the number of dwellings constructed is approximately 162,000 per year, which is equivalent to almost 2 per cent of the existing stock of about 8.2 million dwellings – here it would take 35 years to replace the existing housing stock.

Considerable savings of carbon emissions can be made through improvements to existing houses, however. Energy efficiency measures, water-saving measures and renewable energy technologies can offer significant savings on a home's energy costs and environmental impact. UK government policy is set out in a white paper on energy published in May 2007 (Department of Trade and Industry, 2007). This states that:

> Energy is essential in almost every aspect of our lives and for the success of our economy. We face two long-term energy challenges:
>
> tackling climate change by reducing carbon dioxide emissions both within the UK and abroad; and
>
> ensuring secure, clean and affordable energy as we become increasingly dependent on imported fuel.

The White Paper sets out the government's international and domestic energy strategy in response to changing circumstances, addressing the long-term energy challenges the UK faces and delivering four energy policy goals:

- to put the UK on a path to cutting CO_2 emissions by some 60 per cent by about 2050, with real progress by 2020;
- to maintain the reliability of energy supplies;
- to promote competitive markets in the UK and beyond; and
- to ensure that every UK home is adequately and affordably heated.

Two of those goals relate directly to the housing stock of the country, and if they are to be realized, rapid progress must be made in the field of domestic energy efficiency. In Australia, energy used in buildings is a major contributor to total energy consumption and associated environmental impacts. In milder climates, however, building envelope features may not be as effective in life cycle terms, that is, including the embodied energy of their manufacture (Matthews and Treloar, 2001).

Home insulation

Up to 33 per cent of the heat produced in UK homes is lost through the walls. However, cavity wall insulation is quick, clean and relatively inexpensive to install. It will help create a stable temperature in the home, prevent condensation on the walls and ceilings and can also reduce the amount of heat building up inside the home during summer hot spells.

Solid walls lose heat more quickly than cavity walls, but because they are solid there is no easy way to insulate them. A possible solution to this is external and internal wall insulation. Solid walls can be insulated by applying internal wall insulation. External wall insulation involves adding a decorative weatherproof insulating treatment to the outside of the wall. The thickness of the insulation needs to be between 50 and 100mm and is usually installed where there are severe heating problems or the exterior of the building requires some form of other repair work, providing the opportunity of adding insulation.

Draught proofing can also be effective. In a typical UK home, 20 per cent of all heat loss is through ventilation and draughts and draught proofing is an easy, cost-effective way to reduce heating bills with most materials available from DIY stores. Loft insulation is also a very effective way of reducing heating bills, since as much as a third of space-heating costs could be lost through the roof of a building. The current UK government advice is to insulate the loft to a depth of 270mm.

Insulating the hot water tank can also be effective. Fitting a British Standard 'jacket' to a hot water cylinder will cut heat loss by around 75 per cent and save money on household bills.

Double and secondary glazing of windows reduces heat loss from homes. By trapping air between two panes of glass, double-glazing creates an insulating barrier that reduces heat loss, noise and condensation. Double-glazed windows come in a variety of styles although there may be restrictions on a house due to age and location but fitting double-glazing when existing window frames need replacing will save time and money. In countries with bigger windows, such as Australia, the payback time for installation of double-glazing will be shorter. Table 14.4 provides a summary of energy efficiency improvements from insulation measures.

Energy saving

The replacement of a central-heating boiler can also be effective as these account for around 60 per cent of all domestic CO_2 emissions. Using a high

Table 14.4   Average costs and savings from typical energy efficiency improvements

Measure	Cavity wall insulation	Internal wall insulation[1]	External wall insulation[2]	Energy Saving Trust recommended double glazing
Annual saving (£/yr)	Around £110	Around £365	Around £385	Around £130
Installed cost £	Around £250	£5,500 – £8,500	£10,500 – £14,500	£2,500 – £6,500[3]
Installed payback	Around 2 years			
DIY cost	–	–	–	–
DIY payback	–	–	–	–
Annual CO_2 saving	Around 560kg	Around 1.8 tonnes	Around 1.9 tonnes	Around 650kg

Measure	Loft insulation (0–270mm)	Loft insulation (50–270mm)	Floor insulation
Annual saving (£/yr)	Around £145	Around £40	Around £50
Installed cost £	Around £250	Around £250	Around £1,900
Installed payback	Around 2 years	Around 6 years	–
DIY cost	£50 – £350[4]	£50 – £350[4]	Around £100[5]
DIY payback	less than 1 year to 3 years	1 – 9 years	Around 2 years
Annual CO_2 savings	Around 730kg	Around 210kg	Around 240 kg

Measure	Draught proofing	Filling gaps between floor and skirting board	Hot-water tank jacket	Primary pipe work insulation (visible hot water pipes)
Annual saving (£/yr)	Around £25	Around £20	Around £35	Around £10
Installed cost £	Around £100			
Installed payback	Around 4 years			
DIY cost	Around £100	Around £20	£15	Around £10
DIY payback	Around 4 years	Around 1 year	5 months	Within 1 year
Annual CO_2 saving	Around 120 kg	Around 100 kg	Around 170 kg	Around 60 kg

Notes: [1] Assumes insulating to a U-value of 0.45 W/m²K. [2] Assumes insulating to a U-value of 0.35 W/m2²K. [3] Costs for double glazing are highly variable and dependent on the specific work needing to be done in each home. [4] Loft DIY insulation offers change frequently. Look for a good deal. The less you pay for the insulation the more quickly it will pay for itself. [5] Floor Insulation DIY cost represents the cost of the insulation only.

The costs and paybacks shown are approximate, and are based on a gas-heated semi-detached house with 3 bedrooms and cavity walls. Installed costs assume that installation is undertaken by a professional installer and are subject to a discount from an energy supplier. Some of the savings may be taken in increased comfort.

Source: Energy Saving Trust, 2010.

efficiency condensing boiler with heating controls could save between £190 and £240 a year, and significantly cut a home's CO_2 emissions.

Savings on lighting and appliances assume replacing an average appliance purchased new in 1995 and being replaced with an Energy Saving Recommended model of similar size, and an electricity cost of 10.41p/kWh. Energy-saving recommended bulbs work in the same way as fluorescent lights: an electric current passes through gas in a tube, making the tube's coating glow brightly. Traditional bulbs waste a lot of their energy by turning it into heat but each energy-saving bulb can reduce UK domestic electricity bills by up to £9 a year (Energy Saving Trust, 2010). They also last, on average, up to 12 times longer than ordinary light bulbs. Savings assume replacing a 100W tungsten filament lamp with a 20W Compact Fluorescent Lamp (CFL), an electricity cost of 10.41p/kWh and 1,114 hours of use per year. Hours of use is based on research undertaken into domestic lighting use and is the average usage for the two most used lamps in the average house.

Refrigeration is an area where UK households spend over £1.5 billion worth of electricity every year, on cooling and freezing. Since fridges and freezers are on 24 hours a day, seven days a week, low efficiency appliances cost a lot more to run. Refrigeration products that display the energy-saving recommended logo meet or exceed specified energy efficiency requirements and are backed by the government. The logo is a guarantee that the product will save energy, cost less to run and help the environment.

More than 90 per cent of homes in the UK have a washing machine and 40 per cent have a tumble dryer. Washing machines do, on average, an amazing 274 cycles a year. But the amount of wasted electricity from inefficient machines is exorbitant. This consumption could be cut by up to one-third by using an energy-saving machine. Using a 40°C wash cycle rather than 60°C means you use one-third less electricity. Reduce the wash to a 30°C cycle and the amount of electricity saved (and money) will be even higher: and modern washing machines are just as effective at lower temperatures. Laundry products that display the energy-saving recommended logo meet, or exceed, specified energy efficiency requirements and are backed by the government. The product will save energy, cost less to run and help the environment.

Almost one in three households in the UK now has a dishwasher. A dishwasher does, on average, about 250 cycles per year so an energy-saving model could save about £20 per year in electricity costs. To run a cycle on an inefficient appliance costs around 16p but to run the same cycle on an energy-saving machine will cost only 9p, saving 7p per wash. Energy-saving dishwashers save on water consumption, so are doubly good for the environment! Dishwasher products that display the energy-saving recommended logo meet, or exceed, specified energy efficiency requirements and are backed by the government. Table 14.5 summarizes the savings that can be made by using energy efficient appliances.

Table 14.5   Energy saving possible by use of efficient appliances

Appliance	EU Energy rating	Saving a year (up to)	CO_2 saving a year (up to)
Fridge freezer	A+ or A++	£38	155 kg
Upright / Chest Freezer	A+ or A++	£23	95 kg
Refrigerator	A+ or A++	£13	55 kg
Dishwasher	A	£11	47 kg
Integrated digital televisions	(no EU label for TVs)	£7	24 kg

Note: Savings assume replacing an average appliance purchased new in 1998 with an Energy Saving Trust Recommended model of similar size and an electricity cost of 12.50p/kWh.

Source: Energy Saving Trust, 2010

Table 14.6   UK household water consumption by end use

	%
Toilet	35
Personal washing	20
Kitchen sink	15
Washing machine	12
Wash basin	8
Outdoor use	6
Dishwasher	4

Source: Sustainable Development Commission, 2006

Water technology

Water is a finite resource and severely limited in some parts of the UK, although generally the public perception is that water is plentiful. Households use half of the water publicly supplied in the UK (Environment Agency, 2008). Table 14.6 shows the breakdown of household water use in percentages. The average consumption per capita is 154 litres per day. It is estimated that a reduction of 30 per cent of this consumption is achievable (Sustainable Development Commission, 2006). Mains water has an embodied energy of approximately 0.5kWh/m3 (including pumping, supply and treatment).

Key water saving measures include:

• Metering to monitor demand and raise awareness of waste;
• Use of water efficient fittings – low flow taps and showers, low flush WCs;
• Devices that alter the operation of existing fittings, such as tap inserts;
• Use of water efficient appliances – dishwashers and washing machines;
• Leak detection;

Table 14.7   Cost and benefits of retrofit water efficiency measures

Retrofit measure	Annual savings (% of total household consumption)	Annual savings (£/yr)	Cost of appliance and installation	Payback (years)
Ultra-low flush WC	14.3%	£32.15	£40 – £80 (subsidy)	2.0
Meter on change of occupancy	6% – 9%	£16.86	£71 – £250	9.5
Variable flush retrofit device	7.8% – 8.7%	£18.55	£20 – £40	1.6
Low use shower	3%	£6.75	£30 – £50	5.9
Cistern displacement device	2.2%	£4.95	£0.80 – £2.00	0.3
Low use taps	1.3% – 2.3%	£4.05	£15	3.7
Efficient washing machine	0.7% – 1.4%	£2.36	£20 – £40 (subsidy)	12.7
Efficient dishwasher	0.4% – 0.6%	£1.12	£20 – £40 (subsidy)	26.7
Total	35.7% – 41.5%	£86.79	£217 – £517	4.2

Note: Assumed 4-person household – 616 litres/day: possible 220 – 256 litres saved: average reduced consumption 378 litres/day.

Source: Sustainable Development Commission, 2006.

- Opportunities for grey water and rainwater recycling (water butts);
- Behavioural measures: turning off taps, wider 'water consciousness'.

The costs and benefits of a variety of water-saving measures are shown in Table 14.7. The average price of mains water has been calculated as one penny per ten litres by the UK Environment Agency.

Integrated renewable energy

Further savings are possible through the installation of micro-generation technologies. These systems may be installed in existing buildings and are applicable in all regions of the UK. The costs and benefits of these technologies are listed in Table 14.8. High initial (capital) costs can deter households from investment, therefore, uptake of these technologies is largely driven by grant programmes. As a result, the DTI announced proposals for the *Low Carbon Buildings Programme* (Department of Trade and Industry, 2006). Under phase one, grants totalling £10.5 million were made available to householders and community organizations for micro-generation technology. A further £18 million was made available to public, not for profit and private sector organizations for medium and large scale micro-generation projects. The low carbon buildings programme provided grants for micro-generation technologies to householders, community organizations, schools, the public and not for profit sector and private businesses.

Table 14.8 Costs and benefits of micro-generation energy technologies

Micro-generation technology	Cost	Saving/yr	Cost of savings (£/tonne CO_2 saved)
Micro CHP	£2,500–£3,500	£150	Approx £600
Solar water heating	£2,000–£3,000 for – 4m²	£35–£100	£130–£600
Wind turbine	£1,500–£3,000	£150–£300	£195–£220
Photovoltaic PV	£2,000–£4,000 – 5m²	£32	£550–£1,100
Ground source heat pump	£800–£1,000 per kW heat		£30–£350

Source: Department of Trade and Industry, 2006

Solar water-heating systems comprise solar collectors (evacuated tubes or flat plates) a heat transfer system (a fluid in pipes) and a hot water store (such as a domestic hot water cylinder). A 4m² collection area will provide between 50 per cent and 70 per cent of a typical home's annual hot water requirement in the UK.

Solar photovoltaic (PV) systems generate electricity from sunlight. Small-scale PV modules are available as roof-mounted panels, roof tiles and conservatory or atrium roof systems. A typical PV cell consists of two or more thin layers of semiconducting material, which is most commonly silicon. The electrical charge is generated when the silicon is exposed to light and is conducted away by metal contacts. In Germany, the application of PV is at least 10 times greater than in the UK, both at domestic and commercial level due to a combination of government support and reduced costs of installation of the systems. The reduced costs arise because the large scale installation of PV has pushed prices down sharply. A typical 3kw PV system costs about £17,000 in Britain but less than £10,000 in Germany, where prices have halved in the past 7 years and it is estimated they may do so again in the next seven. The government support is fundamentally due to a policy termed the 'feed-in tariff' (FIT). Anyone generating electricity from solar PV, wind or hydro gets a guaranteed payment of four times the market rate – currently about 35–40p pence a unit (kWh) at 2010 prices for 25 years. This reduces the payback time on such technologies to less than 10 years and offers a return on investment of 8–9 per cent. The cost is spread by generating companies among all users and has added about one cent/kwh to the average bill, or an extra €1.50 (£1) a month.

Feed-in tariffs (FITs) became available in Great Britain from 1 April 2010. Under this scheme, energy suppliers make regular payments to householders and communities who generate their own electricity from renewable or low carbon sources such as solar photovoltaic (PV) panels or wind turbines. The scheme guarantees a minimum payment for all electricity generated by the system, as well as a separate payment for the electricity exported to grid. These payments are in addition to the bill savings made by using the electricity generated on site.

Households receiving the FIT benefit in three ways:

1. **Generation tariff** – a set rate paid by the energy supplier for each unit (or kWh) of electricity generated. This rate will change each year for new entrants to the scheme (except for the first 2 years), but then be continued on the same tariff for 20 years, or 25 years in the case of solar electricity (PV).
2. **Export tariff** – a further 3p/kWh from the energy supplier for each unit exported back to the electricity grid, that is when it isn't used on site. The export rate is the same for all technologies.
3. **Energy bill savings** –savings on electricity bills , because generating electricity to power appliances means not buying as much electricity from an energy supplier. The amount saved will vary depending on how much electricity is used on site.

Domestic FIT installations are likely to have their export deemed (estimated) at 50 per cent in most cases until smart meters are rolled out.

Once household have a micro-generation technology installed they should experience a monthly reduction in their electricity bill and then receive an income from the feed-in tariff (clean energy cash back) provider. If a loan has been taken out to pay for the installation the household will have to make monthly repayments to the loan company but feed-in tariffs are designed so that the average monthly income from the installation will be significantly greater than the monthly loan repayment (with a 25-year loan).

Micro-wind turbines convert wind to electricity – the most common design is for three blades mounted on a horizontal axis, with the blades driving a generator (directly or through a gearbox) to produce electricity. Most systems are mounted on a tall mast, but building-mounted turbines are now starting to come onto the market.

Micro combined heat and power (CHP) – these technologies use natural gas as a fuel but provide electricity as well as heat. The two main systems use either reciprocating engines or Stirling engines. Fuel cells are also an alternative source of power.

Ground source heat pumps use the warmth stored in the ground to heat fluid circulating through pipes, a heat exchanger extracts the heat and then a compression cycle (similar to that used by refrigerators) raises the temperature to supply hot water for heating purposes. Air source and water source heat pumps operate in a similar fashion using temperature differentials in the air and water (these types of heat pump are not quite as efficient as ground source heat pumps).

Biomass stoves and boiler systems can provide space and/or water heating from burning wood (pellets, chips and logs) and non-wood fuels. The biomass fuels are derived from forestry products, energy crops (willow and miscanthus) and waste wood products (sawdust, pallets or untreated recycled wood).

The Renewables Obligation (RO) is the UK government's main mechanism for supporting generation of renewable electricity. Support is in the form of electronic certificates called Renewable Obligation Certificates (ROCs), one certificate being issued for each megawatt hour (MWh) of renewable electricity generated. The price of a ROC is set by the market and could be as much as £40. Zero-carbon content electricity has a value and energy producers have to buy ROCs. This effectively shortens the payback periods for renewable electricity generation schemes.

Readily available heat and power are taken for granted in developed societies. As we become less tolerant to fluctuating temperatures in our homes and more reliant on products requiring electricity, demand for heat and power is likely to grow even in the face of increasing strides being made in greater energy efficiency. Yet the context to this growing demand is one where the UK will no longer be a net exporter of oil and gas, where there is increasing urgency in the need to tackle climate change and rising energy prices are hitting the most vulnerable. Meeting these challenges will require a portfolio of measures, including energy efficiency, renewable energy and other low/zero carbon energy sources. Micro-generation technologies have significant potential as a part of this portfolio.

Rising fuel prices and greater environment awareness are encouraging buyers to pay close attention to a home's running costs and the impact of them on the planet. In the UK, Energy Performance Certificates became compulsory for anyone selling their home after 1st August 2007. When homes are sold or rented, this information must be made available by the seller or landlord to buyers or tenants and making this information available to home buyers will influence property values. In addition, 80 per cent of home buyers want to know if their home is environmentally friendly. New research from the Energy Saving Trust has found that nearly 70 per cent of British residents believe that energy efficiency is important when buying a home (Energy Savings Trust, 2008). Almost half (45 per cent) are willing to pay up to £10,000 more for an environmentally friendly home. Sellers are choosing insulation, modern water-heating boilers and double-glazing over frivolous fixtures and fittings to add real value.

Homeowners are much more likely to adopt the measures outlined above if: a) they believe their actions will be economically beneficial to themselves, and b) the costs can be spread over a period of time during which savings can be made to considerably offset those costs. Of course the problem is how to persuade homeowners to undertake these measures. In Australia, North America and Germany there is an established energy service industry composed of companies that provide consultation and assistance to households and businesses wanting to make their buildings, appliances, industrial processes, and so on, more energy efficient. An Energy Services Company (ESCO) is a firm that

---

Box 14.3   Energy performance certificates

Energy Performance Certificates (EPC) were introduced in the UK to help improve the energy efficiency of buildings. Anyone buying or selling a home now needs a certificate by law. From October 2008, EPCs are required whenever a building is built, sold or rented out. The certificate provides 'A' to 'G' ratings for the building, with 'A' being the most energy efficient and 'G' being the least, with the average up to now being 'D'. Accredited energy assessors produce EPCs alongside an associated report which suggests improvements to make a building more energy efficient.

The EPC is part of a series of measures being introduced across Europe to reflect legislation which will help cut buildings' carbon emissions and tackle climate change. Other changes include requiring public buildings – for example town halls, libraries, hospitals – to display certificates showing the energy efficiency of the building and requiring inspections for air conditioning systems.

Energy performance certificate

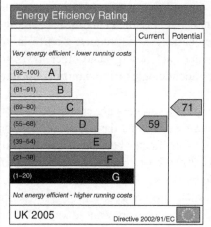

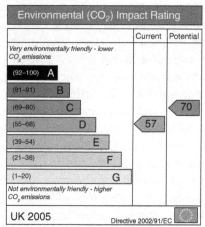

The energy efficiency rating is a measure of the overall efficiency of a home. The higher the rating the more energy efficient the home is and the lower the fuel bills will be.

The environmental impact rating is a measure of a home's impact on the environment in terms of Carbon Dioxide emissions. The higher the rating the less impact it has on the environment.

---

can identify and oversee the installation of energy-saving projects in commercial facilities. After a thorough energy audit the ESCO enters into a contract to reduce energy consumption by a specified percentage through technical efficiency measures (Kellett, 2006). The fee charged is based on the energy savings achieved and the result is reduced energy bills and a reduced environmental impact. Of course applying this model to residential property would be difficult because of the lower cost savings (and therefore lower fees) involved. But there could be scope for this type of arrangement in blocks of apartments or in housing associations for example.

Box 14.4 Retrofit

Retrofitting is the process of making buildings, particularly commercial buildings, more energy efficient. In 2010 London was designated as a Low Carbon Economic Area (LCEA) for energy efficient buildings. London is the seventh area within the UK to be assigned LCEA status. The main ways in which buildings can be retrofitted to improve their environmental performance are:

Maintenance-free lighting retrofits – replacing old bulbs with energy-efficient LED fixtures will help save cash and energy.

Daylight harvesting – installing skylights, more windows, dimmers, motion sensors and timers. Applying practical use of sunlight during daytime hours can reduce energy costs by 20–60 per cent.

Energy-efficient heating, ventilation and air conditioning – retrofits, offer quick payback and large carbon savings.

Solar photovoltaic (PV) systems and wind turbine installations – building owners may be able to receive payment or <u>energy credits</u> from their local <u>utility company</u> if more electricity is generated than necessary. Wind turbines – depending on the region – can reduce electricity bills by 50–90 percent; although they may not receive planning permission in certain areas.

Energy management systems and monitoring devices – which supervise and control energy consumption. Offering consumers detailed information regarding their home energy-efficiency can result in 5–15 percent savings on monthly electricity.

An Energy Service Company (ESCO) is a commercial business (mainly in the USA and Australia to date) providing a broad range of comprehensive energy solutions including design and implementation of energy savings projects, energy conservation, energy infrastructure outsourcing, power generation and energy supply, and risk management. The ESCO performs an in-depth analysis of the property, designs an energy efficient solution, installs the required elements, and maintains the system to ensure energy savings during the payback period. The saving in energy costs is often used to pay back the capital investment of the project over a 5- to 20-year period, or reinvested into the building to allow for capital upgrades that may otherwise be unfeasible. If the project does not provide returns on the investment, the ESCO is often responsible to pay the difference.

The Empire State Building in New York unveiled plans in 2010 for a retrofit to make it a 'green building'. The environmental measures will cost $13 million and are expected to cut the building's energy use by almost 40 per cent, reducing annual bills by $4 million with a payback period of just over 3 years. Its carbon footprint will be cut by 100,000 tonnes over the next 15 years. The retrofit involves renovating the 6,514 windows and installing smart energy technology and smart air-circulation systems. The ESCO involved is Johnson Controls.

For individual households it may well be that the financial sector holds the key. Financial institutions could offer an 'Energy Saving Advance' (ENSA) as a further advance of £5,000–£10 000 over 10 years to existing mortgage holders. This could be made in conjunction with advice on possible grants to offset costs. It would be paid for in large part (if not all) by savings on energy bills and would add value to property by increasing energy efficiency. The risk to the finance providers could be reduced by only offering ENSAs to existing mortgage holders with substantial equity, although as the schemes prove successful (and credit conditions improve) this could be relaxed. In addition there would be considerable public relations benefits for finance companies as they demonstrate environmental credentials by providing ENSAs.

Green commercial real estate

Building characteristics and performance are becoming major determinants of a commercial property's worth and market value. There are public relations benefits for companies occupying buildings that are seen to be 'environmentally friendly' or 'green'. These include branding and reputation advantages, and benefits from being seen to be 'doing the right thing'. Various recent studies also make claims of tangible financial benefits from ownership and occupation of green buildings. These include:

- Energy and water savings of 25–30 per cent;
- Reduced waste;
- Improved indoor environmental quality;
- Increased employee comfort and productivity;
- Reduced employee health costs;
- Lower operation and maintenance costs. (Kats, 2003)

The US green building council (USGBC) makes further claims for the benefits of green buildings – that they consume less energy and fewer resources, saving on average 40 per cent of potable water, cutting waste by 70 per cent and reducing CO_2 emissions by 39 per cent. And the USGBC also claims that green buildings are healthier and that there is a significant association between low ventilation levels and higher carbon dioxide concentrations – a common symptom in facilities with sick building syndrome (see Box 14.5).

It is also claimed that green buildings increase the productivity of workers. Although there is no universally accepted means of measuring office productivity (Haynes, 2007a), the key components are comfort, office layout, interaction and distraction (Haynes, 2007b). Healthier buildings reduce sick time and increase productivity, and natural light, good ventilation, and the absence of organic compounds leads to happier, healthier workers. (Miller et al., 2009).

Research from commercial real estate firm CB Richard Ellis and the University of San Diego's Burnham-Moores Center for Real Estate published a study assessing whether green buildings actually increase worker productivity and the results show that environment can play a role in worker productivity.

Box 14.5 Sick building syndrome

Buildings themselves can be harmful to health and the environment and this has become known as 'sick building syndrome' (SBS). This first came to consideration in the 1970s when reports linked symptoms to the occupancy of buildings that had been deliberately 'air-tightened' to conserve energy during a Middle East oil embargo. In the 1980s, the World Health Organization (WHO) recognized SBS 'in buildings with indoor climate problems'.

Symptoms include irritation of the eyes, nose and throat, neurotoxic or general health problems, skin irritation, fatigue, aches and pains, and sensitivity to odours and nausea. The problems appear to be linked to time spent in a building. There is the potential for long-term health effects especially from biological contaminants such as bacteria, molds, pollen, and viruses. These contaminants may breed in stagnant water that has accumulated in ducts, humidifiers and drains, or where water has collected on ceiling tiles, carpeting, or insulation. Sometimes insects or bird droppings can be a source of biological contaminants. One well-known example of building-related illness is Legionnaires Disease. Building-related asthma may be a particular problem.

Flaws in the heating, ventilation and air-conditioning systems of buildings are often blamed for SBS. Poor exhaust ventilation of ozone, which is a by-product of some office machinery, may also be a factor.

A prominent example was the Inland Revenue offices in Liverpool (demolished in 1995). Its problems were thought to be caused by volatile organic compounds (VOCs) such as formaldehyde (in chipboard and adhesives), organochlorines (in plastics and air fresheners), phenols (in paints, varnishes, plastics) and dust and mites.

According to a US Environmental Protection Agency (EPA) report, illnesses related to indoor air pollution cost over $1 billion each year in medical bills and about $60 billion in lost productivity and sick leave. Because a company's employees are its highest per-square-foot office cost, many companies are designing, renovating, and furnishing buildings with their employees' health in mind. Sick building syndrome is a problem in 30 per cent of new and newly renovated buildings in the USA according to the EPA.

Green building design tries to avoid SBS problems using natural ventilation, solar gain, use of renewable and non-toxic building materials in order to produce efficient, environmentally friendly buildings.

While management is still the largest factor in employee productivity, more than half the tenants surveyed agreed that employees were more productive after they moved to a green building. About 45 per cent agreed workers took fewer sick days (on average, 2.88 days less sick time). There could also be benefits for firms in recruitment and retention of staff from working in green buildings as well as positive impacts on physical and mental health.

The leaders in sustainable property construction are North America and Europe but there are significant opportunities in other economies such as China (Nelson, 2007). Only the USA and UK have a substantial number of certified green buildings – via Leadership in Energy and Environmental Design

(LEED) in the USA; and Building Research Establishment Environmental Assessment Method (BREEAM) in the UK, although similar systems are being developed in Germany, Holland, France, Switzerland, Australia and Hong Kong (Nelson, 2008). Nevertheless in the UK about 98 per cent of commercial stock is existing property and of the 1–2 per cent of new build, only about 7 per cent of offices built annually are BREEAM 'good' or above (Dixon et al., 2009).

Sustainable design and LEED certification may also contribute to market acceptance of higher rent and to a speeding up of the planning process. And having green design features may make it easier to attract capital for development and contribute significantly to property values: these are all fertile areas for empirical research. The LEED programme was developed by the United States Green Buildings Committee and it recognizes performance in key areas including: sustainable sites, water efficiency, energy and atmosphere, materials and resources, indoor environmental quality, awareness and education, innovation in design and regional priority.

There is a growing political consensus in the UK and globally that financial aid to alleviate the recession in the economy should contain a green element (or a 'green new deal'). Governments worldwide have recognized the benefits of using the recession to spend on packages that can help in the move towards a low carbon economy and implement measures that deal directly with transport and the built environment. This has resulted in a variety of initiatives, including funding for making buildings more energy efficient and tax breaks and loans for solar and wind power firms. Governments globally are continuing to legislate to reduce carbon emissions. A variety of measures affecting the built environment are now in place including regulation, green taxes, cap and trade schemes and other measures. The property industry in the UK, for example, is currently coming to terms with the implications of the Carbon Reduction Commitment (CRC), set within the Climate Change Act, 2008 which began in April 2010. The CRC places a mandatory commitment for businesses spending more than £1 million per year on electricity to reduce consumption by using a cap and trade scheme (Dixon, 2009).

Summary

Sustainable development necessarily involves a sustainable built environment and improvements in city design and maintenance. More than half of the world's population now live in cities and large conurbations such as the Hong Kong-Shenhzen-Guangzhou mega-region of 120 million people. The ecological footprint of cities is the total land area necessary to support them. For cities in the developed world this can be a very large area because levels of consumption are very high. If all of the world's people had the same size of ecological footprint as the population of the United States, resource requirements would be more than three times the earth's ability to supply them.

Housing contributes 27 per cent of all UK carbon dioxide emissions. The UK government has a very ambitious requirement for all new houses to be carbon neutral by 2016. Even if this is achieved, however, it does not address the existing stock of houses which is currently replaced at a rate of less than one per cent per year. A range of energy-saving and micro-generation technologies can be adopted to retrofit or 'green' the existing housing stock. Government initiatives such as the 'feed-in-tariff' and Energy Performance Certificates can encourage this process.

Chapter 14: review questions

1. What is meant by the 'ecological footprint' of a city?
2. How can cities become more sustainable?
3. What measures can be taken to make the UK housing stock more sustainable?
4. What is meant by 'sick building syndrome' and what is thought to cause it?
5. What are Energy Performance Certificates?

Contaminated Land and Brownfield Development

After studying this chapter you will be able to:

- Explain why contaminated land is a problem in real estate markets;
- Outline the main features of UK legislation to deal with contaminated land;
- Describe the methods used to remediate contaminated land sites;
- Discuss policy in the UK relating to brownfield land development;
- Outline contaminated land strategy in Europe and the USA.

The problem of contaminated land

Contamination of land occurs when soil contains chemical pollutants and/or physical obstructions that can either harm the wider environment, people, animals and plants or inhibit future uses in, on, over or under the land (Keeping and Shiers, 2004).

Owners and developers of land need to be aware of their potential legal liabilities in respect of environmental issues that can arise because of contamination. Often the contamination originated a considerable time ago (perhaps even hundreds of years) but can continue to cause harm to plants, animals and humans. It is also possible for contamination to cause building materials to fail and to make property unfit for use (for example, sulphates attack concrete and acids and hydrocarbons can damage pipework). Costs of redevelopment of sites are increased because greater care must be taken to protect construction workers and end users from harm that can come from the contaminants. As a result, site values can be reduced and this can be exacerbated by a poor public image and reduced marketability of individual sites and even polluted areas that have become stigmatized by contamination. A contaminated site may remain unused for decades because the cost of clean-up is greater than the value of the land for development.

Contaminated land is usually the result of pollution of the ground by the residues of industrial processes. This can directly affect people who come into contact with the contaminated land. Contamination can also pollute water supplies, or cause vegetation and ecosystem damage. Industrial activities that often result in land contamination include:

asbestos works and buildings containing asbestos; brickworks; chemical works; food processing plants; glass and pottery works; foundries and steel works; munitions sites; paint works; printing works; textile mills, cemeteries, quarries, railway sites; sewage works; landfill sites; airfields; petroleum refineries; scrap yards; gas works; and nuclear power stations.

The decision to remediate a contaminated site is obviously an economic one. It is necessary to make overall decisions on the level of clean-up that may be required and the valuation of damaged resources, option values and intrinsic worth is an important part of this process (Hardisty et al., 1998). Once the decision to remediate has been taken, the question becomes how best to remediate cost-effectively. Evaluation of the economics of a cleanup project is directly linked to the objectives of the site owner, and the constraints within which the remediation must be carried out. After the objectives and any constraints have been identified, a range of possible remedial approaches and technologies can be developed, and each option evaluated on a comparative basis. One of the most powerful tools for comparative options analysis is technical-economic analysis. This combines evaluation of technical feasibility with consideration of capital, operation and maintenance costs over a given period. By constraining remediation alternatives within cost and time boundaries, possible solutions can be evaluated with respect to specific criteria.

Contaminated land in the UK

The UK has a substantial legacy of industrial and chemical contaminants in its land. Sometimes the contaminants may be present naturally, for example radon gas in granite rock areas, but very often they result from human industrial and domestic pollution. In most cases, levels of contaminants are sufficiently low that there is no appreciable risk. However, sometimes there can be significant risks to people or the environment and it is only when such risks exist that land is considered to be contaminated land.

The terms 'contaminated land' and 'brownfield site' convey a perception of risk to developers that may no longer be warranted. The assessment and remediation of these sites is now a major international business. Guarantees and indemnities are available on remediated sites and the economics of development of these sites is attractive. This is demonstrated by the fact that over half of all residential development nationwide is on reused sites. Residential development is the most sensitive end use to which these sites can be put, yet it is now more common than not to build houses on 'contaminated' land. (www.sustainableconstruction.co.uk)

The Department for Environment, Food and Rural Affairs (Defra) has a wide range of policies to tackle land contamination, falling into two broad areas:

- Measures to find and deal with existing contaminated land.
- Measures to prevent more contaminated land being created, including policy and legislation on pollution, waste, water and chemicals.

As we are concerned here with real estate issues we will be considering existing contaminated land problems. In dealing with existing contaminated land, there are two main types of contaminated site for the purposes of Government policy:

- Sites where there is a 'voluntary' solution. Often land is remediated as it is being redeveloped under the planning system, or because land owners want to increase the utility and value of their land. Wherever possible, the government encourages voluntary remediation (as opposed to compulsory remediation under contaminated land legislation). Policy in this area is overseen primarily by the Department for Communities and Local Government (CLG).
- Sites where there is unlikely to be a voluntary solution. This includes contaminated sites which have been developed without being cleaned-up; sites where remediation would be prohibitively expensive; and sites where the person who polluted the land, and/or the current owner, is unwilling to deal with the problem voluntarily. It is mainly on these types of site that contaminated land legislation comes into play.

Defra's interest in contaminated land lies primarily in sites where there is no voluntary solution. In particular, Defra oversees contaminated land legislation (Part 2A of the Environmental Protection Act, 1990), which was introduced to require action in the absence of a voluntary solution.

The government's long-term aim is to work towards a future where all the contaminated land in England has been identified and dealt with but the scale of the task means this is likely to take decades to achieve. The responsibility for dealing with land affected by contamination rests with those who caused it, the owner or occupier of the land or in some cases the person redeveloping it.

Land that is contaminated contains substances in or under the land that are actually or potentially hazardous to health or the environment. Britain has a long history of industrial production and throughout the UK there are numerous sites where land has become contaminated by human activities such as mining, industry, chemical and oil spills and waste disposal. Contamination can also occur naturally as result of the geology of the area, or through agricultural use.

The presence of contamination in the ground does not necessarily mean that there is a problem. In many cases there will be minimal risk from living or working on contaminated ground. Many contaminated sites have been successfully and safely redeveloped to provide high quality housing and working environments. Nevertheless, because there are possible costs and extra risk associated with contaminated land, it will be impaired in value compared with uncontaminated similar sites.

The risk to a proposed development from contaminated land is usually assessed using Source-Pathway-Receptor analysis. This establishes the presence of a chain of events required to present a risk. First, a source of risk is required, which means the discovery of one or more chemical parameters in excess of guidance limits or an excess of soil gas. Once a source is discovered on site, the investigation will analyse the presence of any pathways by which this source can be transmitted to a sensitive receptor. Such pathways include direct ingestion, aerosol exposure, contact and so on.

When a source and a pathway have been established, the final link in the chain is a receptor. A receptor is essentially anything or anyone that can be adversely affected by the contamination. This includes a building's occupants, the fabric of the building itself, landscaping plants, local watercourses and so on. The receptor (and indeed the source) need not be within the boundaries of the site itself. Particularly in areas where the underlying geology is relatively porous, the potential exists for contamination to spread to the site from surrounding areas and to surrounding areas from the site. This means, for example, that a contaminated site may adversely affect the quality of a nearby river by run-off or contamination of groundwater.

In a few cases, some sites are so contaminated that they present an unacceptable risk to human health or the environment. Human exposure to contaminants can be through inhalation of dust or gases, contact with soil or through food grown on the land. Leachates (pollutants draining from the site in liquid form) can pollute groundwater and rivers or ponds. Some contaminants may be corrosive, and some can pose a risk of explosive fire. The effects on human health and on the environment will depend on the type and amount of contaminant involved.

Until recently, contamination usually became an issue only where there was a pollution incident, or where the site was selected for redevelopment through the planning process. Now, under the requirements of Part 2A of the Environmental Protection Act (EPA) 1990, local authorities are required to make assessments of land in their areas to decide which sites are, or could be, causing harm or pollution and to take action to ensure that it is made safe.

This might result in the original polluters, landowners, and other responsible persons (including domestic property owners) becoming responsible for cleaning up a site under the Polluter Pays Principle (PPP). If land is found to be contaminated, it must be restored to a state in which is it 'suitable for use'. The local authority will agree with the responsible persons the degree to which the land should be cleaned-up, in relation to the risk that the land is posing to health or the environment and pollution of watercourses and groundwater.

In the case of redevelopment, the developer will be responsible for ensuring that the site is suitable for its intended use, and in most cases the enforcement of any remediation requirements will be made via formal agreements such as planning conditions and building control. A site affected by contamination may need remedial treatment before it can be redeveloped, and 'Remediation Notices' can be issued under EPA to ensure treatment of land in existing use. There are many ways in which this may be achieved, ranging from 'dig and dump' (taking contaminated soils away to licensed landfill sites) to the use of techniques that treat soil and water to remove, destroy or reduce the amount or potency of the contamination. The choice of approach is very site specific and depends on various factors such as the type of contamination, the physical circumstances of the site, ongoing site use and the regulatory requirements.

In general remedial options fall into one or more of the following broad categories:

- Excavation and containment (removal to landfill: the disposal of material to an engineered commercial void space; deposition within an on-site engineered cell, generally with a view to combining the disposal of waste with the reclamation of land area from the void space; engineered land-raising and land forming, where materials are deposited on the land surface to make a hill or mound above the natural surface level suitably contained).
- Engineered systems (physical containment: designed to prevent or limit the migration of contaminants left in place or confined to a specific storage area, into the wider environment. Approaches include in-ground barriers, capping and cover systems; hydraulic containment and pump-to-contain approaches.)
- Site rehabilitation measures are those used to bring back some measure of utility to a site whose contamination cannot be treated or contained for technical or economic reasons. Examples include growth of grass cover tolerant of contaminants, covering with soil or soil substitute, liming and other cultivation measures.
- Treatment based approaches to destroy, remove or detoxify the contaminants contained in the polluted material (for example, soil, ground water and so on). Using treatment technologies in contaminated land remediation

is encouraged by agencies in many countries, because they are perceived as having added environmental value compared with other approaches to remediation such as excavation and removal, containment or covering/reveg-etation. The added environmental value is associated with the destruction, removal or transformation of contaminants into less toxic forms (Nathanail et al., 2001).

Rivett et al. (2002) reported on a survey of remedial activity in England and Wales over the period 1996 to 1999 which was commissioned by the Environment Agency on data from 367 remediated sites supplemented by fur-ther data from 1,189 contaminated sites. It was found that civil-engineering based remediation techniques dominated and were used at 94 per cent of sites. Disposal to landfill occurred at over 80 per cent of sites but integrated use of multiple techniques was common. Remediation was predominantly of soil (rather than water), was development-based, was designed to protect human health and reflected national development-led and suitable-for-use policies. They recommended:

- regulatory and financial support for innovative remediation techniques and demonstration sites;
- competent use of risk-based approaches to allow pragmatic remediation and effective use of quality guidelines;
- effective guidance on water quality issues;
- post-remediation monitoring to prove effectiveness; and
- the keeping of remediation databases. (Rivett et al., 2002)

The Contaminated Land Exposure Assessment (CLEA) model published by Defra and the Environment Agency (EA) in March 2002 sets a framework for the appropriate assessment of risks to human health from contaminated land, as required by Part 2A of the Environmental Protection Act, 1990. As part of this framework, generic Soil Guideline Values (SGVs) have been derived for contaminants to be used as intervention values. These values should not be con-sidered as remedial targets but values above which further detailed assessment should be considered. Three sets of CLEA SGVs have been produced for three different land uses:

1. residential (with and without plant uptake);
2. allotments;
3. commercial/industrial

The amount of contaminated land in the UK is considerable but estimates vary according to the definition used, from as much as 200,000 hectares to 2,800 hectares under the relatively narrow EPA 1990 definition (Syms, 1999).

Landfill waste disposal sites are a particular problem. Such sites are often close to residential areas. Gas created by the breakdown of organic matter from former landfill sites can become explosive. The gases can be generated for 15 years following the ending of waste tipping and the sites can remain unsafe for up to 50 years. Such landfill gas is usually a mixture of methane, carbon dioxide and oxygen. It can build up in structures close to waste disposal sites and is potentially very dangerous. In Loscoe in Derbyshire in March 1986 a bungalow adjacent to a landfill site exploded when a large fall in barometric pressure occurred. The bungalow was destroyed and others damaged. The nearby waste site had been a brickworks from the mid-nineteenth century to the 1970s and was then used as landfill. After the explosion the gas was extracted and flared off. Similar problems have occurred close to waste disposal sites elsewhere.

Box 15.1   Contaminated land case examples in the UK

Cambridge

In April 2003, contaminants were discovered in the gardens of 25 homes in Littleport, Cambridgeshire. The properties, built near a former gasworks site, were found to contain toxic chemicals including cyanide, mercury, lead, arsenic and cancer-causing benzopyrene.

Initially the council told residents they could be liable for part of the remediation costs because Regal Bourne, the housing developer who originally built the houses, was no longer in business. However, this threat proved unfounded as the local authority and Defra combined to finance the clean up of the site, which finally began in April 2008.

Wolverhampton

Wolverhampton City Council made a declaration on October 21 2009 that twelve households on the site of the former Courtaulds Dunstall Hall Works factory in Wolverhampton, were contaminated. The declaration was made under Part 2A of the Environmental Protection Act, 1990. The council is now investigating who is liable for the contamination, with the intention of making them pay the estimated £1 million remediation bill. It is understood that if those liable can't be found, the Council may make arrangements to do the work itself, meaning that residents should not be faced with the enormous remediation costs themselves.

This case dates back to 2005 when tests were originally undertaken on almost 600 properties on the Farndale Estate in Whitmore Reans. The initial results revealed high levels of the chemical carbon disulphide, used in the manufacture of rayon, and subsequent investigations have confirmed unacceptably high levels in twelve properties. The company conducting the carbon disulphide remediation programme expected the clean-up project which started in spring 2008 to be completed by spring 2010.

Leicestershire

Oadby and Wigston Borough Council confirmed in 2009 that residents of 30 properties in Wigston's Little Hill estate have been given legal notice that their properties are situated on land that is contaminated. The estate is built on the site of the old Great Wigston Gas Works, which formerly extracted gas from coal, a process that left behind chemicals including tar derivatives and lead.

The Council is in the process of identifying who should pay for the remediation of the site and is investigating companies and individuals that have been linked to the site in the past. However, if the search proves unsuccessful, taxpayers or those living in the affected homes could end up footing the bill. Residents are becoming increasingly concerned by the length of time it has taken to conclude the investigations, which began in 2006.

Derbyshire

The Avenue Coking Works in Wingerworth near Chesterfield is a grossly contaminated site, which is to be cleansed of its industrial legacy (colliery, lime and iron works, coking plant, chemical works, gas works) and prepared for mixed use development and green space in a £172.3 million project. A new remediation facility is to be used, a thermal desorption unit, which uses high levels of heat to break down chemicals in soil. At more than 600° C the contaminants become vapour which is further heated to 1,200° C and then rapidly cooled. Other processes of treating material at the site include bioremediation, where soil microbes or bugs are used to break down contaminants, and a water treatment plant. Almost all treated material will be re-used on site. The scheme is the largest funded by the National Coalfields Programme, managed by the Homes and Communities Agency.

Two measures in particular have encouraged the use of brownfield land and clean-up of contaminated land in the UK:

1. Since 2001, businesses can claim relief from corporation tax for land remediation, which means restoring contaminated or long-term derelict land. The rate of relief is 150 per cent of the qualifying cleanup cost. Cleanup expenditure qualifies if all of the following are true:
2. the land is in the UK and was acquired by the business to carry out its trade or property letting business;
3. the land was already derelict or contaminated at the time it was acquired (so if purchasing land 'dirty' from a polluting company, there is benefit to both parties);
4. the dereliction or contamination was not caused by action or inaction of the business or a person connected to the business
5. Relief extends to buildings on the land. Land is contaminated if contamination is present that is causing or has the real potential to cause significant harm. The cost of dealing with natural contaminants (other than Japanese Knotweed, arsenic or radon) does not qualify for relief. The relief is only

available to businesses subject to corporation tax. If the company does not have the profits to offset these allowances they can claim a tax credit equivalent to 24 per cent of actual cost from the Treasury. There is no restriction on the type of development and the contamination does not have to be causing harm – the risk that it might do so in the future is sufficient.

6. Landfill tax exemption if a tax exemption certificate was issued. From 1996 brownfield developers avoided paying the landfill tax for historically contaminated material. This did encourage brownfield development but was felt to encourage 'dig and dump' methods rather than promoting more efficient new technology methods of land remediation and is being phased out and will no longer exist after 1 April 2012.

Contaminated land in Europe

Within Europe, the responses of governments, industry and the public to the problems posed by contaminated land vary from country to country. The member states have different problems, concerns and political systems. Policy-making is dependent on these variables, and it is therefore unsurprising that fiscal policy, legislation and remediation standards for contaminated land vary. Policy aims and actual remediation practices tend to be similar, but there are differences with almost every other aspect of contaminated land (Christie and Teeuw, 1998). The UK was first to use soil trigger concentrations as a decision-support tool in risk assessment and in the adoption of a suitable-for-use policy. Assigned trigger concentrations vary depending on the proposed end use of the land. For domestic developments where risks exist of direct ingestion of soil or consumption of contaminated food grown on the site, the acceptable levels are lower than for commercial or industrial development where these risks are less.

The suitable-for-use approach consists of identifying land where contamination is causing unacceptable risks to human health and the environment, assessed on the basis of the current use and circumstances of the land, and returning such land to a condition where such risks no longer arise. The suitable-for-use approach may give rise to a situation where the same contaminant may be present at the same concentrations at two different sites but because the two sites are being used for different purposes, only one may be considered contaminated. Levels of contamination are, for example, allowed to be higher on the land under a car park than the land used for residential housebuilding.

There are certain fundamental principles on which most European and North American countries appear to agree:

• the need to prevent or limit future pollution;

- the 'polluter pays principle', usually with a mechanism for helping innocent landowners (those not responsible for the contamination);
- the precautionary principle (when there are threats of serious damage, scientific uncertainty must be resolved in favour of prevention);
- the use of a risk-based philosophy for identifying, prioritizing and assessing the need for remedial action.

Throughout Europe there is widespread acceptance that the remediation of contaminated land is a long-term problem. The polluter pays principle is also widely accepted but the extent to which it is enforced in respect of historic contamination varies significantly across member states. Approaches also differ in the extent of protection offered to the innocent landowner and those unable to pay for remediation (Syms, 1997).

The European Integrated Pollution, Prevention and Control Directive has created a uniform framework for avoiding or removing new pollution arising from industrial activity (Nathanail and Bardos, 2004).

Box 15.2 Contaminated land case examples in Europe

Espenhain, Germany

This area is in the former lignite basin near Leipzig. The 300 hectare site was a former chemical plant, briquette factory and two power stations. Contaminants included organic pollutants, metals and waste from lignite mining. At the end of the 1980s, seventy towns and villages had been devastated and Epenhain became the focus of the former German Democratic Republic's environmental movement.

Seven opencast mines and 90 per cent of the lignite processing plants have been closed. There has been a programme of major demolition and decontamination of the works. The reconstruction of the open-cast landscape and the redevelopment of brownfield sites is the objective. At the end of this process twelve lakes with a surface area of more than 40 square kilometres in total will create a 'West-Saxony lake district'. Future land use will be as a regional scale industrial and science park.

Sosnowiec, Poland

This former coal mine of 31.5 acres is in the heavily polluted Silesia region of southern Poland. All industrial facilities of the mine have been dismantled and the reclaimed area has been levelled. The office buildings and storage yard remain and may be re-used. Three out of four pit shafts have been demolished. The pump house remains in operation for safety reasons because the mine is exposed to very high water-related risks. The area is within a main underground water reservoir. The land has been redeveloped for industry, services and housing.

Source: RESCUE: Regeneration of European Sites in Cities and Urban Areas, a research project of the European Commission.

Contaminated land in North America

As with other environmental problems, there was little awareness of contaminated land problems in the USA before the 1960s. Isolated incidents of harmful contamination occurred – notably at Love Canal, New York and Times Beach, Missouri – but it was not until the 1980s that the US Superfund was established in the Comprehensive Environmental Response, Compensation, and Liability Act of 1980 (also known as CERCLA). This created a federal programme to clean-up the nation's uncontrolled hazardous waste sites. Through Superfund, the US Environmental Protection Agency (EPA) and its partners are authorized to address abandoned, accidentally spilled, and illegally dumped hazardous wastes that pose current or future threats to human health or the environment.

The EPA developed new and innovative ways to conduct clean-ups. Important research examined how contamination migrated into groundwater, and new technologies provided improved methods to treat, store and dispose of wastes. The EPA took steps to ensure that communities near hazardous waste sites had a meaningful voice in cleanup decisions, including determining how to reuse land after a clean-up. The Superfund programme also pioneered methods to ensure that the parties responsible for contamination were held responsible for the cleanup.

Superfund evolved into a strong and effective multi-billion dollar programme. By 2005, construction work had been completed at 966 or 62 per cent of Superfund private and federal sites, and work had begun at an additional 422 sites. Superfund's emergency response programme had taken action at thousands of sites to reduce immediate threats to human health. These actions included a substantial role in addressing the 2001 attacks on the World Trade Center and Pentagon, the 2001 anthrax attacks, the Columbia space shuttle

---

Box 15.3   The Love Canal and Times Beach contaminated land incidents

Love Canal was named after William T. Love, who dug a short canal in 1910 to the east of Niagara falls to connect the upper and lower Niagara rivers with the intention of generating electricity. This never happened and the unused canal was turned into a municipal and industrial chemical dump in the 1920s. In 1953 the Hooker Chemical Company covered the canal with earth and sold it to the state for one dollar. In the late 1950s more than 100 homes and a school were built on the site. In 1978, after heavy rain, 82 different compounds, 11 of them carcinogenic, leached out of the soil into the gardens and basements of the homes and school. Residents suffered serious health problems including miscarriages and birth defects. In late 1978, 221 families were moved out and their homes purchased by the state.

Times Beach, Missouri was contaminated by spraying roads to control dust with oil containing dioxins. In 1983 on advice from the Centre for Disease control, the EPA permanently relocated all residents and businesses at Times Beach at a cost of $30 million. It was necessary to thermally destroy 25,600 cubic yards of dioxin contaminated soil.

disaster, and hurricanes Katrina and Rita. Through Superfund's Redevelopment Initiative, former Superfund sites were developed into model airplane fields, airports, major department stores, soccer fields, golf courses, wildlife refuges and many more productive uses. In 2009, demonstrating its commitment to the 'polluter pays principle' the EPA secured commitments from potentially responsible parties to undertake more than $1.9 billion in future cleanup work and to reimburse EPA for $371 million of past costs.

In 2002, in the USA, the Small Business Liability Relief and Brownfields Revitalization Act (Brownfields Law) was passed. This expanded the definition of what is considered a brownfield site so that communities could focus on mine-scarred land, or sites contaminated by petroleum or the manufacture and distribution of illegal drugs. The Brownfields programme encourages development of America's estimated 450,000 abandoned and contaminated waste sites.

Brownfield development

There are many areas in towns and cities that have fallen into disuse. Some have been left as unsightly wasteland or derelict buildings and are known as 'brownfield' land. It can be broadly defined as land which is, or was, occupied by a permanent non-agricultural structure. These sites can have a detrimental effect on the environment and social quality of the area and it is therefore beneficial to redevelop these sites. Much of this brownfield land is contaminated and in past years has often been considered unattractive to clean-up and bring back into beneficial use, especially where there have been alternative 'greenfield' sites available. However, modern technologies and approaches have enabled this kind of land to be brought back into beneficial uses. Reusing urban brownfield and contaminated sites for development is socially, economically, environmentally and culturally important for the development of our cities and regions and a valuable alternative to urban sprawl. Because it is more costly to develop, brownfield land is in less demand than greenfield and so has a lower value. This can be seen in Figure 15.1.

The main method of dealing with brownfield and contaminated sites has been through redevelopment, via the planning process, where the objective of economic benefit is linked to environmental enhancement. The demand for development land has led to the reuse of properties that have been abandoned for a variety of reasons. Many of them are brownfield sites that have deteriorated in different ways, including by contamination. These sites are usually a burden in terms of economic losses and contribute to the deterioration of the quality of life of entire neighbourhoods. They create enormous social problems in addition to severe land, soil and habitat degradation and the rehabilitation and redevelopment of derelict land in general is one of the first priorities of

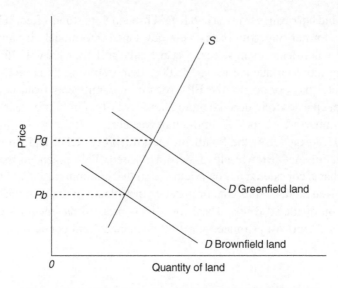

Figure 15.1   The price of greenfield and brownfield land

environmental and spatial planning. The main objective for these sites is to find appropriate new uses and activities, taking into account their economic and social acceptability.

Rehabilitation of brownfields, particularly those which are contaminated, can be an expensive undertaking and requires not only technical solutions but the involvement of financial, regulatory and community stakeholders. Fundamental to this process is the analysis of the risks involved and the development of appropriate strategies, which need to be weighted against the economic and social benefits of brownfield development, to assess the general viability of the redevelopment. In most cases the demand for development land drives the process forward, while sometimes the rehabilitation is grounded on the wish to restore the landscape and the ecology of a region. Brownfield development is, in many cases, essential to attract new business to a locality and for the creation of healthy communities. In effect the development of brownfield land confers external benefits as shown in Figure 15.2.

The external benefits of brownfield land development (removal of unsightly wasteland or derelict buildings plus the preservation of greenfield land) mean the socially optimum amount of brownfield development OM is greater than the private sector determined amount of development ON.

There is little agreement on how much brownfield land there is and where the brownfield sites are located. In April 1998, DETR (Department of Environment, Transport and the Regions) began construction of the National Land Use Database (NLUD), dividing land use into some 51 categories. It is envisaged that once the amount and location of brownfield has been established, initiatives can be devised

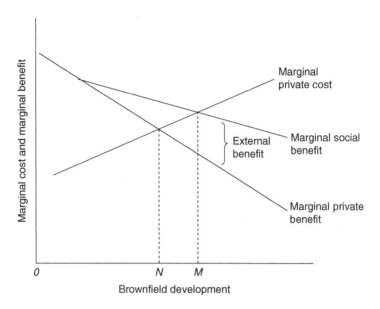

Figure 15.2   External benefits of brownfield land development

and implemented to encourage redevelopment of these areas, particularly where housing demand is high. The Budget for 2008 outlined incentives under the Land Reclamation Tax Relief scheme whereby from April 2009, private developers can qualify for heightened tax relief if they develop on brownfield sites that have been registered on NLUD since 1998 (or demonstrably vacant since then). This new initiative has the potential to unlock some of the most unappealing brownfield sites and allow the developer to qualify for the tax relief.

In 2007, the NLUD–Previously Developed Land (PDL) sites survey unveiled almost 31,000 sites, containing 55,326 ha of land in England. The regions with the most brownfield land are the North West with 18.3 per cent of the total; the South East with 16.2 per cent and Yorkshire and Humberside with 12.5 per cent. The NLUD–PDL classifies brownfield land into five main types:

1. Previously developed land now vacant;
2. Vacant buildings;
3. Derelict land and buildings;
4. Previously developed land or buildings currently in use and allocated in local plan or with planning permission;
5. Previously developed land or buildings currently in use with redevelopment potential but no planning allocation or permission

The aim of the NLUD–PDL database is to provide a consistent, comprehensive, and up-to-date record of all previously developed land and buildings in

England that may be available for development, whether vacant, derelict, or still in productive use. Around 53 per cent of previously developed land in England in the 2007 survey was located in urban areas, as defined by the Department for Communities and Local Government, significantly less than was recorded in 2004. The overall stock also reduced over the same period suggesting that brownfield land reuse policies are working, concentrating new development in urban areas.

In Scotland there are approximately 10,863 hectares of brownfield land which comprises some 8,224 hectares of derelict land and 2,640 hectares of urban vacant land. Vacant land is land which is unused for the purposes for which it is held and is viewed as an appropriate site for development. This land must either have had prior development on it or preparatory work has taken place in anticipation of future development. Derelict land (and buildings) is land which has been so damaged by development, that it is incapable of development for beneficial use without rehabilitation. Land also qualifies as derelict if it has an unremedied previous use which could constrain future development (www.scotland.gov.uk).

The UK Government now wants to bring as much brownfield land as possible back into use and is encouraging the regeneration of previously developed land to limit unnecessary development of greenfield sites and to preserve the countryside. Strict targets have been set to encourage building of the majority of new houses on brownfield land. The percentage of developments taking place on brownfield land rose from 55 per cent in 1989 to 61 per cent in 2004. Government policy is 60:40 brownfield to greenfield sites and local authorities are required to consider using previously developed land before releasing greenfield sites.

The potential liabilities associated with brownfield development have led to developers avoiding such sites in favour of easier and safer greenfield options. However, with careful development, it is possible to turn potential brownfield liabilities into an asset and although policies to encourage the use of brownfield sites before greenfield sites, seem to be successful, there is controversy about the practice of 'garden grabbing'. This arises because, until June 2010, gardens in residential areas were classified as brownfield land, making it easier for builders to get planning permission. About 25 per cent of new homes were built on residential land, mainly gardens in the years up to 2010, whereas before 1997 the Figure was only 11 per cent. In some areas in the south of England including Sevenoaks and South Buckinghamshire more than 70 per cent of new homes were built on gardens.

Valuation of contaminated land sites

In order to effectively value contaminated land sites, information is essential. The highest and best use of the brownfield site may be affected by the contamination, both before and after remediation. The value should take into account residual stigma and potential for third-party liability. It must be established what the site has been used for not just in recent times but throughout its history. A search can be made for previous environmental reports and to discover if the owner/tenant/occupier has complied with environmental legislation and whether there are any discharge consents or abstractions.

It is important to investigate the site as part of the sale and transfer process for four reasons:

1. due diligence;
2. as a tool in the process of redevelopment;
3. to assist in the valuation of commercial and industrial properties for asset and bank valuations; and
4. as part of the process of effective property management. (Syms, 1997)

The lack of information about past uses and land condition is likely to result in one of the following:

- The valuer declining to issue a valuation report until an environmental report has been produced – and costed by a recognized expert;
- The production of a report on the assumption that no contamination exists – that is, highly qualified; or
- The instruction being declined.

Market valuations may be required for many purposes but, in the context of industrial buildings, are most likely to be required for the following:

- As part of the sale and transfer process – either property transactions or business sales;
- For bank finance purposes, for example, to raise working capital; and
- For company asset balance sheet purposes.

A site can first be valued as if uncontaminated, for example, a site of 10,000 square metres and annual rent of £500,000 (£50 per square metre). With a yield of 9 per cent the years purchase (YP) or valuation multiple is 11.1 and so the valuation is £500,000 x 11.11 = £555,000.

Then it is necessary to estimate how much it will cost to clean-up or decontaminate the site. Are there any reports or estimates? How up to date are they? Who prepared them? Who were they prepared for? Can other information be used in lieu of any reports? Is any information obtainable on the decontamination costs for similar sites and historic uses/contaminant profiles? Is there any risk of harm at present or can the decontamination be deferred to a future date? Is there any risk of regulatory action? Comparable costs may be available and the estimated costs of clean-up can be deducted from the uncontaminated value to give a valuation of the contaminated site.

Alternatively, the yield figure could be increased to take account of the impaired value of the contaminated land (thus reducing the YP) but this is fairly arbitrary and therefore may be inaccurate. More detailed and advanced valuation techniques may be required, involving statistical analysis and reference to case studies for evidence.

Summary

Contaminated land occurs where the residues of previous industrial processes such as chemical works and petroleum refineries remain and are harmful to living organisms. In the UK, Defra oversees contaminated land legislation through (Part 2A of the Environmental Protection Act, 1990). Under the definition of contaminated land in this Act, the area of such land in the UK is about 2,800 hectares. Under the widest definitions, however, it is considerably more.

Methods of cleaning up contaminated land sites vary from removal of polluted soil to landfill sites to sophisticated techniques of biological remediation by adding bacteria and other microbes to remove contaminants. Where possible, under the 'polluter pays principle', the original polluter is made to pay for remediation but often, however, they cannot be traced and the developer is responsible for clean up.

Strict targets have been set to encourage building the majority of new houses on brownfield land, in order to limit unnecessary development of greenfield sites and preserve the countryside. In recent years this policy has had some success in the UK in promoting redevelopment of previously developed land.

Chapter 15: review questions

1. Why is contaminated land a problem for property developers?
2. What types of procedure are used to remediate contaminated land?
3. Explain the rationale behind UK government policy on brownfield land development.
4. What is the United States 'Superfund' Programme?
5. Why are waste disposal landfill sites a particular problem in terms of contamination?
6. Explain why there are external benefits from development of brownfield land in the UK.

Part IV
Real Estate Investment

16

Investment in UK Land and Property

After studying this chapter you will be able to:

- Compare the investment characteristics of different interests in real property;
- Describe the various types of investor in property;
- Explain the role of real property investment in portfolio management;
- Explain how property earnings can be capitalized.

Real estate investment

The economist distinguishes two meanings of the word 'investment':

1. expenditure on the purchase of *existing* assets – for example, shares of a company, or an interest in an existing (perhaps tenanted) office block;
2. expenditure on the *creation of new* fixed assets – for example, the construction of North Sea oil rigs, or the development of a new office block.

Thus property investment is an example of the first meaning and property development is an example of the second. There are several types of real estate investment property including:

- residential property investment,
- commercial property investment,
- buy-to-let property investment (including overseas property ownership),
- investment in land purchase.

Residential property investment is the least risky form of investment because the purchase of a residential property by the owner is not only an investment decision but the property also performs the function of providing somewhere to live and is thus a consumer good as well as an investment good. One of the main reasons that people (especially in the UK) engage in home owner-ship rather than renting is because, generally, investment in property is profit-able. By combining the consumer good function of shelter with the investment nature of property purchase, investment in residential property provides a safe and usually profitable dual-use of funds. Moreover, homeowners have an excellent incentive to regard their property purchase as a long-term financial priority because it provides the roof over their family's heads and as a result lenders are often willing to advance up to 90 per cent of the purchase price of a residential property, seeing this as low risk lending. In most developed countries loan to value ratios are in the region of 70–90 per cent as a result (see Chapter 5).

Commercial property investment (see Chapter 17) involves the purchase of multi-family apartments, office buildings, retail space, hotels and motels, warehouses, industrial units and workshops and other commercial properties. The investment usually provides a rental income and the possibility of growth in the capital value of the asset, but commercial property is generally regarded as being more risky than residential and so loan to value ratios are usually in the range of 50–70 per cent.

Buy-to-let investment is the investment strategy of buying a residential prop-erty to be let for profit. Since the mid-nineties in the UK there has been a surge in demand for rental property. Low interest rates and soaring house price growth helped fuel the appeal of buy-to-let, together with changes in legisla-tion, which made it easier for landlords to deal with sitting tenants. Historically, buyers of property to let were surcharged or forced to borrow at commercial rates, and potential rental income was not taken into account for servicing the borrowings. The panel of lenders supporting buy-to-let schemes brought their interest rates into line with the rates for owner-occupation and took rental income into account for servicing the loan. This policy switch was encouraged by the knowledge that professional letting and property management agents were involved in the selection of suitable properties for the rental market, in the selection of tenants and in the management of the properties. This enhanced the creditworthiness of buy-to-let propositions and allowed this form of prop-erty investment to grow until the credit crunch of 2008 cause it to stall. From only 4 per cent of mortgages in 2000, buy-to-let mortgages increased in num-ber to 29 per cent of all mortgages in 2006. By value, in June 2010, buy-to-let mortgages accounted for 12 per cent of all mortgages, the highest proportion since records began (Council for Mortgage Lenders, 2010).

At the height of the boom in property and buy-to-let investment in 2006–7, some investors bought property as 'buy-to-leave' – relying solely on the appre-ciation in value of the property and not renting it out. Clearly if this type of activity became commonplace it would have consequences for communities where there were a number of empty properties.

Box 16.1   Land banking

Building companies and developers tend to keep land banks for several years in order to secure housing supply needs. Some of this land will be held speculatively in the hope that planning zone restrictions will be relaxed in the future. It can take several years to obtain planning permission, especially if there are opposition groups. They can use the land as collateral to obtain loans and need a reserve of land to remain in business – if they run out of land they would have to buy from competitors at higher prices. Many reputable listed commercial building companies engage successfully in land banking for future building projects.

The Land Registration Act of 2002 enabled companies to purchase land sites and easily divide them into smaller plots. The company can then offer these plots for sale to individual investors, often claiming that they may make unrealistic returns. This practice in the UK does not fall under the control of the Financial Services Authority (FSA) although collective investment schemes are regulated. Typically land bankers buy land for less than £10,000 an acre and divide it into plots of 0.1 acres, selling these for £8,000–£20,000 each, making profits of between £80,000 and £200,000 an acre. The selling companies often go into liquidation leaving the buyers with virtually unsaleable plots. In reality, the land may be totally unsuitable for development and have little hope of ever getting planning permission. The land often ends up abandoned and neglected.

In 2008, the FSA ordered UK Land Investments to be wound up as it constituted an unregulated collective investment scheme. UKLI owed £70.8 million to creditors and 4,500 people had bought 5,000 plots of land. The same owner operated Regents Land and St James's Land which continued trading. Several other land banking companies have been put into compulsory liquidation by the Insolvency Service Companies Investigation Branch. As a result of increased regulation, many land banking companies – some still selling UK plots – have moved outside the European Union.

The part of the buy-to-let market hardest hit by the downturn of 2006–8 was that for new inner-city flats. These were often purchased with high mortgages taken out using inflated valuations. This risky and highly speculative part of the market ended with the downturn in prices for city-centre apartments from 2006 onward.

Investment in land purchase can produce reasonable returns because land prices tend to rise over time. Much land investment tends to be carried out by speculators, however. Considerable brownfield land exists, mainly in urban areas, but most of the easier sites that were made available after the decline of heavy and manufacturing industries have already been developed, particularly in the south of the England, although some of this land has severe contamination problems (see Chapter 15). It is possible to make excellent returns by investing in land which then receives planning permission for development, but it is a high risk investment with no guarantee of success. There are three types of land available:

1. National Park land with severe restriction on any type of development;
2. Greenfield land with considerable restrictions on development;

3. Brownfield land with more limited restrictions on development and development on some sites may be encouraged, particularly in areas of regional or local regeneration.

If the planning zones change, then the person who owns the land gains considerably as the zone moves from greenfield to a designated site for development – either retail, commercial or residential. In south-east England, agricultural land might sell for £5,000 an acre, but land with planning permission for residential development in a good location might fetch £1,000,000 an acre. However, the land owner can lose considerably if no planning change is forthcoming. Essentially the land speculator (or 'land banker') is gambling that the area will be re-zoned for development and of course land close to expanding towns and cities is, therefore, likely to be their preferred option.

Real estate investment characteristics

Real estate investments have certain characteristics which affect their performance:

- they are in a fixed location;
- heterogeneity – they are all different;
- they tend to be of high unit value (or large acreages) and this can be a barrier to entry;
- illiquidity – they are among the least liquid of assets;
- information problems – aggregate data has been available in the UK since the 1960s and in the USA since 1978 but in other countries only recently;
- a further information problem is the need for valuers (and subjective valuations) to measure some of the returns on property that arise from increases in capital value.

Because land resources are durable, rights existing in them have a long timescale and, although there may be management costs, no problem exists in storage. Property rights, like stocks and shares, are therefore demanded as investment assets. The real property market can be regarded as a part of the wider investment asset market which also includes company shares or equities and company bonds or government bonds (gilts). It is in the sense of holding assets as a store of wealth that we use the term 'investment'.

The broad objectives of investment are to preserve or enhance the real value of the asset and to receive a flow of income over time. Different interests in real property really represent different bundles of rights. However, like stock exchange securities, they can be classified according to their broad *investment* characteristics: 'equity' interests – for example, freeholds; 'equity-loan' interests – for example, freehold ground rents with significant reversionary prospects; 'loan' interests – such as leaseholds, freehold ground rents with distant reversions, and mortgages.

Freeholds

The holder of a freehold, whether owner-occupier or investor, takes the full financial risk of ownership. If the rent increases – for example, through scarcity or inflation – he gains; if the rent falls – for example, through deterioration of locality – he loses. A freehold is, therefore, an 'equity' interest, equivalent to the ordinary share in a company.

When purchased as an investment, freeholds are usually subject to a lease granted by a previous freeholder. The purchaser receives the rack-rent (full annual rental which a property could achieve were it to be let out to rent) under the lease and the reversion at the end of the lease. But to obtain the full equity interest there must be provision for frequent rent review; otherwise the freehold bears a closer resemblance to a leasehold interest.

Freehold investments usually involve some management: for instance, collecting the rent and ensuring that the tenant observes the terms and covenants of the lease. There may also be maintenance obligations, such as external repairs. Such management costs have to be deducted from the rent received to ascertain the net income.

Like ordinary shares, freeholds differ in quality and this is reflected in their yields. Briefly, the yield, that is the net annual income return expressed as a percentage of the market price of the asset, depends upon:

1. the purchase price;
2. the current rent;
3. the prospect of future rent rises as a result of increased demand for the type of property or because of inflation;
4. the frequency of rent reviews;
5. the type and condition of the property;
6. the strength of the occupier's covenant;
7. management costs,
8. development possibilities; and
9. estimates of future changes in government policy, for example, as regards depreciation allowances.

Demand for prime properties – for example, city-centre shops and modern first-class offices – by institutional investors is keen and they have the funds necessary for what are mostly expensive purchases. As a result, yields on such freeholds are low (shops 7 per cent, offices 6.25 per cent), and often below the yield on long-dated government securities. This *reverse yield gap* implies that the difference is expected to be made good by future rent increases. In contrast, private persons have to consider the cheaper secondary properties. Nor can they overcome the difficulty by borrowing, since insurance companies and merchant banks are reluctant to lend against secondary property. The result is that such properties are sold on a much higher yield (8–11 per cent).

In practice, yields differ slightly on the different types of freehold property. Thus prime shops have a lower yield than offices, while offices' yield tends to be less than that on industrial and residential properties. We can explain this by considering the characteristics of the main types of property.

Shops

Location is all-important in determining the yield on shops. Generally speaking the best high street positions are occupied by the multiples, their values being enhanced by complementarity with one another. The main reasons for the low yield on prime shops are:

- the supply of such sites is limited by purely spatial considerations;
- multiples are willing to pay high rents for these sites;
- the goods sold have a high income elasticity of demand, thereby ensuring growth in turnover; and
- the institutions seek such investments because occupiers have excellent covenants and the rental rate of growth has been the highest of all types of urban development.

Even a short distance from the prime shopping location rents fall off considerably, while potential rent growth is not nearly so good. Hence yields on secondary shops are about double those on prime shops.

Offices

Prime office blocks appeal to the institutions with large funds to invest, because they can often be let to a single tenant providing an excellent covenant, thereby reducing management costs.

During the recessions of the early 1990s and 2007–9, amalgamations of firms, and reduced staff requirements because of the introduction of IT, led to an over-supply of offices, resulting in falling rents, over-renting and reduced prospects for future increases. Furthermore, this has highlighted the problem of obsolescence through technical advances and changes in working practices. Consequently, though the institutions are still buying modern office blocks, it is the property companies which are acquiring the older properties where there are opportunities to add value by management expertise or even redevelopment.

Industrial factories and warehouses

Industrial premises tend to be less popular as investments than other types of property. The reasons are:

- rents are usually more affected by economic depression;
- many factories are built for a special purpose and if they have to be re-let difficulty may be experienced in finding a similar tenant or, alternatively, expense is incurred in adaptation;
- changes in techniques of production and handling goods can make the factory obsolete – for example, greater eave height may be required for fork-lift stacking in a warehouse; and
- the intensive use of industrial premises leads to more rapid depreciation than with other properties, though tax reliefs give some compensation.

The result is that emerging from recession the current yield on industrial premises is about 8 per cent. Nevertheless, there are indications that newly built B1 premises (use for all or any of the following purposes; a) as an office other than a use within class A2 (financial and professional services); b) for research and development of products or processes; or c) for any industrial process; being a use which can be carried out in any residential area without detriment to the amenity of that area by reason of noise, vibration, smell, fumes, smoke, soot, ash, dust or grit) are becoming more popular as investments. These are of simple construction, on the ground floor only, have large clear spaces, roof lighting and office accommodation attached, and are easily adapted to different uses. Furthermore, they can be written off as depreciation for tax purposes, and may carry special tax allowances.

Residential

For a number of reasons residential property usually shows the highest yield:

1. rent increases tend to lag behind the current market rent;
2. costs of management, for example, through frequent rent collection from many tenants, tend to be relatively high; and
3. the cost of repairs, for which the landlord is usually responsible, tends to be heavy.

However, recent relaxation of the legal constraints on rent increases and repossession (see Chapter 5) have made residential property a more attractive investment proposition, particularly for the private investor.

Rural estates

In the UK, the two main types of tenure for farms are tenant farming and owner-occupation. Where a rural estate is let, the landowner (investor) usually provides fixed capital (such as buildings, roads and drainage), while the tenant is responsible for working capital (such as implements, livestock, fertilizers) and labour. But there are no rigid rules. With complete freedom of contract, the arrangement reached would be the one that maximized the joint earnings of the two parties. In practice, ignorance, inertia and even obstinacy of one party may reduce free bargaining.

Tenant farming, once predominant, has declined markedly since the Second World War, and today accounts for less than 20 per cent of all holdings in England and Wales. The Agriculture Holdings Act 1948 made it difficult to give a tenant notice to quit, and the right of succession was extended to relatives working on the farm by the Agriculture (Miscellaneous Provisions) Act 1976. Though a revision of rentals is possible every 3 years, they remain somewhat below the free market level. Investors' income is therefore low, and many farms were sold to owner-occupiers. To halt the contraction in the number of tenanted farms, the Agricultural Tenancies Act 1995 provided for the terms of new farm business tenancies to be decided by free bargaining between landlord and tenant.

Until recently, agricultural land has proved an excellent hedge against inflation, with steady rent increases and above average capital appreciation, chiefly as a result of buoyant demand brought about by:

- rising prices of agricultural products through the EU's Common Agricultural Policy (CAP) and the devaluation of sterling in 1986 and 1992;
- the appreciation in the value of additional sources of income, such as woodlands, mineral workings, sporting rights, which all now form part of the total investment value of an estate;
- the prospect of possible urban development;
- owners who have sold land for development at very high prices reinvesting the proceeds in farmland to take advantage of the 'roll-over' concession for capital gains tax;
- when Britain joined the EU, British farmland was cheap compared with prices in other EU countries;
- a nil rate of inheritance tax on farmland designed to ensure that farms can be passed down through the generations without paying crippling death duties, are now being manipulated by city traders and others as a way to invest in land to soak up their surplus cash, without having to pay inheritance tax;
- the social standing which landownership gives in a rural community, and the satisfaction of walking round a rural estate compared with a block of offices; and
- a rise in the value of the residential and amenity elements of many farms.

All the factors which differentiate real property investments from other investments are accentuated in the rural estate market:

1. not only is each estate unique in its size and position, but it differs in topography and fixed capital;

2. the rural estate market is highly localized; and

3. many estates change hands by private treaty and therefore at undisclosed prices, with demand being influenced by non-economic factors, such as family considerations.

Thus the UK rural estate market tends to be imperfect.

Leaseholds

A freeholder may rent the premises he owns to somebody else. The usual practice is to grant a lease for a fixed number of years in return for a capital sum (a 'premium'), or a rent, or a combination of both. These leases have value and can be exchanged in the market.

At the end of the given period the property reverts to the freeholder, and then the value of the lease to the lessee is zero. Thus if a premium has been paid for a lease, the purchaser should accumulate a sinking fund by putting aside a part of the income received during the period of the loan. Since such sinking-fund provision has to come out of income after tax has been paid, only pension funds and charities, who pay no tax on income, are not penalized. As a result of the restricted market, yields on leaseholds tend to be higher than those on comparable freeholds.

Freehold ground rents

Freehold ground rents (FGRs) refer to the annual payments received on long leases. Originally they were mostly charged on land leased for development, but

---

Box 16.2 Investment in UK farmland

The Church of England, the Crown Estates and many Oxbridge colleges traditionally invest in farmland and in the 1990s City institutions invested heavily. Farmland prices have risen rapidly in the last decade (by 134 per cent according to Savills agricultural land survey, or 164 per cent according to Knight Frank) reaching £5,100 per acre in 2010. Grain prices rose from £65 per tonne in 2004 to £145 per tonne in 2007.
Farming offers relief from taxation:

- Inheritance tax (IHT) – where the property and land are both used for commercial farming, IHT relief is 100 per cent. The farmland must either have been farmed by the owner, or someone on behalf of the owner, for 2 years.
- Capital gains tax (CGT) – there are three types of relief when the property is sold or transferred.
- Income tax – losses can be set against gains made elsewhere (for example, City bonuses) for 5 years.

Farmland prices in the UK are widely expected to double in the next 10 years and in 2010 City investors were buying more arable land than career farmers. Yields are low at 2–3 per cent but farmland is popular because it can be both a tax efficient investment and a 'lifestyle' purchase.

they are now received for flats sold on long leases. Since they are small relative to the full value of the developed site upon which they are secured, the income is certain. Thus where reversion is distant, FGRs are comparable with irredeemable or very long-dated government stock although, being less liquid, yields are higher, particularly if management is involved (as with FGRs on flats). Because of inflation, freeholders granting long leases have insisted on provisions for periodic revision of the ground rent or for profit-sharing or for some combination of both.

When reversion is less than 50 years, an FGR increasingly assumes equity characteristics, for its reversionary value will tend to rise. Its price will tend to be higher if it has a special value to a particular person, such as the current lessee of the property or a property developer who wishes to assemble land for future development.

Mortgages

Mortgages are long-term money loans secured on real property, with interest payments being prior charges. Thus the risk of non-payment of interest or of capital is small. Unlike leaseholds, capital is repaid (although interest-only mortgages were popular with buy-to-let investors before the 'credit crunch' and endowment mortgages were popular in the 1970s and 1980s), and so no sinking fund is necessary. In effect, therefore, mortgages are similar to debentures or government bonds, and their yields tend to move together. On the other hand, because of inflation, mortgages on commercial and industrial properties are less attractive to the financial institutions, who now prefer to retain an equity interest – for example, through part-ownership, sale-and-leaseback or profit-sharing provisions.

Investors in real estate

Investment in real property is carried out by private persons, private trusts and institutions – insurance companies, pension funds, charities, property companies, property bond funds property unit trusts and real estate investment trusts. To some extent each has different objectives, and so their preferences differ.

Private persons

Unlike many other types of investment, such as shares and bonds, property is a tangible asset: if you own a property – or a part of one – you can see your investment. While property valuations can fluctuate, the property is still there. Many private investors feel that they understand property better than other assets, if only because they have the experience of buying their own homes. The considerable sums required for some property investments can, however, act as a barrier to entry for private individuals.

Anybody who purchases a property rather than renting is an investor. The satisfaction or return received should at least equal what could be obtained if, instead, premises were rented and the money invested elsewhere. For example, a person may rent rather than buy a shop either through lack of capital or because it is considered that the money can be more profitably employed in carrying stock, and so on.

Owner-occupiers, for example, shop-owners, farmers and householders, are holding wealth in the form of real property. They enjoy a full equity interest – income or satisfaction from the use of their property, and normally a hedge against inflation.

Other private persons investing in real property usually have only limited funds. Thus their direct investment tends to be restricted to dwellings and secondary shops. Indirectly, however, they can invest in prime shops and offices by buying property bonds or shares in property companies or unit trusts specializing in quoted property companies.

Insurance companies and pension funds

Major institutional investors, such as pension funds and life insurance companies make a sharp differentiation between commercial property and residential property. As a general rule, only commercial property is of interest to UK institutional investors. Residential property ownership is regarded as having much heavier administrative overheads than commercial property, as well as greater political and reputational risk.

Most property is acquired by direct purchase, but because of a shortage of the right type of property, many institutions have participated directly in development, usually in conjunction with development companies, property companies and construction firms. However, insurance companies find it advantageous to own properties directly rather than through shares in property companies because:

1. direct investment in property gives the company more control than an investment in property company shares;
2. a substantial holding of the shares of a property company (necessary to exercise some control) may be more difficult to dispose of than a first-class building;
3. the prices of buildings have tended to be less volatile than the prices of property company shares;
4. the high gearing of a property company is of little advantage to an insurance company, which always holds part of its assets in fixed money terms; and
5. holding shares in a property company represents an inefficient way to invest in property, since corporation tax is deducted from the profit attributable to dividend, whereas the insurance company pays a lower tax rate on life income.

From the early 1980s to 2000, property investment had been an unfashionable area for the institutions. In the 1980s and 1990s, institutional investors tended to reduce their exposure to commercial property. In the mid-1980s the average commercial property holding in pension funds was about 13 per cent but by 1999 the Figure had fallen to just 4 per cent (the same as the average cash holding). Investment in UK and overseas stock markets was preferred as UK equities outperformed UK property in 15 of the final 20 years of the last century.

The institutions' attitude towards property changed considerably when stock markets took a turn for the worse after the technology bubble burst in 2000. Property was rediscovered as an investment category and by the end of 2004, the average pension fund's property holding had risen to 7.0 per cent. Other factors have also helped to increase interest in property investment. Historically low interest rates have made it possible for investors to fund their property purchases largely through borrowing: the rent received has often more than covered the interest payable. For those not wishing to borrow, the high income yield from property is a major attraction. The introduction of a new form of property investment vehicle to the UK, the Real Estate Investment Trust (REIT), has also raised the profile of the sector (see below).

Pension funds now compete strongly with insurance companies and property companies for first-class properties, since the inflation-hedge helps to retain the real value of the accumulated pension funds. The smaller pension funds invest in property indirectly through *pension fund property unit trusts*, whose trust deeds limit membership to pension funds and charities enjoying tax exemption. Such trusts afford the advantages of property investment without management problems. The larger funds, however, prefer to purchase and manage their own properties. The disadvantage of holding shares in property companies is even greater for pension funds than for insurance companies since pension funds do not pay tax on income or capital gains but since 1999 have been unable to reclaim tax credits on shares held.

Charities and trusts

Charities and trusts are concerned not only with income (from which periodic distributions are made) but also with retaining the real value of trust funds. Consequently, although they pay no income tax, they cannot invest entirely in high-yielding securities. For example, the Church Commissioners, who pay clergy stipends from investment income, endeavour to preserve the real value of that income by holding a part of their portfolio in equity interests, including property and farmland.

Unlike most institutional investors, charities receive little 'new' money for investment each year. They are therefore constantly reviewing their existing portfolios to see what possible adjustments could best serve their beneficiaries, both present and future.

Property companies

Property investment and development companies have grown considerably since 1945, largely reflecting the boom in urban redevelopment. Most tend to be highly geared, their capital consisting of a high proportion of loans to ordinary shares. Properties owned provide the security against borrowing, while interest charges are covered by regular rents. High gearing is beneficial to the few ordinary shareholders when profits are good, and it makes it easier to retain control.

Property company shares are traded on the London Stock Exchange (LSE). There are two types of property company:

- Property investment companies such as Land Securities acquire or develop properties and retain them so that the rental can cover running costs, interest charges and dividends. The value of their properties underpins their share values.
- Developer-traders, such as Helical Bar construct or acquire properties and then sell them following completion or refurbishment.

Today many non-property companies, such as Barclay's Bank or Blue Circle, have recognized the additional returns made possible by more active management of their properties. To this end a subsidiary company is formed – for example, Barclay's Property Holdings or Blue Circle Properties.

The larger companies tend to specialize in office blocks or prime shop properties, and a few (such as Slough Estates, now SEGRO) in industrial property. Hammerson specializes in shopping centres. Residential property investment is confined mainly to smaller companies, many of which engage in 'break-up' operations, selling houses and flats to sitting tenants or, when vacant possession is obtained, to owner-occupiers.

Foreign investors

Overseas investment in UK property (particularly in central London) has increased considerably since the fall in property prices through the 2007–9 recession and the fall in the sterling exchange rate. Capital values have fallen by 39.5 per cent since the UK peak in June 2007, according to the leading property index Investment Property Databank (IPD), but this means a fall of up to 60 per cent for buyers in the Eurozone and the USA because of the decline in the pound's value. The UK also tends to have longer leases than continental Europe, 15 years compared to six or nine, and investors are attracted by the income security that this offers during the recession. Much investment is expected to come from German funds – which also took advantage of falling values in the previous recession in the early 1990s – as well as Spanish, Middle Eastern and Far Eastern groups.

Property bond funds and real estate investment trusts (REITs)

Most people wishing to invest in property are faced with the difficulty of having insufficient funds to buy prime property of the kind which has shown the greatest capital growth. The property bond fund, a comparatively recent innovation, partly succeeds in overcoming this problem. Subscribers buy a number of units in a fund which invests the money in first-class property. For example, Allied Dunbar, Friends Provident, Legal & General, Norwich Union and Standard Life have billions of pounds invested in offices, shops and industrial property in the major cities of Britain, and also in Belgium, Holland, France and West Germany: Standard Life alone has 500 properties across Europe with a market value of £8.5 billion. Agricultural estates are also held and, in this way, the holder of property bonds has a wide spread in first-class property, with the value of the bonds varying directly with the value of the properties held. In conjunction with their agents, these funds take an active interest in the management of their properties, revaluing them at fixed intervals.

Already well-established and very popular in many countries overseas such as Australia, the USA, Germany and Japan, REITs or real estate investment trusts were launched in the UK on 1 January 2007. A REIT is a quoted company that owns and manages income-producing property on behalf of shareholders, either commercial or residential. Most of its taxable income (at least 90 per cent) is distributed to shareholders through dividends, in return for which the company is largely exempt from corporation tax. REITs are designed to offer investors income and capital appreciation from rented property assets in a tax-efficient way, with a return more closely aligned with direct property investment. This is achieved by taking away 'double taxation' (corporation tax plus the tax on dividends) of ordinary property funds. The introduction of UK REITs creates an opportunity for a wide range of investors to invest in property as an asset class by creating a more liquid and tax-efficient vehicle.

A REIT can contain commercial and residential property and provides a way for investors to access property assets without having to buy property directly. In the UK, REITs can apply for UK-REIT status, which exempts the company from corporate tax and the introduction of a UK-REIT regime, combined with the traditional strengths of London's capital markets, creates opportunities for the growth of the property investment sector. A UK-REIT enjoys all the benefits of any other company, in addition to the tax advantages. UK resident companies listed on a recognized stock exchange are eligible for REIT status. REITs are required to distribute at least 90 per cent of their taxable profits to investors and companies which qualify as REITs are not subject to corporation tax on their qualifying rental income or chargeable gains. A conversion charge applies to companies adopting REIT status, equal to 2 per cent of the market value of their investment properties at the date of conversion. Nine UK property companies converted to REIT status in 2007, including the five that were

FTSE 100 members at that time: British Land, Hammerson, Land Securities, Liberty International and Slough Estates (now known as SEGRO). The other four were: Brixton, Great Portland Estates, Primary Health Properties and Workspace Group.

REITs receive special tax considerations and typically offer investors high yields, as well as a highly liquid method of investing in real estate. Equity REITs invest in and own properties (thus responsible for the equity or value of their real estate assets). Their revenues come principally from their properties' rents. Mortgage REITs (in the USA but not yet allowed in the UK) deal in investment and ownership of property mortgages. They lend money for mortgages to owners of real estate, or purchase existing mortgages or mortgage-backed securities – their revenues are generated primarily by the interest that they earn on the mortgage loans.

Since their introduction in 2007 in the UK, REIT's have shown disappointing returns (as might be expected given market conditions) but they allow much greater liquidity than direct investment in property with the same effective tax treatment.

Property Unit Trusts

A similar principle operates with those unit trusts which specialize in property (for example, Cornhill Property Share specializing in emerging property markets and off-plan residential investments), but in order to avoid management commitments, such unit trusts use their funds to buy shares in property companies or in companies such as hotels, which are concerned with property.

Building societies

Building societies can be regarded as institutional investors, since they are an important source of loans for house purchase. Their activities are analysed in Chapter 5.

Investment asset yields

Demand for property as an investment asset has a considerable effect on its capital value and, through this, influences the supply of different types of property. We have to ask, therefore, what determines the level of yield on the different types of real property assets? Having answered this question, we can examine the influence of investment demand on the flow of different types of property on to the market.

Two aspects of property yields have to be considered:

1. the *level* of yield, which reflects the relationship with general investment yields and is thus established within the context of national economic trends, government policy and comparative risks;
2. the *pattern* of property yields.

At different times all asset yields move in the same direction; it seems that the 'benchmark' upon which they are based rises or falls. The question we have to answer, therefore, is: how is this benchmark determined?

People can hold assets in many different forms – for example, money, bonds, debentures, shares, land, houses, paintings or antiques. All, except money, yield either a flow of income or direct satisfaction. On the other hand, only money is perfectly liquid: that is, it can be changed into some other form without delay, cost or possible capital loss. The yield forgone by holding money is thus the opportunity cost of being perfectly liquid.

Questions of risk apart, a person will arrange his 'portfolio' of assets according to the emphasis he puts on liquidity as opposed to yield. If he wants complete liquidity, he will hold money; if he prefers some return, he holds other assets. There is a whole variety of assets to choose from. Figure 16.1 shows some examples.

In order to eliminate complications arising because assets differ in liquidity and risk, it is assumed here that the only asset other than money is undated, fixed-interest government bonds. This gives us a model in which there are only two kinds of asset in which wealth may be held – money and bonds (see Figure 16.2).

Let us assume that, at any time, there is a given stock of money and a given stock of bonds available for holding as assets. This stock of money will equal

Money	Building society deposits	Treasury bills (a short-dated government security)	Debentures and mortgage loans secured on real property	Irredeemable bonds and freehold ground rents with distant reversions	Freehold ground rents with early reversions	Shares in companies including REITs	Freeholds

Figure 16.1   Alternative forms of holding assets

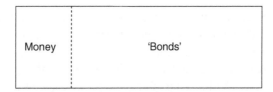

Figure 16.2   Holding assets as either money or 'bonds'

the total supply of money (cash and bank money) in the economy less the amount demanded by persons and businesses for normal buying and selling operations.

The price of bonds, as with other commodities, is expressed in terms of money and, in our simple asset market, equilibrium will occur where, given the stock of money and of bonds and the preferences of the public for holding one or the other, a money price of bonds is established at which the public is willing to hold just the amount of bonds and money available. At any other price there would be no equilibrium. If, for example, the bond market price were below the equilibrium price, demand would exceed supply. In other words, there would still be some people preferring to hold money rather than bonds. As they switched, the price of bonds would rise until nobody wished to switch further. This would be the equilibrium price.

It should be noted that the equilibrium price of bonds can be viewed as the equilibrium rate of interest (yield) on bonds, since the two are inversely related. A 5 per cent bond (that is, one paying annual interest of £5 per £100 nominal value) will in fact be yielding a return of 10 per cent if its price on the market falls to £50. Conversely, should the price rise to £125, the bond yield would fall to 4 per cent.

This simple model explains the determination of the rate of interest, the 'benchmark' for yields on the whole spectrum of assets. It should be noted that it is a 'stock' rather than a 'flow' theory. The justification for this is that neither the stock of money nor the stock of bonds is subject to great variations except over considerable periods of time. The supply of money is controlled by the government; the flow of bonds (new issues by borrowers) is small compared with the existing stock of old bonds. Current borrowing will therefore have little effect on the 'bench-mark' rate of interest and it is the supply from the existing stock of bonds, together with demand, which determines the price of bonds at any one time. The price at which new issues are offered is determined by the current price at which old bonds are being traded. The situation is parallel to that of the housing market (see Chapter 5).

If we now relax the assumption of a single income-bearing asset in the form of bonds and allow that, as in real life, wealth can be held in a range of assets differing in lender's risk, income yield and liquidity, then lender's risk may relate to income or capital. A very short-term investment (say, in a Treasury Bill with only a few weeks to repayment) will be almost completely riskless so far as capital is concerned but provides no guarantee that the money repaid can be reinvested to obtain the same income yield, since short-term rates of interest may have fallen in the meantime. In short, such an asset would be capital-certain but income-uncertain. On the other hand, a long-term investment yielding a fixed money return (such as an FGR) is income-certain but capital-uncertain, since its market value will fall if interest rates generally should rise. Other assets such as shares in speculative mining concerns may be both income-uncertain and capital-uncertain.

What will be the condition of equilibrium for asset prices? Depending on:

(i)   the expected net income yield;
(ii) the degree of risk as regards income and capital;
(iii) liquidity (ease and cost of marketing);
(iv) the asset preferences of the general public with respect to (i), (ii) and (iii); and
(v)   the relative stocks of each asset (including money),

the answer is suggested in our simple money and bonds model. There will be some equilibrium pattern of asset prices and associated yields such that, after taking into account all transaction costs, nobody feels he can gain by switching between assets. With any other pattern some switching will be profitable and prices will change until there is equilibrium.

Real property assets can be included in this asset structure. Like the investor in stocks and shares, investors in real property will appraise an estate or investment for the same qualities specified above. In addition, there may be conditions which apply to property interests in particular, especially possible changes in government monetary and fiscal policy and attitudes to legal constraints and taxes on real property. Therefore a more realistic model of an asset market would include:

- Money (M)
- Treasury Bills (T)
- Debentures or bonds with a fixed repayment date (D)
- Irredeemable bonds (B)
- Ordinary shares (S)
- Mortgage loans secured on real property (Mo)
- Leasehold investments (L)
- Freeholds (FH)
- Freehold ground rents (FGR)

We can deduce a number of propositions from this model:

1. Since money is included in the asset pattern, any change in the economy's total supply of money, unaccompanied by a compensatory change in the transactions demand for money, will alter M. It will thus have a disequilibrating effect on the existing pattern of asset prices.
2. Suppose the monetary authorities were to increase the overall supply of money in the economy by open-market operations. If they buy Treasury Bills, M increases and T decreases; if they buy bonds, M increases and B decreases. In both cases the pattern of asset prices and yields is affected. Therefore, if the monetary authorities buy Treasury Bills, their yield will

fall, and consequent switching operations will reduce all short-term rates. The prices of longer-term assets are also likely to be affected, though the speed and extent of the change will depend on market expectations. If the fall in short-term rates is expected to be reversed in the near future, there will be little profit in switching to long-term securities. In these circumstances, prices of short-term assets may rise considerably without inducing much change in long-term asset prices. On the other hand, if the change in short-term rates is regarded as a shift by the monetary authorities towards a permanent lower level of short-term rates, switching operations will be more pronounced, and long-term asset prices will rise in sympathy.

3. Therefore, expectations, and uncertainty with regard to them, blur the edge of any formal analysis of the asset market. Consider freehold investments as an example. To an investor, a freehold investment has two main aspects – the rent income and a 'growth' element depending on prospects of future increases in rent and capital value. Should monetary policy cause short-term interest rates to rise, the yield factor alone would dictate some switching out of freehold investments, bringing yields into line. But such selling is unlikely if expectations of growth are strong. Such expectations may be due to inflation, and if people think that the monetary authorities' raising of short-term rates is unlikely to be effective in controlling inflation, the prices of freeholds could be pushed up: that is, freehold yields may fall even though short-term rates are rising.

4. The equilibrium pattern of prices will be affected by people's expectations of income from the various assets and their estimate of future capital appreciation. So an institution investing in a freehold showing a current yield of 6 per cent with 5-year rent reviews must anticipate a compound growth in rent of 8.35 per cent per annum over 20 years to match a current return of 13.65 per cent on undated 2.5 per cent Consols.

5. People's attitude to risk will also affect the pattern of asset prices. Thus prices in a market dominated by long-term investors (the proverbial 'widows and orphans') seeking income-certain investments (such as government stock) will be different from one dominated by speculative investors primarily interested in capital gains (such as shares in oil-prospecting companies).

6. Because all assets are, in varying degrees, substitutes for one another, a change at any point affects the equilibrium pattern and will result in switching until equilibrium is restored.

7. The extent of the change will vary according to the degree of substitution, close substitutes experiencing a greater movement than poor substitutes. For example, a switch from irredeemable government bonds to ordinary shares offering prospects of capital growth will lead to a fall not only in the price of bonds but also in the price of, say, FGRs with distant reversions.

Similarly, the rise in the price of ordinary shares will be extended to free-holds since these, too, are likely to be affected by factors favouring capital growth.
8. The prices of intermediate assets will move in sympathy according to their substitutability, on the one hand for government bonds, and on the other for ordinary shares. Eventually a new equilibrium pattern of asset prices will be established where there are no opportunities for profitable switching. Generally, property yields move in line with non-property yields. Of course, this consistency does not imply equality of interest. Differing risks, investors' asset preferences and cost of switching will all be reflected in the final equilibrium pattern of prices and yields.

Property yields

From the above analysis, it follows that in principle it is unrealistic to separate investments in real property from other investments. Although real property assets may incur extra costs of acquisition and management, they are not a homogeneous group of assets different from other assets in the market. Thus investors seeking income stability and certainty will regard FGRs and bonds as good substitutes for each other, while investors looking for capital-growth prospects will see more affinity between shares and freeholds than between shares and debentures. In other words, it is more informative to regroup our assets as follows:

$$[M \quad T \quad \mathbf{Mo}] \qquad [D \quad \mathbf{L}] \qquad [B \quad \mathbf{FGR}] \qquad [S \quad \mathbf{FH}]$$

where the bracketed groups each contain close substitutes having similar yields, and the *real property assets* (in bold type) are interspersed throughout the whole pattern. If, however, we wish to concentrate on property assets, we can extract from the above groups to give their pattern of yields. In real life the above assets would vary considerably even within particular categories – lease-holds, for instance, having different maturity times.

So far we have looked at interest in property as investments competing with other types of asset. But having decided on his broad strategy, an investor has to consider the detailed attributes of *similar* investments. Therefore, those who have decided to invest in ordinary shares must weigh up the respective merits of different companies. Similarly, if freeholds are preferred, a choice has to be made between the different properties being offered on the market. Thus portfolio management consists not only of switching between different types of investment in general but also between particular investments within the same class.

After a disequilibrating event, equilibrium in our 'stock' model of an asset market was restored solely by switching operations. This was justified because the size of the stock of old securities dominates any new flows. In practice, however, we must recognize that flows are continually coming on to the market in the form of new borrowing (which necessitates the issue and sale of new assets). This has two effects. First, flows tend to reinforce the switching of *existing* assets to restore an equilibrium pattern, because any additional supply of new financial claims through borrowing will tend to come from those sectors currently favoured by investors. Second, over a very long period of time, flows on to the market have a cumulative effect on the size of the stock, and thus affect the yield in the long term.

In a perfect asset market:

1. there would be complete knowledge of prices and opportunities prevailing in every part of the market;
2. there would be no barriers, such as dealing costs or day-to-day management obligations, to hamper switching operations or to put pressure on the form new flows (borrowing) should take;
3. assets would be so divisible that they could be bought by many buyers each having a small amount of funds;
4. investors would act solely on the basis of financial gain.

Given these conditions, the asset market would be a single market in which an equilibrium pattern of prices and yields would be established reflecting the size of the stock of different types of asset relative to investors' preferences. In practice, however, perfection is not realized. Therefore, the high denominations in which Treasury Bills are issued mean that they can only be purchased by the institutions. In addition, there are the costs of buying and selling assets: for example, stamp duty, broker's commission, and so on.

With real property assets, imperfections of the market are even greater (see Chapters 2 and 3). As a result, the prices of many real property assets, such as freeholds and leaseholds, may respond only very sluggishly to a change in another part of the asset market. Above all, certain characteristics of real property interests present barriers to investors wishing to move out of stock market assets. Thus, although there is a correlation over time between yields on real property and other assets, those of the former tend to be higher than those of the latter. For instance, FGRs show a higher yield than long-term government bonds, while the yield of multiple shops is higher than that of ordinary shares except when the stock market is disturbed by special events or when the rate of inflation is high.

The main characteristics of real property interests which make for these higher yields are as follows:

1. They are *less liquid*, as there is no central market comparable with the Stock Exchange.

2. They are *less homogeneous*, so that the services of a valuer and solicitor are required, and transactions take time to complete while the title to the property is investigated.
3. They are often *not divisible* into small and uniform units, thereby excluding direct purchase by the small investor (though 'unitization' and REIT's are helping to overcome this difficulty).
4. Most interests *require management*, a function outside the experience and time of many investors. To pay for the services of an agent, a higher yield is required.
5. Real estate is subject to *specific legislation* (such as rent controls, planning requirements) which may increase transactions costs and also uncertainty regarding expected income.

Box 16.3   Yield terminology

It seems odd that yields fall in good markets but this is because demand drives up property prices, which reduces the ratio of rents to capital which is, of course the *yield*. If yields 'harden' they are falling. If they 'soften' they are rising.

The *initial yield* is based on annual actual or *passing rent*. Some retail property pays *turnover rent* where a portion of the payment to landlords is linked to sales. A *headline rent* may disguise concessions such as rent-free periods.

Company reports often use *investment yield* or *yield on present income* to summarize returns on a portfolio and *current* or *running yield* as a snapshot of annual performance. If the term *all risks yield* is used it incorporates risks and the potential for growth, thereby assessing the value of an investment by its yield over a period of time.

A property close to a rent review or lease renewal will be valued by the *reversionary yield* based on the estimated higher (or lower) rent. This will be set according to the estimated rental value or *rack rent* of the property on the open market. In a falling market property may be *over rented* – tenants are paying higher than market rents and they may be willing to pay a *reverse premium* (one-off payment) in order to get out of a lease.

A *gross redemption yield* includes the receipt of a capital sum at the end of the life of the investment.

A *prime yield* is the yield for a fully rented property of top quality in the best location and with the best tenant covenant (most economically secure tenants).

An *equivalent yield* averages the initial and reversionary yield to produce a real income stream over time which is the *internal rate of return* requiring recognition of the time value of money or *discounting*.

A *reverse yield gap* occurs when interest charges are greater than yields for example, a property developer borrows £1 million at 13 per cent on a long term basis, to finance a development which is let to tenants at an annual rent of £80,000 net with 5 yearly rent reviews (8 per cent yield and 5 per cent reverse yield gap).The RYG may be tolerable if the capital value of the property is rising and/or rents are likely to increase.

The previous section has developed a model explaining how yields on property assets are determined over time. While it emphasizes short-term variations, it can also deal with long-term secular changes in yields.

As regards *short-run* yields, it is basically a stock theory: the main influence on the overall yield of assets lies in changes in the demand for money. Therefore, an increased desire to be liquid will result in the yields on all assets rising, including property yields. Let us suppose the initial impact is on undated government bonds: an increase in the demand for money will lead to a fall in the price of bonds and thus a rise in their yield. Bonds will now be cheap relative to property interests, particularly FGRs, thus giving a relatively higher yield. The holders of property interests will therefore tend to switch into bonds. As this occurs, the price of bonds will rise and the prices of property interests will fall, until a new equilibrium set of relative prices is established such that nobody wishes to switch any further.

Two refinements, however, should be noted. First, because of the imperfections of the property market, there may be a time lag before property yields are brought into line with the rest of the market. Second, since the total value of property interests is small relative to stock market investments, changes in demand for the latter are likely to dominate the asset market. Only in abnormal circumstances, for instance, as in 1980–3, is the property market likely to initiate changes in yields.

Once the overall trend of asset yields has been established, variations in the yields between assets can be explained by differences in the demand for the different types of asset and the relative supply situation. For example, the low yields on prime shops and offices are the result of the high demand of institutions coupled with their relatively limited supply.

In the *long run,* the yield on an asset will be affected from the supply side through the accumulation of flows over time. If the price of equities is relatively high (yields low), selling shares will represent the cheapest way for firms to raise capital for expansion. If this continues over a considerable time, the accumulation of these flows will have a significant influence on the stock of equities, so that, other things being equal, their price falls (yield rises).

Asset yields since 1960

Inflation affected asset yields between 1960 and 2000. First, it affected relative yields, people requiring sufficiently high yields on 'money' bonds to allow for a fall in the value of money because of inflation. In contrast, over a long period, equity interests offer some hedge against inflation. At first, ordinary shares were favoured, but investors, particularly the institutions, saw the advantages of prime property. By 1972 the yield on offices was little more than that on equities, and on agricultural land it was lower. This applied only to prime properties, those favoured by institutions and the shortage of these properties tended to force down the yield considerably in comparison with secondary properties, though, as substitutes, these too experienced some fall in yields. Inflation also led to restrictive government measures to protect the balance of payments. Rates of interest rose; earnings on shares and property looked less rosy. In such circumstances yields on assets generally rise.

Political crises, too, tend to produce short-term rises in yields. Not only do they create uncertainty about future earnings, especially as government measures usually involve increased taxation, but people generally seek to be more liquid: asset prices therefore fall. The movement is accentuated if previously a speculative position had been built up. This is illustrated by the events of 1971–4. The Heath government, intent on growth, increased the money supply, which made spending easier – the effect being felt on the asset, house and consumer-durable markets. Asset yields fell, as did the real rate of interest, that is, the nominal rate less the rate of inflation.

But inflationary pressure forced the government to take countermeasures, including, in November 1972, a freeze on business rents which sparked off a liquidity crisis in the property market. When the oil crisis in late 1973 gave a further twist to inflation, pessimism spread to the Stock Exchange. In both markets people had invested in expectation of continually rising prices, and this speculative position led to larger falls than would otherwise have occurred.

The pattern was repeated in the 1980s. High interest rates to combat inflation led to recession in 1979–82. Thereafter until 1987 asset prices recovered strongly, boosted by the growth in national output, a fall in the annual rate of inflation to 2 per cent, the collapse in world oil prices and a fever of 'take-over' bids. But renewed inflation forced the government to raise the rate of interest in stages from 1988 which led to recession in the economy generally, and a severe downturn in the property and construction industries in particular.

As a result of the rate of inflation being held at close to 2.5 per cent since 1995, it is now accepted that the UK has entered a period of low inflation. Residential property prices rose dramatically from 2000 to 2007, however, and there were fears that this could undermine the government and Bank of England strategy on inflation as housing prices soared and homeowners spent from their rapidly increasing equity. The bubble burst with the collapse of the US subprime market in 2007 – the effects of that were discussed in Chapters 5 and 6.

Property yields have fluctuated widely in the last 50 years. They fell sharply during the property booms of the late 1980s and early 2000s. With the fall in property values in late 2007, yields improved. In 2010 yields from UK retail

Table 16.1 Property yields, 1987–2009

Property yields (all property) per cent			
1987	6.0	2002	7.0
1988	5.5	2003	6.0
1989	5.5	2004	5.5
1990	7.0	2005	5.0
1991	8.0	2006	4.5
1992	9.0	2007	5.0
1993	8.0	2008	8.0
1994	7.5	2009	9.0
1995	7.5	**Equities** over the last 20 years had an average yield of 6.9 per cent and over the last 50 years of 7.1 per cent.	
1996	7.5		
1997	7.0		
1998	6.5		
1999	6.5	**Gilts** over the last 20 years had an average yield of 5.6 per cent and over the last 50 years of 2.2 per cent.	
2000	6.5		
2001	7.0		

Sources: Barclays Equity Gilt study (2009); Investment Property Databank (2009); CB Richard Ellis (2009).

investments are at long-term high levels and office and industrial yields are at their highest levels since the late 1990s (see Table 16.1).

In March 2010, CB Richard Ellis reported that the property sector was showing signs of recovery with prime retail yields of less than 5 per cent and secondary retail yield at 6.5 to 7 per cent. Prime offices showed yields of less than 5 per cent also while business parks' yields were 8 per cent plus as were industrial property yields.

The effect on the real property market of the demand for land resources as an investment

Real property interests are wanted for (a) *occupation*, because they yield utility or profit, and (b) *investment* – that is as a means of holding assets – and as such are regarded as alternatives to other types of asset. But investment demand cannot be completely separated from occupation demand, since the amount of rent paid will affect the capital value of the interest just as the size of the dividend paid on an ordinary share affects its price.

Demand and supply in the asset market will generally produce equilibrium prices and yields for all the various assets. There will therefore be a given 'acceptable yield' for each different kind of property interest which, in its turn, will be partly dependent on the yields of comparable stock market assets. In other words, the price of a land resource will depend heavily upon the price of substitute assets in the 'asset market'.

As an example of such a substitute asset, let us take a blue-chip ordinary share, such as Unilever. Such a share has (i) actual current earnings, (ii) prospective earnings and (iii) an inflation-hedge based largely on (ii). People bid in the market for it according to how it compares with other assets, such as gilt-edged stock and alternative blue-chip shares. While the size of the earnings on a Unilever share is relevant, the important point is that such earnings are capitalized at the rate of yield which is acceptable on a Unilever share *compared with other types of asset*. If earnings double, but 'acceptable yield' remains unchanged, the price of the share will double; if earnings remain unchanged, but 'acceptable yield' is halved, the price of the share will likewise double.

It is a similar case with land resources. Office blocks are wanted by investors, chiefly institutional ones. Their current earnings are capitalized at a rate, which reflects their likely future earnings and their inflation-hedge *compared with alternative assets*. This capitalization rate may enhance their value considerably *irrespective of actual earnings* – that is, irrespective of the demand for occupation purposes. Centre Point, a controversial office block development in London, provides an example. Here two factors served to increase its value to at least £45 million in 1972:

1. earnings potential increased as rents rose because of occupation demand for offices; and
2. acceptable yield on prime office blocks fell from 6 per cent to 4 per cent (note also that some of this investment demand may be speculative, driving up the price and lowering the yield still further).

Suppose Centre Point cost £15 million to build (including normal profit) and that potential current earnings were £900,000 a year. Therefore, if the going rate at which office blocks are capitalized is 6 per cent, its capital value would be the same as its cost, £15 million (capitalization factor = 100/6 per cent = 16.66; £900,000 x 16.66 = £15,000,000). If now the rent doubles to £1.800.000, the capital value of Centre Point will increase to £30 million (£1,800,000 x 16.66). Now assume that, with this higher rent, the acceptable yield on office blocks falls from 6 per cent to 4 per cent. The capital value of Centre Point will now be £1,800,000 x 25 (capitalization factor 100/4 per cent = 25) – that is, £45 million.

Changes in the rate at which earnings are capitalized have important effects on the real property market. First, they influence the relative supply of the different types of property. The resources of the construction industry are diverted into office-building rather than into properties, such as rented flats, which are capitalized at a lower rate. Second, they increase the cost to the public sector of its own construction (for example, roads, schools, hospitals) since resources have to be bid away from producing high-priced offices. For this reason, in times of rising property prices, there tends to be a proportionate falling off in gross fixed capital formation in the public sector.

A further influence on real estate markets is the international nature of property investment that has come with the trend towards globalization in economic activity and the 'footloose' nature of corporate service industry headquarters. Such companies may choose to locate where they feel that the host city offers excellent quality premises and a good quality of life for their employees. As a result of these factors, property markets, particularly in major cities, have become increasingly international in terms of owners and occupiers.

Summary

Investment is both purchase of existing assets (for example, property investment) and the creation of new fixed assets (for instance,. property development). Property investment can be made in freeholds, leaseholds, freehold ground rents and mortgages. Occupiers often lease premises in the UK, providing an opportunity for investors to obtain an income from rents as well as growth of capital.

Investors in real property include private persons, insurance companies, pension funds, charities, property companies, foreign investors, property bond funds, property unit trusts and building societies. Property investment is one of a number of possible asset investments that can be made. Other possible investments include government bonds (gilts) and equities (shares) and a portfolio of assets may well contain some of each type of investment. Between 1996 and 2007 in the UK, property outperformed both gilts and equities in terms of return on capital invested.

The demand for land and property as an investment asset has effects on the real estate market including influencing the relative supply of different types of property and bidding resources away from public sector real estate projects.

Property can be an attractive long-term investment – it can provide capital growth opportunities and has frequently performed differently to other asset classes, thus providing portfolio diversification. The low volatility of property returns and its historic low correlation with other asset classes can also be attributed to the fixed and regular rental income (between occupancy reviews) which gives real estate investments income security. The property market also reacts more slowly to economic change than equities and is thus less volatile. The lower volatility of returns means real estate investment can help pension funds better match assets with long-term liabilities.

Chapter 16: review questions

1. What determines the yield on freehold investments?
2. Explain the advantages and disadvantages of the main types of freehold investment.
3. Explain what is meant by 'reverse yield gap'.
4. How has the pattern of UK asset yields changed in the last 50 years?
5. Explain why the yields on real property interests may be higher than those on other assets.

17

The UK Commercial Property Market

After studying this chapter you will be able to:

- Describe the nature of UK commercial property;
- Explain how commercial property markets are interlinked;
- Explain how changes in the user market affect the financial asset market and then the development and land markets;
- Describe and analyse the common features of the downturns in commercial property in the 1970s, early 1990s and 2007–9.

The market for commercial property

In the UK, within the commercial property market, occupiers tend to lease their premises and so ownership and occupation are separated and consequently, there is an investment market in property. Shortages of good quality commercial property space in the UK since 1945, possibly because of a strict planning regime, have kept rents and capital values high making investments attractive. Owner-occupation of commercial space is much more common in the USA and Europe meaning fewer opportunities in their commercial property investment markets.

Property is differentiated from other assets by four main factors:

1. It is a physical asset requiring maintenance and suffering obsolescence;
2. Its income delivery is governed by lease contracts;
3. Its supply is inelastic and is regulated by both central and local government policy;
4. It is not traded in a centralized market – and as every property is unique, it is valued without the benefit of direct reference to quoted trading prices for identical properties.

There are two main ways to invest in commercial property: either by buying property direct in which case the necessary outlay may be very high and management of the building is needed for example, finding suitable tenants, negotiating lease terms, reviewing rents and arranging for repairs (although a property management company can be engaged to do this at some cost); or by buying shares in property-related companies including REITs (see Chapter 16). Both methods of investment in commercial property are influenced by macro-economic variables such as interest rates, unemployment, consumer confidence and the demand for space for production, storage and sales.

The major sectors of the UK commercial property market are:

- Shop units: there are over 500,000 shops in UK; high street shop values range from £100,000 to £5million.
- Retail warehouses and parks: single units have lost popularity to retail parks (typically 75,000–150,000 sq ft and £10 million to £30 million capital value).
- Shopping centres: about 600 shopping centres have been built since the 1960s; they are mostly in city centres typically providing 20–60 additional retail units (values range from £20 million to £100 million). A new generation of 1 million square feet centres (Metro, Gateshead; Lakeside, London; Merry Hill, Birmingham; Bluewater, London; Meadowhall, Sheffield) command values of £500 million – £1 000 million).
- Offices and business parks: traditional town centre offices have been the worst performing UK property sector for 30 years. There is an enormous range of lot sizes:
  - outside London, only the biggest and best buildings are worth more than £20m;
  - in central London there is an active market for lots priced at £100 million plus. Depreciation and obsolescence have badly affected performance as occupier needs have changed.
- Industrials and distribution warehouses: traditional industrial estates have performed surprisingly well – showing resistance to obsolescence. About 300 'high bay' distribution warehouses have been built since the 1980s (100,000–300,000 square feet and £5 million to £25 million). Rents have been held down by 'just-in-time' delivery methods and resulting low stock levels.
- Leisure parks: normally anchored by a multi-screen cinema, themed restaurant, bowling alley, discotheque and other facilities became popular investments in the 1990s; there are only 50 in total, however, and this asset type is dominated by a few developers.
- Hotels, restaurants and inns: although this sector does badly in recession, the budget hotel market (Travelodge, Premier Inns and so on) has expanded in recent years.

Of these, shops, offices and industrial property comprise 80 per cent of the UK commercial property market which, despite falling in value from its peak in 2007 by 44 per cent is still worth in the region of £762 billion in 2010. Half of this is investment property that is rented to tenants. It allows investors to diversify their portfolios and has a low correlation with equities and gilts. Commercial property has shown less volatility than equities and it has longer leases (average 7.3 years) than residential property and consequently more reliable income.

Over the period 1992–2007, UK commercial property returned 11.3 per cent per annum. Between 1997 and 2007, UK residential property delivered the highest returns at 17.8 per cent per annum, and commercial property was the second best asset with an 11.4 per cent per annum return.

Since 1990 there has been a technological revolution that has changed methods of production, selling and distribution. Examples of this include the closure of high street bank branches, the need for high bay warehouse space to cope with just-in-time delivery methods and the separation of manufacturing and office functions by many companies. There is also more emphasis on service provision – corporate restructuring in the property sector is inevitable as a result.

The interlinked nature of commercial property markets

The following analysis, adapted from DiPasquale and Wheaton (1996) and Ball, Lizieri and MacGregor's (2006) *The Economics of Commercial Property Markets* demonstrates the interlinked nature of commercial property markets.

- In the *user market* there is a stock of offices either owner-occupied or rented which is subject to depreciation, requires regular maintenance and could become technologically obsolete.
- In the *financial asset* market offices are financial assets and returns can be compared with other assets.
- In the *development market* office building takes place in response to increased demand for space.
- In the *urban land* market there is competition for land between different uses.

For equilibrium in the commercial property market, all four sub-markets must be in equilibrium. But adjustment processes in office markets can be slow because they are fixed in location, expensive to demolish, long-lasting and held on long leases. Rents do not adjust quickly and supply can not be changed quickly.

Figure 17.1 illustrates all four markets at once. In the user market S and D are the original supply and demand curves. The stock (S) is fixed (perfectly inelastic) and additions to stock net of losses are less than 2.5 per cent per year

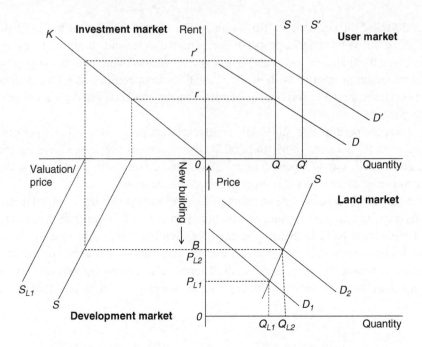

Figure 17.1   The interlinked nature of commercial property markets

(S'). Demand is a determined by the rent in a particular time period t (r_t); the occupying firm's output in that time period O_t; and office space per worker (WS_t):

$$D_t = f(r_t, O_t, WS_t) \tag{17.1}$$

Market equilibrium in the user market (top right diagram of Figure 17.1) is reached at rent r and office stock Q where demand equals supply and the vacancy rate is zero.

Annual net rental flow is multiplied by the inverse of a capitalization factor (K) or initial yield [$YP = 1/K$] to determine its value or market price. The capitalization factor K is determined by valuation rules and by economic evaluation and is the 'all risks yield' (ARY) (see Chapter 16). ARY reflects expected income growth, risk and depreciation.

There is an inverse relationship between the value of a building with a known future rental stream and the rate of interest because when interest rates rise, the future rental stream has a lower value; and when interest rates fall the rents have a higher value. This is shown in the top left diagram of Figure 17.1. The ray K coming out from the origin shows the value of a rental stream at a given capitalization factor K. Note that valuation/price increases from right to left in this graph. The value of the building is the net income derived from letting divided by the capitalization factor:

$$P_t = \frac{Y_t}{K_t} \qquad (17.2)$$

where P_t is the valuation or price of the building, Y_t is the letting income and K_t is the capitalization factor.

Higher interest rates would shift K to the right and lower interest rates would shift it to the left. At rent r the value of the building corresponds to the beginning of the supply curve in the development market – the bottom left diagram of Figure 17.1. If rents rise to r' the value given by the capitalization factor K would rise to the level corresponding to the supply curve S_{L1} in the development market. In this market property developers build new office space either to hold and rent to occupiers or to sell to investors as financial assets.

New development takes place when overall office demand is greater than the existing stock and it is profitable for developers to build new offices. At the point where the value/price given by the intersection of interest rate r and capitalization factor K in the top left diagram meets the beginning of the supply curve S in the development market (bottom left) diagram, existing office values equal their replacement costs. Any higher values – moving left along the x-axis in the top left diagram – induce developers to build and so supply increases along S in the bottom left diagram. Note the direction of increase of new building in the bottom left diagram gives a normal supply curve, that is, supply increases in the development market as values increase once values are greater than replacement costs. Replacement costs include site clearance, construction and land costs. The greater supply of offices in the development market, of course, requires more land for development, affecting the land market (bottom right diagram).

In the land market, offices have to compete with other uses for land; there is a stock of land already used for offices and a flow of land being converted from other uses. The land demand and supply curves show how quantities demanded and supplied change as land prices change. If other factors affecting land demand and supply change the curves shift, for example, if the planning regime becomes less restrictive for commercial property development, the supply curve shifts to the right. If land prices rise, developers can intensify scale of development and substitute capital for land

If we now trace the impact of a rise in demand for offices which causes the rise in rents in the top right user market diagram of Figure 17.1 we can see that:

- rents rise from r to r';
- office building values rise along K in the investment market (top left diagram);

- as values increases, new supply is induced from developers in the development market (bottom left diagram) and quantity B of new offices are built;
- the new supply requires extra land from the land market (bottom right diagram) leading to a shift to the right of the demand curve for land – from D_1 to D_2. This increases land prices from PL_1 to PL_2.

So it is rent that generates equilibrium in the user market ($D = S$ at market rent); in the financial asset market (where it determines capital values); and in the development market (development takes place when stock demand exceeds supply in the user market and rents and capital values rise).

The four markets are back in equilibrium when land prices increase to P_{L2} with Q_{L2} land devoted to office use.

To summarize: rents determined in the user market are translated into asset prices in the asset market. An increase in the demand for space in the user market increases rents. Then asset prices increase and they determine the level of new construction, which determines the available stock of commercial property. The new construction requires land, increasing demand for land and land prices.

If the capitalization rate in the asset market decreased, this would increase the demand for real estate assets, increasing asset prices. Increased asset prices would lead to more construction, increasing the stock of space and decreasing rents.

An increase in construction costs would decrease construction and thus the stock of space, leading to higher rents and asset prices.

In the long run, both demand and supply for offices and land are likely to be more elastic and this model of commercial property markets can be improved by introducing expectations into the demand and supply relations. Then rational agents would base their views of the future on the best available current information (*rational expectations*); user demand for instance is likely to be affected by forecasts of future output and employment rather than current levels (Ball et al., 2001).

The UK commercial property market 1950–89

During the Second World War, what was left of the construction industry could do no more than carry out first-aid repairs to those bomb-damaged buildings still capable of being put to effective use. As a result when the war ended the industry was faced with the mammoth task of reconstructing whole city centres and rebuilding on derelict bomb sites.

The demand for new buildings opened up opportunities for a new breed of property developer, some of whom had originated as estate agents and had the foresight to acquire derelict sites at bargain prices. Initially their activity followed the traditional principle: if the prospective yield of the finished building exceeds the rate of interest at which finance can be borrowed, there is the possibility of profitable development. The shortage of modern office and retail buildings resulting from the war, together with a low rate of interest, meant that their profits were high and attracted other developers.

On completion, the developer could choose either to retain the development or to sell it on to an institution, chiefly an insurance company or pension fund. Both were seeking prime properties for their investment portfolios to take advantage of rising rents and to provide a hedge against an increasing rate of inflation. Initially institutions bought from a developer on a long lease. Later, seeking a share of the profits, they provided the funds for the construction period on a profit-sharing arrangement or even formed a joint company with the developer.

In 1972 the Heath government decided to expand the economy and the money supply was increased. Much of this new money found its way into the property market via the clearing banks, which could now compete openly with the merchant banks. Between 1970 and 1973 bank lending increased from £71 million to £1,332 million, with most of the increase going to property companies.

There was no lack of demand, the institutions were willing to buy all completed developments. Not only was 3.5 per cent an acceptable rate of return on prime property investments but, with a shortage of office space for occupation purposes, rents doubled within 2 years, thereby enhancing capital values still further. Between 1964 and 1974 the value of the Centre Point office block in London soared from £10 million to around £60 million even though it remained empty (see Chapter 16). The price of property freeholds now contained a large element of speculation, with loan repayments not covered by rents in the expectation that deficits could be safely rolled over until covered at the next rent review.

The first check on optimism occurred in November 1972 when, as part of its strategy to combat inflation, the government froze commercial rents. In the following summer a steep rise in the world oil price gave a further twist to inflation and a loss of confidence in sterling. The government's growth policy came to an end.

The rise in interest rates which followed was catastrophic for developers. Buildings under construction fell in value, the situation being aggravated by rising construction costs and completion delays. Worse still, depositors with the fringe banks withdrew their money since they could obtain higher returns elsewhere, for example, in local authority short-term loans. These banks could, therefore, no longer roll over loans to developers.

The storm might have been ridden out had the rent freeze not been renewed. The institutions now reappraised property as an investment, for continually rising rents, upon which their policy had been founded, appeared doubtful. The crisis in confidence, as institutions stopped buying, engulfed both developers and banks, particularly the fringe banks. While property prices were rising, the liquidity risk of borrowing short and lending long for property development and acquisition seemed negligible. Now, when the banks wanted their money back, borrowers could not sell the property against which they had borrowed. But the banks themselves had been far too liberal as regards 'deficit financing' by property companies – lending, for instance, at 14 per cent on controlled residential property showing a current yield of less than 5 per cent. As property prices tumbled, even the original lending base of four-fifths' valuation was not covered.

Many major developers and property companies failed. But, in order to protect depositors and the integrity of the banking system as a whole, most of the fringe banks were rescued by a support operation, known as the 'Lifeboat', mounted jointly by the 'Big Four' clearing banks and backed by the Bank of England.

Anti-property sentiment produced two further blows. First, to deal with the windfall profits made by developers, in December 1973 a development charge on first lettings was imposed. This was a tax on capital gains before they were realized, but it was so ill-defined as to suggest that the Conservative government did not really know what it was doing. Second, in March 1974 a new Labour government came to power. Residential rents were frozen, and there was no easing of the restrictions on business rents. As a result, an orderly property market ceased to exist.

What the government had failed to realize, when introducing its various measures, was the extent to which property had become a vital part of the UK financial structure. The collapse in property prices involved a large part of the City. Not only could insurance companies pay less in bonuses on life and annuity policies but also pension funds could not keep pace with inflation. The value of the assets of many banks also fell. Thus the liquidity crisis in property affected Stock Exchange optimism and share prices tumbled, Worse still, this loss of confidence occurred when world events were revealing the underlying weaknesses of the British economy.

The assumption behind the creation of the Bank of England's 'Lifeboat' was that the crisis was simply a short-term one of confidence: given breathing space, properties could be sold off in an orderly manner, and confidence restored. But, throughout 1974, high interest rates necessitated increased borrowing by the secondary banks, and this forced the sale of property. Consequently, the government, following pressure by the Bank of England and the institutions, announced in December 1974 that control on business rents would end. This partially lifted uncertainty surrounding property values, and confidence in first-class property as an investment was gradually restored.

The property collapse of 1973–4 has been described in some detail because important lessons could have been learned from it. Instead in less than a decade the same basic mistakes were being repeated. Many aspects of the 1973–4 crisis are also similar to the 'credit crunch' collapse of 2007–9, notably borrowing short and lending long for property development and acquisition (which was Northern Rock's business model).

As the institutions once more began to buy prime properties, an orderly property market was re-established by the end of 1975. But the secondary market remained dull, largely because many development and property companies were still selling to repay the banks. In addition, the banks themselves were following a much more conservative lending policy, reinforced by the Labour government's strict control of the money supply.

Regarding development, finance was still available – at a price – for base rate remained high. The difficulty lay in finding projects to give a profitable return on a borrowing rate of around 15 per cent. Moreover, apprehension as to future profitability resulted from (i) doubts as to whether rents would continue to rise at their previous rates, (ii) the uncertainties resulting from the Community Land Act 1975, (iii) the introduction of the development land tax, 1976 and (iv) the recession shortly after the Thatcher government took over in 1979.

The demand for property recovered strongly from the mid-1980s onwards. This was the result of:

1. the rapid rate of growth in the economy;
2. expansion in the service industries;
3. the demand for large modern offices to house information technology equipment and stock market personnel following Big Bang in 1986;
4. the relaxation of planning controls;
5. changes in the User Classes Order 1987, and the advent of business parks, science parks, out-of-town shopping centres and retail warehouses;
6. the explosion of consumer credit and spending.

All this added up to a major increase in the demand for space and in rental growth, encouraging investors to buy buildings at ever-lower yields in anticipation of this continuing.

To respond to the increased demand, property developers needed credit – and this was forthcoming. Initially the banks followed a fairly cautious lending policy, usually limiting loans to about 65 per cent (80 per cent on rare occasions) of the value of the property and for a period of no more than 5 years, with actual advances geared to various stages in the completion of the project. Covenants were tailored to the risk exposure they were prepared to accept and to provide an 'exit' should the development turn sour for some unforeseen reason. The individual development loan was usually in the range of £5 million–£20 million.

One important feature of development schemes in the 1980s was the vast increase in their complexity and size: London Bridge City, Broadgate and

Canary Wharf, were all over 2 million square feet of office space. While a loan of £100 million would be considered on its merits, few banks would accept this degree of risk-exposure on their own and so they usually invited others to join in funding the project. Such a syndicate also allowed small banks to participate in high-quality developments.

As a rule of thumb, banks also limited their risk by restricting their loans on property to some 30 per cent of their total lending, with development funding accounting for about half the property portfolio. Sometimes, as an alternative, risks were spread by insuring the 'top slice' of loan where this was above 60 per cent.

In Chapter 9 the conventional method of financing property development through forward funding by an institution was described. Usually the development was pre-let, thus making it a sound investment even before construction started. Often the buyer was the same institution which had provided the initial finance, for insurance companies and pensions funds were eagerly seeking an equity interest in first-class property, especially easily managed office blocks which, with rising rentals, provided a hedge against inflation and real growth. Property companies, too, often retained some of their developments to increase income from their own investments.

From the early 1980s, however, the institutions became less enamoured with property as an investment and so had no need to seek prime properties for their portfolios. Instead they considered that shares had better growth prospects (which proved true of the early 1980s but meant that they missed out on the property boom of 1985–9). Pension funds, for instance, reduced the proportion of their assets in property from 21 per cent in 1979 to 9 per cent in 1989.

However, the withdrawal of the institutions from financing commercial development did not bring about a decline in construction activity, for the void was filled in various ways, chiefly by the banks where a number of factors tempted them to follow a less-cautious lending policy. The government's change in the method of monetary control (from minimum liquid asset requirements to varying the rate of interest) allowed them to expand their deposits, and financing property development provided a welcome home for their surplus funds. Moreover, the removal of controls on exporting capital by the world's leading economies allowed overseas banks and their financial conglomerates, particularly US and Japanese, to offer loans. In contrast, the merchant banks, so severely mauled in 1974, largely confined their participation to pure investment lending and underwriting, and avoided holding any major element of development debt in their own loan portfolios.

Not only did the replacement of the institutions by the banks in financing development represent a move from investment-led to debt-financed development, but the approach and nature of the developer also changed. With the earlier developer the building was pre-let and the long-term investor was in place before construction started. In contrast, the 1980's developer, often an individual rather than an institution, had as many projects in the pipeline as he could obtain finance to initiate them. During the early part of the boom he found little difficulty in managing to sell at a profit. The bank would then be repaid, and further projects embarked on. Such a developer-trader flourished in the 1980's ethos of free enterprise.

Proposed projects brought forward by euphoric developers met a ready response from the banks, which competed with one another and with foreign rivals by designing new loan packages. The role of the banker changed from that of conservative risk-manager to a target-achieving seller of loans, with the loan officer rewarded with bonus payments. 'Limited recourse loans' restricted the banks' ability to recall debt, and going even further, 'non-recourse loans' isolated a particular project from the overall financial profile of the borrower as to, for example, debt and covenants existing on other projects. This really meant that a parent company could not be called upon to cover any default on a loan by an offshoot company formed simply to carry out a particular development. In effect, the lender, not the borrower, took all the risk and was the loser if the development turned sour.

To make it easier for developers to obtain funds, merchant banks were joined by other financial intermediaries – specialists in 'structural engineering finance'. By 'creative finance' and 'mezzanine' finance, loan schemes were tailored to obtain the maximum initial finance, usually by allowing the difference between interest payments and rental returns to be carried over to the next rent review when it could be paid out of higher rents. As an alternative method to bank lending in raising capital, preference shares were offered to investors. If successful, this source was more attractive than selling ordinary shares at a heavy discount, for this diluted the equity portion.

Between 1985 and 1990 yearly bank lending to property companies increased in money terms from £7 billion, to £38.9 billion with overseas investors (mostly American and Japanese banks) providing some 40 per cent. By 1990 the banks' total property debt amounted to approximately £500 billion. Yet property analysts had previously cautioned that an excess of space over demand, particularly in the office sector, could develop.

The UK commercial property market 1990–2010

Just as there were special factors which stimulated the boom, so other conditions arose which triggered the slump. The banks had looked at property development solely from the supply side, treating developers not as entrepreneurs, but as manufacturers of floor space. Scant regard was therefore paid to the fact that they were lending in a highly speculative market. If, say, the interest charged is 15 per cent and the yield from rents 6 per cent, even if loans cover only 70 per cent of the value of the property, it still leaves a shortfall if rents do not go on rising. Then asset cover is diminished as capital values decline, and the banks find that the escape routes provided by their loan covenants including collateral are insufficient to avoid a loss.

The brake on rental growth affected demand and supply of commercial property. The rate of inflation increased, to 7.7 per cent between 1987 and 1989, leading to wage rise expectations in excess of this. The rate of interest increased in stages, with Bank of England base rate reaching 15 per cent in October 1989. The consequence was a big fall in investment and, as mortgage rates went up to 15.4 per cent, a decline in consumer demand.

Despite the expansion of financial services following deregulation in 1986 there was no great increase in lending. Confidence had been hit by the Stock Market crash in October 1987. Demand for both office workers and office space was reduced by the recession, especially in the City of London. The levying of VAT on rents of new buildings prevented banks, insurance companies and building societies from reclaiming it and the introduction of Uniform Business Rate in 1990 hit the profits of firms, especially retailers (see Chapter 23). The downturn in consumer spending in the economic recession had already hit profits and so, wherever it was possible, retailers reduced their existing floor space.

At the very time that demand was falling for retail and office space, new supply was coming on to the market as developments started in the boom were completed. By the end of 1991 about 30 per cent of City and Docklands office stock was vacant and office rents fell by 20 per cent, with the retail sector also affected. Although London and the South East were worst affected, the effects spread to the rest of the country.

The property market is highly sensitive to monetary conditions and as confidence was damaged in a highly speculative market, there was a wide-spread slump in which the housing market was also affected (see Chapter 5). Developers became saddled with expensive land banks and unlet and even unfinished buildings.

Some property and development companies played for short-term relief from their cash-flow problem by capitalizing interest payments below the line in order to avoid showing a serious fall in profits in their annual accounts. But this 'creative accounting' and any restructuring of borrowing could only afford a breathing space while alternative sources of long-term funds were investigated. The problem was that half-completed buildings, and even build-ings which could not be let, were unsaleable. The resulting fall in asset val-ues left developers with insufficient cover for their borrowing with the banks. Therefore, the choice for the banks was whether to call in the receivers for interest defaulters and to write-off losses or to restructure loans in order to protect the funds already committed until the climate for selling completed developments improved. Generally, though a few major companies were forced into bankruptcy, the banks followed the restructuring course, but at a price to the borrower.

Rates of commercial property return improved from the mid-1990s: 1995 – 3.5 per cent; 1997 – 15.0 per cent; 2000 – 11.5 per cent; 2002 – 10.3 per cent; 2003 – 10.9 per cent; 2004 – 11.5 per cent; and in 2005 – 8.6 per cent. The retail sector showed the highest return in the early years of the decade and office property the lowest. Demand for offices declined after 2001 due to job losses and the technology bust. Commercial property rental growth slowed in 2002 because of weakness in the corporate sector and this reduced capital values in 2003 while at the same time exerting upward pressure on yields.

Property investment in the UK was very strong between 2004 and early 2007 because of explosive growth in cheap borrowing and a strong flow of funds from private investors diversifying from other asset classes into property. From 2001 to mid-2007, capital values of commercial property rose by 53 per cent while rental values rose by only 9 per cent. Yields fell and in 2007 property yields were at an all-time low as a result of the 6-year boom. In mid-2007, HSBC sold their headquarters building on Canary Wharf for £1.1 billion and the 'Gherkin' headquarters of Swiss Re was bought by Evans Randall at a premium of £630 million.

Box 17.1   Canary Wharf

Canary Wharf takes its name from the sea trade with the Canary Islands and until the mid 1960s it was a cargo warehouse at the heart of Docklands. The London Docklands Development Corporation was created in 1980 to regenerate the docklands area (see Chapter 10, Box 10.2).

In 1987 the Docklands Light Railway and London City Airport opened and the Canary Wharf development by Olympia and York began in 1988. This was at the height of a speculative property boom, however, and although the first tenants moved in in 1991, Olympia and York went into administration in the downturn.

By 1993 Canary Wharf had a working population of 7,000 and the Jubilee Line extension had begun. By 1995, when Canary Wharf was sold to an international consortium it was 75 per cent leased. By 1999 the development was 95 per cent let and there was a new Canada Place shopping mall with 90 shops and restaurants. In 2003 a third retail mall opened to take the number of shops, restaurants and bars to 200. A new events venue, the East Wintergarden opened. In 2005 British Waterways named Canary Wharf as its preferred partner in its redevelopment of the Wood Wharf site – 5 million square feet of mixed commercial, residential and retail space.

In 2010 Canary Wharf covers an area of 97 acres and has a working population of approximately 100,000. The showpiece building, 1 Canada Square is 235 metres high, the tallest inhabited building in Britain. Prime rents are about £37.50 per square foot and 96.2 per centof buildings are occupied. More than 60 per cent of the wharf's tenants work in the financial sector.

The sequence of events that led to the 'credit crunch' downturn was outlined in Chapter 6. It is enough to say here that because the financial system was effectively a global entity by 2007, bad risks had spread into many national and international banks. There was a lack of cooperation between banks, which suddenly became reluctant to lend to borrowers and to other banks. The market for mortgage based securities (MBS) closed and bank lending terms on commercial mortgages tightened. Risk premiums rose. Property values fell sharply in late 2007 as the asset bubble burst and there was a significant fall in transaction levels. Office vacancies increased and the difficult financial conditions affected retail sales and construction.

Lower sales and incomes in the wider economy meant that there was reduced commercial real estate demand and a higher vacancy rate, resulting in lower rents and lower commercial property prices. Capital values fell by more than 40 per cent between 2007 and 2010. Unit trusts in property were also hit with the best performers down by 16 per cent and the worst by 60 per cent. Commercial property in the UK came under even greater pressure from 1 January 2009 when Energy Performance Certificates became a requirement for any disposal. The mounting cost of void rates on vacant buildings was another difficulty.

The full impact of the credit crunch on commercial property markets will ultimately depend on the length and severity of the wider recession. The effects in the property investment market were among the first to appear and have already resulted in sharp changes in investment activity and pricing. Construction activity has been very badly hit but the longer-term consequences for development and occupational demand will depend on the effect that the recession has on real economic variables including business investment, employment, consumer spending and retail sales. These in turn will feed through to occupational demand for commercial property, interacting with property supply to determine rental levels. The resulting rental trends will in turn feedback to pricing and decisions in both the development and investment markets.

There are reasons to believe that the credit crunch impact on commercial property will not be quite as severe as the effects of the early 1990s downturn. There is a wider range of investors, especially from abroad: 73 per cent of commercial property purchases by value in central London in 2009 were made by foreign investors – £5 billion in total. The over-supply of office development that occurred in the 1990s has not developed during the credit crunch. The cost of borrowing is very low and yields have increased. Finally, the macroeconomic outlook is improving with lower than expected unemployment and a return to economic growth.

Over the decade 2000–10, commercial property nominal returns were 81.5 per cent – entirely income returns because capital values fell by -4.8 per cent over that period. On an annualized basis, total returns were 6.1 per cent (capital

---

Box 17.2 Tesco – Europe's biggest commercial property company

---

In 2007, Tesco had £28 billion in property assets and made a profit of £139 million from its property division. Tesco even has plans to build 2,000 homes after constructing more than 300 in the last few years. Much of this is affordable housing in mixed-use schemes. Supermarket chains own significant property assets with Carrefour having £20.4 billion in property in 2007, Sainsbury's £8.5 billion; and in the USA, Walmart owns £36 billion of property assets.

---

growth –0.5 per cent; income growth 6.7 per cent). In 2010, commercial property investment offers an attractive income yield and some prospect of capital appreciation in the medium term.

In 2010 there are signs of recovery in commercial property in the UK – Land Securities, Britain's biggest listed owner of offices and retail property, announced in July that it is to spend £350 million on developing Trinity, Leeds, a shopping centre with 750,000 square feet of retail space. Construction of the centre was mothballed in 2008 as the UK economy went into recession. Up to 1,000 construction jobs will be created and 3,000 ongoing retail posts from 2013. However, development finance is still in short supply especially for speculative non pre-let projects.

There are reasons to believe the recovery in commercial property will be different from previous cycles. Most commercial property investment is based on leverage (a large proportion of borrowed funds). The small amount of equity put in provides a big return when asset prices rise. But regulators seem determined to stop the boom and bust of credit markets and of property speculation. The underlying cause of the financial crisis or credit crunch was too much credit, too easily available at a low price. This enabled unsustainable asset price bubbles. If the regulators in the UK and overseas restrict leverage in the financial system this will change the dynamics of the commercial property market and make the creation of asset price bubbles much less likely.

Summary

Commercial property is differentiated from other assets as it is a physical asset requiring maintenance and is governed by lease contracts. It is not traded in a centralized market and supply is inelastic. The major sectors are retail, office and industrial. The commercial property market has four sub-markets: the user market; the financial asset market; the development market and the urban land market. Occupier rents provide the link between the four sub-markets.

Speculative booms, followed by severe downturns occurred in UK commercial property in the 1970s, early 1990s and 2007–9. There are many similarities in the way the asset bubble developed in each cycle. UK commercial property values fell by more than 40 per cent between mid-2007 and end-2009 but in the first quarter of 2010 rents rose by 11.8 per cent and capital values were up by 2.3 per cent. The amount of debt outstanding to lenders from the UK commercial property sector in 2010 was £224 billion.

Chapter 17: review questions

1. What part can commercial property play in investment portfolios?
2. Explain how the sub-markets of the commercial property sector are interconnected.
3. What are the common features of the downturns in commercial property in the UK in the 1970s, early 1990s and 2007–9?
4. Explain the impact of the 2007 credit crunch on UK commercial property.

18

International Real Estate Markets

After studying this chapter you will be able to:

- Explain the advantages and disadvantages of international real estate investment;
- Analyse the growth and scale of international real estate investment;
- Describe the major real estate investment markets of the world;
- Explain the impact of globalization on UK real estate.

International property investment

In the conventional western economic approach the existence of property rights forms the basis of market transactions: the price mechanism allocates scarce resources and there is freedom of enterprise to create wealth. Value in real estate is portable because it attaches to the property rights that enable the use of land to occur, while the land accommodating that use remains fixed. A land-owner holds rights that include: physical possession of the land; the right to derive income from its use; and the right to sell or transfer some or all of those rights and to retain the value of that transfer. Real estate transactions, how-ever, can be complex, prolonged and distinctive. They often extend to weeks or months during which terms can change, and if conducted across international borders, currency exchange rates can change affecting the transaction.

For urban land and buildings, value depends on the profitability of the use to which it can be put and the strength and duration of the right to exclusive enjoy-ment of the benefits of that use – which can vary between countries. Every market has a unique set of obstacles or barriers to entry that can be pitfalls or opportunities; for example, laws favouring tenant rights may be an obstacle to investors and owners but an opportunity for multinational companies and busi-nesses. Despite international efforts to reduce barriers to foreign investment, foreign ownership of real estate in many countries is often subject to specific domestic restrictions and prohibitions, and global investors often utilize specially tailored ownership structures to mitigate such restrictions. There are still significant differences among countries that complicate the process of development, ownership and leasing: local taxation is a problem for owners and investors. Property, income, and capital gains tax vary widely from country to country and sales and transfer taxes such as Value Added Tax (VAT) further complicate both the structural and fiscal position of offshore investments. Local knowledge is vital in many areas of overseas property investment, not least knowledge of the local taxation regime.

The key difficulties of international property investment are:

- information costs – these can be considerable because of different legal systems and variations in methods of valuation between countries;
- cultural barriers and possible restrictions or regulations concerning foreign ownership;
- monitoring and maintenance costs;
- adverse currency movements – both during the acquisition process and at the point of sale when capital value is affected;
- variations in transaction costs (see Chapter 3);
- political instability affecting rents and capital values;
- market inefficiency – especially in smaller markets.

Real estate valuers rely on methods that appear mathematically crude but are widely accepted by professionals – they incorporate qualitative and heuristic factors such as attractiveness of property or popularity of location or the possibility of beneficial change of use. These are the 'rules of the game' which can vary in different countries making international markets uncertain.

Despite the difficulties, considerable international real estate investment takes place although it is difficult to measure because, although records are kept for direct property investment, they are not for special purpose vehicles.

Box 18.1   An illustration of the effect of currency change

A UK individual buys a property in Florida for $300,000. After 2 years it has risen in value to $400,000 and the lady concerned decides to sell in order to take the capital gain of $100,000 less taxes and fees.

During the 2 years of ownership, however, the value of the dollar relative to the pound has changed. When she purchased the property one pound was worth 1.46 dollars (£1 = $1.46) and the purchase was made at 300,000/1.46 = £205,479. At the time of the proposed sale, however, the dollar has fallen to one pound equals 1.95 dollars (£1 = $1.95) and the sale would only be worth 400,000/1.95 = £205,128. The adverse currency movement has wiped out the rise in value of the property.

And corporate acquisitions are often recorded as domestic transactions. In the corporate sector real estate investment takes place for operational or strategic reasons, for example, as a company increases its activities in a country it may need to purchase office space; the purchase of prestigious high quality space may be advantageous for business in that country. International property investment may be made because it offers higher returns than those available in the national market of the investor or because there are not enough opportunities for high quality real estate investment in the home market (this may apply to investors from the Netherlands and Sweden).

International real estate investment also takes place in order to diversify investment portfolios although there is evidence that the correlation between international real estate markets is surprisingly high and international property returns move together. This is largely because in a global economy GNP movements across countries tend to be in the same direction, and real estate is affected by the same fundamental economic variables that affect GNP (Case et al., 2000). The near simultaneous downturns in the office markets of major financial centres such as New York, London and Toronto in the early 1990s and in 2007 confirm this. 'A recent development may be the emergence of a global cycle' – there is a very close correlation between changes in nominal rental values for offices in Boston, London, Madrid, Melbourne, Milan, Paris, Stockholm and Zurich (Lewis, 1994). During the period 1985 to 1994, a large number of countries experienced strong real estate booms that peaked in 1989/1990 followed by severe asset price deflation and an output contraction that lasted until about 1994.

The growth of international real estate investment

With industrialization, large pools of capital arose that could flow among cities, such as, trade surpluses, for example, nineteenth-century British investment in North America; petrodollars of the 1970s into the London property market; Japanese trade surpluses in the 1980s into North American and Australian property; pension funds in North America, south-east Asia, Japan and Europe seeking investment opportunities.

After 1950, urban areas expanded and developers sought capital from sources with greater interest in long-term lending than most banks. The eurocurrency market (the market for investments denominated in currencies other than the one in which the investment is traded) grew in the 1950s to be worth $110 billion in 1970; now $4.0 trillion. Considerable urban and infrastructure development, in both developed and developing countries, required foreign investment.

International real estate investment accelerated in the 1980s keeping pace with globalization and there was a business evolution toward multinational business operations. Financial institutions became dominant as landlords for prime commercial property and growth in international investment practices enabled investors to look outside their own countries for above average performing properties. Floating exchange rates from 1971 had increased foreign exchange risks and led to more international financial instruments, for example, currency futures. Telecommunications and computers enabled stock, option and commodity exchanges to trade globally creating a global financial market (24-hour and instantaneous). Deregulation of financial markets in the 1980s allowed global borrowing and lending and increased diversification of investment and 'prime' real estate began to appear after 1980 in cities throughout the world – not just London and New York.

Globalization of economic activity stimulated widespread urban development. Global cities began to develop – making key economic decisions that allocate capital (human and financial). They are able to influence governments by their investment decisions and they host global corporations, international organizations and cultural institutions. They compete with other global cities for multinational enterprises (MNEs), international organizations and cultural events. In order to compete, global cities need effective and flexible property market institutions and since the late 1980s, there has been widespread foreign ownership of real property in global cities. The free flow of urban economic and property information and free flow of capital created the necessary conditions for a truly global property market. Waves of international investment activity can be identified:

- 1988–90, Japanese investment into the USA;
- 1988–90, Japanese investment into the UK (buying £3.5 billion of UK property);
- mid to late 1990s, German investment into the UK (German funds freed by removal of restrictions and seeking higher returns outside reunified Germany);
- Hong Kong investment into the UK and Canada in advance of the colony's 1997 reversion to China;
- 2000–7, funds from Quatar and Abu Dhabi into the UK;
- 2000–7, Middle East oil revenues into real estate worldwide;
- 2003–7, foreign direct investment into Chinese cities ($5.4 billion, 2005; $15 billion, 2007).

The rapid growth of cross-border investment in commercial property took two forms: direct foreign investment in the private property market to receive a rental income stream and capital appreciation (sometimes as a joint venture with a company in the host country); or indirect investment in publically traded vehicles, for example, property company shares, funding of property projects and purchases of securitized debt.

A 'New International Division of Labour' (NIDL) has contributed to the growth of international property investment. Production is organized and managed on a global scale, tying previously independent local economies into the global marketplace because of:

- the growth of global corporations;
- the dominance of services in advanced economies and decline of goods manufacture because of high wages, environmental controls and rapid technological change;
- services are 'footloose' and quality-of-life driven (security, clean air, clean water, high quality built and natural environments);
- there is now bimodal distribution of job opportunities in developed nations – higher paid managerial and professional jobs, and lower paid semi-skilled or unskilled jobs, resulting in;
- bimodal housing demand, for example, Hong Kong, Vancouver, Toronto where high priced condominiums are being built simultaneously with smaller, more affordable units;
- urban areas are affected by economic shifts in other areas (impacts on goods and services produced and on real estate investment) leading to cyclical volatility;
- migration flows subject local property markets to stress;
- cities are at the centre of the international flow of people, capital and information.

The key parts of the global real estate investment market in 2001 can be seen in Table 18.1.

By 2007, the dominance of the USA in investment grade real estate assets worldwide (worth a total of $17.8 trillion) was being challenged with the EU having more than 36 per cent of the world total and the USA approximately 26 per cent. In the European Union the biggest markets were: UK $1.49 trillion (8.4 per cent of the world total); Germany $1.44 trillion; France $1.16 and Spain $577 billion. Global investment in commercial real estate reached a record total of $930 billion in 2007 (an increase of 29 per cent on 2006). The top five global

Table 18.1   Global real estate, 2001

Real estate market	Percentage share of global investment	$ billion
Australia	1	38
North America	34	1598
South America	1	50
UK	8	361
Continental Europe	27	1262
South East Asia	17	825
Japan	13	600

Source: Steinert and Crowe (2001).

investment targets were still the USA, UK, Germany, France and Japan, but China and Brazil attracted significant inward real estate investment with $15 billion and $14 billion respectively (Cushman and Wakefield, 2008).

Of course the 'credit crunch' and global economic downturn have had a significant effect on international real estate investment since 2007. Equity and derivative markets reacted first with sharp price falls. The direct investment market followed, but more slowly, with transaction volumes falling in the USA, Germany, and UK as investors waited to see the bottom of the market and prospective vendors became reluctant to sell at lower prices.

Large international players who do not need to borrow are taking advantage of falling real estate asset prices and rising yields. In 2010 the low value of sterling made investing in UK real estate attractive. Emerging markets in south-east Europe, Russia, India, Turkey, Ukraine, China and south-east Asia were also attracting international real property investment – because of their high levels of economic growth and favourable demographics for real estate and infrastructure investment.

The real estate market in the USA

In the USA there are two markets: the space (rental) market and the capital (investment) market. The real estate space market determines a property's income stream – this depends on local demand and supply factors. Capital to fund the space markets is:

- private – from banks and life insurance companies and private equity from limited partnerships/corporations and pension funds (while banks and companies may be publicly trade, if the mortgaged debt they issue is *not* publicly traded, the debt is considered *private* debt);
- publicly traded – raised in public auction markets, usually stock and bond markets in New York, with proceeds used to fund real estate investments. Commercial mortgage-backed securities (CMBS) are the main source of publicly traded debt (usually $1 billion in 110–150 loans classified according to risk). REITs are the most common form of publicly traded equity in the USA.

Real estate is now perceived as a viable portfolio investment and real estate markets have become more informationally efficient and liquid. The USA is perceived to be an attractive market for international investors. The total value of all commercial real estate in the United States at 31 December 2007 was $5.3 trillion (Standard and Poors, 2008). Of this retail property was worth $1.9 trillion or 36 per cent; office $1.5 trillion or 29 per cent; apartments $1.3 trillion or 24 per cent; and industrial $191 billion or 4 per cent. The remainder is mainly property in the hospitality sector.

The most popular types of real estate investment in the USA in 2008 were: retail, hotels, industrial, multi-family apartments and then offices. The decline in popularity of office investment reflects the big impact of the credit crunch recession on employment in the financial districts and as a result a fall in demand for office space. Rents fell by about 30 per cent in mid-town New York in 2009 and by 29 per cent in Boston.

More than 90 per cent of REIT investments in the USA are made in commercial real estate equity investments (Seabrooke et al., 2004). The umbrella partnership REIT structure (UPREIT) was introduced in 1993, allowing private real estate partnerships to transfer ownership to an operating partnership controlled by the UPREIT. This had considerable tax advantages and added to the success of REITs in real estate investment, often in non-traditional areas such as healthcare and golf courses.

However, in the US housing market since 2008, there has been a wave of repossessions and the first national decline in house prices since the 1930s. The severe depletion of capital levels of banks involved with mortgage lending or mortgage-backed securities has restricted demand in the market. Fannie Mae and Freddie Mac, the government-sponsored mortgage corporations have made losses in the region of $15 billion. There is a surplus of about 4 million unsold homes and building industry output is down by about 50 per cent with between 1 and 2 million jobs lost.

The real estate market in India

Although India has developed rapidly to become the fifth largest economy in the world (with recent growth rates of 8–9 per cent) its commercial real estate market is only worth in the region of $50 billion in 2010. The economic growth of India has been based on new technological innovation, a booming information technology sector and a very successful hospitality and entertainment sector.

Historically, foreign direct investment (FDI) has been tightly controlled and limited to highly regulated development of integrated residential areas, technology and industrial parks and special economic zones designated by government. The regulations governing FDI in real estate were relaxed in 2005, however, although foreign investors are still prohibited from acquiring property directly and must do so through a joint venture with an Indian partner (minimum capitalization $5 million) or wholly owned subsidiary (minimum capitalization $10 million).

India is a democratic country with transparent property laws but obstacles remain to international investment in real estate:

- the federal government is trying to establish a registry of land titles but a guaranteed land title system has yet to be developed and different states have different laws;

- most transfers of real property are not recorded with the state and so owner-ship of 90 per cent of land in India could be subject to conflicting ownership claims;
- some states have a stamp duty of 10–12 per cent;
- owners of vacant land must either develop the land or risk confiscation of the land by the government.

Indirect investment in completed Indian real estate projects can now be achieved through real estate mutual funds (REMFs), which were authorized by the Securities and Exchange Board of India through an amendment of the rules governing mutual funds in April 2008. REMFs work in a similar way to real estate investment trusts in other countries, but their tax treatment is as yet uncertain. Although the turmoil in global equity markets has affected the near-term prospects for REMFs, they should ultimately provide a necessary source of capital for smaller projects and create a pipeline for the provision of additional liquidity into the Indian real property system.

For a small investor, investing in property will now become affordable, owing to a substantial reduction in minimum investment size. Buying a REMF unit will be far cheaper than buying a small office or residential property. As a result, there are now minimal entry barriers and no leasing or mainte-nance problems and there will be more liquidity as REMFs will be listed on exchanges. REMFs will provide an additional and cheaper source of capital to the industry.

The real estate market in Japan

In Japan, land represents a high percentage of the total value of real estate, and the design life of buildings is relatively short, so depreciation expenses and repair costs are low (Seabrooke et al., 2004). Home ownership rates in Japan are similar to those in other developed countries at 60 per cent (68 per cent in the USA). But there are cultural differences that impact on the Japanese housing market:

- only 6 per cent of Japanese households relocate in any year (16 per cent in the USA) –Japanese workers stay at one company for longer than workers in the USA and Japanese families have a greater tendency to pass their homes on to their children;
- the lower mobility rate in Japan means that annual home sales in Japan are only 0.6 per cent compared to 5 per cent in the USA;
- the ratio of existing homes to new home sales in Japan is 1:5 in Japan and 6:1 in the USA.

Japan's property bubble was a clear example of how fast economic growth combined with loose monetary conditions can lead to an asset price bubble. In Japan, between the 1960s and 1980s, economic growth averaged 8 per cent. Japanese people firmly believed in the 'land myth' because Japan is relatively small in size and there had been no experience of a decline in land value. All Japanese financial institutions regarded land as the best asset for collateral: inheritance tax was much lower on land than on financial assets and so real estate was tax efficient.

Speculation in land markets led to land prices in the six largest cities rising by 180 per cent in real terms in the 1980s. At this time, real estate valuations were based on comparison with similar transactions and rising valuations triggered non-stop buying of land, shares and other assets. Then in the late 1980s monetary conditions were tightened and a long-term economic decline (known as the 'lost decade' by Japanese people) began. In 1991 the bubble burst and real estate prices fell, with a subsequent decline in office demand due to corporate restructuring and a fall in housing demand because of fears about unemployment and because banks were reluctant to lend.

As a result, many companies as well as individuals took years to repay debt. The banking sector also went through major restructuring to solve its bad debt problems. Unlike a stock market crash following a bubble, a real estate crash is usually a slower process, as the real estate market is less liquid than the stock market. Other sectors such as office, hotel and retail generally move along with the residential market, being affected by many of same variables (incomes, interest rates, employment, GNP) and also sharing the wealth effect of booms. Japan's economy enjoyed a slow recovery, helped by both domestic demand and export growth.

Land prices in Japan rose for the first time in 14 years in 2005, a sign of an end to persistent declines in asset prices that have dragged down the economy since the early 1990's recession. There were increases in land prices in urban areas, such as Tokyo, Osaka and Kyoto, while prices in most rural areas remained in decline. The long-term decline in land price levels has led to a trend for foreign corporations to purchase land for investment purposes, basing their valuations on the capitalization of income streams via discounted cash flow analysis. For example, Goldman Sachs paid 60 billion yen for the Yamoto Life Insurance building and AIG paid 70 billion yen for a Japan Energy building. Japanese companies are now also interested in the real estate investment market because prices are low and yields high. Part of this investment market trend is the separation of ownership and management of real estate. The credit crunch recession has stalled the Japanese economic recovery, however. In 2009 urban land prices in the six largest cities fell by 7.8 per cent and overseas real estate investment fell 48 per cent to $19 billion in 2009. The Japanese government has implemented a wide range of monetary and fiscal stimulus measures to try to bring about recovery.

The real estate market in China

In mainland China, until the 1980s, there was no mechanism for the transfer of real estate. Land was either owned by the state or held collectively by village communities and collectively owned land is transferred to state ownership when development takes place. Leases of land are granted for: 70 years for residential use; 50 years for industrial; 50 years for education, science and so on; and 40 years for commerce, tourism and entertainment.

Since the economic reforms of the 1980s, the real estate and construction industries have led economic development. This created demands for construction materials, equipment, plant and machinery and increased employment in over 50 industries (the multiplier coefficient is approximately 1.93 for real estate). Development of real estate also stimulated demand for higher living standards and consumer goods. Economic growth rates consistently above 10 per cent per annum have led to increased demand for offices, industrial space, warehouses, and retail space; and property and construction account for about 10 per cent of China's GDP, excluding the consumer goods that home buying stimulates.

Income levels in China more than doubled between 2003 and 2008 from US$1,200 to US$3,000. This, together with the continuing migration of rural dwellers into cities has increased residential property prices. By 2015 more than half of China's population of 1.39 billion will be living in cities as industrialization attracts people from the countryside. More than 160 cities in China have a population exceeding 1 million, which has brought problems such as low wages, a shortage of affordable housing, an increase in violent crime and a widening gap between rich and poor. However, China has largely managed its mass urbanization without the creation of slums as in India, however. The World Bank expects China's growth rate to slow to 7 per cent a year by 2020 because of relative labour shortages – growth rates have been about 10 per cent a year since 1995.

Poor data means that it is difficult to be sure about Chinese house price trends, however. According to the National Bureau of Statistics of China, prices nationally rose by 12.8 per cent in the year to April 2010. Hot spots were: Sanya (a resort city) 49.3 per cent; Shenzhen 20.9 per cent; Guangzhou 11.3 per cent; Beijing 10.7 per cent and Shanghai 9.0 per cent. The Ministry of Land, however, says that the national house price rise for the same period was 25 per cent. Buying property is appealing in China because the limited financial sector offers few other investment options. People buy homes as a way of saving for the future and this is particularly important in China because the population cannot rely on state pensions and other social security benefits.

In recent years there has been increased foreign direct investment into China ($5.4 billion invested by foreign enterprises in 2005). China overtook the USA as the world's biggest property investment market in 2009 with $156.2 billion invested (the USA slumped 64 per cent to $38.3 billion). Foreign firms pulled out of China in large numbers in the recession leaving considerable office space unlet yet still more under construction. Much retail space is also vacant.

In May 2007 the average price per square metre in central Shanghai was $3,259 with apartments costing $325,901 while the average wage was $332 per month. Some 70 per cent of urban residents in Beijing were unable to buy a house – a mass market Beijing home now costs 12 years of average income according to Credit Suisse. To buy a 100-square-metre home in Beijing, the average household must spend 17 years' income. Local Chinese complain that due to a growing number of foreign workers in the larger cities, who are paid western salaries, the real estate market has inflated and become a bubble and across the country as a whole, home prices are nine times the average income of urban households. The 'one-child' policy means that Chinese parents are able to help their children to buy a new apartment, however, and many Chinese city dwellers live in accommodation provided by their employers. Since the privatization of much of the housing stock in 1998, only 48 million homes have been sold while there are 215 million urban households.

Worried by the increasing speculation in property and the possibility of the market overheating, the Chinese State Council announced measures aimed at cooling the market in April 2010. These included:

- increasing deposits and mortgage rates on second homes to increase the cost of property speculation;
- allocating more land for residential property – 70 per cent of land approved for property development would go to low-income housing, small and medium-sized homes, and shanty-town renovation;
- speeding up plans to introduce tax policies that would influence property purchases and returns including a sales tax on homes sold within 5 years of purchase.

The Chinese property market did slow as a result of these measures with prices across 70 cities falling by 0.1 per cent in June 2010, but the annual rate of increase remained high at 11.4 per cent.

Real estate markets in central and eastern Europe

The development of a functioning real estate market is vital to the development of the economy of a country which is in transition from a command economy to a market economy. Real estate can be used in ways additional to occupancy by the owner. Land can be used as collateral to support borrowings, and in this way the real estate market and the financial sectors become interdependent. This can be both a strength and a weakness for the wider economy. The use of real estate as collateral enables investors to realize part of their wealth in real estate to increase their investments and the property market has played an important part in enhancing the competitive position of capital cities in central and eastern Europe (Keivani et al., 2002).

Investment markets in east-central Europe, notably in Prague, Budapest and Warsaw developed quickly in the 1990s along with significant growth in per capita GDP (despite high inflation and high interest rates). Reorganization of land and its control after the communist era involved privatization programmes and policies to liberalize the market and decontrol rents. The opening up of trade also opened up property markets to foreign demand for real estate assets. The principal central and eastern European (CEE) markets made rapid progress in reducing obstacles to foreign investment in real estate. International firms expanded into the region requiring office and retail space and foreign direct investment was arguably one of the principal driving forces behind the strong economic growth of CEE countries (Adair et al., 2006).

Lack of supply of prime quality office space encouraged development by international companies who financed and traded the assets built. There are still only a small number of investment-quality-grade buildings available, however, and although yields are high the risks of investing in CEE markets are considerable. They include frequently changing tax and legal systems, poorly developed land legislation, an economic infrastructure that is poorly developed compared with more mature real estate markets and few investment guarantees for foreign investors (McGreal et al., 2002).

The CEE region experienced a five-fold increase in foreign direct investment (FDI) inflows between 2003 and 2008, rising from US$30 billion to $155 billion. Russia was the destination which attracted much of this additional investment as its inflows rose from less than $8 billion in 2003 to more than $70 billion in 2008. The credit crunch and recession that ensued coincided with a collapse of FDI inflows to the CEE region. In the region as a whole, FDI inflows were 50 per cent lower in 2009 compared to 2008 (PriceWaterhouseCoopers, 2010).

UK property and globalization

Globalization has increased the free flow of ideas, people, goods, services and capital across borders and has increased the integration of economies and societies. While globalization is not a new phenomenon, some aspects of it going back to the nineteenth century, the current wave of globalization has led to the adoption by a large number of countries of more open economic policies. This has increased international trade in goods and services, and cross-border flows of both capital and labour. Rapid technical progress in the field of information and communications technology has sharply lowered transport and communications costs and has increased the tradability of goods and services. In conjunction with this, economic reform in India and China has enabled their development as low-wage producers of many of the world's manufactured goods and international trade in intermediate inputs and services has grown strongly in the last decade.

International capital flows, particularly foreign direct investment (FDI), have also increased greatly. The UK continues to be an attractive destination for inward investment, although the USA remains by far the single most important source of inward investment, despite its share of inward investment falling over the past 10 years. The EU's share over this period has risen, to over 50 per cent in 2006 when the UK was second only to the USA in terms of FDI inflows. Investment expands the physical capacity of the economy and hence allows economic growth to take place. In an increasingly global economy, there are both more opportunities and competition in relation to attracting globally footloose investment. The Barker and Eddington Reviews examined the investment infrastructure framework and made recommendations with respect o the functioning of the planning system in the UK across transport, energy, waste and water, taking into account, for example, the UK's future transport infrastructure needs (BERR, 2006).

Global value chains have emerged – where firms locate different parts of the production process in different countries according to relative cost structures. The development of global value chains has been made possible by technological progress, making it easier to supply services remotely, to modularize production activities and to manage them remotely. The emergence of global value chains is, in turn, associated with 'offshoring', which involves firms selecting and holding on to the stages in the value chain that they consider to be 'core', whilst relocating the firm's 'non-core' activities to foreign countries or to third parties in foreign countries. The transfer of production, back-offices and research and development centres to developing countries has boosted commercial real estate in many of these countries.

Growth in real estate, renting and business services, which increased its output share by 5.7 per cent (from 19.1 to 24.8 per cent) over the period 1996–2006, has been central to the growth in services (ONS Blue Book). In turn, growth in business services has been central to growth in the broader real estate, renting and business services sector. Business services include a diverse range of activities, from the creative and technical, such as advertising, legal services and computing, to industrial cleaning and call centres. In the past 20 years, business services have doubled their share of UK GDP from 7 to 14 per cent, and account for almost 1.7 million more jobs than previously.

Real estate stays where it is of course, and while its ownership can be international and global firms can target individual property markets in global cities for investment, the assets stay where they are constructed. Investors look beyond their own borders, in part because some home markets are too small or too competitive and do not offer many investment opportunities. Investors try to realize higher returns by taking advantage of inefficiencies or unique opportunities in local markets, while owners seek to expand their existing portfolios of assets and build on the success of their domestic businesses. Securitization and the development of a number of financial instruments has enabled international investors to have liquidity.

Globalization offers increased exposure to alternative markets, more investment choices, and access to global capital markets. For the host country, global investment means increased employment, access to international capital to finance growth and compete internationally, and access to global technologies. Real estate investors have become increasingly international in their outlook over the last decade and the opening up of markets has increasingly led to international development and investment in real estate. With finance and investment capital increasingly mobile, it is possible for investors to achieve higher returns, to widen their investment opportunities, and to diversify internationally as a strategy to reduce risk.

An alternative view to the perception that increasing globalization is inevitable is that the growing importance of services in economic development will reverse the trend to internationalization (Ball, 2007). In the commercial sector, agents are often huge global firms offering a range of services, but in the residential sector, small firms dominate in relatively local markets. Residential buyers and sellers prefer to deal with local agents for reasons of cost, knowledge and proximity. The 'local is best' preference for services may stall the trend towards globalization.

The UK has about 8.4 per cent of the global real estate market, largely in London assets. With a few exceptions there are no limitations on foreign ownership of real estate in the UK. Property may be acquired or occupied by individuals, trustees or companies and it can be acquired as a freehold interest in the land, on a long lease, on a short lease or on licence. However, there are some restrictions on how the owner of an interest in real estate uses or develops the land or building:

- the legal title under which the real estate is held may impose restrictions, for example, a legally binding covenant in a lease limiting the use to which the land may be put;
- planning permission is required for development including alterations to buildings;
- building regulations under public health legislation impose requirements on the way alterations to existing buildings are made and new buildings constructed.

Nor are there any UK exchange controls on inward or outward investment (direct or portfolio), or on the repatriation of income or capital, the holding of currency accounts or the settlement of current trading transactions.

Post credit crunch international property investment

In the credit crunch aftermath financial conditions are still very tight – lenders are reluctant to lend. They prefer to hold on to funds because of rising bankruptcies,

---

Box 18.2   The Dubai real estate bubble

Dubai is one of seven states that make up the United Arab Emirates (UAE). Historically Dubai had an oil-based economy but its oil reserves were in decline after 2000 and it decided to diversify into other areas, especially tourism and commerce. Consequently Dubai embarked upon an ambitious real estate development programme, building a man-made coastline, a series of luxury artificial islands, the world's only 7-star hotel, the world's tallest building, the Burj Dubai, and the world's largest shopping mall. This 6-year boom was based on a 'build it and they will come' philosophy and 17,000 new hotel rooms were built there between 2006 and 2009. From 2006, the Dubai government allowed foreigners to acquire freehold residential titles for designated areas and a wave of buying followed.

Between 2003 and 2007 villa prices increased at an annual rate of about 226 per cent and apartments by about 100 per cent. The population of Dubai was increasing rapidly (it doubled to 1.2 million between 1993 and 2005). In 2007 there was a shortage of supply fuelled by low availability of raw materials and real estate prices rose to the second highest in the world. The economic model focused on developing large areas of desert with foreign money and labour.

Dubai World, which owns the Dubai developer Nakheel, bought assets worldwide and especially in North America borrowing heavily in order to do so. Its liabilities totalled $60 billion out of a total for Dubai of $80 billion. The UK was the largest creditor for more than $50 billion (HSBC $11 billion, Lloyds, Barclays and Royal Bank of Scotland also exposed). The property bubble burst in late 2008 leaving buildings unfinished, debts unpaid and paper fortunes wiped out. Dubai suffered the world's steepest property slump in the global recession. Property prices fell by 50 per cent from their 2008 peak and hundreds of billions of dollars worth of building projects were delayed or cancelled. Developers froze recruitment and made redundancies. Thousands of jobs were lost and migrant workers had to leave (they were not allowed to stay without employment).

Dubai World announced in November 2009 that it could not meet its interest payments and this reduced the share values of British banks by £14 billion. The markets calmed after Dubai World announced that it only needed to postpone payment on half of its debt and the UAE provided liquidity. In late November 2009, however, the Dubai government unexpectedly said it would not guarantee the debt of Dubai World and Dubai's credit rating was ruined. The banks stopped lending and the Dubai stock market fell by 70 per cent (property firms 80 per cent).

Dubai owes $80 billion (148 per cent of GDP) to Abu Dhabi and the UAE and has to cope with falling oil prices and difficulty in obtaining credit. Dubai's debt problems are a hangover from a property bubble that imploded after the financial crisis ruined its ambitious plans to become a magnet for tourists and a regional hub for shipping and entertainment.

---

mortgage defaults and other problems in the economy. As a result, they apply higher interest rates and will only lend to the safest borrowers: borrowing terms were very lax in 2007, but became very restrictive from 2008. In addition, builders and developers are building less because there is less money available and there is over supply of commercial and residential real estate in most mature markets. Unemployment, repossessions of residential property and poor growth conditions look set to hold back real estate prospects for some time.

The world has changed with the severity of the credit crunch recession. Spending by western consumers was the driving force for world economic growth before 2007 but is unlikely to be so again for some time. The demand for commercial real estate is a derived demand which depends on prosperity in national markets creating a need for office, retail, industrial and other space. There is now considerable commercial real estate spare capacity in most of the cities of the developed countries and a return to long-term rates of economic growth will be required before this space is fully taken up. The US and UK commercial property markets have seen a fall in values of 40 per cent plus over the period 2007–9: Canada has fared better with only a 20 per cent fall.

Emerging markets and in particular the Asia-Pacific region seem set to become the preferred investment funds' destination for some time to come. Economic growth has continued at high rates in India and China. Economic growth in Brazil and Russia is likely to result in their property markets recovering at a faster rate than the UK and US markets.

India could attract significant funds: 80 per cent of real estate in India is residential and according to the Tenth Five Year Plan there is a current shortage of 22.4 million dwellings and in the next 10 to 15 years 80–90 million dwellings need to be constructed, most of them for middle and lower income groups. Mumbai and New Delhi are the leading cities. Foreign direct investment into India was $2.8 billion in 2008–9. It is likely that Real Estate Mutual Funds and Real Estate Investment Trusts will boost investment in India.

Asian cities (especially their residential sectors) were identified by the Urban Land Institute and Price Waterhouse Coopers as being the best prospects in 2010 – the top five cities identified were Shanghai (retail, industrial and rental apartments), Hong Kong (retail), Beijing (residential), Seoul and Singapore. For development opportunities, Shanghai, Mumbai and New Delhi were identified as the best prospects.

Summary

Foreign ownership of real estate is often subject to specific domestic restrictions and global investors use specific ownership vehicles (such as joint ventures with domestic companies) to enter such markets. The major difficulties of international investment are currency movements, information costs, variations in transaction costs, political instability and market inefficiency.

Global cities compete with other cities to host international organizations and corporations and in order to do so they need effective, high quality real estate. From the late 1980s there has been widespread foreign ownership of real estate in global cities. The correlation between international real estate markets is surprisingly high suggesting the emergence of a global cycle.

International investment in commercial property can be either; direct in order to receive a rental income and capital appreciation; or indirect in shares and securities. Factors contributing to the growth of international property investment include the growth of global corporations, the dominance of services in advanced economies and the footloose nature of service industries.

The UK is an important destination for international real estate investment with about 8.4 per cent of global real estate assets, mainly in London. Following the global recession it is likely that emerging markets, especially in Asia, will become more important as destinations for international real estate investment.

Chapter 18: review questions

1. Why does international real estate investment take place?
2. Illustrate how currency movement can affect international property investment.
3. What are the main difficulties of international property investment?
4. Explain why there has been globalization of international property markets since the 1980s.
5. What is meant by a 'real estate bubble'?

Part V
The Government and Real Estate

19

Regional Policy in the UK and Europe

After studying this chapter you will be able to:

- Outline the interactions between the UK real estate sector and the European Union;
- Explain the impact of membership of the EU on the property sector of the UK;
- Assess the advantages and disadvantages of eurozone membership for real estate in the UK;
- Describe the main features of UK and EU regional policy.

The European Union

The European Union (EU) is a partnership of 27 democratic countries, working together for the benefit of all their citizens. It aims to promote social and economic progress among its members, common foreign and security positions, police and judicial cooperation in criminal matters, and European citizenship.

The 27 countries in the EU are listed below, by the year they joined:

- 1958: Belgium, France, (West) Germany, Italy, Luxembourg, Netherlands;
- 1973: Denmark, Ireland, UK;
- 1981: Greece;
- 1986: Portugal, Spain;
- 1995: Austria, Finland, Sweden;
- 2004: Cyprus, Czech Republic, Estonia, Hungary, Latvia, Lithuania, Malta, Poland, Slovakia, Slovenia;
- 2007: Romania, Bulgaria.

In 2010 Croatia, Macedonia and Turkey were official candidates to join the EU.

The 27 states provide a common market of some 500 million people, protected from outsiders by common external tariffs. However, the object of the Single European Market (SEM) is, by removing barriers, to allow goods and factors of production to move freely within the EU through the operation of the price system. Only then can the full benefits of the larger market be realized.

Sixteen of the member states of the EU are in the eurozone having the euro as their currency and their monetary policy administered by the European Central Bank (ECB) whose headquarters is in Frankfurt, Germany.

The EU and real estate

Not only does the SEM provide a market equivalent in size to that of the USA, but it should generate a high rate of growth through the economies of scale it offers in finance, production, management ability, research, and so on. These advantages can be secured by the UK development and property companies and investors in property.

Since the demand for property is derived from the services it provides to other industries – manufacturing, retailing and financial services – the large SEM is likely to increase demand for factories, distribution warehouses, shops and offices. And UK developers and property companies should be well-placed for responding to this demand. Not only have they acquired expertise through their operations in the UK, but these have been carried out in the context of the similar high level of income which exists in most European cities.

For the most part, the UK property industry has stayed away from the Continent, mainly because the opportunities existing there can only be exploited by the largest UK companies whose current strategy is to hold large, modern buildings (particularly offices and shops) in prime positions but focused in a limited geographical area.

Nevertheless, among these companies, views differ as to the advantages of positioning operations on the Continent. All are interested in yield and prospective growth in the properties held and stress the demands on management time which the dispersal of operations give rise to. But here the weight which the individual managing directors place on conflicting objectives, and their ability to handle them, are the decisive issues. The leading UK property companies by net worth (2010 estimate) are shown in Table 19.1.

Of these leading companies, only SEGRO and Grosvenor have significant European investments. Hammerson plc, the UK flagship in northern Europe, sold properties and development land held in Australia, the USA and Canada and in 1995 replaced them by purchasing prime retail outlets and offices in France and Germany which, by active management, could add value by development or refurbishment. The company now describes itself as a leading UK real estate company operating in the UK and France (Hammerson.co.uk). Many of

Table 19.1   Leading UK property companies

Company	£ million
Crown Estate	6015
Land Securities	4825
British Land	3200
Hammerson	2950
SEGRO (formerly Slough Estates)	2593
Liberty International	2421
Grosvenor	2388
Cadogan Group	2119
London and Regional Properties	1435
Howard de Walden Estates	1248

the other major UK real estate companies have names that suggest their interests lie within the country, for example, British Land and London and Regional.

The reluctance or hesitancy of even the large property developer companies to expand into Europe has a variety of explanations. First, the initial presentation of the general advantages of the new SEM coincided with the 1990 crash in property as well as a slow return of confidence in the attributes of property as an investment asset. Second, there has been little harmonization of national differences relating to property. Therefore, purchasers of property to let, for example, insurance companies, prefer the 15-year institutional lease with its 5-yearly, upward-only rent reviews to the European 9-year term with a break-option every 3 years and an annual rent review in line with construction costs (France) or the cost of living (Germany). Moreover transaction costs still favour the UK (about 5 per cent) compared with France (17 per cent) and Germany (6 per cent).

EU countries are given considerable flexibility in deciding their own forms and rates of taxation. UK rates are among the lowest in the EU and it has to be admitted that the UK has shown little enthusiasm for harmonization. As a result, the 1989 levying of *VAT* on new non-residential construction was really forced upon the UK by a decision of the European Court of Justice. Similarly, raising the VAT rate in 1991 to 17.5 per cent (and therefore closer to that of all the major EU countries) was really to fund government expenditure rather than the pursuit of a harmonization objective. Indeed the Commission would like VAT rates for each member country to fall within two bands – a standard rate between 14 per cent and 20 per cent (which would include construction and new buildings), and a reduced rate between 4 per cent and 9 per cent for certain essential necessities. It would also like to abolish the zero rate, so that eventually VAT could be applied even to the construction of new dwellings.

Regarding *direct taxes*, the UK has a relatively low rate of *corporation tax* on profits (28 per cent main rate and 21 per cent for companies with less than

£300,000 profit), compared, for instance, with France's 35 per cent, and of *capital gains tax*. Only the UK's *local tax* – the Uniform Business Rate – tends to be higher than the local taxes on income levied by Germany, Italy, Luxembourg and Portugal. The overall EU tax to GDP ratio is high at 39.8 per cent compared to the USA and Japan where it is about 12 per cent lower.

At present, property developers have to adapt to countries' different planning requirements and market operations. For transactions in real property and property assets, markets in the EU are less active (and thus more imperfect) than in the UK. Reasons for this are:

1. a greater preference by occupiers for owning their own property in the EU;
2. the source of long-term finance is bank loans rather than equity capital as in the UK;
3. an adherence to historic values in the accounts, thus masking the returns which are really being earned on capital values;
4. lease terms tend to limit the investor's share of rental growth;
5. portfolio management is impeded by the tax structure and transaction costs which, for example, could in France add 18 per cent to the purchase price. Such factors tend to inhibit property trading and active portfolio management.

Thus, in spite of the globalization of finance, we cannot expect a unified European property market to develop until institutional frictions have been removed. Nevertheless, provided London maintains its pre-eminence in expertise, inventiveness and adaptability it should hold, and even increase, its share of business: for example, there could be scope for banks and building societies to extend their mortgage business in the EU.

It must also be noted that the high equity content of UK property companies leaves them vulnerable to acquisition by continental property companies seeking a higher flow of investment income and economies of scale. Although expansion can be achieved by organic growth, taking over the whole of a company's assets is quicker and economically more efficient, when the net asset value per property share stands at a substantial discount to the market price of the share and the costs of purchasing property direct are high.

The preference of firms on the Continent for owning their own freehold premises reduces the supply of suitable properties in which to invest. There is thus a strong incentive to look elsewhere, merging with or bidding for entire property companies. Offering an attractive price for shares may induce a majority shareholding to accept. Thus, Rodamco (the Netherlands) attempted unsuccessfully to take over Hammerson in 1990. Depreciation of sterling on the foreign exchange market as happened in 2007–10 (Euro up 30 per cent; dollar up 20 per cent) would increase the possibility of such a take-over, since it would be less costly to an overseas bidder.

In addition to (i) firms owning property they occupy, (ii) dealers who acquire development land and properties for trading on, (iii) property companies which develop, refurbish or hold properties to provide a regular cash flow, there is an increasing demand from (iv) institutions, such as insurance companies and pension funds, who wish to hold property long-term as a given proportion of their investment portfolio.

The positive income-elasticity of demand for such services ensures, through the regular premium payments and pension contributions, an increasing flow of funds for investment in order to cover future contractual commitments. Since the top-grade commercial and agricultural properties preferred by these institutions are found in the wealthier countries throughout the world, the EU market for these properties is merely an important part of this highly competitive global market.

In contrast to the limited response of UK property developers to EU opportunities, the international agents who make this market have been dynamic in adapting to its requirements. As a result they have either amalgamated or been taken over, thereby achieving economies of scale. For example, Savills consolidated its growing presence in Asia by joining forces with First Pacific Davies to become FPD Savills in 1997. Savills also acquired a majority shareholding in the Spanish, German and French companies previously trading as Weatherall Green and Smith; Jones Lang Wootton has merged with the US property management group, La Salle Partners; and in May 1998, one of North America's top brokerage and facilities management firms, CB Commercial, merged with Richard Ellis, an international name in commercial real estate to form CBRE. Soon after, it also bought Hillier Parker May and Rowden, another large UK property services firm (Ball, 2007). By 2004, CB Richard Ellis Group Inc. had acquired Insignia Financial Group (US) and gone public with a turnover of $2.4 billion. Cushman and Wakefield based in New York merged with London based Healey and Baker in 1998 to become Cushman Wakefield Healey and Baker. Such integration has enabled these companies to offer a full range of services worldwide as estate agents, consultants, advisers, valuers and possibly in-house accountants and lawyers.

While it would seem that the SEM has not galvanized UK developers and property companies into major activity on the Continent, it has made an impact on the UK itself in a number of ways.

First, the EU now accounts for 55 per cent of Britain's overseas trade. Parallel with this has come an increased two-way, cross-channel movement of people, the Channel Tunnel and a faster direct rail link between London and Paris/ Brussels. Major complementary developments, such as hotels, have followed near the chief east-Kent towns of Dover and Ashford.

Second, it has shifted the regional income balance of the UK still further in favour of London and south-east England to which the newer hi-tech production, linked-services and research have gravitated. This highlights the necessity of improving the motorway and road connections to the industrial north of England.

Third, warehouse development has taken place at strategically based distribution centres, both national and regional. Such distribution centres originated in the 1980s when the retail sector moved its stock-holding operations away from valuable prime High Street sites. These national distribution centres now focus on the Midland triangle, bounded by Birmingham, Northampton and Leicester from which it is possible to serve 75 per cent of the population of England within four hours. Distribution centres for components of manufactured goods are situated further north, having largely resulted through other industries adopting where possible the Japanese 'just-in-time' method of bringing in car components.

In siting both types of distribution centre, the emphasis has been on the convenience and flexibility of road transport. But the environmental costs, such as CO_2 emission, are in future likely to be increasingly targeted by the government which would like to see more traffic being diverted to the rail network. The solution may be the development of swap-body technology enabling trailers to be used on both road and rail. The alternative may be to simply fall back on the restriction of lorry use, as in Austria and Switzerland.

The eurozone

The single currency began on 1 January 1999, with a 3-year transitional period as follows:

- 1 January 1999:
  - exchange rates of member countries' currencies locked irrevocably with the euro;
  - responsibility for the formulation and implementation of monetary policy passed to the ECB, which also decides on exchange rates with outside currencies, manages the reserves and intervenes in the market. It will be the sole issuing authority of the single currency;
  - ECB monetary and foreign exchange operations conducted in euros.
- 1 January 2002: euro notes and coins issued with legal tender became the medium of exchange rather than simply a unit of account. These at first circulated alongside national currencies in participating member countries.
- 1 July 2002: national currencies were no longer legal tender in participating member countries and the euro became the common currency. Responsibility for monetary policy was transferred from the national central banks of 11 EU member states to the ECB in January 1999. Greece joined in 2001, Slovenia in 2007, Cyprus and Malta in 2008, Slovakia in 2009.

There are now 16 European Union (EU) member states which have adopted the euro currency as their sole legal tender. The eurozone currently consists of

Austria, Belgium, Cyprus, Finland, France, Germany, Greece, Ireland, Italy, Luxembourg, Malta, the Netherlands, Portugal, Slovakia, Slovenia and Spain.

The EMU with its single currency represents the most important change in the international monetary system since Bretton Woods in 1944. Yet while the advantage of increased trade through the SEM has been proved, members of the EU must appreciate that the final step of a single currency is a leap into the unknown and fraught with difficulties.

First, there were heavy initial costs of its introduction. Businesses had to alter all their money machines (such as cash dispensers, tills, vending machines). In addition, computer programmes had to be re-calculated to cover the change from the old currency to the euro. Individuals, too, have had to adapt, with wages, salaries, state benefits, mortgages, monetary assets, and so on, being expressed in euros. Since this would be less easy for older persons there is here a psychological cost.

Second, member countries may not be equally sensitive to ECB changes in its 'one-fits-all' rate of interest because they have reached different stages in the trade cycle.

Third, with the impossibility of exchange rate depreciation to lower a country's costs, the alternative – deflation – is only acceptable if labour costs are flexible downwards. If not, prolonged unemployment can result.

Fourth, certain regions which are poor in natural resources or whose basic industry is in terminal decline will have to be given assistance from the EU's Structure and Social Funds. But the danger is that such subsidies, by relieving the pressure to accept lower wages or to move to more prosperous regions, may persist indefinitely.

At present UK politicians, businessmen and academic economists are divided as to whether the UK should join the eurozone, but the 2007–9 recession in the UK has made it less likely that the UK will join. This is because the benefits of controlling interest rates and allowing the pound to depreciate in a recession can be clearly seen and contrasted with the experiences in Ireland, Spain, Portugal, Italy and Greece where the ECB has control of monetary policy.

Those in favour claim that membership of the eurozone would:

1. allow trade to flow more freely according to the law of comparative costs by *eliminating* the *costs* of exchanging national currencies and of exchange rate fluctuations;
2. *increase trade* through the keener competition resulting from the transparency provided by showing all prices in euros;
3. lead to a *lower rate of interest* through the commitment of an independent ECB to controlling inflation;
4. proclaim the UK's commitment to Europe, and so ensure that continuation of *inward investment* by countries outside, for example, Japan, USA;

5. fulfil an essential condition for the *City of London* to maintain its pre-eminence as a financial market in the face of a challenge by Frankfurt;
6. enable the UK to help *shape policies* from within rather than, by delaying entry, having to converge on policies already decided.

Those who oppose membership, however, claim that:

1. the UK would be unable to adjust the sterling *exchange rate* and short-term rate of interest according to the needs of her own economy:
2. the raising of the UK's relatively low *labour cost* through the adoption of EU regulations could undermine her major comparative cost advantage;
3. through its newly granted independence in determining base rate, the Bank of England is equally effective as the ECB in *controlling inflation*;
4. *inward investment* to the UK is not dependent on her being within the EMU, but is mainly determined by her prospective economic growth, relative labour costs, professional expertise, subsidy support, political stability and the use of English as the common language of trade;
5. while for itself the *City of London* would prefer to be in the EMU, it feels that even outside it would, through its proven adaptability and expertise, still retain its leading position in what is now a global market;
6. in place of exchange rate flexibility and interest rate adjustment, macro policy has to rely on *deflation* to stem rising costs even in the face of wage-rigidity and labour immobility (and the resulting unemployment).

With the single currency, every element of money creation is controlled, as to timing, form and amount, by the ECB. The central banks of member countries retain only an advisory role through membership of the European System of Central Banks (ESCB), which simply oversees monetary and foreign exchange markets. Yet they would still be responsible for implementing the ECB's policy decisions.

The impact of a change in the ECB's interest rate may differ between member countries. Much UK borrowing is on variable interest rates and the UK might bear a disproportionately larger share of the burden of adjustment following a rise in the ECB's rate than Germany, whose borrowing is mostly on fixed rates. Moreover, while the reverberations of economic shocks are usually felt by most countries, on occasions a shock may be more specific to a particular country. For the UK this might be the case if there were a considerable fall in the price of oil, or if a major trading partner, such as the USA, ran into serious recession.

With a single currency, where no one member can alone depreciate their currency, realignment has to come about by the deflation of prices, including wages, and then only after a prolonged period of unemployment. Such a policy has in the past proved unacceptable. The UK's inability in 1992 to maintain a fixed ERM exchange rate against heavy speculation illustrates the point. Raising the interest rate to support sterling merely added to the ongoing recession and unemployment.

It is claimed that EMU will generate increased output from which all members will benefit, either directly in increased income, or indirectly through a redistribution from a structural fund of the EU. Such an increase in income should be reflected in additional demand for property by occupiers of shops, offices, factories and houses. For instance, at a minimum it should stimulate cross-border retail trade, similar to that embarked upon by Tesco, and lead to the erection of warehouses at strategically placed distribution centres.

Failure to join the EMU, however, will not preclude UK property developers, property companies and investors from trading freely in the eurozone for all EU members are within the SEM to which the UK is committed. But, in addition to its peripheral cross-Channel location, the UK would be exposed to possible fluctuations in the pound sterling: euro exchange rate, the cost of exchanging currencies and probably a higher rate of interest when borrowing.

By generating growth, EMU should open up new development and investment opportunities in Europe, but the insular attitude of UK real estate companies revealed earlier in this chapter raises the question of whether they want to compete and operate there. Or are there, at least for the time being, more attractive propositions in the home market? As noted previously, in the early 1990s only a few of the larger property-development companies, such as Hammerson and Segro showed any enthusiasm although at that time competition with Europe was on a level playing field since each country had to exchange currencies.

Therefore, while British industry and commerce in general can perceive advantages in UK membership, as far as property development is concerned there is mostly indifference. It should also be noted that, for the present participants, currency exchange costs or exchange rate movements are hardly likely to be important since the spread of their operations between the UK and the eurozone would provide an adequate cash flow in the appropriate currency to cover maintenance costs, ground rents, local taxes, dividend distributions, and so on. Even for further borrowing in euros, properties already held and the company's financial standing would support a direct capital loan in euros.

As we saw earlier, the institutions with funds to invest and their agents would operate very actively and competitively in Europe, which they would probably regard as the most important part of the international market in which they operate.

Financial services is now the UK's largest industry (despite the credit crunch) with most business being concentrated on the City of London and its financial markets. Through the worldwide abolition of exchange controls and revolutionary changes in all forms of communications technology, financial dealings have been transferred from small-scale domestic markets to the large euro-markets centred in London. As a result, during the 1990s, the City expanded its financial business rapidly and in addition acted as a magnet for the head offices of the European operations of multinational companies. Consequently, there are 300,000 persons are now employed within the Square Mile.

It is evident that the fortunes of the City's property market and its financial services industry are directly related. Moreover City of London office development is tied to a rapidly expanding industry, unlike commercial property generally which is linked to the slower-growing economy as a whole.

The City of London would prefer the UK to be within the eurozone for this would make it easier for it to ward off the threat to its business from Frankfurt, already the location of the ECB. But in or out, it feels the worldwide confidence in its markets, expertise and adaptability will enable it to resist the challenge. To this end, therefore, the City Corporation has relaxed its planning restrictions on the height of office buildings and granted permission for the construction of several multi-storey buildings.

UK regional policy in the context of the EU

There is a regional development agency (RDA) in each of the nine English regions. RDAs are responsible for developing and delivering, with regional partners, a Regional Economic Strategy which sets out the economic aspirations of the region and how they are going to achieve them. Each RDA writes its own strategy to make sure that it is related to the region's economy. Scotland, Wales and Northern Ireland have their own agencies for similar functions. Although the European Union is one of the richest parts of the world, there remain striking internal disparities of income and opportunity between its regions. The entry in May 2004 of 10 new member countries whose incomes are well below the EU average has widened these gaps. With enlargement, the area and population of the EU has expanded by 20 per cent while GDP has increased by less than 5 per cent. The GDP of the newcomers varies from about 82 per cent of the EU average in Cyprus to 45–50 per cent in Poland and the Baltic States (Estonia, Latvia and Lithuania).

Regional policy transfers resources from affluent to poorer regions. It is both an instrument of financial solidarity and a powerful force for economic integration. A healthy integrated EU – at both economic and political levels – is possible only if progress is made towards reducing disparities in economic opportunity between regions. The rationale for EU regional policy is:

1. Physical controls are more difficult to operate in the EU context. Not only are they at variance with the objective of greater mobility within the EU,

but firms have the option of relocating in a prosperous region of another member state.

2. The depressed peripheral regions of Scotland, Northern Ireland, Southern Italy and so on, are more distant from the expanding centre of the Community – south-east England through to north-east France and Germany – than they are from the centres of their own countries. This EU 'centre' forms a concentrated market to which industries are likely to be increasingly attracted, thereby adding to its dominance.

3. The EU embraces regions exhibiting wider economic disparities than in any one member state. Moreover, regional problems are more heterogeneous – for example, whereas the UK depressed regions are mainly industrial, Italy and Greece have many depressed agricultural areas.

Such considerations mean that the formulation of an effective EU regional policy is a difficult task. Not only must it respond quickly as new regional problems arise, but it has to be linked with, and be complementary to, the individual nation's regional policy. Indeed EU policy should also coordinate the regional policies of member states, for example a physical control in one country must not be undermined by a firm being able to locate in another country.

It follows, therefore, that regional policy must be handled to a substantial degree at the EU level and be wide-ranging in the measures employed so that one reinforces the others. Above all, to achieve greater equity, it must envisage substantial transfers of income through incentive funds which are additional to and not a substitute for those provided by the member states.

The emphasis of the EU's four Structural Funds is now on regional development programmes rather than on individual projects, and the EU Commission can insist that grants are actually spent in the specified region. These funds are as follows:

1. The *European Regional Development Fund* (ERDF) funds the development and structural adjustment of less-developed regions (such as Spain, Italy, Portugal and Greece) and declining industrial regions (for example, within the UK, Spain and France). The UK's depressed regions are major beneficiaries of the ERDF.

2. The *European Social Fund* (ESF) provides funds to organizations running vocational training and job-creation schemes.

3. The *European Agricultural Guidance and Guarantee Fund* (EAGGF) supports farming in less-favoured or environmentally sensitive areas, and the modernization of infrastructures.

4. The Financial Instrument for Fisheries (FIFG) may support projects which modernize the structure of the fisheries sector, and related industries, and encourage diversification of the workforce and fisheries industry into other sectors. It also aims to promote sustainability within the fishing industry by encouraging a balance between fisheries resources and their exploitation.

Summary

The single European market is equivalent in size to that of the USA and the economic benefits of membership should be reflected in greater derived demand for commercial property. UK property investment companies have not yet made significant investments in continental Europe for a number of reasons, one of which is the differences that exist in treatment of property in other countries.

The UK seems likely to retain its own currency outside the eurozone for some time to come. This will not preclude UK property developers, property companies and investors from trading freely in the eurozone because all EU members are within the SEM to which the UK is committed. But, in addition to its peripheral cross-Channel location, the UK would be exposed to possible fluctuations in the pound sterling: euro exchange rate, the cost of exchanging currencies and probably a higher rate of interest when borrowing.

Regional policy in the UK is coordinated by the regional development agencies, and there are European funds available to support economic development in poorer outlying areas of Europe.

Chapter 19: review questions

---

1. Why might the single European market have benefits for the property sector?
2. Are there disadvantages for UK real estate firms in not being part of the eurozone?
3. Are there advantages for UK real estate firms in not being part of the eurozone?
4. Why does the EU have a regional support policy?

20

The Impact of Government Policy on Real Estate

After studying this chapter you will be able to:

- Explain why changes in the level of economic activity occur and how they affect property markets;
- Explain how property markets affect the macroeconomy;
- Describe the effects of monetary policy on the property sector;
- Describe the effects of fiscal policy on the property sector;
- Analyse aspects of the UK's monetary policy response to the credit crunch recession.

Cyclical instability

The market economy looked at as a whole, is basically unstable, with output fluctuating cyclically over time at fairly regular 7–10 year intervals. The period between 1996 and 2007 in the UK was a longer than normal time without a downturn, but was followed by a severe recession. One major cause of instability is that supply takes time to respond fully to a change in demand so that expectations upon which production decisions were originally based may not be fulfilled. This can occur with both commercial property development and housebuilding. Consequently, there tends to be a property cycle which can vary with the length of the production time lag, being shorter for industrial property than for offices owing to the considerable time taken to plan, construct and dispose of office property (see Chapter 6).

The government's main concern is to dampen down short-term fluctuations in the economy generally in order to maintain the full employment of resources (with labour, as the yardstick, having no more than 4 to 5 per cent unemployment). Success in reducing short-term fluctuations would go a long way towards achieving a steady yearly growth rate of 2 to 3 per cent in the national product of the UK.

An expansion of aggregate demand can be brought about by an increase in aggregate injections – consumption spending, investment, government spending and exports – not matched by an increase in total withdrawals by saving, taxation and spending on imports. Expansion of aggregate demand may originate on the demand side, for example, by an autonomous increase in consumption spending or, on the supply side, for example, by firms granting demands for wage increases which are not matched by an increase in productivity.

In addition, it has to be recognized that today much of the UK production takes place in the context of a global economy. Consequently, recession can be triggered off by events outside the direct control of the government, such as a rise in the world price of oil (1974) or speculation against sterling holding its value against other currencies (1992) or the collapse of the US subprime mortgage market (2007).

While property may not initiate an expansion of aggregate demand, it plays an important role in its subsequent development. In the economy as a whole, any increase in the injections into the economy, such as increased property expenditure, has a multiplier effect which adds still further to the level of aggregate demand. Furthermore, with investment in particular, the upturn gathers momentum through a possible accelerator effect, thereby reinforcing the upswing, but eventually petering out and reversing into a downturn.

The same process is clearly at work in both commercial development and housebuilding. Land use and property market decisions are made on the basis of profitability, used in its wider sense to include maximizing utility. Cyclical movements in the economy therefore give rise to cycles in the real property and construction industries. With commercial property, a buoyant economy will evoke a parallel response from property developers and investors, with the length of the property cycle generated being shorter for industrial buildings, which can be built fairly quickly but depreciate quickly in a depression, and longer for offices which take more time to plan and construct. Thus the macroeconomic background affects not only short-term decisions as to how land resources shall be allocated, but also the rate of development over time. A fast-growing economy will require new and better offices, factories and warehouses. And because growth in the economy is reflected in increased spending power, there is an increase in the demand for new shopping facilities and better housing.

Housing similarly contributes to the cumulative increase in aggregate demand. Changes in demand and supply result in changes in relative prices – the micro effect. But the housing industry is so important that any surge in demand is transmitted to the whole economy – the macro effect. This comes about through dynamic changes in demand and the interaction of the multiplier and the accelerator which raises income in the economy as a whole, with

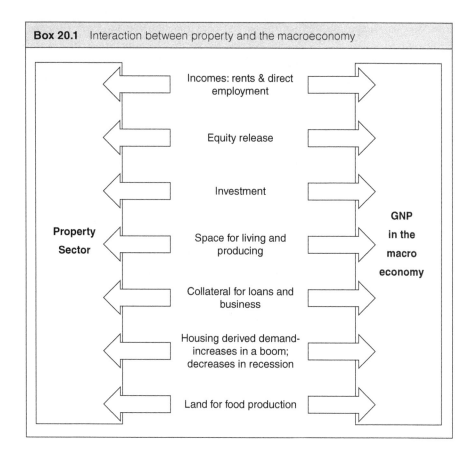

Box 20.1   Interaction between property and the macroeconomy

Property Sector

- Incomes: rents & direct employment
- Equity release
- Investment
- Space for living and producing
- Collateral for loans and business
- Housing derived demand- increases in a boom; decreases in recession
- Land for food production

GNP in the macro economy

a possible further feedback on the demand for housing. We shall examine in particular this dynamic housing demand.

Additional demand for housing may be engendered (as in 1988) by observed rises in house prices (which doubled between 1984 and 1988). Here the house is being bought, not solely as a necessary consumer durable affording shelter and so on, but also as an investment asset which is expected to continue rising in price. More than that, when the price of a house rises, a 95 per cent mortgage represents a high gearing ratio showing an excellent rate of return on the original deposit – the equity stake – especially as an owner-occupied house is exempt from capital gains tax in the UK.

Since home ownership represents over one-half of personal wealth, rising house prices can have a further impact on consumption spending generally. First, because owner-occupiers feel richer, this can induce them to spend on cars and consumer durables – the 'wealth' effect. Second, existing mortgage-holders are tempted to upgrade their housing by moving to larger and newer houses, often requiring new carpets, furniture and garden equipment. Third, and more serious, this additional spending is financed by a personal loan or a second mortgage granted on the strength of the house-price rise. Housing equity withdrawal (HEW) is new borrowing secured on dwellings that is not invested in the housing market (that is, not used for house purchase or home improvements). It has been estimated that this 'equity-extraction' amounted to £61 billion in 1988 at the peak of a housing boom. At the peak of the next boom in 2006 it was almost £50 billion and the impact of falling house prices and the recession can be seen in the figures for 2007: £41.46 billion, 2008 : minus £9.1 billion, and 2009: minus £22.28 billion (Bank of England, 2010). A negative figure for HEW means that households in the UK repaid debt, reducing their mortgage liabilities.

Therefore, house-price inflation has a direct and important effect on the general rate of inflation. Higher house prices encourage the construction of houses. Surplus capacity is soon absorbed, and land prices rise. Eventually bottlenecks appear in labour, materials and components; delivery times lengthen and their prices rise. Thus cost-push inflation may reinforce demand-pull. In addition, the loan-generated demand for houses, by increasing money GNP, results in increased spending overall. Prices in general rise: the initial house-price inflation has spilled out into the wider economy.

Since 1960, the root cause of most recessions has been the UK's inability to control the rate of inflation (the exception is the 2007–9 recession when inflation was relatively low). This has meant that from time to time the government has had to cut back on total spending – in the early years, to protect the balance of payments, later, to maintain the sterling exchange rate. Both monetary policy (raising the rate of interest and credit control) and fiscal policy (adjusting the balance between spending and revenue) were used. This 'stop-go' policy resulted in a period of rising unemployment followed, after easing the restrictions, by a gradual expansion of output and employment.

Monetary policy

Since 1997, the Bank of England's Monetary Policy Committee has undertaken the task of holding inflation in check. This relies on a single weapon – varying the short-term rate of interest, the logic of which is that a change in the short-term rate of interest will affect aggregate demand in a number of ways.

First, a change in the cost of borrowing affects spending decisions in that it alters the relative attraction of spending today as opposed to spending later. Therefore, a rise in interest rates will make saving more attractive, and borrowing less so, and will, as a result, tend to reduce present spending on both consumption and investment.

Second, a change in short-term interest rates alters the cash flow of both creditors and borrowers, having a floating rate for both assets or liabilities. Households receive a floating interest rate on deposits in banks and building societies, while floating rate debtors include households with mortgages and companies running an overdraft. Fluctuations in net cash flow may influence spending.

Third, a change in interest rates affects the capitalized value of certain assets, notably property, houses and stocks and shares. This 'wealth effect' may influence an owner's willingness to spend.

Fourth, pressure on prices may come about through the influence of a change in the rate of interest on exchange rates. For example, a rise in UK domestic interest rates relative to those overseas tends to result in a net inflow of capital and thus an appreciation of the sterling exchange rate. This will lower the prices of imports, and UK products have to compete by reducing their prices.

Since June 1997, there has been a set of clear rules for keeping inflation in check: (i) the Chancellor of the Exchequer sets a target rate of inflation as measured by an increase in the Retail Price Index excluding mortgage payments (RPIX); (ii) the Bank of England, through its Monetary Policy Committee (MPC) of nine members is given sole operational responsibility for delivering this target by varying base rate.

The MPC assembles on the Wednesday following the first Monday in each month to consider the latest data covering a wide range of topics which could bear on the future rate of inflation. These include: recent changes in the money supply, the PSNCR, average earnings, wage settlements, house and asset prices, import and export prices and flows, the sterling exchange rate, investment and consumer spending. On the next day (Thursday), following further discussion, the members of the committee decide, on a simple majority basis, whether base rate should be changed, and, if so, by how much. The Chancellor restates the inflation target each year. It remained at 2.5 per cent, based on the RPIX measure of inflation, from 1997 until December 2003, when it was changed to 2.0 per cent, based on the new Harmonized Consumer Price Index (CPI) measure of inflation.

In recent years, there have been complaints about the willingness of lenders and banks to respond to cuts in the Bank's base rates, resulting in the benefits of reductions not being passed on to borrowers. However, in November 2008 when the global economic crisis led to an unprecedented 1.5 percentage points cut in the base rate, banks such as HBOS, Lloyd's TSB and Abbey all passed on the full 1.5 per cent cut to borrowers with standard variable rate (SVR) mortgages. But banks were said to have warned the Chancellor that following this unexpectedly high reduction, any further cuts would not be passed on in full. In early 2009 the MPC cut base rate to 0.5 per cent, the lowest rate ever in response to the depth and severity of the recession which actually threatened to lead to falling prices. Base rate stayed at this historically low rate for more than a year but banks did not reduce their lending rates accordingly because they felt the need to restore their balance sheets following the financial crisis.

The use of the short-term rate of interest as the sole weapon for control-ling inflation bears heavily on developers and speculative housebuilders, for both are particularly dependent on credit to pay for inputs during the construc-tion period. A rise in short-term rates, by putting up the cost of advances, is felt immediately as profit margins are squeezed; but most buildings under construction will still be completed. Building society and bank lending are also affected. Monthly mortgage repayments eventually rise and the resulting increase in any repayment–income ratio condition will make mortgages more difficult to obtain. Thus housing activity falls (see Chapter 5).

If the rise eventually extends to the long end of the market, the effects are more fundamental for both new construction and the investment market. Since expected yields on real property stretch far into the future, discounting at a higher rate leads to a greater proportionate reduction in their present values than for other types of investment project where costs have to be recouped within about 5 years. This would tend to hold back private-sector development, especially by property development companies, thus affecting the construction industry directly.

In the investment market, the higher yield on government bonds makes them more attractive compared with assets such as mortgages and real property. Particularly for loans against property, therefore, the lending institutions such as insurance companies and pension funds will require a higher return. But with a steady inflow of funds, they have to take a long-term view of infla-tion and the profitability of property interests. Therefore, they may continue to invest in freeholds, either by financing new development or by purchasing existing buildings. Eventually, however, when higher relative returns can be obtained elsewhere, they will push up yields on all real property interests. Such lowering of capital values will discourage new construction by developers.

Nor is the public sector immune from higher interest rates. Local authorities can only afford to raise funds on the same scale by increasing local taxation to cover the higher cost. Reluctance to do this because of its political unpopu-larity means that, instead, they curtail their housing and other construction programmes. Above all, the central government may be forced to contract its spending (see next section).

Fiscal policy

The use of monetary policy to maintain a specified 2 per cent rate of inflation means that the Chancellor of the Exchequer's fiscal policy must be so struc-tured as to be in harmony with the MPC's objective. If, for instance, the MPC considered that government spending would exceed revenue to such an extent that the PSNCR would breach the 2 per cent inflation target, it would simply raise base rate until the inflationary pressure no longer existed.

Box 20.2   Property in a low inflation economy

The success of the MPC in restraining the annual rise in the CPI to 2.0 per cent (except during the crisis of 2007–10, when it diverged slightly) has led to growing confidence that the UK now has inflation under control. This has been reflected in a corresponding fall in the rate of wage increases. During the 1970s and 1980s the property market was to a large extent 'inflation driven'. We, therefore, now have to ask: how is this new situation of low inflation likely to affect the property market? Although the fundamentals of decision making are virtually the same for both the commercial and residential markets, there are differences which call for separate consideration.

Commercial. The yield on a property over the year combines two elements, rent and capital appreciation. In the past both have risen with inflation. Rents rise as increases in money income push up prices; capital appreciation occurs through the capitalization of this higher rent, but also because investors regard property as an excellent hedge against inflation and are prepared to accept a lower rate of return than that obtainable on competing safe assets, in particular, bonds. Now, with yield mostly stripped of the inflation element, the *investor* in real property has to buy mainly on the basis of the margin of rent over cost, with possible capital appreciation having much less influence. Moreover, these sums must be done with extra care, for no longer will there be inflation to cover up a bad deal and there is now a greater incentive to move into gilt-edged stock as this will be more likely to hold its value, or into shares which offer greater liquidity and depending on the profitability of the company, possible capital appreciation.

To achieve this with property, there has been an extension of securitization through bonds, and the removal of legal obstacles to the development of the American method of investing in property through Real Estate Investment Trusts (REITS). This more cautious approach also applies to *lenders* who need to be assured as to the quality of the borrower's covenant and his management skills in recognizing development or refurbishment potential.

The *occupier* of property has also to adapt to the new situation. When, as a result of inflation, rents were continually rising, occupiers were willing to accept a 25-year lease, with 5-year upward-only rent reviews and privity of contract. Indeed between rent reviews, the occupier earned an 'economic rent', and found little difficulty in assigning, possibly at a premium, should he wish to move. Now occupiers need to be more cautious, requiring shorter leases, possibly with a break clause, and to be reluctant to agree to privity of contract.

Residential. Apart from the downturns of the early 1990s and 2007–9, house prices have risen continuously in the UK and owner-occupation has proved to be an excellent inflation hedge. This demand included an 'investment' element in addition to the occupational benefit. At times this expectation of higher prices was magnified by a 'feel good' factor – the 'wealth effect' – especially when mortgages were easily available from building societies and banks. This encouraged people to up-grade their present property by withdrawing some of the equity content of their houses or by spending possible windfalls, for example, through building society conversions or inheritance.

In general, with low inflation people are more likely to rent property rather than buy, especially young people who require mobility. Renting could also be preferred by multi-national companies in providing residential accommodation for their major travelling managers, especially as maintenance, cleaning and other services can be included in the rent.

Within its broad spending and revenue aggregates, there are alternative ways and means in which the Chancellor can increase spending in chosen directions, for example, on health, education and welfare, and still leave a PSNCR which the MPC would consider as being non-inflationary. Balancing adjustments can be made on either the spending or revenue sides, or both. The following are examples of a few recent adjustments which would affect property or the construction industry directly or indirectly.

On the spending side, the opportunities to make cuts are limited since much spending is either contractual or an essential part of the government's commitments in its election manifesto. Only rarely, as with the ending of the Cold War, can there be a substantial cut in regular expenditure; usually the reverse is the case, as with the 1999 Kosovo crisis and the 2003 Gulf crisis and the military commitments to Iraq and Afghanistan. Nonetheless, improved efficiency may reduce expenditure. As a result, a reorganization of the Valuation Office Agency produced a saving in district offices and personnel which kept it on target for a 30 per cent improvement in efficiency between 1995 and 2000.

Opportunities to increase revenue without raising taxation are more available, but mostly only on a one-off or short-term basis. First, in the past the proceeds of the privatization issues of the nationalized industries have been a major means of reducing the PSNCR, but the scope for this is now limited to minor sales, possibly the Post Office, London Underground and British Nuclear Fuels.

Second, to help fund a hospital and school building programme, improve public transport and regenerate depressed areas at an overall cost of £11 billion, the government, through its Property Advisors to the Civil Estate (PACE), has disposed of surplus accommodation and land assets (see Chapter 21). In this way the government is relieved of the necessity to push up long-term interest rates by selling gilt-edged bonds.

Third, following the end of the privatization programme, the government has embarked on a new approach under the banner of the Private Finance Initiative (PFI). In fact this is in essence an extension of the direct selling of Council and New Town dwellings to tenants. This allows Councils to liquidate their housing assets by introducing private capital in the form of the mortgages provided by building societies and banks. Today the PFI is closely connected with the government's property requirements. Instead of itself engaging in capital expenditure on redevelopment or refurbishment of the properties it owns, the necessary capital is brought in by a consortium of property companies, probably backed by institutional funds. This sees the scheme through under contract, and then assumes the role of landlord with a lease of up to 125 years and a rent on agreed terms. What this means is that the government is spending only on the services which the building provides, foremost of which is working space. But other services can be added, such as maintenance, cleaning, information technology connections, and so on (see Chapter 21).

The role of the government in economic growth and distribution of income

So far, government macro policy has been examined in the context of the prevention of short-term fluctuations in economic activity, often referred to as the trade cycle or business cycle. In this context, the main objective is to avoid the unemployment which results from recessions while taking care not to allow an expansion of aggregate demand to bring about inflation. Given this, the UK can reasonably expect Gross Domestic Product (GDP) to grow cumulatively each year by two or three per cent. For the UK, this secular growth has, over the last 50 years, resulted in a threefold increase in real national income – the outcome of investment in capital equipment and technological development, itself the product of research and innovation.

In advanced, market-led economies, such as that of the UK, adequate investment for secular growth can be left to the enterprise of firms responding to market indicators. It is such firms which, over the last 50 years have, by research and application, provided people with cars, air transport, central heating, dishwashers, theme parks, supermarkets and pension funds. With some products, such as agricultural research and farming techniques, television and video recorders, computers, word processors and mobile phones, the rate of growth has been phenomenal. Even defence, a major function of government, incorporates the innovations of specialist electronic firms.

It is submitted, therefore, that government growth policy can be confined to eliminating the short-term hiccups which punctuate the upward secular trend. The most serious consequence of such hiccups is unemployment. Even more important than the loss of income through redundancy is the human unhappiness, and even misery, which may follow the loss of a job – especially the feeling of indefinite rejection through old skills no longer being required. It follows, therefore, that the two immediate objectives of government policy must be the provision of income support and training for new skills.

Policy must also respond to the consequences of secular growth, some of which are not transparent in the bare statistics of GDP, the measure usually chosen to indicate growth over time. First GDP may not provide a true measure of, or even reflect, welfare as distinct from wealth. Secular growth often takes the form of increased leisure which is not included in GDP figures. In any case, it is unsafe to assume that everybody views work as onerous. Thus an across-the-board regulation restricting the working week to 48 hours may actually reduce welfare for those workers who prefer work to leisure. In general, however, leisure-related industries, such as tourism, rambling and hotels, are likely over time to take an increasing proportion of income, and the property and construction industries will respond accordingly.

Second, GDP figures presenting growth of income do not reveal how this increase has been distributed. For instance, retired people relying on state pension for a large part of their income fail to obtain their full share of an increase in growth-related income. Recognizing this, the pressure group 'Age Concern' lobbies for the annual uplift in the state retirement pension to be based on the average earnings index instead of the RPIX, for the former reflects the trend in rising productivity as well as that of price-inflation.

Third, as we have seen in previous chapters, there are costs of economic growth – usually 'bad' or negative externalities – which may not be allowed for in GDP calculations. Examples are: the loss of 'cherished' land for the construction of new roads; noise near busy aircraft terminals; CO_2 emission from road transport. On occasions, action to counteract the 'bads' even increases the GDP figure – for example, the cost of noise abatement and of disposal of the waste of the 'throw away' society. These are mostly environmental negative externalities arising through increasing demands on diminishing resources. The elimination or mitigation of such 'bads' must largely be the responsibility of government.

Most people feel that poverty in the midst of plenty is unacceptable and that all should share in wealth increases. Private giving with this in mind is made to such voluntary bodies as the Salvation Army and the Child Poverty Action Group, and the donors themselves enjoy satisfaction from their generosity. But only the government can effect the scale of redistribution required. This it may do indirectly in pursuing other objectives. Therefore, a 'right to roam' policy benefits in particular those who are fit enough to ramble and have the leisure time to do so.

But most redistribution occurs directly by government expenditure and taxation. Redistribution is a specific objective in money and other benefits which are directed towards certain vulnerable groups, such as the unemployed and lowly paid, the sick and aged. But subsidies, for example to farmers, which have other objectives, for example, the preservation of ancient woodland, also effect income redistribution.

How government expenditure and taxation can achieve a wide range of objectives is analysed in Chapter 22, with the emphasis in particular being directed to their impact on the property market.

The monetary policy response to the credit crunch recession in the UK

The UK, and London in particular, has been hit hard by the impact of the credit crunch. Because there is a greater reliance on the financial sector as a proportion of the economy (both London and the UK as a whole) the impact has been greater than in other countries and cities. As well as the impact on the financial sector, related service industries have also suffered. Law firms, insurance companies, luxury goods sellers, restaurants and airlines have all been affected. Commercial property demand has fallen in line with the drop in business.

The credit crunch has had a negative effect on highly leveraged real estate companies and the banks that finance them, resulting in frozen or renegotiated loan commitments and some forced sales. Lenders have tended to hold onto capital because rising bankruptcies, mortgage defaults and uncertainty make them wary of lending. This has led to higher borrowing rates and a tendency to lend only to the safest borrowers on restrictive terms.

Builders are more cautious and tend to build less since there is less money available. There is an excess supply of commercial and residential space and buyers cannot take advantage because credit is hard to obtain. Unemployment in the UK has increased from 5 per cent to almost 8 per cent and repossessions of homes have increased (although by less than might have been expected because of the historically low level of interest rates).

In 2009, mortgage approvals fell to 1.3 million compared with 3.4 million annually from 2005 to 2007. The Council of Mortgage Lenders warned that removing government support from the financial institutions would choke off lending and raise mortgage costs. That support, however, is to be removed after January 2011 when the institutions are to start repaying £319 billion borrowed from the government in 2007 and 2008. This 'funding gap' is the difference between the amount the banks hold in retail deposits and the sum they have lent. It used to be financed in the wholesale markets (inter-bank lending) but they froze in August 2007 and had to be replaced by government funding (see Chapter 6). The full £319 billion must be repaid by April 2014. In order to pay the money back, the banks and building societies may reduce mortgage availability and make mortgages more expensive.

The government's response to the worst recession since the 1930s has been to borrow and spend to try to prop up the wider economy. Monetary policy has played a vital role in this in two ways. First, the Bank of England reduced its base lending rate from 5 per cent in October 2008 to 0.5 per cent by March 2009 (the lowest rate in its more than 300-year history). This has had limited impact because of the cautious lending policies of the financial institutions and their reluctance to reduce rates to borrowers as discussed earlier.

Second, the Bank of England embarked upon a £200 billion programme of Quantitative Easing of the money supply in March 2009 (this equates to almost £8,000 for every household in the UK). This involves the Bank of England using its computers to create new money which is then injected into the economy in ways designed to get money flowing without causing inflation. They do this by buying assets, usually second-hand gilts from insurers, banks and pension funds. They in turn buy other assets such as corporate bonds making it easier and cheaper for companies to borrow on bond markets and to raise money from rights issues of shares. The LIBOR rate (at which banks lend to each other) has fallen to pre-crunch levels.

The danger of Quantitative Easing is that it could stoke inflation, thereby necessitating interest rate rises to control it. A little inflation could actually

---

Box 20.3   Examples of the effects of government policy on property

The mid 1970s property downturn:

In November 1972, the UK government froze commercial rents as part of an anti-inflation strategy and in 1973 interest rates were raised. Buildings under construction fell in value and the freeze on rents undermined investors' confidence. Many major developers and property companies failed and since property had become a vital part of the UK financial structure, other sectors were badly affected.

The 1989–91 property collapse:

The property boom of the late 1980s was brought to an end by:

- a rise in interest rates (15 per cent by October 1989) to combat inflation. This reduced investment and consumer demand (mortgage rates rose to 15.4 per cent);
- VAT levied on rents for new buildings;
- Uniform Business Rate (UBR) was introduced in 1990 reducing profits (especially retail).

At the same time a large supply of new floor space came onto the market (30 per cent of City/Dockland space was vacant by end 1991).

The 1996–2007 housing market recovery:

House prices rose by an average of 187 per cent across the UK (London 240 per cent) between 1996 and 2007. The average UK house price rose from £62,453 to £194,500, an average of 10.6 per cent per year. Over the same period stock prices rose by 4.6 per cent per year; nominal earnings by 4.2 per cent per year; and retail prices by 2.6 per cent per year. The housing market recovery during this period was due to:

- low interest rates relative to long term averages;
- high employment levels (employment increased by 770,000) 2004–7;
- demographic factors – population increase from immigration, more one person households and so on.

---

be helpful because it reduces the cost of debts – UK consumer debt is more than £1.4 trillion and the National Debt is at least £825 billion. Rising prices effectively make debts smaller. Inflation at rates higher than 3–4 per cent per annum, however, would be disastrous for the long-term future of the economy and possibly for the international credit rating of the UK because it would be seen as a way of avoiding the costs of repaying the debts incurred during the recession. Estimates of total taxpayer liability including lending and insurance schemes for the banks are in the region of £1.5 trillion although the government hopes to get a considerable part of this back when the troubled banks recover.

The UK government has also tried to spend its way out of recession with other temporary measures:

- a stamp duty cut for cheaper properties to help first time buyers and try to stimulate the housing market;
- a VAT reduction from 17.5 per cent to 15 per cent for 1 year to try to encourage spending;
- a £2,000 subsidy to encourage car buying and the scrapping of cars older than 10 years.

The success of these policies remains to be seen. They have certainly been ambitious and unprecedented and the UK acted boldly after initially dithering to the extent that the Bank of England allowed a 'run' on a bank (Northern Rock) to take place for the first time in over 150 years. Other countries, notably the USA, have followed Britain's lead. Signs of emergence from recession began to appear in 2010 and the Organization for Economic Cooperation and Development (OECD) predicted in April 2010 that the UK economy would outpace most G7 rivals including Germany and Japan in 2010. The debt consequences for the government and taxpayers could be severe, however, and they may lead to big public spending cuts and tax increases which will impact on all sectors, not least real estate.

Summary

The level of economic activity in the economy as a whole varies cyclically with a trade or business cycle of 7–10 years. Cyclical movements in the economy cause cycles in property and construction, which are exacerbated by the length of time it takes for property supply to respond fully to demand. Property also influences the macroeconomy. Expenditure on property is part of aggregate demand, equity release can stimulate demand and major construction projects can influence the whole economy through the multiplier process.

Governments use monetary and fiscal policy to control the overall economy and each has effects on the property sector. Monetary policy alters interest rates which affect developers and mortgage payers, while government spending and taxation impact on many parts of the property sector.

Inflation influenced the behaviour of economic agents in real estate during the 1970s and 1980s but the success of the Bank of England in keeping inflation low since 1997 will change behaviour in property markets, affecting lease terms and the relative attractions of renting and buying residential property.

The credit crunch recession of 2007–9 has had a profound impact on real estate markets worldwide and a disproportionate effect in the UK because of its reliance on the financial sector of the City of London. The UK government's response to the recession has been to borrow and spend to try to prevent it becoming a depression. This has widespread taxation, public spending and possibly inflationary consequences that will impact on property.

Chapter 20: review questions

1. How does property contribute to aggregate demand in the economy?
2. What is meant by Housing Equity Withdrawal?
3. Explain how monetary policy change can affect property markets.
4. Explain how fiscal policy change can affect property markets.
5. How did the UK government respond to the credit crunch recession of 2007–9?

21

Government Ownership of Real Estate

After studying this chapter you will be able to:

- Explain why there is government intervention in property markets;
- Describe the different public-sector organizations which have an impact on property;
- Analyse the different ways in which public expenditure can be financed;
- Show how Private Finance Initiatives work;
- Discuss the extent of UK government ownership of real estate.

The provision of goods and services by the public sector

The government can intervene to correct the market's allocation of resources by administrative action, for example, through planning regulation (see Chapter 12), and by fiscal measures, for example, through subsidies and taxes. But 'market failure', as explained in Chapter 2, includes a situation where goods and services, such as defence, would not be provided through the price system because 'free riders' cannot be excluded. Provision of such goods, therefore has to be the responsibility of the government. As shown below, this government provision is often extended in practice to somewhat similar goods.

Economic theory can assist in reaching decisions on: (a) what goods and services should be provided by the government; (b) the extent of such provision in the context of maximizing welfare and, (c) the most appropriate means of financing this provision. We can explain the reasons why the government directly provides goods and services by classifying them as follows:

- *Community goods:* such as defence, police, street lighting, pavements and flood control, cannot be supplied through the price system because of *indivisibility* (there must be a complete supply or none at all) and *non-excludability* ('free riders' cannot be excluded). Thus individuals cannot be charged a price on the basis of use.

- *Collective goods:* which satisfy people's collective needs (for example, parks, motorways, bridges, water supply, refuse collection and drainage), entail such high fixed-capital investment that production takes place under conditions of decreasing cost. Some monopoly element is therefore inevitable, but 'free riders' can be excluded by charging entrance fees, tolls and so on. Given these two conditions, a public body may be able to achieve a more optimal output than a private monopolist.
- *Merit goods:* such as education, health care and housing, are provided by the state because it is felt that they would be inadequately consumed (either, through lack of income or simply spending preferences) if left entirely to market forces. Undesirable external costs, such as an untrained or physically poor labour force, could result. In subsidizing the consumption of such goods, the government redistributes income and so makes a subjective judgement.

The provision of goods and services through the public sector may be undertaken by a government department, state-owned industries, quasi-governmental bodies (variously termed agencies, authorities, boards, commissions, councils or committees) or local authorities. The actual form adopted depends upon both constitutional and economic considerations.

Constitutionally, the *government department* form of organization achieves a high degree of public accountability because the minister in charge is directly responsible to Parliament for all aspects of the department's work. Moreover, the department's finances come under the close scrutiny of the Treasury. Generally speaking, the central government provides those goods and services which are of national importance (such as defence, trunk roads, health care) where most of the cost has to be covered by taxation and where local differences in the standard of provision would be unacceptable. Moreover, the expenditure involved enables the government to consider its effects on stabilizing the economy and, through taxation, on the distribution of income, two objectives which by and large should be left to the central government.

Because the strict accountability of the government department form of organization may conflict with economic efficiency, the *state-owned industries*, for example, the Post Office and Civil Aviation Authority are subjected to less direct accountability. With these the minister concerned exercises control over their broad policies, but not their day-to-day operations. They are fairly free to choose their own pricing policies but have to submit an annual report to Parliament. Thus some accountability is sacrificed in the interests of economic efficiency.

Quasi-governmental bodies have usually been formed to operate particular services where only minimum accountability is required, for example, the National Parks Commission, and the Countryside Agency. In practice the degree of accountability varies, therefore, in their composition, certain official representatives may have to be included; or there may be the simple requirement that an annual report be laid before Parliament. These bodies are usually set up to administer services which have social overtones and where spillover effects are extensive or economies of scale can be secured. A good example is the Environment Agency which administers the whole complex of river basins for water supply, sewerage disposal, angling and so on.

However, the *urban* public sector is mainly concerned with the operations of *local authorities* to whom Parliament delegates functions, chiefly those where economies of scale and spillover effects are relatively weak. Services are divided between the counties and districts on the basis of the optimum scale of operation, the county being responsible for education, police, the fire services, and so on, and the district for personal and environmental services where economies of scale are of less importance. The new unitary authorities cover all functions. Delegating such services to local authorities has certain advantages:

1. those who run local services are local people responsible to local needs and attitudes;
2. it allows close contact between the governed and those who govern;
3. it provides for division of power between Whitehall and town hall, reminding the central government that its decisions must respect local feelings and loyalties;
4. local authorities reduce the burden of central government administration.

If these advantages are to be secured, however, there must be real local *government*, not simply local administration on lines largely dictated by Westminster. This has important implications as regards the way that local authorities raise revenue to finance their activities (see Chapter 22).

Public-sector expenditure

Two problems can be distinguished with regard to public expenditure: (i) its overall size relative to revenue; and (ii) its distribution between individual items. As successive governments have discovered, it is very difficult to reduce expenditure, for the more the government provides by way of welfare services and economic assistance, the greater are the demands of pressure groups for such aid, for example, the Child Poverty Action Group advocating increased child benefits, the National Farmers' Union wanting higher guaranteed prices, and Age Concern demanding higher retirement pensions.

In 2010, total government spending in the UK was projected to be £704 billion, about 49 per cent of GDP. This proportion is very high because of the recession (which reduces government revenues and increases spending) and plans were announced in the budget to gradually bring down this level of government spending and reduce government borrowing. Total UK government borrowing was expected to be £167 billion in 2010, taking the net debt of the country to about 54 per cent of GDP.

Public expenditure has obvious allocative effects, for example, through direct subsidies. But it also influences the *distribution of income*, either indirectly through the services chosen for support or directly through the incidence of subsidies granted: therefore relative expenditure on the different items depends largely on political decisions.

As regards the urban economy, it is the spending by local authorities with which we are primarily concerned. In spite of recent government efforts to reduce local authority spending, for Great Britain, it is expected to increase from £53 billion in 2001, to £183 billion in 2010, largely the result of an extension of services (public services generally tend to have a high income-elasticity of demand), a higher proportion of aged people in the community and the impact of wage-inflation on what are mainly labour-intensive services.

Increases in local government expenditure affect the government's function of stabilizing the economy, since it entails increased borrowing from the central government and more dependence on government grants which now cover 85 per cent of total local authority spending. Both add to the PSNCR (public-sector net cash requirement): so when the government has to take restrictive measures to stabilize the economy, local authorities, too, feel the squeeze.

Government-provided goods and services can be financed by: (a) borrowing, (b) user-charges and (c) taxation. These will be considered in this chapter, while Chapter 22 analyses taxation of real estate more specifically.

Borrowing to finance public expenditure

In practice, the central government's current expenditure is so vast that what would normally be regarded as capital items, for example, the cost of new warships, are covered by the yearly estimates of expenditure as approved by the House of Commons. The same applies to other one-off payments, for example, a grant towards the regeneration of London's dockland or a subsidy to keep British Nuclear Fuels in production despite heavy losses.

However, schemes for which a large amount of up-front capital is required and which can be repaid from future earnings, for example, Network Rail, can be financed by government borrowing. This is particularly true of extensive land development schemes where the government has to take account of a complexity of externalities. An example of such government borrowing is the finance provided through the New Towns Commission to acquire land to build a new town. Largely through the enhanced value of the land when developed, the loan can be repaid by the sale of houses, offices and industrial premises. Nonetheless, the amount which the government can borrow is subject to the demands of the current monetary situation, as revealed by the size of the Public Sector Net Cash Requirement (PSNCR) or Public Sector Net Borrowing (PSNB).

Local authorities borrow both short-term and long-term, the former mainly to cover shortfalls between revenue and current expenditure, the latter to meet the cost of capital projects, such as school and housing construction, and even extensive urban and city centre redevelopment. However, because the central government must retain overall control of public-sector spending, the amount which local authorities can borrow is subject to government approval, and usually in accordance with a projected programme for long-term capital expenditure. Short-term funds are obtained through the money markets, but long-term projects are financed mainly through the Public Works Loans Board, supplemented by issues on the open market.

In the UK, the public sector recorded deficits between 1991–92 and 1997–98 before moving into surplus in 1998–99 and deficits have been recorded since 2002–03. In 2009–10, excluding the cost of interventions to support the financial sector, PSNB – the gap between the exchequer's tax take and its spending – stood at £163.4 billion for the financial year.

The cumulative total of government borrowing over time is public-sector net debt, often called The National Debt. Public-sector net debt, expressed as a percentage of gross domestic product (GDP), was 62.0 per cent at the end of March 2010 compared with 52.9 per cent at end of March 2009 (it was only 36.6 per cent of GDP in 2005). Net debt was £890.0 billion at the end of March compared with £742.3 billion a year earlier.

Public-sector net debt (excluding financial interventions to prop up the failing financial institutions) was £771.6 billion (equivalent to 53.8 per cent of GDP) at the end of March 2010. This compares to £617.0 billion (44.0 per cent of GDP) as at the end of March 2009. At the end of April 2010, net debt was £893.4 billion, equivalent to 62.1 per cent of UK gross domestic product (statistics.gov.uk, 2010). The massive increase is unprecedented historically in peace time and is due to the impact of the recession on the public finances.

User-charges to finance public expenditure

Where they can be levied, charges promote economy in use and achieve equity in that the beneficiary pays. The recent shift towards them aims to avoid increasing taxation to pay for services. Water, currently in short supply, is an example. Where a household pays for it through a charge based solely on rateable value, the marginal cost of water consumed is zero. In contrast, metered water charges means that payment is related to each litre consumed. One other advantage of charges is that they can throw up a valuable guideline for invest-ment. For example, metered water charges reveal demand at the current price, and from this some estimate can be made of future demand.

With community goods, where 'free riders' cannot be excluded, no price can be charged, since nobody will pay when private rights to them cannot be granted and, in this case, the cost has to be covered entirely from taxation. But with other goods, there is a choice between charges, taxation or a combination of both. Here the decision is governed by economic, technical and political considerations.

In the case of collective goods, economic theory can justify public ownership on the grounds of efficiency in the allocation of resources. In addition, when deciding how they shall be financed, the concept of a Pareto improvement is relevant where marginal cost is zero. We can illustrate this with reference to a public garden in the centre of a town. To simplify, let us assume that: (i) people derive pleasure from the flower gardens and would be willing to pay for this benefit; (ii) the garden can be fenced round so that, by excluding 'free riders', a price can be charged; and (iii) the only cost is the initial price, which includes a capitalized sum for future maintenance, giving marginal cost of zero up to the capacity of the gardens to take visitors. The situation is depicted in Figure 21.1, where the *ATC* curve is a rectangular hyperbola and the capacity of the gardens is *OZ* after which more visitors involve serious overcrowding.

If the gardens were provided privately by a monopolist, he would charge *OP*, limiting visitors to *OM*, where marginal cost (OZ), equals marginal revenue, and where total revenue is at a maximum because elasticity of demand equals unity. Suppose now that the gardens were taken over by the local authority By lowering the price to *OP'*, a larger number of people *OM'* could enjoy the

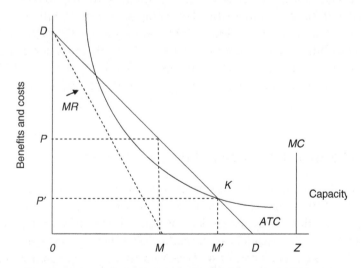

Figure 21.1   Public provision of collective and public goods

gardens at no extra cost, and total costs would be covered by a user-charge of OP' where there are OM' visitors.

Nevertheless it is still possible to effect a Pareto improvement. Where, as in our model, marginal cost is zero (for example, with parks, bridges, motorways and art galleries), enjoyment by an extra person imposes no sacrifice on others. Such 'non-rivalry' means that maximum benefits can be obtained only if such goods are provided by the state at no charge. Therefore, in our example of the garden, if no charge is made, benefits could be increased by $KM'D'$ *at no extra cost* (since marginal cost to OZ is nil). But, because total cost is no longer covered, the garden would have to be entirely tax-financed as with community goods. Likewise, an income redistribution may be involved – from an old lady who rarely goes to the park towards the large family making much use of it.

Technical difficulties may outweigh economic considerations in the method of financing a service. Thus while motorways could be financed by toll charges, the effect on the traffic flow, especially during rush hours, has led the UK to pay for them from general taxation.

Where demand at zero price for a collective service is not likely to be too high and the cost of collecting fees is not disproportionate to the revenue raised, the choice between tax- financing and user-charging could reasonably rest on the question: who benefits from the service? Where the community as a whole benefits – for example, street lighting and bypass roads – tax-financing is appropriate. In contrast, if only certain individuals benefit, the cost is best, and more fairly, covered by individual fees (for example, for public tennis courts and swimming pools), or if a particular group benefits, a special levy can be imposed, for example, street-making charges.

With merit goods in particular, it may be desirable to recognize the uneven distribution of income when considering charges. For instance, charges for essential education would be highly regressive on low-income families with children of school age. Alternatively, the regressive impact of charges can be modified by price discrimination. Thus low-income families are given housing benefits, while persons over retirement age do not pay prescription charges.

Generally, therefore, the choice between charges and taxation is, in practice, likely to be decided politically, especially where income redistribution figures prominently. But the economic constraints on charging less than the free-market price must be emphasized, for an extended demand may impose a heavy burden on taxation generally. The result is that some form of administrative rationing according to need may have to be imposed, for example, the 'points' system for allocating council dwellings. More seriously, hidden rationing may prevail through depreciation of the quality of service provided, for example, state medical services and education. Indeed, this could apply to BBC television, where a possible 'community good' is converted to a 'collective good' by a compulsory legal licence. Through this creation of excludability, the cost falls on TV owners.

In addition, charging for a service at less than its full economic cost leads to pressure for an extension of the service – for example, subsidized public transport and housing – by consumers who benefit most. The minimum necessary condition for this to occur is that benefits are significantly more concentrated or localized than the costs which have to be met.

It should be noted that practical considerations may mean that, over time, methods of covering expenditure may be changed, as the history of road financing illustrates. Tolls were satisfactory when there were few roads, but they had to give way to special levies (for example, road fund revenues) as the government assumed responsibility for a rapidly growing road network. Eventually the Chancellor of the Exchequer realized that expenditure on motor vehicles could be a source of tax revenue, and the idea of road fund gave way to covering the full cost of roads out of general taxation. However, the attributes of user-charges outlined above suggest that a return to toll financing for motorways and, if technical difficulties can be overcome, the introduction of some form of pricing for the use of urban roads (see Chapter 10) may now be appropriate.

User-charges and price discrimination

Even when it has been decided to cover the cost of a service by charges, difficulties may arise where there are relatively very high fixed costs, as with sports centres, public transport, electricity and natural gas, since supply by competing firms would simply mean that none could be financially viable. Moreover, for technical reasons, a monopoly may be necessary. For instance, only one firm can be given the right to acquire land for laying a gas main or for running a water pipe under the roads, while, for public transport, competing firms cannot be allowed to 'skim' the profitable commuter traffic with none providing a service at other times or on other routes.

This necessity of having to create a monopoly because of decreasing costs or of special technical conditions of supply strengthens the case for the provision or supervision of certain services (for example, passenger transport) by the government or local authorities. More than that, it also allows a policy of price discrimination to operate whereby the service can be financially viable without subsidy. Figure 21.2 illustrates this.

If average total cost and demand are as depicted by curves *ATC* and *PD* respectively, it is impossible to cover total cost at a single price, since at all outputs *ATC* will always exceed average revenue. In practice the problem has been overcome in three ways.

1. The difference has been covered by a *subsidy*, either directly, for example, for city transport, or indirectly, through writing off accumulated deficits from time to time, for example, for coal and railways.

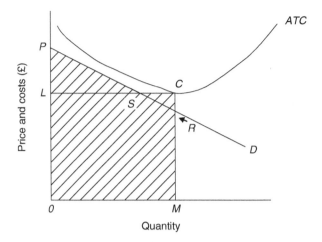

Figure 21.2 The possibility of supply through price discrimination

2. A *standing charge* is levied irrespective of units consumed, for example for electricity and metered water. The standing charge goes to meet fixed costs; the price per unit consumed covers variable costs.
3. The industry is allowed to exploit its monopoly position by *price discrimination*. This is possible where different customers, having a different elasticity of demand for the product, can be kept separate, each being charged the price he is willing to pay. By 'charging what the traffic will bear', total revenue is increased. Such price discrimination by consumer category is used, for example, by the railway operators, where cheap-day trippers, senior citizens and students are charged lower fares than commuters.

The highest degree of charging 'what the traffic will bear' is where the undertaking could discriminate perfectly between every consumer and charge different prices to each. Thus in Figure 21.2, provided $\triangle$ *PLS* is larger than $\triangledown$ *SRC*, the service would be profitable. Although this is impractical, a modified form, 'block pricing', separates additional amounts of the product and charges them at decreasing prices.

Thus in Figure 21.3 total revenue from a single electricity price *OP* would be *POMR*. But if a consumer is charged OP_1 for the first OM_1 units, *OP* for the second block of $M_1 M$ units, and OP_2 for the third block of MM_2 units, the extra revenue realized is shown by the two shaded areas.

Taxation to finance public expenditure

Traditionally, classification of taxes rests on the administrative distinction between direct and indirect taxation. A direct tax is one which is paid directly

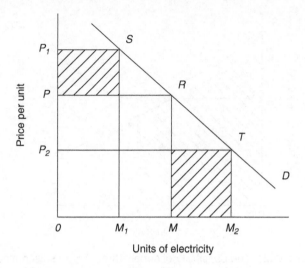

Figure 21.3   Increasing revenue by 'block pricing'

to the revenue authorities by the person taxed – examples include income tax, corporation tax, inheritance tax, local rates, motor-vehicle licence duties. An indirect tax is one which is collected via importers, manufactures, distributors or other intermediaries – for example, customs and excise duties, VAT.

Such a classification, however, is not very helpful in analysing the effects of taxation. Analytically we need to distinguish between: (a) *neutral taxes*, which do not directly affect the relative cost of and the demand for different goods and services, and (b) *selective taxes*, which have effect on demand or supply and thus on relative prices of different goods. To a large extent such a distinction does match up with the administration classification, for most direct taxes have only general effects on the economy as whole. On the other hand, local rates are akin to a selective tax in that they affect the prices of particular properties in both type and location and the price of real property, compared with other goods.

It should be noted, however, that a tax does not have to be 'direct' to be neutral. As a result, a general sales tax (such as a VAT system which taxed *all* goods and services at the same rate) would be neutral because it would simply lower private expenditure (that is, reduce disposable income) by the amount raised by the tax. Since the consumer cannot switch to a cheaper untaxed substitute, relative prices would remain unchanged.

Neutral taxes

Taxes on income

Income tax

In the UK, tax is levied on the net income of persons and partnerships (companies are subject to corporation tax). A high rate of tax on income can be expected to affect 'incentives', but this is by no means clear-cut. Attention is usually focused on its effect on how hard or long people work but it can also penalize risk-taking. Assuming that taxpayers are able to work more in order to earn more income, we can examine how various types of tax may affect their decision.

A poll tax (that is, a tax which does not vary with income) would reduce net income but leave the rate of reward for additional effort unchanged. Such a tax would, if anything, increase the supply of effort, since people might be expected to work harder to make up the income forgone. Any tax based on income, since it reduces total net income, has this 'total income' effect. But an income tax, unlike a poll tax, also alters the 'price' of income in terms of leisure by reducing the financial reward for sacrificing desirable leisure. This 'substitution' effect would therefore work to reduce the supply of effort. Since the two effects work in opposite directions, the net effect will depend on which is stronger. Where the marginal rate of tax is substantially higher than the average, the substitution effect may outweigh the 'total income' effect and so justify the conclusion that a highly progressive income tax inhibits effort more than a proportional or less progressive one. Of course, in the short run, much depends on the extend to which institutional factors (such as terms of employment, insurance and mortgage commitments) allow income to be adjusted to avoid tax.

Even more important for high-income earners is that a high marginal tax rate may reduce the attractiveness of risk-taking. The essence of risk – whether accepting a new job or developing a new product – is that things can go well or badly. A high marginal tax rate tilts the balance against risk. If the gain from a successful outcome is taxed at a high rate, the risk differential is reduced, so that risk-takers choose the safer option.

The disincentive disadvantages of a markedly progressive income tax may be off-set by its 'built-in' stabilizing effect on the economy. Assuming constant government expenditure and tax rates, tax receipts tend to fall in periods of deflation and to rise in periods of inflation, thereby stabilizing budget deficits and surpluses.

Corporation tax

In 1965, the profits tax was replaced by a corporation tax. Under the 'imputation' system adopted in 1973, all profits, whether distributed or not, are taxed at the same rate (28 per cent in 2010, but 21 per cent for small companies up to £300,000 profit a year).

In the short run, a tax on the net income of an enterprise falls on economic surplus or rent, and will not affect price and output decisions. This is true, but not particularly interesting since most of the important problems occur in the long period. Even in the short run, however, problems arise, for example, accounting profits measured for tax assessment may be greater than the true economic net surplus. If they are (for example, through inflation), the tax will fall in part on production costs with consequent contraction in the long period.

Taxes on capital

Taxes on capital can take three main forms:

1. a tax on capital passing at death (inheritance tax);
2. an annual charge on a person's capital (wealth tax);
3. a tax on increases in the value of capital, usually levied when the asset is sold (capital gains tax).

The effects of different taxes depend more on what they are paid out of, rather than what they are levied on. If a capital tax is defined as one which is paid out of capital, no difficulty arises. More usually, however, a capital tax is one which is levied on capital. This gives rise to the analytical difficulty that the tax may be paid out of income – for example, a person may pay out of current income the premium on an insurance policy to cover possible inheritance tax when he dies. Conversely, some taxes assessed on income or on current outlay may be paid out of capital (for example, the car tax and VAT on a new car). A rough-and-ready line of division can be drawn: all taxes tend to be paid out of income except where the size of the tax makes this impossible. When a tax is large and/or abnormal it tends to be paid out of capital irrespective of whether the Inland Revenue regards it as an income tax or a capital tax.

Developing this argument, an annual tax based on the capital values of income-bearing assets may be regarded as an alternative to an income tax on investment income. If, for example, a perpetual investment yielded a rate of return of 5 per cent, the revenue from a capital tax of 2.5 pence in the pound levied on capital values would be the same as that from an income tax of 50 pence levied on income. Given a uniform capitalization factor (number of year's purchase) for all types of investment income, there would be no difference between the two taxes. But obviously a riskier income will be capitalized at a lower number of years' purchase than a well-secured income. For instance, a capital tax of 6 pence in the pound of capital value levied regardless of the use to which the capital is put, would bear least heavily on riskier types of investment. Therefore, the deterrent effect of high rates of income taxation on production would be reduced by the substitution of a tax on capital.

Inheritance tax

In 1986, a capital transfer tax was replaced by the inheritance tax on lifetime gifts. After the first 3 years, tax is paid at reducing rates and no tax is paid if death occurs after 7 years from gifting. There are concessions for small businesses and farms.

Wealth tax

A wealth tax, not currently used in the UK, is an annual charge on a person's capital assets. As an alternative to a tax on capital gains, its great economic advantage is that it does not deter the most efficient use of capital.

Although theoretically plausible, however, a general wealth tax could be difficult to administer because of the need to keep valuations up to date. Also, in the absence of well-defined markets in all types of asset, including property, valuation itself might involve inequity between holders of assets.

Capital gains tax

In strict economic terms, personal 'income' refers to a person's command over economic resources over a given period. So defined, it is the amount a taxpayer could spend during a given period so as to leave himself no worse off at the end of the period than he was at the beginning. Therefore, it includes any growth in the value of wealth over the period as well as of income in its more usual sense.

Interpreting income in this sense of spending power, therefore, argues for a general tax on expenditure (reflecting a command over resources). However, since a tax on *all* spending would require a massive readjustment of the tax system, Britain has preferred the alternative of adding a separate capital gains tax to the existing income-tax structure.

Selective taxes

'Indirect' taxes have to be related to the overall tax structure in their equity and economic efficiency. Since they cannot easily be related to taxpayers' income (even where the commodities to be taxed and the rates of tax are carefully chosen), they tend to be a regressive form of tax, that is, the effective incidence is heaviest on poorer households. Ideally, therefore, indirect taxes should be confined to goods which are not necessities but which are consumed on a broad enough scale to provide the revenue required. The difficulty is that the higher the general standard of living, the wider is the definition of 'necessities'! Moreover, other considerations may be dominant when applying indirect taxes. Therefore, if the disincentive effect of income tax is greater than that of expenditure taxes, some substitution of expenditure taxes for income tax may be desirable.

From the standpoint of economic efficiency, any expenditure tax imposed selectively on some goods and services alters relative prices, brings about a reallocation of consumers' expenditure and distorts the pattern of consumption and production. If that pattern were already ideal, this distortion would result in a less than optimal distribution of resources. This suggests that if economic efficiency is to be combined with equity, expenditure taxes should be levied on goods which have a low price-elasticity of demand (minimizing any reallocation effect) but which also have a high income-elasticity of demand (for these are also likely to be 'non-necessities').

Since selective expenditure taxes distort relative prices, we have to consider their effects in specific sectors of the economy. We do so by examining the *shifting* and *incidence* of such taxes. *Shifting* refers to the possibility that a tax can be 'shifted' on to others by the person who originally pays the tax, while *incidence* refers to its final resting place. But the analysis, although helpful in formulating tax policy, cannot predict precise effects, rather, it is limited to indicating tendencies in terms of 'more' or 'less' relative to the particular time period. Selective taxes affect owners of productive resources, firms and consumers. We consider their impact on each in turn.

With land resources the significant feature is that supply is often only variable after a considerable lapse of time. This applies when analysing the effects of taxes on unimproved land, land bearing specific resources (such as minerals, timber, coal, iron) and improvements to land (for example by buildings, racecourses and so on). Fixity of supply is the feature of non-reproducible resources, such as minerals. Here, since earnings consist wholly of economic rent, the owner must bear all the tax. If he tries to sell the resource, the purchaser will simply capitalize the tax and deduct it from his offer price. This is the basis for the taxation of 'betterment' (see Chapter 22).

'Firms' are situated midway between factors of production and final consumers. The effect of taxes levied on firms will therefore alter economic relationships both in factor markets and in the final product market. As firms respond by changing the extent and direction of their activities, they shift the tax burden – backwards on to factors of production and forward on to final consumers. Which of these two groups will finally bear most of the burden depends on the relative elasticities of consumer-demand and factor-supply. If the elasticity of product-demand is greater than the elasticity of factor-supply, the tax shifting will be mainly backwards, and vice versa. For instance, if a tax is levied on carpets the demand for which is very sensitive to price changes and which are made by firms employing specialists in carpet-making who have no alternative occupation, then, unless the firm is willing to accept lower profits, the wages of carpet-makers are likely to suffer. Conversely, if the demand for carpets is very inelastic and if the factors employed in carpet-manufacture are in highly elastic supply (that is, have alternative occupations to which they can readily turn), the tax is likely to be borne largely by the buyers of carpets.

Taxes levied on firms fall into two groups:

1. *Taxes fixed independently of output.* Local rates, for example, the Uniform Business Rate (UBR), are, analytically, an addition to the fixed costs of the firm and so reduce profits. In the short run, however, this is unlikely to have any effect on supply since marginal revenue and marginal cost are unchanged by the tax. There is thus little possibility of shifting the tax in the short run.

2. But in the long run, if the tax reduces returns in this line of production relative to other lines, supply will tend to decrease and price to rise depending on the

elasticity of demand. Thus part of the tax originally borne by the firm will tend to be passed on to consumers as firms leave this line of production.

3. Furthermore, decreased production reduces the demand for factors of production whose prices therefore fall. Therefore, part of the burden of the tax will be borne by factors of production according to their elasticity of supply in that line of production.

4. *Taxes levied on output.* These taxes can be divided into two types: (a) those levied proportionally to *output*, such as specific taxes on tobacco and beer, and which analytically constitute a *fixed* addition to variable cost per unit; and (b) those which vary more than proportionately with output, for example, an *ad valorem* tax such as VAT, and which by varying with the cost of production, represents a *varying* addition to variable cost per unit of output.

Both types can be analysed in the same way. A rise in variable cost per unit of output means a one-off rise in marginal cost, therefore, output will be reduced and the price of the product is likely to increase even in the short period. But in the long period, productive capacity can be varied, and producers who do not cover total costs will leave the industry, thereby reducing supply. There will thus be an increased tendency towards a higher product-price (net of tax) and a shifting forward of the tax to consumers. Furthermore, reduction of supply will reduce demand for factors, resulting in lower factor-prices and a shifting backwards of the tax if factor-supply is less than perfectly elastic.

As explained above, the burden of taxation may be shifted forward from the firm to consumers. But, consumers themselves, as sellers of labour, can try to shift the burden backwards by claiming higher wages. Similarly, when the burden of tax is shifted backwards on to labour, workers, as consumers of final products, reduce their demand and so tend to shift the burden back again to sellers of final products. The final incidence of the tax as between consumers and producers will depend upon the relative elasticities of supply and demand. The greater the producer's elasticity of supply compared with the consumer's elasticity of demand, the more will the tax be borne by the consumer, and vice versa.

Private finance initiatives (PFI)

The private finance initiative (PFI) was first introduced in Australia in the late 1980s, and was originally applied to toll road and railway projects. A PFI contract is a way for the public sector to obtain new buildings using private investment which is then repaid to the private sector by rental and maintenance charges over a period of time. Since 1992, there have been more than 700 PFI contracts in the UK. Projects such as highways, hospitals, schools, prisons and government offices have been undertaken to provide more than £100 billion of

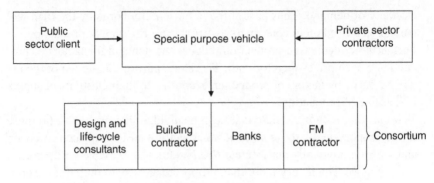

Figure 21.4   PFI structure

development in the UK. In a PFI contract the public and private sectors collaborate (see Figure 21.4) and the procedure is:

- private firms operating in a consortium agree to design, build, finance and manage a public-sector facility;
- in return the public sector client agrees to pay annual charges and/or allows the private sector consortium to reap any profits that can be made over life of the project (30 years or more).

The advantages of PFIs:

- the contractor no longer 'builds and disappears';
- the client drives the project;
- competition reduces inefficiency;
- there is improved flow of information;
- there are incentives to complete on time, within budget and to expected quality.

The disadvantages of PFIs:

- transaction costs are high so only a few firms bid;
- bid costs are often more than £1 million;
- ongoing rental payments can be a burden on public finances.

The debt created by PFI can have a significant impact on the finances of public bodies. In October 2007, the total capital value of PFI contracts signed throughout the UK was £68 billion. However, this Figure is only part of the total liability of central and local government which must pay a further £215 billion over the lifetime of these contracts. The £5.2 billion of PFI investment in Scotland up to 2007 has created a public-sector cash liability of £22.3 billion and the investment of just

£618 million via PFI in Wales up to 2007 has created a public-sector cash liability of £3.3 billion. Annual payments to the private owners of the PFI schemes are due to peak at £10 billion in 2017 and are already stretching constricted public-sector budgets, to the extent that public services could be suffering.

A National Audit Office study in 2003 endorsed the view that PFI projects represent good value for taxpayers' money, but some commentators have criticized PFI for allowing excessive profits for private companies at the expense of the taxpayer. There is also evidence that some PFI projects have been poorly specified and carried out.

Supporters of PFI, however, claim that risk is successfully transferred from public to private sectors as a result of PFI. An example of a successful PFI is the new office accommodation for the Treasury at 1, Horse Guards Road, Whitehall. This was opened by Alan Greenspan, former Chairman of the United States Federal Reserve Board on 25 September 2002. The increased space available in the new building (known as 1HGR) will enable all Treasury staff to work in the same building for the first time in over 50 years. This was achieved through a complete refurbishment of the western end of the building known as Government Offices Great George Street (GOGGS), delivered on budget and ahead of time in a successful innovative value for money PFI project. GCHQ Cheltenham is another successful example of a PFI. This 100,000 square metre building is a major feat in all respects. As the largest PFI project in Europe, the GCHQ's new building will be home to over 4,500 staff, relocating them from 50 different buildings on two existing sites in Cheltenham.

The global financial crisis which began in 2007 presents PFI with difficulties because many sources of private capital have dried up, nevertheless PFI remains the UK government's preferred method for public-sector procurement.

Government ownership of real estate

Government departments and defence forces require offices, land, warehouses and so on, and their transactions are supervised by a coordinating agency, Property Advisors to the Civil Estate (PACE) now part of the Office of Government Commerce (OGC).

The UK government owns a considerable amount of real estate in the UK and overseas. In 2008, the Office of National Statistics estimated the value of the UK assets to be £380 billion. Of this about £240 billion is held by local authorities and the remainder by central government and public corporations. Significant assets are held by the following public-sector areas:

British Waterways: owns 2,000 miles of canals, rivers and supporting infrastructure in England, Wales and Scotland and owns a significant land and non-operational property portfolio close to waterside locations. Rents in

2008–9 were £26.5 million and profits from sales of properties and development sites were £4.7 million. Rental income supports maintenance of the waterways network while profits from sales are reinvested in waterways and the portfolio. Total assets are worth about £450 million.

Defence, Storage and Distribution Agency: has 11 sites providing storage and distribution for the Ministry of Defence. There is no asset valuation as it will probably never be sold but an idea of its scale can be seen from the fact that there are more than 3,300 employees.

High Speed 1 Ltd (HS1): 68 miles of high speed rail line from St Pancras International to the British portal of the Channel Tunnel and all stations along the route. No asset valuation is available but this should become clear when it is sold in 2011. The capital cost of the project was £5.8 billion and it involved 13.7 miles of twin bored tunnels, 3,000 structures, 3 major viaducts and 150 new bridges.

Forestry Commission England: 258,000 hectares of land (2 per cent of total land area) used for timber and recreation. Total assets are worth about £500 million.

Forestry Commission Scotland: net assets of about £156 million.

URENCO: uranium enrichment facility for civil nuclear power production. Assets worth about £2.2 billion.

Public-Sector Spectrum Holdings: mobile communications provider with assets valued at more than £3 billion.

BBC: assets worth about £277 million.

Trust Ports: 50 ports in England and Wales; the largest by turnover is Dover with assets of £132.5 million.

The Tote: horse racing gambling business with 516 shops, turnover of £2.9 billion and assets of £132.5 million.

The Royal Mint: on a 35-acre site in Llantrisant, South Wales with 860 employees and assets worth £53 million.

Dartford Crossing: net proceeds from this public-sector asset were almost £43 million in 2008.

Oil and Pipelines Agency: owns 50 per cent of the UK's oil pipeline (2,500 km) and 46 storage facilities.

Land Registry: assets of £205 million.

NHS Professionals: assets of £18.7 million.

Queen Elizabeth II Conference Centre: worth about £30 million.

Other public-sector concerns with significant assets are:

The Met Office, Ordnance Survey and *National Air Traffic Control Service (NATS)* which has 5,000 employees in three centres.

Box 21.1   The National Assets Register

The first attempt at a list of resources owned by the UK government (apart from the Domesday Book) was compiled in 1997 and updated in 2001when the total asset value was estimated at £270 billion. The most recent register was in 2007when total assets were valued at £330 billion, which is almost certainly an underestimate. It lists all government buildings including 10 and 11 Downing Street (£15 million), embassies overseas, military bases, Edinburgh Castle (nearly £2 million), museums and NHS premises.

The Ministry of Defence is the most valuable of 19 government departments in the register with assets of £93 billion including overseas bases. The Department of Transport has assets worth £81 billion, and the Department of Health, £40 billion.

The government raised £12 billion from asset sales before 2007 and is committed to raising a further £18 billion by 2011. When an asset is sold it seems to raise considerably more than expected, however. Examples of this are four acres of land from the grounds of the British embassy in Bangkok which was sold to a shopping centre for £50 million although the whole embassy was valued at only £8.8 million in 2001; and the stunning £900 million received for Chelsea Barracks in April 2007, at more than £70 million an acre, which was valued at just £58.5 million on the Register.

Box 21.2   British embassies overseas

The Foreign and Commonwealth Office has three prestigious properties in London and one in Milton Keynes. But it also has 4,062 properties in 279 places around the world with a total value of £1.6 billion. £269 million was spent in 2008–9 for the upkeep of these buildings, which are often the most impressive structures in the cities they occupy. They employ 13,000 staff, of whom 2,500 live in staff accommodation. The FCO has a reputation for commissioning good quality architecture.

In February 2010, the National Audit Office (NAO) found that the Foreign Office was 'wasting millions every year on expansive embassy buildings around the world while cutting funding for crucial security measures in high-risk countries'. The NAO criticized the complex management and funding arrangements for the FCO estate and the absence of a clear strategy for its use.

Since 2002, the FCO has spent £250 million on capital projects including the new embassy in Harare, Zimbabwe (£27 million), in Warsaw (£57 million) and in Berlin (£17 million). The embassy in Moscow was renovated at a cost of £14 million (costs increased because of measures necessary to ensure security and freedom from 'bugging').

The FCO sold £61.5 million of assets from its portfolio in 2009–10, however, including the Madrid embassy for £40 million – the new one, further from the city centre cost £16 million. Buildings were also sold in Holland, Argentina, South Africa, the Philippines, Malawi, Canada, Sweden and New Zealand.

Box 21.3   The Crown Estate

The Crown Estate is owned by the monarch of the UK but its revenue goes to the Treasury. As part of a deal struck between George III and Parliament, the sovereign gave up the right to the income from the estate in return for a civil list (annual income from Parliament).

The Crown Estate has two main objectives:

- to benefit the taxpayer by paying revenue from assets directly to the Treasury;
- to enhance the value of the estate and the income that it generates.

The total value of the Crown Estate in March 2009 was £5.7 billion, a fall of about 18 per cent from its peak because of revised valuations during the recession. Since 2000, the Crown Estate's revenue has risen by 70.5 per cent and £1.8 billion has been paid to the Treasury (thecrownestate.co.uk).

It owns an unusually diverse selection of assets, including all the tin, silver and gold mines in the country; 360,000 acres of rural land; 2,000 residential properties from modern flats in Hackney, east London to Windsor Great Park and the smartest town houses around Regent's Park; and 400 commercial properties including a McDonald's in Slough and a Debenhams department store in Worcester.

In 2009, Crown Estates reported £226.5 million in net income surplus which is paid to the government for the benefit of the taxpayer. The land and property is let to around 10,000 tenancies across the UK. The urban portfolio represents 73 per cent of property value (including indirectly held property) and 74 per cent of gross revenue surplus. It includes shops, offices, retail and business parks, industrial sites and residential properties. There are 1,280 units let on monthly regulated or assured tenancies in London. Almost all of the property in London's Regent Street and Regent's Park belongs to The Crown Estate although in July 2010 plans were announced to sell a minority stake in Regent Street.

The marine estate includes more than 55 per cent of the UK's foreshore, tidal river-beds and almost all of the seabed within the 12 nautical miles limit – including rights to all minerals but excluding hydrocarbons. Crown Estate's 146,000 hectares (360,000 acres) is of the largest rural estates in the UK. Rights to all naturally occurring gold and silver – the Mines Royal – belong to The Crown Estate.

The Crown Estate owns over 1,000 listed buildings, 37 per cent of which are Grade 1 and there are over 400 Sites of Special Scientific Interest in the rural and marine estates.

In late 2009, the UK government set up a new Property Unit in the Shareholder Executive to manage state property. The government intends to consolidate the portfolio and in the 2010 budget revealed plans to move 15,000 civil servants out of expensive London properties, including 1,000 Ministry of Justice posts. More joint ventures with the private sector are envisaged in order to develop public property in order to maximize its value.

Telereal Trillium, (the Pears family's investment company Telereal acquired Trillium from Land Securities for £750 million in 2009) has a contract to manage the property portfolio of the Department for Work and Pensions. It has established the department as the government's most efficient user of space and cut its property from 14 million square feet to 10 million square feet. The company has at least £1 billion of equity to invest and is seeking a key role in government plans to make efficiency savings across state-owned properties and maximize the value of the public portfolio. Telereal Trillium also has a contract with DVLA for a major refurbishment of its 400,000 square feet headquarters in Swansea.

Summary

Governments intervene in markets for the provision of community goods, collective goods and merit goods. Public-sector provision of land and property resources takes place through:

- government departments,
- state-owned industries,
- quasi-governmental bodies,
- local authorities.

The finance for the activities of these public sector organizations comes from:

- borrowing,
- user-charges,
- taxation.

Private Finance Initiatives have enabled the government to provide considerable investment in buildings for the public sector in recent years.

The National Assets Register – first compiled in 2007 – provides a comprehensive list and valuation of all public sector assets in the UK. The government of the UK owns a massive portfolio of assets worth in the region of £300 billion.

Chapter 21: review questions

1. What are the reasons for provision of goods and services by the public sector?
2. How are public-sector services financed?
3. How can revenue be increased by price discrimination?
4. What is meant by tax shifting?
5. Describe the extent of UK government ownership of real estate.

22 Taxation of Real Estate

After studying this chapter you will be able to:

- Explain the desirable qualities of a 'good tax';
- Show how direct taxation affects real estate;
- Describe the impact of VAT on real property;
- Analyse the advantages and disadvantages of a land value tax;
- Show how local government is financed in the UK.

The structure of taxation

Taxes can be defined as 'a compulsory levy made by the public authorities for which nothing is received directly in return'. Taxes are the most important source of government revenue as well as a way of transferring resources from the private sector to the public sector. Adam Smith identified four important principles of taxation in The Wealth of Nations (Smith, 1776):

- Equity – the tax should be fair;
- Certainty – the taxpayer should be sure of their liability;
- Efficiency – taxes should not be expensive to collect;
- Convenience – payment of the tax should not be difficult.

Today, however, the main purpose of any tax is usually to raise money although sometimes, as in the case of taxation of harmful products such as tobacco, objectives other than raising revenue may take priority. In the modern era, as far as possible taxes should be:

1. Productive of a worthwhile revenue, which the Chancellor can estimate fairly accurately.

2. Certain to the taxpayer and difficult to evade.
3. Convenient to the taxpayer as regards the time and manner of payment.
4. Equitable in the sense that:
   - the most tax should be paid by those with the greatest ability to pay';
   - impartial between one person and another.
5. Adjustable to changes in policy.
6. Automatic in stabilizing the economy. Thus while, in order to achieve full employment or a stable price level, the Chancellor can adjust taxes in his budget to influence consumer spending, it is helpful if they respond automatically in the desired direction.
7. Harmless to effort and initiative.
8. Consistent with other aspects of government policy. Although the tax structure should not change frequently, individual taxes must be constantly reviewed to promote current government policy. To encourage effort, should income from work be taxed at a lower rate than investment income? Will an indirect tax, by raising the cost of living, increase wage-push inflation?
9. Minimal in their effect on the optimum allocation of resources.
10. Equitable in its distribution of the tax burden. Taxes can be classified according to the proportion of a person's income which is deducted:
    - A regressive tax takes a higher proportion of the poorer person's income than of the richer. Indirect taxes, for instance, which are a fixed sum irrespective of income (for example, television licences), are regressive.
    - A proportional tax takes a given proportion of one's income.
    - A progressive tax takes a higher proportion of income as income increases (Figure 22.1). Thus income tax, which has higher rates above certain limits, is progressive.

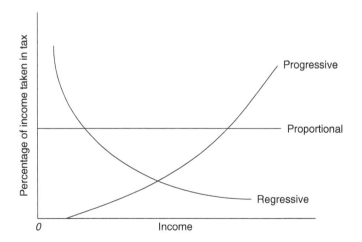

Figure 22.1   The difference between regressive, proportional and progressive taxes

Justification for taxing the rich higher than the poor rests on the assumption that the law of diminishing utility applies to additional income, so that an extra £50 affords less pleasure to the rich person than to the poor person. Thus taking from the rich involves less hardship than taking from the poor. Generally this can be accepted as true, but we can never be sure, simply because there is no absolute measure of personal satisfaction.

Because the objectives of taxation are now so varied and may even be incompatible, no single tax is completely perfect. Consequently, there must be a structure of taxation, combining different taxes which can be varied according to changes in emphasis on different objectives.

Land has long been a source of revenue for governments for many reasons:

- It is a repository of wealth;
- Historically, armed forces were supplied by large estates;
- Until the nineteenth century, estates provided the bulk of British public revenue and landowning classes held the reigns of power;
- Land ownership became synonymous with power and wealth;
- Land is immovable and not easily destroyed;
- The income from land is relatively easy to collect – it can be deducted from rent or the land can be occupied to obtain payment;
- Income from land can be determined accurately in advance;
- Land has a tendency to rise in value in line with increases in population and economic activity.

Direct taxation and real estate

In the case of direct taxes, the taxpayer makes payment direct to the revenue authorities – Her Majesty's Revenue and Customs (HMRC) or the local authority. Usually each individual's tax liability is assessed separately. A direct tax is assessed on, and collected from, the individual intended to bear it, for example, income tax. An indirect tax is not levied directly upon the person on whom it ultimately falls, such as, VAT. While direct taxes may affect incentives to effort and risk-bearing investment, they are basically *neutral* in their effects on individual items of expenditure. Nevertheless, special provisions within the broad tax arrangements may have marginal economic effects, as follows.

Income tax

Interest relief on income tax for homeowners started in 1803. Until 1950, when only 10 per cent of households were homeowners, the cost to the Exchequer was small. But the subsequent increase in ownership led to the qualifying loan being limited to £25,000 in 1974. This was raised to £30,000 in 1983 with the introduction of 'mortgage interest relief at source' (MIRAS), under which the borrower paid the tender interest less the tax relief.

This home-ownership subsidy peaked at £8 billion in 1991, but concern for the PSNCR meant that the rate was subsequently reduced in steps to 10 per cent. On 6 April 2000, when MIRAS was abolished, the Exchequer saved only 1.4 billion a year. Over the previous years, however, this subsidy, by favouring owner-occupiers, effectively moved housing tenure from the rented to the owner-occupied sector (see Chapter 5).

UK Real Estate Investment Trust dividend income is received net of basic-rate income tax (20 per cent in 2010). There is 'rent a room' relief on the income of an individual from letting furnished accommodation which is part of his/her only or main residence. The exemption from income tax applies up to £4,250.

Corporation tax

In the computation of corporation tax (income tax in the case of an unincorporated business) agricultural and industrial buildings enjoy capital depreciation allowances. Commercial and residential buildings, however, can only offset *actual* repair and maintenance costs against tax. As a result agricultural and industrial buildings tend to have a shorter life irrespective of technical considerations, while landlords of residential properties are deterred from making *improvements* to buildings with a limited life.

Inheritance tax

Death duty (or estate duty) was introduced in 1894. It was payable when an estate was transferred on the death of the owner. Inheritance tax was introduced in 1986 and exempts many transfers of assets during the lifetime of the transferee. It applies to transfers on death, gifts made within 7 years of death and lifetime gifts that are not exempt (such as small gifts of less than £250 per year and marriage gifts).

To avoid the break-up of agricultural estates which occurred in the past in order to pay inheritance tax upon the death of a major owner, there is now no tax payable on agricultural land. This relief applies to the agricultural value of the asset only and for the purposes of agricultural relief, a farmhouse, cottage or building must be proportionate in size and nature to the requirements of the farming activities conducted on the agricultural land or pasture in question. When business property is transferred there is a percentage reduction in the value of the transfer. Often this provides full relief.

However, the tax advantage of leaving farm land, rather than other assets, influences demand. A person who wishes to pass on his wealth to an heir may purchase and enjoy the amenity of owning a rural estate for at least 2 years, and can, if he so wishes, carry on the actual farming through a contractor or similar device. Moreover, since exemption from inheritance tax is given for gifts and bequests to certain national institutions such as the National Gallery and the National Trust, it tends to decrease the land available for holding in private hands.

Capital gains tax

Capital gains tax is payable on gains made on the disposal of chargeable assets by chargeable persons. The rate in 2010 was 18 per cent but the parlous state of the public finances makes a substantial rise likely. Individuals have an allowance (that is, they can make capital gains free of tax) of £10,100 in 2010.

Since owner-occupied houses are exempt from Capital Gains Tax (CGT), the owner receives a further 'subsidy' compared with other asset-holders, thereby increasing demand for houses as compared with other assets such as equities, unit trusts and expensive antiques, which are subject to CGT. Moreover, where the gains made on the sale of business assets are fully reinvested in similar business assets within 3 years, the tax may be deferred. This 'roll-over' concession tends to maintain demand for such assets; or, as the holders often put it, they are 'locked in' to such assets.

Stamp duty land tax

Stamp duty is levied on the value of transactions in land and buildings. The bands for the tax year 2010–11 were 0 per cent paid at £0–£125,000, 1 per cent paid on properties costing between £125,000 and £250,000, 3 per cent between £250,000 and £500,000 and 4 per cent for more than £500,000. SDLT is payable on the full amount of the purchase price of the property, thus at current rates a property bought for £400,000 would attract SDLT of £12,000. This has distortionary effects at the thresholds, with sellers and buyers reluctant to pay slightly more than, say, £250,000 because the increase in the rate of SDLT would apply to the whole amount of the purchase price.

The bands were changed in the 2010 budget. First-time buyers can secure a 2-year temporary stamp duty relief up to £250,000, from 25 March 2010. A new 5 per cent threshold above £1 million will also be introduced from 6 April 2011.

The effect on property is that:

1. it discriminates against investment in property as opposed to shares which pay only 0.5 per cent;
2. it depresses overall property values;
3. by increasing purchase costs, it reduces market liquidity;

4. where more accommodation is required, it can make it cheaper to build on one's current house rather than move to a higher-priced house;
5. it has a disproportionate effect on south of England properties, where property prices are highest.

Lease duty is also payable at 1 per cent on the capital value of the lease (found by capitalizing the rent payable over the term of the lease at the discount rate of 3.5 per cent) less the threshold of £150,000.

Development land tax (DLT) and 'planning gain'

Under the Community Land Act 1975, all development land was to be brought under public ownership over a period of about 10 years. In the meantime, 'betterment' was to be collected through a DLT. In theory, as explained below, the tax was sound; in practice, it was a flop, and eventually dropped. But it did provide the background for the concept of 'planning gain'.

From the point of view of economic analysis, a high rate of DLT should have no effect on the supply of land for development since the tax falls on economic rent. This is the return over and above the 'transfer price' which accrues to a factor through fixity of supply. Transfer price covers what the factor can earn in its best alternative use plus any return (often termed 'normal profit') required by the owner to overcome his inertia or inconvenience in effecting such a transfer. This can be illustrated both arithmetically and diagrammatically.

Suppose undeveloped farmland surrounding a town is required for housing. The current-use price is, say £5,000 per acre; this is the transfer price, that is, what another farmer would be prepared to pay for the land for agricultural use. Planning permission is now given for a housing development on 12 acres of a particular farm. As a result the price of these 12 acres rises to £100,000 an acre. Their enhanced development value would equal current market price minus current-use value, that is, £1,140,000. If the rate of development tax on this gain were, say, 60 per cent, the farmer would still be left with £456,0000 (£1,140,000 gain minus £684,000 tax). Thus he can theoretically obtain 91 more acres to replace the 12 sold.

This is shown diagrammatically in Figure 22.2. If no planning permission were required and all the agricultural land surrounding the town were suitable for housing, we can assume that any price above the agricultural price will secure the land for housing. In other words, the supply (S_a) of land is perfectly elastic at OY, that is, at £5,000 an acre. Demand for agricultural land is given by the demand curve D. Any increase in demand for land for housing, XX_1 can be supplied without any rise in price. In other words, because supply is perfectly elastic, the increase in demand to D_1 has no effect on price.

In practice, however, planning permission is restricted to twelve acres, OX and supply curve S_b. Thus the price of these soars above their agricultural-use

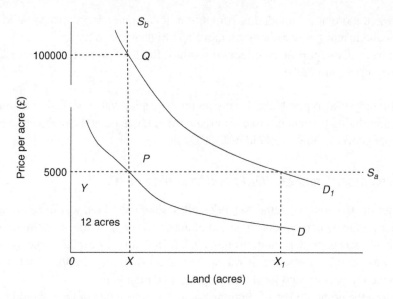

Figure 22.2   Economic rent arising from restricted planning permission

value to £100,000 an acre, OY_1. There is a windfall gain, or betterment, to the farmer of Y_1 YPQ. The whole of this windfall gain can be taxed away without making any difference to the farmer's willingness to supply the land for housing, assuming that his inertia costs were included in the price OY. DLT could thus rise to almost 100 per cent.

In theory, the argument is neat; in practice, it runs up against difficulties. The first is that we do not know for certain how much the farmer will actually require in order to cover his inertia and upheaval costs. Subjective valuations cannot be ignored. He may feel, for instance, that the after-tax £456,000 left to him is insufficient compensation for land which has been in the possession of his family for generations.

A second difficulty is that the theory is essentially static, making no allowance for expectations. The farmer may speculate against a future rate of DLT, refusing to sell if he thinks it might be reduced in the near future, or being more ready to sell if he fears an increase. If there is a lack of voluntary sales, the price of development land will rise (other things being equal), while if compulsory purchase has to be invoked, development will be delayed by the time-consuming procedures of a local public enquiry.

In practice the DLT had high costs of collection relative to yield and a restrictive effect on the supply of land. It was therefore abolished so that betterment is now collected through capital gains tax and 'planning gain'.

Unlike a tax, planning gain has no legal backing and lacks a precise definition. Therefore, we have to fall back on the generally accepted meaning: a benefit, either in cash or kind, accruing to the local authority from the grant of planning consent. The absence of any precise official definition has the advantage of permitting flexibility. But the result is that interpretation of what planning gain should actually cover has widened over the past 20 years.

The early view was that planning gain should relate solely to the external costs of the *actual* development and so should be limited to a contribution to such costs as road access, water supply and sewage disposal, necessary for the development to proceed. Subsequently, planning gain was widened to cover payments on items which may be divorced, both functionally and geographically, but could be considered material to achieving an acceptable balance of uses in mixed developments. For example, this would cover the cost of the developer providing 'social' housing and a library.

Planning obligations (also known as section 106 agreements) under Section 106 of the Town and Country Planning Act 1990 allow a developer to put forward in his application for planning permission a package of what he proposes to build *plus* details of what he is prepared to offer by way of planning gain to cover works which he considers will commend his development to the local authority. But without any precise definition or examples of what planning gain should be limited to, the procedure regarding planning consents often followed a course which was highly suspect. Such obligations can prescribe the nature of development (for example, requiring a given portion of housing is affordable), compensate for loss or damage created by a development (for example, loss of open space), or mitigate a development's impact (for example, through increased public transport provision). Planning obligations should be directly relevant to the proposed development.

On the one hand, the developer offers a level of inducement, which on occasions might be little short of a bribe, to cajole the local planning authority, to give consent. There seemed to be no limit to the nature of such offers. For instance, in 1992 Sainsbury, in its application for a superstore at Plymouth, offered benefits costed at £3.66 million for items which included a tourist information centre, an art gallery display, a bird-watching hide and access to a nature reserve! On the other hand, many local authorities saw their role of ruling on planning applications as a means of collecting betterment – a unilateral imposition of what was virtually its own DLT in order to fund functions, such as social housing, normally financed from general taxation. To this, the government, which had cut grants to local authorities in order to reduce the PSNCR, seemed to turn a blind eye.

In practice, 'betterment' would be split between the developer and the local authority by a process of bilateral bargaining or negotiation, depending on the assessment of the strengths of the opposite side. If agreement is reached, the developer gets his planning consent without going through a lengthy and costly appeal procedure, and the local authority obtains its social affordable housing, and so on. At times, however, the local authority may overplay its hand, and the developer withdraws. This happened in 1998 when Berkeley Homes pulled out of a scheme to convert an office building into 24 flats because Camden Council would not compromise on its demand for £420,000 by way of commuted compensation for not including six affordable flats, that is 25 per cent of the scheme.

The above arrangement has given cause for serious concern. Meetings may be held in secret, thereby eliminating the transparency essential for democratic control. More than that, it can undermine confidence in the planning system as there is only a thin line between planning gain and selling planning permission. The planning gain may become a bribe by the developer to persuade the council to ignore or overrule technical considerations, when, for example, affordable social housing is accepted irrespective of the excess traffic it might generate on already congested local roads.

There are two methods by which what has been described as 'the only lawful form of corruption left in the United Kingdom' can be brought under control. First, an aggrieved third party may appeal to the courts, though in practice the courts have been liberal in their interpretation of what is acceptable. Second, the Minister may decide that 'enough is enough'. This happened in what is known as the Tesco-Witney case. In 1994–5, Tesco tried to ease its application in Witney by offering to wholly fund a link road to ease traffic problems in the town centre; the roads concerned would barely have been affected by the building of the store. The local authority had previously decided to build a link road, but at a considerable distance from the Tesco site, in order to relieve traffic congestion. In spite of the fact that the foodstore was unlikely to generate more traffic than other permitted users of the site, Tesco offered to fund this road.

The Secretary of State refused planning permission, thereby overruling the view of his planning inspector at the local public inquiry. Tesco appealed, and eventually the House of Lords had to decide: (a) whether Tesco's offer comprised a 'material consideration'; (b) if so, did the Secretary of State fail to have regard to it? The Lords also threw out the appeal, ruling that, while there was some element of material consideration in Tesco's offer, the Secretary of State had, after due consideration, given little weight to it in arriving at his decision.

This decision can be regarded as a milestone in defining the section 106 conditions which a local planning authority may impose when deciding on a planning application and the obligations which may be accepted by the developer. Even though there will be further legal challenges, the Tesco case is a step towards restoring the integrity of the planning system and in reversing the planning gain bonanza which had come into being.

In theory, councils are allowed to make Sainsbury's or Tesco pay for road-widening so their lorries don't cause congestion; or make Barratt Homes build a few affordable houses so that a new estate is not only executive homes. In practice, commercial interests have paid for schools, libraries, fire stations, community centres, cricket pavilions and have sometimes just handed over cash. In 2005, the Labour government issued a circular saying that 'planning permission may not be bought and sold'. Since agreements are usually made in secret, it is hard to be certain whether councils have taken this on board.

In 2007, the government scrapped a plan to introduce Planning Gain Supplement (PGS). The decision about the controversial levy, under which increases in land value would be taxed after planning permission is granted, came after months of lobbying by the building industry. If you wonder why commercial chains have been allowed to take over our towns and cities, and why smaller versions of big supermarkets have been allowed to locate where they will have adverse effects on local shops, planning gain is a big part of the explanation. Even if councils have the power to resist the developers most do not have the will, since they raise about £1 billion a year from planning gain (see also Chapter 12).

The impact of Value Added Tax (VAT) on real property

All goods and services are classified by HMRC as VAT 'standard-rated', 'zero-rated' or 'exempt' supplies. The standard rate was 17.5 per cent of the value of the supply in 2010 but rose to 20 per cent from 4 January 2011. Zero-rated supplies have a notional charge of 0 per cent but input tax can be recovered. Exempt supplies do not attract any VAT and there is no credit on inputs. VAT is intended to be a tax on final consumers, and not on economic intermediary producers. Therefore, suppliers of standard-rated and zero-rated goods and services can reclaim all the VAT they pay on their inputs (for example, raw materials, components, office supplies). 'Exempt' indicates a liability to VAT, not an exclusion. The essential point is that with 'exempt' goods the supplier cannot reclaim VAT paid on inputs.

If VAT were levied at the standard rate on all goods and services, it would be a neutral tax. But the different categories described in Table 22.1 mean that its incidence is different between certain goods.

Until 1989, the construction and sale of new buildings was zero-rated, while rents were exempt. In 1988 the European Court of Justice ruled that only residential construction could be zero-rated, though all other rents could continue to be exempt. Accordingly, the government enacted that, from 1 April 1989, VAT must be paid at the standard rate on all *new* non-domestic buildings and civil engineering works, and on the sale of freehold or leasehold non-domestic building land as soon as construction begins.

Rents would remain 'exempt'. But this posed the major problem of how the developer, if he retained the building as an investment or the purchaser of the new construction (the landlord/investor), could recoup the VAT paid on the construction. Here the government made a concession which has important implications for real property. The developer or landlord could become a

Table 22.1   VAT on land transactions

Land transactions are:

Standard rate	S
Zero rate	Z
Exempt	E
Exempt with an option to tax	E/O
Commercial/industrial land/buildings	
Freehold land sale	E/O
Sale of freehold new buildings	S
Grant of leasehold interest	E/O
Civil engineering work	S
Construction work new building	S
Demolition services	S
Repairs etc. existing building	S
Residential land/buildings	
Sale of freehold land (by housing association or individual)	E
Sale of freehold land (by other)	E/O
Sale of freehold by person constructing	Z
Grant of lease of more than 21 years	Z
Construction work on new building	Z
Demolition	Z
Repairs etc.	Z

taxable supplier by charging VAT at the standard rate on rent. This is known as the 'option to tax' (OTT) and is exercisable unilaterally by the landlord (with a lease or licence) or by the vendor (in the disposal of land or buildings).

Supplies of land and buildings, such as freehold sales, leasing or renting, are normally exempt from VAT. This means that no VAT is payable, but the person making the supply cannot normally recover any of the VAT incurred on their own expenses. However, you can opt to tax land. For the purposes of VAT, the term 'land' includes any buildings or structures permanently affixed to it. You do not need to own the land in order to opt to tax. Once you have opted to tax all the supplies you make of your interest in the land or buildings will normally be standard-rated. And you will normally be able to recover any VAT you incur in making those supplies.

It should be noted that exercising the OTT for both current and future leases lasts for at least 20 years (although it can be revoked within three months). Any subsequent sale is automatically standard-rated, although a new owner would be entitled to decide afresh whether to exercise the option. Nor can the option be exercised piecemeal – it has to apply to the whole building. Consequently, where a building is multi-let, the owner cannot vary the OTT according to the particular VAT liability of different tenants.

It is likely that developers retaining properties and other landlord-investors will exercise their OTT when the new building is bought (the developer who retains his construction has to pay VAT by 'self-billing'), but VAT can be recovered on a building so extensively refurbished or subsequently refurbished that it is considered to be a 'new' building, and thus subject to tax. Nor, with one possible exception, will the OTT affect the rent obtainable. With industrial and retail property, the occupiers can reclaim the VAT on rent as an input. The same applies to offices let to accountants, lawyers, surveyors and similar services whose supplies are standard-rated.

The one major exception is services whose supplies are mainly 'exempt' – chiefly banks, insurance companies, pension funds, building societies and finance companies. In this case, the owner of the property would have to look at the likely future tenant of the building and ask what effect the OTT might have on the rent at which it could be let, and therefore, on its capitalized value. The OTT does increase input tax recovery but it may have a negative impact on tenants who are dealing with largely exempt supplies such as finance, insurance and education.

Local taxes based on property

The merits of local property taxes should be examined against the overall objectives of local government. If it is judged that in providing certain services local *government*, as opposed to mere local *administration*, has advantages, then local people must be allowed to make their own decisions as to the type of service they prefer and be responsible for raising the necessary revenue. In this respect, taxes on property have many advantages.

First, they promote local autonomy and accountability. By having a clear base and giving local authorities their own source of revenue, property taxes afford a degree of financial independence from the central government. Moreover, by being raised on a local basis with the rate determined annually, they make local authorities responsible to local people. However, such accountability is limited, in that only residential property is directly linked to the electoral process: no local voting powers are enjoyed by commercial and industrial property, though political influence may be exercised through pressure groups, such as the local Chamber of Commerce.

Second, local property taxes are generally accepted. Having been levied for nearly 400 years, they conform to the view that 'an old tax is no tax'. Moreover in form they are simple, easily understood and appear equitable in that property benefits from local services, and those occupying the largest properties tend to be the richer members of the community. Third, there is certainty of yield. Not only are property taxes difficult to evade, but being based on fixed property any increase in the rate of tax cannot easily be shifted geographically (unlike a sales tax where people can shop in a cheaper area). Only in the long term can occupiers respond to high rates by moving to another area.

Fourth, property taxes have administrative advantages in that, once rate-able or capital values have been assessed, the rate is easily calculated and can be adjusted when additional revenue is required. Furthermore costs of collection are relatively economic, being less than 2 per cent of yield. Fifth, since a property tax is a lump-sum tax on housing, it penalizes under-occupation and thereby provides an incentive to let rooms or move to a smaller property.

In spite of these advantages, however, local property taxes are not without criticism. First, because domestic rates are a selective tax on a particular good, there is a loss of welfare compared with a direct tax which raises the same amount of revenue. Furthermore, a tax on housing services could be considered illogical in the light of the government's policy of subsidizing housing as a merit good.

Second, local property taxes, like all selective outlay taxes, distort market prices and therefore, at least in the long period, have allocative effects. In order to show this we will assume:

1. there is a competitive free market in housing;
2. houses are homogeneous;
3. all houses are rented on a weekly tenancy;
4. no rates are being levied initially;
5. the demand for rented housing is depicted by the D curves as shown in Figure 22.3 (a) and (b).

Initially the rent paid is OR (Figure 22.3(a)). If rates are now imposed on the tenant on an *ad valorem* basis, the demand curve shifts to D_t. In the short

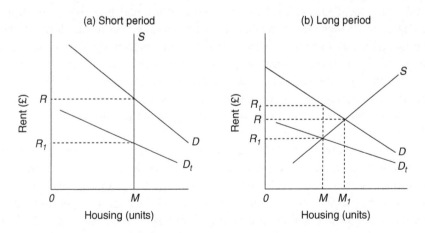

Figure 22.3   The effect of the imposition of rates on rents and the supply of housing

period, the stock of rented houses is fixed, and the new rates will be borne by landlords for net rent will fall from OR to OR_1 unless the tenant is under a long-term contract to pay exclusive of rates. In the long period, however, the supply of houses is more elastic since, assuming no planning consent is required, owners will adapt them to other uses or simply not replace them as they wear out, switching to lower-taxed and more profitable forms of investment. This means that some of the rate burden is now passed on to the tenant, the extent depending upon the relative elasticities of supply and demand. Thus in Figure 22.3(b) RR_t of the rate of burden is shifted forward to the tenant, and RR_1 backwards to landlords, the total rates paid being $R_t R_1 \times OM_1$. Furthermore, rented housing decreases by MM_1.

It should be noted, however, that if the new rates result in improved local services, especially education, roads and transport facilities, there could be an increase in the demand for property in the area, the demand curve shifting to the right. As a result the impact of the rates on the landlord is partly offset by a rise in rents so that rented housing will not decrease by as much as MM_1. Furthermore, when the rate system itself is made selective by varying the poundage between different types of property (for instance, when agricultural land pays no rates and domestic buildings pay at a lower rate than businesses) there are additional allocative effects.

Third, the yield from property taxes lacks buoyancy – the result of the narrowness of the tax base together with its rigidity in the face of inflation. Concentrating on a single form of wealth – property – allows other types, such as works of art, jewellery and antiques, to escape tax. Consequently, a rise in local government expenditure results in a considerable increase in the rate-poundage. Though, as we have seen, this promotes accountability, it hampers progressive authorities who wish to extend their services. Again, though the yield from such taxes as income tax and VAT automatically increases with inflation, the rise in property prices takes time to be reflected in higher taxable values because revaluations may, through administration difficulties, be continually postponed. Worse still, local government services tend to be labour-intensive so that the yearly rate-poundage increase tends to be proportionately higher than the rate of inflation, which in the past has led to periodic outbursts of discontent.

Fourth, local property taxes tend to be regressive and inequitable. Not only do poor people tend to spend a higher proportion of their income on housing, but the tax levied may be unrelated to ability to pay. Nor is there any direct link between the property tax and local services used. A pensioner, for example, has little call on education or refuse collection. However, rate (or council tax) rebates do help to offset the burden for poorer persons. In any case, the rating system must be viewed in relation to the overall national fiscal structure where more progressive taxes and free social benefits can compensate.

Similar considerations of equity apply to business undertakings. No rates are levied on agricultural land and buildings. On the other hand, small firms probably find what is virtually a lump-sum tax more onerous than large firms that have a higher turnover, while a rate increase imposes a heavier burden on those forms of production which are building-intensive, such as retailing, compared with those which are labour-intensive and machinery-intensive, such as light industry. Fifth, groups bearing the lowest rate burden, such as householders, especially those on housing benefit or with children at school, tend to press for more goods and services to be provided by local authorities, since others bear a larger proportion of the costs.

Sixth, local property taxes accentuate relative differences in local authorities' resources. Often the authority with a low rateable value has more to spend on new infrastructure, housing and education, and is thus forced to levy a high rate-poundage. This means that the rates paid on similar properties can vary from one part of the country to another, and even between different parts of the same urban concentration. Such 'fiscal zoning' has allocative consequences, households and firms tending to move to those areas where the rate-poundage is lowest. Although inequalities between districts may be corrected by central government equalization grants, this may be only at the expense of undermining local autonomy.

It is usual for local property taxes to be levied *ad valorem (by value)*; but the tax base chosen may be net annual value, capital value or site value.

Net annual value

When the basis of assessment is net annual value (NAV), it is likely to be determined as follows. First, a gross annual value – the yearly rent that the property might reasonably be expected to be let for on a determined date – is given to the property, and then statutory deductions are made for maintenance and insurance to give the NAV. Compared with a site value base, NAV has certain advantages. First, because the base includes buildings as well as land, the yield is higher, especially for properties whose building cost is a high proportion of the total cost. Second, it is easier to assess, since in a free market rentals can be calculated by comparison with similar properties.

On the other hand, NAV has significant defects. First, because the tax falls on buildings as well as on land, it tends to be more regressive for houses, which are occupied by poor persons as well as rich. Second, NAV is not neutral concerning building improvements, for these are taxed. In the long period, therefore, capital tends to move to untaxed uses, an owner-occupier, for example, preferring to buy antique furniture rather than build a garage. Third, apart from the above problems of principle, NAV may, as the experience of the UK has shown, involve practical difficulties. Therefore, rent control and the loss of part of the private rented sector has meant that, in assessing rentals, evidence of free market rentals was confined to about 2 per cent of a sector, which accounts for only 15 per cent of total dwellings. Moreover, anomalies occur: not only is agricultural land de-rated with a severe loss of possible revenue to rural authorities, but relieving charities of rates penalizes those authorities (such as Westminster, Oxford and Cambridge) that contain a high proportion of charities within their boundaries, especially as the NAVs are included in the valuation list which the central government uses in assessing its 'needs' grant.

Capital value

On this case, the tax is the value of the premises if sold freehold in an open market, given a willing seller. Provided the capital value is equal to the NAV capitalized at the relevant rate of interest, it will produce an equivalent base for taxation as NAV. In practice, however, marginal divergencies between the two methods may have allocative effects. If potential-use value is included in capital value, vacant and underdeveloped sites pay more tax than under NAV, thus accelerating redevelopment, discouraging non-occupation of buildings and stimulating greater use of existing property.

Other variations in assessing capital values may affect the rate of renewal of property, particularly dwellings. Capital-value assessments in the USA, for example, allow for the state of repair and length of life of the property and for risk of rental default. Such factors lower the capital value of such property as slum housing even though net returns relative to gross yields are high since little is spent on upkeep. Therefore, the tax base is smaller than it would be if net returns were capitalized to obtain the capital value, and it is suggested that the resulting tax advantage tends to retard urban renewal.

Land value taxation or site value rating

Land value taxation is a method of raising public revenue by means of an annual *ad valorem* tax on the rental value of land. Advocates say it would replace, not add to, existing taxes and, if properly applied, land value tax (LVT) could support a range of social and economic initiatives, including housing, transport and other infrastructural investments.

The value of every parcel of land in a country would be assessed regularly and the land value tax levied as a percentage of those assessed values. 'Land' means the site alone, not counting any improvements. The value of buildings, crops, drainage or any other works which people have erected or carried out on each plot of land would be ignored, but it would be assumed that all neighbouring properties were developed as at the time of the valuation; other things being equal, a vacant site in a row of houses would be assessed at the same value as the adjacent sites occupied by houses. The valuation would be based on market evidence, in accordance with the optimum use of the land within the planning regulations. If the current planning restrictions on the use were altered, the site would be reassessed.

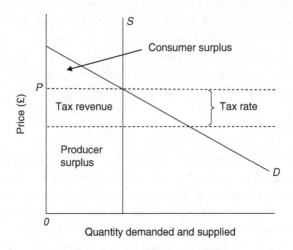

Figure 22.4   The effect of a land value tax

LVT does not have distortionary effects on output, because it is payable regardless of whether or how well the land is actually used. Because the supply of land is inelastic, market land rents depend on what tenants are prepared to pay, rather than on the expenses of landlords, and so LVT cannot be passed on to tenants. The only direct effect of LVT on prices is to lower the market price of land. So LVT can be justified for economic reasons because if it is implemented properly, it will not deter production, distort market mechanisms or otherwise create welfare losses the way other taxes do. The situation is shown in Figure 22.4.

Land value taxation (LVT) (or site value rating) is an *ad valorem* tax on the value of land. The idea behind site value rating (SVR) as the basis of assessment is that the tax falls only on the land element of real property, that is, the open market value of the site on the assumption that it is currently available for its most profitable use. Thus, compared with an NAV or capital-value base, the buildings are not taxed, but potential value is taxed (Figure 22.5).

As the basis of a property tax, LVT/SVR has certain advantages. First, it has strong moral backing in that it is closely associated with taxing 'betterment'. The argument is founded on Ricardo's theory of economic rent (Ricardo, 1817): since land is fixed in supply, its value is determined solely by demand, LVT/SVR is a tax on this demand-determined value and is thus a means by which 'betterment' can be returned to the community. Moreover, because sites are, for spatial reasons, fixed in supply, the tax falls entirely on economic rent with no effect on supply.

Second, LVT/SVR should improve the efficiency of land use. Because site value is the sole tax base, it is in effect a lump-sum tax which is levied

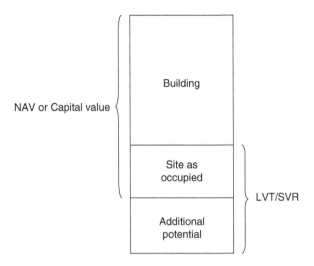

Figure 22.5 Comparison of the incidence of NAV, capital value and LVT/SVR on buildings and land

irrespective of how the site is used, the value of the building on it, or whether the buildings are improved. That is, LVT/SVR is neutral in the type of use, intensity of use and improvements. There is therefore, an incentive to develop sites to their most profitable use, since the burden of the given tax would then be spread over higher gross receipts. Even if speculators continued to hoard land – vacant central sites and agricultural fringe land – LVT/SVR would ensure that they had to pay towards the cost of public services provided. Furthermore, the improvement of existing buildings would be encouraged. Thus LVT/SVR should speed up the renewal of inner-city areas.

Third, LVT/SVR could have benefits for housing. In the short period, the rate burden would tend to shift to central sites and away from suburban houses. Figure 22.6 shows that under LVT/SVR, (a) will pay rates on one-half of the original base, whereas (b) will pay on only one-quarter. In the long period, the more intensive use of central sites should, given no change in the demand for land resources, reduce the demand for and therefore, the price of peripheral land, the main source for new housing.

Fourth, LVT/SVR should produce external benefits. Given no change in the demand for land resources, its impetus towards the redevelopment of central sites would reduce city sprawl. On the other hand, this could be accompanied by external costs – increased city-centre traffic congestion and the loss of open space, such as large private gardens and centrally situated recreational facilities, which could be taxed out of existence. Planning regulation, however, could partly deal with such costs.

Fifth, LVT/SVR would reduce 'fiscal zoning' since, in the long run, the movement of business and people to 'low-rate' areas would be self-defeating

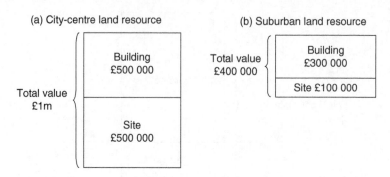

Figure 22.6   The incidence of land value tax or site value rating

in that it would simply raise site values there. Sixth, LVT/SVR should promote objectivity in making planning decisions. Because the NAV-system rates both buildings and land, the local authority has a built-in reason for approving a proposed development through the higher rateable value which would result. With the building element removed by LVT/SVR, planning decisions can follow a consistent policy based solely on environmental considerations.

Nevertheless though LVT/SVR has advantages, it faces objections on principle and difficulties in implementation. First, the true site value can only be ascertained when there is *competition* for a *vacant* site, because only then will the most profitable use under present conditions be indicated. At other times indirect methods of valuation have to be used, and these give rise to difficulties in ensuring accuracy and uniformity. Comparability is the safest method, but even so the personal judgement of the valuer cannot be eliminated when allowing for differences in the size and position of sites. Moreover, the difficulty of isolating the site element from any value resulting from improvements or the enterprise of the owner could provide scope for challenge, appeals and litigation. But if the residual method is used, the valuer has to assess the most profitable use and ultimately the cost of the building which will secure this. In short, the specialized expertise of all types of developer has to be embodied in the official valuer. Moreover, unless there were detailed local plans for the site, he would also have to make assumptions about the most profitable use likely to be allowed!

Furthermore, precise identification by the planning authority of permitted development covering the use and type of building for every site would be a departure from the current practice of broad structure plans. Not only would it lead to rigidity, but it would increase centralized decision making. Policy would have to stipulate whether site value should be assessed on short-run or long-run potential. If the latter, 'hope' value would be relevant. But this is a 'floating' value in that it cannot settle on all possible properties when development actually takes place. Therefore, to attribute a long-term potential value to all properties would involve double counting. Furthermore, it would, in effect, be a tax on income since the owner could do nothing to recoup that part of the tax based on potential. The site value assessment would be greater than the capitalized current net return from the site. This means that the incidence of the tax no longer falls entirely on betterment, and, by impinging on current resources, exaggerates a failure of the NAV system, in that it may be unrelated to the taxpayer's present capacity to pay.

Moreover, by assessing potential site values, LVT/SVR would not only tax increased value before it was realized, but would tax an increase in value which might *never* be realized. For one thing, there could be several interests in the land resource with no individual owner being able to redevelop because he could not acquire the other interests. For another, even though the land resource was taxed for a number of years on potential development value, that potential might be lost before it could be realized because of a change in planning policy or development elsewhere (for instance, a new hypermarket). And apart from planning restrictions, such encumbrances as long leases and private covenants would have to be taken into consideration in estimating site value.

As shown above, therefore, LVT/SVR could penalize the owner who has to postpone development in order to acquire adjoining land or complementary interests for a comprehensive scheme. In so doing, it could encourage piece-meal development detrimental to satisfactory town planning. It is also the case that assessment of site value can only be provisional when the environment is constantly changing. For instance, a new motorway would improve accessibility, but site values may not rise if the motorway increases the supply of sites. Moreover, the betterment may be thinly spread and accompanied by 'worsement' in the areas from which people move. Therefore, a period of at least 5 years may have to elapse following the completion of the motorway before there is reliable evidence of the resulting change in site values. However, once site values have been determined they will not be subject to the many assessment changes which under NAV follow structural alterations and additions.

While the inclusion of the potential value of vacant and underdeveloped sites may provide an initial tax base equal to NAV, LVT/SVR could prove less onerous if building costs increased relatively to site values, for example, through a shift in shopping from city centres, where sites are fixed in supply, to out-of-town hypermarkets, where alternative sites are available.

Though LVT/SVR would be paid by owners instead of by occupiers, in the long period its incidence for particular uses can be passed on to occupiers according to the relative elasticities of demand of occupiers and the elasticity of supply by owners. Inasmuch as the tax would be paid by owners but hidden in rents, LVT/SVR tends to weaken the link between local taxation, and representation and accountability. Against these difficulties must be set the fact that owners are fewer in number than occupiers, making the tax easier to collect.

Box 22.1 Claims made for land value tax

Equity or fairness:

Land (unlike goods and services) has no cost of production. If an ample supply of land of equal desirability were available everywhere, there would be nothing to pay for its use. In reality, land acquires a scarcity value owing to the competing needs of the community for living, working and leisure space. Therefore, land value owes nothing to individual effort and everything to the community at large. Because of differences in positional advantages, fertility or natural resources, some locations are more desirable than others. Demand for access to these features gives land its rental value. Land value taxation, being assessed on these values, is fair in its incidence.

In effect, failing to tax land value can be seen as being unfair, and this is especially evident in cases such as the announcement of a new transport hub or park, where surrounding land values escalate overnight simply by virtue of government plans, not by individual initiative.

It is hard to evade or avoid LVT – land cannot be hidden, removed to a tax haven or concealed in an electronic data system.

It can revitalize marginal areas:

Economic activity is handicapped by distance from the major centres of population. Conventional taxes such as VAT and those on transport fuels cause particular damage to the more remote areas of the country. Land value tax, by definition, bears lightly or not at all where land has little or no value, thereby stimulating economic activity away from the centre – it creates what are in effect tax havens exactly where they are most needed.

Less urban sprawl:

Land value taxation deters speculative land holding. Thus dilapidated inner-city areas are returned to productive use, reducing the pressure for building on greenfield sites. The necessity to pay the tax obliges landowners to develop vacant and under-used land properly or to make way for others who will.

Moderation of real estate bubbles:

Speculation in land value is often the cause of unsustainable booms which result periodically in damaging corrective slumps. Land value taxation, fully and properly applied, takes the speculative element out of land pricing.

Reduction of other taxes:

Hong Kong is perhaps the best modern example of the successful implementation of a high LVT. The Hong Kong government generates more than 35 per cent of its revenue from land taxes. As a result they can keep their other taxes rates low or non-existent and still generate a budget surplus.

Finally, in weighing up the pros and cons of introducing LVT/SVR into the UK, we have to remember that because the uncertainties in assessing site values would give rise to considerable challenge by owners, a transition period of several years might have to elapse before it could become fully operative. In the meantime it might not provide a predictable basis for financing local services.

The strength of LVT/SVR (already operative in such countries as Denmark, Australia and New Zealand) lies in the incentive it provides towards development and improvement. It has particular merit, therefore, for underdeveloped countries. On the other hand, in the UK the main need is to direct development into the best channels, an aim which is probably more effectively achieved by planning requirements. Moreover, the other objective of appropriating betterment for the public purse can, as an alternative, be achieved by a capital gains tax and planning gain.

Present finance of local government in the UK

UK local government finance now has four elements:

1. The Uniform business rate (UBR);
2. Government grants;
3. Charges;
4. Council tax.

The uniform business rate (UBR) – a national non-domestic rate

Prior to 1 April 1990, businesses were subject to the same rate poundages as domestic hereditaments and, as such, business rates had four main defects. First, they bore no direct relationship to ability to pay, for they were harder on building-intensive users and afforded no rebates for firms suffering a serious fall in profits. Second, being fixed arbitrarily by the local authority, they changed considerably over time through a change in the political party in power. Third, they could vary markedly between different authorities. Fourth, they carried no accountability restraint on the local authority since businesses, although paying some 60 per cent of the local rate revenue, enjoyed no local vote. This allowed high-spending local authorities to off-load a large proportion of the necessary financing on to businesses located in their areas.

On the other hand, business rates are easy and cheap to collect and do ensure that firms contribute to local expenditure on collective services, such as police, roads, street lighting and open spaces. In addition, it is probable that rates form only a small percentage of total costs. Moreover, they are tax-deductible (from profits).

In 1990 the response of the government to the weaknesses of the business rate was to take away the power of the local authority to levy it. A new rating list was compiled by the valuation officer appointed for each charging authority (the district borough or city council), using an unchanged formula of a notional rental value – what the premises could be let for *less* rates and taxes, insurance and maintenance expenses.

A rate (now known as 'the multiplier') is set for England and Wales by the Department of Communities and Local Government. If the rateable value of a business property, in England, was £20,000, and the local authority was calculating the 2010–11 business rates bill, it would multiply it by 41.4p to get a total for the year of £8,280. If the business is entitled to any form of rate relief, this sum is then adjusted to reflect that, making a final total for the rates bill. The multiplier usually changes each year in line with inflation. In England, since 1 April 2005, a small business rate relief scheme has been in operation. Eligible businesses who apply to their local authority to be part of the scheme can have their liability calculated using the small business multiplier (40.7p in 2010–11). Dependent on their rateable value, they may also be eligible for a further discount on their bill. The City of London is able to set a different multiplier from the rest of England (slightly higher in 2010–11).

Revaluations of the rating list take place every 5 years, the next being in 2015. At each revaluation the UBR is reset to ensure that in real terms the revenue from business rates is unchanged following the revaluation. The product of the new rate is paid into a national pool and then distributed to local authorities in proportion to their adult populations. There are separate pools for England and Wales. It is doubtful whether businesses, while still relying on local authorities for services, will find their needs treated with more respect now that they are paying a national rather than a local tax. Indeed, when businesses paid the *local* tax, their Chambers of Commerce were listened to and could exert influence. Thus 'accountability' could be less under the UBR.

What is likely to be the effect of increased rates on rents? In the short period, only if the demand for a firm's product is completely inelastic can the whole of a rate increase be passed on to the consumer through higher prices. Since the firm has to sell in competition with other firms, it is likely that it will have to bear most of the increase. In the long term when a rent review is due, a firm may be able to pass some of the higher cost on to the landlord by a rent reduction, depending on the relative elasticities of demand and supply. However, any such fall would reduce capital values and so apply a brake on future development. Moreover, where rateable values for out-of-town superstores have undergone a more than proportionate increase than town-centre shopping, there could be a shift back to the latter, thus reinforcing planning policy.

Taxes on commercial property, such as the UBR, also have an effect on investment in property relative to plant and machinery which is not subject to such a tax (Evans, 2004). The effect is illustrated in Figure 22.7.

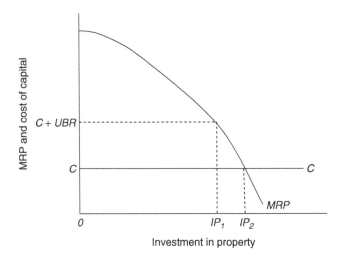

Figure 22.7 The impact of UBR on investment in commercial property

In Figure 22.7 the impact of the imposition of the UBR on commercial property reduces investment in property from IP_1 to IP_2. Without the UBR, investment in property would take place to the point where the added value from each additional unit of investment or marginal revenue product (MRP) is equal to the cost of that investment represented by the cost of capital (the line CC). The imposition of the UBR raises CC to $C+UBR$ reducing investment in property from IP_1 to IP_2.

Government grants

Government grants, together with the UBR distribution, now provide about 80 per cent of local authorities revenue. They:

1. offset the defects of the rating system by transferring more of the burden to general taxation;
2. assist local authorities with services of national concern, for example, roads, police, education;
3. ensure a minimum standard in the provision of such services;
4. encourage local authorities to provide services above the minimum required; and
5. assist in special emergencies, such as floods.

The basis upon which grants are made must achieve their objective without destroying local control or initiative, or committing the government to excessive expenditure. Therefore, though grants based on a *percentage* of cost or of so much per *unit* encourage local authorities to spend more than the bare minimum, they make it difficult for the government to control its own spending.

A *block* grant – a single, annual lump sum to be used at the local authority's discretion – avoids this, but only at the risk of discouraging those authorities who are keen to improve and develop services since extra expenditure has to be covered locally. The result is that today there are two main types of grant:

- Grants in aid of specific services – calculating the grant on a percentage basis, for example, police (50 per cent), highways (50–75 per cent according to the class of road), encourages high standards but necessitates careful central audit to ensure that spending is not wasteful. Therefore, a grant of so much per unit, irrespective of whether standards above the minimum are provided, is easier to administer.
- The revenue support grant – This is a 'needs-related' block grant (revised in 1980) designed to compensate authorities for differences in the cost of providing other services at a standard level. The government fixes the aggregate level of grant, based on its own estimates for each category of service. It is paid to local authorities on a per capita basis according to the government's estimate of their needs with reference to its Standard Spending Assessments. 'Needs' are calculated on a formula covering a number of factors, such as the rate resources of the authority, the density of population and the number of young and old people in the area.

However, providing a high proportion of local authority revenue through grants can give rise to problems. First, local councils tend to lose their autonomy because central government determines most of their spending. Second, it lessens the accountability of councils to those paying local taxes. Third, it may create difficulties for the government in its stabilization policy, for any reduction can bring it into conflict with the local authorities.

User charges and fees

Charges have the advantage that those who benefit from the service pay at least a part of its cost, as with rents for housing, admission fees to swimming pools, and planning applications. But while some trading services (especially lotteries) make a profit, most local government activity is concerned with providing community, collective and merit goods whose cost has to be covered mainly from taxation, either central or local (see Chapter 21).

Raising revenue by increased charges is limited to a few services, such as sports centres, allotments, planning applications, building control, libraries. At times it has been suggested that education, the major spender, could be treated in a special way. Vouchers to a certain value would be issued by the central government to parents who would then 'spend' them at the school of their choice, perhaps supplementing them from their own resources if they so wished. This would relieve the local authorities of the cost of education (so that the rate yield was adequate for remaining services) and achieve accountability to parents through the price system.

Council tax

The amount by which the area authorities' spending exceeds revenue from the previous three sources has to be covered by levying a council tax on households.

In essence it is a reversion to the old rating system, but instead of a notional annual letting value, for which market evidence was deficient, it is based on the 1 April 1991 capital value of the property – what it would have sold for on that date. The council tax band of a property is not related to its current market value. This is because, by law, council tax valuations are based on the price a property would have fetched if it had been sold on 1 April 1991. For Wales, the valuation date is 1 April 2003. The Valuation Office Agency (VOA) determines the council tax bands of the 23.2 million domestic properties in England and Wales. To allow for the difficulties involved in making a precise valuation of each individual dwelling, values are divided into eight bands – A to H – with all households in the same band paying the same amount of tax, but increasing upwards to H, whose payment band is treble that of band A and double that of D. There is a 50 per cent discount for unoccupied dwellings and second homes. There is no provision for a general revaluation, but a future sale or a change in the locality, such as a new nearby motorway, may afford grounds for a revaluation.

Council tax is regressive because it is not proportional to either property values or incomes and the rate charged is higher on lower value properties than it is on higher value properties (note that this does not mean that the actual amount payable is higher on lower value properties). For single residents there is a 25 per cent discount, but people exempt from the council tax are ignored for the purpose of determining the single-person discount. Exempt people include: students, student nurses, apprentices, youth trainees, those on income support, the severely mentally handicapped and elderly dependent relatives.

In Scotland a similar system operates to that in England and Wales, but the Scottish Government believes that the council tax is fundamentally unfair and should be abolished and replaced with a fairer local income tax based on ability to pay (Scotland.gov.uk, 2010).

The future of local authority finance

Many attempts have been made to find a tax, which is fair, reserved for local revenue, practicable and cheap to collect, ensures the authority's accountability to local voters and harmonizes local autonomy with the central government's macroeconomic policy requirements. Suggested new sources all lack one or more of these attributes.

Not only would *revenues assigned from national taxation* (such as motor-vehicle duties) be inadequate for the poorest authorities, but their transfer could force the government to increase its other taxes to make good lost revenue. A *local sales tax* would be difficult to superimpose on VAT and in such a small country as Britain could be undermined by people shopping in areas where tax rates were low. A *payroll tax* would similarly induce firms to locate in low-rate areas, apart from leading to the replacement of labour by capital and being inflationary.

The Layfield Committee (Layfield, 1976) favoured a local income tax. But this faces the technical problem of running a local income tax in conjunction with Britain's accumulative PAYE system. Not only would revenue have to be split between national and local government on each pay day rather than yearly as under other systems, but the tax could be levied where a person works, rather than where he lives. In view of these difficulties and the necessity to avoid capricious differences in local income tax rates, a local income tax system might simply result in assigning some of the national income tax revenue to local authorities. This could clash with a government's aim of reducing the basic rate of tax.

An alternative proposal, that the central government could accept full financial responsibility for services of national importance, such as education, police and social services, would simply further weaken provision of services according to local preferences and circumstances.

With central government grants contributing 75–80 per cent of local authorities' finance, however, there is a need for new sources of revenue. These are required to restore the autonomy that local authorities have lost through the loss of direct revenue as a result of rate-capping, capital spending controls, the switch to housing benefits, and the transfer of the non-domestic rate to the central government. Moreover, with only 20–25 per cent of revenues raised locally, a rise in local authority expenditure, which is not financed by central government, would require a larger than proportionate rise in council tax which would be unpopular. If you wonder why planning permission was granted for an infill development on someone's garden in your already overdeveloped locality, the pressure on council tax finance could be the answer.

Summary

Direct taxes are mainly neutral in their effects on property, but they can have marginal economic effects; for example, mortgage interest relief via income tax and exemption from CGT have encouraged home ownership; and capital allowances against corporation tax for agricultural and industrial buildings shorten their life.

The impact of indirect taxes and in particular VAT on property is complex and the OTT may affect exempt and non-exempt occupiers in different ways.

Land value tax or site value rating has many advantages and has been adopted successfully in several countries, notably Hong Kong.

Planning gain is a benefit accruing to a local authority from the granting of planning consent. Developers may offer inducements to local authorities in the form of provision of amenities such as roads or parks in return for planning permission for their scheme.

Local property taxes promote local autonomy and accountability. They are equitable in the sense that larger properties (which tend to be occupied by the richer members of the community) pay larger local taxes. They are difficult to evade and easy to collect and calculate.

Chapter 22: review questions

---

1. Consider the current rates of stamp duty land tax; explain whether this tax is regressive, proportional or progressive.
2. Why is a land value tax unlikely to distort the allocation of resources?
3. How might a land value tax reduce the frequency of speculative real estate bubbles?
4. What are the main types of taxation used to finance local authorities' expenditure?
5. Consider the system of council tax; explain whether this tax is regressive, proportional or progressive.

References

Adair, A., Allen, S., Berry, J. and McGreal, S. (2006) 'Central and Eastern European property investment markets: issues of data and transparency', *Journal of Property Investment and Finance*, 24: 3, pp. 211–220.

Adams, D. (1994) *Urban Planning and the Development Process*, London: Routledge.

Ball, M. (2007) 'Localisation versus globalisation: some evidence from real estate services organisations', *Journal of Housing and the Built Environment*, 22: 1, pp. 91–106.

Ball, M., Lizieri, C. and MacGregor, D. (2001) *The Economics of Commercial Property Markets*, London: Routledge.

Ballard, G. and Howell, G. (2003) 'Lean project management', *Building Research and Information*, 31: 2, March, pp. 119–33.

Bank of England (2010) 'Housing equity withdrawal', available at www.bankofengland. co.uk/statistics/hew/2010/jun/index.htm.

Barker, K. (2006) 'Barker review of land use planning, interim report – Analysis', London: HMSO. Available at www.barkerreviewofplanning.org.uk

Barclays Equity Gilt study (2009) available at: *www.barcap.com/*.

Barras, R. (1994) 'Property and the economic cycle: building cycles revisited', *Journal of Property Research*, 11, pp. 183–97.

BERR (2006) 'Globalisation and the UK Economy' Department for Business, Enterprise and Regulatory Reform, February.

Case, B., Goetzmann, W. N. and Rouwenhorst, K. G. (2000) 'Global Real Estate Markets – Cycles and Fundamentals', National Bureau Economic Research Working Paper No. W7566. Available at SSRN: http://ssrn.com/abstract=227635.

CB Richard Ellis (2009) available at CBRE.co.uk.

Christie, S. and Teeuw, R. M. (1998) 'Varied policy of European states on contaminated land', *Environmental Impact Assessment Review*, 18: 2, March, pp. 175–97.

Coase, R. (1960) 'The problem of social cost', *Journal of Law and Economics*, 3 (October), pp. 1–44.

Council for Mortgage Lenders (2010) available at: www.cml.org.uk/.

Crook, T., Currie, J., Jackson, A., Monk, S., Rowley, S., Smith, K. and Whitehead, C. (2002) *Planning Gain and Affordable Housing: Making It Count*, Joseph Rowntree Foundation, York.

Cullingworth, J. B. (1963) *Housing in Transition: A Case Study in the City of Lancaster, 1958–1962*, London: Heinemann.

Cushman and Wakefield (2008) press release 1 February, London, available at www.cush-wake.com/cwglobal.

DCLG (2007) 'Building a Greener Future: policy statement', available at www.communities.gov.uk.

DCLG (2008) 'Definition of Zero Carbon Homes and Non-Domestic Buildings: consultation,', available at www.communities.gov.uk.

DCLG (2009) *'Zero Carbon for New Non-domestic Buildings: consultation on policy options',* available at www.communities.gov.uk.

DCLG (2010) 'Code for Sustainable Homes: a cost review' available at www.communities.gov.uk.

Defra (2006) 'UK Climate Change Programme', available at www.defra.gov.uk/environment/flooding/manage/climate.htm.

Department of Trade and Industry (2003) 'Our energy future – creating a low carbon economy', available at www.dti.go.uk/energy/whitepaper/.

Department of Trade and Industry (2006) 'Low Carbon Buildings Programme', available at www.dti.gov.uk/energy/sources/sustainable/microgeneration/index.html.

Department of Trade and Industry (2007) *Energy White Paper: Meeting the Energy Challenge*, Norwich: HMSO.

Department for Transport (2009) 'Britain's Transport Infrastructure. Adding Capacity to Heathrow: Decisions Following Consultation', available at www.dft.gov.uk.

DETR (1999) *Towards an Urban Renaissance: Report of the Urban Task Force*, DETR, London.

DiPasquale, D. and Wheaton, W. (1996) *Urban Economics and Real Estate Markets*, New Jersey: Prentice Hall.

Dixon, T. (2009) 'Property in the Economy: Sustainability and Corporate Real Estate', RICS (rics.org/propertyintheeconomy).

Dixon, T., Ennis-Reynolds, G., Roberts, C. and Sims, S. (2009) *Demand for Sustainable Offices in the UK*, London: IPF Research.

DOE (1977) *Policy for the Inner Cities* (Cmnd 6845), London: HMSO.

Donaghy, R. (2009) 'One Death is too Many – Inquiry into the Underlying Causes of Construction Fatal Accidents', Report to the Secretary of State for Work and Pensions, July.

Economist (2005) Special Report 'The Global Housing Boom'.

Energy Saving Trust (2008) 'Energy Efficiency and the Code for Sustainable Homes', available at www.energy savingtrust.org.uk.

Energy Saving Trust (2010) 'Energy saving assumptions', available at www.energysavingtrust.org.uk/Energy-saving-assumptions.

Environment Agency (2008) 'Water resources in England and Wales –current state and future pressures', available at www.environment-agency.gov.uk.

Estates Gazette (1974) *Digest of Building Land Prices* (in conjunction with the House Builders Federation Advisory Service), London.

Evans, A. W. (2004) *Economics, Real Estate and the Supply of Land*, Oxford: Blackwell.

George, H. [1879] (1937) *Progress and Poverty* (3rd edn) London: The Henry George Foundation.

Hardisty, P., Bracken, R. A. and Knight, M. (1998) 'The economics of contaminated site remediation: decision making and technology selection', London: *Geological Society, Engineering Geology Special Publications*, 14, pp. 63–71.

Harford, T. (2006) *The Undercover Economist*, London: Abacus.

Harvey, J. and Jowsey, E. (2004) *Urban Land Economics* Palgrave Macmillan, Basingstoke.

Haynes, B. P. (2007a) 'Office productivity: a theoretical framework', *Journal of Corporate Real Estate*, 9, pp. 97–109.

Haynes, B. P. (2007b) 'An evaluation of office productivity measurement', *Journal of Corporate Real Estate*, 9, pp. 144–55.

HMSO (1973) 'Widening the choice: the next step in housing' (Cmnd 5280) presented to Parliament by the Secretary of State for the Environment and the Secretary of State for Wales by command of Her Majesty, London.

Horne, R. and Hayles, C. (2008) 'Towards global benchmarking for sustainable homes: an international comparison of the energy performance of housing', *Journal of Housing and the Built Environment*, 23, pp. 119–30.

IMF (2003) *When Bubbles Burst*, Chapter II, International Monetary Fund.

Investment Property Databank *(2009) available at: www.ipd.com/marketdata.*

JonesLangLaSalle – www.jll.com.

Kats, G. H. (2003) *Green Building Costs and Financial Benefits*, Massport, MA: Massachusetts Technology Collaborative.

Keeping, M. and Shiers, D. E. (2004) *Sustainable Property Development, A Guide to Real Estate and the Environment*, Oxford: Blackwell.

Keivani, R., Parsa, A. and McGreal, W. S. (2002) 'Institutions and urban change in a globalising world', *Cities*, 19: 3, pp. 183–93.

Kellett, J. E. (2006) 'Energy service companies – a route to more sustainable Australian cities?' *Australian Journal of Environmental Management*, 13: 4, pp. 226–33.

Kim, K-H. and Renaud, B. (2009) 'The global house price boom and its unwinding: an analysis and a commentary', *Housing Studies*, 24:1, pp. 7–24.

Layfield, F. (1976) 'Report of the Committee of Inquiry into Local Government Finance' (Cmnd 6453), London: HMSO.

Levitt, S. D. and Dubner, S. J. (2005) *Freakonomics – A Rogue Economist Explores the Hidden Side of Everything*, London: Allen Lane (Penguin).

Lewis, M. K. (1994) 'Banking on Real Estate', Discussion Papers in Economics No. 9416, University of Nottingham.

Martin, A. and Scott, I. (2003) 'The effectiveness of the UK landfill tax', *Journal of Environmental Planning and Management,* 46: 5, pp.673–89.

Marshall, A. [1890] (1920) *Principles of Economics*, (8th edn), London: Macmillan.

Matthews, T. and Treloar, G. J. (2001) 'Net energy analysis of double glazing for residential buildings in temperate climates', *Structural Survey*, 19: 4, pp. 201–8.

McCutcheon, R. (1988) 'Technical and economic efficiency in the UK building industry 1965–1977', *Habitat International*, 12: 1, pp. 117–28.

McGreal, W. S., Parsa, A. and Keivani, R. (2002), 'Evolution of property investment markets in Central Europe: opportunities and constraints', *Journal of Property Research*, 19: 3, pp. 213–30.

Miller, N. G., Pogue, D., Gough, Q. D. and Davis, S. M. (2009) 'Green buildings and productivity', *Journal of Sustainable Real Estate*, 1: 1, pp. 65–89.

Monbiot, G. (2006) www.Monbiot.com/archives/2006/09/21/an-87-cut-by-2030.

Monk, S. and Whitehead ,C. M. E. (1996) 'Land supply and housing: a case study', *Housing Studies,* 11: 3, July, pp. 407–23.

Muellbauer, J. (1990) 'The great British housing disaster', *Roof,* May–June, pp. 16–20.

Muellbauer, J. and Murphy, A. (2008) 'Housing markets and the economy: the assessment', *Oxford Review of Economic Policy*, Oxford: Oxford University Press.

Nathanail, J., Bardos, R. P. and Nathanail, P. (2001) 'Contaminated land management: ready reference', Richmond, Surrey: EPP Publications and Land Quality Press in association with Environmental Technology Limited and Land Quality Management Ltd at the University of Nottingham.

Nathanail, P. C. and Bardos, P. (2004) *Reclamation of Contaminated Land* , Chichester, England: Wiley & Sons.

Nationwide House Prices Index (nationwide.co.uk/hpi/historical.htm).

Nelson, A. (2007) 'The greening of US investment real estate-market fundamentals, prospects and opportunities', RREEF Research Number 57, November.

Nelson, A. (2008) 'Globalization and global trends in green real estate investment', RREEF Research Number 64, September.

Newman, P. W. G. and Kenworthy, J. R.(1989) 'Gasoline consumption and cities', *Journal of the American Planning Association*, 55: 1, pp. 24–37.

ONS Blue Book (2010) available at www.statistics.gov.uk.

ONS (2010) 'Output and Employment in the Construction Industry' available at www.statistics.gov.uk.

Pigou, A. C. (1913) *Unemployment*, London: Williams and Norgate.

PriceWaterhouseCoopers (2010) 'Foreign direct investment in Central and Eastern Europe. A case of boom and bust', March, available at www.pwc.com.

Reilly, W. J. (1931) *The Law of Retail Gravitation,* New York: Knickerbocker Press.

RICS (1994) *Understanding Property Cycles,* London: RICS.

Ricardo, D. ([1817] (1978) 'Principles of political economy and taxation' (3rd edn, 1821) in Marc Blaug (ed.) *Economic Theory in Retrospect,* (3rd edn), Cambridge and New York: Cambridge University Press.

Rivett, M. O., Petts, J., Butler, B. and Martin, I. (2002) 'Remediation of contaminated land and groundwater: experience in England and Wales', *Journal of Environmental Management*, 65: 3, July, pp. 251–68.

Salem, O., Solomon, J., Genaidy, A. and Minkarah, I. (2006) 'Lean construction: from theory to implementation', *Journal of Management Engineering*, 22: 4, October, pp. 168–75.

Scotland.gov.uk (2010) available at www.scotland.gov.uk/topics/government/local-government/17999/local-income-tax.

Seabrooke, W., Kent, P. and How, H. H. (eds) (2004) *International Real Estate – An Institutional Approach,* Oxford: Blackwell.

Shorrock, L. D. and Utley, J. I. (2003) *Domestic Energy Fact File 2003*, Watford, UK: Building Research Establishment.

Smith, A. [1776] (2008) *An Inquiry into the Nature and Causes of the Wealth of Nations: A Selected Edition*, Kathryn Sutherland (ed.), Oxford: Oxford Paperbacks.

Standard and Poors (2008) 'S&P/GRA Commercial Real Estate Indices' available at: www.standardandpoors.com/

statistics.gov.uk (2010) 'Statistical bulletin: public sector finances, April 2010', available at www.statistics.gov.uk/pdfdir/psf0510.pdf.

Steinert, M. and Crowe, S. (2001) 'Global real estate investment: characteristics, optimal portfolio allocation and future trends', *Pacific Rim Property Research Journal*, 7: 4, pp. 223–39.

Sustainable Development Commission (2006) *STOCK TAKE: Delivering Improvements in Existing Housing*, London: SDC.

Syms, P. M. (1997) *Contaminated Land, the Practice and Economics of Redevelopment*, Oxford: Blackwell Science.

Syms, P.M. (1999) 'Redeveloping brownfield land: the decision-making process', *Journal of Property Investment and Finance*, 17: 5, pp. 481–500.

UN (2009) *World Economic Situation and Prospects 2009*, Sales No. E.09.II.C.2, released in January 2009. available at http://www.un.org/esa/policy/wess/wesp.html.

Wackernagel, M. and Rees, B. (1996) *Our Ecological Footprint*, Canada: New Society Publications.

WCED (World Commission on Environment and Development) (1987) *Our Common Future*, New York: Oxford University Press and United Nations.

Winch, G. (1998) 'The growth of self-employment in British construction', *Construction Management and Economics,* 16, pp. 531–42.

Index

Printed and bound by CPI Group (UK) Ltd, Croydon, CR0 4YY